THE SOUTH IN CONTINUITY AND CHANGE

THE SOUTH IN CONTINUITY AND CHANGE / *edited by* John C. McKinney and Edgar T. Thompson

sponsored by The Southern Sociological Society *and* The Center for Southern Studies, *Duke University* / *published by* Duke University Press, *Durham, North Carolina* / 1965

© 1965, Duke University Press

Library of Congress Catalogue Card number 65-19448

Printed in the United States of America
by the Seeman Printery, Inc., Durham, N.C.

PREFACE

A great many people have assisted in the process of developing this volume. It was first envisaged in 1962 and undertaken as a project of the Committee on the Profession of the Southern Sociological Society. Meyer F. Nimkoff, the President of the Society, issued the initial challenge by suggesting that the Committee attempt to do something about the prevailing "image" of the South. This was, of course, a very large and difficult challenge. The Committee decided that one thing that might constitute a valuable contribution with respect to the problem would be to instigate and develop a comprehensive volume analyzing and assessing the state of the southern region at this period in time. President Nimkoff and his successors in the presidency, Selz C. Mayo and Bryce F. Ryan, each encouraged the idea and the project as it was developed during the period 1962-1964.

Organized on the basis of a rotating membership, the Committee included the following members during the time in which the project was planned and developed: Alvin L. Bertrand (Louisiana State University), Raymond V. Bowers (University of Georgia), Lee M. Brooks (University of North Carolina), Lewis M. Killian (Florida State University), Charles B. Nam (U. S. Bureau of the Census), Bryce F. Ryan (University of Miami), Charles Bowerman (University of North Carolina), Joseph H. Fichter (Loyola University of New Orleans), William E. Cole (University of Tennessee), and John C. McKinney (Duke University). Individually and collectively these people contributed significantly to the formulation and conduct of the project. In addition, the informal advice of Joseph J. Spengler (Duke University) and Rupert B. Vance (University of North Carolina) was invaluable with respect to delineating the problem areas and selecting appropriate authors.

As the planning proceeded and the volume took on a definite format with a specified and committed authorship, the Southern Sociological Society decided by vote of the membership formally to sponsor the volume. Simultaneously, events were taking place at Duke University leading to the establishment of the Center for Southern Studies in the Social Sciences and Humanities. Space, facilities, and personnel were provided at Duke in order to maintain and carry the project to its proper conclusion. *The South in Continuity and Change* thus emerges under the joint sponsorship of the Southern Sociological Society and the Center for Southern Studies, Duke University.

It should again be noted that many people have been helpful in one way or another in the development of the volume, but there are some whose contributions should be especially acknowledged. Alvin L. Bertrand and William E. Cole read the manuscript and submitted many constructive criticisms. Mrs. Barbara Reitt and Mrs. Linda Gerber rendered valuable editorial assistance. Mrs. Minna T. Mitchell supplied secretarial assistance over a long period of time. Finally the very major contribution of Mrs. Sandra F. Mascitelli, Research and Editorial Assistant for the project, must be acknowledged. Mrs. Mascitelli bore the primary responsibility for the day-to-day management of the problems related to the transformation of an idea into a volume, and for the "grass-roots" editing of this volume. Our special thanks to all of these people for giving their time, energy, and talent.

John C. McKinney
Edgar T. Thompson

Durham, North Carolina
Summer, 1965

CONTENTS

INTRODUCTION

There are books that survive as antiques. There are other books that are so immediately contemporary that they are read and forgotten in short order. There are yet other books that rise so far above the preoccupations of any place and time that they become placeless and timeless.

The South has produced books which qualify, or approach qualification, for each of these three types. We cannot hope that this book merits inclusion among the books of the last type—no symposium is ever likely to achieve this eminence—and it is not likely ever to become a collector's item as is the case with books of the first type. But there is reason to hope that it goes well beyond the books of the second type, and that at least some of the chapters included herein will engage the attention of students of the South for many years to come.

Forerunners of this book and standing out in the vast literature on the South are a number of symposia and books which have appeared from time to time. Three of these deserve mention. A thoughtful book written by twelve southerners, most of them literary men, and entitled *I'll Take My Stand* (Harpers, 1930), looks nostalgically toward the past. They were agrarians protesting industrialization and they yearned for a return to a Golden Age before Progress had reared its ugly head. After thirty years the book continues to appeal powerfully to those who entertain an image of the Old South which never really conformed to all the facts and especially the unlovely ones. Another important symposium on the South was edited by William T. Couch and published by the University of North Carolina Press in 1933 under the title, *Culture in the South*. Its roots are in the southern counterpart of the Populism of the 1890's and in the spirit of the New Deal of the 1930's. This book remains as a significant resource, and has stimulated subsequent studies and reports on aspects of southern life. At least fourteen topics discussed in it are also treated in the present volume and one writer, Rupert Vance, is a contributor to both. Mention must also be made of Howard W. Odum's *Southern Regions of the United States*, published in 1936 (University of North Carolina Press), a massive survey and inventory of the South's resources and problems. Without the dedicated hard work

of Odum and his students, the state of social science in the South
would today be much the poorer.

The volume presented here takes cognizance of the past, ex-
amines the present, and looks to the future in anticipation of further
integration of the southern region into the mainstream of American
life. We believe it is the first general symposium on the South to
offer a body of substantive materials from the perspective of social
theory; the theory in this case has to do with the general problem
of continuity and change. This theoretical perspective is presented
and specified in some detail in Chapter I, in the form of an analysis
of continuity and change within the framework of a structural-
functional view of society. The volume may be thought of as a set
of related analyses loosely articulated within the structural-functional framework, and oriented toward the persistent problems of
continuity and change. The preceding implies that the South, as a
region, is herein viewed as a social system. This is in full recognition that in many of the most fundamental ways it is merely a
subsystem of American society, and that in examining southern life
we are indeed examining a variant form of American society. It is
this fundamental feature that has all too frequently been obscured
by the literary and historical traditions of writing in their emphases
on the idiosyncrasies and differences of the South.

It is further implied that the tendency to view the South as a
colorful land peopled by a variety of picturesque types of humanity
—Negroes, crackers, creoles, mountaineers, sharecroppers, planters,
Klansmen, and political demagogues—and characterized by poverty,
ignorance, backwardness, agrarianism, and extreme forms of resistance to change, gives a greatly distorted and grossly inadequate
picture of this sector of American society. There is a basic similarity
throughout American society of those fundamental social institutions which organize the life of man and direct his capabilities in
the continuing process of solving his problems and achieving his
aspirations. The tendency to overlook this critically important fact
is a consequence of the preoccupation with the very observable but
far more superficial differences in the manifestations of these institutions. This volume attempts to examine both the extent to which
the southern region is similar to and involved in American society,

and the extent to which it is characterized by its own cultural modes, regional problems, and organization.

Until very recently, it has been customary to think of the South as a culturally passive area where people assumed that what had always been would always be. Unlike the urban North, where change initiated from within seems almost to have been the very life principle of the society itself, change in the feudal and agrarian South has appeared as something forced from without in the form of market fluctuations, federal law and programs, and northern carpetbaggers. The South has seemed to live inside its people like an instinct. In contrast, the Middle West and New England have appeared to exist in the inhabitants of those areas more like a habit. Time, intruding events, and new surroundings can break a habit, but an instinct is unbreakable and unchangeable. As in the case of many other alleged instincts, however, what we apparently have had in the perspective and posture of the South is really a deeply ingrained habit. For this region, like other parts of the society, and indeed, like other parts of the world, is seething with active and frequently contradictory movement.

The present South exists in one of those moments of time in which deep concern in it for the continuity of traditional values, clashing with equally deep concern for advance toward specific as well as general goals, has produced wide discrepancies and imbalances between the verbal and the real situation. Techniques for institutional self-preservation are being devised to counter movements and strategies looking toward change. There have been many such periods in the history of mankind which to the peoples most immediately involved have been, of course, profoundly disturbing. Yet it has been in just such times of ambiguous social situations that students have realized their finest opportunities for discerning a little more clearly what society, the business of living together, is all about. These historical turning points have contributed immeasurably to the advance of all the social sciences. We learn most about society as it moves and changes, especially when these changes are speeded up. Social change is clearly a major theme in southern life.

In the view presented in this volume, change exists primarily, but not entirely, in continuity. The assumption is that the persistence of social structure and of cultural patterns present the primary clues as to what the South will be like in the foreseeable future. The changes already under way and the sectors within which they are taking place constitute together the best available base line from which to view the development of the future. When one considers the South from the earliest days to the present, one notes that there has been a clearly discernible structural continuity; yet there are many significant differences in the kinds of social, political, and economic arrangements prevailing in contrast to even the very recent past. Where does the change come? This is an empirical question and within this volume it has been approached in that manner. Chapters II through XXI present analyses of continuities and change in specific sectors or aspects of the southern region. Chapter XXII constitutes a general interpretation of the prevailing patterns of change against the background of the established social order. Collectively, the various analyses presented in this volume constitute a bench mark appraisal of one region as a social system in continuity and change within the framework of the broader society.

John C. McKinney
Edgar T. Thompson

Duke University

THE SOUTH IN CONTINUITY AND CHANGE

I. CONTINUITY AND CHANGE IN SOCIO-LOGICAL PERSPECTIVE / John C. McKinney

Clearly visible changes are taking place with discernible impact in the South. Demographic and ecological change, economic development, urbanization, elaboration of transportation and communication facilities, innovation in agricultural enterprise and style of life, the expanded role of scientific research and development, industrial and technological change, political transitions, increased differentiation of the occupational structure, alterations in race relations, and the expanding scale of enterprise and scope of responsibility of education are sectors within which change is not only visible but of general concern. They are all of functional relevance to the persistence and development of the South as a region.

However, these changes are taking place within the well-established framework of a social order. The primary institutions persist, and in the most fundamental ways the old modes of behavior survive in modified form. Beliefs, values, and sentiments from out of the past are perpetuated in a more differentiated role and institutional structure. With its more highly differentiated and complex social organization, the increasingly heterogeneous South of today maintains a stability of behavioral form and social relationship even as new social perspectives and arrangements continue to evolve. The South, of course, is not unique in this respect, since this is a characteristic of all persistent social systems. Indeed, it is merely an example of the dual problem that societies, and sociology as the study of society, have faced throughout their histories. The problem of the relationship between social order and change is persistent, and it is not only a problem of vast practical significance to any social system, but constitutes the highest level theoretical and empirical problem of the academic disciplines concerned with social life. Before the specific analyses of salient aspects of the South in continuity and change are undertaken in the following chapters, a brief analysis of the sociological perspective with respect to the general phenomena of continuity and change would seem to be in order.

1

The behavioral sciences in general approach the analysis of the behavior of living organisms through an "action" frame of reference.[1] Behavior is perceived as it takes place in situations, is conducted in terms of anticipated states of affairs, is motivated, and is normatively regulated. In other words, human beings act in situations including relevant aspects of the physical and social world, orient their behavior toward objectives or goals, expend energy or effort in carrying out their action and hence demonstrate "motivation," and conduct themselves in an orderly fashion, thereby indicating "regulation" or the normative orientation of behavior.

Sociology is just one of the behavioral sciences and as such has its own particular focal point of analysis. The fundamental datum for the sociologist is interaction. In the generic sense, interaction refers to reciprocal and interdependent behavior between two or more components in a situation. Traditionally, sociologists restrict their attention to interaction among human beings. This type of interaction is unique in that it takes place through communication by means of symbolic behavior. For interaction to take place, there must be a plurality of persons, there must be reciprocal action between them, and communication through signs and symbols must take place. Moreover, interaction has a "duration" or time dimension, and this is a continuity possessing a past, present, and future. Insofar as a future is necessarily involved, an anticipated state of affairs (consequences, goals, or ends) in part determines the character of the ongoing action. Consequently, interaction will have an "object," whether or not it is in view by the participating actors or by an independent observer, which cannot lie in the separate behaviors of the individuals involved, but lies in the reciprocal action itself. Therefore, interaction cannot be explained

1. For representative contributions to the delineation of the action frame of reference, see: Talcott Parsons, *The Structure of Social Action* (Glencoe: The Free Press, 1949); Florian Znaniecki, *Method of Sociology* (New York: Farrar and Rinehart, 1934); R. M. MacIver, *Social Causation* (Boston: Ginn, 1942); and Talcott Parsons and E. A. Shils (eds.), *Toward A General Theory of Action* (Cambridge: Harvard University Press, 1951). For historical delineation, see R. C. Hinkle, "Antecedents of the Action Orientation in American Sociology Before 1935," *American Sociological Review*, 28 (October, 1963), 705-715; and for recent critical commentary, see J. F. Scott, "The Changing Foundations of the Parsonian Action Scheme," *American Sociological Review*, 28 (October, 1963), 716-735.

solely in terms of unit acts performed by participating actors, but stands as a legitimate order of existence in its own right.

Having postulated the preceding with regard to action and interaction, it is necessary to propose further that interaction can develop certain uniformities over time and hence become systematized by the structuring of action. Structure refers to the established patterns of interaction that tend to persist. Expressed differently, structure is a general term having reference to all those attributes of interaction which enable one to view the relationships involved as composite or complex wholes made up of interdependent parts. In brief, behavioral systems emerge out of interaction, and we typify these as social systems. Just as all other disciplines of scientific orientation, sociology is concerned with the orderliness or uniformities involved in its particular class of phenomena, and it finds this order in the social system. The problems that cluster around the development, maintenance, and modification of that order may all be typified as problems of social change.

The social system is the central notion of what is commonly referred to as structural-functional theory.[2] Parsons has defined the social system in bare essentials as consisting of "a plurality of individual actors interacting with each other in a situation which has at least a physical or environmental aspect, actors who are motivated in terms of a tendency to the 'optimization of gratification' and whose relation to their situations, including each other,

2. "Structural-functionalism" is in most respects indistinguishable from general sociological theory. Its primary importance apparently lies in the fact that it focuses attention on social systems. Much of the critical literature refers to "structural analysis," "functionalism," "structural-functionalism," and "social systems analysis." These must all be understood as all of a piece. We view them as a continuity of development with systems analysis presupposing the contributions of the necessary but less developed forms of analysis. In brief, structural-functionalism is viewed as incipient systems analysis.

For representative presentations of many of the major theoreticians contributing to this development, see: Talcott Parsons *et al.* (eds.), *Theories of Society* (2 vols.; Glencoe: The Free Press, 1961); and C. P. Loomis and Z. K. Loomis, *Modern Social Theories* (Princeton: D. Van Nostrand, 1961). For a "classic" presentation, see Talcott Parsons, *The Social System* (Glencoe: The Free Press, 1951). For relevant views, see R. K. Merton, *Social Theory and Social Structure* (rev. ed.; Glencoe: The Free Press, 1957); Walter Buckley, "Structural-functional Analysis in Modern Sociology," in Howard Becker and Alvin Boskoff (eds.), *Modern Sociological Theory* (New York: Dryden Press, 1957); Kingsley Davis, "The Myth of Functional Analysis as a Special Method in Sociology and Anthropology," *American Sociological Review*, 24 (December, 1959), 757-773; Bernard Barber, "Structural-Functional Analysis: Some Problems and Misunderstandings," *American Sociological Review*, 21 (April, 1956), 129-135; and Harold Fallding, "Functional Analysis in Sociology," *American Sociological Review*, 28 (February, 1963), 5-13.

is defined and mediated in terms of a system of culturally structured and shared symbols."[3] Stating it somewhat differently, Sorokin indicates that the social system exists in the "meaningful interaction of two or more human individuals . . . by which one party tangibly influences the overt actions or state of mind of the other."[4]

In the abstract sense, a social system may be perceived at any level—from the direct, face-to-face, personal interaction of two actors up to the indirect, enormously interlinked, and impersonal interaction of a society. The concept of the social system can be used to make explicable and intelligible the behavior involved in such diverse spheres as familial, community, educational, religious, occupational, political, and military organizations. Or it can be used in a more concrete and localized sense to analyze such social entities as a specific family, fraternity chapter, rural school, friendship clique, factory, platoon, program, etc. A part of the efficacy of the concept lies in the fact that the analytic observer is able to move from the particular to the general and back again. It is equally legitimate to examine both American society and the relationship of a physician and his patient as behavioral social systems. With equal justification, one can turn his attention to the Catholic Church or to a concretely representative component of that church by means of the concept of systems. When the term "region" is used in the sociological rather than strictly geographical sense, one is in effect imputing at least some of the characteristics of system to it and thereby distinguishing it as an entity within a broader context. When one speaks of the South in other than the locational sense, the implication is that there are certain behavioral and interactive patterns that make it visibly different from other regions, despite the fact that, in the most fundamental ways, people living in the region are part of the broader society.

When the behavior of many people living together is examined as a system of relationships, it is found to be orderly; it has a pattern. It is the pattern, not the people, which is termed "society." Society is a tissue of reciprocal activity, differentiated into a variable number of systems, some of them quite distinct, highly structured, and persistent, others not so directly traceable but instead amor-

3. Talcott Parsons, *The Social System*, pp. 5-6.
4. P. A. Sorokin, *Society, Culture, and Personality* (New York: Harper and Brothers, 1947), p. 40.

phous and transient, and all are interlinked to such a degree that one sees different systems according to the perspective taken. Whatever system one is viewing, however, whether it be the "master" system (society) or any of its component subsystems (region, community, family, etc.), the elements which constitute it as a social system remain the same. That is, society and its parts are not made of different stuff; on the contrary, certain persistent elements appear at any level of orderly interaction. As a consequence, these elements may be conceived of as being organic components of social systems and thus be utilized as the basis for analysis of social behavior in general.

A distinction must be made between the social system as an intellectual construct or "model" and social systems as "going concerns." All systems of "real life," e.g., a particular society, community, corporation, or family, are open systems. They are interacting with their environment, which includes other social systems, in many and varied ways. Empirically we recognize that these "interactive foci" or "relational clusters" which we view as social systems are always involved with and interlinked with other social systems. Their autonomy and isolation are always relative rather than absolute, and *de facto* they are always, to varying degrees and in widely varied ways, a part of a more extensive network of social relationships within which they are nested. For purposes of analysis, however, it is necessary to assume that in the application of the intellectual construct "social system" to particular real life systems, the operation of the system is affected only by specifiable conditions previously established in the environment and by relations among the elements of the system obtaining at the time of the analysis. The domain of relevance of the construct social system is on the one hand broad enough to encompass all relational clusters conceivable as social systems despite variations in type, and on the other hand always so delimited that it never completely or perfectly represents the complexities, actualities, and uniqueness of any social system as an active going concern. There is nothing unusual about this, since it is in the nature of all constructs and analysis. However, a failure consistently to recognize this has resulted in the imputation of certain difficulties to sociological analysis, particularly with reference to the problem of conceptualizing and explaining social change, that are not inherent in sociological analysis but, on the contrary, are reflective of the stage of development of that analysis. This matter will be examined in greater detail after further explication of the social system.

For most purposes, the most significant analytical unit of the social system is the role, of which role expectations are the primary ingredient. Role may be defined as that organized sector of an actor's orientation which constitutes and defines his participation in an interactive process.

Each individual is involved as a participant in a plurality of patterned interactive relationships. This participation revolves around the two reciprocal perspectives inherent in interaction. Each participating individual is an object of orientation, and insofar as this object significance derives from the individual's position in the social relationship, it is a status significance. Each individual is also oriented toward other actors, and in this capacity is not an object, but is acting and therefore acting a role. The structure of the social system is composed of a network of reciprocal role relationships.

Roles, of course, vary in their degree of institutionalization and the degree to which they are common to members of the society at large. A pattern governing action in a social system may be considered institutionalized insofar as it defines the main modes of the legitimately expected behavior of the persons acting in the relevant social roles, and insofar as conformity with these expectations is of structural significance to the social system. Parsons conceives of institutions as constituting the main link between social structure and the actor, in that they are at the same time related both to the functional needs of actors and to those of the system.[5] The link centers on the normative-voluntaristic aspect of the structure of action. The roles that individuals play in a social system are defined in terms of goals and norms. From the point of view of the actor, his role is defined by the normative expectations of the members of the group as they are formulated in the cultural tradition.

These expectations are always an aspect of any situation within which an actor is acting. His conformity or deviation brings conse-

5. Talcott Parsons, *Essays in Sociological Theory* (Glencoe: The Free Press, 1949), pp. 34-36.

quences in the form of approval and reward or condemnation and punishment. These expectations are not only aspects of culture; they are internalized as aspects of the actor's personality. In the process of socialization, the actor internalizes, to varying degrees, the standards of the group; they become motivating forces in his own conduct independent of external sanctions. The relation between role expectations and sanctions is a reciprocal one. Sanctions to the actor are role expectations to alter, and vice versa. Their institutionalization is always a matter of degree based upon the factors affecting the actual degree of sharing values and standards and those determining the motivational commitment to the fulfilment of expectations. Institutional behavior cannot be conceived of in terms of a rational model or self-interest terms, but it can be said that any individual can seek his own self-interest only by conforming to some degree to the institutionalized expectations. In social structure, then, one has a system of patterned expectations defining the *proper* behavior of actors in specified roles. This system is positively enforced both by the individual's own motives for conformity and by the sanctions of others. These well-established patterns of expectations in the perspective of a social system are our institutions. These institutions constitute the structurally stable element of social systems, and their prime function lies in defining the roles of the constituent individuals. Viewed functionally, institutionalized roles constitute the mechanisms by which varied human tendencies become integrated into a system capable of dealing with the problems of a society and its members.

2

Of all the critical charges leveled at the structural-functional or systems analysis approach, the most persistent and most frequently voiced charge is that this approach is indifferent to or incapable of handling change or problems of change. For instance, in a recent survey of theories of change, Martindale has suggested that theorists working from that perspective have "treated social and cultural change as of little general significance."[6] The most cursory review of the literature would indicate that this charge is manifestly off

6. Don Martindale, *Social Life and Cultural Change* (Princeton: D. Van Nostrand, 1962), p. 2.

the mark, or at least seriously overstated. Its significance lies not in its validity, but in the fact that this view is not at all uncommon.

In a recent polemic advancing the "historicist" position and advocating the primacy of a "conflict" model in the assessment of change, Dahrendorf claimed that recent theoretical approaches in sociology have tended to analyze social structure in terms of immobility and have consequently assumed a utopian image of society. He suggests that overconcern with the social system has dulled our vision of change and stunted our problem consciousness. He comments that: "The extent to which the social system model has influenced even our thinking about social change and has marred our vision in this important area of problems is truly remarkable."[7]

In arguing the case for historical analysis, Bock has expressed the view that structural-functionalism is inadequate as an approach to the analysis of change on the basis of its premise that processes of change are deducible from an analysis of order or structure. He asserts that this premise or conviction stems from a reluctance to accept time and place events as classifiable data for the study of both persistence and change. Being hampered by an orientation that encourages the derivation of sources of change from the nature of the thing changing, structural-functionalism is not oriented toward the discernment of sources of change in happenings. Rather, Bock takes the view that "Processes of change are conceptual arrangeabilities of events."[8]

In criticizing the adequacy of the functional approach in dealing with social change, Geertz made the following succinct comment: "The emphasis on systems in balance, on social homeostasis, and on timeless structural pictures, leads to a bias in favor of 'well-integrated' societies in a stable equilibrium and to a tendency to emphasize the functional aspects of a people's usages and customs rather than their disfunctional implications."[9]

7. Ralf Dahrendorf, "Out of Utopia: Toward a Reorientation of Sociological Analysis," *American Journal of Sociology*, 64 (September, 1958), 126. For a similar view, see Evon Z. Vogt, "On the Concepts of Structure and Process in Cultural Anthropology," *American Anthropologist*, 62 (February, 1960), 18-33.

8. K. E. Bock, "Evolution, Function, and Change," *American Sociological Review*, 28 (April, 1963), 229. For a more detailed exposition of the historical view, see his provocative *The Acceptance of Histories* (Berkeley: University of California Press, 1956). Also see Howard Becker, *Through Values to Social Interpretation* (Durham: Duke University Press, 1950).

9. Clifford Geertz, "Ritual and Social Change," *American Anthropologist*, 59 (February, 1957), 32.

Critics have also claimed that structural-functional analysis is couched in terms too general to explain the specific directions of change in any concrete society. Moreover, they aver, such specificity is beyond the province of structural analysis; such a mode of analysis can explain any concrete change only by reference to broadly general and hence inconclusive and inadequate causes or to forces or factors external to the system.[10]

In his editorial introduction to the recent Loomis and Loomis analysis of the sociological theories of Howard Becker, Kingsley Davis, George C. Homans, Robert K. Merton, Talcott Parsons, Pitirim Sorokin, and Robin Williams, Moore made the following cogent comment on the "style" of their approach:

> There are here no radical behaviorists, who "have made up their windpipes that they have no minds," or attitudes and aspirations. Yet they strike me as a rather "conservative" group with regard to the larger shape of things social. Fearing, perhaps, the "group mind" fallacy, the theorists seem to depict society as a kind of by-product of mindless functional necessities plus mindful and moti-vated individual actions almost solely at the interpersonal level. The "common value system" attributed to societies seems to have no politically powerful spokesmen, although we know better. And the values seem not to include deliberate, planned, and large-scale social change. The reality of such change tends to be treated as "exog-enous," an unpredicted datum, and the equilibrium model used to trace through systemic consequences. The pursuit of consequences is not a trivial kind of labor. However, it does fall short of large issues—issues of scientific predictability as well as such practical questions as human survival and the capacity to tolerate change at explosive velocities—presented in the factual world of contemporary experience. Social revolutions no longer just happen, if they ever did. They are planned and executed, despite the real resistances that equilibrium models of society help to identify but not to protect.[11]

Since many of the most productive and distinguished theorists of our era are referred to in the preceding comment, it is indeed re-

10. See, for instance, Ralf Dahrendorf, op. cit., pp. 115-127; K. E. Bock, "Evolu-tion, Function, and Change," pp. 229-237; R. P. Dore, "Function and Cause," American Sociological Review, 26 (December, 1961), 843-853; Wayne Hield, "The Study of Change in Social Science," British Journal of Sociology, 5 (March, 1954), 1-10; David Lockwood, "Some Remarks on the Social System," British Journal of Sociology, 7 (June, 1956), 134-146.

11. W. E. Moore, "Editorial Introduction," to C. P. Loomis and Z. K. Loomis, op. cit., p. xxiv.

vealing with respect to the current state of affairs in sociological theory.

In recent years, a series of analyses and commentaries has appeared in the literature that may be typified as "revisionist" or "constructive" with respect to the capabilities of structural-functional theory in handling change. These have ranged from quite defensive statements with respect to underestimation of present capability to suggestions for reformulations and new syntheses within the framework of existent theory. Implicitly or explicitly these analysts have accepted the main trend of the development of sociological theory, and they have been exploring ways of extending and specifying theoretical capabilities with respect to problems of change.

In a recent analysis, Cancian focused on the problem of "formalizing" functional analysis in order better to adapt it to handling change. This analysis was based on the earlier presentation by Nagel of a formal definition of functional systems which, in turn, was based on Merton's explication of "manifest and latent" functions. Nagel did not explicitly consider the problem of functional analysis of change. His formal definition of a functional system, however, provided Cancian with a basis for outlining several specific ways in which functional analysis can be utilized in the study of change. Moreover, it led to the conclusion that most of the arguments about the so-called static nature of such analysis are based on semantic confusion and unimaginative and incorrect methods.[12] Fundamentally the burden was placed on the further development of methodology.

On the basis of an analysis of the social and political structure of traditional, centralized empires and of the development of religions within them, Eisenstadt has argued that the institutionalization of any social system creates possibilities for specific and definable types of change, which develop not randomly but in specific directions primarily set by the process of institutionalization itself. "Our major point is that the institutionalization of any social system—be it political, economic or a system of social stratification

12. Francesca Cancian, "Functional Analysis of Change," *American Sociological Review*, 25 (December, 1960), 818-827. Also see Ernest Nagel, "A Formalization of Functionalism," in his *Logic Without Metaphysics* (Glencoe: The Free Press, 1956), pp. 247-283; and R. K. Merton, *op. cit.*, pp. 19-84.

or of any collectivity or role—creates in its wake the possibilities of change."[13] He reiterates the long-established but frequently overlooked view that this creates the possibility of "anti-systems," or groups developing within the system with negative orientations toward its premises and values. Eisenstadt indicates that while the nature and strength of such anti-systems will vary, as between different institutional (i.e., religious, economic, etc.) systems and between different types within each, and while they often may remain latent or inactive for prolonged periods of time, they nevertheless constitute important foci of change under facilitative conditions.[14] Perhaps the primary achievement of the Eisenstadt analysis was the effective illustration of the combination of systematic institutional analysis with the analysis of change in showing that the explication of change is inherent in the examination of concrete societies or parts thereof as social systems.[15] Hence again pointing out that a systematic structural analysis is a prerequisite for anything approximating a compelling analysis of change.

As indicated previously, Bock is primarily a critic of the structural-functional approach. In his critique, however, he has issued the fundamentally important reminder that structure is also a temporal phenomenon. "Processes of persistence of tradition and processes of change in tradition are alike historical processes."[16] In a similar noting of the "ahistorical" character of modern sociology and sociologists, Shils makes the comment that: "On the whole, it may be said that neither concrete empirical sociology nor theoretical sociology has been especially well endowed with a 'sense of the past.' "[17] He takes note of a deficient appreciation of pastness as evidenced in the predominant conception of modern society as cut loose from tradition. In this he is critical of the relative absence of

13. S. N. Eisenstadt, "Institutionalization and Change," *American Sociological Review*, 29 (April, 1964), 235.

14. *Ibid.*, p. 246. See also A. W. Gouldner, "Reciprocity and Authority in Functional Theory," in Llewellyn Gross (ed.), *Symposium on Sociological Theory* (Evanston: Row Peterson, 1959), pp. 241-247; and Gideon Sjoberg, "Contradictory Functional Requirements and Social Systems," *Journal of Conflict Resolution*, 4 (June, 1960), 198-258.

15. S. N. Eisenstadt, *op. cit.*, pp. 235-247. See also W. E. Moore, "A Reconsideration of Theories of Social Change," *American Sociological Review*, 25 (December, 1960), 810-818.

16. K. E. Bock, "Evolution, Function, and Change," p. 236.

17. E. A. Shils, "The Calling of Sociology," in Talcott Parsons *et al.* (eds.), *Theories of Society*, p. 1427.

any sociological treatment of the nature and mechanisms of tradition. He goes on to make the following provocative comment:

> Pastness as the property of an object, of an individual action, of a symbol, or of a collectivity, has not yet been accorded a place in sociological theory. It need not remain so; and the correction of the formulations of the theory of action in a way that would do it justice should not be a hard task. The adaptation of the larger theory will be harder. Like much in the general theory, it will depend as much on a matrix of sensibility as on the deductive powers.[18]

Despite the superficial similarity of their approaches and the concurrence of opinion as to the inadequacy of treatment of "the temporal factor" in contemporary sociological theory, Bock and Shils actually take radically opposed positions with respect to the corrective. In the final analysis, Bock is advocating a reconversion of sociology into "history" and historical procedure. Shils, on the other hand, is suggesting the necessity of incorporating and coming to grips with the temporal dimension in systematic theory.

In a recent serious attempt to achieve a new synthesis of theoretical approaches to change, van den Berge tried to show that both functionalism and the Hegelian–Marxian dialectic present one-sided, but complementary and reconcilable, views of society. By an examination of what he conceives of as the basic postulates of functionalism and the dialectic, he imputes certain strengths and weaknesses to each which suggest a reformulation of both in minimal form. Van den Berge sees the problem as one of arriving at a theory of society that achieves an adequate balance between stability and the various sources of change, between consensus and conflict, and between equilibrium and disequilibrium. After primarily examining the Parsons' version of structural-functionalism and the Dahrendorf version of the dialectic, he concludes that the two theoretical approaches show promise of a fruitful synthesis.[19]

One of the points of convergence suggested by van den Berge is that functionalism and the dialectic share an evolutionary notion of social change. Bock has referred to the functionalist's return to evolutionism. This is an inaccurate appraisal, for structural-functionalism never left the broad framework of evolutionary thought.

18. *Ibid.*, p. 1428.
19. P. L. van den Berge, "Dialectic and Functionalism: Toward a Theoretical Synthesis," *American Sociological Review*, 28 (October, 1963), 695-705.

A distinction must be made between the discrediting or destruction of specific evolutionary formulations or theories (organicism, uni-linear development, progress, etc.) in which structural-function-alism has played a fundamental role, and abdication of the general evolutionary view which structural-functionalism has never done. Indeed, in its evolution from earlier more fragmentary forms, social systems analysis has historically taken the evolutionary view seriously. The massive two-volume *Theories of Society*, representa-tive of the major individual contributions toward a theory of society and accompanied by relevant commentary, clearly indicates this historical stance. More important with respect to the problem under consideration here, Naegele makes the following summarizing com-ment: "The combination of an interest in the conditions of stability with an interest in the direction of transformation of social arrange-ments is made possible by the distinctions, implicit or explicit, made by the thinkers represented in this Reader."[20]

This assembly of the classical theoretical approaches to society (in the *Theories of Society* volumes), however, carries a theme that is even more centrally relevant to the problem of a sociological perspective for continuity and change. That theme, which per-sistently runs through this literature constituting the foundations of sociological theory, is that of the complication of society and the inadequacy of any one model for its representation. Sociologists should not have to be reminded of the complexity of societal life, but in effect that is what this compilation does. Of course, this has particular relevance to the conceptualization of change. Change as variously conceptualized in cycles, spirals, straight lines, ascend-encies, discontinuous alternation, and dialectic zigzags leaves us with a sense of inadequacy and a low predictive ability. We have witnessed the downfall or limited applicability of the global, com-prehensive, simplifying theories. The sweeping, broad-gauge, evolu-tionary or cyclical theories have provided a relatively poor fit to data and have been of little explanatory value with respect to the changes of primary concern in contemporary life. An almost total rejection and abandonment of single-factor explanations, uniform determinisms, and external (non-social) causes have also occurred.

20. K. D. Naegele, "Introduction" to Part V, "Social Change," in Talcott Parsons *et al.* (eds.), *Theories of Society*, p. 1213.

The rich and colorful vocabulary of change—e.g., "growth," "decay," "progress," "development," "lag," "attrition," "revolution," "flux"—has been shown to be sadly deficient with respect to many problems of change. The complexity of society and its processes of change remain even more visible today against the backdrop of these historical efforts to capture change conceptually in one model or another.

With regard to this problem, Moore remarks that:

> Between the global theories, which explain too little because they attempt too much, and the relativistic position that views all change as unique, there is a large middle territory. Within that spacious terrain one may note the standardized internal dynamics of groups of various types, and identify the sources, forms, directions, and rates of change in types and segments of social systems. If the resulting theory is not exactly simple, neither is it wholly simple-minded.[21]

This statement leads us to the crux of the problem responsible for the rapid recent increase of anxiety, pessimism, and self-deprecation characterizing the many critics and revisionists of contemporary sociological theory. On the one hand, structural-functionalism—e.g., incipient social systems analysis—has dominated the theoretical scene for several decades. The main drive, positive effort, and successful achievements of sociological theory have been concentrated in the buildup toward the capability of systems analysis. On the other hand, the theoreticians who have been most explicitly and continuously involved in that buildup have given limited specialized attention to the problem of transformation of systems, e.g., to problems of continuity and change. The primary concentration has been on the structure of social systems, secondary attention has been devoted to function, and limited attention has been paid to change per se. The theoretical drive toward systems analysis has contributed to a paradoxical situation in the discipline. First of all, it is from the perspective of this buildup (along with the accompanying empirical accumulation) that the deficiencies, distortions, and general inadequacies of all extant theories of change have been noted. Secondly, the positive achievements of systems analysis make possible, and sensible, all of the current rash of criticism pointing out deficiencies in the handling of problems of

21. W. E. Moore, "A Reconsideration of Theories of Social Change," p. 811.

change. Theoretical concentration has been on the system per se, and yet, in the eyes of many, if not most, sociologists, the problem of change constitutes the fundamental problem of society. Therefore, the view prevails that any theory of society or its aspects or components should be competent to deal with problems of change. This raises the question as to whether social systems analysis (and its historical antecedents—structural analysis, functionalism, and structural-functionalism) is really as feeble (currently and potentially) in the area of change as it is reputed to be and leads us to further consideration regarding this approach. We will examine this problem by setting forth what appear to be the basic postulates of social systems analysis.[22]

3

Societies may be looked at holistically as systems of interrelated parts. Hagen has described the historical development of systems analysis as follows:

As judged by the history of the physical, biological, and social sciences, study in any field is apt to begin with a none-too-ordered description of phenomena in the field, followed by a cataloguing of them on bases that seem to make sense. As understanding grows, the systems of classification become more closely related to the functioning of interacting elements. Gradually, generalizations about functioning are reached which are useful in predicting future events. As the generalizations gain rigor, they take the form of analytical models of the behavior of the elements being studied. They take the form that is of systems. When they do, a great increase in rigor and power is achieved.[23]

This is, in effect, a statement of an evolutionary view of the methodological development of the scientific disciplines. The developing capability of sociology with respect to the fruitful utilization of the intellectual construct "social system" is simply an aspect

22. It is not suggested that these are *the* basic postulates in any absolute or exhaustive sense. It is suggested, however, that any more extensive or refined listing would have to include these or variant forms of them accounting for the sectors which they represent. Attention is also directed toward the list of postulates ascribed to structural-functionalism by van den Berge. There is considerable overlap in the two sets, although our concern is more directly with social systems. See P. L. van den Berge, *op. cit.*, p. 696.

23. E. E. Hagen, *On the Theory of Social Change* (Homewood: Dorsey Press, 1962), p. 4. Also see his "Analytical Models in the Study of Social Systems," *American Journal of Sociology*, 67 (September, 1961), 144-151.

of the broadly based extension of capability of the whole complex of scientifically oriented disciplines. The further extension of that capability is a necessary working assumption.

Any degree of complexity in a society implies that there are interactive foci within it which also may profitably be looked at as systems. The concept of the social system can be used at any level from the dyadic relationship to the society at large. It is the structuring of the interaction so that it has some minimal degree of autonomy and social organization that justifies this flexible use of the notion of system.

All real-life systems are "open" systems in that they always have interchanges and relationships with other systems and the environment in general. Some degree of closure is characteristic of all systems, and they vary widely in the extent to which they are closed. None, however, is entirely closed. All systems are relational foci clustered within a larger network of relationships. As such they are accessible, to varying degrees, to input through the linkages outside the system. The phenomenon of diffusion constitutes the most obvious case.

Social systems have a temporal dimension. Social systems are constituted out of symbolic interaction. Interaction has a duration or time dimension, and this is a continuity possessing a past, present, and future. As these interactions are stabilized into institutional arrangements, the structure of the interaction can persist independent of any particular individuals. It is this persistence through time that gives our social institutions a degree of control over the future of any social system. A social system always projects both ways from the present. Goals, objectives, aspirations, and institutionalized ways of doing things constitute the core of projection into the future. Tradition, custom, accumulated knowledge, established values, and our institutional arrangements constitute the projection into the past. For any persistent social system the projection into the past tends to be much greater (of longer duration) than any reasonably predictable projection into the future. In other words, our goals and aspirations with respect to the future tend to be for the short run, in contrast to the long run of history. This in itself is ample enough reason to require the inclusion of the past as a factor in general sociological formulations.

Social systems have a dialectic dimension. There are conflicts and contradictions inherent in social structure. The very old tradition of typing societies or relationships antithetically, e.g., *Gemeinschaft und Gesellschaft,* sacred-secular, mechanical-organic, etc., is reflective of a recognition of the coexistence of fundamentally different principles of social organization and normative order within the same system.[24] The primary utility of these polar-type labels does not lie in the ability to attach one or another of them to a system as a blanket description; rather, it lies in the fact that through the paired opposites one can remain sensitized to the alternatives (and the range they encompass) persistent within the system. Predominant institutionalization of one alternative does not dispel its counterpart. The presence of incipient or established anti-systems within a social system constitutes a fundamental dynamic of change.

Social systems vary along the dimension of structural and functional differentiation. Again our lead comes from the polar typologies. All of them, e.g., rural-urban, primitive-civilized, status-contract, developed-underdeveloped, etc., carry with them the notion of the direct relationship between differentiation and complexity. The greater the differentiation the greater the complexity of the system. The greater the complexity the greater the probability of further differentiation. In his "milestone" work on social change, Smelser makes the following reference to differentiation:

> This implicit concept underlies much of our discourse about social development. We seldom ask, however, whether the *very process* of passing from a less differentiated to a more differentiated social structure possesses definite regularities, and whether the sequence itself produces phenomena which can be analyzed systematically. It is my assertion that such regularities do exist, and can be extracted from societies in flux.[25]

The work that Smelser has done along these lines to date has had a significant impact upon our notions of general structural change. *A given state of the social system presupposes all previous states,*

24. See J. C. McKinney and C. P. Loomis, "The Typological Tradition," in J. S. Roucek (ed.), *Contemporary Sociology* (New York: Philosophical Library, 1958), pp. 557-582. For a different but related perspective, see Reinhard Bendix and Bennett Berger, "Images of Society and Problems of Concept Formation in Sociology," in Llewellyn Gross (ed.), *Symposium on Sociological Theory,* pp. 92-118.

25. N. J. Smelser, *Social Change in Industrial Revolution* (Chicago: University of Chicago Press, 1959), pp. 1-2.

and hence contains them, if only in residual or modified form.
This might well be referred to as the principle of structural continuity. Social process is the dynamic aspect of any given social relation. If a social system is a network of social relations, it is also a flow of relationships through time. It follows, then, that history is a continuity of such relationships, an evolutionary process in which, similar but not identical to the organic world, nature makes no leaps and in which the most difficult act is the attempt to break with the past. As long as the system persists, rather than moving into extinction, factors of both endogenous and exogenous change have operated within the framework of social order characterizing the system.

Change is immanent in the social system. Sorokin has commented on the principle of immanent change as follows:

> As long as it exists and functions, any sociocultural system generates consequences which are not the results of the external factors to the system, but the consequences of the existence of the system and its activities. As such, they must be imputed to it, regardless of whether they are good or bad, desirable or not, intended or not by the system. One of the specific forms of this immanent generation of consequences is an incessant change of the system itself, due to its existence and activity.[26]

Change is inherent in social systems since they are action systems. A great deal of behavior is future-oriented in the sense that it is directed toward objectives, gratifications, and the achievement of aspirations. At the level of individual behavior and role relations it involves many confrontations, recombinations, and adaptations. At a more complex level, one can refer to the inherently unstable condition of a social system consequent upon imperfect socialization and social control, ambiguities and looseness of role specification, conflict between institutions organized on different orientational bases (e.g., religious, economic, political, etc.), and the process of structural differentiation. Moreover, one can again note the conflict and change rooted in the process of institutionalization when it is viewed as a social form of problem-solving.

All systems are subject to exogenous (extra-systemic) change.

26. P. A. Sorokin, *Social and Cultural Dynamics* (Boston: Porter Sargent, 1957), p. 639.

Here again reference is to the fact that all persistent social systems are open systems. This means that no social system is entirely in control of its own present and future. By virtue of its interrelationships and interdependencies with other systems, and by virtue of its existence within a general environment, a social system is subject to "inputs" and "influences." The specification and tracing out of these is essentially an empirical task and one of fundamental importance in the assessment of rate and direction of change within a system.[27]

Social systems tend to persist in a moving equilibrium. Davis makes the succinct comment that: "It is only in terms of equilibrium that most sociological concepts make sense. Either tacitly or explicitly anyone who thinks about society tends to use the notion. . . . It is usually phrased in static terms, but as soon as the element of time is added it alludes to a moving equilibrium."[28] The model of the dynamic equilibrium has change built into it, although not to the degree that is satisfying to those seeking a theory of change. However, it appears to be not only logically necessary, but empirically correct to speak of the equilibrating tendency of social systems. Moreover, it seems empirically warranted to speak of a long-range tendency towards integration within systems. Dysfunctions, tensions, stress, deviance, variance, inventions, innovations, diffusions, and differentiation itself tend to be dealt with by the established institutional structure and normative order. Adjustive or adaptive responses are made within the system, and hence change tends to occur gradually (in the historical sense of time), although by no means evenly in all sectors of the system. The very fact that a system is always differentiated to some degree implies that change will not take place with the same degree of probability in all sectors. We are empirically well aware of the fact that change tends to take place much more rapidly in the area of technological development than in the ideological sphere, in economic affairs in comparison to religious, etc. The assumption is typically made in the equilibrium model that any change has repercussions through-

27. For an extensive examination of the research in diffusion, see Elihu Katz, M. L. Levin, and Herbert Hamilton, "Traditions of Research on the Diffusion of Innovation," *American Sociological Review*, 28 (April, 1963), 237-252. For an exploration of the "linkages" of systems, see C. P. Loomis, *Social Systems: Essays on Their Persistence and Change* (Princeton: D. Van Nostrand, 1960).
28. Kingsley Davis, *Human Society* (New York: Macmillan, 1949), p. 634.

out the system. This must be understood as a working assumption and not a mechanical law. The direction, rate, and degree of dependent change are empirical problems with respect to any change. The repercussive assumption merely directs attention to the assessment of consequences; it does not in itself indicate anything about the extent of interdependencies involved in any particular change. This remains primarily an empirical problem, although it would undoubtedly be of considerable help to have a more systematic map of the primary sources of change.

The preceding premises and postulates relate to social systems analysis, and only partially to its intellectual precursors, e.g., structuralism, functionalism, and structural-functionalism. To use an evolutionary phrase, the discipline of sociology has now reached a stage in its development wherein it is clearly on the threshold of systems analysis. This is only possible because of the varied contributions of the many "feeder" or subsidiary lines of thought which are convergent with structural-functional theory at the systems level. The historical concentration on the delineation of structure and the widely varied attempts to explicate functionalism must be understood primarily as a phase in the development process of the discipline.

Parsons, for example, takes a much more optimistic view of the disciplinary capacity to deal with problems of change today than at the time he wrote *The Social System*. On the basis of sociological developments in the past few years, he now believes that the problems of social change are

> soluble in empirical-theoretical terms. Above all we have at our disposal a conceptual scheme which is sufficiently developed so that at least at the level of categorization and of problem statement it is approaching the type of closure ... which makes *systematic* analysis of interdependencies possible. We can define the main ranges of variability which are essential for empirical analysis, and the main mechanisms through which variations are propagated through the system. We can quantify to the point of designating deficits and surpluses of inputs and outputs, and here and there we come close to specifying threshold values beyond which equilibrium will break down.[29]

29. Talcott Parsons, "Some Considerations on the Theory of Social Change," *Rural Sociology*, 26 (September, 1961), 238.

4

It is clear that we now have the theoretical ability (or potential), and in many cases the methodological and empirical ability to deal with conflicts, contradictions, deviance, variance, strain, dysfunction, innovation, invention, diffusion, adaptations, and repercussions within the loose framework of structural-functional analysis. As structural-functionalism is, through time and effort, tightened up and transformed into a full-blown style of social systems analysis, one can assume that approaches to these disparate types of problem and change can be better articulated. However, at least for the foreseeable future, one cannot assume that this will result in a general theory of change. On the contrary, the greater likelihood is the fuller development of complementary models of social change, in effect a pluralism of change models all related in one way or another to the structure and function and the maintenance and development of social systems. These will have to reflect the several premises listed above with respect to change and systems analysis, and not merely the equilibrium premise. It may well be that the prime indicator of a movement up to the level of a genuine systems analysis will be that of the developed capacity to handle change in terms of the requirements implicit in the several systemic premises.

One approach and potential model complementary to the well-established equilibrium model is that which is based upon the premise of structural continuity. The lead here comes from Radcliffe-Brown. "The characteristic of any persistent system is that it maintains through a certain lapse of time its structural continuity. The structure of a system is the specific set of relations between its units. The continuity of that structure . . . is a dynamic continuity."[30] The basic assumption is that the past, present, and future are inextricably bound together.[31] Our experience is always experience in passing, which involves extension into other experiences. What has just happened, what is going on, and what is appearing in the future are all implicated in the present situation and give it its

30. A. R. Radcliffe-Brown, *A Natural Science of Society* (Glencoe: The Free Press, 1959), p. 25.
31. This assumption is explicitly developed and elaborated in the work of G. H. Mead. See especially *The Philosophy of the Present* (Chicago: Open Court Publishing Co., 1932).

unique character. There is an interpenetration of what we are going
to do and what we have done into what we are doing. Our ends are
as truly real as our means. Such a view is entirely consonant with
"action" theory.

In passage from the past into the future, the present is constituted by that which is both old and new. This also holds for the
relations between members of a system. For example, a person
belongs to a given social system and has his character conditioned
by his relations to members in that system; when he moves into a
new system, he will carry over something of the nature of the members of the old into the process of readjustment to the new. In a
community the members will carry over their characters as determined in the old order into the readjustment entailed in social
change. A classic example of this is the repeated re-establishment of
an essentially old structure after a purportedly dramatic revolution has taken place in a society.

In this view, change exists primarily, but not entirely, in continuity. The persistence of social structure and cultural patterns
presents the primary clues as to what the South, when viewed as a
social system, will be like in the foreseeable future. The changes
already under way and the sectors within which they are taking
place together constitute the best available base line from which
to view the development of the future. If one considers the South,
from the earliest days to the present, one can see it is still in many
respects the same society. There has been structural continuity, and
yet there are many differences in the kinds of social, political, and
economic arrangements prevailing today in contrast to any earlier
epoch. Where does the change come? We would say that it does not
come precisely anywhere, but literally everywhere. Where one
draws the line is always to some extent arbitrary. This is the familiar
problem that always has to be faced in all history and projection of
social development. Nevertheless, on theoretical grounds it is possible to avoid purely *ad hoc* concerns with change by using the
structural elements of the social system as the primary referents
in the assessment of the significance of change. Moreover, on empirical grounds it is possible to assess saliency.

5

Clearly we do not have a general theory of change if what is meant by this is a theory that will encompass enduring shifts of a whole society from one state to another state. Moreover, such a theory is not "immanent." It is at this point that a statement made by Moore is relevant. "The mention of 'theory of social change' will make most social scientists appear defensive, furtive, guilt-ridden, or frightened. Yet the source of this unease may be in part an unduly awe-stricken regard for the explicitly singular and implicitly capitalized word 'Theory.' "[32] The absence of a theory with a capital "T" may be discomforting, but in no sense is it catastrophic. Several theoretical approaches to change have been developed, and each in its own way is extremely useful. None of them has been more than partially exploited either methodologically or empirically. These theories concern subprocesses of change within and between systems, and none of them claims to encompass the general phenomena of change as such. These subprocesses or aspects of change are of great importance in their own right. Empirically the absence of anything resembling a general theory is neither as important nor as devastating as one might be led to believe by the self-effacing posture of many sociologists with respect to change. Sociology has provided a number of fairly high-level, empirically based, and interdependent propositions concerning social change.[33] It is obvious that we have many treatments of change in the literature which are satisfactory in an empirical sense, as well as theoretically respectable. These are treatments of limited or specified changes within the general system. They represent theorizing with a small "t," and they refer to changes in limited sectors of societal life. In a recent survey, Boskoff described some of these theories and their areas of relevance.[34] The point here is that the search for a theory of social change may continue to contribute a fearsome challenge for the discipline of sociology and to fire the imagination of particular

32. W. E. Moore, "A Reconsideration of Theories of Social Change," p. 810.
33. For a brief, succinct, and yet comprehensive review of established generalizations related to social change, see W. E. Moore, *Social Change* (Englewood Cliffs: Prentice-Hall, 1963). Also note Bernard Berelson and G. A. Steiner, *Human Behavior: An Inventory of Scientific Findings* (New York: Harcourt, Brace and World, 1964), especially pp. 613-619.
34. Alvin Boskoff, "Social Change: Major Problems in the Emergence of Theoretical and Research Foci," in Howard Becker and Alvin Boskoff (eds.), *Modern Sociological Theory*, pp. 260-302.

sociologists, but the absence of such a theory does not deter the sociologist from treating change within systems and between systems in meaningful and theoretically useful ways. Moreover, it is precisely knowledge of change of this order and at this level which is actually or potentially of direct use to those in policy-making and implementation positions with respect to the planning, instigation, and execution of change. The kinds of change that planners and "change agents" are interested in are the kinds of change that sociologists and other social scientists are theoretically and methodologically capable of dealing with.

6

This brings us to another set of considerations. These relate not to the sociologist's ability to theorize about and conduct inquiry into change, but to his role in the management of change. As indicated previously, the problems that cluster around the development, maintenance, and modification of the order characteristic of social systems may all be typified as problems of social change. These are not only problems of theoretical and empirical significance to the sociologist, they are also constitutive of the social problems perceived by and of concern to the members, or some segment of the membership, of society. It is here that the routine or bread-and-butter concerns of the sociologist, indeed all social scientists, and the moral and practical concerns of the public become mutually implicated.

Historically many sociologists have raised serious questions about the nature of the relationship between social scientists and society and the mutual responsibilities involved therein, perhaps none more provocatively than Louis Wirth. Wirth consistently expressed the view that social science cannot be and should not pretend to be disinterested in the problems of the world. It was his contention that a completely disinterested social science could not exist, since the values, beliefs, and rationalizations of the scientist not only influence his choice of frame of reference and problem area, but also influence the selection of relevant data, recording of observations, theoretical and practical inferences drawn, and the manner of presentation of results.[35] Wirth held the view that "with-

35. See Louis Wirth, "Preface" to Karl Mannheim, *Ideology and Utopia*, trans.

out valuations we have no interest, no sense of relevance, or significance and consequently no object."[36] Moreover, more than most sociologists, Wirth was aware of the consequences of ideas. He held that no matter how objective or disinterested one attempts to be, he cannot escape the fact that "every assertion of a 'fact' about the social world touches the interests of some individual group, one cannot even call attention to the existence of certain 'facts' without courting the objections of those whose very *raison d'être* in society rests upon a divergent interpretation of the 'factual' situation."[37]

Consequently, whether the social scientist likes it or not he is involved with practical problems of the ongoing world; and since he is involved, he not only should but must be responsible for the consequences of his research. The implication of this position is that the task of science, particularly social science, should be to help solve the crucial social problems facing man as he lives in this world. Wirth's position was that until social scientists find a method of obtaining answers to critical problems, they cannot expect society to support their endeavors.

Whether or not the individual sociologist accepts the Wirth point of view, and it is clear that many do not, the fact remains that the discipline of sociology, and the other social sciences, has something of value to offer the society which it studies. What it has to offer consists in the aggregate knowledge it has of the structure and function of society and the problems that confront society in its efforts to maintain and develop itself in the process of change. It is clear that this knowledge lies in the public domain, not only nationally, but internationally. Consequently, whether or not the individual scholar wishes to be at the direct service of mankind, it is evident that the aggregate knowledge to which he has contributed is at such service.

If society, and of course any of its component social systems, is to maximize its probability of successfully coping with the problems

---

Louis Wirth and E. A. Shils (New York: Harcourt, Brace, 1936), pp. xii-xxxi; and Louis Wirth, "Ideological Aspects of Social Disorganization," *American Sociological Review*, 5 (August, 1940), 472-482.

36. Letter from Louis Wirth to Gunnar Myrdal, September 29, 1939. Reprinted in part in *American Dilemma* (New York: Harper and Brothers, 1944), II, 1063-1064.

37. Louis Wirth, "Preface" to *Ideology and Utopia*.

confronting it, then it must utilize the best available knowledge in coming to grips with those problems. Coping with problems of continuity and change in part is dependent upon the ability to anticipate, which in turn is based upon the ability to mobilize relevant knowledge. It has long been recognized that the most rational way of confronting the future and the changes involved in it is to plan for it and thus attempt to gain at least some degree of control, however minimal, over the events yet to come. The existent and developing knowledge of the social sciences thus constitutes the basic underpinning of the activity now institutionalized as social planning.

7

"To plan or not to plan is no real issue. Planning even of economic affairs has existed at all levels of our national life, both public and private, since the beginning of our history."[38] Planning is a normal and universal human activity which is manifest in different forms and explicit in varying degree in all persistent social systems. Planning is essentially the attempt to resolve the problems of the future by assessment of future consequences, as implicated in the activities and events of the present and our experience of the past. The process of planning is the process of delaying, organizing, and selecting a response appropriate to the anticipated situation in terms of the known alternative possibilities. Planning, just as any case of mobilization and utilization of knowledge, lies inside the process of conduct. It may be thought of as a process of pointing out; to plan for something is to distinguish it before acting. In this sense planning, insofar as it involves some social unit or organization, is the social analogue of thinking at the individual level. Although a universal human activity, it has become explicit and institutionalized as an activity in its own right only in certain types of social systems. The continuum on which these types fall can be described in terms of the broad polar types, *Gemeinschaft* and *Gesellschaft*.[39]

The mainstream of history of Western society has been one of transition from *Gemeinschaft* to *Gesellschaft* form of organization.

38. C. E. Merriam, "The Possibilities of Planning," *American Journal of Sociology*, 49 (March, 1944), 397.
39. Ferdinand Tönnies, *Community and Society: Gemeinschaft und Gesellschaft*, ed. and trans. C. P. Loomis (East Lansing: Michigan State University Press, 1957).

Essentially this is a move from the relatively undifferentiated, homogeneous, and simple to the more differentiated, heterogeneous, and complex form of general social organization. Clearly this move to the *Gesellschaft*-like social structure has not eliminated the *Gemeinschaft*-like basis and mode of organization of many institutional complexes within the broader and more differentiated societal framework. On the contrary, the persistence of many *Gemeinschaft*-like structures, e.g., family, friendship cliques, accounts for a major dimension of differentiation within the increasingly complex society.

A part of the price for that transition is the loss of the integration characteristic of the *Gemeinschaft* structure. Since the modern sociologist perceives himself primarily as an analyst of society and not as a utopian remodeler of society, then it makes no sense merely to urge a "return to *Gemeinschaft*." A "back to *Gemeinschaft*" movement would be as impotent as most nativistic and romantic movements. The sociologist, perhaps above all others, is convinced that change has to take place within the framework of the existent social structure. This obviously means that the integration of knowledge characteristic of our *Gemeinschaft* era is unattainable. It does not necessarily follow, however, that integration of a different order, integrated knowledge compatible with the present social structure, cannot be obtained. In its various forms and in its reliance on various subspheres of knowledge, planning in effect constitutes the social device for the attainment, however imperfectly, of the integration of existent knowledge and social structure. It is for this reason that planning has become an explicit, visible, and specialized activity within the *Gesellschaft*-like system and within the many subtypes of component social systems clustering toward that end of the polar continuum.

The relationship, in the general if not the operational sense, between planning and structural continuity is clear. Planning involves the attempt to maintain and develop social systems, and hence may be regarded as a rational component of structural continuity. In the small-scale system the planner may simply be one person, whereas in the large-scale system the planner may be an organization in its own right. Whatever the scale of these variations, planning itself, as a type of human activity, can be viewed best as a method of extrapolation. It is a way of speculating as to what a result may be, and then justifying the speculation by means of the result. The most substantial grounds upon which to base such a speculation consist in as complete knowledge as possible of the existent structure, knowledge of the present system as linked to the past. Projections on this basis are little theoretic leaps, but they require an understanding of the social system for which the plans are being made.

In this view planning is neither ivory-tower speculation, intellectual star-gazing, nor utopian thinking. Essentially it is a practical and instrumental activity. Its criteria and style are pragmatic. Although concerned with the instigation, management, and realization of change, it has no general or theoretical problem of change. Critical dissatisfaction with existent theories of change, as described earlier, are matters of irrelevance to the planner and the planning operation. As institutionalized to a high degree in sectors of modern society, planning is always for the short run or for what might be called a "specious present." In the historical sense of time, planning confines itself to very brief periods despite the use of such euphemisms as "long-range planning." Such planning typically has reference to periods in the range of five, ten, or in rare instances, twenty years. Moreover, there is no shortage of basic knowledge and no necessary shortage of data for the conduct of planning for change. On the contrary, there is a vast underuse and frequent misuse of existent relevant knowledge and data. In this regard it is suggested that sociology, like its sister social sciences and despite its theoretical deficiencies with respect to change, has a perspective to offer the planner. However commonplace, pedestrian, and non-esoteric this perspective may seem, it would appear to be essential to the planning process and hence utilitarian.

8

The preceding analysis has been essentially a bimodal exposition. On the one hand it has been an analysis of the prevailing theoretical stance with respect to continuity and change in social systems. On the other hand it has briefly explored the role of the sociologist in the task of lending specific directions to that change. With regard to the former, emphasis has been placed on the fact that we have now reached a stage of development where we are at least on the threshold of systems analysis. This does not imply the immanence of any satisfactory general theory of change. On the contrary, it appears that pluralism is to be the state of affairs for the foreseeable future, and that we will have diverse models which have descriptive and explanatory power with respect to various types or spheres of change. The linkage of the models within the general framework of systems analysis will constitute an important area of articulation in its own right and presumably lead to further theoretical refinements with respect to coping with problems of continuity and change.

Social systems have no more important problem than that of change. Social systems develop by adjusting themselves to the problems before them. How can order and structure be preserved in a system and yet have the necessary changes take place? To bring about change is seemingly to destroy the existent order, and yet systems must change, for change is implicit in the action that constitutes society. How can society find a method for changing its own institutions? The answer here is in the pragmatic tradition. The view is taken that planning is a natural type of behavior and is manifest in even the most elementary forms of persistent social life. In the *Gesellschaft*-like or instrumental system, planning is elevated to the status of a method. When it is incorporated as a method of society and its component social systems, we should look upon it as the method for securing the changes most appropriate to the existent and anticipated problems. As a method, however, it can have no thrust or effectiveness independent of the substance provided by the various fields of knowledge, particularly the social sciences. In this respect the special contribution of sociology lies in the area of the analysis of social structure and continuity.

With regard to the second mode, the role of the sociologist in the management of change, it has been suggested that existent theoretical approaches, methodologies, and accumulative empirical work are quite adequate for the planning process as it is institutionalized to varying degrees in diverse systems. Indeed, it would appear that there is a vast underutilization of available social scientific knowledge as various social systems, through planning, evaluation, decision-making, and implementation, attempt to determine and manage to some greater degree their own futures.

This volume on the South in continuity and change is envisaged as being relevant to both modes of the preceding analysis. It may be thought of as a set of related analyses loosely articulated within the structural-functional framework, in the sense that as a region the South is herein viewed as a social system. This is in full recognition that in many of the most fundamental ways it is merely a subsystem of American society, and conversely, is merely a context for many fundamental subsystems, e.g., states, communities, families, etc., existing within it as a regional system. In this sense, this work constitutes a rough cognitive map of the South as it is at this moment in time. This is a specious moment, however, in that there is some projection back into the past and some explicit, although more frequently implicit, projection into the future.

It is in this sense, as a cognitive map, that this volume may be relevant to the second mode of analysis. It is not suggested that the South, as a social system, can or will engage in any extensive planning or program instigation at the regional level. This has not been a characteristic of regions within American society, and regions have not been articulated in a fashion that such action is likely to occur in the foreseeable future. On the other hand, the South constitutes a referent of fundamental importance in the planning for change that is occurring at many levels within the society. As policy is formulated at the national level, either by the federal government or any of its functional agencies, or by private organizations, e.g., industrial corporations, eleemosynary foundations, etc., the South as a regional system with particular characteristics and forms of continuity and change must be taken into account if such policy is to achieve optimum realization. At the opposite extreme of more purely local planning, organizations, both public and private, e.g., states, communities, business firms, academic institutions, etc., find that the South constitutes a domain of relevance for the consideration and establishment of realistic goals and operations. As a regional system the South serves as the context, and hence supplies both implementive and limiting conditions, within which local plans and operations must make sense if they are to have any chance of success.

Problems typified as those of social change vary in scope, level, and degree of social significance. As attempts to cope with them are formulated, and gains rather than losses are sought for in the process of change itself, the South repeatedly appears, not only as a useful but as a necessary referent in the planning process. As a bench mark appraisal of one region as a social system in continuity and change, this volume may be useful in the planning process at levels varying from local to national as that process touches upon the problems and developmental potential of the South.

II. THE CHANGING REGIONAL CHARACTER OF THE SOUTH / H. H. Winsborough

This chapter represents an attempt to delineate the changing place of the South within the division of labor of the nation as a whole. As such, it focuses on the concept of region as a tool in the analysis of the areal distribution and organization of functions within a society. As used in this chapter, region is based on some structural or functional differentiation of an area rather than on strictly environmental characteristics on the one hand or cultural characteristics on the other.

1

The idea that the surface of the earth can be divided into regions seems to have a great deal of intuitive appeal. A word appears in most principal languages to designate an uninterrupted area possessing some unity or sameness.[1] The concept of region also has a fruitful intellectual history in geography, economics, and sociology. As the social sciences have attempted to come to grips with the spatial structure of society, the regional concept has played a larger and larger part in developing explanatory schemes. Some writers argue that this role is assigned by default, because the nature of areal units within the system is so complex that no satisfactory alternative is readily available.[2] Others contend that the regional concept has sufficient flexibility and present utility to warrant its retention.[3]

This diversity of attitudes has led the proponents of the regional concept to clarify its logical status. The following is a widely accepted statement:

> A region is not an object, either self-determined or nature-given. It is an intellectual concept, an entity for the purposes of thought, created by the selection of certain features that are relevant to an areal interest or problem and by the disregard of all features that are considered irrelevant.[4]

1. Preston E. James and Clarence F. Jones (eds.), *American Geography: Inventory and Prospect* (Syracuse: Syracuse University Press, 1954), p. 21.
2. Otis Dudley Duncan, Ray P. Cuzzort, and Beverly Duncan, *Statistical Geography* (Glencoe, Illinois: The Free Press, 1961), pp. 14-28.
3. Donald J. Bogue, "Population Distribution," in P. M. Hauser and O. D. Duncan (eds.), *The Study of Population* (Chicago: The University of Chicago Press, 1959), pp. 393-397.
4. James and Jones, p. 30.

Within the social sciences, then, it seems most reasonable to regard the regional concept as a tool to be used in exploring the way society is organized in space. Because the regional concept has this nature, we shall not attempt in this chapter to delineate a single region called the South. Clearly the area one might like so to designate will vary from subject to subject and from problem to problem. Since most of the data in this chapter come from official statistics, we shall use the Census definition of the South as a region and then, turning the problem around, investigate the changing regional character of the South as so described. *Figure 1* presents the Census definition of the regions of the United States and of the divisions that make up the regions.

2

In order to begin to try to understand the changing place of the South within a rapidly changing larger system, it may be wise to consider what the regional concept has taught us about the spatial organization of society. The attempt to use the regional concept has led to many attempts to formulate a technical definition. In the process, many kinds of regions have been described. In general they fall within two types:

> No matter what criteria are involved in defining them, geographic regions of all kinds may ... be grouped under two heads according to whether they are *uniform* or *nodal*.
> Uniform regions are so throughout. The uniformity is not complete, for there is always a certain range of characteristics permitted by the criteria, and there are irrelevant differences which are disregarded. But within the limits set by the criteria, regions of this kind are uniform. . . .
> Nodal regions are homogeneous with respect to internal structure or organization. This structure includes a focus, or foci, and a surrounding area tied to the focus by lines of circulation. . . . Internally nodal regions are marked by diversity of functions that goes far beyond the range of minor variation permitted in uniform regions.[5]

Within the social sciences, this distinction provides an important insight into the way in which a society is organized in space. The distinction implies that the areal division of labor within society, insofar as it is regionally organized, may be of two types. On the one

5. *Ibid.*, p. 34.

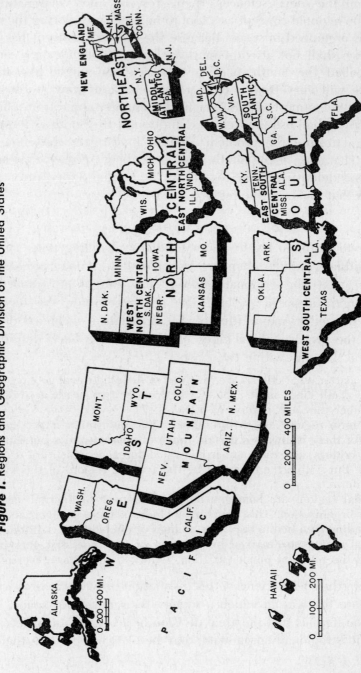

Figure 1. Regions and Geographic Division of the United States

Source: U.S. Bureau of the Census, *United States Census of Population, 1960, United States Summary, Number of Inhabitants,* PC(1)-1A (Washington, D.C.: U.S. Government Printing Office, 1964), p. S2.

hand it may be the result of the specialization of an area in the production of some good or service. On the other hand, it may be the result of an internally diverse but internally organized pattern of activities. Since the South has been discussed from the point of view of both kinds of regions, we will begin by investigating the changing regional character of the South from the point of view of first one and then the other of these regional types.

3

Uniform regions would seem to perform specific functions—the production of manufactured goods, the raising of grain, the growing of cotton—for the system as a whole or, at least, for a subsection of the system. It seems likely that the development of such a region will depend on some relative locational advantage of the area for the industry forming the region. Unless there is a reasonable relative proximity to necessary resources, consumers, or the development of external economics of scale, it is difficult to explain the concentration of functions within one area. Let us begin our investigation, then, of the changing functional specialization of the South by considering *Table 1*, which presents the percentage of the labor force in each of eight broad industry groups by region from 1880 to 1960.[6]

The early specialization of the South in agriculture is very apparent from *Table 1*. In 1880 three-fourths of the southern labor force was engaged in agricultural pursuits. In all regions the proportion in agriculture declines rather dramatically over the period, reflecting a basic change in the character of the American economy. The South has shown a relative, but decreasing, specialization over the whole of the period. The pattern in the North Central Region is somewhat similar but with an earlier shift to manufacturing. *Figure 2* presents the changing place of agriculture in the various regions in somewhat more detail.[7] In this figure each state's concentration in agriculture is presented as a percentage of the United States average for the year. From 1870 to 1890 all southern states demonstrate a similar degree of concentration in agriculture.

6. The data in *Table 1* for 1950 and before are taken from Simon Kuznets, Ann Ratner Miller, and Richard A. Easterlin, *Population Redistribution and Economic Growth: United States, 1870-1950*, Vol. II: *Analysis of Economic Change* (Philadelphia: The American Philosophical Society, 1960), p. 70. Data for 1960 are taken from the U.S. Census of Population, 1960.

7. *Figure 2* is taken from Kuznets, Miller, and Easterlin, p. 47.

Table 1. Percentage of Labor Forces in Each Industry, by Region, 1880-1960.

	Northeast					South				
	1880	1900	1940	1950	1960	1880	1900	1940	1950	1960
Agriculture	23.3	14.4	4.5	3.1	2.0	75.4	65.5	32.0	19.6	9.3
Forestry and fisheries	0.4	0.3	0.2	0.2	0.1	0.3	0.6	0.4	0.4	0.3
Mining	2.2	2.9	1.9	1.3	0.6	0.3	1.2	3.0	2.9	1.0
Construction	8.1	8.5	6.1	5.9	5.5	2.3	2.9	5.1	6.8	7.4
Manufacturing	25.7	25.9	30.9	32.6	33.6	4.6	6.3	15.3	17.5	21.5
Transportation, etc.	6.6	8.1	7.3	7.9	6.9	2.3	4.0	5.3	6.5	6.6
Trade, finance, etc.	13.8	17.1	21.6	22.7	22.2	4.4	6.4	15.0	19.1	23.7
Services and public adm.	19.7	20.5	23.9	23.8	24.4	11.1	12.7	21.6	24.6	27.4
Not reported	0.1	2.3	3.7	2.7	4.8	0.0	0.4	2.2	2.6	3.8

	North Central					West				
	1880	1900	1940	1950	1960	1880	1900	1940	1950	1960
Agriculture	54.5	40.2	18.4	13.1	8.1	28.8	29.6	15.0	9.6	6.1
Forestry and fisheries	0.1	0.1	0.1	0.1	0.1	0.9	0.5	0.4	0.4	0.3
Mining	1.1	2.2	1.2	0.9	0.6	16.2	9.3	2.9	1.4	1.1
Construction	5.6	6.4	5.2	5.4	5.6	7.5	6.8	6.8	7.8	7.1
Manufacturing	10.5	12.0	25.0	28.7	30.3	9.5	10.1	15.3	16.9	21.4
Transportation, etc.	4.7	6.9	7.1	7.8	6.8	7.3	9.7	7.8	8.2	7.2
Trade, finance, etc.	9.1	14.1	20.1	21.3	21.7	12.6	14.7	23.2	24.1	23.7
Services and public adm.	14.3	16.9	20.5	20.2	22.8	17.0	18.6	26.2	29.2	28.9
Not reported	0.1	1.2	2.5	2.5	4.0	0.1	0.8	2.4	2.4	4.2

In the Northeast, by contrast, involvement in agriculture is considerably lower and much less uniform. The North Central Region has an early, rather homogeneous concentration in agriculture, but the decreasing homogeneity of states begins more quickly than is the case for the South. After about 1890, however, homogeneity of the South also decreases. By 1950, southern states demonstrate a considerable variability of concentration in agriculture, and they would be relatively intermixed with states from other regions in a rank ordering of relative concentration in agriculture.

Relative to agriculture, the picture presented here is one of a southern area which, in the early years, might well be classified as a uniform region having a special function which it performs. The degree to which this function is performed for the nation as a whole is, perhaps, somewhat uncertain, since the amount of subsistence farming is uncertain. In spite of this uncertainty, however, it seems likely that in the latter part of the nineteenth century the South behaved as a homogeneous region, with this regional specialization declining over the twentieth century.

What kinds of functions have taken over from the agricultural ones in the South? This question can be partly answered by returning to *Table 1*. Important increases have taken place in manufacturing, trade, finance, etc., and in services and public administration.

The increasing involvement in manufacturing seems especially interesting. The proportion of the southern labor force in manufacturing has risen from 4 per cent in 1890, a figure which was less than for any other region, to almost 22 per cent in 1960. The 1960 concentration in manufacturing is, of course, less than in the Northeast or the North Central Region, but at a level similar to that of the West. Further, the kinds of manufacturing engaged in have undergone some interesting shifts over the period. *Table 2* presents the percentage of U.S. employment in selected manufacturing industries which are located in the South. These industries are grouped by the degree of importance of natural resource inputs to the industry.[8] Thus, first-stage resource users depend rather heavily on raw material inputs. Second-stage resource users depend most heavily on inputs from first-stage industries. The last column displays industries for which resources have the most indirect significance. This classification of industries by stage of resource use, though somewhat crude because of the degree of aggregation of the industry groups, probably suffices to demonstrate the direction of change.

In 1879 an average of 15 per cent of workers in first-stage resource-user industries were located in the South. By 1947 the figure had risen to 36 per cent. Thus, as early as 1879 the South showed some involvement in these industries. From 1879 to 1947 the degree of concentration increased considerably. In 1879 the South claimed

8. This grouping is done by inspecting the input-output relationships for the component industry groups. These relationships were derived from the summary of the 1947 input-output table presented in Harvey S. Perloff, Edgar S. Dunn, Jr., Eric E. Lampard, and Richard F. Muth, *Regions, Resources, and Economic Growth* (Baltimore: The Johns Hopkins Press, 1960), pp. 677-680. Where an industry group seemed too evenly divided between two categories, it has been left out of the analysis.

Figure 2. Proportion of Labor in Agriculture Relative to United States Average.

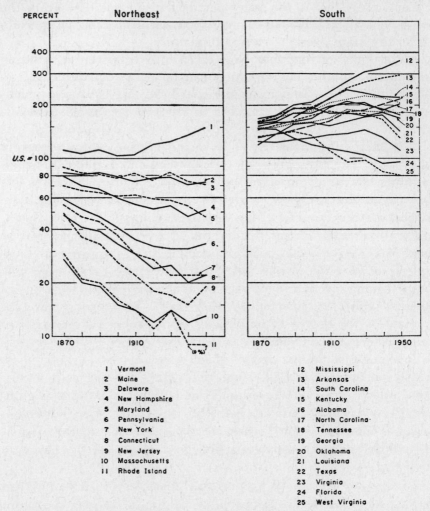

1	Vermont		12	Mississippi
2	Maine		13	Arkansas
3	Delaware		14	South Carolina
4	New Hampshire		15	Kentucky
5	Maryland		16	Alabama
6	Pennsylvania		17	North Carolina
7	New York		18	Tennessee
8	Connecticut		19	Georgia
9	New Jersey		20	Oklahoma
10	Massachusetts		21	Louisiana
11	Rhode Island		22	Texas
			23	Virginia
			24	Florida
			25	West Virginia

a very small percentage of the national labor force in second-stage resource users. By 1947, however, the South had an average of 23.2 per cent of the national labor force in these industries. Industries for which resources have the most indirect significance, on the other hand, showed little concentration in the South in 1879 and demonstrated little change by 1947.

The general picture for the South is of a region shifting away from specialization in extractive types of endeavors to manufactur-

by States 1870-1950

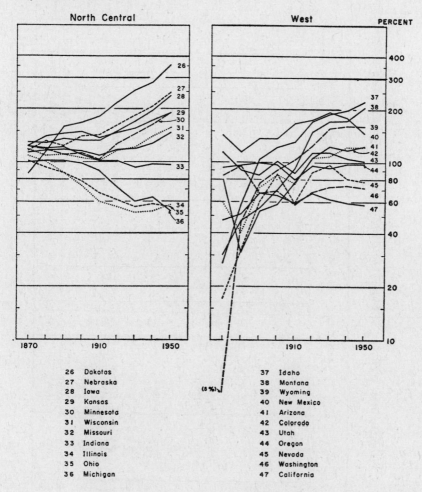

North Central

West

PERCENT

26	Dakotas
27	Nebraska
28	Iowa
29	Kansas
30	Minnesota
31	Wisconsin
32	Missouri
33	Indiana
34	Illinois
35	Ohio
36	Michigan

37	Idaho
38	Montana
39	Wyoming
40	New Mexico
41	Arizona
42	Colorado
43	Utah
44	Oregon
45	Nevada
46	Washington
47	California

(5 %)

ing activities which have some strong resource tie. There is, perhaps, some indication of greater freedom from resource location in the relatively rapid rate of increase in second-stage resource users, but first-stage users in 1947 still demonstrated the greatest tendency to concentrate in the South.

The continuity aspect of social change seems fairly clear in the development of manufacturing in the South. Over time, the location of a significant extractive function in the South has made it an

Table 2. Percentage of Average of Wage Earners, 1879 and of Employees, 1947 in Selected Manufacturing Industries Employed in the South.

First-stage resource users

Industry	1879	1947	Change
Food and kindred products	12.5	22.5	10.0
Tobacco manufacturing	28.9	57.8	28.9
Forest products	14.7	44.4	29.7
Products of petroleum and coal	12.5	34.6	22.1
Stone, clay, and glass products	6.6	20.1	13.5
Mean	15.0	35.9	20.9

Second-stage resource users

Industry	1879	1947	Change
Paper and allied products	3.3	22.1	18.8
Chemicals and allied products	4.7	28.4	23.7
Rubber products	0.0	8.3	8.3
Textiles	3.9	34.0	30.1
Mean	3.0	23.2	20.2

Industries for which resources have the most indirect significance

Industry	1879	1947	Change
Printing, publishing, and allied products	7.0	14.4	7.4
Leather and its mfg.	3.6	10.4	6.8
Machinery except transportation	5.4	5.1	-0.3
Transportation equipment	6.7	9.5	2.8
Mean	5.7	10.0	4.3

attractive location for first-stage resource users. Second-stage users seem to have found location in proximity to first-stage users convenient in order to minimize transportation costs for inputs. Perhaps this tendency is augmented by the increasing development of external economies of scale.

This review of the functions performed in the South tends to suggest an area which was originally a uniform region but which has been moving to perform a more and more heterogeneous set of functions for the larger society. These newly undertaken functions, however, are related to the previous function performed in their tie to resources. Thus, changes presently underway are closely constrained in their tie to resources and therefore by the nature of the previous structure of the southern economy.

But what of the South as a nodal region? In the next section we will first consider the nature of nodal regions. Then we will investigate the South's claim to status as a nodal region.

4

Nodal regions seem to be fairly separate subsystems within the society as a whole. Apparently this designation was first used to describe metropolitan regions with their internally diverse functions organized around the central city. The von Thünen isolated city-state seems the prototypal description.[9] In this description the urban core is surrounded by a zone of agricultural production which is, in turn, surrounded by a zone of natural resources.

It is clear that the concept of a nodal region might be extended beyond the single metropolitan area. A considerable amount of recent research suggests that cities may be organized in a hierarchical fashion somewhat similar to the organization chart of a bureaucracy. One branch of such a hierarchy might, for some purposes, be regarded as a nodal region.[10] In such a branch, the set of cities and their hinterland are to some extent focused on the highest order place, demonstrate a diversity of functions, and probably cover a continuous area.

9. Johann Heinrich von Thünen, *Der Isolierte Staat in Beziehung auf Landwirtschaft und Nationalökonomie* (Berlin: Wiegandt, Hempel and Parey, 1875), *passim.*

10. For a discussion of ideas involved in the notion of an urban hierarchy see Otis Dudley Duncan, W. Richard Scott, Stanley Lieberson, Beverly Duncan, and Hal. H. Winsborough, *Metropolis and Region* (Baltimore: The Johns Hopkins Press, 1960), pp. 46-82.

Historically, two rather separate lines of thought have led to the notion of a hierarchy of cities. One approach derives from central place theory, a theory purporting to describe the location of towns and cities on an uninterrupted plane. According to this theory towns at each level of the hierarchy should be equidistantly spaced on the plane, and they should produce a characteristic good or service consumed in lower-order places within the city's "chain of command." This good or service, called a central good, is produced in all places of higher order but in no places of lower order.[11]

The second line of thought which has led to the notion of a hierarchy of cities focuses on the concept of metropolitan dominance. In attempting to describe the influence which a large city exerts over its hinterland, human ecologists have borrowed the concept of dominance from their colleagues in biology. In general, dominance is thought to attach to the organism or unit which controls the conditions under which other organisms or units must function. Within the metropolitan community, this type of control is likely to come about in two ways: First, decision-making units locate in the city and influence, by their authority, the functioning of the hinterland units. Secondly, those functions which are strategically placed in the division of labor so as to influence many other functions—for instance, the lending of money—locate in the metropolis. It was realized quite early in the use of the notion of dominance that some cities have influence over others which, in turn, are influential over still others.[12]

The notions implied in central place theory and in the dominance idea are not necessarily separate. Rather, it seems as though the notion of dominance specifies the special kinds of central services provided in the upper reaches of the hierarchy, and considers the consequences of such provision.

The data in *Table 1* indicated a fairly steady and impressive increase in the proportion of the southern labor force in trade,

11. For a summary and bibliography of central place theory see Brian J. L. Berry and Allan Pred, *Central Place Studies, A Bibliography of Theory and Application* (Philadelphia: Regional Science Research Institute, 1961).

12. For a more detailed description of the notion of metropolitan dominance see Amos Hawley, *Human Ecology* (New York: The Ronald Press, 1950), pp. 220-222. See also, Donald J. Bogue, *The Structure of the Metropolitan Community* (Ann Arbor: University of Michigan Press, 1949); and R. D. McKinzie, *The Metropolitan Community* (New York: McGraw-Hill, 1933).

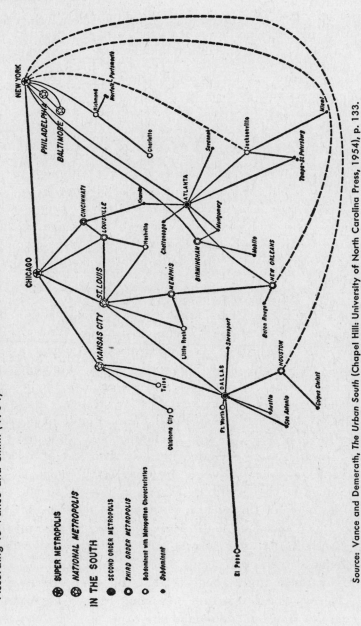

Figure 3. Metropolitan Organization of the South, with Order of Dominance and Major Lines of Integration, According to Vance and Smith (1954)

SUPER METROPOLIS

NATIONAL METROPOLIS

IN THE SOUTH

SECOND ORDER METROPOLIS

THIRD ORDER METROPOLIS

Subdominant with Metropolitan Characteristics

Subdominant

NEW YORK

PHILADELPHIA

BALTIMORE

Richmond

Norfolk-Portsmouth

Charlotte

CHICAGO

CINCINNATI

LOUISVILLE

Nashville

Knoxville

ATLANTA

Chattanooga

Montgomery

Savannah

Jacksonville

Tampa-St.Petersburg

Miami

ST. LOUIS

MEMPHIS

BIRMINGHAM

Mobile

NEW ORLEANS

KANSAS CITY

Little Rock

Baton Rouge

Tulsa

Shreveport

HOUSTON

Oklahoma City

DALLAS

Ft. Worth

Austin

San Antonio

Corpus Christi

El Paso

Source: Vance and Demerath, *The Urban South* (Chapel Hill: University of North Carolina Press, 1954), p. 133.

finance, etc., and services and public administration. Since these industries contain many activities which can be regarded as nodal or indicative of dominance, this finding may suggest that, as the shift from extractive activities to a more heterogeneous set of activities has taken place, there has been a concomitant increasing development of nodal structures within the South.

In 1954, Vance and Smith made an attempt to classify southern cities by their order of metropolitan dominance.[13] They further indicated "major lines of integration" between the metropolises. The resultant pattern is presented in *Figure 3*. Although the authors are not clear about the meaning of lines of integration or how they were derived, the connections seem related to major transportation routes. The study seemed to indicate two major nodal points within the South: Atlanta and Dallas. It seems to be through these major nodes that much of the South is interlinked with the rest of the nation.

In 1960, Duncan conducted a study which provided some additional information on "major lines of integration" between cities in the United States.[14] Using information from the Federal Reserve System records of the Interdistrict Settlement Fund, they were able to present a picture of the flows of commercial and financial payments and receipts between each of the head offices and branch zones of the Federal Reserve System. *Figure 4* presents Interdistrict Settlement Fund Gross Flows of $100,000,000 or more for four weeks in 1957 excluding New York and Chicago. These two cities were excluded because their net of relationships is so complex as to make the picture unwieldy.

Focusing on the South in *Figure 4*, one is struck with the similarities between this picture of the net of relationships and that presented by Vance and Smith. Here, too, we find two major nodes in the South, Dallas and Atlanta, although the relative degree in connectedness of the two seems reversed.

Both of these studies suggest that the South presently has a fairly vigorous nodal structure consisting of two important nodes rather than a single predominant one.

13. Rupert B. Vance and Sara Smith, "Metropolitan Dominance and Integration," in *The Urban South*, ed. Rupert B. Vance and Nicholas J. Demerath (Chapel Hill: The University of North Carolina Press, 1954), pp. 134-144.
14. Duncan *et al.*, pp. 105-158.

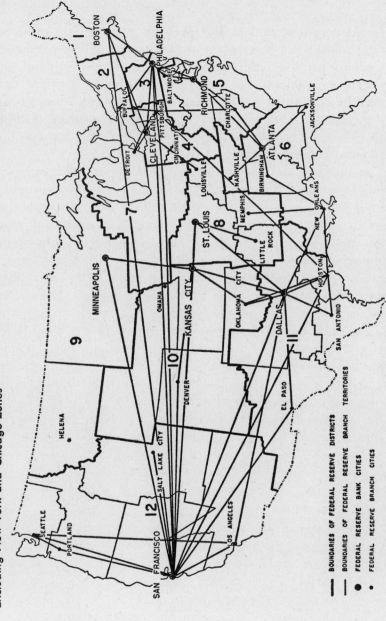

Figure 4. Interdistrict Settlement Fund Gross Flows of $100,000,000 or More (Total of Four Weeks in 1957), Excluding New York and Chicago Zones

Source: O. D. Duncan et al., *Metropolis and Region* (Baltimore: Johns Hopkins University Press, 1960), p. 155.

5

The evidence presented in the previous sections led us to argue
that the South is not presently a uniform region but has become two
somewhat separated nodal regions. Since these two kinds of regions
may seem separate and distinct typological forms, it might be wise
to consider something of the relationship between them insofar as
it is pertinent to the transition that has taken place within the
South. This discussion may give us some basis for speculation
about future changes in the South.

The uniform and the nodal are two important ways of conceiving of the areal division of labor when it is organized regionally.
There is little reason, however, to think that these modes of organization are mutually exclusive. It seems likely that any uniform
region may have properties of an independent subsystem for
maintenance purposes while a nodal region may well perform some
kinds of special functions. In dealing with cities as related to
regions, this principle seems generally accepted. Thus, Duncan
describes some cities as specializing in manufacturing and at
the same time having "metropolitan" functions for a hinterland.[15]
Isard and Kavesh have presented a methodology based on input-
output analysis for investigating the interrelationships between the
two aspects of the division of labor.[16] Morrissett has investigated
the necessary minimum level of various kinds of maintenance activities within cities of various sizes in order to estimate the
amount available for special-function production.[17] Further, there
is evidence that areal division of labor in society does not necessarily operate regionally. For the homogeneous region this proposition seems clear. It is not necessary that a relatively location-free
industry demonstrate concentration within one area or that an area
will have locational advantages necessary to produce specialization.
For nodal regions, the argument is not clear. A strict interpretation
of central place theory would lead one to the notion that any area
of land could be regarded as a nodal region with focus on some
large city. If no other central place intervenes to organize the area

15. *Ibid.*, pp. 248-275.
16. Walter Isard and Robert Kavesh, "Economic Structural Interrelations of
Metropolitan Regions," *American Journal of Sociology*, 60: 152-162.
17. Irving Morrissett, "The Economic Structure of American Cities," *Papers and
Proceedings of the Regional Science Association*, 4: 239-256.

under consideration, it will be organized under the largest city in the system. Working within the dominance derivation of an urban hierarchy, however, Pappenfort has conceptualized the problem in a fashion which leads to a different implication for the existence of regions:

> A "community"—whether the concept is applied to plants, animals, or human beings and their institutions—by definition is not a discrete entity. It is an identifiable set of symbolic relationships which necessarily are involved with and have implications for other such identifiable sets. Several or many such communities constitute an ecological "field" which is the fundamental unit of analysis. Hypotheses and methods used in the study of several communities or even a single community need to be predicated upon a process of abstraction from the more inclusive area.[18]

By using this formulation Pappenfort has been able to demonstrate that proximity to two large cities has a joint influence on the location of branch plants of manufacturing establishments. This finding suggests that a hierarchical arrangement of towns in terms of dominance may be too simple a model of the complex web of relationships. One might suppose that the net of relationships would become even more complex with the development of more inexpensive communications systems, especially ones having to do with the transmittal of records and information. Thus, one might suspect that the development of interlinked computers and data-transmittal facilities might lead to a more complex relationship between the location of decision-making apparatus and the location of those places influenced by the decisions.

The foregoing seems to lead to a crude fourfold typology of functional relationship of an areal part to the whole of the system:

		Does the area in question specialize in the production of some good or service which it "exports" to the remainder of the system?	
		Yes	No
Does the area in question manifest "nodal" organization?	No	Type 1	Type 4
	Yes	Type 2	Type 3

18. Donnell M. Pappenfort, "The Ecological Field and the Metropolitan Community: Manufacturing and Management," *American Journal of Sociology,* 64: 380-385.

Type one areas specialize in the production of some commodity but are not nodally organized. This type of organization is basically an anomalous one. By virtue of its specialization, a homogeneous region must ship much of its product outside of the region and may import many of the other things it uses. It also seems likely that there must be many lines of communication and channels of authority interlinking the region and the rest of the system—with the nature of the function performed in the region determining the amount and kind of such interlinkings. For regions of this kind the very homogeneity of the area, which indicates its unity, implies its immersion in the larger system.

Insofar as it is stable, a type one structure might come about in several, special ways. On the one hand, if the commodity produced in the uniform region doesn't play an important part in the economy of the area, it may not strongly constrain the hierarchical structure of relationships. Thus, heterogeneity of other, more important, functions in the area may lead to the uniform region's overlying the boundaries of several separately organized nodal regions. On the other hand, if the commodity is used in only a few other locations, the centers of decision-making and influence may be located at the site of consumption.

Neither of these situations seems to apply to the early South. We may speculate that, during the period in which the South could be regarded as a uniform region, there was some kind of nodal organization (at least nascent) dealing in the collection and distribution of farm products and serving as a channel of control over goods and services "imported" to the South. Thus, one might be more inclined to view the South, during its period as a uniform region, as a type two area.

Type two areas qualify as regions on both counts. They specialize in the production of some commodity which is shipped to the larger system, but at the same time they are nodally organized. Such areas seem like small, exporting nations within a larger nation. Such a characterization of the South would have seemed applicable.

One is inclined to speculate, however, that the nature of the nodal organization within this type of area is rather different from that of a type three area. Within a type two area the node seems more like the organizational focus of a commensalistic group rather than a center of dominance within a symbolically organized group. Thus, one might be inclined to expect such a node to behave like a trade union or a manufacturing association, focusing its attention on the national scheme and attempting, in its mediation between the region and the nation at large, to maximize the relatively clear-cut regional best advantage.

In type three areas, however, which are internally organized but not allocated a single function in the national division of labor, one might expect the node to invest more effort in adjusting the internal relationships between the symbolically related parts of the area.

One is tempted to say that the South has moved from a type two area to a type three area or, rather, two type three areas. One might also expect the nodal activities to have concomitantly changed the nature of their character. Perhaps the increase in "nodal" types of functions noted in *Table 1* represents a transition to the more complex dominant nodal organization as opposed to the rather simpler commensalistic nodal organization. Since it seems likely that at least Atlanta, of the present southern metropolises, has served both roles, it would be instructive to investigate its changing nodal character over the past 100 years.

Type four areas admit of the possibility that the area in question is a random selection of contiguous units and therefore has a small chance, in itself, of being uniformly or nodally organized. That the South did not become such an area during its transition from extractive to processing specialization is probably indicative of the strength of the "continuity" feature of social change. The possibility that the South might become a type four area seems to this writer to rest on a rather different set of chances, however—one which involves the possibility that, in the country as a whole, nodal organization might become less important. This possibility seems to rest on the proposition that nodality, the location of many decision-making functions and many influential functions in one city, is a result of external economies of scale accruing to the information-collection process necessary for decision-making. It seems possible that, as the technology of data collection and transmission becomes cheaper, the advantages of informal sharing of information and impressions will be lessened in the face of what may seem to be unwieldy amounts of precise data. Thus, the advantages of common location for decision-making may lessen in importance and such functions find a more deconcentrated location pattern equally satisfactory.

6

In summary, we have been able to trace the changing place of the South in the areal division of labor of the nation from that of a uniform region dealing in extractive functions to an area with a more heterogeneous set of functions to perform. These newer functions, however, demonstrate some continuity with the past in their relative dependence on resource location. We have also been able to suggest a changing character of the internal organization of the South. We have speculated that the character of southern regional metropolises has shifted from a focus on adjusting the relationships between the commensalistically organized area and the outside world to dominant points focusing attention on adjusting the increasingly complex internal division of labor. These transitions seem to make the place of the South in the internal division of labor in the nation as a whole rather more similar to that of other areas within the nation.

III. CONTINUITY AND CHANGE IN SOUTHERN MIGRATION / C. Horace Hamilton

1

The traditional role of the South as a major supplier of the nation's population is changing, and the tide of migration from the South is slowing down. Nevertheless, some important historical trends are continuing, and the influence of migration trends of the past is still strong both within and outside the South.

With regard to migration—its volume, direction, and characteristics—the South can no longer be considered a homogeneous region, and neither can it be considered altogether unique in the nation. National social, economic, and cultural forces are rapidly modifying the nature and volume of migration to, from, and within the South. Industrialization, the technological and scientific revolution in agriculture, urbanization, metropolitan growth, communication and transportation, rising incomes and levels of living, rising educational levels, birth control, and the development of social institutions are national influences which have swept across the South; consequently, they have played a large part in modifying and redirecting migration trends.

Although migration from the South has attracted most attention and is admittedly of very great sociological significance, several other aspects of Southern population movements are also of considerable importance. These other aspects are: (1) the high rates of population movement within the South between both states and local areas, and from rural to urban areas; (2) the substantial and growing movement into southern states from other regions; (3) the white–non-white differentials in migration within, to, and from the South; (4) the high correlation between formal education and migration; (5) the continuing role of migration in the adjustment of young people to changing economic opportunities; and, finally, (6) the impact of changing fertility levels and patterns on migratory movements in and out of the South. All these aspects of the subject will be factually documented and discussed in this chapter.

2

The large variations in migration to and from the South, viewed in historical perspective, seem to be closely related not only to the

character of the South's early colonial and almost wholly agricultural economy but also to the growth and industrialization of
the nation's economy, and to great wars, national economic depres-
sions, and booms.

The development of the early agricultural economy of the South
under colonialism set the stage for the plantation type of land
tenure and for the rapid growth of a large rural population consisting of white migrants from the Old World and black slaves
from Africa. The invention of the cotton gin, the availability of a
foreign market for cotton, and later the development of a textile
industry in America were the big factors that enabled the South to
become the center of world cotton production.

But before the days of agricultural mechanization cotton was
produced with human and animal labor. The fact that the processes
of cotton production were suitable for the use of children and
women in the fields as choppers and pickers encouraged high birth
rates and large families—a factor which later led to a surplus youth
population and, hence, to heavy out-migration. Only high death
rates among infants and children prevented the surplus from rising
higher.

The Negro family, slaves before the Civil War, became the
sharecropper family after the war. A growing white population
developed independent family farms on the uplands but others
became sharecroppers and tenants on plantations and on smaller
land holdings. In the days before soil exhaustion and the boll weevil,
cotton production very quickly met the world effective demand
for cotton. As old areas in the southeastern states declined because
of soil erosion and overcropping, new cotton producing areas
opened up in the Southwest—especially in Texas and Oklahoma.

Although the market for cotton grew, the availability of a large
supply of cheap labor and land permitted production to grow even
faster. Population increase was even more remarkable and inevitably migration of surplus population from the South had to occur.
Fortunately, for at least two centuries before 1900, the American
frontier offered an economic opportunity for surplus agricultural
workers of the South and East. On the other hand, large areas in
the South also attracted migrants from cotton areas, and new types
of farming and ranching developed. Lumbering and mining pro-

vided employment for a growing number of workers. However, some sources of employment were not very rewarding. Poverty pockets developed in many of the poor land areas, in the red hills of the Piedmont, and in the cutover lands of the Southern Appalachians. Tobacco production began very early and developed rapidly in Virginia and the Carolinas. Tobacco has always required a heavy labor input, and its production was closely associated with the sharecropper-tenant system of land tenure.

The growth of small towns and cities in and out of the South also provided some opportunity for the surplus population from southern farms. However, it was not until the late 1800's and the early 1900's that the total urban influence was strong enough to absorb a significant amount of the surplus farm population. Before 1900, the net migration from the South never exceeded 900,000 for any decade.

3

In the first decade after the Civil War, net migration from the eleven southeastern states reached about 300,000. *Table 1* shows the trend in migration from not only the eleven-state Southeast but also from the seventeen-state Census South as well.[1] After 1880 net migration from the Southeast increased slowly reaching 872,000 in the 1900-1910 decade. Between 1870 and 1910 Negroes comprised about one-third of the net out-migration—about the expected proportion in terms of population. Gross out- and in-migration numbers are unknown but must have been much larger.

In the World War I decade, 1910-1920, net migration from the South jumped to 1,200,000 of which 577,000 were non-white. Then in the 1920's the price of cotton dropped, the boll weevil cut cotton production in the deep South, and business and industry boomed in the North and West; and, as a result, net out-migration rose to 1,700,000, 50 per cent higher than in the preceding decade. The increase in Negro net out-migration was relatively greater than that among the white population, being 977,000 as compared with only 778,000 for the whites.

1. The eleven southeastern states are: Virginia, North Carolina, South Carolina, Georgia, Florida, Kentucky, Tennessee, Alabama, Mississippi, Arkansas, and Louisiana. Other states making up the Census South are: Delaware, Maryland, West Virginia, Texas, Oklahoma, and the District of Columbia.

Table 1. Net Migration to and from the United States South by Color and Decade, 1870-1960 (in 1,000's).

Decade	Total South			Southeast (11 states)		
	Total	White	Non-white	Total	White	Non-white
1870-1880	+ 11	+ 82	− 71	− 304	−205	− 99
1880-1890	− 411	−328	− 83	− 515	−405	− 110
1890-1900	− 143	+ 52	− 195	− 849	−537	− 312
1900-1910	− 274	− 77	− 197	− 872	−605	− 267
1910-1920	−1,088	−566	− 522	−1,219	−642	− 577
1920-1930	−1,576	−704	− 872	−1,704	−778	− 926
1930-1940	− 756	−349	− 407	− 651	−188	− 463
1940-1950	−2,137	−538	−1,599	−1,880	−365	−1,515
1950-1960	−1,403	+ 53	−1,457	−1,078	+381	−1,459

Sources: (1) 1870-1940: Lee, Miller, Brainerd, and Easterlin. *Population Redistribution and Economic Growth in the United States; Methodological Considerations and Reference Tables* (Philadelphia: American Philosophical Society, 1957); (2) 1940-1960: U. S. Bureau of the Census. *Current Population Reports,* Series P-25, No. 247 (April 2, 1962).

In the decade of the Great Depression, 1930-1940, the lack of non-agricultural jobs in the North and West cut net out-migration from the South by two-thirds—dropping to 651,000. Yet it was in this period that employment in southern agriculture began a precipitous decline which is still in process. Lack of effective demand for cotton and tobacco products, low prices, crop control programs pushed both white and Negro farmers off the land into the towns and cities and out of the South.

In the late 1930's, agricultural mechanization, New Deal programs, and economic recovery were major factors contributing to rural-urban migration within the South and to migration from the South. High fertility rates in the South before 1930, especially in rural areas, had resulted in a large surplus of youth. Having few promising opportunities for employment in any region, this large contingent of southern young people was backed up on the land and in the South. Had there not been a national depression, a much larger percentage of these youth would have left the South during the 1930's.

During the 1930-1940 decade the Negro share of net migration rose to about two-thirds. The number of southern Negro tenants and sharecroppers began to decline—dropping from a high of 699,000 in 1930 to 507,000 in 1940. The number of Negro farm owners dropped from 182,000 to 173,000 in the same period. The

number of white tenants and sharecroppers declined a smaller percentage—from 1,092,000 to 943,000, but the number of white farm
owners increased from 1,234,000 to 1,371,000.

It was in the World War II decade, 1940-1950, that net migration from the South reached an all-time high of 2,135,000, of which
three-fourths were non-white. Not only the war but several other
factors converged to influence heavy out-migration. A big factor
was the continued mechanization of agriculture and the consequent
decreasing number of tenants and sharecroppers. During the
1940's the total number of tenants and sharecroppers in the South
dropped from 1,449,000 to 905,000. Continuing a trend begun in
the 1930's, the number of farm owners increased slightly—both
white and non-white—but the number of white tenants and sharecroppers decreased from 943,000 to 540,000, and the number of
Negro tenants and sharecroppers dropped from 507,000 to 366,000.
About 75 per cent of farm youth reaching maturity left the farm.

Strangely, it was in the 1940-1950 decade that migration from
the South showed signs of slowing down and even reversing its
direction in some southern states. As *Table 1* shows, the out-migration among the white population reached its highest peak in the
1920-1930 decade, while the non-white out-migration reached its
highest peak in the 1940-1950 decade. Five of the seventeen southern states, including the District of Columbia, gained population
by migration. Leading the list was Florida with a net migration gain
of 578,000, 31 per cent of its 1950 population. Other states gaining
migrants during the 1940's were: Texas and Maryland, 270,000
each; Virginia, 168,000; and Delaware, 21,000. The District of
Columbia gained 49,000 migrants. These are all peripheral states in
which large cities and metropolitan areas were developing.

During the 1950-1960 decade the net migration from the seventeen-state South dropped from 2,137,000 to 1,403,000, and in the
eleven southeastern states from 1,880,000 to 1,078,000. With respect
to color, the net migration volume changed from a net out-migration of 365,000 whites to a net in-migration of 381,000. The non-
white net out-migration dropped from 1,515,000 in the 1940's to
1,454,000 in the 1950's. Also, four states, including the District of
Columbia, gained non-white migrants and five states gained white
migrants. Florida, which had gained 578,000 migrants in the 1940's,

Table 2. Net Migration to and from the South by Color, State, and Division. 1950-1960 and 1955-1960.*

(All figures rounded to the nearest 1,000)

State and Division	Total		White		Non-white	
	1950-60	1955-60	1950-60	1955-60	1950-60	1955-60
Total South	−1,403	+ 55	+ 53	+334	−1,456	−279
South Atlantic	+ 648	+540	+1,189	+640	− 542	− 99
East South Central	−1,465	−311	− 844	−192	− 619	−119
West South Central	− 588	−174	− 292	−113	− 295	− 61
Delaware	+ 64	+ 17	+ 58	+ 15	+ 6	+ 2
Maryland	+ 320	+ 87	+ 284	+ 77	+ 36	+ 9
Dist. of Columbia	− 158	− 82	− 213	− 96	+ 54	+ 14
Virginia	+ 15	+ 43	+ 84	+ 60	− 70	− 17
West Virginia	− 446	−137	− 406	−129	− 40	− 9
North Carolina	− 328	− 77	− 121	− 34	− 207	− 43
South Carolina	− 222	− 45	− 4	+ 3	− 218	− 48
Georgia	− 214	− 43	− 9	− 2	− 204	− 41
Florida	+1,617	+777	+1,516	+744	+ 101	+ 32
Kentucky	− 390	−108	− 374	−102	− 15	− 5
Tennessee	− 273	− 80	− 216	− 67	− 57	− 13
Alabama	− 368	− 52	− 144	− 12	− 224	− 40
Mississippi	− 434	− 71	− 110	− 11	− 323	− 60
Arkansas	− 433	− 66	− 283	− 41	− 150	− 25
Louisiana	− 50	− 7	+ 42	+ 15	− 92	− 22
Oklahoma	− 219	− 73	− 192	− 67	− 26	− 6
Texas	+ 114	− 28	+ 141	− 20	− 27	− 8

*The 1950-1960 data include population migrants under 10 years of age in 1960. The 1955-1960 data do not include children under 5 years of age in 1960.

Sources: (1) U.S. Bureau of the Census, *Current Population Reports,* Series P-25, No. 247, April 2, 1962. (2) U.S. Bureau of the Census, *U.S. Census of Population: 1960, Subject Reports, Mobility for States and State Economic Areas,* Final Report PC(2)-2B, Tables 16 and 18.

gained 1,617,000 during the 1950's, and 100,000 of this gain were non-white. Louisiana moved from the "out" to the "in" column in the migration of white population. The District of Columbia, reflecting a nationwide metropolitan pattern, continued to lose white and gain non-white migrants.

In the latter part of the 1950-1960 decade, migration to the South apparently increased and migration from the South decreased. Evidence of this interesting trend is found in the 1960 Census data relating to the state of residence in 1955. These data are summarized in *Table 2,* which shows in parallel columns the net migration by states for the entire 1950-1960 decade and similar data for the period 1955-1960. Except for the under-five age class in which the net migration loss was only 35,000 for the entire decade, the two types of data are comparable. Had migration been uniformly distributed over the decade, the net migration during the latter half should have been about one-half of that during the entire decade. But, as *Table 2* shows, the net migration during the 1955-1960 period in most states was much less than the expected 50 per cent.

For the South as a whole (seventeen states) there was a net in-migration of 55,000 in the 1955-1960 period as compared with a net out-migration of 1,403,000 for the entire period. These figures do not include migration from abroad. The comparisons by color are more interesting. The five-year white net in-migration was 344,000 as compared with a net gain of only 53,000 during the entire period; whereas, there was a net loss of only 289,000 non-whites during the

Table 3. Native Population of the Conterminous United States by Place of Birth and Place of Residence, by Color, 1940, 1950, and 1960, South and Non-South Compared.

	1940	1950	1960
Total population	119,515,740	138,072,605	163,066,380
Living in the South	40,934,449	45,937,580	52,597,842
Born in the South	38,727,962	42,522,110	47,509,383
Born outside the South	2,206,487	3,415,470	5,088,459
Living outside the South	78,581,291	92,135,025	110,468,538
Born in the South	4,752,658	7,411,900	9,865,368
Born outside the South	73,828,633	84,723,125	100,603,170
Born in the South	43,480,620	49,934,010	57,374,751
Born outside the South	76,035,120	88,138,595	105,691,629
White population	106,325,345	122,808,695	144,437,728
Living in the South	30,959,202	35,708,465	41,484,853
Born in the South	28,816,273	32,401,395	36,552,574
Born outside the South	2,142,929	3,307,070	4,932,279
Living outside the South	75,366,143	87,100,230	102,952,875
Born in the South	3,204,047	4,818,775	6,616,632
Born outside the South	72,162,096	82,281,455	96,336,243
Born in the South	32,020,320	37,220,170	43,169,206
Born outside the South	74,305,025	85,588,525	101,268,522
Non-white population	13,190,395	15,263,910	18,628,652
Living in the South	9,975,247	10,229,115	11,112,989
Born in the South	9,911,689	10,120,715	10,956,809
Born outside the South	63,558	108,400	156,180
Living outside the South	3,215,148	5,034,795	7,515,663
Born in the South	1,548,611	2,593,125	3,248,736
Born outside the South	1,666,537	2,441,670	4,266,927
Born in the South	11,460,300	12,713,840	14,205,545
Born outside the South	1,730,095	2,550,070	4,423,107

Source: U.S. Bureau of the Census, *U.S. Census of Population, Subject Reports, State of Birth:* *1940*, Tables 20, 21, 22, 23, 24; *1950*, Tables 13, 14, 15, 16, 17; *1960*, Tables 18, 19, 20, 21, 22.

five-year period as compared with a loss of 1,456,000 during the entire decade. Florida's heavy in-migration apparently continued in the latter half of the decade at about the same rate as the first half.

Lumping together the states which lost migrants during the decade, the net loss of the latter half of the decade (758,000) was less than a fourth of the net loss for the entire decade (3,374,000). In this comparison, the District of Columbia (which lost migrants during the decade) is included with Maryland, Virginia, Delaware, Florida, and Texas as states gaining migrants because it is the center of a large metropolitan area which spills over into Maryland and Virginia, and the remaining eleven states are classed as "losing" states. Texas is the only southern state that gained migrants in the first part of the decade (about 142,000) and lost in the latter half of the decade.

What is the explanation of the great change in the rate of migration out of the South? Is it due to the recession in the latter part of the 1950's, or is it a part of the longer downward cycle of migration which began in the 1940-1950 decade? Until more and later data become available, it can only be surmised that both long- and short-range cycle factors were influencing the out-migration trend during the 1955-1960 period.

Evidence that migration to the South from the North and West is speeding up and is already a significantly large movement is found in the state-of-birth data in recent censuses.[2] *Tables 3* and *4* show data compiled from the last three United States Censuses of Population. Briefly summarized, these data show that the population of the South, born in the non-southern states, is increasing more rapidly than is the southern-born population residing in the non-southern states. The decade rates of change of these two migrant cohorts were:

Migrant cohort	Per cent increase	
	1940-1950	1950-1960
Southern-born migrants living in the North and West	56.0	33.1
Non-southern-born migrants living in the South	54.8	49.0

2. U.S. Bureau of the Census, *U.S. Census of Population: 1960, Subject Reports, State of Birth*, Final Report PC(2)-2A.

Table 4. Per cent Changes and Per cent Distribution in Native Population of the Conterminous United States by Place of Birth and Place of Residence, by Color, 1940, 1950, and 1960, South and Non-South Compared.

	Per cent change			Per cent distribution		
	1940-1950	1950-1960	1940-1960	1940	1950	1960
Total population	15.5	18.1	36.4	100.0	100.0	100.0
Living in the South	12.2	14.5	28.5	34.2	33.3	32.3
Born in the South	9.8	11.7	22.7	32.4	30.8	29.1
Born outside the South	54.8	49.0	130.6	1.8	2.5	3.1
Living outside the South	17.2	19.9	40.6	65.7	66.7	67.7
Born in the South	56.0	33.1	107.6	4.0	5.4	6.0
Born outside the South	14.8	18.7	36.3	61.8	61.4	61.7
Born in the South	14.8	14.9	32.0	36.4	36.2	35.2
Born outside the South	15.9	19.9	39.0	63.6	63.8	64.8
White population	15.5	17.6	35.8	100.0	100.0	100.0
Living in the South	15.3	16.2	34.0	29.1	29.1	28.7
Born in the South	12.4	12.8	26.8	27.1	26.4	25.3
Born outside the South	54.3	49.1	130.2	2.0	2.7	3.4
Living outside the South	15.6	18.2	36.6	70.9	70.9	71.3
Born in the South	50.4	37.3	106.5	3.0	3.9	4.6
Born outside the South	14.0	17.1	33.5	67.9	67.0	66.7
Born in the South	16.2	16.0	34.8	30.1	30.3	29.9
Born outside the South	15.2	18.3	36.3	69.9	69.7	70.1
Non-white population	15.7	22.0	41.2	100.0	100.0	100.0
Living in the South	2.5	8.6	11.4	75.6	67.0	59.7
Born in the South	2.1	8.3	10.5	75.1	66.3	58.8
Born outside the South	70.6	44.1	145.7	0.5	0.7	0.8
Living outside the South	56.6	49.3	133.8	24.4	33.0	40.3
Born in the South	67.4	25.3	109.8	11.7	17.0	17.4
Born outside the South	46.5	74.8	156.0	12.6	16.0	22.9
Born in the South	10.9	11.7	24.0	86.9	83.3	76.3
Born outside the South	47.4	73.5	155.7	13.1	16.7	23.7

Source: See Table 3.

As of 1960, 5,088,000 people born in the North and West, just under 10 per cent of the total southern population, were living in the South. These figures do not include either foreign-born or the population for whom state of birth was not reported. On the other hand, 9,865,000 southern-born people, under 9 per cent of the non-southern population, were living in the North and West.

Although there are still many more native southerners living outside the South than there are native non-southerners living in the South, the South is more highly saturated with "Yankees" and "Westerners" than the other way around. Thus, there is a realistic,

Table 5. Migration to, from, and within the South by Color, 1955-1960 (Excluding Population Abroad in 1955 and Population Whose 1955 Residence Was Not Reported).

Migration	Population in 1,000's			Per cent		
	Total	White	Non-white	Total	White	Non-white
Population 5 years old and over	47,352	37,740	9,612	100.0	100.0	100.0
Non-movers	23,100	17,924	5,176	48.8	47.5	53.8
Movers, within county	14,953	11,402	3,551	31.6	30.2	36.9
Migrants, within southern states	4,297	3,802	495	9.1	10.1	5.2
Migrants, between southern states	2,512	2,245	267	5.3	5.9	2.8
Migrants to the South	2,490	2,367	123	5.3	6.3	1.3
Migrants from the South	2,435	2,033	402	5.2	5.4	4.2
Net migration to the South	56	334	−279	0.1	0.9	−2.8
Population in 1955, less deaths between 1955 and 1960.*	47,296	37,405	9,891	100.0	100.0	100.0

*The 1955 population, used as the basis for computing per cent migration from the South, is equal to the 1960 population 5 years old and over minus net migration to the South.

Source: U.S. Bureau of the Census, *U.S. Census of Population: 1960, Mobility for States and State Economic Areas*, PC(2)-2B, Tables 16 and 18.

demographic basis for the belief that southern social life and culture is as much or more subject to outside influences than is the culture and social life of non-southern states. This statement is not relevant here to the influences of foreign cultures by way of international migration. There are, of course, relatively more people of foreign birth and parentage in the North and West than in the South.

The state-of-birth data also show that the migration of non-white northern- and western-born people to the South is extremely small as compared with the corresponding migration of white people born in the North and West. The migration of the Negro out of the South is almost a one-way street. Surprisingly, the total of southern–non-southern migration (in both directions) among white people is relatively larger than the corresponding migration among Negroes. Data on net migration of whites and Negroes out of the South do not reveal this interesting aspect of population movements in America. More data and discussion of this white–non-white differential are found in other sections of this chapter.

4

In the analysis of interregional migration with respect to the South, we are in danger of overlooking the relatively great and socially significant migration within the South, consisting of: (1) migration between counties within states; and (2) migration between states within the South. As *Table 5* shows, the first of these migration components, between 1955 and 1960, involved 4,297,000 migrants and the second involved 2,512,000—making a total of 6,809,000 migrants. This within-South migration exceeds the total of inter-regional migration (4,925,000) by 1,874,000.

The ratio of within-region migration to total population is higher in the South than in the Northeast and North Central Regions, but somewhat lower than in the West. The data below show the comparison clearly:

Region	Population	Migrants within region	
		Number	Per cent
Northeast	40,024,689	4,169,749	10.4
North Central	45,613,713	5,222,269	11.4
South	48,548,666	6,808,896	14.0
West	24,816,743	3,873,594	15.6

Confirming the generalization made in the last section regarding white–non-white migration differentials, *Table 5* also shows that white people are more mobile than Negroes. Negroes in the South do have a higher rate of movement (from house to house) within counties than do white people, but only about one-half the rate of white migration across county, state, and regional boundaries. Even gross migration of whites from the South exceeds that of the non-whites—5.4 per cent as compared with 4.2 per cent. The gross in-migration rate of whites to the South is almost five times that of the non-white population—6.3 per cent as compared with 1.3 per cent.

Lumping all migration streams together, the data of *Table 5* show that the ratio of migrants to total population (in the South) for the 1955-1960 period was about twice as high in the white as in the non-white population—27.7 per cent as compared with 13.5 per cent.

Table 6. Migrants to and from the South by Class of Destination and Origin, 1955-1960 (in 1,000's, rounded**).

State and Division	Migration from southern states by region of destination			Migration within states	Migration to southern states by region of origin		
	Total*	South	Non-South		South	Non-South	Total*
Total South	9,244	2,512	2,435	4,297	2,512	2,490	9,299
So. Atlantic	4,281	1,351	1,067	1,863	1,463	1,496	4,822
E. So. Central	1,865	567	532	766	443	345	1,554
W. So. Central	3,097	594	835	1,669	605	649	2,923
Delaware	49	18	25	6	22	37	66
Maryland	480	127	132	220	199	148	566
Dist. of Columbia	193	139	55	—	67	44	111
Virginia	811	218	195	398	243	213	855
West Virginia	341	95	134	112	37	55	204
North Carolina	680	214	135	331	168	104	603
South Carolina	349	134	78	137	111	57	305
Georgia	702	227	112	363	195	101	659
Florida	676	179	203	295	422	736	1,453
Kentucky	488	101	194	194	64	123	380
Tennessee	530	184	150	197	151	102	450
Alabama	470	163	99	208	136	74	419
Mississippi	376	119	90	167	92	46	305
Arkansas	356	95	124	137	71	82	290
Louisiana	453	124	81	249	139	59	447
Oklahoma	516	119	175	221	95	126	442
Texas	1,772	255	455	1,062	300	383	1,744

Total columns include migration within states.
**Excludes persons living abroad in 1955 and persons whose 1955 residence was not reported.
Source: U.S. Bureau of the Census, *U.S. Census of Population: 1960, Subject Report, Mobility for States and State Economic Areas,* Final Report PC(2)-2B, Table 16.

The social and economic significance of the white–non-white migration differential lies in the fact that white workers have a wider range of economic opportunities than do non-white workers. When it comes to changing jobs and climbing the socioeconomic status ladder, Negroes find themselves in a caste-like social structure. This situation is a complex one consisting of traditional race attitudes as well as of objective conditional factors, such as poor education, low income, farm tenancy, and so on.

Migration from community to community, from state to state, from region to region, and mobility from occupation to occupation are important means of social and economic adjustment which

Table 7. Net Migration to, from, and within the South 1955-1960 by Color (in 1,000's).*

State and Division	Total		White		Non-white	
	Within the South	To and from the Non-South	Within the South	To and from the Non-South	Within the South	To and from the Non-South
Total South	—	56	—	+334	—	—279
South Atlantic	+112	+428	+ 99	+540	+13	—112
East So. Central	—124	—187	—103	— 89	—20	— 98
West So. Central	+ 12	—186	+ 4	—117	+ 8	— 69
Delaware	+ 4	+ 13	+ 3	+ 13	+ 2	—
Maryland	+ 71	+ 15	+ 60	+ 18	+12	— 2
Dist. of Columbia	— 72	— 10	— 87	— 9	+15	— 1
Virginia	+ 25	+ 18	+ 27	+ 33	— 2	— 15
West Virginia	— 59	— 78	— 57	— 71	— 2	— 7
North Carolina	— 46	— 30	— 36	+ 2	—11	— 32
South Carolina	— 23	— 22	— 4	+ 7	—19	— 29
Georgia	— 32	— 11	— 12	+ 10	—20	— 20
Florida	+243	+533	+206	+538	+37	— 5
Kentucky	— 37	— 71	— 37	— 65	—	— 6
Tennessee	— 33	— 48	— 39	— 29	+ 6	— 19
Alabama	— 27	— 25	— 16	+ 4	—10	— 29
Mississippi	— 28	— 44	— 11	—	—16	— 44
Arkansas	— 24	— 42	— 22	— 19	— 2	— 23
Louisiana	+ 15	— 21	+ 17	— 2	— 2	— 20
Oklahoma	— 24	— 49	— 25	— 42	+ 1	— 7
Texas	+ 45	— 73	+ 33	— 53	+11	— 19

*Excludes people living abroad in 1955 and people whose 1955 address was unknown.
Source: U.S. Bureau of the Census, U.S. Census of Population: 1960, Subject Reports, Mobility for States and State Economic Areas, Final Report PC(2)-2B, Tables 16 and 18.

white people in an open-class society can take advantage of provided they have the personal qualifications. Negroes, on the other hand, even if they have the personal qualifications, have a more limited range of employment opportunities than do white workers. The fact that Negro workers do not have a wide range of occupational choices explains their relatively low rates of geographic mobility. Movement is facilitated only if jobs are freely available.

The extent to which intraregional migration exceeds interregional migration, for nearly all southern states, is shown in Table 6. Only in Delaware and Florida does gross interregional migration exceed intraregional migration. Net migration, intraregional and interregional, for the southern states by color, is shown in Table 7. It is interesting to note from the data of Tables 6 and 7 how southern states "import" population from sister states, and "export" population to both southern and non-southern states. This fact shows that the redistribution of the South's population, like that of the nation, occurs somewhat indirectly in steps and not by direct migration, as net change and net migration figures seem to imply. The amount of direct migration from southern farms to northern and western cities is probably quite low.

5

Migration is highly associated with age. Many studies have shown this relationship but the most recent and useful information on the subject is found in a 1960 United States Census report showing movement and migration by sex, color, and single years of age for the entire country.[3] Some of these data, presented in condensed form in *Table 8*, show: (1) the highest rates of migration for all sex and color groups are found among young people from 18 to 22 years of age; (2) the migration rates of children under 16 years of age are highly correlated with the migration rates of adults about a generation (28-30 years) older; (3) white people, male and female, migrate at substantially higher rates than do non-white males and females; (4) there is very little difference in the migration rates of males and females, but at certain ages one sex or the other does have the higher rates.

Although these data are national in scope, they are useful in evaluating southern migration which has already been shown to be higher than in the Northeast, North Central, and somewhat under that of the West. Regional data on migration by single years of age are not published as yet.

Estimates of net migration from the South during the 1950-1960 decade, shown in *Table 9*, also show the close association between age and migration. Highest rates of net out-migration during the decade were reached by white males, aged 15-19, and by white females, aged 10-15, in 1950. The peak rates for non-white males and females are in the 15-19 age class. Over the decade these age classes average about five years older—assuming that migration is distributed evenly. Females usually begin migrating about three years before males.

3. U.S. Bureau of the Census, *U.S. Census of Population: 1960, Subject Reports, Mobility for States and State Economic Areas*, Final Report PC(2)-2B.

Table 8. Per cent of the United States Population by Single Years of Age Moving from One County to Another Between 1955 and 1960.

Age in 1960	White		Non-white	
	Male	Female	Male	Female
Total	18.7	17.4	10.8	9.8
5	24.0	23.6	10.7	10.7
10	17.7	17.5	7.6	8.1
15	14.1	14.5	8.4	8.5
16	13.5	13.8	8.9	8.5
17	15.8	14.8	10.3	10.4
18	29.2	27.5	16.0	16.0
19	36.9	32.8	21.9	19.6
20	37.8	34.8	23.8	23.2
21	36.3	35.4	24.4	23.0
22	36.0	36.1	24.9	22.7
23	36.6	36.3	24.5	21.9
24	35.7	36.0	23.8	20.0
25	33.6	35.6	21.3	18.5
26	34.0	33.5	20.4	17.8
27	34.2	31.6	20.8	15.6
28	33.4	29.4	18.5	15.0
29	31.7	27.5	17.4	13.7
30	29.8	25.3	16.1	12.7
35	22.0	19.6	11.7	9.5
40	17.3	15.2	9.6	7.1
45	13.4	11.7	7.3	6.3
50	11.2	10.4	6.3	6.0
55	9.4	9.4	5.8	4.9
65	8.6	9.3	4.7	4.9
75	7.8	8.2	4.6	4.0
85+	8.9	9.8	6.2	7.1

Source: U.S. Bureau of the Census, *U.S. Census of Population: 1960, Subject Reports, Mobility for States and State Economic Areas,* Final Report PC(2)-2B, Table 3.

It is interesting to note that after ages 30 to 35 the direction of white net migration is *to* the South. Among the older non-white population, net migration also turns to the South, but only after 60 years of age. This phenomenon of net migration to the South after middle age is interesting, because it reflects a change in the relative social and economic advantages of southern over non-southern living as people grow older. Perhaps the keen struggle for survival and advancement in the urban North and West is just too much for many former migrants. Some may be coming South to retire or to work in a more leisurely environment and in a milder

Table 9. Net Migration Rates to and from the United States South, 1950-1960, by Age, Sex, and Color.

Age in 1950	Age in 1960	Total	White		Non-white	
			Male	Female	Male	Female
Total	Total	− 2.2	− 0.4	0.0	− 8.9	− 9.4
Births 1955-1959	0-4	− 0.5	− 0.6	−0.7	0.0	− 0.5
Births 1950-1954	5-9	− 1.9	− 0.6	−0.8	− 5.4	− 5.5
0-4	10-14	− 3.1	− 1.1	−1.2	− 8.5	− 9.2
5-9	15-19	− 3.2	+ 0.1	−2.0	− 9.5	−10.7
10-14	20-24	− 8.1	− 3.3	−4.3	−21.3	−21.9
15-19	25-29	−10.1	− 6.9	−3.9	−26.1	−24.9
20-24	30-34	− 5.8	− 3.4	−1.3	−19.5	−18.1
25-29	35-39	− 3.1	− 1.4	−0.2	−13.5	−11.7
30-34	40-44	− 1.3	0.0	+0.5	− 8.3	− 7.6
35-39	45-49	− 1.0	0.0	+0.8	− 6.0	− 7.0
40-44	50-54	− 0.1	+ 0.5	+1.8	− 4.5	− 6.3
45-49	55-59	+ 0.9	+ 1.7	+3.1	− 4.3	− 6.4
50-54	60-64	+ 3.0	+ 3.5	+5.6	− 4.7	− 5.1
55-59	65-69	+ 7.8	+ 8.8	+7.2	+ 4.8	+ 9.3
60-64	70-74	+ 8.7	+10.5	+6.7	+ 9.6	+ 9.9
65 up	75 up	+ 1.1	+ 5.6	+3.6	−10.9	−15.8

Source: Computed by the use of Census Survival Ratios and other data provided by the United States Bureau of the Census.

climate. Others may be returning to claim and exploit inherited wealth and still others may be enterprising Yankees looking for good business opportunities which have been overlooked by native southerners.

Unfortunately the data of *Table 9* may leave a false impression that Negroes are more mobile than white people; but, as pointed out earlier in this paper, Negroes are less mobile than white people. They only seem to be more mobile than white people because of the nature of net migration statistics. The gross migration of Negroes back to the South is relatively much smaller than that of white people, whereas the gross migration of Negroes from the South is only slightly less than that of white people.

6

It has long been thought, and it seems quite likely, that heavy migration to or from a community, a state, or a region, will affect the *quality* of the area's population to some degree. *Quality* in this respect is defined to include a wide range of biological, psychological, and cultural traits which are not so easy to define or to measure as are the purely demographic characteristics such as age, sex, color, and marital status.

In spite of the difficulties involved, there is a growing body of literature on the subject. Interest in the subject has been kept alive by the availability of new Census data on formal education of migrants. Several papers on educational characteristics of southern migrants have appeared.[4]

This writer, using the survival rate method, has analyzed rural-urban and other internal migration in the major geographical regions of the United States for the decade 1940-1950 with respect to educational selectivity. The results of this study have been only partially and inadequately presented in two papers cited above. Other results of this analysis are to be published soon in a book on migration and mental health.[5] The general results of this 1940-1950 analysis may be briefly summarized as follows:

1. There has been some educational selection in net migration to and from the South, but the extent of the selection does not appear to be great enough or of a kind which could seriously either impair or improve the *quality* of the population either biologically or culturally.

2. To the extent that educational selection in migration to and from the South has occurred, the net result seems to confirm the hypothesis that the losses have been relatively greater at the extremes than at the middle of the educational grade scale. During the 1940-1950 decade, the South held and even gained population

4. Noel P. Gist, C. T. Pihlbald, and C. W. Gregory, *Selective Factors in Migration and Occupation* (Columbia: University of Missouri Press, 1944). C. Horace Hamilton, "Educational Selectivity of Rural-urban Migration: Preliminary Results of a North Carolina Study," in *Selected Studies of Migration Since World War II* (New York: Milbank Memorial Fund, 1958), pp. 110-122. C. Horace Hamilton, "Educational Selectivity of Net Migration from the South," *Social Forces*, 38 (October 1959), 33-42. Elmer H. Johnson, "Methodological Note on Measuring Selection in Differential Migration," *Social Forces*, 33 (March 1955), 289-292. Paul H. Landis, "Educational Selectivity of Rural-urban Migration and Its Bearing on Wage and Occupational Adjustments," *Rural Sociology*, 11 (September 1946), 218-232. T. Lynn Smith, *Population Analysis* (New York: McGraw-Hill Book Co., 1948), Chapter 19, "The Selectivity of Migration." Dorothy Swain Thomas, "Selective Migration," *Milbank Memorial Fund Quarterly*, 16 (October 1938), 403-407. George L. Wilber and James S. Bang, *Internal Migration in the United States, 1940-1957. A List of References*, State College, Mississippi Agricultural Experiment Station, Sociology and Rural Life Series No. 10, October 1958.

5. C. Horace Hamilton, "Educational Selectivity in Internal Migration." Contribution to *Migration and Mental Health*. Ed. Mildred Kantor (St. Louis: Washington University, 1965), pp. 166-195.

having an eighth-grade education and even up to the eleventh
grade of high school, and tended to lose population with less than
eight and more than eleven years of formal education.

3. However, the extent and direction of migration varied by age
as well as education and color. Statistically speaking, there was a
significant interaction between age, color, and education. Among
white people, at ages below 30 years, the South lost at the high and
low levels and gained in the middle of the educational scale. Among
young non-whites, however, the heaviest losses by migration occurred at the higher educational levels.

4. The most interesting and significant finding of all was that
among the older age classes net migration by education was definitely favorable to the South. This was most noticeable among
middle-aged and older white migrants, but tended in the same
direction among the Negro migrants. Above age 30, for example,
the South enjoyed a net in-migration of college graduates along
with a shift of the higher net out-migration rates to the lower school
grades. Even at the middle and older ages, however, the South
appeared to be gaining eighth graders at a faster rate than college
graduates. The comparative advantage of the eighth grader in the
South as compared to the non-South is no doubt due to the predominance of rural and small town occupations in the South.

Nevertheless, it is significant to note that a person with less than
an eighth-grade education is, for some reason, finding it either
easier to get work in the non-South or possibly more difficult to
return to the South once he has left. A young educated migrant, on
the other hand, does evidently find it easier to return to the South.
Possibly his family and property ties are strong in the South, and
also, many young migrants from the South may not have found the
social and economic climates of the North and West to their liking.
Having a college education does at least give them a greater range
of choices, whether in leaving or in returning to the South. With the
continuing urbanization of the South, the number and range of
opportunities available should attract even more non-southerners
and ex-southerners back to the region.

With the publication of the detailed 1960 United States Census
volumes on migration, a wealth of new material on educational
selectivity in internal migration has become available. Some of these

Table 10. Interregional Net Migration. Southern Gains and Losses by Age, Sex, and School Years Completed, 1955-1960.*

Age	Total	School years completed						
		Under 5	5-7	8	9-11	12	College 1-3	College 4
White Male								
Total	+19,748	− 6,155	− 2,111	+ 7,018	+13,395	+13,140	+ 2,251	+ 7,790
25-29	−51,939	− 1,548	− 3,672	− 4,613	− 6,580	−13,991	− 8,667	−12,868
30-39	+ 8,595	− 2,285	− 2,004	− 1,110	+ 3,453	+ 9,869	+ 2,265	+ 1,593
40-49	+18,596	− 2,055	− 954	+ 1,897	+ 6,229	+ 8,249	+ 3,160	+ 2,070
50-64	+44,496	− 267	+ 4,519	+10,844	+10,293	+ 9,013	+ 5,493	+ 4,601
White Female								
Total	+85,257	− 4,004	− 956	+13,557	+22,127	+42,047	+10,347	+ 2,139
25-29	−17,030	− 962	− 2,078	− 2,053	− 1,773	− 4,873	− 3,210	− 2,081
30-39	+15,710	− 1,863	− 2,520	− 969	+ 3,644	+14,507	+ 3,032	− 121
40-49	+21,625	− 1,842	− 1,895	+ 1,714	+ 5,718	+13,644	+ 3,244	+ 1,042
50-64	+64,952	+ 663	+ 5,537	+14,865	+14,538	+18,769	+ 7,281	+ 3,299
Non-white Male								
Total	−48,541	− 6,666	− 9,777	− 6,622	−10,715	− 8,282	− 3,169	− 3,310
25-29	−20,627	− 1,125	− 2,741	− 2,295	− 5,563	− 5,261	− 1,965	− 1,677
30-39	−16,747	− 2,333	− 3,725	− 2,465	− 3,879	− 2,129	− 907	− 1,309
40-49	− 7,261	− 1,844	− 2,151	− 1,203	− 900	− 664	− 203	− 296
50-64	− 3,906	− 1,364	− 1,160	659	− 373	− 228	− 94	− 28
Non-white Female								
Total	−60,130	− 5,263	−12,298	− 8,626	−14,841	−11,102	− 3,734	− 4,266
25-29	−21,814	− 504	− 2,240	− 2,089	− 6,484	− 6,062	− 2,108	− 2,327
30-39	−19,438	− 1,136	− 4,082	− 2,933	− 5,199	− 3,677	− 1,083	− 1,328
40-49	−10,271	− 1,361	− 3,093	− 2,095	− 2,063	− 924	− 323	− 412
50-64	− 8,607	− 2,262	− 2,883	− 1,509	− 1,095	− 439	− 220	− 199

*Excludes population living abroad in 1955 and persons whose 1955 residence was not reported.
Source: U.S. Bureau of the Census, U.S. Census of Population: 1960, Subject Reports, Lifetime and Recent Migration, Final Report, PC(2)-2D, Table 8.

Table 11. Net Migration Rates to and from the South by Age, Sex, and Color, 1955.*

	School years completed	Age in 1960				
		Total	25-29	30-39	40-49	50-64
White male	Total	+0.2	− 4.1	+0.3	+0.7	+1.6
	Under 5	−0.7	− 2.7	−1.2	−0.8	−0.1
	5-7	−0.1	− 2.6	−0.5	−0.2	+0.7
	8	+0.6	− 4.1	−0.4	+0.6	+2.2
	9-11	+0.7	− 2.7	+0.6	+1.2	+2.1
	12	+0.7	− 3.7	+1.4	+1.5	+2.6
	College 1-3	+0.3	− 5.5	+0.8	+1.4	+2.7
	College 4+	−0.8	− 6.7	−0.4	+1.1	+2.4
White female	Total	+0.8	− 1.2	+0.5	+0.8	+2.1
	Under 5	−0.6	− 2.4	−1.4	−1.1	+0.2
	5-7	−0.1	− 1.8	−0.7	−0.4	+0.9
	8	+1.1	− 1.9	−0.4	+0.5	+2.8
	9-11	+1.0	− 0.6	+0.6	+1.0	+2.5
	12	+1.5	− 0.9	+1.3	+1.8	+3.7
	College 1-3	+1.1	− 2.2	+1.0	+1.3	+2.6
	College 4+	+0.3	− 2.1	−0.1	+0.6	+1.8
Non-white male	Total	−2.4	− 7.0	−2.9	−1.3	−0.6
	Under 5	−1.0	− 2.6	−1.8	−0.9	−0.4
	5-7	−1.7	− 4.2	−2.3	−1.3	−0.7
	8	−3.1	− 7.1	−3.7	−2.1	−1.2
	9-11	−3.6	− 7.6	−3.4	−1.3	−0.9
	12	−4.7	−10.2	−3.3	−1.8	−1.0
	College 1-3	−5.1	−11.6	−0.5	−1.6	−0.4
	College 4+	−5.5	−14.2	−0.9	−2.0	−0.3
Non-white female	Total	−2.5	− 6.1	−2.7	−1.6	−1.3
	Under 5	−1.0	− 2.0	−1.3	−1.0	−0.9
	5-7	−1.8	− 3.4	−1.3	−1.4	−1.3
	8	−2.9	− 5.2	−3.3	−2.4	−1.9
	9-11	−3.2	− 6.0	−2.9	−1.9	−1.6
	12	−4.0	− 7.7	−3.3	−1.7	−1.4
	College 1-3	−4.8	−11.1	−3.9	−2.0	−1.5
	College 4+	−4.4	−11.4	−3.9	−1.7	−1.0

*Excludes population living abroad in 1955 and persons whose 1955 place of residence was not reported.

Source: U.S. Bureau of the Census, *U.S. Census of Population: 1960, Subject Reports, Lifetime Recent Migration*, Final Report PC(2)-2D, Table 8.

new data have been analyzed only recently and are made available here for the first time. This new data based largely on the Census volume on lifetime and recent migration[6] provide a means for analyzing gross as well as net interregional migration by age, sex, color, and educational level. These data relating to southern migration and some of the most interesting results are shown in *Tables 10,*

6. U.S. Bureau of the Census, *U.S. Census of Population: 1960, Subject Reports, Lifetime and Recent Migration*, Final Report PC(2)-2D.

Table 12. Migration of Youth, 25-29 Years of Age, to and from the South by Sex and Color, 1955-1960.*

	School years completed	Number of migrants			Migration rate (%)		
		In	Out	Net	In	Out	Net
White male	Total	+143,043	+194,982	−51,939	+11.7	+15.9	− 4.1
	Under 5	+ 1,616	+ 3,164	− 1,549	+ 2.9	+ 5.6	− 2.7
	5-7	+ 6,021	+ 9,693	− 3,672	+ 4.4	+ 7.1	− 2.6
	8	+ 8,496	+ 13,109	− 4,613	+ 7.9	+12.1	− 4.1
	9-11	+ 23,314	+ 29,894	− 6,580	+ 9.8	+12.6	− 2.7
	12	+ 44,105	+ 58,096	−13,991	+12.3	+16.1	− 3.7
	College 1-3	+ 21,971	+ 30,638	− 8,667	+14.6	+20.4	− 5.5
	College 4+	+ 37,520	+ 50,388	−12,868	+21.0	+28.3	− 6.7
White female	Total	+126,071	+143,101	−17,030	+ 9.4	+10.6	− 1.3
	Under 5	+ 1,031	+ 1,993	− 962	+ 2.6	+ 5.0	− 2.4
	5-7	+ 4,261	+ 6,339	− 2,078	+ 3.7	+ 5.5	− 1.8
	8	+ 6,722	+ 8,775	− 2,053	+ 6.4	+ 8.3	− 1.9
	9-11	+ 23,844	+ 25,617	− 1,773	+ 7.6	+ 8.1	− 0.6
	12	+ 52,664	+ 57,537	− 4,873	+10.0	+10.9	− 0.9
	College 1-3	+ 20,397	+ 23,607	− 3,210	+14.4	+16.7	− 2.2
	College 4+	+ 17,152	+ 19,233	− 2,081	+17.8	+19.9	− 2.1
Non-white male	Total	+ 8,947	+ 29,574	−20,627	+ 3.3	+10.8	− 7.0
	Under 5	+ 409	+ 1,534	− 1,125	+ 1.0	+ 3.6	− 2.6
	5-7	+ 859	+ 3,600	− 2,741	+ 1.4	+ 5.7	− 4.2
	8	+ 700	+ 2,995	− 2,295	+ 2.3	+10.0	− 7.1
	9-11	+ 2,364	+ 7,927	− 5,563	+ 3.5	+11.7	− 7.6
	12	+ 2,592	+ 7,853	− 5,261	+ 5.6	+17.0	−10.2
	College 1-3	+ 1,178	+ 3,143	− 1,965	+ 7.8	+20.9	−11.6
	College 4+	+ 845	+ 2,522	− 1,677	+ 8.3	+24.8	−14.2
Non-white female	Total	+ 8,139	+ 29,953	−21,814	+ 2.4	+ 8.9	− 6.1
	Under 5	+ 141	+ 645	− 504	+ 0.6	+ 2.6	− 2.0
	5-7	+ 570	+ 2,810	− 2,240	+ 0.9	+ 4.4	− 3.4
	8	+ 593	+ 2,682	− 2,089	+ 1.5	+ 7.0	− 5.2
	9-11	+ 2,357	+ 8,841	− 6,484	+ 2.3	+ 8.7	− 6.0
	12	+ 2,767	+ 8,829	− 6,062	+ 3.8	+12.2	− 7.7
	College 1-3	+ 956	+ 3,064	− 2,180	+ 5.6	+18.1	−11.1
	College 4+	+ 755	+ 3,082	− 2,327	+ 4.2	+17.0	−11.4

*Excludes population who lived abroad in 1955 and population whose 1955 place of residence was unreported. Out-migration rates are based on the South's 1955 population, excluding deaths during the 5-year interval and in-migration rates are based on the South's 1960 population.

Source: U.S. Bureau of the Census, *U.S. Census of Population: 1960, Subject Reports, Lifetime and Recent Migration,* Final Report PC(2)-2D, Table 8.

11, and 12. A close study of these data leads to the following generalizations with regard to educational selection in migration to and from the South in the 1955-1960 period.

1. *Selection against the South's educational level occurs primarily and most heavily among young people and particularly among young Negroes.* In other words, better educated youth are more likely to leave the South than are the poorly educated. How-

ever, an exception is noted among young white females whom out-migration tends to select from the extremes of the educational scale; but the differences are small here.

2. *Above 30 years of age educational selection in migration adverse to the South declines and even changes to a favorable selection in several age-sex classes.* This tendency confirms the findings of earlier studies reviewed above. Among both white males and females, 30-39 years of age, net migration to the South becomes positive at educational levels from the ninth grade through the third year in college and the net out-migration of college graduates is so small as to be insignificant. However, the net migration at lower grade levels remains negative for both males and females between 30 and 40 years of age. Among Negroes, in the 30-40 age range, selection against the South is similar to that among younger Negroes.

3. *At the higher age levels migration tends strongly to be favorable to the South's educational structure.* For example, in the case of white men, 60-64 years of age, the South had a net loss of persons with less than a fifth-grade education and gained less than 1 per cent in the 5–7 grade class; but the South gained from 2 to 3 per cent from school grade eight upward. A similar situation may be noted among white females. Among the older non-white males and females, net migration losses occur at all educational levels—somewhat higher in the middle grades than at the extremes.

Analysis of gross in- and out-migration among young people, 25-29 years of age, shown in *Table 12*, points up two important aspects of educational selection which may be summarized as follows:

4. *Confirming other findings discussed earlier in this paper, white persons are more mobile than non-white persons at every grade level.* The higher rates of migration among the white population are found among both *in-* and *out-*migrants.

5. *The percentage distributions by educational level of in–migrants and out-migrants are almost identical.* One group is about as well-educated as the other. Among both groups, however, there is a high positive association between education and rate of migration. The selective process in migration to and from the South, therefore, operates against the South when gross out-migration

exceeds gross in-migration; and, conversely, in favor of the South when gross in-migration exceeds gross out-migration. This is not so obvious as it sounds because even if out-migration exactly balanced in-migration, selection could operate against the South or any other area if the correlation between education and migration rates were negative in the case of in-migration and positive in the case of out-migration. The amount of educational selection against or in favor of any area, therefore, will depend not only on the amounts and directions of migration but also on the size and directions of the correlations between education and migration.

7

Changing fertility rates in the South relative to those in other regions of the nation are having and will continue to have a bearing on the volume of migration to and from the South. At one time the southern states had higher birth rates than most of the non-southern states, but this is no longer true. In 1960, ten of the seventeen southern states had lower age-adjusted birth rates than the average for the nation. In the case of the white population, twelve southern states had lower adjusted birth rates; but among non-white people only five southern states had lower adjusted birth rates than the national non-white average.

These changing fertility patterns mean simply that the South no longer can be expected to have a surplus white population to be siphoned off to man the businesses and industries of other regions. Other regions of the nation will be forced to raise their own baby crops.

The situation is different among southern Negroes. Their fertility is still high relative to southern whites and to non-southern Negroes. However, these differentials may not continue for long. The rising living and educational levels among Negroes all over the nation will tend to depress their birth rates, and should the changing patterns follow the changes which have occurred among white people, then the time will come when migration from the South of the best educated Negroes will be balanced by migration back to the South of equally well-educated Negroes—a situation which has already been approximated for the white population.

8

The general effects of migration on the southern population can be inferred from the trends and differentials which have been discussed. Although it appears that migration from the South has passed its peak and will gradually decline, the South's total population cannot be expected to grow as rapidly as that of the nation during the next fifteen or twenty years. The decline in the South's agricultural labor force will almost certainly continue, and it is unlikely that southern cities will be able to absorb the population moving off farms and out of rural areas. Another factor is that, in the short run, only a very small decrease in the fertility of southern Negroes can be expected; and hence, population pressure will continue to operate as a causal factor in out-migration. Coupled with this fact is the low rate of Negro in-migration which leaves a high net migration as the inevitable result.

On the other hand, although a number of southern states will continue to lose white population by migration, it can be reasonably conjectured that the next two decades will see a more substantial reversal of out-migration of white people from the South.

If the age-specific birth, death, and migration rates of the past ten years should continue during the 1960-1970 decade, the population of the South would increase by 15.0 per cent as compared with a prospective increase of 18.4 per cent for the non-southern states.[7] By sex and color, the prospective population changes during this decade are:

Sex and Color	South	Non-South
White male	15.5	16.0
White female	16.9	17.2
Non-white male	9.9	39.2
Non-white female	10.7	42.6

Obviously, as the above data show, a very small shift in the direction of net migration of white people to or from the South could bring about a rate of southern population growth somewhat in excess of that of the non-southern states. On the other hand, it would require a very great reversal of out-migration of Negroes to

7. C. Horace Hamilton, "The Negro Leaves The South," *Demography I,* 1 (1964), 273-295.

equalize the growth rates of southern and non-southern non-white populations.

Migration to, from, and within the South will continue to serve as a means of redistributing population and workers, both geographically and occupationally. The great metropolitan areas of the South will continue to grow, and states with large rural populations will continue to lose population to such peripheral states as Texas, Florida, Maryland, Delaware, and Virginia. On the other hand, even the urban and metropolitan populations of the rural states will continue to grow at the expense of migration from rural areas.

Migration will also continue to serve as a means of redistributing the labor force of the South among occupations and industries. As during the past twenty years (1940-1960) the greatest increases will occur in the middle-status low- and moderate-income occupations: craftsmen, operatives, and clerical and kindred workers. Percentage increases in these occupations among Negroes, in spite of out-migration, will be equal to and possibly greater than among the white population.

In the upper-status white-collar occupations (professional, technical, managerial, and proprietorial, and kindred occupations) the increase among whites will be greater than among Negroes—that is, if the trends of the past two decades should continue. This trend is related to the fact that the net migration of Negroes from the South is relatively much heavier among educated Negroes than among educated whites. The only prospect for this situation's changing lies in the success or partial success of current efforts to change employment practices relating to Negro workers. Even if some success should occur in upgrading the occupational status of southern Negroes, it might have very little total effect on the occupational structure unless southern changes were relatively greater than those in the non-southern states—which seems unlikely. The changes would have to be great enough to reverse the relatively heavy out-migration of educated Negroes.

Overall, the prospects for the South's retaining its well-educated population are good. The migration of older well-educated white people back to the South is substantial but not yet great enough to counteract the even heavier net out-migration of young well-educated white people.

If white and non-white populations are combined it must regrettably be predicted that the educational level of the South's population will likely continue to be adversely affected by net migration. The only way to change this general trend is to develop in the South opportunities for employment in occupations, industries, and businesses that require a well-educated labor force. It will also require an upgrading of southern schools, colleges, and of the quality of education in general. It will also involve an increase in high school and college attendance which can only come about by lowering costs, especially college tuition and fees, and in a great increase in the motivation to become educated.

IV. URBANIZATION IN THE SOUTH / Leonard Reissman

1

Urbanization in the South before 1940 was not a particularly significant activity. Cities were growing, to be sure, but at a leisurely pace compared with urbanization in the country at large. The South probably would have maintained a relatively slow pace were it not for the catalyst provided by events that were soon to follow. The year 1940 is stressed here in order to impress upon the reader the fact that the South has come a long way in a short time in urbanization. Prior to 1940 the South could fairly be described, with one or two states excepted, as a predominately rural region here and there dotted with cities. The most apparent evidence for that conclusion was the heavy rural concentration of the South's population. In that year, when a majority of Americans lived in urban places, defined by the Census Bureau as those containing a minimum of 2,500 persons, the majority of southerners lived on farms or in small towns. In 1940 when one out of every three Americans lived in a city of one hundred thousand people or more, only one out of every eight southerners did. To express the difference another way, there were more people living in the three metropolitan areas of New York City, Chicago, and Philadelphia in 1940 than in all of the so-called urban places in the eleven states of the Confederate South combined.

Such Census figures adequately convey the predominately rural settlement of the South's population. Some interpreters, on the contrary, have read those population figures to suggest that a strong urbanizing trend was taking place in the region before 1940.[1] However, the push for urban growth had to come from outside the region, as the subsequent decade showed. Even so, there is more to urbanization than the growth of cities, and when these additional

1. Such seems to be the interpretation offered by T. Lynn Smith in his essay, "The Emergence of Cities," in *The Urban South*, ed. R. B. Vance & N. J. Demerath (Chapel Hill: University of North Carolina Press, 1954), pp. 24-37. To do so, however is to underemphasize the importance of other rural features as are discussed in the essay. Furthermore, as Smith himself noted, "Were it not for the fact that urbanism in the South has always been overshadowed by the national trend, increases in urban centers in southern states would have received more attention" (p. 29). The comparison must inevitably be made between the South and the rest of the nation.

facets of the urban process are considered, then the dominating rurality of the region prior to 1940 is plainly evident. The South's economy, for one thing, from cotton and tobacco to textiles and petro-chemicals was agricultural and rural—at best, a builder of small towns. None of those economic activities required or could support large cities the way heavy industry and manufacturing would. With few exceptions, southern cities functioned primarily to answer the subsidiary needs of an agricultural economy: shipping and warehouse facilities, commercial and credit resources, and entertainment and leisure activities.[2] Intimately tied to that economy was a biracial society that had been frozen into shape by decades of tradition and supported by converging institutional sanctions. This racial caste system by itself did not commit the region to rurality, but its origins in the plantation system of the ante bellum South endowed the caste system with a powerful social inertia that bound the economy to agriculture. The Negro chained the South to agriculture. He provided cheap labor and discouraged technological innovations which would have required scarce capital. The majority of the South's population, the Negro included, was committed to an agricultural, labor-intensive economy as part of its cultural heritage. To make this rural encirclement complete, the South had built a fortress of tradition that was meant to protect the biracial social system. The fortress remained almost impregnable for decades. With so great a proportion of Negroes in the population, southern whites were forced to maintain a complex set of traditions, beliefs, and institutions in order to perpetuate the status quo. Under those circumstances, social changes, especially those implicated in urbanization, were rejected because they might disturb the social balance. In the hierarchy of southern values, change was given a low priority because it might threaten southern society. This attitude suggests that white southerners believed their social arrangements to be highly fragile and that they could be maintained only by constant surveillance. Nor was there any strong attraction exerted by southern cities that might have set the South down the path to change. Few economic appeals to rural residents were exerted by southern cities. Those persons who might have wanted

2. Rudolf Heberle, "The Mainsprings of Southern Urbanization," in *The Urban South*, pp. 9-10.

or felt they had to escape from the land generally tended to leave the region entirely. For all of these reasons, then, the South was held in a tight grip of rurality.

The rural traditions in the South did not weaken appreciably during the decades from 1900 to 1940, a period when the country as a whole was being virtually transformed by urbanization and by the inevitable changes that accompanied it. Compared with the national average, the South consistently showed a lower per capita income, a higher incidence of illiteracy, a lower level of economic productivity, and a lower proportion of people living in cities. These conditions, in one way or another, were the costs of maintaining southern rural traditions: traditions supported by a powerful historical momentum, unleavened by any significant immigration into the region, and left relatively unchallenged by a continuous departure of population out of the region, including among others, those who might have questioned or challenged the traditions.[3] On the contrary, the South was a "seedbed" supplying population to the rest of the country, as Odum had remarked some decades earlier. Even as late as 1951, Danhof found 45 per cent of outstanding southern-born business leaders pursuing careers outside the South.[4]

There was little reason to expect social changes to originate in the relatively small elites that dominated the power structures in southern states. Southern traditions protected an aristocratic social structure as well as the rurality and biracialism mentioned before, and all three supported one another in the same social complex. Compared with most other regions in the country, the South supported a steeply pyramidal stratification structure: a small, white elite at the apex, a relatively small urban-based middle class, both atop a wide base that contained most rural whites, an urban proletariat, and almost all Negroes. Such stratification systems, typical of traditional and rural societies everywhere in the world, lacked a large middle class which is typically the initiator and instigator for

3. In 1960, it was significant to note that 13 per cent of American-born residents of all cities in the country having populations of at least 250,000, were born in the South. The proportion born in the South was higher than for any other region among those urban residents born in states other than where they were living at the time of the Census.

4. Clarence Danhof, "Business Leadership in the South," *The Journal of Business of The University of Chicago*, 39: 130-137, April, 1951.

social changes in its own behalf. In our own history it was the class that possessed the motives and the talents that were the prerequisites for change. Without the middle class, urbanization and all of the changes associated with that process had but little support in the South. Once again tradition—in this case an aristocratic type of social stratification—kept the South from making major social changes.

It was not that the South lacked cities. The region was dotted with cities that boasted histories as long as any city in the country. Charleston, New Orleans, St. Augustine, Mobile, and Norfolk to mention the oldest, had been founded anywhere from twenty to two hundred years before the Revolution. Nor could it be said that the region was geographically isolated as was true of the plains or mountain states. The South was crossed by major interior waterways and was freely exposed to world trade through its Atlantic and Gulf ports. Furthermore, the South could boast of a variegated cultural heritage that stemmed from Spanish, French, German, Irish, English, Portuguese, Italian, and American origins. Each had played some part in the development of the institutions and the culture of southern states. In short, the South possessed some of the necessary preconditions for urbanization to occur, but economics, biracialism, and aristocratic stratification structure, and rural traditionalism combined to blunt or repel most of the forces that would have resulted in urbanization and social change.

For all of their cosmopolitanism, southern cities remained subordinate to the more numerous, more populous, rural sections of the region in the decades before 1940. Politically, the cities were outnumbered and outvoted in state legislatures controlled by rural representatives, much as was the case in many state legislatures in the country. The difference in the South, however, was that the cities were politically weaker than in the North and did not generally build political machines to concentrate their power. Economically, southern cities were dependent upon agriculture so they had but little leverage to win concessions on the political front. Socially, southern cities generally remained isolated from the greater part of southern society. Urban attitudes and urban values remained encapsulated within the city's boundaries long after they had infused the beliefs of most Americans elsewhere. Furthermore, illiteracy and strong rural control combined to keep those attitudes and values from impinging too strongly on those who lived outside the city. Southern cities grew during the forty years from 1900 to 1940, but they did not flourish and did not alter the urban-rural balance in their favor until somewhat later.

Left alone, untouched by urban developments and by the social changes taking place elsewhere in the nation, the South probably would have continued much as it had even beyond 1940, the last year of the region's clearly dominant ruralism. There had been some urban changes before 1940, of course, but compared with the nation as a whole those changes were minimal and simply served to keep the South in the same relative position. For example, from 1900 to 1940 the proportion of people living in southern cities lagged constantly from 20 to 25 per cent behind the national average. That lag can be viewed as symbolic of the general reluctance of southern society to change from ruralism to urbanism, to admit and to incorporate the broad social changes that were implicated in urban development.

But 1940 marked the eve of significant social events whose effects upon southern society are still far from over. The year can be taken to mark the end of a way of life for most of the region that had been followed fairly consistently for more than a century. To be sure, changes such as those to be described do not suddenly spring full-blown, but 1940 can be taken as a clear point for their appearances. The social changes that followed were in many ways the first, sustained, and broad consequences of urbanization that the South had experienced; in their own way, they were even more significant than the Civil War. Certainly compared with the changes that had gone on before 1940, the changes that came after were especially significant and extensive. In the fullest meaning of the word, these were *urban* changes because they built new cities, expanded older cities, increased the urban invasion into the rural countryside and the rural mentality, and in general increased the power of the cities in southern society. Given the entrenched rural traditions, such changes had to be massive and they were: World War II, the space and missile programs, the increased demand for higher education, the growth of commercial air transportation, the U.S. Supreme Court decisions on school integration in 1954 and on urban representation in 1962, and last but by no means least, the mushrooming of an organized Negro militancy intensely dedicated to racial equality. Taken together these events comprised a force for social change too large and too insistent for the South to withstand as it had done more or less successfully in the past. The South, in effect, lost the initiative. It could no longer choose the kinds of social changes it would allow, although it was to take a decade before many southerners would begin to appreciate the significance of that fact; some still do not. The results of those changes were to explode the South into the urban era within the short space of twenty years, or about three times faster than it took for most other regions in the nation to accomplish a similar urban transformation. It is impossible in this essay to explore these events in any great detail, but their relevance for the analysis of urbanization in the South can be indicated briefly.

The war exposed millions of rural southerners to ideas and experiences they had never encountered, through contacts with non-southerners and with urbanites both in this country and abroad. No one can say with certainty what the effects were of that exposure, but it is plausible to assume that it cracked, if it did not destroy, the traditional outlook and perspectives of a great many rural southerners. Many could not, and did not, return again to their former way of life, and even those who did must have retained some residue of their experiences. To be sure, there must have been large numbers of rural southerners who remained almost untouched by their experiences during the war or who returned to the region believing even more strongly in what they had always believed. The point to be stressed, however, is that for millions of persons the war was a leavening experience that tested their traditional values and traditional beliefs in a new setting. Add to this the fact that non-southerners also underwent similar experiences, encountering a region of the country that was new for many of them. Some of this latter group returned to the South later as civilians and initiated one of the most important immigrations into the region that the South had had for decades.

The space program, coupled with the nuclear and electronic technology that is required, built new cities in the South and provided a substantial economic basis for many of the older cities that was new and different; most importantly, this was a basis that was independent of rural control because it had little to do with traditional economic relationships. This urban aspect of the economic changes in the South must be stressed. Southern cities, with a few exceptions such as Birmingham and Mobile, had been bypassed by the major industrial developments in the U.S. at the beginning of this century. Southern cities thereby lost a major opportunity to achieve economic dominance, such as had marked the careers of cities in other regions of the country. The new industrial revolution of the 1950's and 1960's, however, gave the southern cities a second chance for economic growth. Oak Ridge and Huntsville were the immediate consequences of that revolution, and very shortly the effects were felt even in the older cities of the South as well. The high input of federal and private capital associated with the new technology was concentrated, as such things are, in the cities. This infusion of capital has been of decisive importance in creating a new urban-rural balance in the region, for the cities have gained a large measure of economic independence. Increased wealth and economic opportunities, in turn, have attracted rural southerners to move to the cities where earlier they had little reason to do so. Once such urban migrations begin they tend to develop their own momentum, and such has been the case in the South since 1940.

The new technology, with its emphasis upon research and development, demanded a variety and a large number of professional skills. One important consequence of all this has been to introduce a substantial middle class into the region and, necessarily, a middle class based in the cities. The effects on the stratification structure have been revolutionary in their own way, supplying southern cities with a sizeable middle class as the agent for a number of subsequent social changes. A major prerequisite for change that the South had lacked, therefore, was now supplied. For one thing, the expansion of the middle class introduced a politically and socially active element into the former aristocratic and elite-dominated structure. State and local politics soon began to feel the impact of the restructuring of the urban class system. Vocal pressure groups arose, greater discussion of and interest in politics occurred, and, in general, the level of political involvement was raised. The process

is by no means over yet. Concomitantly, there has been a growing
pressure for higher education not only to train the needed professional talent but also to satisfy the educational expectations of a
growing middle class. As one result, southern colleges and universities have expanded and have begun to play a greater role in
regional developments than before. And, as such spiraling developments go, educational expansion and improvement in its turn has
served to attract more middle-class persons into the region.

The great postwar expansion of commercial air transportation
also had its effect upon urbanization in the South. Above all, perhaps, it has served to tie major southern cities into an integrated
transportation web with cities throughout the country and the
world. It is worth remembering that the railroad net, as well as
the subsequent highway net that tended to parallel it, was oriented
primarily east to west. Air transportation shifted the axis, or at any
rate, made it less important. With its greater fluidity, air transportation almost overnight has brought the South back again into a national transportation network from which it had been more or less
excluded since 1869 when the first transcontinental railroad was
completed. In their own way, too, the requirements of the airlines
have built cities to serve as great transportation hubs as, for example, Atlanta, Miami, Houston, and New Orleans. Such developments not only opened up the South but also emphasized the cities
as the points of contact.

More than anything else, perhaps, the decisive factor in the
South's urbanization has been the heightened frequency and success of Negroes demanding changes. Most of the protests, necessarily, have centered in southern cities where Negro organizations
could find sufficient support and be relatively free from intimidation. Just as important, however, has been the fact that the protests
have served to break the mold of rural southern traditions. At the
same time they have exposed a large proportion of the Negro population to what are in essence urban values and urban aspirations.
The Negro population has rejected the place that rural southern
society had insisted it fill, and thereby too, the Negro has helped to
break the chain that bound him and the South to rurality. As much
as anything else associated with the Negroes' militancy has been the
rapidity with which changes have been demanded and won. The

Negro can justly claim that he has waited for more than one hundred years to be given a measure of equality, but it is also true that most of the changes have been effected in less than ten years. By any reckoning this is an astoundingly short period for changes of such scope to be effected. As with the other urban developments that have been described, so too in this instance the South has lost the initiative to accept or reject the changes confronting it. The decisions by the federal judiciary and by other federal agencies have made mandatory the changes in traditional racial practices in the South. There is no doubt that the Negro population will make significant gains in the long run as a result of their successful demands for equality up to now and the demands they will yet make in the future. But even in the short run, the Negro population stands to make significant improvements in its economic position by opening up opportunities in employment and education. The migration of significant numbers of the Negro population to the cities since 1950 is at least one indication of how powerful is the Negroes' desire for economic improvements. At the same time, the Negro urban migration is itself a consequence of greater economic opportunities available in the cities. Sooner or later, even the political voice of the Negro population in urban affairs must become louder. Not that Negro urban ghettos or other forms of segregation will disappear at once, but the urbanizing Negro has already introduced an important dimension into southern society, which had long been structured to disregard it.

The changes that have been described have not taken place uniformly throughout the region. The southern states have responded differently to urbanization and to the changes it has entailed. Additionally, there are variations even between sections within a single state. One result has been to destroy whatever social homogeneity the region may have possessed at one time. It is now abundantly clear, for example, that Florida and Texas are as different from Mississippi and Arkansas as states are likely to be; between those extremes the remaining seven states in the region can be graded. It is not feasible to undertake a detailed documentation in support of that generalization, but since these are essentially urban or urban-associated changes, it might suffice simply to mention the extent of urbanization in the eleven southern states and take that as indicative of the differences between them. In 1960, when 70 per cent of all Americans lived in urban places, only Florida and Texas contained a larger urban proportion, 74 and 75 per cent respectively. Louisiana with 63 per cent urban came reasonably close to the national average. The remaining states, on the other hand, were more rural. Alabama, Georgia, Tennessee, and Virginia grouped around a 50 per cent urban-rural division of their populations. Most rural of all the states were Mississippi, Arkansas, and North and South Carolina, each of which contained some 40 per cent of their population in urban places. These differences, I am suggesting, can be taken as indications that the earlier, southern, regional unity has been fragmented insofar as urban growth implies a number of important social changes. The states that have remained predominately rural thus far have withstood some of the major social changes that have taken place. But in so doing, such states have widened the gap between themselves and the remaining urbanizing states. Change has meant the end of regional unity and the creation of a new kind of national unity on different bases and along new lines.

2

The far-reaching social changes that have been described are all features of the process of urbanization that the South has been experiencing during the last twenty years or so. The process originated in and was initiated by social forces from outside the region, but the changes have caught up the South in their momentum and deeply implicated the region. Consider as one example A. J. Youngson's analysis in which he has attributed the force of economic changes within the South to the American economy as a whole.[5] Atomic power was the result of military pressure; the development of new uses for aluminum drew the Aluminum Company of America into the South; the discovery by a Savannah chemist in 1934 that pulp from southern pine could be used in the manufacture of newsprint, rayon, lacquer, and cellulose products encouraged the movement of some industries into the region to take

5. A. J. Youngson, *Possibilities of Economic Progress* (Cambridge: Cambridge University Press, 1959), pp. 259 ff. Especially Chapter XI, "The Acceleration of Economic Progress in the Southern U.S., 1929-54."

advantage of the large supply of southern pine. "Not all expansion, of course, was of this nature," Youngson went on to note:

> As innovations reduce the cost of some products, more income becomes available to be expended in other directions, and some demand rises, therefore, in fields where no innovations have occurred. Rising demand for Georgia peaches or vacations in Florida is likely to be a reflection of cost reductions in other spheres. When necessities are cheapened in one sector or one region of the economy, demand for luxuries elsewhere may arise. Thus the luxury sector or region benefits from changes elsewhere with which, originally, it had nothing to do. Much economic development in the South has been of this nature too.[6]

Not only have such changes come from outside the region, but just as importantly, the changes frequently have had immediate urban consequences. The best example of that dual feature in change is the redistribution of urban representation in state legislatures to which reference was made earlier. At this writing (December, 1963), only South Carolina and Arkansas of the eleven states in the South have not taken any action as yet to redress the underrepresentation of cities in the state legislatures as a direct result of the U.S. Supreme Court decision in the Tennessee case of 1962 (*Baker* v. *Carr*). The remaining nine states have increased the number of urban representatives either by court decree or by the threat of it. It is too soon to assess fully the consequences of that momentous decision, but it is patently obvious even now that the urban South must benefit from it. The greater political power that has been given to the cities, sooner or later, means a more decisive role for them in setting future policies in the states.

Fortunately, it is possible to consider other facets of the urbanizing process in the South at this time without waiting for the many changes to develop their full consequences. It requires, however, a willingness to read meaning into the patterns of urban development. I have already indicated that urbanization is related to the changes that have been taking place so that the connection should not be considered too novel. The last twenty years have been sufficient to permit significant population shifts toward the cities to take place. Such population shifts provide a concrete measure of the effects of change on the South. In other words, urban migration

6. *Ibid.*, p. 260.

and the urban constellations that have been produced are the results of the social changes that the South has been experiencing since 1940. People migrate to the city for many reasons, and in this case the reasons have been supplied by the changes the South has experienced. Indeed, it is just that kind of relationship between change and migration that is included in the very concept of urbanization.

The analysis of urbanization today in the South, however, must begin with a recognition of the main outlines of urban developments in the U.S. Taken as a whole, the nation experienced at least three distinct stages in its urban development. From approximately 1880 or so until 1930 the very large cities in the country expanded more rapidly than did the smaller cities. These were the decades of the million-plus cities, which seemed to attract even greater numbers of immigrants from year to year. In the decade that followed, from 1930 to 1940, a period of urban consolidation seemed to set in. It was as if the very large cities had reached a saturation point and started to level off, if not in absolute numbers then at least in their rates of growth, while the cities of less than one million showed an increased rate of growth. The decade from 1940 to 1950 brought the beginnings of the metropolitan shift, which really had started soon after the war. Population had begun to leave the central city in significant numbers and to settle in the urban fringe—the suburbs. In the decade beginning in 1950, the metropolitan shift had assumed major proportions as the very large cities lost population to the cities of less than one-half million located in the periphery. Hence, the million-plus cities that contained 12 per cent of the nation's population in 1940 accounted for only 10 per cent of the population by 1960. During the same period, 1950-1960, the cities of ten thousand to five hundred thousand population increased from 31 to 38 per cent the proportion of the total U.S. population that they contained. Sooner or later this centrifugal dispersion of urban population to smaller but more numerous concentrations reached a point where those concentrations adjoined one another.

This kind of expansion has produced a pattern of metropolitan growth known as conurbations—that is, an almost continuous urban sprawl spreading out from one or more metropolitan centers. Three major conurbations have been evident for some time: in the North-east, extending from Boston to Washington, D.C., and slightly be-yond; in the Midwest, from Milwaukee south around Lake Michi-gan and Chicago and in an easterly swath as far as Detroit; and in the Far West, as a bulging band dropping down from San Francisco to Los Angeles. Those three conurbations between them included one out of every three Americans in 1960. America has changed from the million-plus cities typical of the 1930's to the million-plus conurbations of the 1960's and later.

This redistribution of population was recognized formally by the Census Bureau in 1950 when it created the classification, "standard metropolitan area," somewhat revised in 1960 to the "standard metropolitan statistical area." The SMSA is defined by the Census Bureau to include at least one city of fifty thousand persons or more and all of the adjoining territory according to a series of special definitions meant to identify the effective metropolitan unit. As the Bureau explained, the SMSA classification was needed because "it is necessary to consider as a unit the entire population in and around the city whose activities form an integrated social and economic system."[7]

There is little doubt that the expanding SMSA, linked eventually to similarly expanding SMSA's, has created gigantic conurbations that are the dominating urban pattern for the country for the next decade or so. There are some experts who contend that a "hollow-ing-out" process is going on by which population is being pushed into the conurbations at the borders of the U.S., leaving the center of the country relatively underpopulated.

These recent developments of metropolitan areas and conurba-tions are especially significant for the South. For one thing, if the hollowing-out hypothesis is correct, then the South is a likely re-cipient of future immigration. For another, the South has shown signs of adopting the pattern of conurbations since it was current at the time the region seriously entered urbanization. This is under-standable, for the forces that have created suburban expansion and conurbations are as effective in the South as elsewhere. Finally, we are a national society to the extent that political, economic, and

7. U.S. Bureau of the Census, *U.S. Census of Population: 1960, Number of Inhabitants, United States Summary*, Final Report PC(1)-1A (Washington, 1961), p. xxiv.

social changes are national in their scope and impact. The South
has become integrated into the nation in such a way that the region
is no longer able to avoid or evade the consequences of those
changes. On all three counts, then, the South has become involved
in a pattern of national urbanization and it would seem to be an
inevitable result that the South will resemble the national metropolitan pattern more and more within the next decade.

It is not accidental, therefore, that urbanization in the South
from at least 1960 onward must be seen as a process of *metropolitan*
rather than simply city growth and expansion. For that reason, the
population trends we should consider are those in the standard
metropolitan statistical areas rather than in the southern cities
per se. A second purpose to be served by considering SMSA's and
conurbations is to disassemble the South as a region and look at its
effective urban components—to separate, as it were, those sections
which belong together as part of the metropolitan pattern. The
unity of the region—politically, socially, economically, and ecologically—is a thing of the past. The new urbanizing forces that have
been acting on the South since 1940 have fragmented the region
irreparably. What we can now observe is a transition period during
which a new coalition of metropolitan sections in the region will
emerge: that is, conurbations that will transcend existing state and
local boundaries and that will seriously rearrange the urban ecology
of the South.

3

In order to project the character of these metropolitan trends concretely, I would suggest the existence of five major metropolitan
conurbations and two lesser metropolitan complexes that divide the
South into new constellations. The conurbations and complexes
have been formed by geography, economics, population, and the
forces that have been described earlier. These areas are specified
in *Table 1* and graphically shown in *Figure 1*.

These conurbations and urban chains contain over seventeen
million people and include almost 40 per cent of the total population living in the South. There can be little question about the importance of these massive concentrations for the future of the South

Table 1. Metropolitan Conurbations in the South: 1960.

Conurbations & standard metropolitan statistical areas

Gulf Coast Conurbation	Western Inner Core Conurbation
(Population: 3,451,228)	(Population: 3,199,285)
Houston	Dallas
Galveston-Texas City	Ft. Worth
Beaumont-Port Arthur	Abilene
Lake Charles	Austin
Baton Rouge	San Antonio
New Orleans	Laredo
Mobile	Corpus Christi
Pensacola	Waco
	Tyler

Atlantic Coast Conurbation	Carolinas Conurbation
(Population: 3,448,131)	(Population: 1,879,072)
West Palm Beach	Charlotte
Ft. Lauderdale-Hollywood	Greensboro-High Point
Miami	Durham
Orlando	Raleigh
Tampa-St. Petersburg	Winston-Salem
Jacksonville	Roanoke
Savannah	Asheville
Charleston	Greenville
	Augusta
	Columbia

Eastern Inner Core Conurbation	Nashville-Memphis chain
(Population: 3,194,274)	(Population: 1,336,427)
Atlanta	Nashville
Knoxville	Memphis
Chattanooga	Little Rock-N. Little Rock
Huntsville	Ft. Smith
Gadsden	
Birmingham	*Shreveport chain*
Tuscaloosa	
Montgomery	(Population; 661,846)
Columbus	Shreveport
Macon	Monroe
	Jackson
	Texarkana

if only because of the large proportion of the region's population that is involved.[8]

8. There may be some question, however, about the validity of the outlines I have drawn of the conurbations. There is no information available to establish objectively the social and economic unity of each conurbation, hence I have relied upon geography, the linkage between SMSA's by the national highway net, and personal impressions. Others might question some of the places that have been included in each metropolitan complex. Yet, I believe most persons would agree that the general idea of the conurbations is valid as applied to the South and that the major designations are correct even though there might be some difference of opinion about the particular SMSA's included under each designation.

Figure 1. Major Conurbations and Standard Metropolitan Statistical Areas of the South, 1960.

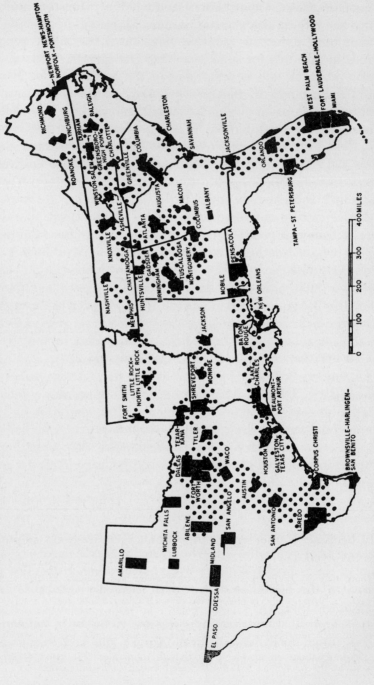

Source: Adapted from U.S. Bureau of the Census, *U.S. Census of Population: 1960, Selected Area Reports, Standard Metropolitan Statistical Areas,* Final Report PC(3)-1D, p. vi.

The Gulf Coast Conurbation is hinged at Houston and New Orleans, the largest cities in the pattern. Shipping, petro-chemicals, and aluminum reduction facilities have been the major economic activities in this area for some time, but the growth of installations for space research and development in the last few years has contributed importantly to the new economy of this conurbation. A significant immigration of population has followed and the conurbation has spread geographically. It is at present the largest conurbation in the South, and the indications point to its continued growth.

The Atlantic Coast Conurbation is heavily concentrated in southern Florida. There might be some question whether it extends as far north as Savannah and Charleston as *Figure 1* shows. The question cannot be answered at this time but it seems plausible to project a heavy population concentration along the Atlantic seaboard to which South Carolina's coastal cities will belong. This conurbation, however, is not part of the much larger eastern conurbation that now ends around Newport News and Norfolk-Portsmouth, Virginia. It is doubtful whether such a linkage will occur in the near future, because there is as yet no reason for large population concentrations along the Atlantic coast to spread south below the Washington, D. C., metropolitan area.

The conurbation that has been called the Eastern Inner Core is centered on Atlanta. Atlanta's economic prominence has been built upon its central role in commercial air transportation and upon its commercial and banking facilities. Atomic research in Tennessee and space research in Huntsville, Alabama, also have contributed to the importance of this conurbation, which is very likely to gain in importance in the future.

A Western Inner Core Conurbation is centered around Dallas and Fort Worth, and it has attracted to it most of the other metropolitan areas in the northeastern quadrant of Texas. The completed and projected superhighway network makes clear the linkage of these metropolitan areas to one another. It is a fast growing area in the South, and it would seem likely to continue its growth in the future.

The Carolinas Conurbation is distinguished by a collection of relatively small metropolitan areas. Unlike the first four conurbations, the Carolinas lacks a clearly dominant center. It contains

fewer people than the other conurbations even though it includes
the greatest number of SMSA's. Such dispersal is the result of the
area's economy; tobacco and textiles do not build large cities but
tend instead to spread population out in a series of small factory
towns.

The two remaining metropolitan chains are lesser conurbations
in the South. It is impossible now to predict their future with any
accuracy, for they can move in one of two directions: either they
will be bypassed in the future and remain relatively static, or they
will become incorporated into the major conurbations near them.
Hence, the Shreveport chain may become linked to the Fort Worth-
Dallas conurbation. The Nashville-Memphis chain may also divide,
with the Tennessee part being pulled into the Atlanta orbit, while
the Arkansas part is left to itself. One would want a few years more
to pass before making any predictions for either of these metropolitan complexes.

A major point to be emphasized is that the metropolitan pattern that has emerged in the South resembles the national pattern.
A related point also needs to be reiterated. The metropolitan conurbations in the South mean the end of the region as a homogeneous unity and the creation of a new alignment in which the older
boundaries and older loyalties have less functional meaning. For
most of the South this will come to mean, as it already has in some
cases, the development of new chains of common interest and outlook. If this prediction is correct, then Alabama, for example, is
likely to find itself divided into two separate conurbations: Mobile
tied into the Gulf Coast Conurbation and the northern section of
the state aligned with the conurbation centered on Atlanta. A
similar division could be seen to exist for Louisiana with the northern and southern portions of the state tied into different urban
networks. The creation of such divisions, with all of their economic
and social consequences, might well come to mean that southern
states will encounter increasing internal political conflicts as the
needs of different sections of the state come more and more into
conflict.

It should be stressed that these metropolitan constellations represent more than just an abstract neighborliness based on geographic proximity. Rather, they have reference to an emerging

pattern of functional unity within the conurbation that is reflected in common political and economic interests as well as in a whole range of social conditions common to the conurbation. The existing legal and administrative boundaries, it is safe to say, will continue to stay for some time even though they will become increasingly dysfunctional. In this respect, unfortunately, the South will share the same problems and frictions that have been monotonously repeated in the older metropolitan conurbations elsewhere.

Some southern states that were least responsive to the broad changes that have been described, notably Mississippi and Arkansas, quite likely will be bypassed by these metropolitan developments. They are generally under-urbanized to begin with, and in some measure they belong to the lesser metropolitan chains, as shown in *Figure 1*. The SMSA's within those states probably will soon reach their maximum growth and then remain relatively isolated and static. One sign of that condition is even now apparent in the fact that Mississippi and Arkansas each lost population during the decade 1950-1960, 700,000 and 123,000 respectively. Since those figures are net losses, it is very likely that the out-migration from both states was considerably higher than those figures indicate. Mississippi's future, however, seems somewhat brighter than that of Arkansas in view of the NASA facility that is planned for Mississippi's Gulf Coast region.

The position and role of the Negro population in all of these developments deserve special attention. More than any other single feature, the changes that have taken place in the Negro population in the South reflect the depth and character of the trends that have been described. There is no question that Negro migration since 1940 has been of great significance in the South's urbanization. Before that time, the needs of an agricultural economy and the traditions of a biracial society combined to tie the bulk of the Negro population to the farm and the small town. Negroes had but little incentive to migrate to the city. Poverty, lack of skill, and a sense of psychological security bound the large proportion of Negroes to the rural birthplace. When in 1940, three out of every ten southerners was a Negro, it was almost as difficult for the South to urbanize as it is for underdeveloped areas throughout the world today to improve their standard of living, and for about the same reasons. The resources of the South simply were insufficient to support any major urban changes, the more so when such changes had to occur within the restrictive requirements of southern racial traditions. Southern states might have prided themselves on allocating such a high proportion of their scarce income for education and welfare services, but they received few concrete benefits from such costly expenditures as long as they insisted on keeping their traditions intact. One might as well praise the efforts of a pianist who has played a difficult concerto with one hand tied behind his back: the performance was astonishing but unnecessarily difficult.

The broad urbanizing changes that the nation has initiated in the South have also meant critical changes for the Negro population, which in turn, has accelerated those changes even more by its responses. Most noticeably, the Negro has been leaving the South, and within the South he has been moving to the cities. Only thirty years ago, the eleven states in the Confederate South contained 70 per cent of the entire Negro population in the country. At present, that proportion has dropped to around 50 per cent and undoubtedly will continue to decrease still further. As part of that same trend of migration, the Negro has been moving to the cities in such significant numbers that even southern Negroes are now predominately urban residents. Hence, even such states as Arkansas and Mississippi, both of which had a net loss of more than one hundred thousand Negroes from 1950 to 1960, still have shown a net gain of Negroes in their metropolitan areas during the same period. So too in every one of the southern states, the Negro urban migration has been increasing since 1940.

A feature of the urban migration by the Negro within the South has been the absence of any clear segregation of the Negro to the central city and the white to the urban fringe, as has become generally typical for the rest of the nation. As can be seen from the figures in *Table 2*, in Florida, Louisiana, Tennessee, and South Carolina, the Negro gains in the metropolitan fringes have been larger than in the central city. To those states must be added Texas, which tends to extend the city limits rather than to create separate suburban places. Where the major population growth during the decade 1950-1960 has been in the central city, then the fringe growth has been low for Negroes as well as for whites, as can be

Table 2. Population Changes in States and Standard Metropolitan Statistical Areas, by Race: 1950-1960.

State	Percentage change in white population			Percentage change in Negro population		
	State	Central city	Fringe	State	Central city	Fringe
Alabama	9.8	34.4	15.7	*	17.5	− 1.9
Arkansas	− 5.9	12.9	44.4	− 8.6	10.2	8.3
Florida	87.6	47.8	149.1	45.9	43.2	105.3
Georgia	18.3	36.4	45.6	5.6	32.2	7.1
Louisiana	21.4	11.5	89.6	17.7	29.1	39.1
Mississippi	5.6	60.3	5.0	− 7.3	26.8	− 4.2
North Carolina	14.0	42.7	8.4	6.5	27.4	− 5.1
South Carolina	19.9	6.6	56.8	.9	6.4	33.3
Tennessee	7.8	5.3	38.1	11.1	17.2	43.8
Texas	24.5	49.2	24.2	21.3	64.1	14.0
Virginia	21.7	39.3	14.9	11.4	39.6	−21.7
The South	24.1	37.0	46.4	8.9	34.7	20.7

*Less than .1
Source: U.S. Bureau of the Census, *U.S. Census of Population: 1960, Selected Area Reports, Standard Metropolitan Statistical Area,* Final Report PC(3)-1D (Washington, 1963), Table 1.

seen in the cases of Virginia, Alabama, North Carolina, and Mississippi. Georgia, and possibly Arkansas, have come closer to the national pattern than most other southern states, although the growth of population in the central cities in Georgia has been almost as large as in the fringe.

4

The changes in the South in the last twenty years have done much to alter every feature of its social landscape. This author is well aware of the glibness with which observers have been ready to attribute a new look to the South. Too often one encounters the clichés about "the new South" or "the changing South." Not to be forgotten are the events of 1962 and 1963 in which sections of the South responded almost as usual to Negro protests and demonstrations. The significant point even in this connection, however, is that so many sections responded so differently than before. Birmingham's violence was counterbalanced by the saner responses in Dallas, New Orleans, and Atlanta. The South has changed significantly from what it was. Federal activity, national economic and political trends, and the organized and militant spirit of the

Negro population coupled with its urban migration, have combined to crack, if not to destroy, the traditional southern resistance to change.

The effect, as described here, has been to bring the South closer to the national pattern of urban and metropolitan developments. The gap in 1960 was narrowed enough, in fact, to expect that the South will go more or less as the nation goes in the next few decades to come. In many ways, the fact of population redistribution is indicative of the deeper social, economic, and political changes that the South has begun to experience. As noted earlier in this essay, urbanization involves not only a change in locale but also a change in attitudes, values, and institutions.[9] It is evident even now that the South has begun to leave behind the traditions, economy, and social structure that have held the region in a tight rural grip for so much of its history. The rural South has become, and will increasingly become, a complex series of metropolitan conurbations, which will make out-of-date the older regional and rural conceptions of the South.

9. Since writing this essay I have come across a book by William H. Nicholls, *Southern Tradition and Regional Progress* (Chapel Hill: University of North Carolina Press, 1960) with which I am in substantial agreement. Nicholls contends that southern traditions account in substantial part for the lag of industrial-urban development in the South, and he goes on to specify the components of tradition as follows: "(1) the persistence of agrarian values, (2) the rigidity of the social structure, (3) the undemocratic nature of the political structure, (4) the weakness of social responsibility, and (5) conformity of thought and behavior" (p. 15). These are important and relevant components of southern culture and social structure. The difference between Nicholls' prognosis and the one suggested here, I believe, is, as I have argued, that the South has lost the initiative for dictating the social changes that will occur. Probably more than ever before, the region has been caught up in national developments and, therefore, its future patterns of development will come to resemble those that are current nationally. Hence, when Nicholls contends, "The very lateness of the South's economic development offers a real opportunity to avoid some of the excesses of Northern industrial-urban growth; with proper foresight and planning, the South can still avoid them" (p. 9)—I can only applaud the sentiment expressed but must remain much less sanguine about the possibilities of achieving them in reality.

V. SOUTHERN ECONOMIC TRENDS AND PROSPECTS / Joseph J. Spengler

> The end of the state is the good life.
>
> ARISTOTLE, *Politics*, III, 9.

> We live in a rich society, which nevertheless in many respects insists on thinking and acting as if it were a poor society.... The ultimate sources of our large and growing wealth ... are to be found ... in the accumulation of capital and application of technical progress by corporate enterprises and the acquisition of increasing skill and knowledge by individuals—the accumulation of human capital.
>
> H. G. JOHNSON, *Money, Trade and Economic Growth*, pp. 166, 180.

The term South, as used in this chapter, usually embraces the East and West South Central states (except Oklahoma) and Virginia, the Carolinas, Georgia, and Florida. Occasionally it denotes all three southern divisions of states, when data available for the South thus defined yield inferences applicable to the Old South. The central concern here is the movement of income in the South and the behavior of factors underlying this movement.

1

In his introductory essay Professor McKinney suggests that the South may be viewed as an interaction system in which the forces making for stability have produced structural continuity despite the strength of change-producing forces. It is true that the economy of the South has manifested continuity; its physical environment has persisted and some of its interaction systems have proved stable despite recurring instability in others. There may even be some warrant for dealing with the "economy" of the South as if it were a subsystem of the national economy; certainly so doing helps us to surmount various analytical difficulties.

Suppose that, with P. A. Samuelson, we define an economic system as one consisting

of a designated set of unknowns which are constrained as a condition of equilibrium to satisfy an equal number of consistent and independent equations [which] are implicitly assumed to hold within a certain environment and as of certain data.[1]

The economy of the South does not conform closely enough to this description to be designated an economic system. While its physical environment has remained fairly constant, the economic significance of this environment has changed, as have many socioeconomic aspects of the southern economy. Moreover, much of the change undergone by the southern economy is not of the sort entirely determined by the conditions which completely and systematically defined that economy at earlier points in time. The South's behavior has at most resembled that of a "dynamic and historical" system subject to autonomous and exogenous changes as well as to changes flowing out of the system itself.

For analytical reasons, however, we shall proceed at times as if the South were an economic system. Then we can estimate roughly how economic interaction within the South responds to changes affecting its price and income structures and the external relations of these structures. We shall assume that in the main the South's economic decision-makers, its entrepreneurs, its suppliers of productive factors, and its households, or consumers, seek to maximize something: the entrepreneur, his longer-run profits; the factor-supplier, his return therefrom (given his tastes for leisure and security); and the household, or consumer, his "ordinal preference scale of quantities of consumption goods and services." We shall even assume that these decision-makers act as if the society in which they live is equipped with a social policy in keeping with its degree of opulence.[2]

Even though the South is not accurately describable as an economic system, it is characterizable as an economic region. For, though shot through with heterogeneity, it still is homogeneous enough. Its members have enough environmental and other ele-

1. *Foundations of Economic Analysis* (Cambridge: Harvard University Press, 1947), p. 19; also see pp. 21-22. Compare also J. R. Hicks, *Value and Capital* (London: Oxford University Press, 1948), chap. 5.
2. On such policy see H. G. Johnson, *Money, Trade and Economic Growth* (Cambridge: Harvard University Press, 1962), chap. 9. On the theory and nature of adjustment within a regional framework see Walter Isard, *Methods of Regional Analysis* (New York: John Wiley & Co., 1960); G. H. Borts and J. L. Stein, "Regional Growth and Maturity," *Schweizerische Zeitschrift für Volkswirtschaft und Statistik*, XCVIII (1962), 290-321; J. R. Meyer, "Regional Economics," *American Economic Review*, LIII (March, 1963), 19-54; A. C. Anderson, "Den Amerikanska Södern-En Region I Omvandling," *Svensk Geografisk Arsbok*, Lund (1955), 199-231.

ments in common and they have experienced enough similar problems to meet the requirements of the region-oriented economist if not also the more rigorous specifications of the factor analyst.[3] Moreover, the states composing the South have shared sufficient politico-military, racial, demographic, agricultural, and industrial history to develop a quite common outlook. It is this common history and common experience that have helped give continuity to the South as an economic region and so have conditioned the pace of economic change and income growth in the South.

2

In times past physical environment has been treated as the major source of product outside labor. This view, especially manifest in politico-military and Malthusian analyses, had much plausibility when 70-90 per cent of the labor force remained in agriculture and the imputed product of labor was relatively low. Even today this view is not entirely without merit. One cannot wholly disregard the South's physical environment when analyzing its economic past or its prospect; for, since environment is a means, its economic significance changes whenever man's wants or capacities change. Indeed, the future welfare, both eudaemonic and economic, of the southern people depends greatly upon their ability to exploit environmental opportunities emerging in the South.

While the South's physical environment has remained quite stable, the economic significance of this environment has changed, sometimes notably. The outside limits set by this environment to what is attainable at any time, given the current composition of aggregate demand and technology, have been shifted, sometimes inwardly but mostly outwardly. The relative contribution of natural resources to production has diminished, in part as a result of greater economy in the use of raw materials. Moreover, technological change has enlarged the range of raw-material substitutes as well as the amount of economically utilizable raw stuff and thus has

3. Margaret Hagood, in "Statistical Methods for Delineation of Regions Applied to Data on Agriculture and Population," Social Forces, XXI (March, 1943), 287-296, finds that Florida and Texas are marginal members of the contiguous "South" and that West Virginia might be a marginal member. Small portions of the South belong in economic areas centered outside the South. See D. J. Bogue and C. L. Beale, Economic Areas of the United States (Glencoe: The Free Press, 1961); H. M. Mayer, "Urban Geography and Urban Transportation Planning," Traffic Quarterly, XVII (October, 1963), 626-630.

enabled man to escape constraints formerly imposed by particular scarcities, and improvements in transportation have extended the area whence raw materials may be drawn. Finally, with increase in per capita income, the proportion of it spent upon imputed outputs of environment (i.e., land and other natural resources) other than recreation has tended to fall, though the absolute amount of such expenditure has increased and the aggregate demand for space and raw materials has grown somewhat more rapidly than population.[4] It is mainly out of population change and income growth, together with progress in public health, technology, and communications, that opportunities to capitalize on the South's physical environment will flow.

Among the prospectively fruitful elements in the South's physical environment one may include the South's proximity both to some foreign markets[5] and to the North and East where live about 45 per cent of the nation's population. The degree to which proximity to markets is favorable varies, in respect to specific industries, directly with transport costs and inversely with economies of scale, the significance of which may be declining relatively to that of transport costs. Of much greater importance is the South's endowment of water, space, and climate, the economic significance of any one of which is often enhanced by the copresence of the others.

As population and income grow, water requirements increase, and water, at one time exemplar of the economist's "free good," becomes a limitational or "bottleneck" factor. In some parts of the United States, dearth of water is already constraining expansion of output and living standards, and water is having to be allocated with increasing care.[6] The South (exclusive of most of Texas) lies

4. See J. J. Spengler, ed., *Natural Resources and Economic Growth* (Washington, D. C.: Resources for the Future, 1961); also H. J. Barnett and Chandler Morse, *Scarcity and Growth* (Baltimore: Johns Hopkins Press, 1963). For an earlier interpretation of the South's environment see A. E. Perkins, *The South: Its Economic Geographic Development* (New York: John Wiley & Sons, 1938). Many issues dealt with in my paper are treated in a fine collection of essays which appeared when this study was in the process of publication. See M. L. Greenhut and W. T. Whitman, eds., *Essays in Southern Economic Development* (Chapel Hill: University of North Carolina Press, 1964).

5. In 1960 the South exported about $2,978 million of manufactures and about $1,656 million farm commodities. These figures are based upon unpublished estimates prepared by the U.S. Department of Commerce. See also note 79 below. In a news release on January 15, 1965, Secretary of Commerce Luther H. Hodges put exports of southern manufactures at $3,241 million, or 17.7 per cent of the nation's exports of manufactures.

6. C. C. Bradley, "Human Water Needs and Water Use in America," *Science*,

in the humid East which, along with the Pacific Northwest, enjoys a "generally large continuously available supply of water."[7] This water is required for irrigation, manufacturing, power generation, municipal use, on-site use (for wildlife, ponds, soil conservation), and above all, to absorb or carry off wastes. Even in the East by 1980 these requirements, though heavier in the North than in the South, will approximate "40 per cent of the maximum flow that could be made available and about four times the daily flow now available 95 per cent of the time."[8] Since requirements in the West will then be approximating the maximum dependable flow, the South as well as the Pacific Northwest will enjoy a differential advantage over the West in respect of water. Southern agriculture and recreation in particular may profit, for since the value of water when scarce is much lower when used in agriculture and recreation than when utilized in cities or in manufacture, westerners will divert it increasingly to urban and industrial uses.[9] Relative plenitude of water should also facilitate beautification of southern cities and countrysides, now too often as much of an eyesore in the South as in the North or even as in India and Pakistan. Abundance of water may also act in combination with the South's relatively favorable climate to accentuate advantages flowing from its comparative abundance of land.[10]

CXXXVII (October 26, 1962), 489-491; also Roger Revelle, "Water," *Scientific American*, CCIX (September, 1963), 92-109.

7. H. H. Landsberg *et al.*, *Resources in America's Future* (Baltimore: Johns Hopkins Press, 1963), pp. 259, 380-381; David W. Miller *et al.*, *Water Atlas of the United States* (Port Washington, L. I., New York: Water Information Center, 1962), Plates 3, 7, 9-10, 13, 38.

8. Landsberg, *et al.*, *op. cit.*, p. 381. On withdrawals by state see Miller, *op. cit.*, Plates 31-36, 39-40. On factors affecting availability and efficiency of use of water see E. A. Ackerman and G. O. G. Löf, *Technology in American Water Development* (Baltimore: Johns Hopkins Press, 1959), Parts II-III.

9. Nathaniel Wollman estimates that in New Mexico an acre-foot of water used in manufacture or by municipalities is about sixty times as valuable as one used in agriculture and about ten times as valuable as one used in recreation. See *The Value of Water in Alternative Uses* (Albuquerque: University of New Mexico Press, 1962).

10. The South is well adapted to agriculture as well as to military training. The growing season is considerably longer in much of the South than in the states to the North, the temperature is more moderate and equable, there is less snow, and average frost penetration is much lower. See Miller, *op. cit.*, Plates 5-6; U.S. Bureau of the Census, *Statistical Abstract of the United States: 1962* (Washington, D. C., 1963), pp. 177-180 (hereinafter cited as *Statistical Abstract*). On aspects of the role of climate see E. L. Ullman, "Amenities as a Factor in Regional Growth," *Geographical Review*, XLIV (1954), 122 ff; V. R. Fuchs, *Changes in the Location of Manufacturing in the Central States* (New Haven: Yale University

The South is better endowed with space than most states situated to the North, its population density of 34-80 per square mile falling far short of that in most northern states. Moreover, even though population density is higher in the South than in states west of the Mississippi (except California), the South is more abundantly supplied with water than most and equipped with a better climate than many. Because the South's land-man ratio is relatively high and its population is less concentrated than that to the North,[11] even its urban inhabitants have relatively good access to space, demand for which tends to rise with income (when space is to be had) and especially with the development of motor transport and the expansion of the demand for recreation. For population density within cities, especially in the central portion, tends to increase with size of a city,[12] and so does difficulty of access to the immediate countryside where some recreation facilities are situated.[13] Southern cities have not, however, capitalized as they might on their lower density;[14] they have made too little provision for

---

Press, 1962), pp. 92-95, 100-101, 104.   On military expenditure see *ibid.*, pp. 149-151, 163.

11. In 1960, according to the Census for that year, about 58 per cent of the South's population was urban and 13 per cent lived in cities over 250,000; in the United States the corresponding percentages were 69.9 and 22.   Of the South's population, 46 per cent were in Standard Metropolitan Statistical Areas, though 78.7 per cent remained in places below 100,000; the corresponding percentages for the nation were 66 and 71.5.   See note 18 below.

12. See Fuchs, *op. cit.*, pp. 93, 103. Average density in 1950 rose from 1,695 per square mile within the boundaries of cities of 2,500-5,000 through 5,075 for those of 50,000-100,000 to 14,105 for those of a million and over.   See Marion Clawson *et al., Land for the Future* (Baltimore: Johns Hopkins Press, 1960), pp. 77-95, 520-525.   Data gathered for the Census of 1960 produce a similar pattern. U.S. Bureau of the Census, *U.S. Census of Population: 1960, I, Characteristics of the Population,* Pt. A, p. xiii. It does not follow, however, that land used per person was (say) about three times as high in places of 2,500-5,000 as in places of 50,000-100,000, for not all land within city boundaries is used (Clawson *et al., op. cit.*, p. 95), in part because of relative undertaxation of idle land. Increase in city size not only tends to reduce the land-man ratio; it also increases the relative monetary price of land and so produces a substitution effect against land.

13. Let A represent the area of a circular city whose population is proportional to A, or Πr^2, where r is the radius and also the index of difficulty of access to the region surrounding A; then r increases as the square root of A. In actuality, since population increases more rapidly than A, difficulty of access may increase somewhat more rapidly than $\sqrt{A}$. On the role of land in recreation see Clawson *et al., op. cit.*, chap. 3; Landsberg *et al., op. cit.*, chap. 11.   Also Sebastian de Grazia, *Of Time, Work and Leisure* (New York: Twentieth Century Fund, 1962); F. S. Chapin and S. F. Weiss, eds., *Urban Growth Dynamics* (New York: John Wiley & Sons, 1962), chap. 11 on city livability.

14. Density is somewhat lower within southern cities in given size ranges than in northern and eastern cities. Clawson *et al., op. cit.*, pp. 90, 520-525; also U.S. Bureau of the Census, *U.S. Census of Population, 1960, I, Characteristics of the Population,* pp. 1-40-49.

municipal and county parks even as southern states have made too little use of their park potential.[15] In the South, therefore, as elsewhere, urban as well as rural land is not being put to its best uses. Urban land misuse, artificial crop control, bribing landowners not to cultivate, and replacing land by creeping concrete command far more political and commercial support than does optimizing land use.[16]

Although much of the South's farm population remains to be urbanized,[17] the predominance there of relatively small cities may enable the South to escape the "urban sprawl" and "squeeze" and permit it to optimize the size and internal organization of its cities.[18] As yet most southern cities remain free of heavy pressure to economize on space, usually at the expense of amenities. Southern city planners have done little, however, to take advantage of their favorable spatial situations.

15. Clawson *et al.*, *op. cit.*, pp. 156-158; *Statistical Abstract: 1962*, pp. 203, 205. On aspects of urban land use see Lowden Wingo, Jr., ed., *Cities and Space* (Baltimore: Johns Hopkins Press, 1963).

16. On adverse effects of current national land policy upon land and resource use, see J. F. Timmons, "Land and Water Resource Policy," *Journal of Farm Economics*, XLV (February, 1963), 95-108. According to Don Bogue the addition of one member to the urban population in 1929-1954 was accompanied by the conversion of 0.17-0.26 acres of rural land to urban land. See *Metropolitan Growth and the Conversion of Land to Non-Agricultural Uses*, Studies in Population Distribution, No. 11 (Oxford, Ohio: Scripps Foundation, 1956).

17. By the close of the century, the number of farm operators, 3.7 million in 1960 (of whom about two-fifths were in the South), will have declined to between 0.6 and 1.0 million. See G. S. Tolley and H. W. Hjort, "Age-Mobility and Southern Farmer Skill—Looking Ahead for Area Development," *Journal of Farm Economics*, XL (February, 1963), 15, 24-25; also Edward Higbee, *Farms and Farmers in an Urban Age* (New York: Twentieth Century Fund, 1963). This trend, while conditioned by the age composition of farm operators, 87 per cent of whom are over thirty-four and hence not very mobile, is reinforced by the failure of the 61 per cent of operators selling below $5,000 of produce to supply more than 12 per cent of all produce sold, or to average as much as $1,300 net cash farm income from produce sales of $2,500-5,000. See J. V. McElveen, "Farm Numbers, Farm Size, and Farm Income," *Journal of Farm Economics*, XL (February, 1963), 7-11. Of the South's 1.48 million farm operators, only 23 per cent or 0.34 million sold more than $5,000 of produce, according to the 1959 Census of Agriculture. About 85 per cent of the nearly 966,000 non-white operators in the South sold less than $5,000. Many low-income farmers, white and non-white, supplement their farm incomes with wage or salary income.

18. See Edward Higbee, *The Squeeze* (New York: William Morrow, 1960); W. H. Whyte, Jr., *et al.*, *The Exploding Metropolis* (Garden City, N. Y.: Doubleday, 1958), esp. chap. 5. The pattern of southern cities reflects the effects of motor transport as do western cities which developed after the motor car came into general use. See R. B. Vance and N. J. Demerath, eds., *The Urban South* (Chapel Hill: University of North Carolina Press, 1954), pp. 144-147. Of the South's thirty-eight cities of 100,000 or more in 1960, only one has close to a million inhabitants, four have around a half million, and five have between 300 and 500 thousand, but there were eleven urbanized areas of over 500,000 inhabitants and eight with 250,000-500,000. However, see note 11 above.

What constitutes an optimum size city varies with city type. Both net productivity per worker and the per capita cost of urban services rise as city size increases, the former until a limit is reached and the latter perhaps without limit. Other costs and disadvantages, only some of which assume explicit monetary form,[19] increase with city size. The availability of cultural amenities subject to great economies of scale also increases with city size. In general, a city may be said to be of optimum size when the total marginal cost of additional population balances the marginal economic or "welfare" yield of such addition; this principle is compatible with a range of optima, however.[20] Indeed, some hold that optimum city size falls largely if not wholly within the range fifty thousand to five hundred thousand inhabitants. Even given this range, a very large fraction of a nation's population could get assembled into a small number of cities.[21] Optimum city sizes have tended to be exceeded, largely because city builders have failed to take all costs of size, public and private, as well as all benefits of smaller size, into

19. A case in point is the time cost of journeying to and from work, which tends to vary with city size and for which workers apparently are little compensated (though it has been argued that this cost is at least partly shifted to the employer and then to the consumer in the manner of an excise on work). See Lowden Wingo, Jr., *Transportation and Urban Land* (Washington, D. C.: Resources for the Future, 1961), pp. 59-62. De Grazia, *op. cit.*, p. 73, puts the average time cost at 8½ hours per week, with the cost much higher in large than in small cities. See also Leo F. Schnore, "The Separation of Home and Work: A Problem for Human Ecology," *Social Forces*, XXXII (1954), 336-343; E. J. Taafe *et al.*, *The Peripheral Journey to Work: A Geographic Consideration* (Evanston: Northwestern University Press, 1963); K. K. Liepman, *The Journey to Work* (New York: Oxford University Press, 1944), chap. 2, esp. pp. 50-56. According to L. K. Loewenstein, "Commuting and the Cost of Housing in Philadelphia," *Traffic Quarterly*, XVII (April, 1963), 302-319, the cost of journeying to work is both considerable and inversely related to site rent. The U.S. Census of 1960 reports mode of transport and where workers lived and went to work, but not in a form to permit a good estimate of the time absorbed by journey to work.

20. It is not easy to locate the optimum both because changes in size effect various functions differently and because it is not always easy to estimate costs and advantages. See Otis Dudley Duncan, "Optimum Size of Cities," in J. J. Spengler and O. D. Duncan, eds., *Demographic Analysis* (Glencoe: Free Press, 1956), pp. 372-385; R. M. Lillibridge, "Urban Size: An Assessment," *Land Economics*, XXVIII (November, 1952), 341-352; W. H. Ludlow, "Urban Densities and Their Costs...," in Coleman Woodbury, ed., *Urban Redevelopment: Problems and Practices* (Chicago: University of Chicago Press, 1953), Part II.

21. Lillibridge, *op. cit.*; Ludlow, *loc. cit.*, pp. 153-158; Colin Clark, "The Economic Functions of a City in Relation to Size," *Econometrica*, XXXIII (April, 1945), 97-113. On city size and function see A. K. Philbrick, "Areal Organization in Regional Geography," *Papers and Proceedings*, Regional Science Association, III (1957), 87-98. Of the respondents queried in Durham and Greensboro, North Carolina, not quite one-fifth wanted to live in a place of over 100,000. See Chapin and Weiss, *op. cit.*, pp. 374-376, 390.

account.[22] Optimum sizes would be more nearly approximated in the South were they made objects of public and private policy.

3

We turn now to trends in per capita income, the best single indicator of the performance of the southern economy. The South has been doing badly for at least a century. Back in 1840 per capita income was 60 per cent higher in the West South Central states than in the nation, 84 per cent as high in the South Atlantic states, and 85 per cent as high in the East South Central states. In 1880 (and presumably during the fifteen years following the Civil War), the comparable percentages were 60, 45, and 51, and they continued at these levels for at least twenty more years, in 1900 approximating 61, 45, and 49. Under the impact of World War I, however, these relatives rose notably in two of the southern regions, becoming 72, 59, and 52 by 1920 only to fall back to 62, 55, and 50 by 1930. In the later 1930's, recovery again set in until by 1950 these relatives had risen to 81, 71, and 61. This upsurge reflected the favorable impact of World War II and its immediate aftermath upon labor mobility and the demand for southern output; but it did not suffice to reduce the absolute spread between southern and non-southern average income, nor did it continue in sufficient strength to improve the South's relative position notably.[23]

Data presented in *Table 1* indicate that between 1929 and 1963 per capita income, expressed in current dollars, rose appreciably more rapidly in each southern state than in the United States. This improvement merely reduced the margin of the South's inferiority; it did not move southern incomes up in the national income structure. In 1962 the twelve southern states fell among the fifteen lowest in per capita income, with nine falling in the nine

22. Uneconomic subsidies, together with disregard of costs and gains, often prevent the emergence of optimum producing decision-determining cost-benefit ratios. For example, were gasoline taxed in keeping with its congestion-producing cost in urban areas, say at 33 cents per gallon, urban congestion would be reduced and population would be dispersed. See A. A. Walters, "The Theory and Measurement of Private and Social Cost of Highway Congestion," *Econometrica*, XXIX (October, 1961), 676-699.

23. See R. A. Easterlin, "Interregional Differences in Per Capita Income, Population and Total Income, 1840-1950," in W. N. Parker, ed., *Trends in the American Economy in the Nineteenth Century* (Princeton: Princeton University Press, 1960), pp. 85-89, 139-140. Also E. S. R. Booth, "Interregional Income Differences," *Southern Economic Journal*, XXXI (July, 1964), pp. 44-51.

Table 1. Per Capita Personal Income, Absolute and Relative, in Selected Years.*

State or area	1929		1940		1950		1960		1963		Per cent change 1929-1963
United States	703	(100)	595	(100)	1,491	(100)	2,217	(100)	2,443	(100)	247
Florida	521	(74)	513	(86)	1,287	(86)	1,967	(89)	2,111	(86)	305
Virginia	435	(62)	466	(78)	1,234	(83)	1,850	(83)	2,066	(85)	375
Texas	478	(68)	432	(73)	1,339	(90)	1,917	(86)	2,046	(84)	328
Georgia	350	(50)	340	(57)	1,017	(68)	1,610	(73)	1,865	(76)	433
North Carolina	334	(48)	328	(55)	1,012	(68)	1,561	(70)	1,813	(74)	443
Kentucky	391	(56)	320	(54)	958	(64)	1,536	(69)	1,789	(73)	358
Tennessee	377	(54)	339	(57)	995	(67)	1,538	(69)	1,776	(73)	371
Louisiana	415	(59)	363	(61)	1,087	(73)	1,605	(72)	1,768	(72)	326
Alabama	324	(46)	282	(47)	869	(58)	1,462	(66)	1,656	(68)	411
Arkansas	305	(43)	256	(43)	807	(54)	1,338	(60)	1,598	(65)	424
South Carolina	270	(38)	307	(52)	882	(59)	1,379	(62)	1,584	(65)	487
Mississippi	285	(41)	218	(37)	733	(58)	1,168	(53)	1,379	(56)	384

*Source: U.S. Department of Commerce, Personal Income by States Since 1929 (Washington, D.C.: U.S. Government Printing Office, 1956), pp. 142-143; idem, Survey of Current Business, XLIII (August, 1963), 9; Survey of Current Business, XLIV (April, 1964), 13.

lowest positions; thirty-three years earlier eight of these nine had fallen among the nine lowest, with all twelve falling among the seventeen lowest, even as in 1963.

What income-retarding influences checked the rise of southern incomes? To this question we cannot supply answers at local levels; the required research has not yet been done, only the brilliant inquiries of William Nicholls being available. He found that in the Upper East Tennessee Valley men early saw that only manufacturing and not agriculture offered real promise; not for them was "the anti-industrial, agrarian philosophy which dominated most of the ante-bellum South" and continued long after the 1860's to depreciate the business man and retard economic progress in much of the South.[24] In the progressive counties of the Upper Tennessee Valley, imported capital and managerial skills played a major role, supplementing the development-favoring influence of the relatively superior (though often transient) natural resources found in these counties. Of perhaps paramount significance was the "quality" of the population found in these counties, partially reflected in its emphasis upon educational expenditure and some family limitation.[25] Farther east in the Southern Piedmont, where ante bellum agrarianism had also deterred industrial development, a combination of circumstances continued to retard industrial development until late in the nineteenth century when, under the aegis of industrially oriented leaders, an economic renaissance was set in motion.[26]

Great income disparity is still found in southern states. Within each state, for example, family (or individual) income in the economic area with highest incomes usually is about 2-3.5 times as high as the corresponding income in the area with lowest incomes.[27]

24. "Some Foundations of Economic Development in the Upper East Tennessee Valley, 1850-1900," *Journal of Political Economy*, LXIV (August and October, 1956), 277-302, 400-415; "Relative Economic Development of the Upper East Tennessee Valley, 1850-1950," *Economic Development and Cultural Change*, V (July, 1957), 299-324; *Southern Traditions and Regional Progress* (Chapel Hill: University of North Carolina Press, 1960).

25. Nicholls, "Some Foundations...," pp. 414-415.

26. Anthony M. Tang, *Economic Development in the Southern Piedmont 1800-1950* (Chapel Hill: University of North Carolina Press, 1958).

27. See U.S. Bureau of the Census, *U.S. Census of Population: 1960, State Economic Areas*, Final Report PC(3)-1A. Per capita income has been found to vary more within each of seven southern states than among the states themselves. See F. H. Hanna, ed., *Regional Income* (Princeton: Princeton University Press, 1957), pp. 114 ff. See also, U.S. Bureau of the Census, "Socio-Economic Characteristics

These disparities, of course, reflect other underlying disparities, occupational, industrial, rural-urban, racial, and so on. For example, urban incomes are higher than rural. Thus white urban males in 1960 received about 2.3 times as much as their rural-farm counterparts, and urban non-white males about 2.8 times as much as their rural-farm counterparts. White urban males received nearly twice as much income as non-white urban males while white rural-farm males received nearly 2.4 times as much as their non-white counterparts. Disparities of the sort described are encountered elsewhere in the United States as well as in the South.[28] While redistribution of population, together with new investment, etc., will tend to reduce these disparities, much income disparity will persist, in the South as elsewhere. Forces making for the convergence of incomes and the reduction of inequality, while always present, are not powerful enough to overcome the fundamental individual differences which underlie inequality in an open, mobile society.

4

The relative lowness of southern incomes has had its origin in the South's economic and cultural history, with factors acting in combination to retard the expansion of output and income. These factors vary considerably from state to state. They may be grouped largely under five heads: (1) demographic composition; (2) shortage of complements to labor; (3) occupational composition of the labor force; (4) industrial composition of those engaged in manufacturing; (5) quality of the population and the factors governing quality.

1. Because the South's age composition is slightly less favorable than the nation's, the ratio of the South's labor force to its population is slightly lower. In 1960, 69 per cent of the nation's population and 67 per cent of the South's population were fifteen or more years old. Moreover, slightly smaller fractions of the South's

of the Population: 1960," *Current Population Reports*, P-23 (July 31, 1964), 4. Hereinafter these reports are cited by series number and date only.

28. U.S. Bureau of the Census, *U.S. Census of Population: 1960, Detailed Characteristics*, Final Report PC(1)-1D, pp. 1-735 ff. Of the South's families, 32 per cent, about double that in the remaining regions receive less than $3,000 cash income per year and hence fall in the "poverty" category. See *Annual Report of the Council of Economic Advisers* (Washington, D. C., U.S. Government Printing Office, 1964), p. 71.

males and females, fifteen or more years old, were in the labor
force than the 77.4 per cent of the nation's males and 34.5 per cent
of the nation's females, aged fifteen or more years. The corresponding percentages for the three southern divisions were 75.2
and 33.5, with most southern states reporting slightly lower percentages. The resulting fractions of the population in the labor force
in 1960, 36.9 per cent in the South and 39 in the nation, were somewhat higher than the corresponding percentages reported in 1950,
about 34.9 and 38.3.[29]

2. Both agriculturalists and non-agriculturalists are less well-
equipped with land and other forms of physical capital in the South
than elsewhere. This condition is associated with the relatively slow
growth of capital per head in the South in the past, a consequence
in part of a too high rate of population growth.[30] Because of the
relatively slow growth of capital the growth of both wages and
output per worker is retarded, and the capacity of southern industry to absorb excess farm labor is restricted.[31] In 1959 the average value of land and buildings for all farms was 49 per cent higher
in the nation than in the southern divisions; the corresponding percentage in 1950 was 58. For commercial farms the corresponding
excess in 1959 was 36 per cent, with only Texas and Florida reporting averages above the national level.[32] Comparable data are
not available, on a regional basis, for the non-agricultural sector
of the economy. Indirect evidence indicates, however, that the
capital-labor ratio is lower in the South than elsewhere, in part
because relatively more of the South's non-agricultural labor force
is employed in industries with relatively low capital-labor ratios.[33]

29. The 1960 fractions are based on 1960 Census data. The 1950 fractions are
from U.S. Senate, Report of Committee on Banking and Currency, Selected
Materials on the Economy of the South (Washington, 1956), p. 9.

30. Borts (op. cit., p. 302) estimates that the capital-labor ratio grew faster in
low-wage than in high-wage areas in 1929-1948 but not in 1919-1929 or 1948-1957.

31. Geographical differences in agricultural wages are closely associated with
differences in output per agricultural worker. See W. D. Weatherford, Geographic
Differentials of Agricultural Wages in the United States (Cambridge: Harvard
University Press, 1957), pp. 44-48; also pp. 66-71 on the tendency of agricultural
wages to move with industrial employment and wages as industrialization progresses.

32. U.S. Bureau of the Census, U.S. Census of Agriculture: 1959, II, chap. 10,
pp. 1036, 1168. See also E. O. Heady, Agricultural Policy under Economic Development (Ames: Iowa State University Press, 1962), chap. 7; also Weatherford, op. cit.,
p. 46.

33. H. S. Perloff et al., Regions, Resources and Economic Growth (Baltimore:
Johns Hopkins Press, 1960), chaps. 31-32. L. E. Galloway, "The North-South

Even given direct data, it is difficult to determine the imputed product of capital. Presumably, a 1 per cent increase in capital per worker will increase output per worker 0.2-0.4 per cent, and it may also facilitate technical change and so make possible an even greater increase in output per worker.

3. The occupational composition of the South's labor force is comparatively unfavorable; it includes a relatively large number of workers in employments in which average income is relatively low. The relevant data are summarized in *Table 2*.[34] The data on male median incomes in column 8 indicate roughly how income varies with occupational category. Comparison of columns 5-7 with column 1 as well as with column 4 (which describes projected labor requirements as of 1975) indicates that the South is undersupplied with white-collar workers and oversupplied with blue-collar and private household service workers as well as with agriculturalists. The data in columns 3 and 4 indicate that the South's unfavorable occupational composition is associated in part with its racial composition. The data in column 9, suggesting how education and occupational level are associated, support the argument developed below that undereducation is responsible in part for the unfavorableness of the South's occupational structure.

While the lowness of agricultural earnings depresses overall average income even more in the South than elsewhere,[35] relative lowness of earnings in most other employments depresses overall earnings appreciably only in some states. Thus, while average earnings were lower in trade and government than in most employ-

Wage Differential," *Review of Economics and Statistics*, XLV (August, 1945), 270.

34. This table is based on U.S. Department of Labor, *A Report on Manpower Requirements, Resources, Utilization, and Training* (Washington, 1963), esp. pp. 143, 44, 100, 158; Stella P. Manor, "Geographic Employment Changes, 1950-1960," *Monthly Labor Review*, LXXXVI (January, 1963), 9; *Statistical Abstract: 1962*, p. 336. For data relating to non-whites see also M. A. Kessler, "Economic Status of Non-White Workers, 1955-1962," *Monthly Labor Review*, LXXXVI (July, 1963), 504-515. See also Section 4 below.

35. In 1961, average annual earnings per full-time employee in agriculture, forestry, and fishing, $1,758, was only 36 per cent as high as the corresponding average for all employment, $4,857; yet in 1959 the fraction of the labor force engaged in agriculture was about 1½ times as high in the three southern divisions as in the nation; in 1950 it was about 1.9 times as high. *Selected Materials*, p. 86. For 1959-1960 the reported data differ but the ratio remains around 1.5. See U.S. Bureau of the Census, *U.S. Census of Population: 1960, Detailed Characteristics*, Final Report PC(1)-1D, Tables 210, 259; or *Manpower*, pp. 179-181, and *Statistical Abstract: 1962*, pp. 215, 236.

Table 2. Occupational Composition, United States and Southern Divisions Together with Income and Schooling.

| | Occupational composition, U.S. | | | | Occupational composition of regional employment, 1960 | | | Male median income 1960 | Median years of schooling 1962 |
| | 1962 | | | 1975 | South Atlantic | East So. Central | West So. Central | | |
	All	White	Non-white	All, projected					
Total	100.0	100.0	100.0	100.0	100.0	100.0	100.0	5435	12.1
White-collar workers	44.1	47.3	16.7	47.8	40.1	34.7	41.9	—	—
Professional and technical	11.9	12.6	5.3	14.2	10.7	9.2	11.0	7228	16.2
Managers, officials proprietors	10.9	11.9	2.6	10.7	8.6	7.7	10.0	6922	12.5
Clerical workers	14.9	15.8	7.2	16.2	13.5	11.0	13.4	5328	12.5
Sales workers	6.4	7.0	1.6	6.7	7.3	6.8	7.5	5998	12.5
Blue-collar workers	35.8	35.4	39.5	33.4	39.2	39.4	36.1	—	10.4
Craftsmen and foremen	12.8	13.6	6.0	12.8	13.3	12.7	13.5	5905	11.2
Operatives	17.7	17.5	19.9	16.3	20.0	20.6	16.5	5030	10.1
Non-farm laborers	5.2	4.3	13.6	4.3	5.9	6.1	6.1	3956	8.9
Service workers	13.0	10.6	32.8	14.3	13.2	13.0	13.5	—	10.2
Private household	3.5	2.1	14.7	—	4.7	5.1	4.2	—	8.7
All other	9.5	8.5	18.1	—	8.5	7.9	9.3	4209	10.8
Farm workers	7.2	6.8	11.0	4.5	7.5	13.0	8.7	—	8.7
Farmers	3.8	4.0	2.7	—	4.0	8.4	5.2	2210	8.8
Laborers	3.3	2.8	8.3	—	3.5	4.6	3.5	1843	8.5

Source: Columns 1-4 and 9 are from Report on Manpower, pp. 143, 44, 100, 158; columns 5-7 are from Manor, op. cit., p. 9; column 8 is from Statistical Abstract 1962, p. 336. See footnote 34.

ments, the proportion of the labor force so employed varied appreciably by state, much as did the relative number engaged in better-paying employments (e.g., mining, transportation, utilities). Even in services, the average pay in which is depressed (especially in the South) by low earnings in household and personal service, there is considerable interstate variation both within the South and elsewhere.[36] Comparison of average weekly wages in the South, by major industrial category, with averages elsewhere revealed southern wages to be 9-29 per cent lower,[37] in part because rates of pay for similar work remained lower in the South than elsewhere. Among the conditions responsible for this differential is the presence of excess or low-paid labor in agricultural areas, continually fed by a relatively high rate of natural increase, which in the absence of sufficiently heavy emigration from the South tends to press more heavily upon the wages of unskilled than upon those of skilled labor.[38]

4. Value added by manufacturing per employee as well as hourly wage rates of production workers in manufacturing are lower in the South than elsewhere, both because these rates are lower within than outside the South and because southern manufacturing includes a relatively large number of low-income industries.[39] In 1958, in the South, 53 per cent of workers in manufacturing received less than $1.50 per hour straight time wages;

36. For data on occupational composition and pay see *Statistical Abstract: 1962*, pp. 224, 337.

37. *Selected Materials*, p. 26, also p. 90. Representative of recent evidence of the relative lowness of wages in the South are Fuchs, *op. cit.*, pp. 165-167; U.S. Department of Labor, *Employment and Earnings Statistics for States and Areas*, Bulletin No. 1370 (Washington, D. C.: 1963), pp. xxx-xxxv; K. J. Hoffmann, "Job Pay Levels and Trends in Metropolitan Areas, 1962," *Monthly Labor Review*, LXXXVI (February, 1963), 147, 149-150; C. M. O'Connor, "Wages in Fertilizer Plants 1962," *Monthly Labor Review*, LXXXVI (February, 1963), 164-165; Martin Segal, *Wages in the Metropolis* (Cambridge: Harvard University Press, 1960), pp. 32, 46, 48, 53, 55, 62, 67, 74, 84; R. M. Lichtenberg, *One-Tenth of a Nation* (Cambridge: Harvard University Press, 1960), pp. 48-56. Teachers' salaries also are lower in the South than elsewhere; *Statistical Abstract: 1962*, p. 127.

38. Segal, *op. cit.*, p. 21. Out-migration has helped to alleviate this pressure, especially in the East South Central Division where population in 1950-1960 grew much more slowly (0.5 per cent per year) than in the South Atlantic (2.0) and West South Central states (1.5). Even so the ratio of southern to non-southern wages has remained lower among unskilled than among skilled workers, e.g., see T. P. Kanninen, "Wage Differences Among Labor Markets," *Monthly Labor Review*, LXXXV (June, 1962), 619.

39. *Selected Materials*, pp. 21-22, 27. Textiles, apparel, and lumber, among the six lowest-paid manufacturing industries in the South, accounted for about 45 per cent of all employment in southern manufacturing in 1954. *Ibid.*, pp. 21-22, 27. See also U.S. Department of Labor, *Employment and Earnings Statistics, passim*.

the corresponding percentage for the United States was 27 per cent.[40] The corresponding percentages in 1962 for non-metropolitan workers in manufacturing and non-manufacturing industries, respectively, were about 62 and 68 in the South and 27 and 59 in the North Central states.[41] The comparative lowness of these rates reflects the inferior training of the population, the pressure of an excessive agricultural population, and the continuing predominance of slowly growing, low-wage industries despite the relatively rapid growth of construction, trade, finance, and government.[42]

5. Both average income in the South and capacity to increase it are depressed more by lack of training in the population than by any other condition, especially in the rural white population and in the non-white population, rural and urban. Consequently range of skill, levels of aspiration, and motivation are very low. The unfavorable impact upon non-whites of neglect of investment in personal improvement (or "capital") and of resulting personal deficiencies is evident in their occupational composition, their proneness to unemployment,[43] and the comparative lowness of the incomes of non-whites, even when superficially as well educated as whites.[44] It is evident also in the inability of Negroes to fill many of the positions becoming open to them as discrimination abates.[45]

40. Statistical Abstract: 1962, p. 235.
41. U.S. Department of Labor, news release, June, 1963.
42. Selected Materials, pp. 21, 87-88; Manor, op. cit. Evidence of the pressure of numbers on jobs is to be had in the heavy out-migration from both southern rural areas and the South, and in the greater rate of decline in agricultural employment in southern than in non-southern divisions in 1950-1960.
43. See Table 2, columns 2-3; also Kessler, op. cit., Table 1-2. Since 1950 unemployment has been about twice as high among non-whites as among whites. Ibid., Table 3-6 and Charts 1-2. See "Socio-Economic Characteristics of the Population: 1960"; also M. R. Cramer, "Aspirations of Southern Youth: A Look at Racial Comparisons," Research Previews, XII (March, 1965), 1-11.
44. The ratio of non-white to white income (53-55 per cent of white income on a family basis), with years of schooling given, ranges from 0.63 among those with less than eight years of elementary education to 0.85 for those with four or more years of college. Ibid., Tables 9-10. See also Selected Materials, pp. 31-32. In the South, median non-white family income in 1961 was 43 per cent of median white family income for all income-receivers; the corresponding percentage for full-time workers was 50, and for farm families, 42. See U.S. Bureau of the Census, Current Population Reports, Consumer Income Series P-60, No. 39 (February 28, 1963), p. 26. Were the ratings of Negro college students on tests and in civil service examinations published, they would reveal how underdeveloped a world is that of Negro education. The indisposition of Negroes to become business men may also be associated with circumstances of the sort underlying the lack of effective education in much of the Negro population. See note 45.
45. Careful statistical studies of the actual supply-demand relationship are not available. See, however, Louis E. Lomax, "Young Negroes Aren't Ready," Saturday Evening Post, September 21, 1963, pp. 14-17 and reports in the United States News

The unfavorable impact of insufficiency of education among those reared in rural areas is evident in the low productivity of many southern farms as well as in the limitations of the job opportunities open to migrants from southern rural areas.

Degree of education is quite highly correlated with accessibility to well-paying employment. Such correlation is suggested by a comparison of column 9 in *Table* 2 with columns 1, 4, and 8; it is clearly demonstrated in reports on income and education which show how income rises with years of schooling.[46] A minimum amount of education is usually essential to carrying out specific job requirements. It is estimated, for example, that as of 1950, 7.45 per cent of our labor force needed a college education or better; 25.49 per cent required a high school education while 44.69 per cent could get along with ten years of schooling; only about 22.4 per cent would get along with seven years or less of schooling.[47] In 1960, persons twenty-five years and older with less than eight years of schooling formed 30.1-43.4 per cent of the population in southern states (other than Florida) but only 22.6 per cent of the nation's population. The median school year completed by southern

& World Report, July 15, 1963, pp. 56 ff., July 22, 1963, pp. 40 ff., August 12, 1962, pp. 28 ff., and August 19, 1963, pp. 58 ff. For a comparative study see Nathan Glazer and D. P. Moynihan, *Beyond the Melting Pot; The Negroes, Puerto Ricans, Jews, Italians and Irish of New York City* (Cambridge: The M.I.T. Press, 1963). Evidence presented in recent Senate hearings indicates, however, that in the relatively discrimination-free Armed Forces, Negro military personnel have fared better than in the civilian economy. In the economy at large, however, "the relative position of the Negro has not improved" in the past twenty-two years; non-whites remain concentrated in low-paying jobs, benefiting less from advanced education than whites, and experiencing lower incomes, especially in the South, when their education is roughly comparable to that of the whites. U.S. Senate, Committee on Labor and Public Welfare, Subcommittee on Employment and Manpower, Hearings, *Equal Employment Opportunity* (88th Congress, First Session, July 24-August 20, 1963), pp. 322-388, 433-455, 493-494. See also Gary Becker, *The Economics of Discrimination* (Chicago: University of Chicago Press, 1957).

46. See Kessler, *op. cit.,* Table 8; Tables 9, 27-28, in *Current Population Reports* cited in note 44 above; Denis F. Johnston, "Educational Attainment of Workers, 1962," *Monthly Labor Review,* LXXXVI (May, 1963), 512-515; *Selected Materials,* pp. 30-32. Education also makes for upward occupational mobility. See O. D. Duncan and R. W. Hodge, "Education and Occupational Mobility: A Regression Analysis," *American Journal of Sociology,* LXVIII (May, 1963), 629-644.

47. R. S. Eckaus, "Higher Education as an Investment in People," in S. J. Mushkin, ed., *Economics of Higher Education* (Washington, D. C.: U.S. Government Printing Office, 1962), pp. 120-121. Eckaus also estimated that about 42 per cent of all jobs required preparation of 1-4 or more years; about 21 per cent could be mastered in a month or less. On the impact of underinvestment in southern education, see M. R. Colberg, "Human Capital As A Southern Resource," *Southern Economic Journal,* XXIX (January, 1963), 157-166.

individuals, twenty-five years old and over, ranged, among whites, from 9.5 in Arkansas to 11.6 in Florida, and among non-whites, from 5.9 in South Carolina to 8.2 in Kentucky. The corresponding medians in the South in 1950 were 8.5-10.9 among whites and 4.6-7.3 among non-whites; in 1940, 7.8-9.5 among native whites, 3.9-6.2 among Negroes, and 4.5-7.5 among rural farm people. By 1960, the median for all southern rural farm people had become 8.4, and the rural farm non-white median had risen to 6.4. Even so, the non-white and rural rates remain too low, given the requirements of many types of industry.

The adverse effect of the South's underinvestment in education was accentuated in the past by the concentration of so much of this underinvestment in the population of primary and secondary school age.[48] For the "rate of return" on investment in education, somewhat higher for high school than for college educational investment, has been highest on investment in elementary schooling. The average return on investment in college education may not be much higher than the return on other forms of investment.[49] Indeed, the marginal return on investment in college education could be lower than that in other forms of capital, since this type of investment causes many young people to stay in school longer than necessary, given their lack of "natural ability" and "interest."

Nothing has been said of South–non-South wage differentials; the South's wage structure is not a deterrent to income growth but

48. The degree of concentration is suggested roughly by data showing that, whereas about 34.5 per cent of the population of the United States twenty-five years and older in 1950 had completed at least a high school education (and in two-fifths of the instances, one or more years of college), a much lower percentage of the South's population had gone that far in the school system. In the South the corresponding percentage ranged from 18.9 in South Carolina through 29.1 in Virginia to 35.9 in Florida (much of whose population had been born and educated outside the South). Computed from *Selected Materials*, p. 30. Southern education still lags behind that of the nation, though not quite so far as in the past. Among those aged seven to thirteen, southern enrollment is virtually on a par with national enrollment, and among those aged fourteen to seventeen it is only 4 per cent below the national rate; but in the age group sixteen to twenty-four southern enrollment remains 16 per cent below the national level. See U.S. Bureau of the Census, *Current Population Reports*, Series P-20, No. 126 (September 24, 1963), p. 11. Even if enrollment rates are similar, there may be differences consequent upon differences in quality of teaching personnel and equipment.

49. See Fritz Machlup, *The Production and Distribution of Knowledge in the United States* (Princeton: Princeton University Press, 1962), pp. 112-117. Many aspects of "investment in human beings" are treated in the supplement to the *Journal of Political Economy*, LXX (October, 1962), which includes papers by T. W. Schultz and his co-workers who have given much attention to this form of investment.

tends to facilitate it just as the relative weakness of southern unionization often serves to attract industry. Even were southern labor
exploited, resulting excessive profits might stimulate local capital
formation and attract capital from the outside. Wages are lower in
the South than in the nation both because low-wage industries
predominate and because wage earners, especially those in the
lumber industry or otherwise lacking in skill, are paid less in the
South than elsewhere for similar work. Moreover, since 1947 there
has not been so marked an improvement in the South's relative
position as there was in 1929-1947.[50] In general, the industries experiencing the largest employment gains in the South between 1929
and 1954 have been relatively low-wage industries, although since
1947 the East South Central Division has been attracting relatively
high-wage industries.[51] The relative lowness of southern wages
appears to be associated closely with the South's relatively low
overall capital-labor ratio, though this ratio may have risen per-
ceptibly since 1954. It is not attributable to the performance of
southern workers, for under similar conditions their output often
exceeds that experienced outside the South.[52] Should the wage-
productivity ratio be increased appreciably more in southern than
in non-southern industry, the expansion of non-agricultural employment in the South would be retarded.

Heavy emigration from the South has made for the improvement of southern average income, but it has not eliminated (mainly
rural) underemployment which remains more than twice as high
in the South as elsewhere. This emigration has counterbalanced the

50. See V. R. Fuchs and R. Perlman, "Recent Trends in Southern Wage Dif-
ferentials," *Review of Economics and Statistics*, XLII (August, 1960), 292-300;
Galloway, *op. cit.*, pp. 264-265. See also Lloyd G. Reynolds and Cynthia H.
Taft, *The Evolution of Wage Structure* (New Haven: Yale University Press, 1955),
pp. 84-92, 146, 150, 159-160, 326-327; Kanninen, *op. cit.* On unionization see
Fuchs, *op. cit.*, pp. 91-92, 94-95, 102.

51. Fuchs and Perlman, *op. cit.*, pp. 296-297; this discussion relates only to the
South Atlantic and East South Central states. See also J. E. Moes, *Local Subsidies
for Industry* (Chapel Hill: University of North Carolina Press, 1962), pp. 199-214;
Fuchs, *op. cit.*, pp. 115, 171-174; M. L. Greenhut, *Plant Location in Theory and in
Practice* (Chapel Hill: University of North Carolina Press, 1956), pp. 129-135;
U.S. Department of Labor, *Employment and Earnings Statistics*. Tables 1-9. Of the
nation's interdivisional shift in manufacturing employment in 1929-1954, about one-
third was associated with the presence of inexpensive labor, mostly in the South,
and about one-third with the pull of natural resources and raw materials, a pull
present only in some southern states. These two forces also attracted indirectly some
demand-oriented manufactures. See Fuchs, *op. cit.*, p. 250, also 115, 171-174.

52. Galloway, *op. cit.*, pp. 270-272; also see note 65 below. Apparently production functions, by industry, do not vary markedly in space.

flow of rural migrants to southern cities; it has thus kept conventional unemployment at the national level and has reduced pressure upon wages in employments requiring little skill. In the 1950's non-metropolitan state economic areas in the three southern divisions gave up 4,124,000 migrants, of whom 2,334,000 came from areas only 0-24.9 per cent urban, while the metropolitan areas added 2,719,000, over 400,000 of them outside the South as herein defined, though within the three southern divisions. Of the 3.3 million net emigrants from nine southern states,[53] 53 per cent were non-white. These migrants left (as did over 2.4 million in 1940-1950) presumably because they expected to find elsewhere greater opportunity than the slowly growing southern economy was likely to provide.[54] Their removal is inadequate, however, to correct underemployment or to overcome the lowness of the overall southern capital-worker ratio; capital from external as well as internal sources is required.[55] Moreover, insofar as migration carries out more people with skill and training than come to the South, it reduces the region's capacity for development,[56] badly equipped as the South is with skilled personnel.[57]

53. Virginia experienced a net immigration of 14,000; Texas, of 114,000, and Florida of 1,617,000. Of these only 101,000 were non-white. See U.S. Bureau of the Census, *Current Population Reports*, Series P-23, No. 7 (November, 1962), and *Statistical Abstract: 1962*, p. 40.
54. On the response of migrants to income and other differences see Fuchs, *op. cit.*, pp. 101-104; R. L. Raimon, "Interstate Migration and Wage Theory," *Review of Economics and Statistics*, XLIV (November, 1962), 428-438; L. A. Sjaastad, "Relationship Between Migration and Income in the United States," in *Papers and Proceedings*, Regional Science Association, VI (1960), 37-64; Phillip Nelson, "Migration, Real Income and Information," *Journal of Regional Science*, I [2] (1959), 43-74; F. T. Bachmura, "Man-Land Equalization Through Migration," *American Economic Review*, XLIX (December, 1959), 1004-1017. J. D. Tarver has estimated that about 72 per cent of white and 40 per cent of non-white state net migration is explainable by economic variables. "Predicting Migration," *Social Forces*, XXXIX (March, 1961), 210-211. Negroes seem to have been the only low-income migrants highly disposed to move relatively long distances. See A. M. Rose, "Distance Migration and Socio-Economic Status of Migrants," *American Sociological Review*, XXIII (August, 1958), 420-423.
55. E.g., see G. H. Borts, "The Equalization of Returns and Regional Economic Growth," *American Economic Review*, L (March, 1960), 319-346; Galloway, *op. cit.*, pp. 270-272. On southern underemployment, see R. B. Glasgow and E. L. Baum "Considerations for Planning Economic Development of Rural Areas," *Journal of Farm Economics*, XLV (December, 1963), 1083-1090; F. T. Bachmura, "The Manpower Development and Training Act of 1962," *Journal of Farm Economics*, XLV (February, 1963), 61-72.
56. C. H. Hamilton reports considerable economically adverse selectivity in "Educational Selectivity of Net Migration From The South," *Social Forces*, XXXVIII (October, 1959), 37-42. H. S. Shryock, however, reports the South a gainer. See his "The Efficiency of Internal Migration in the United States," in Louis Henry and Wilhelm Winkler, eds., *International Population Conference* (Vienna: Christoph Reisser's Söhne, 1959), p. 688.
57. Scientists form 0.6 per cent of the nation's labor force. Yet, only in Louisiana

5

We turn now to the elimination of barriers to income growth in the
South. Of the corrective steps indicated, the stepping up of capital
formation will prove easiest. Large southern firms now have access
to funds on terms as satisfactory as are to be had by large firms
elsewhere, and firms of intermediate size probably are in nearly
as favorable a situation, given that labor and markets are to be had.
Bank rates on short-term business loans, which are generally smaller
in size, do not appear to be much higher in southern than in most
northern and eastern cities.[58] If, with the supply prices of funds and
perhaps also of capital equipment as such not much above the
national level, capital will flow into the South as long as it is more
productive there than in the North and East. Presumably this is the
situation, for capital is flowing into the South on balance, though
the amount has not yet been accurately determined. Moreover,
should national investment be falling short of saving at "full employment," increase in national investment would elevate the flow
of capital into the South. Such a stepping up of the rate of national
investment would also increase labor mobility and facilitate the
training and employment of many of those who today are "structurally" unemployed.

How much additional labor will be available for employment in
the South in the next ten to twenty years is conjectural, coming as
it does from three variable sources. There is first the natural increase of persons of working age, but net emigration must be de-
ducted from this. Second, there are the equivalents of the currently
unemployed. Third, there may be several or more million relatively
young and mobile people transferable out of agriculture, personal
service, and other activities involving underemployment, especially
in the many counties that have lost population in the past ten to
fifteen years. The South should, therefore, be well supplied with
increments to its labor force in the near future.[59]

and Texas is so high a fraction found and only in Virginia do engineers form as
large a fraction of the labor force as is found in the nation, 1.2 per cent. See
National Science Foundation, *Profiles of Manpower in Science and Technology*
(Washington, D. C., 1963), pp. 30-33.

58. E.g., see *Federal Reserve Bulletin*, XLIX (August, 1963), 1107; also Green-
hut, *op. cit.*, pp. 135-137; H. C. Carr, "A Note on Regional Differences in Discount
Rates," *Journal of Finance*, XV (March, 1960), 62-68; George Macesich, "Interest
Rates On The Periphery And In The Center Of Economic Development," *Southern
Economic Journal*, XXVIII (October, 1961), 138-147.

59. See labor force projections in U.S. Department of Labor, *Manpower*, pp.

The quality of the South's labor force will have much to do with her capacity to attract capital and elevate output per head. Fortunately, the educational composition of the population is improving, though school retardation remains high, especially in the non-white population among whom the high school dropout rate is still about double that among whites.[60] In 1960, median years of school completed in the South by persons aged fourteen to twenty-five, twenty-five and over, and fifty to fifty-four, respectively, were as follows: for all males, 10.1, 9.1, 8.6; for non-white males, 9.0, 6.4, 5.6; for all rural farm males, 9.0, 7.8, 7.7; and for rural farm non-white males, 7.9, 4.7, 4.6. Similar trends obtain in the female population. School enrollment data bear out these trends. Enrollment is practically at the national level among southern whites and non-whites aged seven to thirteen years. Among southern whites and non-whites aged fourteen to seventeen years, the respective enrollment rates are 3 and 7 per cent below the national average, with the deficiency about as great in the urban as in the rural population. Among southern whites aged eighteen to twenty-four years the enrollment rate is 13 per cent below the national level, and among southern non-whites, 25 per cent below. Urbanization, it is interesting to note, does not serve to elevate the rate among southern non-whites aged eighteen to twenty-four, though in other regions as well as among southern whites, enrollment is higher in urban than in rural communities.[61]

The trends described, while salutary, may not be salutary enough. Given an emerging age of automation and artificially high and employment-curtailing wage rates, there could come into being a growing "internal proletariat,"[62] white and non-white, lacking in the will, skill, and flexibility essential to continuously serviceable activity in a complex, dynamic, opulent society. Such outcome is best guarded against through the state's supplementing the family's

179-198. These may underestimate the potential labor supply of the South because they neglect labor on the margin of transference from low-paying to better-paying employments.

60. U.S. Bureau of the Census, *Current Population Reports,* Farm Population (P-27), No. 32 (June 15, 1962), and 1960 Census data on education.

61. Data for 1960 are reported in U.S. Bureau of the Census, *U.S. Census of Population: 1960, Characteristics of the Population, U.S. Summary,* Final Report C and D. Enrollment data for 1960 and 1962 are reported in U.S. Bureau of the Census, *Current Population Reports,* Series P-20, No. 110 (July 24, 1961), and No. 126 (September 24, 1963).

62. Compare A. J. Toynbee, *A Study of History,* V (London: Oxford University Press, 1939), 58-193.

responsibility for educating its young members adequately by performing functions most families are incapable of doing. The state must provide for counselling the young and inducing them to undertake studies essential to economic and financial survival; it must ease the pressure that earnings foregone puts on the young to drop out of school; it must readjust educational offerings to the needs of a technologically dynamic society; and it must make the young aware of "the severity of the demands that life in the opulent society makes on those who participate in it."[63] These objectives probably can be achieved at no great increase in cost to individuals and community, in the South or elsewhere. For the length of time most students spend in school can be cut to ten or eleven years at the same time that the amount of training communicated to the educable student is greatly increased, and corresponding economies and improvements can easily be achieved in colleges and universities.[64] Greater attention must be given also to on-the-job training and its equivalents, a function which, despite its great and growing importance, may not be receiving the attention it deserves.[65]

That the qualitative composition of the South's population is improving is suggested by comparison of its 1950 with its 1960 occupational composition. The relative importance of agricultural employment declined slightly more rapidly in the South than in the nation while that of professional employment increased slightly more rapidly even as did that of non-household service workers, sales workers, and clerical workers. Craftsmen, foremen, and operatives increased relatively in the South while declining in the nation,

63. See Johnson, op. cit., pp. 189-190, 192, on the incapacity of the typical family and current educational arrangements to fit the young for life in an uncertainty-ridden economy.

64. On the economies attainable in American education, see Machlup's penetrating analysis in op. cit., pp. 120-144. "The way to get better-educated people in the United States is to make them learn faster, study more intensively, so that a greater percentage of those whose minds will have been stretched through intensive work in earlier years can benefit from a likewise somewhat improved college education." Ibid., p. 144.

65. See ibid., pp. 57-64; Jacob Mincer, "On-the-Job Training: Costs, Returns, and Some Implications," Journal of Political Economy, LXX (Part 2, October, 1962), 50-79. Mincer finds (ibid., p. 62) "that, in the male half of the world, on-the-job training—measured in dollar costs—is as important as formal schooling." Under similar educational and working conditions, southern workers are as productive as workers in any other region. Indeed, according to the testimony of a number of employers supplied to southern state bureaus concerned with the promotion of industrial development, the performance of the southern worker often is superior to his similarly situated counterpart elsewhere.

apparently because manufacturing was developing more rapidly in the South. Moreover, the relative number of laborers declined slightly less rapidly.[66] In industrial structure, too, the South improved relatively in 1950-1960, developing faster than the nation in construction, finance, and trade, in transportation, communication, and public utility activities, and in professional activities and public administration, though not in business service and entertainment. Employment in manufacturing also grew more rapidly, in all two-digit durable categories except lumber and in all two-digit non-durable categories except textiles (employing 15.1 per cent of all southern manufacturing workers) which declined 1.3 per cent.[67]

No attempt is here made to determine to what extent the South has participated in the increase in the proportion of the nation's labor force engaged in knowledge production which rose from only 10.7 per cent in 1900 through 21.6 per cent in 1930 to 31.6 per cent in 1959.[68] Data presented in the preceding paragraph suggest, however, that for some time the rate of increase in this component has been slightly higher in the South than in the nation. Such a trend is highly advantageous to the South for, as Machlup finds, the demand for labor engaged in knowledge production increased faster than that for other types of labor in the 1950's. Moreover, there is underway in the United States "a continuing movement from manual to mental, and from less to more highly trained labor."[69]

Manufacturing has played a major role in the transformation of the twelve-state southern economy which in 1958 provided 18.4 per cent of the nation's employment in manufacturing instead of 12.9 as in 1899 or 14.8 as in 1929.[70] Manufacturing is of primary importance because, even though it should provide relatively less employment in the future than now, it will probably remain the main arena of applied science and the agency most capable of continually transforming its output and thereby sustaining high income elastic-

66. Based on Manor, *op. cit.*, p. 9.
67. Based on U.S. Bureau of the Census, *U.S. Census of Population: 1960, Detailed Characteristics*, U.S. Summary, Final Report PC(1)-1D, pp. 1-563-564, 1-726-727; *U.S. Census of Population: 1950*, Vol. 2, Part I, pp. 1-405-406. The South gained relatively in textiles, since elsewhere employment in textiles declined notably.
68. Machlup, *op. cit.*, pp. 384-385.
69. *Ibid.*, pp. 394, 396-397.
70. The percentages are based on U.S. Bureau of the Census, *U.S. Census of Manufactures: 1958*, I, *Summary Statistics*, pp. 1-47-49. The twelve southern states included 27.8 per cent of the nation's population in 1900 and 25.8 per cent in 1960.

ity of demand for manufactures in general. The expansion of manufacturing, which has created about 1.8 million jobs in the South
since 1929 and thus has facilitated the creation of perhaps twice as
many jobs in more or less complementary activities, has made possible, along with out-migration, the transfer of millions out of agriculture, and it will facilitate the final equilibration of agriculture.
Between 1929 and 1954 most southern states attracted mainly low-
wage industries in which wages formed a large fraction of costs;
in some states, however, especially Florida and Texas, natural resources and climate drew new enterprises.[71] Expansion of southern
income as of southern manufacturing employment took place, however, under unfavorable conditions, in that most of it was centered
in slow-growth sectors of manufacturing.[72] Even so, according to
the 1962 *Annual Survey of Manufactures*, the South's relative position improved in 1947-1962, with its manufacturing employment
increasing about 41.7 per cent while that of the rest of the United
States increased only about 12.9 per cent.

Expansion has continued to take place despite the shortage, in
parts of the South, of growth loci, of points about which economic
activities tend to cluster, drawn there principally by economies of
agglomeration, availability of labor, good transfer relations, and
satisfactory physical and socioeconomic environments. Thus in
1950-1960, marked growth took place only in a few of the economic
regions situated wholly in the South (or nearly so) and only in
some of the South's sixty-five standard metropolitan statistical areas,
of which forty-two are situated in five states and only thirteen are
found in five others. Of the thirty-three such areas which grew 30
or more per cent (while the nation's 212 areas grew 26.4 per cent),
twenty-one are in three states, Texas, Florida, and Georgia. Of the
South's forty-eight economic regions only eight experienced net
immigration in the 1940's *and* 1950's, while thirty-five experienced
net emigration both decades. Only nineteen (of which seven are in

71. Fuchs, *op. cit.*, pp. 23-25, 125, 205-222, 235-236, 239, 250-257. See also
Wilbur Zelinsky, "A Method For Measuring Change in the Distribution of Manu-
facturing Activity: The United States, 1939-1947," *Economic Geography*, XXXIV
(April, 1958), 95-126, esp. pp. 119-126.

72. E. S. Dunn, *Recent Southern Economic Development* (Gainesville: University
of Florida Press, 1962), pp. 8, 34-38; Robert E. Graham, "Factors Underlying
Changes in the Geographic Distribution of Income," *Survey of Current Business*,
XLIV [4] (April, 1964), 15-32, esp. 20-27. Also Chapin and Weiss, *op. cit.*, pp. 104-
117, 463-464.

Texas) grew more than 12 per cent in the 1950's when the nation's population was growing 18.5 per cent.[73]

Among the South's needs, therefore, besides a great increase in personal and physical capital, may be an increase in the number of growth points around which to locate rapidly growing manufacturing and other activities. For eventually, close to nine-tenths of all employment will be situated in urban centers. While local governments are limited in what they can do to bring new loci into being, they can provide particular stimuli as well as attractive entrepreneurial and living environments. Tax incentives appear to be of secondary importance unless appropriately formulated.[74] Subsidization is profitable generally only when there is unemployment or "underemployment in the vicinity of the enterprise."[75] Not much can be done locally to circumvent monopolistic behavior associated with absentee ownership.[76] Careful research may, however, identify suitable fast-growing manufactures as well as potential loci whose comparative advantages can be counted upon to attract enterprise and capital and help increase the South's share of rapidly expanding activities.

Of great importance is the extent to which the South succumbs to unemployment-generating legislation and to industry-wide wage-fixing arrangements. Investment in the South will proceed at something like an adequate rate only if wage rates remain commensurate with productivity and at levels making investment in the South sufficiently attractive to enterprise. Efforts to fix wages in given industries at the same level in the South as in the Far West or the

73. See U.S. Bureau of the Census, *Current Population Reports*, Series P-23, No. 7 (November, 1962). On the character of southern cities, see O. D. Duncan *et al.*, *Metropolis and Region* (Baltimore: Johns Hopkins Press, 1950), esp. Part IV. The proportion of the population in declining urban centers was much lower in the South than elsewhere. See R. M. Northam, "Declining Urban Centers in the United States, 1940-1960," *Annals of the American Association of Geographers*, LIII (March, 1963), 54-56.

74. Tax incentives are reported as of both primary and secondary importance in Michigan. See Eva Mueller *et al.*, *Location Decisions and Industrial Mobility in Michigan 1961* (Ann Arbor: University of Michigan Press, 1961), pp. 12, 16, 24-25, 28, 35-40, 55, 61. See also Greenhut, *op. cit.*, pp. 137-139; Fuchs, *op. cit.*, pp. 88-89; J. S. Floyd, *Effects of Taxation on Industrial Location* (Chapel Hill: University of North Carolina Press, 1952), chap. 1. While most of these writers dismiss tax incentives as unimportant, Moes tries to identify the conditions under which they may be effective. *Op. cit.*, chaps. 3-4 and Appendix II.

75. Moes, *op. cit.*, pp. 171-172, 186-189, 196-198, 229-237.

76. G. W. Stocking, *Basing Point Pricing and Regional Development* (Chapel Hill: University of North Carolina Press, 1954), pp. 149-152, 154-155, 191-194.

North will slow down the rate of expansion in the South and thus work to the disadvantage of those in lower-paying employments. Minimum-wage fixation will tend to make for unemployment, especially in regions with a large unskilled labor force, by elevating required rates above what employers can afford to pay, given the low productivity of much of the South's population. In the South, as in the nation, the wage-productivity ratio is tending to rise faster among the less skilled than among the more skilled components of the labor force. In consequence, employers are inclined to substitute more skilled for less skilled labor and to reduce the requirement of the latter through mechanization and automation. This tendency makes for relatively high unemployment in regions where, as in the South, the comparative number of less skilled persons is higher than in the nation as a whole. It is incumbent upon the South, therefore, to keep its wage as well as its price structure flexible. Deviations from this policy will produce far more *unseen* ill effects than *seen* good effects.

The South's prospect is now decidedly better than it was ten to fifteen years ago. For a predominant agriculture is no longer so great an incubus; even in states where much deruralization remains to be achieved there are areas of promise.[77] Moreover, the industrial composition of a number of states besides Florida and Texas now permits more rapid growth (e.g., Louisiana and Georgia), or is on the verge of doing so (e.g., Alabama, Kentucky, Tennessee and Arkansas).[78] Furthermore, trade within the South has become far more important than the South's trade with other regions and foreign countries,[79] with the result that it is now easier than formerly for a potential activity locus to become an expanding economic base adequate to supply required goods and services

77. E.g., the Piedmont Crescent area of the Carolinas. See Chapin and Weiss, *op. cit.*, pp. 114-117.

78. See Dunn, *op. cit.*, pp. 42-46; Fuchs, *op. cit.*, pp. 290 ff. At present Mississippi appears to offer less promise than other southern states. On Georgia's short-run prospects see Henry Thomassen, "A Growth Model for a State," *Southern Economic Journal*, XXIV (October, 1957), 123-139.

79. L. H. Moses, "A General Equilibrium Model of Production, Interregional Trade, and Location of Industry," *Review of Economics and Statistics*, XLII (November, 1960), 373-397, especially 383-387. But see on some of the South's weaknesses C. D. Harris, "The Market as a Factor in the Localization of Industries in the United States," *Annals of the Association of American Geographers*, XLIV (December, 1954), 315-348.

hitherto imported.[80] The South's incomes should, therefore, approach incomes elsewhere more rapidly than in the recent past, especially if full employment is restored within and outside the South.

It is doubtful, however, that convergence will manifest itself as fully within the South as between the South and the non-South. Certainly the inquiries of economic geographers do not suggest accelerating convergence.[81] The South's main urban and related centers are, as has been noted, unevenly distributed; of the fifty American cities described as "major" in a recent study, sixteen are located in the South, but with ten in three states (Texas, Tennessee, and Florida) and none in four states (Arkansas, Mississippi, and the Carolinas).[82] This uneven distribution of large urban centers may not be disadvantageous in the long run, given the possibility of developing other distribution patterns and the advantages associated therewith. There exist, for example, other centers or areas (e.g., the Piedmont Crescent) about which growth can be very satisfactorily oriented; and there appear attainable a variety of patterns of population distribution which yield both economies of conglomeration and attractive living conditions. Still there are now operative forces which are adversely affecting many existing urban centers, among them some of significant size. Thus, with the improvement of transport, "the resultant clustering of functions to achieve economies of scale, produces more rapid growth of the larger places, and slower growth, stagnation, or decline of smaller central places which offer fewer goods and services."[83] This tendency is accentuated by the uneven incidence of the costs of such conglomeration, many of which apparently are not incident upon the decision-makers initially responsible for excessive conglomeration.

80. Such a base may be of considerable relative magnitude, however; e.g., the Los Angeles SMSA exports directly 27 per cent and indirectly 9 per cent of its output of goods and services. See C. M. Tiebout, *The Community Economic Base Study* (New York: Committee for Economic Development, 1962), pp. 33-37. See also Duncan *et al., op. cit.,* pp. 77 ff.; Homer Hoyt, "The Utility of the Economic Base Method in Calculating Urban Growth," *Land Economics,* XXXVII (February, 1961), 53 ff.

81. E.g., see Harris, *op. cit.;* A. K. Philbrick, *op. cit.,* and "Principles of Areal Functional Organization in Regional Human Geography," *Economic Geography,* XXXIII (October, 1957), 299-336, esp. pp. 329-336; Zelinsky, *op. cit.*

82. Duncan *et al., op. cit.,* Part IV.

83. Mayer, *op. cit.,* pp. 619-620; also Duncan *et al., op. cit.,* Parts I-II; Northam, *op. cit.,* pp. 58-59; R. Vernon, *Metropolis 1985* (Garden City: Doubleday, 1963), chap. 5.

In the immediate future, however, even though steady expansion of the South's total internal market will make for growth of its output and income, uneven distribution of growth loci will sustain interstate disparity in growth and this disparity may in turn intensify uneconomic interstate and intrastate competition for industry.

It is advisable, in view of what has been said, that the impact of prospective changes in both economies of scale and transport costs be assessed. Economies of scale make for industrial and demographic concentration, whereas increase in transport costs makes for decentralization. When economies of scale are ascendant in an industry (e.g., in tobacco, textiles and apparel, machinery, transportation equipment), the South can attract it only if it can attract it in sufficient quantity to generate these economies. When, on the contrary, transport costs are rising, especially in respect of long hauls and finished goods, many activities tend to be dispersed in keeping with the distribution of consumers and consumer demand. The South's capacity to attract industry may, therefore, be expected to rise with increase in transport costs.[84]

It is particularly advisable that the significance for the South of the revolutionary developments now taking place in communication be correctly assessed. These should make for dispersal of economic activities and population both to the South and within the South toward smaller communities. Indeed, the South appears to be one of the nation's regions best situated to capitalize on these revolutionary changes. One outcome might be a partial remedying of a fundamental defect in the South's current industrial structure, a relative dearth of industrial activity in which research and development play an important role. Research and development are of much greater significance in manufacturing than in other lines of activity, though far more important in some branches of manufacture than in others. The South, as has been indicated, has only about two-thirds as large a fraction of its labor force engaged in manufacture as has the non-South. Moreover, manufacturing employment in the South is heavily concentrated in industries in which expenditure on research and development is very low. A large

84. I have benefited through study of Benjamin Chinitz's paper on "Transportation and Decentralization of Manufacturing," National Bureau of Economic Research conference, April 26-27, 1963.

fraction of this employment—over two-thirds in 1947—remains in textiles, apparel, food products, lumber, and tobacco in which the ratio of research and development expenditures to sales is slightly to markedly below one-third of the national average for all manufacturing.[85]

Given the trends under way or in prospect, it is advisable that an independent Institute for the Study of Southern Growth and Prospects be set up, not to attempt to modify essentially non-modifiable trends but to assess what these trends are and enable the South to make appropriate industrial and other adjustments thereto as well as avoid the evils which presently encompass many metropolises.

85. For ratios by types of manufacture, see J. W. Kendrick, *Productivity Trends in the United States* (Princeton: Princeton University Press, 1961), p. 182. It should be noted, however, that research and development expenditures are very high in relation to sales only in industries engaged in the production of aircraft, missiles, electrical equipment, and communication; and in these (which account for 59 per cent of all such expenditures) the companies concerned finance only about 20 per cent whereas all other companies finance about 76 per cent. See *Annual Report of the Council of Economic Advisers* (January, 1964), p. 107, on 1961 expenditures. In short, the federal government is the major source of research and development funds, and the South is relatively short of the industries to which these funds flow. Only a small fraction of these funds is devoted to basic research. Too much of the taxpayer's money turned over to the now dominant military-industrial complex is wasted, and little of that not wasted contributes to the generation of industry in the South or to the resolution of its problems. On aspects of this very important, albeit uncritically handled problem, see Paul D. Foote, "Government-Financed Research, Basic and Applied," *Proceedings of the American Philosophical Society*, CIX (April, 1965), 57-62.

VI. TRENDS IN SOUTHERN MONEY, INCOME, SAVINGS, AND INVESTMENT / Joe S. Floyd, Jr.

As Professor Spengler has suggested in his essay on southern economic trends,[1] southern per capita income has been growing at a rate higher than that of the nation. With this growth in personal income, the savings of southerners have increased. As recently as 1940, for example, the per capita liquid dollar savings of the southern people was only $66.48, as compared to $339.70 for the nation. Since 1940, however, dollar savings of southerners have increased by about 600 per cent as contrasted with only 174 per cent for the nation.[2]

1

Just as there is a wide difference between per capita incomes within the various southern states, there is also a large difference in dollar savings. In 1940, for example, the per capita liquid savings of the people of Arkansas was only $38.66, while the per capita liquid savings of Virginians was $122.00. These figures for the various southern states, the South, and the nation, are shown in *Table 1*.

From this table it will be noted that in 1940 Virginia was the only southern state with per capita savings in excess of $100, and even this figure is dwarfed by the national average of $339.70. By 1960, however, the southern state with the lowest per capita savings was Mississippi with only a little more than $270. However, all but four of the southern states had per capita savings in excess of $400. And the southern state with the highest per capita savings, Florida, had a figure which was 88 per cent of the national average.

2

In a less advanced society where the economy is based primarily upon extractive industries such as fishing, forestry, and agriculture, the level of per capita savings is low. Even these meager savings are typically not held in the form of cash or assets which can easily

1. *Infra.*
2. For the dollar amounts of liquid savings in the U. S., the South, and individual southern states see *Table 1*.

Table 1. Liquid Savings in the United States 1940-1960 (Per Capita Savings).

	1940	1950	1960	Per cent change 1940-1960
Alabama	$ 45.86	$118.84	$ 324.72	606
Arkansas	38.66	112.15	326.83	720
Florida	92.74	301.85	839.56	803
Georgia	54.59	180.82	439.00	700
Kentucky	94.94	184.96	447.13	370
Louisiana	89.90	209.11	472.27	402
Mississippi	39.58	88.14	272.18	580
N. Carolina	64.46	193.06	419.21	561
Oklahoma	69.22	182.39	517.76	650
S. Carolina	41.09	132.93	320.58	680
Tennessee	72.26	201.36	480.08	560
Texas	54.24	157.28	472.11	770
Virginia	122.00	247.83	453.78	270
Total South	66.84	179.75	467.70	600
Total Non-South	445.83	872.85	1104.13	147
Total U.S.	339.70	681.73	930.92	174

Sources: *Savings and Loan Fact Book, 1961; 89th Annual Report of Comptroller of Currency; House Documents, 1st Session 82nd Congress, No. 11; Savings and Loan Annals, 1951; Monthly Labor Review of U.S. Bureau of Labor Statistics, 1951, Vol. 73; Statistical Abstract of U.S., 1952; Statistical Abstract Supplement, Colonial Times to 1957; 79th Annual Report of Comptroller of Currency; House Documents, Vol. 21, 1st Session 77th Congress; Savings and Loan Annals, 1940; and Monthly Labor Review of U.S. Bureau of Labor Statistics, 1940, Vol. 51.*

be converted into cash. The farmer holds his savings in the form of land, buildings, and a few hand tools. The fisherman puts his savings in boats and gear as the forester puts his in a saw and ax. In addition, such primitive economies are typically characterized by a high degree of self-sufficiency within the family unit. Much of their production is for use by the producing unit itself and little is sold outside this unit. Thus the actual cash income is very small, and, consequently, money savings are insignificant.

Since real savings are embodied in capital goods, i.e., the tools, farms, and boats, they cannot be transferred. The only way that these investments can be liquidated is by use, and the resulting immobility is reflected in a lack of flexibility in economies of this type. When it comes, change is necessarily slow. Movement of capital between alternative uses is difficult if not impossible.

With the development of more modern societies based upon manufacturing and trade, the need for a medium of exchange is urgent. At first hard money and subsequently bank credit replaces barter; self-sufficiency breaks down and money income replaces real or goods income. With this development, financial institutions arise to serve first as custodians, and, subsequently, as creators of the stream of money and credit.

To show the relative self-sufficiency of the South as recently as 1949, a single illustration will suffice. In that year over one-third of southern farm income was obtained from products consumed at home and the rental value of farm-owned and -occupied houses.[3] Over half of the farm income in Alabama, Virginia, and Georgia was obtained in this non-cash fashion, and the proportion of this type of income to total farm income exceeded 45 per cent in three other states.[4] In that year, farm income was over 13 per cent of total southern personal income, and non-cash farm income exceeded 4 per cent of total southern personal income.

In sharp contrast, during that same year, 1949, non-cash income was only 26 per cent of total farm income of the states outside of the South. Also, farm income was only 6 per cent of the total personal income of these non-southern states. Thus, the importance of the non-cash income is further reduced.

By 1961, non-cash farm income was less than 25 per cent of farm income in the South. In only one state, Virginia, was non-cash farm income as high as 40 per cent of total farm income. In that year, farm income was only 6 per cent of total southern personal income, while non-cash farm income was only 1.3 per cent.[5]

3

With this movement away from self-sufficiency and toward a specialized, interdependent, money economy, has come the development of southern financial institutions. Historically, the larger southern agricultural, mercantile, and manufacturing interests which required financing had sought accommodation from the large financial interests of the North and East. Southern banks, savings and loan associations, and life insurance companies were small and ill equipped to handle large capital transactions.[6] Even the bonds

3. U. S. Department of Agriculture, *Supplement to the Farm Income Situation for July, 1962* F I S 187, August 1962.
4. *Ibid.*
5. *Ibid.*; personal income data from the U.S. Department of Commerce, *Survey of Current Business*, Washington, D. C.
6. For a discussion of the adequacy of southern capital resources see C. B. Hoover

of the state and local governments in the South were underwritten by banking houses outside the South.[7] The comparative shortage of savings and the resulting scarcity of money capital tended to raise interest rates in the region.

Some measure of the growth of southern financial institutions may be obtained from *Tables* 2 and 3. These tables provide a measure of the increase in time and demand deposits of commercial banks and savings accounts at savings and loan associations during the period 1940-1960. It will be noted that these financial assets grew at a much more rapid rate in the South than elsewhere in the United States.

Examining first the data in *Table* 2, which indicate the volume of deposits in commercial banks within the South, the rapid growth in these financial resources is immediately evident. While demand deposits were not included in the computation of the liquid savings of the region because of the familiar argument that such deposits result from the credit creation function of commercial banks rather than through real savings,[8] their growth reflects an expansion of trade and commerce. In a modern industrial society, such deposits are the principal medium of exchange;[9] therefore, the growth is indicative of an increase in commercial activity.

The growth in demand deposits for the South as a whole is best evidenced by the fact that demand deposits within the South are almost 20 per cent of the national total today as contrasted with only 10 per cent in 1940.[10] When calculated on a per capita basis

and B. U. Ratchford, *Economic Resources and Policies of the South* (New York: The Macmillan Company, 1951), pp. 165-194. Also see C. T. Taylor, "The South's Capital and Credit Needs: Problems and Solutions with Particular Reference to Capital Expenditure by Industry," paper presented at the 28th annual meeting of the Southern Economic Association, Atlanta, Ga., November 21, 1958 (mimeographed). An early evaluation of the banking resources of the South is provided by Brant Bonner, *An Analysis of the Condition of Banks in the Southeast, 1920-1940* (unpublished doctoral dissertation, University of North Carolina, Chapel Hill, 1942).

7. C. T. Taylor, "Southern vs. Non-Southern Underwriting of Municipals," *The Southern Economic Journal*, XXIV (October, 1957), pp. 158-169.

8. This line of reasoning suggests that demand deposits of commercial banks result from the making of loans and investments by the banks because banks are not required to hold 100 per cent primary reserves against deposits. The lending process results in deposit creation. For an elaboration of this point see Lester V. Chandler, *The Economics of Money and Banking* (New York: Harper and Brothers, 1959), pp. 58-59.

9. *Ibid.*, pp. 27-28.

10. U.S. Comptroller of the Currency, *Annual Reports of the U.S. Comptroller of the Currency*, Washington, D. C.

Table 2. Demand and Time Deposits in Commercial Banks throughout the South, 1940 and 1960.

State	Millions of dollars				Dollars Total per capita		Per cent growth 1940-1960
	1940		1960				
	Demand	Time	Demand	Time	1940	1960	
Alabama	$ 174.8	$ 103.5	$ 1,073.2	$ 578.5	$ 98.24	$505.61	414.7
Arkansas	116.7	47.6	675.9	287.9	84.28	539.56	540.2
Florida	248.3	85.5	2,598.8	1,172.4	175.92	761.62	332.9
Georgia	258.4	124.7	1,494.7	689.3	122.64	556.16	353.5
Kentucky	268.4	139.4	1,282.3	471.7	143.31	577.32	302.8
Louisiana	263.8	111.3	1,403.1	661.8	158.68	633.98	299.5
Mississippi	102.9	70.5	641.1	314.5	79.40	438.72	452.5
North Carolina	234.5	117.8	1,357.1	619.3	98.64	433.79	339.8
Oklahoma	238.1	73.5	1,441.7	480.7	133.37	825.67	619.1
South Carolina	107.3	34.7	606.0	169.2	74.74	325.36	335.3
Tennessee	254.7	171.1	1,390.6	976.8	146.03	663.68	454.5
Texas	989.2	208.3	6,326.4	2,033.6	186.68	872.68	467.5
Virginia	271.6	271.0	1,439.5	1,154.9	202.63	654.00	332.8
Total South	$ 3,519.7	$ 1,558.9	$ 21,730.4	$ 9,510.6	$137.21	$640.16	466.6
Total United States	$33,491.7	$25,750.0	$110,446.5	$63,273.5	$448.24	$968.75	216.1
South as a percentage of U. S.	10.51%	6.05%	19.68%	15.03%	30.61%	66.08%	

Sources: for time deposits, Savings & Loan Facts Book—1961; for demand deposits (1960) Federal Reserve Bank as quoted in the County & City Data Book, U.S. Department of Commerce, 1962, and (1940) Annual Report of the Comptroller of the Currency 1940 (all active banks, including national, state [commercial] savings, and private banks).

Table 3. Total Assets of Savings Associations throughout the South, 1940 & 1960.

State	Savings associations assets in millions of dollars		Assets per capita in dollars	
	1940	1960	1940	1960
Alabama	$ 13.9	$ 423.0	$ 4.91	$129.49
Arkansas	14.6	278.8	7.49	156.08
Florida	55.2	2,904.9	29.4	586.66
Georgia	30.0	953.6	9.6	241.84
Kentucky	113.5	834.7	39.89	274.74
Louisiana	93.8	839.2	39.68	257.66
Mississippi	9.0	265.6	4.12	121.92
North Carolina	98.5	1,237.3	27.58	271.62
Oklahoma	64.5	653.5	27.61	280.68
South Carolina	27.3	572.7	14.37	240.37
Tennessee	27.0	664.2	9.26	186.20
Texas	95.2	2,222.9	14.84	232.04
Virginia	51.6	619.9	19.27	130.07
Total South	$ 694.1	$12,370.3	$18.75	$253.48
Total U.S.	$5,674.3	$62,104.2	$42.93	$346.33
South as a percentage of U.S.	12.23%	19.92%	43.68%	73.19%

Source: *Savings and Loan Fact Book, 1961.*

the combined demand and time deposits within the South rose from only 30 per cent of the national figure in 1940 to approximately two-thirds in 1960.[11] Since the per capita liquid savings in the South was not quite half of the national figure in 1960, it is evident that the deposit resources are growing more rapidly than liquid assets.

Turning to the data for individual states, which are also shown in *Table 2,* the group of states located in the western part of the South experienced the most rapid increases. In some instances, as in the case of Arkansas, the rapid percentage gain may be attributed to the extremely low figures which prevailed in the base year (1940). For other states, like Texas and Oklahoma, however, the rapid growth in deposits per capita seems to be attributable to economic growth generally.

In *Table 3* the assets of savings and loan institutions in the South are shown. For the most part these institutions are mutually operated[12] and are local in nature without extensive systems. Their

11. *Ibid.*
12. Mutual operation means that the shareholders (depositors) own the institu-

assets are held principally in the form of first mortgage loans on urban real estate. Their funds are provided by their shareholder whose claims against the association represent a liability much like the time deposits of banks. Growth in these specialized institutions represents both accumulation of funds in the area immediately surrounding the association as well as expansion of construction activities within the same area. Such expenditures typically help to support economic activity in the construction and related industries.[13]

An examination of the data on *Table 3* reveals a striking growth in the assets of southern savings and loan associations over the period 1940-1960. This growth, both in absolute dollars and in relationship to the U. S. totals, is best demonstrated by the fact that the assets of southern savings associations grew from 12 per cent of the total assets of all U. S. associations in 1940 to almost 20 per cent in 1960. On a per capita basis, assets of southern associations were 44 per cent of the national figure in 1940 and 73 per cent in 1960.

Turning to figures for individual states, it is evident that the amount of savings and loan assets was negligible in 1940 in a number of southern states.[14] On a per capita basis, these assets were less than $10 in Georgia and Arkansas. Reference to *Table 2*, which shows time deposits, indicates that savings and loan assets were extremely small relative to time deposits in 1940. By 1960, however, savings and loan assets were over $250 million in every southern state, and in Florida and Texas they exceeded $2 billion. On a per capita basis, savings association assets exceeded $120 in every state and were $586 in Florida. The growth of the Florida associations

tion. The only equity funds are reserves created over time from income. Only Texas of the southern states permits organization of savings and loan institutions with stock ownership. Of 6,300 savings associations currently in operation, only about 600 are stock associations. For a review of the industry's recent growth see Joe S. Floyd, Jr., "The Savings and Loan Industry: Its Growth and Prospects," paper presented at annual meeting of the Southern Section of the American Finance Association, Atlanta, Ga., Nov. 9, 1962 (mimeographed). For recent data concerning the industry see the annual issues of the *Savings and Loan Fact Book*, U. S. Savings and Loan League, Chicago, Ill.

13. While most savings and loan association loans are for the construction or purchase of single family dwellings, other types of loans are also made. A limited number of loans are made using industrial and commercial property as collateral while modernization and home improvement loans also are made.

14. The assets of these associations are approximately equal to their deposit (shareholders accounts). Since in mutual associations the reserves belong to the shareholders the total asset figure is meaningful in a savings sense.

is indicative of the support they gave to the building boom in this rapidly growing area.[15]

Savings and loan association assets in the South were only half the size of time deposits in 1940. By 1960, however, savings and loan assets exceeded time deposits by almost $3 billion. Also it should be noted that savings assets exceeded time deposits in eight of the thirteen states of the region.[16] In 1940 savings association assets were substantially smaller than time deposits in every southern state.

4

It should be understood that capital moves into the South from elsewhere in the nation in a number of ways. In some cases there may be a transfer of savings accounts or time deposits, but in other instances investments have been made in the South by financial institutions located elsewhere. While it is impossible to measure accurately the total flow of capital into the South from sources outside the region, these resources have contributed significantly to southern economic development. In this sense, the South is an underdeveloped nation with free access to the capital markets of the North and East. For example, life insurance investments in the South increased from $441 million in 1939 to $26,419 million in 1961.[17] Between 1947 and 1961, life insurance assets invested in the South increased by over 250 per cent as compared with a rate of increase of only 180 per cent in the states outside the South.

In 1939 only 19 per cent of the assets of the largest life insurance firms in the nation[18] were invested in the South. By 1961 this percentage had increased to 30. Between 1948 and 1961, two categories of life insurance investment in the South, mortgages other than home mortgages and real estate ownership, increased by 400 per cent and 500 per cent respectively. Comparable investments outside

15. The construction activity in Florida reflected population growth of that state. The association between population growth and the increases in assets of savings and loan associations has been developed by Dr. Leon Kendall. See his *The Savings and Loan Business: Its Purposes, Functions, and Economic Justification* (Englewood Cliffs, N. J.: Prentice-Hall, 1962).

16. While many factors were at work here it appears that the management of the savings and loan associations were more aggressive than the managements of commercial banks. See J. S. Floyd, Jr., *op. cit.*

17. These figures were obtained from the *Record of Life Insurance Investments*, which is published annually by the Life Insurance Association of America.

18. *Ibid.*

the South rose by 275 per cent and 225 per cent over the same period.[19]

In the past there has been considerable apprehension concerning the activities of large national financial institutions, such as life insurance firms, in the South. The allegation has been made that such institutions tend to draw premium income from the region while these funds are invested elsewhere. One measure of this relationship between income and investment is the ratio between the investments made by life insurance firms in the South and the amount of their reserves computed from the amount of their insurance policies in force within the region. A ratio of this type, equal to 100 per cent, would indicate that the investments in the region were exactly equal to reserves maintained against policies sold in the region. Ratios higher than 100 per cent would indicate that investment exceeded policy reserves. While detailed data are not readily available for each southern state, the ratios for the three regions which include the southern states under review suggest that insurance companies are investing far more in the region than the reserves which result from policies written within the area. The precise ratios for 1961 are 140 per cent for the South Atlantic Region, 180 per cent for the East South Central Region, and 232 per cent for the West South Central. Such ratios suggest a large inflow of capital to the South from other regions.[20]

It should be understood that other types of capital have been invested in the South in addition to the categories enumerated above. Such institutions as pension funds, investment companies, and private industrial corporations along with investment by private individuals have played a role in the expanding economy of the South. One measure of total investment in the productive resources of the South is found in the annual dollar amount of investment in manufacturing corporations within the area. As recently as 1947, the total annual investment in manufacturing within the region was $1,160 million. By 1961 this total had increased to $2,210 million.[21]

19. An unpublished study by Winston C. Beard indicates that the ratio of investments to reserves in Arkansas was equal to 258 per cent in 1956. See "The Effects of State Investment Requirements for Life Insurance Companies," an unpublished manuscript by Winston C. Beard, College of Business Administration, University of Arkansas.

20. *Record of Life Insurance Investment, op. cit.*

21. From the 1947 *Census of Manufacturers* and the 1961 *Annual Survey of Manufacturers.* U. S. Department of Commerce, Washington, D. C.

Put in a slightly different manner, the annual investment in manufacturing in the South was only 19 per cent of the national total
in 1947, but by 1961 the southern share had risen to 24 per cent of
the national figure.[22] This investment is made possible by reinvest-
ment of profits of industrial corporations as well as investment by
individuals and financial corporations in enterprises within the
region.[23]

5

What has been the result of this increase in money savings in the
South together with this inflow of money capital from outside the
region?[24] One extremely important result has been that the prevailing rates of interest have fallen.

While regional interest rate data are incomplete, it is apparent
that effective rates of interest paid on loans made by national banks
in the South were high in 1920. In six of thirteen states of the South,
this effective rate exceeded 9 per cent in that year.[25] The national
average in that year was 8.75 per cent. Ten years later the highest
effective interest rate prevailing on national bank loans in the South
was only 7.7 per cent and only three other southern states had
effective interest rates on national bank loans in excess of 6 per
cent.[26]

Beginning in 1937, more complete information concerning effective interest rates on loans is available for the member banks of
the Federal Reserve System.[27] These data are shown in *Table 4* for
the three Federal Reserve Districts which include the bulk of the
southern states. To facilitate comparison, the average effective loan

22. *Ibid.*
23. Much of the new investment made by manufacturing firms comes from "internal" sources. High among these sources are reinvested profits. For an evaluation of sources of long term capital for industry see Joe S. Floyd, Jr., and Luther H.
Hodges, Jr., *Financing Industrial Growth: Public and Private Sources of Long Term
Capital for Industry*, Research Paper 10, School of Business Administration, University of North Carolina (Chapel Hill, N. C., 1962). Large multi-plant national
firms make profits in one region and invest them in others adding to capital mobility.
24. In an attempt to augment private capital sources, a number of southern
states and municipalities have used public funds for industrial lending. For an
evaluation of this development, see Floyd and Hodges, *op. cit.*, also Joe S. Floyd, Jr.,
"Federal, State, and Local Government Programs for Financing Industrial Development," *Proceedings of Fifty-fifth National Tax Conference* (Miami Beach, 1962).
25. See the *Annual Reports of the U. S. Comptroller of the Currency*, Washington,
D. C.
26. *Ibid.*
27. For an early presentation of these data see Hoover and Ratchford, *op. cit.*

Table 4. The Difference between the Percentage Rate of Return on Loans Made by Member Banks of the Federal Reserve System in Districts Five, Six, and Eleven, and the Average Return for the System as a Whole.

Year	All districts	District 5	District 5 as a % of all districts	District 6	District 6 as a % of all districts	District 11	District 11 as a % of all districts
1937	4.0	5.1	127.5	4.8	120.0	6.1	152.5
1939	4.2	4.9	116.7	4.8	114.3	5.7	135.7
1941	4.0	4.7	117.5	4.7	117.5	5.5	137.5
1943	3.5	4.2	120.0	3.8	108.6	4.2	120.0
1944	3.2	3.7	115.6	3.4	106.3	3.8	118.8
1945	3.0	3.5	116.7	3.3	110.0	3.5	116.7
1946	3.2	3.7	115.6	3.6	112.5	3.9	121.9
1947	3.6	4.0	111.1	4.0	111.1	4.4	122.2
1948	3.8	4.4	115.8	4.4	115.8	4.6	121.1
1950	5.56	5.48	98.6	6.02	108.3	6.85	123.2
1951	5.63	5.52	98.0	6.03	107.1	6.88	122.2
1952	5.77	5.72	99.1	6.26	108.5	6.92	119.9
1953	5.79	5.85	101.0	6.29	108.6	6.80	117.4
1954	5.71	5.80	101.6	6.19	108.4	6.49	113.7
1955	5.84	6.04	103.4	6.35	108.7	6.50	111.3
1956	5.91	6.09	103.0	6.35	107.4	6.53	110.5
1957	6.16	6.31	102.4	6.68	108.4	6.93	112.5
1958	6.17	6.32	102.4	6.70	108.6	6.90	111.8
1959	6.31	6.52	103.3	6.90	109.4	6.92	109.7
1960	6.46	6.57	101.7	6.91	107.0	7.26	112.4
1961	6.41	6.46	100.8	6.83	106.6	7.09	110.6
1962	6.53	6.68	102.3	6.93	106.1	7.23	110.7

Source: Federal Reserve Bulletin, "Member Bank Operating Ratios."

rates for all member banks in the U. S. are shown in this table; the rates for the Atlanta, Richmond, and Dallas districts are shown as a percentage of the all-district (national) average.[28] While the absolute level of rates has varied considerably over the period 1937-1962, reflecting conditions in the national money and capital markets, the difference between interest rates in the southern districts, compared to the nation, has decreased markedly. At the end of the period, the largest absolute difference between loan rates for member banks in the South and similar rates for all member banks was only .7 per cent. This was the margin in the Dallas district; the Richmond and Atlanta districts had a differential of only .15 per cent and .4 per cent, respectively.[29]

28. These data were obtained from the Research Department of the Federal Reserve Bank of Richmond.
29. *Ibid.*, Federal Reserve Districts are not coterminous with states. The principal

Certainly bank lending rates are not indicative of all rates of return on capital. It is possible that differential between prevailing interest rates on long-term loans and equity capital might display a wider gap than that shown for member bank loans. But the narrowing of the gap between bank loan rates in the South and the nation is indicative of the general pattern of interest rates. And this narrowing gives support to the general thesis that with the growth of southern savings and the inflow of capital from other regions, rates of return on capital investment in the region are being brought into line with the rates of return that prevail elsewhere in the nation.

6

What is the significance of this growth in liquid savings and the resultant strengthening of southern financial institutions? Certainly such developments should not be construed in such a way as to suggest that the South might soon be able to become self-sufficient. Much of the growth in the South may be attributed to capital inflows from other parts of the country, and these continued inflows are vital if the future growth of the region is to be assured.

Future capital inflows, together with increasing amounts of southern savings, will make possible large investments within the region. These investments may take a number of possible forms. Increased use of modern farm machinery and modern farm methods may result. Erection of new and modernization of old manufacturing facilities may be expected. Creation of new modern transportation and communication facilities of both public and private types awaits such investment stimulus. In short, the creation of a modern, complex, industrial, agricultural, and commercial society in which workers may expect large money incomes is dependent upon an adequate volume of investments in the region.

Even a cursory examination of the economic needs of the South reveals the vital need for this additional capital investment.

southern districts are Richmond (which includes Virginia, North and South Carolina, as well as Maryland, West Virginia, and the District of Columbia), Atlanta (which includes Georgia, Florida, Alabama, and portions of Louisiana, Tennessee, and Mississippi), and the Dallas district (Texas and portions of Louisiana, Oklahoma, and Arizona). The St. Louis district includes parts of Mississippi, Arkansas, and Tennessee, but the bulk of the district is outside of the South. For a map showing their districts see *The Federal Reserve Bulletin*, Board of Governors of the Federal Reserve System, Washington, D. C.

Measures to restore the fertility and productivity of southern land require substantial investment in drainage, fertilization and other measures. Many southern industries, especially the large textile industry, must be modernized in order to meet competition from at home and abroad. A very large segment of southern industry—not only textiles but also apparel, food, and related products and certain parts of the furniture and wood products industries—is "labor-intensive." This type of industry tends to employ large quantities of unskilled and semiskilled workers and comparatively small amounts of capital. Inevitably such industries are "low-wage," for by their very nature worker productivity is low.

The future growth of the South is dependent upon an up-grading of these industries, together with the development of new scientific industries which require a high order of worker skills and offer relatively high per worker wages. Large amounts of capital investment are needed in the up-grading process. Modern machines can, and will, invade the labor-intensive industries; thus it is necessary that those industries acquire both the capital goods necessary and also that the human capital in worker skills be increased. The South has received real stimulus in the growth of its scientific industries both in Florida and along the Gulf Coast. The large government and private expenditures in connection with the national space program have resulted in the erection of expensive facilities and the migration of skilled workers into many parts of the South. It is important that the region build upon this foundation.

Future growth in southern money incomes and savings will further strengthen southern financial institutions. Capital available from these institutions, as well as other sources, will further reduce prevailing interest rates in the region. Low interest rates in turn will stimulate business managers to undertake additional investment. Clearly the historic pattern of capital scarcity and high interest rates which prevailed in the South over such a long period has been broken. Consequently, more rapid growth of southern incomes, savings, and investment appears likely in the future.

VII. TRANSPORTATION AND COMMUNICATION / Daniel O. Fletcher

The importance of the transportation and communication network to the economic and social development of a region can hardly be overstated. People are joined together both by communicating over distances and by traveling between locations. Economic development can only occur when products are able to move freely between different locations, allowing regional specialization and the large-scale production that comes with large markets. Without efficient transportation and communications, the population of a country is broken up into small isolated groups, self-sufficient, dependent on their own resources, and usually out of touch with the world.

For many years the South was isolated, in two senses. First, individual local communities, or even families, were isolated from their neighbors. Second, the region as a whole was separated from the rest of the United States. Both of these forms of isolation meant that the South was different from the rest of the country. The lack of transportation facilities inhibited economic growth and made it difficult to ship products out of the area. The lack of communications facilities inhibited the social development of the area, or at least led to a social development differing from that of the rest of the nation. In part, this isolation continues in the South, but it is rapidly breaking down, and it is breaking down because of the development of transportation and communications in the area.

If this isolation, both locally and regionally, is really disappearing, it may solve many of the problems of the South. For instance, the economic development of the area will accelerate. On the other hand, these changes will lead to further problems. The society of the South is being transformed by its contacts with the rest of the nation. Change is often painful and the breaking down of old barriers is no exception. The development of more rapid and efficient transportation and communications is basic to these changes.

This chapter asks several questions about the transportation and communications network of the South. Does it weld the region into a unit or is the area a group of isolated localities? Does the network attach the South to the rest of the nation, or does it leave the South a separate entity? Is the transportation and communications system of the South growing with the region? Is it growing at the same rate as the system in the rest of the United States, or better? Is the quality of the facilities improving? Is the network of sufficient size and is it growing at a sufficient rate to provide for the economic and social development of the region?

The "South" has many meanings. In some sense it is merely a way of thinking. For purposes of this paper, the South will be defined as Southern Territory, unless otherwise stated. This is one of the five major railroad rate-making territories in the United States. It includes all of the states of Florida, Mississippi, Alabama, Georgia, South Carolina, North Carolina, Tennessee, the southern half of Virginia, and the part of Louisiana east of the Mississippi River. Thus it includes most of the former Confederate states and one border state. *Figure 1* illustrates the territorial divisions of the country. Texas, Louisiana, Arkansas, and Oklahoma form Southwestern Territory to the west. West Virginia and northern Virginia are part of Official Territory, made up basically of northeastern states. In the transportation field, "The South" has meant Southern Territory for many years. The area has its own rates and classification structure. It is served by its own railroads and by regional airlines. Therefore, this paper will define the South as Southern Territory, recognizing that several "southern" states are excluded. When it is appropriate other states, particularly West Virginia and the rest of Virginia, will be added.

Traditionally, the transportation network has been built around the railroad. Today, the highway system is probably of equal importance. Beyond these two, the South possesses excellent inland waterways and several good deep water ports. In passenger transport, the airlines are becoming leaders. Communications in the 1960's can almost be equated with the telephone, at least as far as personal and business communications are concerned. However, the influence of mass communication via radio, television, and the printed word cannot be ignored. These are the institutions whose growth in the South we are going to examine, dealing first with transportation and then communications.

Although not as crucially important as they once were, the railroads are still the basic skeleton of the transportation network of the nation. They are also the best documented of all the modes.

Figure 1. Railroad Rate-Making Territories

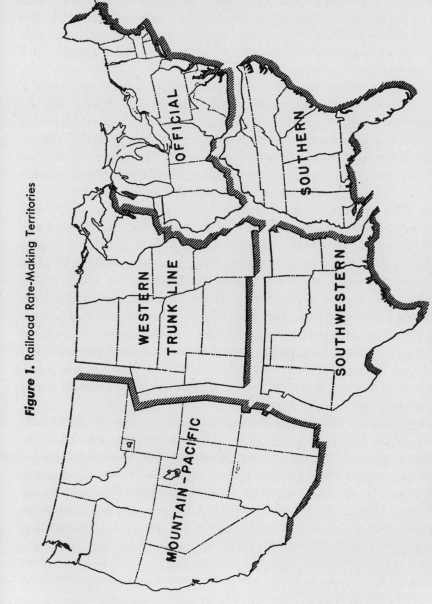

Source: U.S. Interstate Commerce Commission, Bureau of Transport Economics and Statistics, Carload Waybill Statistics, 1961 (Washington, D.C.: U.S. Government Printing Office, 1962), Statement TD-1 cover.

While it is difficult to discover the makeup of highway freight traffic, rail traffic is measured and analyzed in great detail by the Interstate Commerce Commission. Since 1947, the Commission has collected every waybill numbered 1 or with a number ending in 01. This procedure gives the Commission's Bureau of Transport Economics and Statistics a 1 per cent sample of waybills on Class I railroads (those with operating revenues of over a million dollars a year). The Bureau then publishes annual summaries of these data.[1] From these statistics it is possible to analyze the composition, origin, and destination of freight traffic on the railroads.

The territorial data show the relationship of the South to the other territories shown in *Figure 1*. In 1961, the latest year for which data were available in February, 1965, more tonnage originated in Southern Territory than terminated there. The largest part of these totals was intraterritorial in nature, but more tonnage was shipped out of the territory ("exports") than was received ("imports"). This excess of exports was almost entirely in the category "Products of Mines," which counts heavily in tonnage figures, but less importantly in terms of value. In the "Manufactures and Miscellaneous" category, the South was still a net importer. In "Forest Products," the area exported slightly more than it imported. In the other categories of traffic, "Products of Agriculture," and "Animals and their Products," the region imported slightly more than it exported.

These results correspond to the traditional view of the South as a buyer of industrial goods and a producer of raw materials. The pattern holds through all the available waybill statistics back to 1947, when they were first published. However, there has been a steady shift in the size of the import-export gap in manufactured and miscellaneous goods. While inward shipments of commodities in this class increased some between 1947 and 1961, exports to the rest of the nation increased markedly. This, of course, is a reflection of the increased industrialization of the South.

1. U.S. Interstate Commerce Commission, Bureau of Transport Economics and Statistics, *Carload Waybill Statistics*, 1947 to present (Washington: United States Government Printing Office, annual). Due to a change in compilation techniques, the 1961 issue was the latest published by February, 1965. Other data in this chapter are as of the time of writing (August, 1963). In most cases, new data were available by publication, but none changed overall patterns or conclusions significantly.

The other categories of traffic held about the same relative import-export positions throughout the period 1947-1961. That is, Southern Territory exported more than it imported in trade via railroad with the rest of the United States, this excess being made up of Products of Mines. Small import balances in animal and agricultural products and a small export balance in forest products persisted. Agricultural exports from the South showed a marked instability over the years, varying as much as 15 per cent from year to year. Both total imports and exports grew considerably and steadily from 1947 to 1961, but the distribution of these totals remained basically the same.

Which of the other rate territories were the major trading partners in these transactions? For shipments from the South, the answer is simple. Official Territory, made up of northeastern states, received far and away the largest part of shipments from Southern Territory in all of the years for which data are available. This is also true for all of the five divisions of traffic.

Imports to the South show a more complicated pattern. Again, Official Territory leads in total shipments and in the categories of manufactured goods, agricultural products, and products of mines. Southwestern Territory was a growing second in all the years from 1947 to 1961, being of particular importance in agricultural products. Mountain-Pacific Territory has continued to be the leading shipper of forest products to the South, although in total these are not large. Western Trunk Line Territory was the leader in sending animal products to the South.

In summary, Southern Territory is a net exporter of commodities by railroad, but most of this excess is from mines. The region continues to be an importer of manufactured goods. The two contiguous territories, Official and Southwestern, are the main trading partners. Several elements of change are evident, however. Total shipments and receipts are rising, and the South is cutting the import gap in manufactured goods. The South is increasing trade with territories other than Official Territory, the traditional partner. Thus the South is becoming more closely tied economically with the rest of the nation and with areas farther from its boundaries.

In the territorial statistics, the largest tonnage is the Southern to Southern movement—that is, the intraterritorial shipment of commodities. Looking at the most recent state-to-state statistics, the leading originating states were Kentucky, Florida, and Virginia. The smallest shippers were Mississippi and South Carolina. The most important trading partners for the states were generally the neighboring states, as would be expected. This means that the most important receivers of shipments from Kentucky were all outside the South (Ohio, Illinois, Indiana, and Michigan). For Florida, Georgia and Alabama ranked first and second as trading partners, but were followed by Illinois and Ohio. Every southern state, even such Deep South states as Alabama and Georgia, did significant business with states outside the South. This fact reinforces the conclusion reached in discussing territorial data that the South is bound firmly to the rest of the nation by economic ties. These ties lend importance to the levels of rail rates, both within the Southern Territory and between southern and other territories, in comparison with rates in the rest of the United States.

The question of rate differentials between Southern Territory and the rest of the country, especially Official Territory, became an important political issue just before World War II. Much popular attention was focused on this matter as the basis for the lack of southern industrial development. Some students of the South have contended that the differences were not as great as many thought, at least in more recent times, and that the differences were not as important as they appeared.[2] Nevertheless, the controversy has a long history and a firm hold on popular opinion. It is certainly true that rates in Southern Territory were higher for many years. By the beginning of the post-World War II period, and especially after the *Class Rate Decision* of 1945, there is evidence that this discrimination was disappearing.[3] This decision of the Interstate Commerce Commission set the stage for the equalization of rates and led to the Uniform Freight Classification as a replacement for the old territorial classification systems.

The difficulties of any attempt to compare rail rates in one section of the country with rates in another section are indeed formid-

2. C. B. Hoover and B. U. Ratchford, *Economic Resources and Policies of the South* (New York: Macmillan, 1951), pp. 78-79.

3. U.S. Interstate Commerce Commission, *Class Rate Investigation, 1939*, 262 ICC 447, 701 (Washington, D. C.: U.S. Government Printing Office, 1945). For an excellent discussion of this issue up to 1947, see William H. Joubert, *Southern Freight Rates in Transition* (Gainesville: University of Florida Press, 1949).

able. Since the advent of the Uniform Freight Classification at least one problem is eased, for goods should be classed uniformly across the country. However, a simple comparison of class rate scales is useless, for the majority of traffic moves on commodity or exceptions rates. Freight tariffs are complex documents made up of many individual rates set between thousands of pairs of individual cities. There is no simple "price list" that can be set down for comparison purposes. The basic concept of rate making, the distance scale of rates, is so altered by departures for specific shipments that it is of no use.

It is possible, of course, to compare individual rates on specific goods between two points the same distance apart in two different territories, such as Southern and Official. Even this comparison is difficult, due to the problem of finding sets of stations similar distances apart and with similar cost conditions. A more serious objection to this type of matching is that anything can be proved if the right goods and stations are picked. This happened in many of the Interstate Commerce Commission cases concerning Southern rate differentials. Much time was spent on "horrible examples," where the Southern rates were definitely higher than those in the North. Equally "horrible" instances could probably have been found to prove the opposite case. These differences exist within any territory as well as between them.

Since 1947, the Interstate Commerce Commission's series of waybill statistics has provided information on the average revenue per hundred pounds of freight actually shipped. These data cut through the maze of differing tariffs and give a true indication of rate levels actually charged. From the information collected in the waybill sample, the Bureau of Transport Economics and Statistics of the Interstate Commerce Commission constructs indexes of average freight rates on carload traffic by commodity class and by geographic territory. These index numbers give a good indication of changes in rate levels from year to year.

Based on the first year's results, the Bureau of Transport Economics developed a set of index numbers comparing intraterritorial rates on the various commodity groups for 1947.[4] These comparisons

4. U.S. Interstate Commerce Commission, Bureau of Transport Economics and Statistics, *Comparison of Average Rates Charged on Intraterritorial Carload Freight* (Washington: U.S. Government Printing Office, 1950).

Table 1. Comparison of Freight Rates, 1947 (Southern Territory Rates Equal 100).

	Official	Western Trunk Line	South-Western	Mountain-Pacific
All commodities	104±0.8	100±0.8	98±1.6	105±1.2
Agricultural products	91±3.0	100±5.2	92±2.1	99±3.0
Animals and their products	86±4.0	87±2.5	101±1.8	106±3.3
Products of mines	108±2.4	99±1.3	92±2.8	110±2.7
Products of forests	128±4.3	104±3.9	102±2.5	112±4.2
Manufactures and miscellaneous	99±1.0	102±0.9	102±1.3	101±2.0

Source: U.S. Interstate Commerce Commission, Bureau of Transport Economics and Statistics, *Comparison of Average Rates Charged on Intraterritorial Carload Freight* (Washington: U.S. Government Printing Office, 1950), p. 21.

did not show that the Southern Territory suffered under appreciably higher rates than the rest of the nation, particularly Official Territory. These results are summarized in *Tables 1* and *2*. Rates in Southern Territory were practically identical with those in Official Territory, with the exception of rates on agricultural and animal products. Rates on manufactured goods, the center of the former controversy, were so close to Official rates that the minor difference could easily be sampling error. From this well-documented study, one can conclude that southern rail rates were little higher than other territorial rates in 1947.

The question remains as to what has happened to freight rates since 1947. Here the Interstate Commerce Commission Freight Rate Index series is useful.[5] Relevant parts of this series are in-

Table 2. Southern Territory Rates, 1947.

	As per cent of Official Territory Rates	As per cent of five territory averages	Rank among five territories
All commodities	97±0.7	98.5	4
Agricultural products	110±4.7	103.6	2
Animals and their products	116±4.7	104.2	2
Products of mines	93±1.9	98.7	4
Products of forests	78±2.6	91.5	5
Manufactures and miscellaneous	101±1.0	99.2	3 (tie)

Source: U.S. Interstate Commerce Commission, Bureau of Transport Economics and Statistics, *Comparison of Average Rates Charged on Intraterritorial Carload Freight* (Washington: U.S. Government Printing Office, 1950), p. 21.

5. U.S. Interstate Commerce Commission, Bureau of Transport Economics and Statistics, *Indexes of Average Freight Rates on Railroad Carload Traffic, 1948-1961* (Washington: U.S. Government Printing Office, 1963).

cluded in *Table 3*. From these figures, it appears that the Southern Territory rates on all commodities have risen less than the national average increase for all commodities since 1947.

In comparison with rates within Official Territory, rates within Southern Territory rose slightly less. On all commodities, the increase in Official Territory amounted to 28 per cent of the 1948 level, while in Southern Territory it amounted to 20 per cent. On the crucial manufactured goods, the difference is striking. Rates within Official Territory rose 28 per cent between 1948 and 1961, while within Southern Territory these rates rose only slightly over 5 per cent.

Rates between Southern and Official Territories were crucial in the prewar controversies. Unfortunately, good comparisons on interterritorial rates are not available for 1947. Such rates are constructed, in sometimes complicated fashion, from the territorial rates. Since 1948, according to *Table 3*, interterritorial rates on all commodities rose more on Southern to Official than on Official to Southern movements. Most of this increase, however, was concentrated in products of mines and products of forests, where Southern rates were lowest. (See *Tables 1* and *2*.) For manufactured goods, the percentage increase was the same for Official to Southern as for Southern to Official traffic. Therefore, Southern Territory is at least holding its own in this category of rates.

It appears that the South can no longer claim to be severely handicapped by higher freight rates than in states to the north. Some very recent changes, such as the low rates on wheat filed by the Southern Railroad in 1963, are quite favorable to southern development. Rates do not seem to be a barrier to the economic integration of the South with the rest of the nation.

A modern highway system is rapidly replacing the railroads as the basic transportation network in the United States. While some goods must still be carried by railroads and many other goods are carried more cheaply by water carriers, the highways are becoming the core. The slogan of the truckers, "If you've got it, a truck brought it," is close to the truth. In passenger travel, the highway is even more in the ascendency, accounting for over 90 per cent of intercity passenger miles in private or commercial vehicles. The highway as a form of transportation is especially important in

Table 3. Freight Rate Indexes 1948-1961 (1950 = 100).

Year	Within Southern Territory					Within Official Territory		Official to Southern		Southern to Official					U.S.
	All commodities	Agricultural prod.	Products of mines	Products of forests	Manufactures & misc.	All commodities	Manufactures & misc.	All commodities	Manufactures & misc.	All commodities	Agricultural prod.	Products of mines	Products of forests	Manufactures & misc.	All commodities
1948	95	96	94	94	97	91	92	92	92	91	94	90	90	92	93
1949	101	101	100	98	104	99	100	100	100	98	99	97	97	98	99
1950	100	100	100	100	100	100	100	100	101	100	100	100	100	100	100
1951	102	101	101	104	102	103	103	101	101	102	100	102	102	102	102
1952	109	107	107	112	109	110	111	108	109	109	105	108	112	111	102
1953	112	112	109	116	113	111	113	111	112	112	108	111	115	115	109
1954	109	111	107	114	108	109	109	107	107	112	108	110	115	113	111
1955	106	109	104	113	105	107	107	105	106	109	108	107	115	109	109
1956	108	108	106	116	108	112	112	108	109	112	112	110	121	111	108
1957	112	105	110	121	112	119	123	115	116	118	116	116	129	117	112
1958	111	104	108	119	113	123	127	117	118	118	107	119	134	116	118
1959	106	100	102	117	109	120	123	114	115	115	104	117	128	112	121
1960	104	96	100	119	104	118	120	110	111	112	103	114	124	108	116
1961	104	96	101	123	102	117	118	107	107	111	100	115	123	107	114

Source: U.S. Interstate Commerce Commission, Bureau of Transport Economics and Statistics, Indexes of Average Freight Rates on Railroad Carload Traffic (Washington: U.S. Government Printing Office, 1963).

developing and unifying a region because of its ability to reach everywhere. Together with private automobiles, highways open up every hamlet and almost every farm to the outside world.

In terms of mileage, the South has made impressive gains in hard-surfaced rural roads since World War II. In the ten-state southeastern section of the country (Southern Territory plus Virginia and West Virginia), total rural road mileage has increased from 565,147 miles in 1945 to 595,573 miles in 1961. In 1961, however, about 76 per cent of these roads were surfaced compared to 52 per cent at the beginning of 1945. In both these years, the South was slightly ahead of the national average in this respect. Through December 31, 1962, there were 2,072 miles of Interstate highways completed in the ten-state area.[6] This Interstate system, of course, was nonexistent in 1945.

All of these roads, non-surfaced, surfaced, and divided four-lane highway, have their uses. The Interstate system is primarily meant for long-distance travel, and the spacing of the interchanges prevents much local travel. The bulk of traffic is on the other surfaced roads and non-surfaced roads, providing access to even the more remote rural areas. Growth in any of these categories is important, but for all-weather use, a surface is needed. The upgrading of non-surfaced roads shown is therefore of great importance to the development of the South.

Often the placement of surfaced roads is such that new roads are situated in areas already served and the remotest rural areas are forgotten. It is natural that the state road commissions should place new roads near the population centers. Roads are needed there and, furthermore, the taxpayers who live there want to see the product of their taxes. The result is that underdeveloped sections of the state, such as Appalachian regions, often receive small shares of state funds. Yet it is in these remote areas where new roads, even of a low grade, would do the most to further economic and social development.

A large share of the cost of road construction is borne by the federal government, up to 90 per cent in the case of Interstate highways. In fiscal 1963, the federal government paid 70.5 per cent of

6. U.S. Bureau of the Census, *Statistical Abstract, 1964* (Washington, D. C.: U.S. Government Printing Office, 1964), p. 559.

the total cost of those highways in the South that were eligible for aid.[7] There are considerable sums appropriated by the federal government for use in the South, but still unspent. Some of this money is for projects approved, but not under construction, and some is for projects not yet planned. Some southern states have been somewhat slow in developing plans to meet federal approval. It is also necessary for the states to obtain their portion of the cost. Even when funds are available on a 90/10 federal-state split, some states have been hard pressed to raise the necessary money.

Present disbursement of federal funds is based on a formula originated in the 1920's. This formula allocates funds on the basis of population, road mileage, and area of the individual state in relation to the totals for the United States as a whole. The formula is inflexible enough to prevent any special treatment of a single area in the name of economic development. The suggestion has been made, and should be encouraged, that funds be allotted for developmental highways on the basis of need, rather than use. These roads would be built in areas where there are few roads, few towns, and little population. They would open up the hitherto inaccessible areas to economic development and social integration with the rest of the South. Such roads would be particularly useful in such areas as the Appalachian regions. To use federal funds for such purposes, however, would require a departure from the time-honored formulae for disbursement of money to the states.

The building of local roads has traditionally been a function of state and local governments. The ten-state southern area increased total spending of state funds on highways from $268 million in 1945 to $1.8 billion in 1961.[8] The major source of this money was the tax on motor fuels. By 1962, a seven cent per gallon tax on gasoline had been imposed in all southern states, except for Georgia where the tax was six and a half cents. In some states this was an increase over 1945, but in most it meant only a one cent increase from prewar levels.[9] With expenditures rising so rapidly, this minimal increase in motor fuel taxes means that the general taxpayer is bearing more of the burden of providing highway facilities. When it is recognized that highways contribute to the welfare of everyone in a state, not

7. *Ibid.*
8. U.S. Bureau of the Census, *Statistical Abstract, 1947*, p. 492, and *1963*, p. 562.
9. *Ibid., 1963*, p. 564.

just those who actually drive on the highway, this division of the burden may not be unjust.

As important as roads to the maintenance of an effective highway system are the vehicles that operate over them. Between 1945 and 1961, total motor vehicles registered in the ten southeastern states increased from 4.4 million to 14.4 million, an increase of well over 200 per cent. This represents an increase from 168 vehicles per thousand people to 418 vehicles per thousand people. The rate still lags slightly behind the national average, which is just over 421 vehicles per thousand of population. Effective operators' licenses in the South also lag slightly behind the national average. In the South there were 448 licenses per thousand persons; in the United States there were 485, according to the 1960 Census.[10]

The fact that the South still trails the national average in number of vehicles and drivers' licenses is not the important fact in these figures. The important fact is that the number of automobiles and of licensed operators has increased so tremendously since World War II. The revolutionary impact of this increase in mobility on the social organization of the nation is too well known to be belabored here. Suffice it to say that the change has been dramatic, especially in the formerly more isolated areas. Local isolation has been all but obliterated by the family car.

In 1962, there were 2,364,000 trucks and buses registered in the ten southeastern states.[11] This figure includes both private vehicles and those operated by common carriers of passengers and freight. Private trucks are particularly important in the transportation of agricultural products such as the citrus crops from Florida. As no motor carriers of agricultural goods are subject to Interstate Commerce Commission regulation, data on their use are almost nonexistent. However, we do know that private trucks carry large volumes of traffic, especially higher valued goods where speed of delivery is important.

Highway common carriers are grouped geographically in a slightly different fashion from the railroad groupings. Southern Region is very close to the railroads' Southern Territory, for it includes the states of Virginia, Kentucky, Tennessee, North Carolina,

10. U.S. Bureau of Public Roads, *Highway Statistics, 1945,* p. 16 and *Highway Statistics, 1961,* p. 19.
11. U.S. Bureau of the Census, *Statistical Abstract, 1963,* p. 569.

Mississippi, Alabama, Georgia, South Carolina, and Florida. In
1961, the latest year for which official figures are available, 86 Class
I common carriers of general freight reported to the Interstate
Commerce Commission from the Southern Region. A Class I motor
carrier is one with gross operating revenue of $1 million or over.
These carriers operated 5,573 trucks, over 12,000 truck tractors, and
over 20,000 semi-trailers in intercity service and carried some 21
million tons of freight. In addition, the Interstate Commerce Commission reported 65 common carriers of other than general freight
in the Southern Region in 1961, operating 393 trucks, 3,322 tractors
and 5,689 semi-trailers. These carriers moved about an equal number of tons, but for many fewer miles.[12]

Turning to the smaller companies, one finds many carriers
operating a smaller number of vehicles, but still contributing an important transportation service. There were 222 Class II carriers of
property in the Southern Region in 1961 (those with gross operating
revenues of between $200,000 and $1 million annually). Carriers of
this class are often of very small size. In total, they operated 1,386
trucks, 3,752 tractors, and 5,830 semi-trailers in 1961. Some of them
are common carriers of general freight and some are contract carriers. The majority, however, are common carriers of special items,
concentrating their efforts in well-defined areas of traffic. These
small operators serve to illustrate the great flexibility and mobility
afforded by highway transportation. In addition, the private truckers' role must be re-emphasized. Anyone with a truck and a cargo of
his own goods can move it by highway to any destination he desires.

In passenger travel the family automobile, the counterpart to
the private truck, is dominant. Slowly, but surely, the railroads are
relinquishing their historic role as carriers of passengers. Part of the
slack is taken up by public buses. At the end of 1961, there were
twenty Class I passenger carriers in the Southern Region, although
a few large interstate companies dominated the industry. These carriers operated 2,295 vehicles and carried a total of 43,022,757 passengers on intercity routes in 1961.[13] However, the private automo-

12. U.S. Interstate Commerce Commission, Bureau of Transport Economics and
Statistics, *Transport Statistics, 1961*, Part 7 (Washington: U.S. Government
Printing Office, 1962).
    13. *Ibid.*

bile now accounts for about 90 per cent of intercity passenger miles in the United States.

In the highway field, the United States is growing more and more dependent on private vehicles, especially in the passenger field. While this development has brought tremendous mobility to most individuals, it has left a few stranded. Those too old, too poor, or too infirm to drive find that public transportation has almost disappeared. The traditional common carrier, holding itself out to serve all, is no longer able to operate profitably. The transition to a private motor car system as the basis for passenger movement actually contributes to the isolation of small segments of the population. As private trucks become more important for the movement of goods, the same fate may overcome certain small businesses, unable to provide private trucks for their own shipments. This does not detract, however, from the contribution of highway transportation in breaking down local isolation and knitting even the back country parts of the South into a whole.

The southeastern part of the United States is particularly fortunate in the possession of navigable waterways and deep water ports. The inland waterways afford cheap transportation, especially for heavy bulk goods. They also force the railroads to charge lower rates to meet the competition. This was dramatized in 1963 when the Southern Railroad proposed rate cuts averaging more than 60 per cent on large-volume shipments. The Interstate Commerce Commission modified this request, and, at the time of writing, the matter is still before the courts.[14] Even the Commission, however, was willing to allow considerable reductions, and the incident illustrates the benefits of a system of navigable rivers. Ocean ports, of which the South has many, allow the region to take an active part in foreign trade, a tradition of the South from its earliest days.

The most important inland waterways in the United States serve the South, beginning with the Mississippi River. In addition, the Tennessee, the Kanawha, the James, the Warrior, and other rivers, as well as the Gulf Intracoastal Waterway, serve the area. All of these have shared in the tremendous postwar surge of shipping on the inland waterways of the country. Total ton-miles generated on the Mississippi increased to about four times the 1945 total in 1961.

14. *Washington Post*, July 16, 1963, p. A24.

Preliminary figures for 1962 and the first half of 1963 show a continued increase, of 11 per cent from 1961 to 1962 and of another 9.5 per cent to the first half of 1963.[15] The other southern inland waterways have experienced similar increases in traffic, with the Warrior-Tombigbee System showing the greatest percentage gain.

These increases are largely the result of great strides in the technology of water transportation made since World War II, principally in tugboat power. No freight could have moved, of course, without large expenditures of money by the federal government on these waterways. The federal government spent about $100 million[16] during fiscal 1962 on navigable waterways and harbors in the South. This includes the South Atlantic Division, Lower Mississippi Valley Division, and the Norfolk District of the North Atlantic Division. In addition to the money spent on navigation projects, another large sum is spent on flood control projects each year. Without these expenditures, commerce on the inland rivers and through the ocean ports would be impossible.

Bulk commodities are the greatest part of water shipments. These goods are peculiarly adapted to the slow, but cheap, transportation afforded by barges. In 1962, bulk petroleum products made up 44.1 per cent of the tonnage on the Mississippi River. Grain and grain products accounted for 17.3 per cent; iron, steel and other metals, 9.1 per cent; coal and coke, 6.8 per cent; and sugar, molasses, chemicals, sea shells, sulphur, and other commodities made up the remainder.[17] This composition is typical of most waterway cargoes. Many of the products of the South, from mines and wells, are particularly well suited for water transportation. Although there are no reliable figures on the origination and destination of shipments by water, the geographic location of the waterways dictates that much of the traffic moves between the South and other states, principally to the north.

The ocean ports of the region have also experienced a great increase in traffic, in coastal as well as in foreign trade. Coastal

15. U.S. Army, Corps of Engineers, *Annual Report, 1945*, Part II (Washington: U.S. Government Printing Office, 1946), and U.S. Army Corps of Engineers, *Waterborne Commerce of the United States, Calendar Year 1961* (Washington: U.S. Government Printing Office, 1963), and American Waterways Operators, Inc., *Weekly Letter*, July 27, 1963 and August 24, 1963.

16. Calculated from figures in U.S. Army, Corps of Engineers, *Annual Report, 1962*, Part II (Washington: U.S. Government Printing Office, 1963).

17. American Waterways Operators, Inc., *Weekly Letter*, August 24, 1963.

traffic in general cargo has declined greatly in the United States since World War II. However, the bulk cargoes, especially petroleum, have increased. As an example, Wilmington, North Carolina, originated 11,000 tons of coastal shipments in 1945 and received 589,000 tons. In 1961, Wilmington shipped even less, but received over 3,000,000 tons, almost all petroleum products. Some alcohol, coal tar products, chemicals, and clay made up the remainder.[18] The pattern of increasing bulk shipments found on inland waterways persists for coastal traffic in all southern ports.

In 1961, over 46 per cent of American export tonnage left the country from ports located south of Baltimore and east of the Texas state line. If Texas is included, this percentage jumps to 64. Only about 14 per cent of American imports entered the country through southeastern ports, however; 19 per cent, if Texas is included.[19] The importance of these ports to the South and to the nation is obvious.

The composition of the foreign trade out of southern ports varies with the location of the port. Generally the products of the region dominate exports. In 1961, tobacco, wood pulp, iron and steel scrap, cotton, cotton goods, lumber, and paper were important exports. Further south, naval stores were important. To the north, grains and coal are very important in Norfolk's export trade. The grain, of course, is not a product of the region, but is shipped in from further west. On the Gulf Coast, petroleum exports are of great size.

Prominent in the imports through southern ports are the products of South America, such as bananas, coffee, and asphalt. Raw materials for southern products, such as raw tobacco and molasses, are also important. In addition, southern ports received rolled steel, petroleum, sulphur, pulpwood, vehicles, and a large amount of fertilizers from abroad.

The South's ports connect the area with the wider economy of the world. Insofar as they serve products from other parts of the United States, they also serve to integrate the economy of the South with that of the nation as a whole. They are one additional tie that binds the southeastern area into the total United States.

18. U.S. Army Corps of Engineers, *Annual Report*, Part II, 1945; and U.S. Army Corps of Engineers, *Waterborne Commerce, 1961*, Part I.
19. Calculated from data in U.S. Bureau of the Census, *Statistical Abstract, 1963*, p. 600.

Long-distance passenger travel in the United States is increasingly served by commercial airlines. In the South, several trunk lines, such as United Airlines and Eastern Airlines, connect the region with the rest of the country. Local carriers, such as Piedmont and Southern, serve the smaller cities within the area.

The crucial factor in providing commercial service is the availability of local airports. The city airport is now the source of civic pride that the local union railroad terminal once was. In 1962, the ten southern states could boast of a total of 897 airports of all sorts, compared to 732 airports on January 1, 1946.[20] The quality of fields has also been improved, as longer and stronger runways, more passenger handling facilities, and ground maintenance plants have been added. From the beginning of the Federal Aid Program in 1946 through 1961, the federal government contributed almost $100 million to the building of airports in the ten southeastern states. State and local authorities added approximately another $100 million to these projects.[21] In addition, local grass fields have been built and expanded.

One good measure of air traffic activity is the Federal Aviation Agency's report on contacts with planes by airport control towers and traffic control centers.[22] This report states that the Southern Region (North Carolina, Tennessee, Mississippi, Alabama, Georgia, South Carolina, and Florida) accounted for 16 per cent of the total United States departures in 1962. The Atlanta Air Route Traffic Control Center ranked fourth in the United States in activity of all sorts in 1962, following New York, Chicago, and Washington.[23] The Atlanta airport control tower ranked sixth in the United States in scheduled air carrier operations in 1962, and Miami ranked eighth.[24]

Passenger departures by air in the ten southeastern states were almost three times as many in fiscal year 1962 as they were ten years earlier. Almost ten million passengers enplaned in these states in fiscal 1962. Over one-third of these left airports in the state of Florida. Georgia also recorded heavy activity. Mississippi contrib-

20. *Ibid., 1946,* p. 529; *1963,* p. 591.
21. *Ibid., 1963,* p. 591.
22. U.S. Federal Aviation Agency, *FAA Air Traffic Activity, Calendar Year 1962* (Washington: U.S. Government Printing Office, 1963).
23. *Ibid.,* p. 13 and 17.
24. *Ibid.,* p. 41.

uted only just over 150,000 to the total.[25] Again one notes the great diversity in the development of the several southern states.

The Federal Aviation Agency's peak day traffic survey for fiscal 1962 shows seven southern cities (Memphis, Nashville, Greensboro, Raleigh, Atlanta, Miami, and Jacksonville) exchanging ten or more direct instrument flights with cities in the northeastern part of the United States.[26] Other southern cities were served by flights connecting through these key airports. The speed and convenience of these flights makes Atlanta and New York as close business partners as Atlanta and Macon were only a few years ago.

Although air cargo service is still only a small fraction of total freight movement, its growth has been rapid. By 1962, total air freight and express originated in the ten southeastern states had increased to almost four times the 1952 total, or about 83,500 tons.[27] The increase has been particularly rapid in the past few years. Almost half of the total originated in Florida, which is one of the leading air cargo shippers in the nation. The valuable, perishable produce of Florida is a particularly good candidate for air shipment, and this was recognized early in the development of air cargo. In this way, valuable shipments can reach any market in the nation within a few hours.

Private aircraft were, until recently, playthings of the rich or the foolhardy. Now general aviation includes an increasing number of business planes and embodies an important secondary transportation system. In 1962 almost 11,000 privately owned planes were active in the ten southeastern states.[28] According to the Federal Aviation Agency, the greatest amount of general aviation activity is found in the West, but Fort Lauderdale, Florida, otherwise a small airport, ranked twelfth in the country in 1962 for general aviation activity.[29]

25. Calculated from data in U.S. Department of Commerce, Civil Aeronautics Administration, *Air Commerce Traffic Pattern, Calendar Year 1952* (Washington: U.S. Government Printing Office, 1953) and U.S. Federal Aviation Agency and Civil Aeronautics Board, *Airport Activity Statistics* (Washington: U.S. Government Printing Office, 1963).

26. U.S. Federal Aviation Agency, *En route IFR Air Traffic Survey, Peak Day Fiscal Year 1962* (Washington: U.S. Government Printing Office, 1963), p. 113.

27. Calculated from data in U.S. Civil Aeronautics Administration, *Air Commerce Traffic Pattern, 1952* and U.S. Federal Aviation Agency and Civil Aeronautics Board, *Airport Activity Statistics, 1963*.

28. U.S. Bureau of the Census, *Statistical Abstract, 1963*, p. 591.

29. U.S. Federal Aviation Agency, *FAA Air Traffic Activity, 1962*, p. 44.

The implications of the great growth of air travel are mostly in
the realm of the integration of the South into the rest of the nation.
The airplane does not break down local isolation in the sense that
the automobile does. Private light planes may perform this function
in the West and in Alaska, but in the South they do not, as yet. The
great increase in air traffic is both a symptom and a cause of the
economic and social growth of the South since World War II.

In the unification of the region, personal communications play a
prime role. The telephone is the basic tool of personal communications today. The presence of a telephone instrument, or two or
three, in most American homes has accomplished a social revolution as important as that caused by the family automobile. The
telephone has brought neighbors closer, has brought help when
needed, and has relieved the isolation of the farmer and the housewife. The South still lags behind the nation in the number of phones
in relation to population, but its progress since World War II has
been dramatic.

There is a great range in number of telephones per one thousand
people within the South. In 1945, Mississippi had 33.53 residential
telephones per one thousand people, and South Carolina had 31.24.
At the other extreme, Tennessee, Virginia, and West Virginia had
over 75 per thousand. Even the highest of these averages, however,
was well below the national average of about 118 residential telephones for every thousand persons in 1945.[30]

By 1961, these averages had increased to a range of 150 to 227
residential phones per one thousand population. Mississippi was the
lowest of the southern states, with South Carolina next. The highest
average was in Tennessee, followed by West Virginia and Georgia.
The national average was still considerably higher than any of these
states, however. Statistics on local calls per person show some of
the southern states leading the national average. Alabama, Georgia,
Tennessee, and West Virginia all recorded more local calls per
person in 1961 than the United States average.[31]

Available data do not distinguish between intrastate and interstate toll calls. Total long distance calls increased between two and

30. Calculated from data in U.S. Bureau of the Census, *Statistical Abstract,
1947*, pp. 466-467.
31. Calculated from data in U.S. Bureau of the Census, *Statistical Abstract,
1963*, p. 517.

three times in the southern states between 1945 and 1961. Some of
these calls were relatively local in nature, between neighboring
towns. Others, however, were between points in the South and
points in the rest of the nation. While the former contributed to the
unification of the South, the latter contributed to the integration
of the region into the nation as a whole.

Mass communication may well be the most important instrument for the joining of the South to the nation. As of January 1,
1962, the eleven southeastern states, including West Virginia, had
119 television stations in operation. In 1945, of course, there were
no television stations. The same states had 201 FM radio stations,
also nonexistent in 1945. Even the number of AM radio stations
increased rapidly from 1945 to 1962.[32] The South still lags behind
the rest of the nation, however, in television sets owned. In 1962,
85 per cent of the families in the South owned television sets, as
against 90 per cent for the nation as a whole.[33]

The significance of these figures lies in the tendency of radio
and television broadcasts to standardize the culture of the nation.
Almost everyone watches one of three or four programs on a
Saturday night, whether they live in South Carolina or in California.
This is because of the network system of program generation that
dominates television at the present time. The stars of the popular
television shows do not speak with a southern accent, or a New
England accent, or a Midwestern accent, unless the role happens to
call for it. The stories are not set in the local region, nor do they
concern the mores of the local region. In this way the "popular
culture" of the country is becoming more uniform and the South
merges with the other sections of the country in a common pattern.
In the past, when entertainment and leisure activities were purely
local in nature, local customs and local accents developed. In the
future, it is not unlikely that regional differences will be eliminated
and one national personality will emerge.

What has our examination of the transportation and communication network of the South shown us? Within the region the tools
to break down local isolation are in existence. The growth in the
number of telephones, the increase in the media of mass communi-

32. *Ibid.*, 1963, p. 521.
33. *Ibid.*, p. 523. The figure refers to percentage of wired homes.

cations, the increase in mileage of paved roads, and the great growth in automobile ownership have served to break down local isolation and widen the local community beyond its former borders. The integration of the region into the country as a whole is shown by the increasing rail traffic with other regions, the Interstate highway system, the increasing use of the airplane for long-distance passenger travel, the long-distance telephone system, and the spread of mass broadcast communications originating outside the South.

The region has made great strides economically. The great increase in rail shipments, especially manufactured goods, and the increased exports from its ports show this. The gain has been uneven, however, and areas of underdevelopment remain. Mississippi and South Carolina seem to lag behind the other southern states in most aspects of economic development. The same is true of parts of the other states, especially mountainous areas. The presence of an excellent system of waterways, ports, and highways indicates future economic development is likely.

For many pages we have been discussing the South, a distinct region within the United States. The discussion of transportation and communications leads one to ask if the concept may not be dated. Certainly the economic separation of the South from the rest of the nation is becoming indistinct. Socially the erasure of sectional lines may be slower, but full use of the transportation and communications tools available will, in time, lead to the same results.

VIII. TECHNOLOGICAL CHANGE AND THE SOCIAL ORDER / E. William Noland

About three decades ago, the Southeast[1] was labeled by a certain well-known phrasemaker of that period as "the Nation's No. 1 Economic Problem." The Southeast of 1930, described so accurately and poignantly by the late Howard W. Odum, was different from the other regions of the country, for many the object of ridicule, for southeasterners a special project for uplift. "With five cent cotton and ten cent meat, how in the world can a poor man eat"[2] told the story of how so many people in this region faced economic problems which must have appeared to them to be insurmountable.

The major foci of this chapter are four: (1) an examination of the Southeast of the past three decades and of today; (2) a description of the principal features of the new technology, particularly automation; (3) observations on how well the two, the new Southeast and the new technology, will fit; and (4) a regional comparison of "susceptibility" to automation. The third of these will focus on answering two questions: (a) what will the Southeast do for the new technology, encourage or resist it; and (b) what will the new technology do for the Southeast, save it or be so differentially successful throughout the nation as to increase the present gap between this region and the remainder of the country? Here seeming paradoxes arise: the characteristics of the Southeast which currently impede technological change may eventually be helped by it; on the other hand, the factors which make for an easy entrance of automation may, in turn, make of the process something other than that from which real social and economic gains may stem, at least initially.

1. The regional breakdown used here is that of Howard W. Odum in *Southern Regions of the United States* (Chapel Hill, North Carolina: The University of North Carolina Press, 1936). It runs as follows: *Northeast*—Maine, New Hampshire, Vermont, Massachusetts, Rhode Island, Connecticut, New York, New Jersey, Pennsylvania, Delaware, Maryland, / West Virginia; *Southeast*—Virginia, South Carolina, North Carolina, Georgia, Florida, Kentucky, Tennessee, Alabama, Mississippi, Arkansas, Louisiana; *Southwest*—Oklahoma, Texas, New Mexico, Arizona; *Midwest* (Middle States)—Ohio, Indiana, Illinois, Michigan, Wisconsin, Minnesota, Iowa, Missouri; *Northwest*—North Dakota, South Dakota, Nebraska, Kansas, Montana, Idaho, Wyoming, Colorado, Utah; *Far West*—Nevada, Washington, Oregon, California.

2. George L. Simpson, Jr., "The South at Midcentury" (unpublished manuscript, University of North Carolina), Chapter 1, p. 5.

1

Obviously only the broadest outlines of what has happened to the Southeast during the past three decades and appears to be in the offing can be given here. The factors in the change which are usually considered to be more good than bad—helping the region catch up to the remainder of the nation—are many. Let us briefly examine some of them.

From 1930 to 1960, the number of farm people dropped 55.6 per cent, from 12,211,000 to 5,416,000. In 1930, the Southeast had 40 per cent of the nation's farms, of an average size of 71 acres; by 1959 the average farm was nearly twice as large—138 acres.[3] During the last three decades the industrial work force has doubled and now earns six times as much. In that time, per capita income grew 343 per cent, from $368 to $1,604. It was half that of the nation in 1930; 72 per cent of the nation's figure in 1960.

Three-fourths as much cotton is now grown in the Southeast as in 1930, but on one-fourth as much acreage.[4] Only three-tenths of the people were urban in 1930; by 1960 more than half were living in towns and cities.[5] During this period the Southeast increased its urban population by 155.8 per cent; the nation, by 81.7 per cent. No longer is the Southeast the "seed bed" for the nation: in 1940, the birth rate in the Southeast was 25.3, compared with 19.4 for the entire country; by 1960, this differential had been almost wiped out, for the two birth rates stood at 24.5 and 23.7, respectively.[6] In education, in the school year 1929-30 the amount spent per pupil in the Southeast was only 47.1 per cent of the national figure; by 1957, this per cent had grown to 69.9.

World War II had an obvious impact on the life of the Southeast. There was a large infusion of cash money, a substantial increase in non-farm jobs, and a spirit of change engendered by wartime activities. But the Southeast did not corral its share of wartime industrial expansion: manufacturing employment did not grow as rapidly (43.4 per cent) as in the nation as a whole (50.0 per cent); its industrial mix in 1945 was practically the same as in 1940; and the curtailment in the building of roads, schools, hos-

3. *Ibid.*, Chapter 1, p. 8.
4. *Ibid.*, Chapter 1, p. 6.
5. *Ibid.*, Chapter 1, p. 18.
6. *Ibid.*, Chapter 1, p. 21.

pitals, and public buildings, characteristic of wartime to be sure, was even more pronounced in the Southeast than elsewhere.[7]

It is the post-World War II period, appropriately defined as beginning in 1947, that must be viewed as that time segment of the last three decades of greatest significance in the *ambitions* of the Southeast to catch the rest of the nation. Textiles now employ substantially less of the total work force: the drop has been from 29.4 per cent of total employment in 1947 to 22.5 per cent in 1958.[8] Tobacco provides a substantially similar picture of employment decline. There is an easily recognized variety of income sources; in 1957, for example, only 6.2 per cent of the income of the Southeast was from farming.[9] The improvement in the ability of the region to attract capital investment is substantial. In education, between 1949 and 1958, expenditure per pupil in average daily attendance increased 77.3 per cent, to compare with the national figure of 67.3 per cent.[10]

Thus we see that the Southeast has pursued certain basic goals —higher income, diversified industry, meaningful education, healthful living, an attractive urban life. But progress is relative and the rest of the nation is not standing still. On the national level there are many new potentials, new achievements. So the Southeast is faced with the difficult task of catching up with a nation which itself is changing more rapidly than ever before. Let us examine next, therefore, the progress the Southeast has *not* made.

Measured by employment figures, the Southeast has made the more rapid gains in the "soft" industries—food, textiles, apparel, lumber, furniture, tobacco. Here it has outstripped the rest of the nation 35 per cent to 20 per cent. But "soft" industries pay low wages and low salaries—and in the Southeast they tie up three-fifths of the region's manufacturing employment compared with only one-fourth in the nation. The furniture worker in the Southeast gets less than two-thirds the national average for furniture workers (i.e., $3,195 *vs.* $4,873). Four of these industries are declining industries—tobacco, textiles, apparel and lumber—a fact which can profit the Southeast, to be sure, but only if efforts further to diversify

7. *Ibid.*, Chapter 3, p. 12.
8. *Ibid.*, Chapter 3, pp. 17-19.
9. *Ibid.*, Chapter 3, p. 22.
10. *Ibid.*, Chapter 3, p. 23.

manufacturing are successful. Fifty-five per cent of the nation's total employment increase went to the "hard" industries—metals, machinery, transportation, and instruments—but the corresponding figure for the Southeast was only 23 per cent. In fact, the region showed a net loss in the primary metals and instruments industries. In the machinery industry, since World War II the Southeast has added only 10,000 workers while the nation has added 155,000. Even in the "middle range" of industries—pulp, paper, paper products, chemicals and chemical products, printing and publishing, petroleum, coal and coal products, rubber products, leather and leather products, and stone, clay and glass products—the Southeast has not quite held its own in employment increase—13.5 per cent to 17.0 per cent for the nation.[11]

More evidence of the long, hard road the Southeast has yet to travel is obtained by comparing its progress with that of the other two hinterland areas of the country—the Southwest and Far West. One measure of the dynamic quality of a region is a comparison of its percentage of the nation's employment at a given date with the percentage of new employment it has been able to corral since that time. In 1929, the Southeast had 12.5 per cent of the nation's total manufacturing employment, and received in the next three decades 15.7 per cent of the new, an "improvement index" value of 1.26. Corresponding values for the Southwest and Far West, however, are 2.41 and 2.29, respectively. In salaries and wages, the Southeast in 1929 had 8.1 per cent of the nation's total and has received 11.3 per cent of the new, for an improvement index value of 1.40. Corresponding figures for the Southwest and Far West are 2.05 and 1.73, respectively. In Value Added by Manufacture, the index value for the Southeast is 1.45; for the Southwest and Far West, 2.35 and 1.82, respectively.[12]

Further help in understanding the position of the Southeast relative to other regions is found in a searching look at what George L. Simpson, Jr., has chosen to call the economic heartland of our country—the financially and industrially well developed areas of the Mideast and Midwest.[13] The major backbone of these two regions runs from Boston to New York, to Pittsburgh, then across the Mid-

11. *Ibid.*, Chapter 4, p. 6.
12. *Ibid.*, Chapter 7, p. 5.
13. *Ibid.*, Chapter 7, p. 4.

west to Chicago. Here one finds produced a wide variety of goods and services, a decisive market advantage, great technological advance, a strong and continually improving transportation system, ready financing, and technical services in good supply. It is this section of the country which in the twelve-year period from 1947 through 1958 outshone all other regions in Value Added by Manufacturing and in Expenditures for New Plants and Equipment. To these regions the Southeast still must play second fiddle; it is a hinterland which has grown and for a while likely will have to grow only by a "filling in" process. New products tend to be started in the heartland, are nourished along, and, when they find sufficiently wide acceptance to permit volume to grow, are "farmed out" to the hinterland. Actually, there is little manufacturing in the Southeast for end use in that region. All regions must compete in the national market, so advantage to the Southeast takes place only when national price, quality, and convenience are equalled or bettered.

A dramatic illustration of the difficulty under which a hinterland region operates, again provided us by Professor Simpson, is found in the case of the synthetic organic chemical industry, which has had substantial growth in the Southeast and Southwest. The work of this industry may be divided into two steps: the first is carried out by the manufacturer who combines raw material and fuel to make a basic chemical. For this raw materials are of prime importance, and on the Gulf Coast of Texas and Louisiana there has been, for instance, cheap natural gas as fuel, power, and raw material. But the price of natural gas has risen, so from this stage on likely we can expect the establishment of new plants on a major gas line farther north with access to water transportation. The second step involves converting the basic chemical into products useful to industry or the consuming public. Here the market is of the essence. Consequently, this type of plant will be located near population and manufacturing centers—the central East Coast, the Chicago area, San Francisco, Los Angeles. It is an uphill fight to develop "linkages" of production around the basic chemicals. It is true, of course, that the chemical manufacturers supplying the textile industry in the Southeast located near that industry—but the textile industry is a declining one!

The post-World War II per capita income picture for the Southeast is one depicting little if any gain relative to that of the remainder of the country. In 1947, it was 67 per cent of the national average but by 1960 had climbed to only 72 per cent of that figure (helped considerably, of course, by Florida's 89 per cent).[14] Some of the reasons seem clear: high component of farm income; concentration in low wage industries (e.g., textiles, apparel); continued high number of Negroes in personal services; a variety of wage differentials; and provision by the region of services only for itself. While it is true that the per capita income figure for the Southeast (as a per cent of that of the nation) grew 20 per cent in the last three decades, three-fourths of that gain came between 1930 and 1945, due in large measure to the injection of federal money into the economy—the greatest domestic Point Four Program in history. In fact, the Southeast's per capita income as a per cent of the national figure has grown only two points during the last decade.

Much of the answer to low income doubtless lies in better education, and in this the picture for the Southeast is not a rosy one. Walter Crosby Eells' twenty-point index of educational adequacy (ten items on education per se, ten on matters relating to education) reveals that in the period 1957-1959, all but two of the states of the Southeast ranked in the bottom quartile (Florida was twentieth; Virginia was thirty-fifth).[15] In the period 1952-1956, the Southeast had 22 per cent of its pupils in grades 1-5 drop out of school; the corresponding figure for the nation was 16 per cent. This figure for grades 5-9 compared to the nation was even more discouraging: 18 per cent against 6 per cent. And in grades 8-12, the Southeast lost 42 per cent to compare with the national figure of 32 per cent.

Despite desegregation and other efforts to enhance the lot of the Negro in the Southeast, his present status provides little room for satisfaction anywhere. The personal income of the non-white at the end of the 1950's was substantially less than half that of the white; in fact, the situation during that decade actually grew worse in that the personal income of the non-white was relatively less in 1960 than in 1950. The Negro's lack of success in securing high

14. *Ibid.*, Chapter 4, p. 15.
15. *Ibid.*, Chapter 10, p. 7.

paying jobs is seen, for example, in the dramatic and conceivably typical story told by the U. S. Employment Security Commission in North Carolina in 1959.[16] Of the 1,876 placed in professional or managerial positions, 25, or 1.3 per cent, were Negro. The corresponding figure for clerical and sales was 1.59 per cent; for skilled, 9.3 per cent; for semiskilled, 11.2 per cent. Of course, in service and in the unskilled category, the picture was the reverse: 78.4 per cent of service employees were Negro, as were 66.3 per cent of the unskilled-and-other category. However, the validity of any argument that the recent history of Negro employment is about to be repeated is threatened by the current sudden upsurge in Negro aggressiveness throughout the country. During the past year sit-in demonstrations have resulted in tremendous gains for the Negro in his struggle for desegregation of public facilities (e.g., restaurants).[17] It is conceivable, therefore, that such a cataclysmic change is upon us in this area that the above description of the plight of the Negro during the 1950's will be astonishing news to readers of this account only a few years hence. This is not to argue, however, that this spectacular progress of the Negro currently underway will go uncontested, or that all resistance to desegregation will vanish overnight. For a while it will be hard to prevent race riots; and especially in areas with a high percentage of Negroes, it is likely for several years that subtle ways to circumvent the law will be invented. The rapidity and peacefulness with which this sudden transition will take place will depend in very large measure on the wisdom of Negro leaders, the willingness of whites to work with them at the grass roots level, and the posture of government, especially federal, with respect to the problem.

2

Let us turn now to the new technology, the most significant aspect of which is automation. Automation, according to Floyd C. Mann and L. Richard Hoffman, is the application of control devices of a feedback nature to provide self-regulating production processes.[18]

16. *Ibid.*, Chapter 11, p. 33.
17. As this is being written (August, 1963) we are about to experience a mass march on Washington, D. C., in support of President Kennedy's civil rights legislation, a principal feature of which is provision for non-discrimination in employment.
18. For one of the better research reports on automation, see Floyd C. Mann and L. Richard Hoffman, *Automation and the Worker* (New York: Henry Holt and

W. S. Buckingham, Jr., points out that automation involves four major principles—mechanization, feedback, continuous process, and rationalization.[19] Peter Drucker sees automation as "the use of machines to run machines,,"[20] while William E. Drake claims that "in its most fundamental sense automation calls for not only the machines and power which characterized the first Industrial Revolution, but the programming and control which characterize the new."[21] John Diebold, inventor of the term, calls automation a new concept, a new set of principles, new self-regulating systems for solving new operational problems and for arriving at decisions that could not be reached without such an innovation.[22] Edwin G. Nourse claims that "under this principle [automation], electric mechanisms make it possible to conduct more elaborate, more economical and more precise continuous productive operations be-cause the outcome of the process controls the process itself, starting, altering, or stopping it so as to make it produce a desired result."[23]

Despite this high degree of consistency in definition of automation, perhaps no phenomenon in the history of modern civilization provides one with less basis for uncontrovertible conclusions regarding its effects. Neither its worth nor the price we shall have to pay for it has been accurately assessed; similarly focused research has produced seemingly contradictory results. Much of what has been written about it is highly speculative. Consequently, it is difficult at this stage of development to separate the good, the bad, and the controversial in automation. Such categorization obviously is the product of the interplay of value judgments, lack of clean-cut definitions and objective measurement, a dearth of imaginative and valid research, and the inevitable truism that what is one man's meat is often another man's poison. Nevertheless, there are aspects of automation commonly agreed to be more good than bad, others adjudged more bad than good, and still others, probably com-

Company, Inc., 1960). Here one finds a realistic discussion of what automation is, the areas of its impact, and a detailed account of social change in two power plants.

19. W. S. Buckingham, Jr., "Automation, Employment and Economic Stability," in *Automation and Society*, ed. H. B. Jacobson and J. S. Roucek (New York: Philosophical Library, 1959), Chapter 19, pp. 231-233.

20. P. F. Drucker, "Promise of Automation," *Harper's* (April, 1955), p. 41.

21. William E. Drake, "Automation and Education," in *Automation and Society*, Chapter 23, p. 263.

22. John Diebold, "Automation as a Management Problem," *ibid.*, Chapter 26, p. 313.

23. Edwin G. Nourse, "What's New About Automation," *ibid.*, Chapter 16, p. 197.

posing the largest of the three categories, about which no firm conclusions regarding merit can be reached. Consequently, let us look at workers, management, unions, the family, the community, and the economy at large in this framework.

The worker. Among the advantages automation is supposed to provide the worker are job enlargement and job rotation, greater safety, better health, and less physical fatigue.[24] On the negative side fall displacement of workers, tension from having to tend expensive machines, feelings of less job security born of fewer positions and less job "visibility," and greater isolation at the work place.[25] Controversial items include a recognition that job upgrading often calls for greater intelligence, the shorter work week may provide leisure which will not be well spent,[26] new machines likely will create sticky problems in job evaluation,[27] and there may arise the tendency to retire older workers even earlier.

Management. From the standpoint of management, those who

24. For two of the best discussions of the contributions of automation to the worker, see International Labor Office, *Report of the Director General*, Part I: "Automation and Other Technological Developments" (Geneva: International Labor Office, 1957), especially p. 79. M. Crozier and G. Friedmann, "The Social Consequences of Automation: Foreword," *International Social Science Bulletin*, 10 (1958), 7-16. It should be noted here that William Faunce in a study of the automobile industry, "Automation in the Automobile Industry: Some Consequences for In-Plant Social Structure," *American Sociological Review*, 23 (1958), 401-407, refutes many of the contentions found in the first two references.

25. G. P. Shultz and A. Weber, "Technological Change and Industrial Relations," in H. G. Heneman *et al.* (eds.), *Employment Relations Research*, Association Publication No. 23 (New York: Harper & Brothers, 1960), pp. 190-221. This article presents both the positive and negative impacts of automation on work and working conditions; it is a rather complete bibliography of studies dealing primarily with the effects of automation on industrial organization and union-management relations. Also, for more skepticism about the effects of automation, see H. Winthrop, "Some Psychological and Economic Assumptions Underlying Automation," *American Journal of Economics and Sociology*, 17 (1957-58), 399-412, and William A. Faunce, "Automation and Leisure," in *Automation and Society*, p. 297.

26. See William A. Faunce, "Automation and Leisure," pp. 297-309; H. Winthrop, "Some Psychological and Economic Assumptions Underlying Automation, II," *American Journal of Economics and Sociology*, 18 (1958-59), 69-82; E. William Noland, "Technology's Impact on Culture and Work," chapter 4 in *The Changing American Population* (New York: Graduate School of Business, Columbia University, and the Institute of Life Insurance, 1962), p. 74. See also John Diebold, "Automation: Its Impact on Business and Labor" (Washington: National Planning Association, 1959), p. 39, for comments on Erich Fromm's skepticism regarding the role of more leisure in increasing one's sense of insecurity, and on David Riesman's notion that many Americans look upon additional leisure as "a threat, a problem, a burden, or a hazard."

27. See H. H. Punke, "Social and Educational Problems of Automation and Longevity," *Journal of Educational Sociology*, 30 (1957), 402; James Stern, "Implications of Automation," paper read at the American Association for the Advancement of Science, Atlanta, Georgia, December, 1955.

espouse the cause of flatter organizational structures are finding in automation a boon to their orientation. From flatter organizations come fewer supervisory levels, a wider span of control, and better vertical communication because messages do not have as far to travel. As a result, supervision will be less close and a kind of self-supervision will ensue, a change supposedly welcomed by both supervisor and supervisee. Emphasis will be on the manager's having perceptual rather than manual skill;[28] there will be a premium on constructive imagination; decisions will be more rational due to the availability of more data bearing on them; and businessmen will have more time to participate in community affairs. But, in a negative sense, automation may upset company security programs; straight time wages will return to plague those who like the piece rate system;[29] the retraining of all workers will be costly and of older workers especially difficult; and performance, both individual and organizational, will be difficult to measure.[30] Controversial features relative to the impact of automation on management include the outmoding of present job grading systems, the growth in importance of seniority in allocating employment, and changes in the nature of supervision. With respect to the last, the crucial question seems to be: Will the supervisor become more a technical specialist or a "human relations" expert?[31]

The labor union. A content analysis of newspaper discussions of labor unionism *vs.* automation would probably indicate that labor unions oppose automation more than they favor it. Likely the labor union argument used most frequently and publicized most widely is the threat of unemployment. However, many labor leaders and writers on the subject of the union's justified posture relative to automation are not completely negative toward this aspect of the

28. For an insightful and imaginative set of propositions on relationships between technology and administrative processes, see J. D. Thompson and F. L. Bates, "Technology, Organization, and Administration," *Administrative Science Quarterly,* 2 (1957), 325-343. See also J. R. Gass, "Research into the Social Effects of Automation," *International Social Science Journal,* 10 (1958), 76; and Crozier and Friedmann, *op. cit.,* p. 12.

29. A. Braunthal, "The Trade Union Movement Faces Automation," *International Labour Review,* 76 (1958), 550.

30. Noland, *op. cit.,* p. 71. Also, for a list of twenty-four company characteristics associated with technical progressiveness, see C. F. Carter and B. R. Williams, "The Characteristics of Technically Progressive Firms," *Journal of Industrial Economics,* 7 (1959), 87-103.

31. M. Crozier and G. Friedmann, *op. cit.,* p. 11; Noland, *op. cit.,* pp. 72-73.

new technology. Almost as if labeling automation inevitable, Walter Reuther confesses: "We have said many times that we welcome automation and that we are going to encourage the expeditious development of this technology. . . ."[32] Yet in another place Reuther implores management to accept the responsibility of seeing that "economic and material factors are brought into balance with moral, social, and human values."[33]

On the assets side, unions likely will welcome the greater sophistication in collective bargaining techniques and procedures automation will bring, the greater possible bureaucratization and the greater chance for them to become, with the scattering of workers spatially, a more needed unifying and socializing force.[34] On the liabilities side, the union may become less "visible" to the rank-and-file member if, as is supposed to be true under automation, collective bargaining takes place at the higher reaches of both management and union; if automation makes workers more nearly professional in outlook and if professionals identify less with labor unions than non-professionals, unions may suffer;[35] the new types of workers automation creates may make for jurisdictional and membership disputes among unions. A controversial phenomenon is the trimming down of number of employees. Will this mean fewer union members and if it does, will fewer members necessarily mean a weaker union? Furthermore, if automation requires workers to be better educated and if, as some research to date indicates, the better educated unionists are the most active, might not unions become even stronger?

The family. Greater business and residential decentralization, made much easier by recent improvements in electric power transmission technology and the appearance of light-weight fabricating materials, has both good and bad features for the family.[36] There

32. Walter P. Reuther, "Labor's Stake," in *The Challenge of Automation*, paper delivered at the National Conference on Automation (Washington, D. C.: Public Affairs Press, 1955), p. 45.

33. *Ibid.*, p. 49. See also Braunthal, *op. cit.*, p. 542.

34. For a discussion of what the labor union may mean anew for workers, see *International Labor Office Report of the Director General*, p. 93.

35. See Kermit Eby, "Labor and Automation," *Current History*, 36 (1959), 334, for the plea that labor unions need to concentrate on organizing technicians, clerks, and other white-collar workers.

36. U. S. Congress, Joint Economic Committee, *New Views on Automation*. Papers submitted to the Subcommittee on Automation and Energy Resources. (Washington: U. S. Government Printing Office), 1960. Statement by Walter P. Buckingham, p. 71.

promises to be less crowding, and the journey to work will require a
shorter time and, therefore, likely be easier. Perhaps for the first time
the choice between urban and suburban living will be a real one. On
the other hand, such decentralization is fraught with the strains
which inevitably accompany displacement of companies and the
people who work in them. Automation is likely to speed up the
present trend toward a shorter and shorter work week. The father
(and the mother, too, if she works) can be at home more of the
time. What this may mean for family stability and changes in child-
rearing practices remains to be seen.[37]

The community. The advantages accruing to a community under
automation are substantially the sum total of advantages accruing
to its residents. However, the challenges and, therefore, the problems are many. One-industry communities will be hit hard, at least
temporarily, when its only industry automates.[38] Decentralization
creates tax problems for municipal governments and income problems for renters of commercial property; it adds in many ways to
the cost of providing goods and services and places a huge premium
on management efficiency and planning.[39] Automation is sure to
mean a substantial revamping of the community's educational system:[40] at the lower levels book learning will take on new importance; dropouts cannot be tolerated; a college education will become essential for a wider variety of job types; adult education
programs will take on new meaning; and our indirect producers
(e.g., teachers, lawyers, priests) may have to discard some of the
features of their traditional laissez faire orientation in favor of
appropriate engineering principles.[41]

The economy. At the level of the overall economy, protagonists
of automation claim for it cuts in direct labor costs, increases in

37. See Faunce, *op. cit.*, for a discussion of the likely impact of the father's having
more time to spend at home.

38. For a dramatic story of what can happen under such a circumstance, see
W. F. Cottrell, "Death by Dieselization," *American Sociological Review*, 16 (1951),
358-365.

39. For a good treatment of the problems caused when industries are moved from
one community to another, see S. H. Ruttenberg, "Economic and Social Implications
of the New Technology," *Monthly Labor Review*, 83 (1959), 164.

40. For good descriptions of the specifics of such needed change, see M. P.
Moffatt and A. G. Rich, "Implications of Automation for Education," *Journal of
Educational Sociology*, 30 (1957), 268-274; H. H. Punke, *op. cit.*, pp. 398-404;
William E. Drake, *op. cit.*, pp. 263-265.

41. Drake, *op. cit.*, p. 266.

output, rises in productivity, improvements in quality of products, and the creation of new types of industry.[42] Firms whose production process is of the continuous-flow type (e.g., petroleum, communications) or whose process entails reactions too fast for mere human surveillance (e.g., chemicals) are particularly amenable to automation.[43] Some types of companies, however, cannot afford automation and should not attempt it—those where the traditional form of mechanization and mass production prevail[44] (e.g., mining; agriculture), those which manufacture in lots of twenty-five or less, and those that must redesign their products frequently.[45]

The most controversial economy-wide items are two—wages and employment. It seems likely that automation will put substantial stress on the wage structure, for automated firms will be able to pay more and, as a result, the bargaining situation will be upset.[46] This is held by some to be the most objectionable aspect of automation. Since wage rates depend on marginal productivity, if the automated industries drain large amounts of capital from non-automated ones, workers will be released and the capital-labor ratio in the non-automated industries will fall. The net result will be a decline in marginal productivity, and, concomitantly, wage rates as well (even though average productivity for the economy and national income may actually rise).[47]

The net impact of automation on employment is held by some to be good; by others, bad. One report, on employment changes between 1953 and 1960, paints a picture of fewer workers in certain basic industries (e.g., food and beverage; textile; oil refining and coal products) but increases in production all along the line.[48] In the period from 1947 to 1959, employment in the coal industry dropped by one-half yet production doubled, and railroads during

42. Melvin J. Vincent and Jackson Mayers, *New Foundations for Industrial Sociology* (Princeton, New Jersey: D. Van Nostrand & Company, Inc., 1959), pp. 341-351.

43. Diebold, "Automation: Its Impact on Business and Labor," pp. 29-30.

44. J. R. Gass, *op. cit.*, p. 79.

45. Diebold, "Automation as a Management Problem," p. 322; also W. S. Buckingham in *New Views on Automation*, p. 72.

46. Gass, *op. cit.*, p. 72.

47. Yale Brozen, "Automation's Impact on Capital and Labor Markets," *Automation and Society*, chapter 24, pp. 286-287.

48. *New Views on Automation*, statement by George Meany, p. 539. Also Victor R. Fuchs, "Fallacies and Facts About Automation," *New York Times Magazine Section*, April 7, 1963, p. 27.

that period increased production 65 per cent while employing 10 per cent fewer people.[49] Another compilation of production and employment figures develops the theme that while production personnel suffer, professional and white-collar employees and employment overall gain through automation. In a specified period and employment area, production personnel decreased in number by 2 per cent while professional and white-collar workers increased by 58 per cent. Overall employment rose 10 per cent and total production was up 34 per cent.[50]

For those who fear that automation is about to take place devastatingly fast, Yale Brozen offers solace. The cost per person is too high (and, relatedly, the availability of money too low) for this to happen. Automation cost Commonwealth Edison (Chicago) $5,000 per displaced person, Fairless Steel works (near Philadelphia) $100,000 per man-year saved, and Cross Transfer Machine $90,000 per man reduction in work force. In fact, if all the money set aside for new equipment in American industry in 1956 had been used to reduce the number of people employed, no more than 700,000 workers would have been displaced. Furthermore, most displaced workers, continues Brozen, are reassigned within the same company.[51] Also, the net supply of savings in excess of what is required to equip added workers runs from $10 to $15 billion a year. If this amount were used to automate manufacturing industries, which employ one-fourth of the total number of workers, it would take at least thirty and perhaps as much as fifty years to automate these manufacturing operations completely.[52]

3

Let us examine current southeastern impediments to automation. Unskilled and semiskilled workers, of which the Southeast has more than its share, will be turned out of jobs in relatively large numbers, at least in the early stages. The dearth of technical training schools will render the initial employment and retraining tasks brought on

49. Robert J. Myers, "Social Ramifications of Automation," address presented at Commencement Week Seminar, University of Pittsburgh, June 9, 1961, pp. 5-6.

50. From U. S. Department of Commerce Data, quoted by Roger W. Bloz, "Trend in Manufacturing Industries due to Automation Technology," in *New Views of Automation*, p. 19.

51. Brozen, *op. cit.*, p. 285.

52. *Ibid.*, pp. 287-288.

by automation particularly troublesome. The Southeast has a greater relative shortage of scientists, technicians, and skilled laborers than other regions—and the out-migration of such people continues. To the extent that automation strengthens labor unions and labor unions are strengthened by having their members well educated, the typical southeastern laborer offers little encouragement. The high level of homogeneity of the southeastern work force, especially as measured by nativity and parentage, about which many southeastern managers brag, may be more of an impediment to automation than a boon. Automation will require managers to know not only the natural sciences and engineering but the social sciences as well—and many would find it hard to argue that the average sophistication of the southeastern industrialist is higher than that of his counterpart in other regions!

If one adopts the position that the supervisor's job will be made harder technically (and perhaps easier in the "human relations" sense) by automation, then the low level of technical training from which the Southeast has long suffered will stand in the way. Low wages are a deterrent to automation, since a principal reason for automating is the elimination of high labor costs. The initial financial burden of process and plant conversion is often so high as to make it prohibitive in many southeastern companies. Furthermore, among the industries in which automation appears to be taking place most rapidly are many in which the South to date has not held its own—automobiles, steel, communications, chemicals, electrical, and such service types as banking and insurance.

In some respects the Southeast is a friend to automation. Automation requires fewer personnel for a given amount of production and provides for the creation of new, more highly skilled jobs for which new types of workers must be trained. Continued out-migration and a tempered rate of natural increase might eventually produce a work population where quality will be a more appropriately descriptive term than quantity. The creation of the need, relatively, for fewer but more highly skilled workers, the essence and magic of automation, is a goal toward which the Southeast should strive. In short, to the extent that the Southeast can and will furnish a sophisticated, well-trained work force, automation will be able to find its proper niche.

With this brief discourse on how the Southeast impedes automation in some ways and aids it in others, let us turn now to a consideration of what automation likely will do for the Southeast. The effect of some of the factors in the situation seems clear; the probable impact of others, however, is debatable relative to the balance between help and hindrance. Homogeneity of the work force and, therefore, of the population at large will be reduced by automation—and thereby will disappear some of the debilitating effects of a long and potent inferiority complex ethnocentrically expressed. The higher educational level necessarily preliminary to a substantial amount of automation will benefit the Southeast in ways which only intellectual change can bring. Labor unions, possibly smaller in actual membership, will be more mature and more nearly understood, thanks to a better educated and less defensive leadership and to a wise population overall. New companies will spring up, with the optimism and challenge that reside in freshly created endeavors: new places in which to start new workers and new managers in new ways of making new things. Although the trend toward further urbanization will continue in the Southeast, under the impact of automation it may take place at a slower rate, for this technological giant will permit, and even encourage, industrial, and hence residential, decentralization. Consequently, it seems likely that a larger proportion of the population will in a very real sense be given the choice between urban and suburban living. Some industries, currently finding it difficult to compete with foreign products or substitute domestic ones (e.g., textiles), may be saved by automation. Others, with a labor force declining due to mechanization (e.g., tobacco), may, through automation, be able to speed the inevitable loss of jobs for many and thereby free them for retraining for other jobs while they are still young enough to learn and adjust. Automation will do much to provide the high skill and challenging jobs many young people have left the Southeast to find elsewhere. Automated industries can pay higher wages, surely a major consideration as the Southeast continues its struggle to catch up. Within the plant, to the extent that supervisory jobs will be made easier by automation through well-developed standard operating procedures, the supervisors will welcome it.

But the impact of automation on the Southeast has its negative aspects. One-industry communities will be particularly hard hit by layoffs occasioned by the sudden automation of the plant providing its sole major payroll. Automation will not be the answer to needed agricultural reform, for here the traditional type of mechanization cannot be displaced, at least for a long time. The improvements in working conditions automation is supposed to provide may be less meaningful in the southeastern context: in general southeastern workers are newer to industrial jobs than workers elsewhere (with the possible exception of the Southwest and parts of the Northwest), a fact which makes them see industrial employment as relatively easy compared to the farm labor of their early years and/or of their fathers. Consequently, some of the assumed advantages of automation—less close supervision, job enlargement, job rotation, job upgrading, more leisure—may have little effective appeal. In fact, beginning workers sometimes welcome relatively close supervision, and the low I. Q. of some southeastern workers might make job upgrading painful. In short, perhaps many southeastern workers, partly because industrial work is relatively new to them, are not as resistant to the so-called bad of industrial employment ("They never had it so good!"), and are not as insistent on having the so-called good.

On balance, automation and the Southeast of today in so many ways appear to present an insoluble paradox. Automation requires a skilled labor force, widespread scientific training, a generally high level of education, and heavy capital investment—all commodities in short supply in this region. Some argue that the Southeast actually is losing ground in the race to catch up with the rest of the nation.[53] The position taken here is that in those characteristics favoring automation the Southeast is doing relatively well but that in consideration of its comparatively poor position no farther back than, say, 1950, it still has a long way to go. The fear that automation is sure to take place devastatingly fast must be dispelled—and dispelling it is feasible, for automation requires long periods for planning, designing, and building specialized machines.[54] Close management-union consultation is essential—for the

53. Simpson, *op. cit.* This is one of the trenchant themes of the manuscript.
54. Diebold, "Automation: Its Impact on Business and Labor," pp. 19-21. Also, for a discussion of the costs of automation in addition to the initial one, see Noland, *op. cit.*, p. 74.

introduction of new machinery, the shifting of workers, retraining, discharge, for changes in job evaluation and wage scales.[55] A strike may be more nearly disastrous in an automated plant than in a non-automated one.

Communities must immediately face their responsibility—for security of displaced workers and for the revision of educational programs.[56] Substantial progress has been made in the Southeast in the direction of better municipal government, zoning and long-range planning, schools, housing, and recreational facilities. Even climate and scenery as industry enticers have corralled their share of attention. The Southeast has recently furnished us almost a plethora of industry hunters, but the payoff for their efforts is likely to be only a limited one at best. Such an approach is only the first step—and can be quite a superficial one at that. When a sociologist reads in the newspaper of an industry-hunting mission to New York, or Chicago, or even Europe, and then looks around him, I suspect he finds it easy to recall Henry Grady's famous description of the Georgia funeral: the wagon that hauled the coffin was made in Chicago, the coffin itself in Louisville; nails in the coffin had been manufactured in Pittsburgh, and the funeral garment had come from Massachusetts. The Southeast furnished only the hole in the ground. This is not true today, of course. However, the Southeast in some respects continues to furnish just the hole in the ground. This time the hole is for buildings, to be sure—but these buildings are so often built by others, financed by others, and operated and managed by people trained outside the Southeast.

Governments will have to recognize and shoulder the responsibilities peculiar to them—provision of monies for the automation of appropriate small- and medium-size plants (through tax advantages to the private investor and generous depreciation return), for in-plant apprenticeships, on-the-job training, special educational programs, encouragement of individual self-education, relocation of displaced persons, and to stimulate the development of new industries in distressed areas. Even a National Automation Planning Board to serve as a central clearinghouse of knowledge of automation has been suggested.[57]

55. *International Labor Office Report of the Director General*, p. 94.
56. Braunthal, *op. cit.*, pp. 545-548.
57. For a comprehensive treatment of obstacles to innovation, see Meyer

And perhaps more important than any of these is the proper role of the Southeast in national politics. The major part the federal government can play in helping the Southeast take advantage of the new technology must be recognized. The Southeast must so deport itself in the political arena as no longer to be taken for granted: instead of the "solid South" of the past it needs to be—and there are signs that it is on its way to becoming—a "doubtful Southeast." This is simply an important facet of the cultural heterogeneity the Southeast needs.

4

Let us turn now to a consideration of differential acceptance and adoption of automation among the various regions of the United States. Are not the factors making for and impeding automation the same everywhere, except in different amounts or degrees? The answer is in the affirmative, to be sure, yet it seems reasonable to argue that the rate at which automation is taking place and will take place differs, perhaps substantially, as one goes from one part of the country to another. In fact, the six major regions of the United States as defined here may already differ significantly in the extent to which they have subscribed to and implemented the new technology. Conceivably many causative factors enter the picture and, although one is hampered by the dearth of research on the point, there may be some merit, in the type of speculative approach a paper of this sort at the present time has to be, in examining some of the probabilities.

The percentage of workers in a work force who are unskilled is a factor negatively related to the ability of a region to automate. Automation calls for more than the skills learned in vocational programs, to be sure, so doubtless there are those who claim that the higher the percentage of young people enrolled in such programs the fewer the students in other curricula (e.g., college preparation) leading to the type of training automation is sure to require as skill and analytic requirements rise. This may be true, but a sounder argument seems to be that the greater the incidence of vocational programs the greater the awareness of significant tech-

---

Nimkoff's list in F. R. Allen, *Technology and Social Change* (New York: Appleton-Century-Crofts, Inc., 1957), p. 71. Also, for a discussion of what can be done to cushion the impact of automation, see Noland, *op. cit.*, p. 77.

nological change and that, while such programs are in themselves inadequate to meet the needs for highly skilled personnel, they are a necessary preliminary step and/or a measure of technological awakening. Where professional, technical, and kindred workers are found in good supply one also finds a climate conducing to a more rapid adoption of automated processes.

Related to the job qualifications makeup of a work force is the phenomenon of internal migration. The question of what kinds of people migrate, especially in relation to their usefulness under automation, is an unanswered one. There are many seeming paradoxes. Keeping in mind our focus on factors promoting automation, let us raise some questions about migration which seem to be meaningful. Is a region which loses unskilled and uneducated Negro workers to another region through failure to provide jobs for them better or worse off by virtue of their leaving? What is the net effect on the region into which they migrate? Do the same questions asked about migrating white workers have the same answers? If automation requires fewer but better workers and a region loses its poorest, is it not helped by such out-migration? And is not the recipient region handicapped commensurately? Furthermore, is a region experiencing a huge out-migration of poorly qualified workers likely to find itself more able to keep its best people and more likely to entice well qualified outsiders into the fold? Or, conversely, do the best migrate (with the conceivable exception, on balance, of management people)? That is, does a region which attracts people in large numbers have a dynamic quality, an acceptance of the new, which makes for the rapid spread of automation? All in all, the crucial question seems to be: has in-migration raised or lowered the overall worker qualification average of a community or region?

If one sees in heterogeneity of population—measured by such variables as locality of birth, nativity and parentage, color, job diversification, political behavior—a force making for change in the *status quo*, those regions of highest heterogeneity will automate the fastest. Rate of adoption of automation and heterogeneity of population both appear to be significantly positively associated with industrialization, and with one another.

Since non-whites are on the average not as well educated as whites and since educational level of work force is related to ease of adoption of automation, it would appear that the percentage of population that is non-white is a significant variable.

Since automation will not capture us overnight, will require better and differently educated workers, and will depend upon the willingness of the working population to accept the new, the relative youthfulness of the population of a region appears to be of considerable importance for the adoption of the new technology. The percentage of people in a region currently under, say, twenty years of age may be highly positively associated while the percentage of people over fifty-five may he highly negatively correlated with the propensity and ability of that region to automate.

The beginning costs of automation are particularly high: the prospect of many companies' failing because they cannot afford the initial outlay is real. Perhaps the best measure of a company's ability to corral the money necessary to automate is its past history of expenditures for new plant and equipment. Many, perhaps most, small industries cannot afford automation and should not attempt it, so a disproportionately large number of small companies in a region would tend to impede automation. Industrial diversification is likely to favor automation, since the relative costs a community must pay for it are distributed more nearly equitably: initial unemployment can be devastating in a one-industry community when it automates; some types of automation need other types nearby to support or feed on them; and the retention of some industries nonautomated makes for a desirable job mix and a softening of the shock a high degree of automation may bring in terms of needs for retraining people, modifications of value systems, and overall economic, social, and political adjustment. If one assumes that industrialization inertia is real, that regions that have industrialized most rapidly recently will continue to set the pace, that the new technology negates industrial saturation, then rate of industrialization among regions, as measured, say, by percentage of total employment found in manufacturing, should be positively associated with the rate of adoption of automation among them.

Perhaps the most meaningful variable in any discussion of the propensity of a region to automate is its present industrial makeup. Those regions whose indigenous raw materials, proximity to markets, favorable labor situation and the like, have made them the most appropriate areas for the adoption of continuous-flow production industries, the "natural habitat" of automation, have a head start on other regions in subscribing to this new technology. Regions already heavily involved in such types of business (e.g., automobiles, chemicals, steel, communications, petroleum, electrical, banking, insurance) are likely to outdistance other regions, at least for a while.

Farming, an endeavor which has lent itself effectively to a high degree of mechanization, is not given to automation in the strictest meaning of the term. Therefore, those regions which remain most dependent on agriculture as a source of income appear to be, in turn, those very regions in which automation will take place least rapidly. This assumes, of course, that, as argued earlier, industrialization begets more industrialization, that the new industrialization will be as closely associated with urbanization as the old, and that rurality impedes automation. Even if these assumptions are in some measure fallacious (e.g., rurality may favor decentralization, a bedfellow of automation), it seems reasonable to assume that for a while those regions whose farm income is still a relatively large segment of total income will be the regions where automation is least likely to get an early effective foothold.

One finds it easy to argue that the rate at which automation will take place will depend more on the quality of the job done in revising our educational systems than on any other single factor. Automation will require new and different educational emphases and a concomitant willingness on the part of communities to pay the price for such change. Therefore, support for education, measured, say, by expenditure per pupil and for teachers' salaries, might be a valid indicator of the commitment of a region to doing those things educationally that automation will require.

Now let us rank our six regions on the variables we have just discussed, and arrive at an overall score from which to predict their present relative "susceptibility" to automation. To do this we shall, of course, make certain basic assumptions.[58] We shall assume

58. The dearth of knowledge about automation, its impact and implications, has required us—perhaps permitted is a better word—to make certain assumptions which some doubtless will want to challenge. The significant point to make here, however, is that if our assumptions are valid, our six regions will adopt automation differentially according to the scores derived from *Tables 1* and *2*.

that progress in automation is positively associated with (1) percentage of elementary and secondary school enrollments in vocational programs; (2) percentage of professional, technical, and kindred workers; (3) heterogeneity of population; (4) youthfulness of population—percentage nineteen and under; (5) expenditures for new plant and equipment; (6) industrial diversification; (7) percentage of work force employed in manufacturing; (8) incidence of continuous-flow production industries; and (9) support of education. We shall assume it to be negatively associated with (1) percentage of work force that is unskilled; (2) extent of in-migration; (3) percentage of population that is non-white; (4) percentage of population over fifty-five years of age; (5) relative number of small industries; and (6) percentage farm income is of total income.

Ranking the six regions on each of the fifteen variables (1 means "most favorable" to automation, 6 stands for "least favorable"), summing their rankings to arrive at a composite score from which a summary ranking is obtained, one gets the following picture (*Table 1*)[59]: the Northeast in 1960 had that combination of characteristics most favorable to the adoption of automation (low score of 33); the Midwest barely nosed out the Far West for second place (scores of 43 and 46, respectively); the Northwest in 1960 offered automation the least encouragement (score of 68), while the Southwest and Southeast placed fourth (score of 61) and fifth (score of 64), respectively. One should note that no region had a monopoly on high ranks or low ranks.

The Northeast, with top automation proneness ratings on eight of the fifteen items, appears to have only the handicaps of a less youthful population than the other regions and a position of less than average favorableness relative to white–non-white population distribution. The Midwest's automation potential lies principally in its favorable position relative to industrial diversification, incidence

59. Some readers may want to quarrel with the way the variables used are defined and measured, and, in fact, the overall methodological scheme employed here. Obviously the rationale for weighting the fifteen items equally is open to question, yet in the absence of a basis for doing otherwise the approach appeared to be a justified beginning. Furthermore, this is no brief for these variables being the only ones associated with automation. In short, the scheme employed here is recognized as conducing at best to rough approximations and of being only suggestive of a challenging prediction problem relative to likely interregional differences in the rate of growth of automation in the near future.

of small industries, percentage of employment in manufacturing, and labor force composition at the lower skill levels. Its two major handicaps are its relatively older population and, surprisingly, its comparative dearth of professional, technical, and kindred workers. The Far West has a heterogeneous population, supports education well, and has more than its share of professional, technical, and kindred workers, farm-free income and continuous-flow production industries. Its chief impediments to automation are its relatively high proportion of unskilled workers and small industries.

The remaining three regions, the Southeast, Southwest, and Northwest, group closely relative to their automation proneness and, measured by sums of rankings, are well below the other three regions in their inducements to the new technology. Fifteen points separate the third-place region, the Far West, from the fourth-place region, the Southwest, while the entire range represented by the bottom three regions is only seven.

The Northwest ranks lowest among the six regions on six of the fifteen automation promoters. It is the "don't fence me in" region, with heavy dependence on agriculture and little attention to industrialization. With but one exception (its population is the least non-white), it ranked no higher than third in characteristics conducing to automation. The Southwest's principal weaknesses are its relatively low level of industrialization as measured by employment in manufacturing and industrial diversification. Its strengths are the youthfulness of its population and its good supply of professional, technical, and kindred workers.

The Southeast, next to the bottom on this overall measure of readiness for automation, has five 6's and three 5's in its rankings. Its current weaknesses stem principally from its having been so long a region poor in financial resources for education and industrial promotion. Its chief rays of hope are its youthful population, its political awakening (there are numerous indications that it is no longer a taken-for-granted "solid South"), and a position relative to the incidence of small industries better than is commonly believed.

Another approach to predicting the spread of automation is to examine the trend of the regions on each of the variables for which comparable data were obtainable at two different times. Conceivably one region, A, at a given time may have a combination of characteristics more favorable to automation than another region, B, yet an examination of what has recently been happening in these two regions may provide some valuable insights. Actually region A may have had a comparatively favorable position for, say, ten years yet gives no indication of doing anything about it by way of actual adoption of automation. On the other hand, region B, at present less well endowed and having arrived only recently at a position as favorable as it now has, may have come a long way in the period under study and, under such momentum, may be strongly inclined to exploit its recently acquired automation-inducing wares energetically. With this assumption, let us now examine the trend over a decade (in most instances, from 1950 to 1960, although in some cases the data are for 1947 and 1958) of fourteen of the fifteen variables used above (item 5 in *Table 1*, political behavior, is omitted here because comparable 1950 data were unavailable). Added to these fourteen is "net gain or loss through civilian migration," bringing the total to fifteen variables (see *Table 2*).

One immediately notes that the Southeast, a long-time laggard in industrialization, has placed first (score of 39) among the six regions in favorableness to automation of recent development (i.e., during the decade of the 1950's). The Northwest is second (score of 47) and the third place region, the Southwest, is close behind, with a score of only 51. The Far West and Northeast tie for fifth place (scores of 58), while the Midwest finishes last (score of 62).

This table (*Table 2*) tells us that the three regions least given to automation at the present time—the Northwest, Southeast, and Southwest—made substantial strides toward catching up to the top three during the 1950-1960 decade. Leader of the parade is the Southeast with six 1's and four 2's to its credit. Although its progress is meager during this period as measured by the indexes of industrial growth per se (e.g., industrial diversification; expenditures for new plant and equipment), the improvements in the nature of its work force relative to automation adoption (younger, more heterogeneous, better educated, more highly skilled) appear to be quite significant. However, obviously one must guard against overoptimism in such an analysis: progress is relative to the base from which it is computed—and in 1950 the Southeast had so far to go!

Table 1. Ranking of Regions of the United States on Current Susceptibility to Automation, Using Fifteen Variables Assumed To Be Associated with It.

Variable	Regions					
	Northeast	Southeast	Southwest	Midwest	Northwest	Far West
1. Unskilled workers	1	6	4	2	3	5
2. Enrollment in vocational programs	1	5	6	2	3	4
3. Professional, technical, and kindred workers	3	6	2	5	4	1
4. Heterogeneity—nativity and parentage	1	6	5	3	4	2
5. Heterogeneity—political behavior	1	2	5	3	6	4
6. Non-white population	4	6	5	3	1	2
7. Youthfulness of population—19 and under	6	1	2	4	3	5
8. Population 55 years of age and over	5	2	1	6	4	3
9. Expenditures for new plant and equipment	1	5	3	2	6	4
10. Incidence of small industries	3	2	4	1	6	5
11. Industrial diversification	2	4	5	1	6	3
12. Employment in manufacturing	1	4	6	2	5	3
13. Continuous-flow production industries	1	5	4	3	6	2
14. Farm income	1	4	5	3	6	2
15. Support of education	2	6	4	3	5	1
Total of rankings	33	64	61	43	68	46
Relative position derived from total rankings	1	5	4	2	6	3

Sources: See footnote 60.

On balance, in terms of present characteristics ("the bird in hand"), the older economies industrially promise most for automation (i.e., the Northeast, first place; the Midwest, second place), while in terms of potential as measured by what has been happening during the past decade, the newer economies industrially (i.e., the Southeast, Northwest, and the Southwest) have the most to offer. The Far West requires special attention here: strictly speaking it is neither an old nor a new economy industrially. The development of California, the most important industrially of the states in its region, during World War II and since has helped place the Far West at present (*Table 1*) above the average (i.e., third place) with respect to inducements to automation; its fourth position in the trend analysis (*Table 2*) reflects the broad base it already had in

1950, the beginning of the decade under study, compared with the Southeast, Northwest, and Southwest.

Finally, if we assume that present readiness for automation (*Table 1*) and recent trends in the development of factors favoring it (*Table 2*) are equally important, we can arrive at a "final" evaluation of the relative susceptibility to automation of our six regions (*Table 3*).[60] With this rationale, the Northeast will automate most

60. *Unskilled workers.* Data source: U.S. Bureau of the Census, *U.S. Census of Population: 1950*, Vol. II, *Characteristics of the Population*, Part I, *U.S. Summary*, Table 58, p. 105; and *U.S. Census of Population: 1960, General Social and Economic Characteristics*, *U.S. Summary*, Final Report PC(1)-1C, Table 105, p. 248. Measure computed: percentage of unskilled workers in work force.

Enrollment in vocational programs. Data source: U.S. Bureau of the Census, *Statistical Abstract of the United States, 1953*, Table 192, p. 146, and *ibid., 1963*, Table 156, p. 136. Measure computed: enrollment in vocational programs as a percentage of elementary and secondary school enrollments.

Professional, technical, and kindred workers. Data source: *Characteristics of the Population, 1950*, Table 79, p. 131; and U.S. Bureau of the Census, *County and City Data Book, 1962* (a *Statistical Abstract* supplement), Table 1, p. 4. Measure computed: percentage of this category of workers in the work force.

Heterogeneity—nativity and parentage. Data source: U.S. Bureau of the Census, *U.S. Census of Population, 1950*, Vol. IV, *Special Reports*, Part 3, Chapter A, *Nativity and Parentage*, Table 6, pp. 20-44; and *County and City Data Book, 1962*, Table 1, p. 2. Measure computed: percentage of foreign-born and native of foreign or mixed parentage.

Heterogeneity—political behavior. Data source: *County and City Data Book, 1962*, Table 1, p. 2. The data used were: votes cast for leading candidate, presidential election of 1960. Political heterogeneity is defined here as degree of disagreement in political voting. A high degree of political heterogeneity is found where votes are split evenly among many political candidates. In the national election of 1960 the only significant division of votes was between just two parties, the Democratic and the Republican. Some states in all regions gave a majority of their votes to the Democratic candidate and the remaining gave a majority to the Republican candidate. Determination of degree of political (voting) heterogeneity of a region runs as follows: all states in a region giving a candidate, either Democrat or Republican, less than 52 per cent of the total votes are classified as "heterogeneous" states. The remaining states (those giving a candidate, either Democrat or Republican, at least 52 per cent of the total votes) are divided into Democrat-winning states and Republican-winning states. The closer the number of the two "kinds" of states come to being equal, the greater is the degree of heterogeneity of the region. For example, the Northeast had three Republican-winning states and six Democrat-winning states in the 1960 election, while the Northwest had nine Republican-winning and no Democrat-winning states. In this case, therefore, the Northeast was more heterogeneous than the Northwest (if, of course, the remaining heterogeneity of the two regions—importance of states classified as heterogeneous—balanced). The combination of percentage of states in a region classified as heterogeneous (i.e., giving less than 52 per cent majority to either party) and the balance between Republican-winning and Democrat-winning states provided the measure of political heterogeneity. The formula is:

$$I = N - \overline{(R - D)} + H$$

where I = index of political heterogeneity; N = number of states in the region; $\overline{R - D}$ is the absolute value of the difference between the number of states giving a majority of more than 52 per cent of the votes to the Republican candidate and the number of states giving a majority of more than 52 per cent of the votes to the Democratic candidate; and H = number of heterogeneous states in the region rapidly, with the Far West and Southwest close behind in that order. The reasons here vary widely. The likely success of the Northeast is due to its already high level of education, population heterogeneity, and industrial development and diversification, despite its disadvantage relative to population age.

The Far West, handicapped by an unfavorable picture relative to small industries, vocational schools, and expenditures for new plant and equipment, profits from a young and heterogeneous work population, good education, light dependence on farm income, and

---

(i.e., not giving as much as 52 per cent of the votes to either candidate). The less $\overline{R - D}$, the greater the heterogeneity. This is taken care of in the formula by subtracting this quantity, $\overline{R - D}$, from N, the number of states in the region. Also, the larger the value of H, the greater the heterogeneity, hence the plus sign joining the two parts.

Non-white population. Data source: U.S. Bureau of the Census, *Characteristics of the Population, 1950,* Table 59, p. 106; and *General Population Characteristics, 1960, U.S. Summary,* Final Report PC(L)-1B, Table 55, p. 163. Measure used: percentage of non-whites in the population.

Youthfulness of population—19 and under. Data source: *Characteristics of the Population, 1950,* Table 63, pp. 112-114; and *General Population Characteristics, 1960,* Table 59, p. 167. Measure used: percentage of population under 20.

Population 55 years of age and over. Data source: for 1950, *Characteristics of the Population,* Table 64, p. 115; for 1960, *General Population Characteristics,* Table 60, p. 173. Measure used: percentage of population 55 and over.

Expenditures for new plant and equipment. Data source: U.S. Bureau of the Census, *U.S. Census of Manufactures, 1947,* Vol. III, *Area Statistics,* Table 4; and *ibid., 1958,* Table 4. Measure used: expenditures for new plant and equipment.

Incidence of small industries. Data source: *U.S. Census of Manufactures, 1947,* Vol. II, *Statistics by Industry,* Table 4; and *ibid., 1958,* Table 4. Measure used: percentage of industrial establishments employing less than 100 people.

Industrial diversification. Data source: *Characteristics of the Population, 1950,* Table 83, p. 135; and *General Social and Economic Characteristics, 1960,* Table 132, p. 281. Also *U.S. Census of Manufactures, 1947,* Vol. II, *Statistics by Industry,* Table 4; and *ibid, 1958,* Table 4. Measure used: scattering of workers among employment categories.

Employment in Manufacturing. Data source: *U.S. Census of Population: 1960, U.S. Summary,* PC(1)-1C, Table 106, p. 249. Measure used: percentage of workers employed in manufacturing.

Continuous-flow production industries. Data source: *U.S. Census of Manufactures, 1947,* Vol. II, *Statistics by Industry,* Table 4; and *ibid., 1958,* Table 4. Industries chosen: transportation equipment, primary and fabricated metals, petroleum and chemical, electrical machinery, financial, insurance, and real estate. Measure used: their employment as percentage of total employment.

Farm income. Data source: *Statistical Abstract, 1953,* Table 312, p. 284, and *Statistical Abstract, 1963,* Table 442, pp. 330-331. Measure used: farm income as percentage of total income.

Support of education. Data source: for expenditures per pupil, *The Book of the States, 1952-53* (Chicago, Ill.: The Council of State Governments, 1953), IX, 250; and *ibid., 1962-63,* XIV, 317. For teachers' salaries, *ibid., 1952-53,* IX, 252; and *ibid., 1962-63,* XIV, 314. Measure used: average expenditures per pupil and average teachers' salaries. Ranking of regions was obtained by assigning equal weight to expenditures per pupil and teachers' salaries.

Net gain or loss through civilian migration. Data source: *County and City Data Book, 1962,* Table 1, p. 3. Measure used: gain or loss as a percentage of population in 1950.

Table 2. Ranking of Regions of the United States on Automation-Adopting Potential, Based on Trends[1] in Fifteen Variables Assumed To Be Associated with It.

Variable	Regions					
	Northeast	Southeast	Southwest	Midwest	Northwest	Far West
1. Unskilled workers	3	2	1	5	4	6
2. Enrollment in vocational programs	5	1	4	2	3	6
3. Professional, technical, and kindred workers	6	1	3	4	2	5
4. Net gain or loss through civilian migration	3	2	5	4	1	6
5. Heterogeneity—nativity and parentage	4	1	3	6	5	2
6. Non-white population	4	1	2	5	3	6
7. Youthfulness of population—19 and under	5	1	6	3	4	2
8. Population 55 years of age and over	4	6	5	2	3	1
9. Expenditures for new plant and equipment	3	4	2	6	1	5
10. Incidence of small industries	4	5	2	6	1	3
11. Industrial diversification	1	6	4	2	3	5
12. Employment In manufacturing	1	2	4	5	6	3
13. Continuous-flow production industries	6	2	1	5	4	3
14. Farm income	6	4	3	5	2	1
15. Support of education	3	1	6	2	5	4
Total of Rankings	58	39	51	62	47	58
Relative position derived from total rankings	5	1	3	6	2	4

[1]The trend period used is 1950-60 except in the case of items 9, 10, and some of 13, where the time interval is 1947-58.
Sources: See footnote 60.

a good start in continuous-flow production industries. The Southwest compensates for its low enrollment in vocational schools and its lack of support for education by having its share of professional and technical people, a good position relative to non-automatable small plants, and raw materials (e.g., oil) for the development of continuous-flow production industries.

The Midwest and Southeast, strikingly different regions in many respects, tie for fourth place. The Midwest, high in vocational school enrollment, industrial diversification, and support of education, suffers from a relative dearth of professional and technical people, high population homogeneity, an influx of workers of questionable

Table 3. Ranking of Regions of the United States on Automation-Adopting Potential, Based on Assumption of Equal Importance of Current Readiness and Recent Developmental Trends, Using the Fourteen Variables Common to Both Bases of Analysis.

Variable	Regions					
	Northeast	Southeast	Southwest	Midwest	Northwest	Far West
1. Unskilled workers	1	5	2	3–1/2	3–1/2	6
2. Enrollment in vocational programs	3	3	5–1/2	1	3	5–1/2
3. Professional, technical, and kindred workers	5–1/2	4	1	5–1/2	2–1/2	2–1/2
4. Heterogeneity—nativity and parentage	2	3	4	5–1/2	5–1/2	1
5. Non-white population	5	2–1/2	2–1/2	5	1	5
6. Youthfulness of population—19 and under	6	1	5	3	3	3
7. Population 55 years of age and over	6	4–1/2	2	4–1/2	3	1
8. Expenditures for new plant and equipment	1	5–1/2	2	4	3	5–1/2
9. Incidence of small industries	3–1/2	3–1/2	1	3–1/2	3–1/2	6
10. Industrial diversification	1–1/2	6	4–1/2	1–1/2	4–1/2	3
11. Employment in manufacturing	1	2–1/2	5	4	6	2–1/2
12. Continuous-flow production industries	3–1/2	3–1/2	1–1/2	5	6	1–1/2
13. Farm income	2	4–1/2	4–1/2	4–1/2	4–1/2	1
14. Support of education	2	4	5–1/2	2	5–1/2	2
Total of Rankings	43	52–1/2	46	52–1/2	54–1/2	45–1/2
Relative position derived from total rankings	1	4–1/2	3	4–1/2	6	2

Source: The entries in *Table 3* are obtained by averaging corresponding entries in *Tables 1* and *2*, then ranking averages. Obviously item 5 in *Table 1* and item 4 in *Table 2* are omitted for they do not appear in both tables.

qualifications overall, and a less favorable position relative to the incidence of continuous-flow production industries than one would assume to be true. The Northwest, last place "winner," is so relatively free of urbanization-industrialization demands that automation is an understandably—and justifiably—scarce phenomenon. It is a region of sparse population and little manufacturing, of land suited to agriculture and grazing. There is little there to automate.

The Southeast still suffers from lack of industrial diversification, its large number of unskilled workers, and its financial inability to expand industrially. But the youthfulness of its population, its recent progress in professional training and attention to education overall, its general improvement in quality of work force through more technical training and the loss through out-migration of many incompetent workers, combine to make this region one capable of substantial progress toward the adoption of automation. Much of the needed potential and the challenge are present; whether or not the South will meet that challenge remains to be seen.

IX. THE CHANGING OCCUPATIONAL STRUCTURE OF THE SOUTH* / Richard L. Simpson and David R. Norsworthy

Jobs and workers, like other social positions and their incumbents, can be seen as occupying a three-dimensional space. They are located *vertically* in a hierarchy of *strata*. They are located *horizontally* in *sectors* representing different economic functions. Strata and sectors are thus portions of "social space." Finally, jobs and workers are located in *geographic* space.[1] In this chapter we shall present some highlights of the occupational structure of the South in 1960 and its changes since 1940, with special attention to how its sector (horizontal) structure has affected its stratum (vertical) structure, to the racial composition of strata, and to ways in which sector and stratum composition affect individual workers' opportunities. The "South" under discussion will be Odum's Southeast unless otherwise indicated.[2] Strata will be represented by the Alba Edwards Census occupational groupings unless otherwise indicated.[3] Sectors will be represented sometimes by Census industry groupings and sometimes by Colin Clark's primary, secondary, and tertiary groupings.[4]

1

The South's persistent economic lag behind the rest of the nation is seen not only in low incomes, but also in underrepresentation of southern workers in the higher occupational strata. This in turn has reflected a continuing overconcentration in agriculture, relative to

* We are indebted to Carl Harter, Ida Harper Simpson, and Charles R. Wingrove, who did most of the compilation of Census data; to Angell G. Beza for suggestions which helped us in compiling and interpreting the Census data; and to Harriet L. Herring for critical comments on an early draft. The Burlington-Graham community research was performed pursuant to a contract with the United States Office of Education, Department of Health, Education, and Welfare.

1. This formulation is taken, with slight change in terminology, from Pitirim A. Sorokin, *Social Mobility* (New York: Harper, 1927), pp. 3-9. See also Theodore Caplow, *The Sociology of Work* (Minneapolis: University of Minnesota Press, 1954), pp. 59-61.

2. Alabama, Arkansas, Florida, Georgia, Kentucky, Louisiana, Mississippi, North Carolina, South Carolina, Tennessee, Virginia. See Howard W. Odum, *Southern Regions of the United States* (Chapel Hill: University of North Carolina Press), 1936.

3. Alba M. Edwards, *Comparative Occupational Statistics for the United States* (Washington: U. S. Government Printing Office, 1943).

4. Clark's sectors are composed chiefly of agricultural, manufacturing, and trade and service occupations, respectively. Colin Clark, *The Conditions of Economic Progress* (3rd ed.; London: Macmillan, 1957).

other parts of the United States, and an underconcentration in secondary and, until recently, tertiary activities. Rupert Vance in 1945 detailed the sector imbalance of the South's economy and saw a need for both industrialization and out-migration.[5]

About a decade later, Lorin Thompson wrote optimistically of sector shifts in the southern economy during the 1940's.[6] As evidence of welcome change, Thompson could cite swifter movement out of agriculture in the South than elsewhere. He also showed that manufacturing and tertiary employment were absorbing most of the loss from agriculture. By 1950 the South had reached virtual parity with the rest of the nation—61.1 per cent of its workers vs. 62.7 per cent of non-southern workers—in trade, service, and other non-manufacturing activity. Its surplus in agriculture, forestry, and fishing (21.3 per cent vs. 9.0 per cent) was balanced by a deficit (17.6 per cent vs. 28.3 per cent) in manufacturing.[7]

By 1960 the South had passed the rest of the United States in non-manufacturing industries (67.1 per cent in the South vs. 63.9 per cent elsewhere), had partially narrowed the gap in manufacturing (22.1 per cent vs. 30.4 per cent), and had continued to reduce its surplus in agriculture, forestry, and fishing (10.8 per cent vs. 5.7 per cent).[8]

The amount of concentration in secondary and tertiary activities does not, however, tell the whole story, for these gross sector categories conceal substantial variation in occupational stratum composition. Harriet Herring in an extensive statistical analysis has shown that the South has specialized in the less desirable types of manu-

5. Rupert B. Vance, *All These People* (Chapel Hill: University of North Carolina Press, 1945), pp. 140-153.

6. Lorin Thompson, "Urbanization, Occupational Shift and Economic Progress," in Rupert B. Vance and Nicholas J. Demerath, eds., *The Urban South* (Chapel Hill: University of North Carolina Press, 1954), pp. 38-53.

7. *Ibid.*, p. 41. Thompson's figures refer to Odum's Southeast plus Oklahoma and Texas. His three categories do not correspond to Clark's primary-secondary-tertiary sectors since Thompson includes mining and construction in the category with trade and service industries.

8. U.S. Bureau of the Census, *U.S. Census of Population: 1960, General Social and Economic Characteristics, U.S. Summary,* Final Report PC(1)-C, Table 92; and Table 62 in the following state reports: PC(1)-1C, 2C 5C, 11C, 12C, 19C, 20C, 26C, 35C, 38C, 42C, 44C, 45C, 48C. In these figures we have retained Oklahoma and Texas in the southern category, and mining and construction in the category with trade and service industries, for comparability with Thompson's 1950 figures. In all of our use of occupational or industrial classifications we have omitted the "not reported" categories. Because of the variable accuracy of censuses, some imprecision is thus introduced. However, this imprecision will have little effect on *relative* changes or regional comparisons, with which we are chiefly concerned.

Table 1. Selected Secondary and Tertiary Sectors in the South and Non-South, 1940 and 1960.

	1940			1960		
	Per cent of non-agricultural employed workers[a]		South's surplus or deficit (South–Non-South)	Per cent of non-agricultural employed workers[a]		South's surplus or deficit (South–Non-South)
Sector	South	Non-South		South	Non-South	
Non-durable goods manufacturing	17.7	15.0	+2.7	16.6	12.6	+4.0
Durable goods manufacturing	10.0	15.2	−5.2	10.4	18.5	−8.1
Transportation, communication, and utilities	8.1	8.9	−0.8	7.3	7.8	−0.5
Retail trade	16.2	17.9	−1.7	15.9	16.8	−0.9
Wholesale trade and finance	5.8	7.8	−2.0	7.3	8.8	−1.5
Professional and related services	8.9	9.6	−0.7	12.2	13.4	−1.2

[a]Base for percentages excludes "industry not reported." Percentages do not add to 100 since not all industries are shown.

Source: U.S. Bureau of the Census, *U.S. Census of Population: 1960, General Social and Economic Characteristics, U.S. Summary,* Final Report PC(1)-C, Table 92; and Table 62 in the following state reports: PC(1)-1C, 2C, 5C, 11C, 12C, 19C, 20C, 26C, 35C, 42C, 44C, 48C.

facturing.[9] Southern manufacturing industry in 1940, for example, had only one salaried worker for each 12.5 wage earners; in no other region was the ratio less than 1 to 6.7.[10] The regional disparity remained in 1960 and was especially pronounced in professional and technical jobs; professional and technical workers ranged from a fifth of all workers in aircraft and parts, an industry relatively lacking in the South, to a hundredth of all workers in textiles and apparel goods, a predominantly southern industry.[11] Perloff and associates have documented the differing effects of different industries on state income levels; they find, for example, that fabricating industries and business services are associated with high state income.[12] Therefore in evaluating the effects of gross sector shifts, one needs to know what types of industries are involved.

How has the South fared in the kinds of secondary and tertiary

9. Harriet L. Herring, *Southern Industry and Regional Development* (Chapel Hill: University of North Carolina Press, 1940).

10. *Ibid.,* pp. 8-9.

11. U.S. Bureau of the Census, *U.S. Census of Population: 1960, Characteristics of the Population, U.S. Summary,* PC(1)-1, Introduction, p. lxxiii.

12. Harvey S. Perloff, Edgar S. Dunn, Jr., Eric E. Lampard, and Richard F. Muth, *Regions, Resources, and Economic Growth* (Baltimore: The Johns Hopkins Press, 1960), p. 602.

Table 2. Occupational Stratum Composition of Selected Secondary and Tertiary Sectors, United States, 1960.

Sector	Stratum			
	Professional and managerial (%)	Clerical, sales, craftsmen, and foremen (%)	Manual other than craftsmen (%)	Total[a] (%)
Non-durable goods manufacturing	11.3	33.8	54.9	100.0
Durable goods manufacturing	14.1	37.7	48.2	100.0
Transportation, communication, and utilities	12.9	46.7	40.3	100.0
Retail trade	21.0	48.0	31.0	100.0
Professional and related services	59.9	17.7	22.5	100.0
Wholesale trade and finance	21.6	62.7	15.6	100.0

[a]Excludes "occupation not reported."
Source: U.S. Bureau of the Census, *U.S. Census of Population: 1960, Detailed Characteristics, U.S. Summary,* Final Report PC(1), Table 209.

sectors it has developed? Not very well, as *Table 1* and *2* show. *Table 1* compares the relative size of selected secondary and tertiary sectors in the South and the rest of the country in 1940 and 1960. (The base for the percentages excludes the primary sector. If this were included, the South vs. non-South ratios would be slightly less than the ones shown for 1960, and markedly less in 1940.) The most notable regional differences were in manufacturing. In comparison with manufacturing in the rest of the country, the South's economy in 1940 was weighted toward non-durable goods and away from durables; and these disparities grew larger during the twenty-year period. Regional differences in the tertiary sectors shown were smaller; compared with the rest of the country, the South was slightly deficient in all of them. Its deficit grew during the twenty years in professional services and shrank in the others.

Table 2 shows occupational stratum composition within the same six sectors in 1960. Within the manufacturing and non-manufacturing categories separately, the sectors are arranged in order of increasing southern underrepresentation in them in that year. The picture thus presented is not a happy one for the South. Non-durable goods manufacturing—the only one of the sectors in which the South was overrepresented, and one in which its over-concentration had grown since 1940—was last among the six sectors in the percentage of its workers who were professional and managerial, and first in blue-collar workers below the craft level. Among the tertiary sectors, the more workers above the bottom manual level a sector had, the more underrepresented the South was in it. A similar relationship existed between southern underrepresentation in a sector and percentage of the sector's workers who were in the top, professional and managerial, category. The professional service sector was a partial exception to this pattern, since it had by far the largest proportion of high-status workers but was outranked in southern underrepresentation by wholesale trade and finance; but this highly desirable sector was the only one in the tertiary group in which the South's underrepresentation increased during the twenty years.

It is thus apparent that the South has lagged behind the nation in the kinds of secondary and tertiary sectors it has developed, and that the lag was not disappearing between 1940 and 1960. From this we would expect the South's occupational structure to overrepresent the lower strata, and it does. Vance has written that in 1940 the South had an occupational structure which was seriously out of balance with other regions.[13] *Table 3* shows this imbalance for occupational groups arranged in order of increasing representation in the South in 1940. Clerical workers were least represented relative to their non-southern total in 1940, followed by craftsmen and foremen. At the other end of the scale, the South had between two and three times its share of farmers and farm laborers.

By 1960, as *Table 3* indicates, the occupational position of the South had undergone significant improvement. No stratum was deficient by as much as 30 per cent, and several of the middle strata had almost reached par with other regions. The overconcentration of farmers and laborers had been greatly reduced. Not all of the South's relative change had been favorable, however. Southern overconcentration had increased in three of the lowest non-farm strata: private household workers, laborers, and operatives. Private household workers and laborers lost ground relative to other strata in the South as elsewhere, but less rapidly. The number of operatives grew rapidly in the South while barely keeping up with general population growth elsewhere, so that the South moved from

13. Vance, *op. cit.*, p. 144.

Table 3. Comparative Occupational Structure, South and Non-South, 1940 and 1960.

Occupational group	Region	1940		1960	
		Per cent of employed persons[a]	South's percentage/non-South's percentage x 100[b]	Per cent of employed persons[a]	South's percentage/non-South's percentage x 100[b]
Clerical	South	5.4		11.7	
	Non-South	11.0	49	16.0	73
Craftsmen, foremen	South	7.6		12.9	
	Non-South	12.6	60	14.5	88
Professional	South	5.4		9.6	
	Non-South	8.7	63	12.3	78
Sales	South	4.8		7.1	
	Non-South	7.5	64	7.7	92
Service	South	5.1		8.2	
	Non-South	7.7	67	9.0	91
Managerial	South	5.9		8.5	
	Non-South	8.7	68	8.9	96
Operatives	South	14.8		20.3	
	Non-South	18.9	78	19.1	106
Total employed		100.0	100	100.0	100
Non-farm laborers	South	8.0		6.2	
	Non-South	6.8	119	4.8	130
Private household	South	7.2		5.2	
	Non-South	4.0	177	2.2	232
Farmers	South	21.4		6.0	
	Non-South	9.0	239	3.6	166
Farm laborers	South	14.4		4.3	
	Non-South	5.1	281	1.9	226

[a]Excludes "occupation not reported."
[b]Calculated on the basis of proportions correct to four decimal places.
Source: U.S. Bureau of the Census, *U.S. Census of Population: 1960, General Social and Economic Characteristics, U.S. Summary,* Final Report PC(1), Table 89; and Table 59 in the following state reports: PC(1)-1C, 2C, 5C, 11C, 12C, 19C, 20C, 26C, 35C, 42C, 44C, 48C.

a sizeable deficit of operatives in 1940 to a slight surplus of this group in 1960. Clearly the South was far from overcoming its occupational maldistribution in 1960, despite marked progress. Overall occupational development in the nation is indicated particularly in the growth of professional and technical occupations, and in these the South had closed the regional gap somewhat by 1960 but still had a sizeable deficit.

2

It has long been fashionable, but nonetheless accurate to say that there are many Souths. Comparative Census data on the states of the South vary sufficiently to call into question the very reality of a homogeneous region in 1960. Initially ranking the states from most to least agricultural, we discovered that they could be placed with little ambiguity in four groups according to the distribution of 1960 employment in agriculture, manufacturing, and tertiary industries (*Table 4*). The three most agricultural states also had the lowest proportions in tertiary employment (*Table 4* does not show this since it presents only one type of tertiary employment, professional services); these were named "primary" states. The next most agricultural states, the Carolinas, stood out as having very high proportions of employment in manufacturing; these were named "secondary" states. Three states were medium in all three main sectors; we called these "unspecialized." Finally, three states had low proportions in agriculture and high proportions in tertiary activity, hence received the designation "tertiary" states.

As *Table 4* indicates, this sector classification of southern states corresponds in a general way to differentials among them in non-agricultural stratum composition; but it is the secondary states, not the primary states, which come off worst in this comparison. The percentage of employment that was white-collar was highest in the tertiary states, lowest in the secondary states, and intermediate in the primary and unspecialized states. The only exception to this pattern was Mississippi, a primary state with a lower percentage of white-collar workers than the Carolinas. If instead of all white-collar workers we consider only the upper white-collar strata— professionals and managers—the pattern remains and the exception disappears, with Mississippi slightly ahead of the Carolinas. The same pattern of white-collar proportions remains when we examine the number of white-collar workers as a percentage of all non-agri-cultural workers; uniformly the tertiary states had the highest per-centages and the secondary states the lowest.

Moreover, in a general way though with several exceptions the same picture emerges in comparing the states in the number of

Table 4. Aspects of Sector and Stratum Composition within Individual Southern States, 1960.

States by sector type	Per cent of employed persons in selected sectors[a]				White-collar as per cent of total employment	White-collar as per cent of non-agricultural employment	Craftsmen and foremen as per cent of non-agricultural manual employment
	Agriculture	Non-durable manufacturing	Durable manufacturing	Professional and related services			
Primary							
Mississippi	20.6	10.2	8.9	9.8	30.0	37.7	21.5
Kentucky	14.5	10.6	10.6	10.7	35.7	41.8	26.3
Arkansas	14.2	9.5	10.6	10.5	33.9	39.5	22.7
Secondary							
North Carolina	13.0	22.5	9.2	9.6	32.0	36.8	22.2
South Carolina	11.8	25.3	6.8	9.5	30.8	34.9	21.0
Unspecialized							
Tennessee	10.8	16.2	9.8	10.6	36.5	40.9	24.5
Alabama	9.4	12.8	13.7	10.1	34.6	38.2	24.1
Georgia	8.4	17.5	8.8	9.6	36.4	39.8	21.9
Tertiary							
Virginia	7.4	13.1	9.3	11.2	42.2	45.6	27.4
Louisiana	6.4	10.0	5.6	11.9	39.5	42.2	23.9
Florida	5.5	6.9	6.2	11.1	45.3	47.9	29.2

[a]Horizontal totals do not add to 100 per cent since not all sectors are shown.

Source: U.S. Bureau of the Census, U.S. Census of Population: 1960, General Social and Economic Characteristics, Final Report PC(1), Tables 59 and 62 in the following state reports: 2C, 5C, 11C, 12C, 19C, 20C, 26C, 35C, 42C, 44C, 48C.

craftsmen and foremen—the top blue-collar category—as a percentage of all blue-collar non-agricultural workers. The two secondary states were low but were joined by Mississippi and Georgia, and the two highest-ranking states were tertiary, but the tertiary state of Louisiana was not among the leaders.

These facts support the prevailing view that tertiary industries are generally the most desirable. At the same time they underscore the warnings by Perloff and associates, Herring, and others against regarding all manufacturing industries as uniformly desirable. The two most industrialized states in the region, North and South Carolina, have specialized in textiles, an industry which employs few white-collar workers and a high ratio of semiskilled to skilled workers. As a result even Mississippi has outdone them in occupational stratum composition outside agriculture.

3

Historically, the South's low ranking in occupations has been due in no small part to the large proportion of the region's Negroes in servant, unskilled, and farm labor and tenant occupations.[14] *Table 5* indicates that the concentration of Negroes[15] in the lower strata had by no means disappeared in 1960, although some changes since 1940 were discernible. The table arranges the region's occupational strata for each sex in order of increasing concentrations of Negroes in them in 1940. Among males there were large deficits of Negroes in the managerial, clerical, craft, and professional strata in 1940. In the managerial and clerical-sales categories, for example, Negroes were only 3.2 per cent of the employed males, although they were 27.8 per cent of employed southern males in all occupations combined. The 1940 deficits of Negro women, who constituted 43.4 per cent of all southern working women but less than half this percentage of the higher-ranking strata, were even larger than the Negro male deficits; and Negro women were also grossly underrepresented among operatives.

By 1960 all of these large Negro deficits had been reduced, the small Negro deficits of male operatives and female service workers

14. See Vance, *op. cit.*, p. 143 for a discussion of this.

15. Throughout our discussion we shall speak of "Negroes" although our statistical data are for "non-whites." The two are all but synonymous in the South and the occupational situation of Indians, who make up a large share of the non-whites other than Negroes, is not much different from that of Negroes.

Table 5. Per Cent of Employed Southern Male and Female Workers in Different Occupational Strata Who Were Non-white, and Non-white Surplus or Deficit, 1940 and 1960.

	1940		1960	
Occupational stratum	Non-white as per cent of all civilian employed	Non-white deficit or surplus: per cent non-white in stratum minus per cent non-white among all civilians employed of each sex	Non-white as per cent of all civilian employed	Non-white deficit or surplus: per cent non-white in stratum minus per cent non-white among all civilians employed of each sex
Males				
Managerial	3.2	−24.6	2.6	−17.4
Clerical, sales	3.2	−24.6	4.8	−15.2
Craftsmen, foremen	10.5	−17.3	9.4	−10.6
Professional	10.8	−17.0	6.7	−13.3
Operatives	19.9	−7.9	22.3	+2.3
Total males employed	27.8	0.0	20.0	0.0
Farm	35.5	+7.7	33.8	+13.8
Service	39.6	+11.8	42.5	+22.5
Laborers	56.3	+28.5	54.0	+34.0
Private household	90.6	+62.8	77.4	+57.4
Females				
Clerical, sales	2.1	−41.4	2.6	−23.5
Managerial	8.4	−35.1	6.7	−19.4
Craftsmen, foremen	9.3	−34.2	10.2	−15.9
Operatives	12.8	−30.7	12.6	−13.5
Professional	17.4	−26.1	16.0	−10.1
Service	40.2	−3.3	39.7	+13.6
Total females employed	43.5	0.0	26.1	0.0
Laborers	45.1	+1.6	41.5	+15.4
Farm	71.9	+28.4	59.7	+33.6
Private household	87.4	+43.9	85.2	+59.1

Source: U.S. Bureau of the Census, *U.S. Census of Population: 1960, General Social and Economic Characteristics*, Final Report PC(1), Table 58 in the following state reports: 2C, 5C, 11C, 12C, 19C, 20C, 26C, 35C, 42C, 44C, 48C; *U.S. Census of Population: 1940, The Labor Force*, PC(3), Table 13, Parts 2, 3, 4.

had become Negro surpluses, and the small surplus of Negroes among female laborers had become a large one. (The 1960 deficits and surpluses are given in the right-hand column of *Table 5* and are measured against the smaller percentage of the southern labor force which Negroes constituted in 1960 than in 1940.) All of these shifts can be taken to mean improved occupational status for Negroes. Even their movement into operative, laboring, and service jobs was probably a step up from farming, in view of Negroes' low position within southern agriculture.[16] Even after these shifts, however, Negroes remained heavily concentrated in the lower strata; and as Glenn has noted, such upgrading of Negro occupations as did occur in this twenty-year period took place mainly during the war-time decade of the 1940's and slowed down in the 1950's.[17]

Table 6 looks at the same facts in a different way, and it also leads to a gloomy conclusion about the racial composition of southern occupational strata. This table shows the percentages of workers in each race and sex group in 1940 and 1960 who were in the various occupational categories, and, for men and women separately in each year, the proportion of employed Negroes who were in each category as a percentage of the proportion of employed whites who were in the category. The occupations are again arranged in order of increasing Negro concentrations in them in 1940.

By this measure used in *Table 6*, the largest underrepresentations of Negro men in 1940 were in clerical-and-sales and managerial jobs. Negro men were also heavily underrepresented in the professional and skilled craft categories, and somewhat underrepresented among operatives. Negro men were overrepresented in farm, service, laboring, and private household occupations. By 1960 the Negro male deficit had been somewhat lessened in the clerical-and-sales and craft categories but was substantially unchanged in managerial and professional work. The Negro male surplus in farming increased during the twenty-year period by our index, since a larger proportion of white than of Negro farmers left southern agriculture. Negro men moved from a deficit to a surplus among operatives, and increased their lead over whites in service and laboring jobs. As was noted earlier, movement into even these low strata is probably an improvement when it takes Negroes out of the kinds of agricultural employment generally available to them in the South. An additional bright spot is the rapid movement of Negro men out of domestic service.

16. More extensive discussion of racial polarization in certain occupations is presented by Munro S. Edmunson and David R. Norsworthy in "Industry and Race in the Southern United States," to appear in a UNESCO symposium on the effects of industrialization upon race relations edited by the Institute of Race Relations, London. The Negroes' position in southern agriculture is discussed in Gunnar Myrdal, *An American Dilemma* (New York: Harper, 1944), pp. 230-250.

17. Norval D. Glenn, "Changes in the American Occupational Structure and Occupational Gains of Negroes during the 1940's," *Social Forces*, 41 (1962), 188-195; see p. 189.

Table 6. Occupational Distribution of Non-white and White Southern Workers, by Sex, 1940 and 1960.

Occupational group	Race	1940		1960	
		Per cent of employed persons[a]	Non-white percentage/ white percentage x 100[b]	Per cent of employed persons[a]	Non-white percentage/ white percentage x 100[b]
Males					
Clerical, sales	non-white	0.9		3.0	
	white	10.8	9	14.9	20
Managerial	non-white	0.8		1.4	
	white	9.4	9	13.2	10
Craftsmen, foremen	non-white	3.7		8.9	
	white	12.0	31	21.3	42
Professional	non-white	1.3		2.7	
	white	4.3	31	9.4	29
Operatives	non-white	10.1		23.6	
	white	15.7	64	20.6	115
Total male employed		100.0	100	100.0	100
Farm	non-white	53.6		23.3	
	white	37.6	143	11.4	205
Service	non-white	7.0		11.8	
	white	4.1	170	4.0	296
Laborers	non-white	20.2		24.5	
	white	6.0	334	5.2	470
Private household	non-white	2.4		0.8	
	white	0.1	2506	0.1	1373
Female					
Clerical, sales	non-white	0.8		3.1	
	white	28.3	3	41.2	8
Managerial	non-white	0.6		1.0	
	white	4.8	12	4.9	20
Craftsmen, foremen	non-white	0.1		0.4	
	white	0.8	13	1.2	32
Operatives	non-white	5.1		9.0	
	white	26.9	19	22.0	41
Professional	non-white	4.3		7.8	
	white	15.7	27	14.3	54
Service	non-white	8.0		20.6	
	white	9.2	88	11.0	186
Total female employed		100.0	100	100.0	100

(Table 6 Cont.)

Occupational group	Race	1940		1960	
		Per cent of employed persons[a]	Non-white percentage / white percentage x 100[b]	Per cent of employed persons[a]	Non-white percentage / white percentage x 100[b]
Laborers	non-white	0.9		0.9	
	white	0.9	107	0.5	201
Farm	non-white	24.1		7.8	
	white	7.2	333	1.9	420
Private household	non-white	56.1		49.4	
	white	6.2	902	3.0	1626

[a]Excludes "occupation not reported."
[b]Calculated on the basis of proportions correct to four decimal places.
Source: U.S. Bureau of the Census, *U.S. Census of Population: 1960, General Social and Economic Characteristics*, Final Report PC (1), Table 58 in the following state reports: 2C, 5C, 11C, 12C, 19C, 20C, 26C, 35C, 42C, 44C, 48C; *U.S. Census of Population: 1940, The Labor Force*, PC(3), Table 13, Parts 2, 3, 4.

The ratios of Negro to white representation in women's occupations given in *Table 6* are harder to interpret, since our method of arriving at this index shows an increase for Negro women in every occupational stratum.[18] Therefore it may be more instructive to look at the absolute percentages of Negro and white women in the various occupations from which the ratios were derived. These show less marked shifts for women of both races than occurred among men, mainly because fewer women than men in 1940 were in agriculture and therefore fewer left it for other occupations during the twenty years. A substantial shift of white women into clerical and sales occupations (from 28.3 per cent to 41.2 per cent) was accounted for principally by decreasing white female concentrations in the operative, farm, and domestic servant categories. A large exodus of Negro women from agriculture and a smaller exodus from domestic service led to small percentage increases of Negro women in the clerical-and-sales, managerial, craft, operative, and professional categories, and to a large shift (from 8.0 per cent to 20.6 per cent) of Negro women into service jobs.

18. This is arithmetically possible since our index measures the proportion of all Negroes as a *percentage* of the proportion of all whites in each stratum, rather than the *difference* between the two racial percentages in each stratum. Thus, for example, in clerical and sales jobs, Negro women increased from 0.8/28.3 or 3 per cent to 3.1/41.2 or 8 per cent of the white percentage, even though their absolute percentage gain was only from 0.8 to 3.1, or 2.3, while the white percentage gain was from 28.3 to 41.2, or 12.9.

A striking fact about Negro women's occupations in the South is their continued concentration in domestic service. Thompson could report in the early 1950's that the number of private household workers in the South was declining,[19] and Anderson and Bowman wrote in 1953 of "the vanishing servant" in the South.[20] Among women, however, even in the boom of the 1940's the decline was greater in areas outside the South than within the South, and from 1950 to 1960 the number of private household workers actually increased in every one of the eleven southern states. In three Gulf Coast states—Florida, Louisiana, and Mississippi—as well as in Arkansas, the increase was 40 per cent or more.[21] These increases in the 1950's largely offset the decreases of the 1940's, and in the same three Gulf states plus another, Alabama, there were absolute increases in the number of women employed in private households between 1940 and 1960.[22] In the South as a whole, nearly half of all Negro women workers in 1960 were still in domestic service.

From the various data we have presented we can conclude that southern men and women of both races improved their occupational distribution during the twenty years preceding 1960, but that whites maintained their advantage over Negroes. Whether the Negro's relative position improved only slightly or actually became worse depends on what index of racial imbalance is used. The data are consistent with Norval Glenn's interpretation of racial shifts in occupational stratum composition in the nation as a whole: upward occupational movement of Negroes occurs only when it will not displace white workers.[23] The movement of Negroes out of farming was chiefly into blue-collar jobs; and even the overall expansion of the South's white-collar and craft strata benefited mainly, though not only, whites. White males declined in absolute numbers only in

19. Thompson, *op. cit.*, p. 47.
20. C. Arnold Anderson and Mary Jean Bowman, "The Vanishing Servant and the Contemporary Status System of the American South," *American Journal of Sociology*, 59 (1953), 215-230.
21. Stella P. Manor, "Geographic Changes in U. S. Employment from 1950 to 1960," *Monthly Labor Review*, 86 (1963), pp. 1-10.
22. U.S. Bureau of the Census, *U.S. Census of Population: 1960, General Social and Economic Characteristics*, Final Report PC(1)-C, Table 59 in the following state reports: 2C, 5C, 11C, 12C, 19C, 20C, 26C, 35C, 42C, 44C, 48C. In Alabama and Louisiana the net increases were the resultants of very small Negro decreases somewhat more than matched by white increases.
23. Glenn, *op. cit.*

agriculture and domestic service, which Negro males were also leaving. The ratios of percentages of Negro female employment to percentages of white female employment within the various strata, shown in *Table 6*, might seem to suggest that Negro women displaced white women in the professional, operative, and laborer categories, where Negro percentages rose while white percentages fell. In absolute numbers, however, white female employment in these strata grew rapidly as more white women entered the labor force. Total female employment grew so fast from 1940 to 1960 that both white and Negro women could increase their employment at various levels.[24]

As this is written, active campaigns are under way in many southern cities to open up non-traditional jobs to Negroes by ending discriminatory hiring practices. These will undoubtedly have an effect on Negro stratum distribution, but it is too early to say how much effect or how soon. On the other side of the coin, genuine (as distinct from token) desegregation of public schools might make it harder for Negroes to become school teachers,[25] and the end of discrimination in other economic spheres might have similar consequences for Negro professional, business, and white-collar workers who have been sheltered from white competition in the segregated Negro economy. Thus the eventual occupational effects of the civil

24. In any discussion of the effects of ascriptive qualities on occupational stratum composition, sex is as important a consideration as race, since women, like Negroes, suffer disadvantages. We have nevertheless not attempted to compare male with female occupational distribution, although some pertinent data are given in *Tables* 5 and 6. We have not discussed this topic because consideration of it is complicated by two factors. (a) Within major Census occupational categories the jobs held by men and women are very different, the men's jobs being generally the better ones. On this see Theodore Caplow, *op. cit.*, pp. 230-247. Any sex comparison using major Census groupings would be misleading since it would show women far outnumbering men in the higher (white-collar) strata. As an extreme example, in 1940, 4.3 per cent of white men and the same percentage of Negro women were in the "professional" category, but it would be absurd to infer from this that the job opportunities for white men and Negro women were the same. For this reason meaningful sex comparisons would require the use of finely detailed occupational categories. (b) The South's large agricultural population makes sex comparisons additionally suspect because the concept of employment as "gainful employment" leaves out a number of farm wives who are by no means economically idle but who do not appear in the Census reports as "employed." Other farm wives *are* economically unproductive in varying degrees, like many urban wives; these are chiefly the wives of the more prosperous farmers. We know of no accurate way to correct for these vagaries of classification using available data.

25. Richard A. Lamanna summarizes a number of discussions of this problem in "The Role of the Negro Public School Teacher in the Process of School Desegregation" (Ph.D. dissertation, University of North Carolina, 1965).

rights movement of the 1960's may be substantial but cannot be foretold.

4

We have seen that the sector composition of a state has a marked effect on its stratum composition. Sector composition also appears to influence the ability of Negroes to move up from the bottom strata. Some effects of sector composition on the vertical mobility opportunities of Negroes can be illustrated by comparing their occupational shifts between 1940 and 1960 in two Deep South states which are contiguous but differ sharply in sector composition. The states are Mississippi, the most rural and primary state in the region, and Louisiana, one of the region's most urban and tertiary states.

The comparison makes use of four occupational categories which constitute a status ordering of a rough sort, at least for Negroes. The top stratum consists of all white-collar workers and craftsmen; this grouping combines several Census categories, in all of which Negroes have traditionally been underrepresented. Then come operatives and service workers (other than domestic servants), followed by non-farm laborers and domestic servants. At the bottom are farmers and farm laborers; to include farm owners and tenants in a bottom stratum is perhaps inaccurate for whites but generally accurate for southern Negroes, since the farms they own are mainly the poorest ones and tenancy for them has usually meant share-cropping.[26]

Table 7 shows the absolute numerical changes from 1940 to 1960 in the four strata by race and sex in the two states. Louisiana gained more workers than Mississippi in the two upper strata even though it lost fewer farmers; the Mississippians who left agriculture were relatively likely to migrate out of the state, creating a net loss in employment, whereas Louisiana experienced a sizeable gain in employment.

In both states white employment grew while Negro employment fell. These changes reflected Negro out-migration, which was especially large in the case of Mississippi. (The increase in Negro female employment in Louisiana resulted from growth in the per-

26. Myrdal, *op. cit.*

Table 7. Redistribution in Occupational Classes in Two Deep South States, 1940 to 1960, by Color and Sex.

Occupational Class	Race	Numerical change in employment (in 1,000's)[a]			
		Louisiana		Mississippi	
		Male	Female	Male	Female
White collar and craftsmen	white	+150	+89	+75	+48
	non-white	+15	+9	+8	+5
Operatives and non-domestic service workers	white	+50	+17	+33	+30
	non-white	+30	+22	+18	+12
Non-farm laborers and domestic service workers	white	−5	+1	−2	+2
	non-white	+2	0	−8	0
Farmers and farm laborers	white	−80	−3	−92	−5
	non-white	−83	−17	−139	−43

[a]Lack of complete comparability between 1940 and 1960 employment data introduces some lack of precision in these data, but the relative magnitudes of various employment changes can be accepted.

Source: U.S. Bureau of the Census, *U.S. Census of Population: 1960, General Social and Economic Characteristics,* Final Report PC(1), Table 58 in the following state reports: 20C and 26C; *U.S. Census of Population: 1940, The Labor Force,* PC(3), Table 13, Part 3.

centage of Negro women who were employed, which was more than sufficient to offset the out-migration.) The pattern of mobility into and out of occupational strata was also dissimilar for Negroes and whites. More Negroes than whites left agriculture, especially in Mississippi, but fewer Negroes than whites entered the two higher non-farm strata. Indeed, in both states the white gains were nearly ten times the Negro gains in the top category, craftsmen and white-collar workers. These trends show clearly what is already well known, that Negroes move out of the South because not many of them can move up very far within the South.

There remains the task of discerning whether the two states had different trends during the twenty years in the racial disparity of occupational stratum composition. This task is achieved by comparing the percentages of employed whites and Negroes who were in each stratum (as was done for the entire region in *Table 6*) and noting the deficit or surplus of Negroes, for each sex in each state, in 1940 and again in 1960. The results of this comparison appear in *Table 8.*

As the small positive numbers in *Table 8* show, the Negro surplus in Louisiana agriculture had almost disappeared by 1960

Table 8. Relative Net Occupational Mobility of Whites and Non-whites in Two Deep South States, 1940 to 1960, by Sex.

| Occupational class | Year | Differences between non-white and white percentages employed in occupational classes (non-white minus white) | | | |
| | | Louisiana | | Mississippi | |
		Male	Female	Male	Female
White collar and craftsmen	1960	−46	−63	−44	−49
	1940	−36	−59	−28	−50
Operatives and non-domestic service workers	1960	+13	+13	−3	−11
	1940	−3	−10	−4	−20
Non-farm laborers and domestic service workers	1960	+23	+48	+13	+47
	1940	+14	+54	+7	+36
Farmers and farm laborers	1960	+9	+2	+29	+14
	1940	+25	+16	+24	+35
Total difference (absolute value):	1960	91	126	29	14
	1940	78	139	63	141

Source: U.S. Bureau of the Census, *U.S. Census of Population: 1960, General Social and Economic Characteristics,* Final Report PC(1), Table 58 in the following state reports: 20C and 26C; *U.S. Census of Population: 1940, The Labor Force,* PC(3), Table 13, Part 3.

though it had been fairly substantial in 1940. In the lowest non-farm occupations in Louisiana, an increase in the Negro male surplus (of laborers) was almost matched by a fall in the Negro female surplus (of domestic servants).[27] In the middle non-farm occupations, Negroes of both sexes gained, so that by 1960 a Negro surplus existed among operatives and non-domestic service workers. But in the top category Louisiana's Negroes, already grossly underrepresented in 1940, were more so (by this index) in 1960. Their relative loss among craftsmen and white-collar workers was greater for men than for women, but the racial differences remained greater among women than among men.

Negroes in Mississippi, unlike those in Louisiana, had not by 1960 overcome a sizeable employment surplus in agriculture. The surplus of Negro female agricultural workers fell but was still 13 per cent, and the surplus of Negro men in farming actually grew, despite heavy out-migration of the Negro farm population. The

27. See footnote 22 and the earlier discussion of domestic servants. The number of Negro and white domestic servants in Louisiana changed very little, and the Negro surplus fell mainly because a relatively constant number became a smaller percentage of the enlarged total Negro female employment in Louisiana.

surpluses of Negro men and women in non-farm labor and domestic service grew; in the case of women, this trend was opposite to that previously noted in Louisiana. As in Louisiana, Negroes gained in Mississippi at the level just above labor and domestic service; but in Mississippi their gains were smaller and did not bring them to parity with whites in these occupations. At the top, Negro males lost ground in Mississippi but Negro females did not.

Do these figures show more occupational gains for Negroes in the tertiary than in the primary state? The answer is a clear "yes" if we make the reasonable assumption that greater success in moving into operative and service occupations from previous laboring and farm categories represents a greater gain; in this respect Louisiana's Negroes outdid those of Mississippi. However, the answer is less clear if one expects to find the Negro making more progress at skilled and higher levels in a state which has become relatively empty of agricultural employment. The proportion of Negroes among those moving into the top class was *not* greater in Louisiana. Moreover, the absolute value of the total difference between racial percentage distributions—an index of racial polarization in occupations obtained by adding the differences for the four occupational levels regardless of their signs—was greater in Louisiana than in Mississippi for both males and females in 1960.

Thus it cannot be said unequivocally whether Negroes shared more fully in the overall gains of the period in the tertiary state of Louisiana or the primary state of Mississippi. Their position relative to whites in the top level of occupations became worse in both states, to about the same degree; in the next level it did improve faster in Louisiana. It appears that as overall sector and stratum composition improve, whites take the lion's share of the expansion in the higher strata. The gains filter down to Negroes, who move into manual occupations from which whites are moving up but which represent improvement for Negroes.

5

We turn now to a further illustration of the effects of sector shifts on movement between strata. We shall report some findings of a study by Norsworthy of a southern textile community in which rates of individual vertical mobility rose sharply after a modern electrical machinery plant came to town. The community is the adjoining cities of Burlington and Graham, in Alamance County, North Carolina. The data on work careers are from interviews conducted in 1959 with 265 randomly selected white male workers in the community.[28]

Burlington-Graham and surrounding Alamance County have experienced two major expansions of occupational sector composition in this century.[29] A cotton mill had been established on a creek near town in 1837, and several mills were built within Burlington-Graham in the 1880's, but these were comparatively small and the area remained chiefly agricultural. Overall industrial development of the community received its greatest impetus in the 1920's with the coming of Burlington Mills, which was established in 1923 and opened its first rayon dress goods plant in 1927. Thereafter the community became increasingly dominated by textiles and hosiery manufacturing, which grew rapidly and provided nearly all its industrial employment until after World War II. The most recent sector expansion began in 1946 when a Western Electric plant making electronics and radar equipment was established in Burlington.

This plant grew slowly at first, employing just nine hundred and fifty workers in a community of slightly over thirty thousand population in 1952, but by 1959 Western Electric employed an estimated four thousand workers in a community of about forty thousand.[30] Not all of these lived in either Burlington or Graham, and many of them were women, but the plant nevertheless accounted for a major share of the community's male employment. Precise statistics on the industry composition of the community's total employment are not available, but the composition of our randomly drawn block sample of white male interviewees is probably reasonably indicative. In this sample, 31 per cent of the men worked in textiles and 17 per cent in electrical machinery manufacturing.[31]

28. The full study is reported in David R. Norsworthy, "Mobility Effects of Industrial Growth: Structural Change and Work Experience in a Southern Piedmont Community" (Ph.D. dissertation, University of North Carolina, 1961). Most of our discussion in this section is based on this source.
29. Information on the industrial and population growth of the area is taken from the U. S. Census and from James E. Payne, "Burlington-Graham: A Study of Urban Development" (M.A. thesis, University of North Carolina, 1952).
30. The 1952 Western Electric figure is from Payne, op. cit., p. 10. The 1959 figure is from an interview with a company official.
31. The sample may have underrepresented textile workers and overrepresented

Thus since World War II the community had moved from an even greater reliance on the textile industry than prevailed in the Carolinas as a whole to greater diversification, with a sizeable concentration in the kind of modern industry the South has traditionally lacked. The shift had major effects on work opportunities for men in the community, a few of which we will discuss. Similar effects might be anticipated in other southern communities where similar sector changes occur.

One result of our research is to question some pessimistic views of textile work which have been prevalent in writings about mill communities. A number of studies have reported that once a person enters textile work he is not likely to leave it, and that his children are apt to follow him into the mill and stay there.[32] From some writings one gets the impression that mill work has mysterious inherent qualities which stamp themselves on mill workers, destroying their initiative and making them and their descendants unable to leave the protective environment of the mill village.[33] Our findings do not bear out this impression.

Of our 265 workers, 155 had worked at some time in textiles. However, only 32 of these 155 had worked *only* in textiles, and presumably some of these 32 would leave textiles eventually. The other 123 of the 155 either worked now in textiles but had previ-

---

electrical workers, but not in a way which distorts conclusions about the comparisons between them. A discussion of sampling procedures and possible sample biases is given in Norsworthy, *op. cit.*

32. Studies of textile workers and their communities in the Carolinas are reported in Jennings J. Rhyne, *Some Southern Cotton Mill Workers and Their Villages* (Chapel Hill: University of North Carolina Press, 1930); Herbert J. Lahne, *The Cotton Mill Worker* (New York: Farrar and Rinehart, 1944); Harriet L. Herring, *The Passing of the Mill Village* (Chapel Hill: University of North Carolina Press, 1949); and J. Kenneth Morland, *Millways of Kent* (Chapel Hill: University of North Carolina Press, 1958). A national study also finds textile workers more attached to their occupation and industry than most kinds of workers: Herbert S. Parnes, *Research on Labor Mobility: An Appraisal of Research Findings in the United States* (New York: Social Science Research Council, 1954), p. 87. Morland returned in 1958 to the town he had first studied in 1948 and found that the occupational aspirations of mill-village youth had risen but that the limitations of the setting militated against their achieving their ambitions; see J. Kenneth Morland, "Educational and Occupational Aspirations of Mill and Town School Children in a Southern Community," *Social Forces*, 39 (1960), 169-175.

33. Jennings J. Rhyne after studying five mill villages in Gaston County, North Carolina, in the late 1920's referred to textile workers as a "hereditary occupational group" (*op. cit.*, p. 156) and wrote of the "development of a social type" (pp. 209-212). He found that the social life of mill workers was almost wholly with other mill workers (p. 175) and that their children customarily quit school at age fourteen to work in the mills (p. 201).

Table 9. Background Characteristics of Burlington-Graham Workers by Industry and Level of Occupation.

Background characteristics	Industry and level					
	Textile mfg.		Electrical mfg.		Other	
	Manual (%)	Non-manual (%)	Manual (%)	Non-manual (%)	Manual (%)	Non-manual (%)
Totals						
Number of workers	(61)	(22)	(21)	(24)	(48)	(84)
Percentages	100.0	100.0	100.0	100.0	100.0	100.0
Age						
34 or less	38.9	36.3	81.9	41.7	29.2	41.7
Education						
High school graduate	16.4	57.1	81.0	100.0	14.3	81.7
Childhood residence						
Alamance County						
Farm	15.0	4.8	9.5	4.3	16.7	4.9
Non-farm	36.7	38.1	47.6	8.7	35.4	31.7
Not Alamance County						
Farm	30.0	23.8	19.0	17.4	14.6	23.2
Non-farm, N.C.	13.3	9.5	19.0	21.7	16.7	25.6
Non-farm, other state	5.0	23.8	4.8	47.8	16.7	14.6
Industry and occupational level of father						
Textile manufacturing						
Manual	40.0	50.0	57.1	21.7	21.3	18.3
Non-manual	1.7	4.5	0.0	4.3	2.1	3.7
Other non-agricultural						
Manual	13.3	13.6	19.0	34.8	44.7	18.3
Non-manual	11.7	9.1	9.5	21.7	10.6	36.6
Agriculture	33.3	22.7	14.3	17.4	21.3	23.2

Source: David R. Norsworthy, "Mobility Effects of Industrial Growth: Structural Change and Work Experience in a Southern Piedmont Community," (Ph. D. dissertation, University of North Carolina, 1961), pp. 102-103.

ously done something else, or (more frequently) had once worked in textiles but were now doing something else. This rate of sector mobility is substantially higher than the rates reported in the earlier studies, and it suggests that mill workers are entirely capable of moving into other occupations, once the opportunity presents itself. Earlier findings of a tendency to cling to the occupation have reflected the fact that cotton mill workers, and studies of them, have been concentrated in small undiversified communities which offered few alternatives.

Some related conclusions emerge from an examination of char-

acteristics and social backgrounds of workers in our sample
(*Table 9*). We divided jobs into four sectors which fit the facts of
life in Burlington-Graham: agriculture, textiles, electrical machinery manufacturing, and everything else. The textile workers in the
sample were more likely than other workers to have farm backgrounds. This was to be expected. What was *not* expected was that
the men most likely to have textile-worker fathers were not the
textile workers, but the blue-collar workers in electrical machinery
manufacturing. These latter workers were also more likely than
those now in textiles to have grown up in Burlington-Graham or
in towns and villages in the surrounding area of North Carolina,
some of which are classical "mill villages." Also noteworthy is the
greater youth of the blue-collar electrical machinery workers.

The findings suggest a three-generational pattern in which the
coming of the electrical plant had turned the textile mill into a
way station between the farm and the more advanced industrial
sector; no longer was textiles a dead end. In the ideal-typical case,
a farmer has a son; the son moves to Burlington or some smaller
town, where he becomes a textile worker; he in turn has a son who
goes into the more advanced industrial sector.

This diversification of work sectors has an effect on vertical
mobility, but the full effect is delayed. At first it is felt mainly by
younger workers who move from the lower occupational strata in
other sectors into the suddenly expanded middle strata in the advanced sector. (As *Table 10*, below, shows, it is the middle strata
that expanded most in the Burlington-Graham sector shift.) The
older workers derive little mobility advantage from the sector shift
since they are unequipped by training and experience to take advantage of it, or they may be discriminated against in hiring by the
new industry. The very top levels of managers and of professional
people such as engineers in the newly expanded sector are at first
filled by in-migrants from outside the area, since local people lack
the advanced skills needed for these top positions.[34]

Table 10 gives further comparisons of textile and electrical
workers; it presents less detail than *Table 9* in the hope of suggesting the patterns with greater clarity. The electrical workers

34. Data in Norsworthy, *op. cit.*, suggest this. *Tables 9* and *10* do not show it
directly since our sample subcategories are too small for the needed cross-tabulations
to be presented.

Table 10. Careers of Textile and Electrical Workers Compared.

Career and personal characteristics	Textile workers	Electrical workers
Hollingshead status level[a] of present job (per cent in each level)		
1, 2 (high)	9.6	13.0
3, 4, 5 (medium)	43.4	65.2
6, 7 (low)	47.0	21.7
Total N	(83)	(46)
Intergenerational mobility		
Per cent upward mobile[b]	34.6	54.5
Total N	(81)	(44)
Mobility from previous job		
Per cent upward mobile[b]	49.3	66.7
Total N (excludes workers whose present job was their first one)	(69)	(42)
Job stability		
Per cent who had held same job throughout career	15.9	6.7
Total N	(82)	(45)
Age		
Per cent 34 or less	38.3	60.9
Total N	(81)	(46)

[a]This is the Index of Occupational Status described in A. B. Hollingshead and F. C. Redlich, *Social Class and Mental Illness* (New York: Wiley, 1958), pp. 359-368. Levels 1-2 are upper white-collar, 3-4 are lower white-collar, 5 is skilled manual, and 6-7 are semiskilled and unskilled manual.

[b]Upward mobility is defined as movement to a higher level in Hollingshead's seven-level Index of Occupational Status.

were more likely than the textile workers to have jobs in the upper and, especially, the middle strata. They were more likely to have moved up in occupational status, in comparison with their fathers and also with their own previous jobs,[35] and they were less likely to have held only one job throughout their careers. The electrical workers had thus experienced more job and stratum mobility in spite of the fact that they were younger men than the textile workers.

35. A previous report on this study shows that, although upward mobility rates usually vary directly with size of community, Burlington-Graham (and Raleigh) have recently had higher rates of upward mobility than were found in studies of larger cities such as Oakland, California, or Indianapolis, Indiana, or in national surveys of industrial nations such as Sweden, Britain, and Japan. The reason presumably is the more recent sector and stratum diversification of Burlington-Graham. See Richard L. Simpson, "Occupational Careers and Mobility," in F. Stuart Chapin, Jr., and Shirley F. Weiss, eds., *Urban Growth Dynamics* (New York: Wiley, 1962), pp. 400-420. Earlier studies are summarized and interpreted in Seymour Martin Lipset and Reinhard Bendix, *Social Mobility in Industrial Society* (Berkeley and Los Angeles: University of California Press, 1958).

Some aspects of this pattern are likely to change, however, when the full effects of sector and stratum differentiation—including further growth of the tertiary sector—are felt. Once the initial vacuum in the middle strata is filled, upward mobility into these jobs will probably become less frequent than it was immediately after the electrical plant arrived, though it should remain more frequent than when textiles almost completely dominated the community's industrial scene. A new generation of locally reared workers, some of them the sons of today's middle stratum, will be better able to compete for the top stratum of managerial and professional jobs, mainly through advanced education; hence there should be less need to import people for the upper stratum. The situation as a whole will be much improved over the days of textile dominance, with more opportunities for local workers to move into middle- and upper-level jobs, though with less movement from the bottom to the middle than in the early phase of industrial diversification.[36]

This is, in fact, what seems to have happened in Norristown, Pennsylvania, a city of similar size, when it experienced similar sector changes earlier in this century. Sidney Goldstein reports considerable mobility of locally reared workers into the middle levels in the early period of Norristown's industrial development, but fairly heavy in-migration to staff the higher-ranking occupations —as in Burlington-Graham more recently.[37] As Norristown settled down to a more stable pattern of sector diversity, rates of mobility of its locally reared workers into the higher strata rose and there was less need to bring in outsiders to fill these positions. Rates of mobility by locals into the middle strata became fairly stable at moderately high levels. This is what we are predicting for Burlington-Graham, and this is what we would predict for any southern community which experiences the same kind of sector expansion. The Burlington-Graham findings, like other data given earlier in this chapter, clearly indicate that the *kinds* of industry an area has largely determine its occupational composition and the career opportunities of its people.[38]

36. This analysis somewhat oversimplifies the situation but does not distort it in any essential way. A fuller analysis is given in Norsworthy, *op. cit.*

37. Sidney Goldstein, *Patterns of Mobility, 1910-1950: The Norristown Study* (Philadelphia: University of Pennsylvania Press, 1958), pp. 124-195.

38. For a discussion of increased rates of vertical mobility and changing class structure in the South, and of the broader consequences of the growth of modern

This survey of recent occupational change in the South may seem to have struck a pessimistic note. The more the South changes, the more it stays the same, persistently backward in comparison with other American regions. It is still the most agricultural region, though less so than in the past, and its farmers are the nation's poorest. In the shift it has made toward the national norm it has specialized in the kinds of manufacturing and services which provide the fewest craft, white-collar, and professional jobs. Its whites, still in control of its economy, have reaped most of the fruits of its progress; southern Negroes are in some ways more disadvantaged than ever in the region's occupational structure.

There is, however, good reason for optimism and for a sense of accomplishment. While the South is still a long way from catching up with the nation, it has markedly upgraded its occupational structure in an absolute sense. Instead of 29 per cent of its workers, as in 1940, 50 per cent of its workers in 1960 were in white-collar and skilled craft occupations. In 1940, 36 per cent of the South's employment was in agriculture. The figure in 1960 was barely more than 10 per cent, and the difference represents an almost unmixed blessing for the region; for almost any occupation is an economic improvement over southern agriculture except for the prosperous elite of farmers who, ideally, would be left to run large farms. The hard fact is that agriculture has always been, for most southerners in it even more than for the farm population elsewhere in the United States, not just a horizontal sector of the nation's economy but a stratum, at the bottom. Further departure from the land will take place and is to be welcomed.

Beyond this the picture becomes more complicated. Not all manufacturing industry is equally desirable, and not all tertiary activity is superior to manufacturing in the occupational strata it produces. It is clear that random industry-hunting is not the wisest policy for the South; in the long run some kinds of industry may do more harm than good if they divert the region's capital and manpower from the kinds of industry which bring greater wealth and provide more high-status jobs. Neither is diversification of economic activity necessary, past a certain point. The addition of only

industrial sectors for the life styles of workers, see Rudolf Heberle, "The Changing Social Stratification of the South," *Social Forces*, 38 (1959), 42-50.

one limited sector produced, in the Burlington-Graham community we studied, greater opportunity for upward occupational mobility than has been found in other places much more diversified but with a lesser rate of expansion in the most desirable sectors. The condition which is most fundamental for maximizing workers' opportunities is that the economic sectors in which high occupational strata predominate be expanding faster than the sectors whose jobs are concentrated in the lower strata. The community case study we presented attests that when this condition is met, southern workers can take full advantage of the resulting opportunities.

X. CHANGE AND RESISTANCE TO CHANGE IN THE SOUTHERN LABOR MOVEMENT / Donald F. Roy

With more immediately pressing matters drawing public attention, interest in the southern expansion of American labor unions seems to have receded. The relinquishing of headlines to the turbulencies of race relations, to disquieting developments in international affairs, and the gathering belligerencies of war on poverty does not mean, however, that fears, hopes, and uncertainties in regard to the union problem have been laid to rest. Submerged for the time being by competitive apprehensions, but not far beneath the surface, lie strong fears of unionization.

Folk-dread of the labor union Minotaur is, of course, not shared by those who are most immediately involved with advancing the labor movement. Union organizers and officials are notably immune. Theirs is an apprehension of a contrary and perhaps more realistic nature. Their shudders are elicited not by dreams of a huge, devouring monster, but by an image of a dwarf, and a frail one at that. They see the southern union movement as stunted, and have fears that arrested development may be permanent.

Detached observers note that the work force of the South is underorganized. In a study published in 1957, Leo Troy set forth an invidious comparison of rates of union organization: In 1953, 17.1 per cent of the non-farm labor force in a bloc of twelve southern states belonged to labor unions; for the nation as a whole, the percentage was 32.6.[1] In a later study based on the same data, Troy set up "hypothetical standards" to show that union membership in the South was 57.7 per cent of what it would have been had southern industry been organized at the rate prevailing in the rest of the country.[2] "Given the national percentage of industry, organization, and composition of employment in 1953, total Southern membership could be increased by about ¾, or about 1¼ million above the

1. Leo Troy, *Distribution of Union Membership Among the States, 1939 and 1953* (New York: National Bureau of Economic Research, 1957). The twelve southern states are: Alabama, Arkansas, Florida, Georgia, Kentucky, Louisiana, Mississippi, North Carolina, South Carolina, Tennessee, Texas, and Virginia.
2. Leo Troy, "The Growth of Union Membership in the South," *The Southern Economics Journal*, 24 (April, 1958), 413-414.

level prevailing in that year."[3] Few union officials would disagree
with Ray Marshall, who wrote in 1960 that "the South remains one
of organized labor's most serious organizing problems."[4] A year
later, Robert Cooney pointed out that "The South today remains a
'new frontier' for organized labor, even though 80 years have passed
since the first organizing campaign in that region."[5]

There was a flurry of "frontier" settlement during the 1940's,
when American labor unions were enjoying a general boom in
membership. During the period 1939-1953, while union membership in the nation as a whole was increasing from 6,517,700 to
16,217,300, a gain of 148.8 per cent, membership in the twelve
southern states was advancing from 591,500 to 1,700,500, a gain of
187.5 per cent.[6] With a national growth of nearly ten million new
members, and a southern growth of 1.1 million, the South increased
its percentage of nation-wide union affiliation from 9.1 to 10.5.[7] The
South fell behind the nation as a whole, however, in percentage
increase of the non-agricultural labor force unionized; the respective percentages were 6.2 and 11.1, from 10.9 per cent to 17.1 per
cent, and from 21.5 per cent to 32.6 per cent.[8] From examination of
these 1939-1953 comparisons we may be permitted the crude but
succinct generalization in regard to growth of the labor movement:
As the nation goes, so goes the South. In fact, N. M. Douty said
just about that in 1946: "During the past 60 years union organization and membership in the South has risen with every major upsurge of organized labor activity nationally."[9]

In recent years union membership on the national scene has
been in ebb. According to a report of the Bureau of Labor Statistics
of the U. S. Department of Labor, a peak membership of 17,500,000
was reached in 1956. A drop from this peak resulted in a loss of
500,000 members by 1960.[10] The membership growth trend since

3. *Ibid.*, p. 420.
4. Ray Marshall, "Some Factors Influencing the Growth of Unions in the South,"
*Industrial Relations Research Association: Proceedings of the Thirteenth Annual
Meeting,* 1960 (Madison, Wisconsin: 1961), p. 166.
5. Robert B. Cooney, "The Modern South: Organized Labor's New Frontier,"
The American Federationist, 68 (May, 1961), 15.
6. Leo Troy, "The Growth of Union Membership in the South," p. 409.
7. *Ibid.*, p. 410.
8. *Ibid.*, pp. 412-413.
9. H. M. Douty, "Development of Trade Unionism in the South," *Monthly Labor
Review,* 63 (October, 1946), 555.
10. U.S. Department of Labor, Bureau of Labor Statistics: *Directory of National*

the early 1950's has been variously referred to as "stability," "stagnation," "saturation," and "plateau."[11] Solomon Barkin, onetime Research Director for the Textile Workers Union of America, and author of *The Decline of the Labor Movement*, considers "crisis" not too strong a word to use "for the cessation of the trade union movement's expansion into new areas and its decline in numerical strength."[12] If shrinkage of membership has been slight, less than 3 per cent, the contraction is becoming ever greater in relation to the expansion of population in general and the labor force in particular. The plateau is sinking in relation to the surrounding terrain. Our latter-day Spengler of the labor movement explains that the shrinkage is "due primarily to attrition of jobs in unionized occupations, a continuing loss that is greater than the minor gain in recruitment."[13] The attrition of jobs appears especially impressive in certain employment categories, such as the mining industries, where 60 per cent of the production jobs were eliminated from 1947 to 1959, railroad and bus employment, where 40 per cent of the jobs were lost, and textile mill products, where the cut was 30 per cent.[14] To offset such losses and to advance in step with the rising labor force, unions would need to extend membership to as yet unorganized groups and industries. Leaders of the American labor movement appear to be in agreement that "the essential task of organizing the unorganized" is "the greatest unresolved trade union problem."[15]

Computations based on membership estimates provided the Bureau of Labor Statistics by state AFL-CIO bodies in 1961 indicate that the growth of southern unions continues generally to follow the national pattern. During the plateau years, 1953 to 1960, the South increased its percentage of nation-wide union affiliation by little more than a percentage point, from 10.5 per cent to 12

and International Labor Unions in the U.S., 1961, Bulletin #1320 (Washington, D. C.: Government Printing Office, March, 1962), p. 47.
11. H. P. Cohany, "Membership of American Trade Unions, 1960," *Monthly Labor Review,* 84 (December, 1961), 1299.
12. Solomon Barkin, *The Decline of the Labor Movement* (Santa Barbara, California: Center for the Study of Democratic Institutions, 1961), p. 62.
13. *Ibid.,* p. 62.
14. *Ibid.,* pp. 10-11.
15. "What's Behind the News and What's Ahead: Labor," *Fortune* (February, 1962), p. 199.

per cent.[16] Thus the South, in a national comparison, remains underorganized. And, with recognition that organizing is labor's most pressing problem, Marshall's reference to the South as labor's most serious organizing problem gains significance.

1

The purpose here is not to allay uneasiness about the growth of unions, though soothing effects may emerge as a by-product of this discussion, nor to try to foretell what appears to be a highly problematical future. This will be an attempt merely to point out, in groping, provisional designation, the events and circumstances that seem to be bound up with the status and prospects of organized labor in the South. What happenings appear to have salient influence on the growth of southern unions? What doings, goings on might be specified as facilitating conditions? As inhibiting conditions? With present or portending efficacy, by design or by happenstance, what augments the union movement? What tends to stunt it?

Explanatory epithets that spring first to mind are "industrialization" and "cultural lag." The former is said to beget union movements and nurse them along, the latter to delay their hatching and retard their growth. Since the South has been undergoing industrial development, it will necessarily undergo an eventual burgeoning of labor unions, either as an unavoidable evil or as a guaranteed dawning of a bright new day for the wage slave, depending upon the tilt of one's outlook. In accordance with this presumption, unions have appeared on the southern industrial scene, and if their emergence has seemed feeble and halting, almost wraithlike, more on the order of something going out than something coming in, then the follow-through term cultural lag may serve to account for the unimpressive velocity of the movement and to certify its direction. If development seems not merely sluggish, but questionably overdue, the prolonged retardation may be explained by reference to the South as a region known for the durability of its lags. Although the inevitable may be delayed, like race mixing and Judgment Day, it is still the inevitable.

16. *Directory of National and International Labor Unions in the U. S., 1961*, pp. 52-53.

Such a "creeping immanence" explanation of the birth and slow development of southern unionism is a simple one, but it does represent a considerable advance, in credibility if not in complexity, over such comparably unpretentious interpretations as "Unions are the work of the Devil" or "They spring full-blown from the ear of a carpetbagger." The linking of unions with factories has some history to back it up; so does association of factories with cultural lags, of one sort or another. There is the industrial history of England to read about, and the industrial past of the American North to point to. What happened before will happen again; so we can extrapolate. Destiny, like the Outline of History, comes in big chunks. We can hop from lump to lump, like Eliza crossing the ice, as we move imaginatively into the future.

Glenn Gilman,[17] who concerns himself with the prospects of labor organization in the southern textile industry, maintains this simplicity of lumpen analysis by using a brace of explanatory labels that have the blessing of sociology, if not history. The switch in credit for stunted union growth is from cultural lag to "folk society." The labor movement can't make headway in folk-type societies, such as the South; it flourishes in another kind of arrangement, the "mass society," which is found north of the Mason-Dixon line. The two types of society are constituted by different complexes of social interaction, the latter form contrasting conglomerations of goodies and baddies like plum pudding and coyote bait. The main union-repellent ingredients of folk society seem to be (a) sympathetic rapport between management and employees, based on a common background of custom, and (b) informal community pressure on management to preserve the folksy harmony. With such protection, mill hands don't need labor unions; in fact, they give union organizers the horse laugh or get indignant and tell them to peddle their leaflets somewhere else. On the other hand, mass society lacks the old-timey rapport based on custom; it has formal rules, regulations, and laws, with police and the courts to enforce them. Since an impersonal management and an indifferent community do not seem to give a tinker's damn about the industrial workers, the latter, to ensure protection of their rights, welcome

17. Glenn Gilman, *Human Relations in the Industrial Southeast* (Chapel Hill: University of North Carolina Press, 1956).

the organizer as a friend in need. The organizer in turn welcomes the workers, and his international union expands accordingly.

In the exchange of one concept for two, cultural lag for folk society and mass society, explanation seems to show a net gain, without getting entangled in the complexities, complications, and contrarieties that painstaking observation usually reveals. Even to avoid the stigma of cultural lag should constitute a benefit. From the point of view of the members, better to belong to a society that is incompatible with the growth of labor unions than to one that is falling behind in noticeable ways. Furthermore, the social interaction of folk society seems to carry an aura of "honor system"; not to need laws, cops, or labor unions speaks pretty well of any society.

However, the gain is in doubtful coin as far as explanation is concerned. The noting of negative cases, which stand out in any casual inspection of the actual state of affairs on the southern industrial scene, would indicate that adequate description calls for a closer scrutiny with more discriminating linguistic tools than observation through the stellarscope of a polar typology could provide. The logical contrariety shows immediately when attention is drawn to the fact that unions do exist, if they do not prosper, in the reputedly union-repellent southern folkways. And it shows when it is noticed that the North, under the supposedly union-encouraging mass ways, also poses a "some are . . . , some are not . . ." challenge to further investigation.

Just as impressive to the casual observer is the contrariety evident in the showing of hands on the occasion of National Labor Relations Board "elections" in southern manufactories—such elections serving as formal and decisive procedures to determine whether or not the workers of particular industrial establishments wish union affiliation. The vote in each instance indicates that some do, some do not. Although the "noes" usually have it in these special ballotings, in some cases the vote is excitingly close. Thus, it would appear that folksters and massites are mixing it up, not only in the same region, but in the same town, and, indeed, on the same production line. If folkways fail to breed true to type, if they produce pro-union mill hands along with anti-union mill hands in a confused admixture, like the commingling of pigs and chickens in a barnyard, then their antithetical combination with mass ways

as an explanatory device would be of questionable utility. It would
seem that any attempt to specify the influences affecting the development of the union movement in the South would call for
procedures considerably more discriminative, if less dashing, than
running up a couple of conceptual flags. Instead of stereotyping
large hunks of quasi-located environment with "ideal type" labels,
a taxonomic operation that hypostatizes while it compresses, a more
cautious kind of investigation might start with attempted disen-
tanglement, dissection, and detailed examination of activities and
environments that have definite location in time and space.

This unravelling of contextural entanglement is aided, in its
early phases, at least, by an available store of observations, reflections, and meditations that have accumulated, if that be the word,
over many years. Sources of ideational supply range from voices
of experience to just hearing voices. The degree of emotional attachment to theories seems to vary from that which one would
expect to find in a planetarium to the objectivity of a cat with his
tail in a slammed icebox door. This help comes for the most part in
the form of single-factor determinisms; a few presentations recognize a multiplicity of influences. One of the most bandied-about
pet theories could be regarded as a popularized version of the folk
society notion; crudely put, the industrial worker is happy as is, so
blandishments of union seducers from Yankeeland are to no avail.
A strikingly contradictory explanation, one of strong conviction in
union circles, is that the worker is unhappy with the *status quo*,
but is scared that he'll be fired if he dabbles in union activity.
Another contrasting pair of interpretations locates the source of
union difficulty in the personality of the southern workman. Assertion that this man is ruggedly independent in psychic construction,
culturally if not congenitally deaf to those who would lure him
from his proud self-reliance, is countered by an insistence that the
claimed nine hundred thousand square miles of southern Walden
Pond is strictly a mirage, that the southern blue collar adorns a
head so beaten down into it and so completely "brainwashed" that
it is unable to recognize self-interest when it is spelled out in the
most cogent, most simply-worded leaflet.

One of the more detached analyses was offered decades ago by

Weyforth,[18] in his multifactoral discussion on "the organizability of labor." Weyforth saw low-skilled workers as harder to organize than the highly skilled because their "strategic position" for control of the labor supply is less favorable. Those low in skill form a large, common labor pool; they are in relatively unrestricted competition with each other for available jobs. Weyforth also saw size of industrial organization as a major factor handicapping union organizing; he pointed to the "strategic strength" for controlling job supply possessed by "trusts." In their control over a large number of factories, the heads of large organizations can restrict substantially the "area" of alternative job opportunities to their employees. Furthermore, a well-organized employers' association could approximate the strategic strength of the trust in controlling job supply.

Mitchell and Mitchell,[19] also analysts of labor problems, have shared Weyforth's emphasis on labor supply as a critical factor. In their view, the South will not be unionized until further industrialization of that region takes up the slack in labor surplus.

More recently, Marshall[20] has presented a multifactoral listing of influences on the growth of the southern labor movement. His accent on the negative produces a close approximation to the assortment of "hindrances" to union expansion later catalogued by Barkin.[21] The latter offers three categories of hindrances, namely "outside impediments," "internal impediments," and "obstacles to growth from non-union workers." Not only could the generalities of Barkin's presentation be provisionally accepted as applying in the South; that region is singled out for special mention as an area of organizing difficulty.

The internal impediments are those having to do, in the main, with inadequacies of organizing procedures; union officials and organizers aren't going at it with maximum effectiveness possible under otherwise discouraging circumstances. The outside obstructions are provided by employer anti-union tactics, including (a) the

18. William O. Weyforth, *The Organizability of Labor* (Baltimore: The Johns Hopkins Press, 1917).
19. George S. Mitchell and Broadus M. Mitchell, "The Plight of Cotton Mill Labor," in J. B. S. Hardman (ed.), *American Labor Dynamics* (New York: Harcourt, Brace and Company, 1928).
20. Ray Marshall, *op. cit.*
21. Solomon Barkin, *op. cit.*

installation of "human relations" programs to win employee good will, and (b) "outright anti-union appeals," meaning knocking unions by spoken and printed word. Outside obstructions also lie in national and state laws and National Labor Relations Board orientations unfavorable to unions. Social conditions, such as post-depression prosperity of industrial workers and cessation of New Deal pro-labor attitudes of the national government, add to union difficulties from external sources of supply. The third category, "obstacles from non-union workers," features apathy toward unionism as a formidable stumbling block. Certain kinds of workers are especially refractory: women, Negroes, low-wage service workers, and white-collar workers. The southern textile workers, with whom Barkin has had years of disheartening professional experience, might like to embrace the union movement, but they don't dare; the quantity and quality of pressures on them to withhold union membership read like a list of Job's afflictions. Those encouraging delay include, in addition to employers, town merchants and professionals, the church, the newspaper, and, at times, the police. Also, the southern mill hand carries but a vague image of unionism, has had little experience with indigenous formal social organization as preparation for independent action, and can look to little or no support from a "liberal, intellectual middle class." Furthermore, his life is complicated by the color issue and he has difficulty in finding alternate employment, in case he incurs employer disapproval, which he almost surely will if he flirts too seriously with unions.

With these findings, lugubrious from the point of view of leaders of a southern labor movement, Barkin stresses the necessity for improvement in organizing procedures. The growing point of the union movement is the organizing campaign. In the main, the building of union membership hinges on campaign victories. The decisive moment of the campaign comes, of course, with the NLRB election, when hitherto unaffiliated workers decide whether to accept or decline union membership. If election results show a majority of "yeas," a new local is formed; if the "nays" predominate, there is no growth in membership. Unions thus grow in chunks, campaign victory by campaign victory. Yet this is not the whole truth. In those states possessed of right-to-work laws, unions cannot move automatically from election win to total unionized shop. Members may be added, one by one, by continuation of persuasive processes, after the local union has been established. Membership may also drop off, as far as dues paying is concerned, and contributions may fall off to impressive lows. Thus there may be "plenty of room for improvement" or deterioration in the local situation after election victory. Also, local unions may grow or decline qualitatively with changes in intensity of identification with the organization and its principles. Or, election victory may not result in lasting establishment of a local union if the factory or mill involved closes down. And there are cases on record that show that management's failure to bargain in good faith may bring union election victory to naught. In the latter type of situation the process of appealing NLRB decisions to ever higher courts may stretch over so many years that the onetime local union membership has melted away.

This expansion by chunks or not at all is a peculiarity of labor union growth not shared by other social movements, such as those involved with matters of religious creed, reform, or protest. Unions can't add members here and there, few in numbers but strong in convictions, who band together to meet in each others' homes regardless of what the neighbors think, or who can pick up their belongings and move to wherever the colony has been established.

Nor can the union win new adherents through mere processes of selling, like the Fuller brush man may win customers, steady or otherwise, and herein lies another peculiarity of the movement. Representatives may have to sell, but they sell under conditions of vigorous counter-selling. As they offer potential members encouragement to join, someone else is trying to discourage joining, or has been coaching, in advance, resistance to union sales talk. It is not news that management groups, in general, are not favorably inclined toward unions, and that southern management, in particular, has a decided distaste for organized labor. Thus, union proselytizing involves not just two parties, but at least three: salesman, potential customer, and sales-discourager. In many campaigns, more than one product-knocking group becomes actively involved.

During the course of an organizing campaign the web of influences linked to union growth may become manifest. The campaign, as a sort of processual gateway, where facilitating and inhibiting forces converge and interact, thus bears watching. It is in the campaign that merchants, professionals, churches, newspapers, the unemployed, Negroes, police, and other groupings or segments of the population show most clearly the thrust of their impact on union fortunes. It is in the campaign that the lure of competing and/or conflicting affiliation possibilities for the mill hand is made evident: urgings to join the white race, the South, Christianity, and the United States of America. The groups that boost such affiliations may make their influence known, too. From campaign to campaign, over a span of time, the emerging or waning of influences is made apparent. New societal developments indicate their relevance to union prospects as they affect success or failure in the organizing process.

As a guest of the TWUA-CIO, I have had the opportunity to observe, in close-up view, a few organizing campaigns conducted in the upper South. This undertaking came to center chiefly on trying to account for the outcomes of campaigns. Perhaps my perceptions, intuitions, and speculations, restricted as they have been to a limited sector of the textile industry, may contribute to an understanding of the more general situation confronting the southern labor movement. Such a contribution, based on a casual but time-consuming "Ernie Pyling" on fighting fronts rather than a sharply designed questionnaire thrust at the heart of the problem, can claim little beyond the mere opening up of a subject. Since nobody else wants to open it up, perhaps that is value enough for the time and effort expended.

One may see the organizing campaign, that spearhead of the southern labor movement, as a struggle between management groups and union groups over interactional structures. In a given campaign, two groups lock horns in attempts to maintain or to alter social situations describable in terms of "social distance," including under that general concept dimensional distinctions of cultural, political, economic, and psychological as well as more narrowly "social" distances. The fight centers on the affiliations of the worker group, its nearness and farness in relation to the warring labor and management groups. In the organizing campaign both sides organize and both sides disorganize. They try to build or strengthen their own bonds with the workers at the same time that they try to destroy, weaken, or prevent the development of worker affiliation with the opposition. Both stake out the same claim over the same social territory; and for help in pounding and pulling stakes they cultivate or activate supporting groups: churches, business groups, other unions, police, lawmakers. Thus, the nucleus of labor and management troubadouring and cat-calling spreads to a wider field of intergroup relations.

Of course, changes have been going on within an evolving web of intergroup relations long before an organizing campaign is initiated. Just as the NLRB election may be seen as a phase of a larger event, the campaign, so may it be seen, in turn, as a phase of a still larger development, the evolution of employee-management relations within a changing setting of intergroup relations. With the blind forces of change that constitute the historical spinning out of the industrial revolution come the more immediately pre-campaign manipulations of the situation by union and management, processual interferences in the form of strengthening intergroup bonds and weakening those of the opposition. The beginning of a specific campaign may then mark an acceleration in the rate of change, at least an attempted acceleration, as the adversaries, neither content to let "nature take its course," struggle for control of situational "levers" at "strategic points of intervention."[22] The drift of evolution becomes application of human intelligence to compel or to prevent change. So many are the possible points of intervention, so various are the possibilities for attack, defense, and counter-attack, so multiform of terrain the scattered battlefields, that any attempt to predict the future state of the system, general or local, would be mere guesswork, extrapolation, or wishful thinking. In the words of Cassirer, who points to our incapability of anticipating the future development of civilization, "Human action is known only in its realization; only when realized are we aware of its living possibilities. Prior to its realization it is not restricted to a fixed and clearly delimited sphere of possibilities; indeed, its work is precisely that of seeking and creating ever new possibilities."[23]

A glance at reputed evolutionary changes in worker-management relations in the southern textile industry would seem to indi-

22. C. Wright Mills, *The Sociological Imagination* (New York: Oxford University Press, 1959), p. 131.
23. Ernst Cassirer, *The Logic of the Humanities* (New Haven: Yale University Press, 1961), p. 37.

cate development of conditions favorable to growth of labor union organization. A widening "gulf" between mill hands and mill management since World War I has been described by Cash.[24] This widening cleavage could be depicted in terms of shifting values along dimensional lines of the intergroup relationship. The growing gap would feature changing measures of consensus, or "cultural distance," and association, or "social distance." Other dimensions for provisional consideration as elements of distance in a metrical construction for analytic description of changing worker-management relations might include "power," "status," "service," "affection," and "dependency." The last-named would incorporate the shifting labor-market situation.[25]

During the past few decades, at least, textile management has been moving "up and out" of mill and community in the manner described by Warner and Low[26] in their attempt to account for the successful strike in and unionization of Yankee City's shoe industry. The movement has been from factory and village to "market square," meaning consolidation of manufacturing establishments under absentee top-management groups who exercise remote financial and policy control from a central locus. This exodus of top management has also represented establishment and strengthening of various outside connections that are now part of the web of influence affecting local management-worker relations. Along the channels of command emanating from remotely located authority has come the rationalization of work and work relations, wave after wave of efficiency procedures locally applied by professionally trained line executives and staff functionaries. These developments have, of course, been sparked by advance in the technology of manufacturing and transportation.

The combination of interactional features assigned to folk society in the folk-mass dichotomy might be more aptly labeled "benevolent paternalism." It all reads like "Life on the Old Manor,"

24. W. J. Cash, *The Mind of the South* (New York: Alfred A. Knopf, 1941), p. 261.

25. A discussion on these possibilities for construction of metricizable dimensions of intergroups relations may be found in my unpublished "The Labor Union Organizing Campaign: Toward Functional Analysis of Structure and Process in Intergroup Relations," a revised version of a paper read at the April, 1963, meeting of the Southern Sociological Society.

26. W. Lloyd Warner and J. O. Low, *The Social System of a Modern Factory* (New Haven: Yale University Press, 1947).

not like the folk societies described by anthropologists. The older order, characterized facetiously by union officials as "The mill by the rill and Uncle Ben on the hill," appears, indeed, remindful of the descriptive materials set forth by such historians as Funck-Brentano[27] and De Tocqueville[28] in depiction of manorial life during the "Ancient Regime" of eighteenth-century France. Although the "down on the farm" interaction between blue-blood country squire and his common clay serfs maintained rigid status and power distances it also featured informal give-and-take in the daily round of work, and jolly Saturday night festivities at the old manse when field hands joined the boss and his family at eating, swigging, singing, lute plucking, and general chummy relaxation.

The up-and-out movement of southern mill management and the replacement of Uncle Ben with college-trained officials has meant a shift in the quality of association from shirt-sleeved informality toward impersonal business relationships. It has meant, also, growing dissensus, as the application of means to increased efficiency has violated norms traditional to the work situation. The "stretch-out" is a case in point. The imposition of greater work loads on mill hands, it may be assumed, has been received by workers as a tipping of the balance of service reciprocity decidedly in favor of management. It is a prime source of worker disaffection in southern textile mills. As distance has developed, management has been the deviant group; mill workers have been the "homebodies." They have been the last to reaffiliate, to join or to threaten to join unions.

The Uncle Bens of yesteryear have not been long gone. They live in the fond memories of middle-aged and elderly mill hands who reminisce and make invidious comparisons in moments of relaxed conversation during organizing campaigns. One once-upon-a-time mill owner and manager was remembered with deep affection by several of his former employees as they recalled his kind deeds and apparent genuine affection and concern for them and their children during their times of personal trial and tribulation. As each conversationalist related his own especially remembered

27. Frantz Funck-Brentano, *The Old Regime in France* (New York: Longmans Green and Company, 1929).
28. Alexis De Tocqueville, *The Old Regime and the French Revolution* (New York: Doubleday Anchor Books, 1955).

experience with heartfelt praise for the never-to-be-forgotten "friend in need," his listeners would nod in solemn understanding and agreement. They agreed also in their condemnation and distrust of the incumbent manager and his "hatchet man" efficiency expert. In another conversational setting, union officials told with mixed amusement and dismay of the refusal of the workers of a Georgia mill to consider union affiliation as long as a certain beloved patriarch, a retired former owner of the manufactory, still lived. "He's retired, but it would break his heart if he heard that we joined a union," they said. After the death of this aged Uncle Ben, a union was voted in.

When management moves up and out, benevolent paternalism seems characteristically followed by one of two types or patterns of relationships. These successor types may be labeled "pseudo-paternalism" and "coercion." They become especially evident in the kinds of managerial activities evoked by the challenge of an organizing campaign.

Labor union organizers have a name for the kind of management-to-worker action characteristic of pseudo-paternalism: "sweet stuff." The "human relations" program of the kind considered by Barkin as providing obstacles to organizing should be so classified. In my own field observations, the application of sweet stuff has not had, however, an institutionalized look. The appearance has been of something whipped up on the spur of the moment with arrival of unexpected guests. The kind of sweet stuff distributed only during organizing campaigns, such as "love letters" from a top executive newly pining for his employees, or one-night-stand "Ol' Buddy" speeches from company presidents on election eve, probably would not yield the dimensional measures characteristic of pseudo-paternalism. Should classification of relationships be refined beyond my immediate intention, the quickie sweet stuff might be called "phony pseudo-paternalism."

In true pseudo-paternalism, management-worker dissensus has developed in regard to various matters, but the workers perceive the situation as one of consensus. Management words and gestures, through contrived public relations, or "dramaturgy,"[29] appear

29. Victor Thompson, *Modern Organization* (New York: Alfred A. Knopf, 1961), pp. 138-151.

representative of the old bonds of a genuinely personal nature; and workers perceive the relationship as one of "friendship." As Goffman[30] would put it, there is "role distance" in the behavior of management; and workers are "taken in." Management, like the philandering husband, has changed, but the stay-at-home spouse has not yet perceived this change.

In a coercive type of relationship, dissensus is recognized by both workers and management. Interaction is impersonal and mutually perceived as such. Negative sanctions are inflexibly applied by management upon discovery of disservices perpetrated by workers in the form of union activity. Employees are fired for detected or strongly suspected union leanings; there are warnings, threats, predictions of such counter-disservices in advance. Worker interest in union activity is thus checked not by positive sentiments toward management, but by fear of unemployment in a job-market situation of extreme dependency. With a large, visible labor surplus ready to snap up payroll vacancies, the mill worker does not have the alternative of affiliation with another employing group. As one scared pro-union worker put it, "What would I do for a living, pick wild blackberries?"

In a coercive relationship workers practice role distance. With hostilities covered up, the situation may give the appearance of harmony to the casual observer. Below the smooth surface of apparent continuity, the apparent equilibrium of the interactional system, major changes may be taking place.

The alienation of workers from management doesn't imply affiliation with the campaigning union. A break in one relationship isn't necessarily followed by a bond in another. Workers may be classified as satisfied or dissatisfied with the *status quo*. Those who find themselves alienated from management may or may not find union membership appealing. Those who are union-inclined may or may not dare to develop union affiliation. Those who dare to "go union," may or may not dare to declare themselves openly and work for the cause.

Union organizers are usually called to an organizing situation by workers who want a union and who assure union officials that

30. Erving Goffman, *Encounters* (Indianapolis: The Bobbs Merrill Company, 1961).

a majority of fellow workers share this desire. In order to win a necessary majority of votes, organizers, with the help of pro-union "actives," will try to convince the less enthusiastic that establishment of a local union constitutes a vital step on the way toward effective solution of the "management problem." In this persuasion process organizers try to articulate, widen, and develop alienation. By the use of printed leaflets, passed out at mill entrances, by house calls, and by mass meetings, union representatives point up and discuss various and sundry injustices having to do, in the main, with wages, work loads, lack of fringe benefits, and insecurity of employment. But increasing the distance between workers and management is not enough. At the same time workers must be brought closer to the union. The organizing task is more than de-acculturation and de-socialization; it is also re-acculturation and re-socialization.

In the attempt to develop worker-union consensus, organizers place themselves unequivocally on the side of higher pay, lighter work loads, more paid holidays, and job security—which is, of course, the side of the workers. Union affiliation is urged as a connection productive of service in regard to the desired values. Attempts to achieve perceived consensus cover a range of mores wider than factory matters. Organizers "key in" with norms that define general respectability. Leaflets and speeches feature pithy blessings by the prominent and impeccable, such as presidents of the United States and national senators. At mass meetings qualified gentlemen of the cloth give their blessings in person, and union speakers may spike their delivery with Biblical references. Organizers who feel that their dexterity with the scriptures is less than adequate can at least avoid conspicuous transgression of the mores by refraining from the social glass in public. The concern is, of course, for establishing and maintaining a broad base of moral consonance from which to project a program of worker re-acculturation in regard to values more central to the business of the union movement. The problem is to prevent a diverting of worker attention from the cultural closeness of worker-union concord on higher wages and reduced work loads to a distance-producing judgment that whatever the objective merits of more pay and less work, they represent in this instance crafty proselytizing of the devil. The problem is also sometimes wistfully conceived as one of reducing the antagonism of other groups in the community, or at least neutralizing, if not winning over, church, professional, and merchant groups who might otherwise serve as auxiliaries to management in the campaign struggle over worker affiliation. The problem, in its finer points, is also one of how much of the labor movement ideology and eschatology to soft pedal, or to jettison, in order to protect moral flanks against diverting and possibly devastating verbal raids.

Just as the union attempts to weaken management's bonds with the workers while at the same time it tries to build its own, so does management essay an antithetic strengthening and weakening of connections. By means of sweet stuff and promises of more sweet stuff to come, by employment terminations and portents of more terminations in the future, management draws attention to the desirability of its services, especially its payroll service, and to a demand for reciprocity in the form of adherence to codes of anti-unionism. Prevention or destruction of worker-union connections characteristically features the kind of name-calling that promises maximum effectiveness in putting the union beyond the moral reach of the workers. While union organizers, speakers, and leaflet writers stake out claims of respectability, value by value and norm by norm, management challenges these claims. The polar words that provide the ammunition for this challenge tag the union with a variety of ascriptions, relationships, and alliances, each one of which carries extreme disrepute; in combination they represent a depreciation that is massive. These designations link unions with race mixing, Yankee carpetbagging, godlessness, and communism. By implication, employment of such derogations points to pre-eminently worthy management affiliates: the White Race, the Confederacy, Christianity, and the United States of America. The industrial worker is invited to join these groups, or rather, to reaffirm and solidify already established memberships.

In several observed campaigns, workers received in the mail copies of a periodical entitled *Militant Truth*. To emphasize the principles and points of view expounded in its columns, this little magazine carried representations of the American flag and the Bible in the upper corners of its front page. To help readers weigh the pros and cons of joining unions it featured factual reporting and editorializing concerning the atheistic and communistic tendencies of nationally prominent union officials. Interviewed workers denied subscribing to the periodical and stated that management had denied subscribing for them. However, it was noted by union officials, as well as workers, that such mailings tended to come only during the course of organizing campaigns. During one campaign anonymous leaflets got into circulation; they presented a drawing of a drooling, ape-like creature of Negroid features, carrying a carpet bag with a "CIO" label. Its caption read: "I've come down here to organize you bastards."

The union's organizing task is one of re-socialization as well as re-acculturation. Indeed, in instances that have come to my attention, it is one of socializing from scratch. In the South there seem to be few, if any, already organized groupings of any appreciable size and cohesiveness to be incorporated en bloc into the union. The kind of experience reported by union officials in regard to the organizing of immigrant groups in northern cities, such as the "selling" of Italian immigrant leaders who then "delivered" their constituencies, does not occur in southern campaigns. Management's movement up and out of mill and community leaves southern workers without leadership. Groups that were once functionally relevant under traditional management's paternalistic leadership have disintegrated. No other basis for cohesion, for the rise of leadership, has appeared, and social isolation has become the lot of whatever small groupings have developed. Such isolation is especially striking in industrial communities where management-worker relations are strongly coercive. In one observed campaign, management's firings were so numerous and so effective that workers were extremely reluctant to communicate union sentiments with each other, even in such small neighborhood groupings as car pools. Union talk could not be developed, and organizers had to communicate with these workers on an individual basis, by house calls. Of course, mass meetings were out of the question. Such paralysis of communication is quite understandably to management's advantage. The voting situation on election day is so "scary," claim the organizers, that unless the worker can receive his ballot under conditions of strongly felt cohesion, he is likely to be afraid to vote union. Technically speaking, the organization of a union follows victory at the polls; actually, to win such victory, organization must precede the voting.

Thus, in their struggles to advance their movement in the South, labor union officials are faced with formidable difficulty, regardless of the quality of the worker-management bond. In some mills, where a paternalistic type of relationship is still maintained, it is virtually impossible to induce workers to cast votes for the union, Where management does draw away from its employees to establish pseudo-paternalistic or coercive types of relationship, workers either continue to perceive the shattered ties as still intact, or, in their lack of group cohesion, are easy to intimidate from developing interactional bonds under union leadership.

2

To speculate on the future prospects of the labor movement in the South is largely to speculate about possibilities of changes in inter-group relations affecting the outcome of organizing campaigns. Union fortunes will continue to be bound up in a struggle with management over the situational levers, and feeding into battles of wits and resources will be the blind forces of evolutionary change over which neither side will be able to exercise more than partial control.

When a longer and wider view is taken, possible future influences that now appear as separately evolving may be considered. Also, possibilities for manipulation of levers now overlooked may be examined. Some of these possibilities would appear likely to enter the campaign process as influences favorable to the union cause; others might be noted in advance as management assets. The balance in the long run, when both presently overlooked or eventually emerging influences are appraised, appears to be in favor of management. Since the long run, in this age of accelerating rate of change, presses ever harder on the short run, seems even to threaten to infiltrate it, unions will have to proceed vigorously with whatever immediate advantages lie within their grasp if the southern labor movement is not to come to a halt.

The expansion of unions in the South will depend, first of all, on changes in management's employee policies and the quality of management-worker cohesion that such changes bring about. Effective managerial procedures include a great variety of types of sweet stuff, ranging from "Successful Officers"[31] paternalism at the level of supervisor-worker relations to plantwide participation programs on the order of the "Scanlon Plan."[32] They include increasing material benefits to workers without regard for closeness in consensus, association, affection, or decision-sharing. With high pay and superficial communication, "alienation" can be "loyalty."[33] There are so many ways to skin a cat in regard to improving the management-worker relationship that it seems as if only the most obtuse management would resort to firing and threat of firing to keep the union out.

If management fails to accentuate the positive to develop cohesion with employees, but relies instead on reductive measures to hold workers in the interactional fold, then, in their attempts to win worker support unions would be faced with the difficult task of overcoming the fear of being fired, as well as rendering ineffective the mud-slinging that is sure to accompany intimidation practices. Union expansion would depend on improvement in campaign tactics. It would also depend on development and application of greater political influence for changing legislation and administrative practice at the national and state levels.

If the migration of industry from northern states brings unions, which, in some instances, it has done, then the organized workers might be used, across union lines, to reduce the fears of unorganized workers and to break the negative images of unions that they carry. This kind of organizing assistance has shown itself to be instrumental to union victory in several textile campaigns of recent years.[34] The upswing of TWUA campaign fortunes since 1961 may or may not be a straw in the wind portending massive breakthroughs in the near future.

During the course of one organizing campaign, I noted that the

31. David G. Mandelbaum, *Soldier Groups and Negro Soldiers* (Berkeley: University of California Press, 1952), pp. 15-25.

32. Frederick G. Lesieur (ed.), *The Scanlon Plan* (New York: John Wiley and Sons, 1958).

33. Chris Argyris, *Understanding Organizational Behavior* (Homewood, Illinois: The Dorsey Press, 1960).

34. "2-1 Vote Wins 637 in South: Dixie Belle Rug Workers Score Major Triumph," *Textile Labor*, 23 (December, 1962), 24 and 21. "Anatomy for an Election," *Textile Labor*, 24 (January, 1963), 3-5. Irving Kahan, "When the Spirit of Unionism Hit Canton," *Textile Labor*, 24 (November, 1963), 3-5.

unorganized workers listened with great respect to organized workers of other local industries. One worker told me in a group situation, when organizers were not present, "They [the organizers] shouldn't tell us what big wages they're getting in those northern factories. It doesn't make us for the union; it just makes us mad at the North. We know they're always getting the best of everything anyhow. But when one of our own friends or kinfolk who is a union man tells us what he is making, we listen to him." Assistance from organized labor might come in the form of pressure for revision of labor legislation. Thus far, such pressure has been vainly applied. A curbing of managerial methods of discouraging employees from engaging in union activities would reduce a major union handicap in the organizing process. However, if unions have reached a plateau of strength at the national level, as Barkin indicates, then further aid in the form of legislation might have to wait for an increase in strength that only further organizing can bring. Likewise, help at the state level, in the form of repealing right-to-work laws, would seem to depend on further organizational gains. Help from the national labor movement may come through pressures on the executive branch of the national government for shifts in the policy of the NLRB. Union officials regard NLRB decisions in regard to claims of unfair labor practices, such as the firing of employees for union activity, as critical to the success of organizing campaigns. According to union officials, the trend in NLRB policy has shown decided improvement since 1961, the year of a special investigation into the work of the NLRB by members of a House labor subcommittee.[35]

It is interesting to speculate on possible future linkages between the now rapidly developing Negro movement for civil rights and the now all-but-halted southern labor movement. Traditionally, the large Negro population segment has had a depressing effect on union organizing in the South. Although white jobs have been protected from the large Negro labor surplus by the color bar, that surplus has afforded a potential threat to the southern white worker. Not only have white workers and management found basis for consensus in their mutual rejection of the Negro; threat of possible job

35. "Not a Chance with the Boss, with the NLRB," *Textile Labor*, 22 (June, 1961), 3-5. "Dixie Workers Blast NLRB; Situation Called 'Shocking'," *Textile Labor*, 22 (June, 1961), 24 and 19.

replacement by the Negro has added to worker fear of risking managerial displeasure. And, by pre-empting low-status jobs the Negro has withdrawn from the white labor market the alternative jobs that might have provided employment insurance to those who would risk firing for union activity. Should the Negro emerge from occupational limbo to take industrial jobs now considered white, he may respond less fearfully to invitations for union affiliation. The confidence gained from battle experience on the picket lines and in marches in regard to his own social movement may be a critical factor here. The training that the working-class Negro is now permitted to receive in his fight against strong opposition may serve him later on in other struggle-group participations. So progress of the labor movement during the immediate years ahead may depend greatly on how union leadership handles the race question.

No attempt to appraise labor's future in the South can overlook the strongly negative promise of the accelerating pace of automation. A correlatively accelerating shrinkage of jobs may leave little left to organize. The migration of industry into the South may turn into a mere migration of automated machines. The Negro may finally emerge from occupational outer darkness into a world of no work.[36] Thus, if management's hold-the-line tactics can stall the further development of the southern labor movement until the installation of automated factories and the economy of abundance that such technological advance may bring, then that movement may never reach the height of the plateau achieved in northern and western regions.

Management's ultimate victory may be but a Pyrrhic one, however, if the problems that could have been solved in co-operative interaction at the "infra-structural" level get absorbed within the activities of centralized national government.[37] The waning of power of business and industrial management groups may follow soon upon the checking of labor's thrust, with decision-making eventually relinquished to the benevolent authoritarianism of a rising "meritocracy."

36. Gerard Piel, *Consumers of Abundance* (Santa Barbara, California: Center for the Study of Democratic Institutions, 1961).
37. Bertrant De Jouvenel, *On Power* (Boston: Beacon Press, 1962).

XI. SOUTHERN AGRICULTURE IN A COMMERCIAL ERA / C. E. Bishop

The dynamic character of the U. S. economy creates a need for continuous adjustment in the structure of its economic sectors. Economic development in agriculture is accompanied by improvements in technology, by changes in the kinds and amounts of resources employed, and by alteration in the number, size, and jobs performed by firms. In the process the incomes of persons employed in agriculture are affected importantly. This chapter discusses briefly the nature of agricultural adjustment, indicates how agricultural development has affected the competitive position of the agriculture of the southern region, and outlines some implications of further development.

1

Economic development makes its impact in agriculture through technological improvements in the production and marketing of farm products. The adoption of these improvements increases the productivity of agriculture, alters the costs of producing farm products, and creates opportunities for improvement in the organizational structure of agriculture.

Initially, agricultural development places emphasis upon biological innovations—upon the selection and breeding of improved varieties and strains of crops and livestock. Scientists concentrate upon identifying, adapting, and developing plants and animals with greater yield and product quality potentials. A major objective is to achieve increased production. Increased production is desired to meet food and fiber needs and to make it possible to release labor for the production of non-farm products. Biological innovations have been very successful in increasing the productivity of land and in making it possible for a man to produce greatly increased quantities of marketable products.

Chemical innovations in agriculture, like biological innovations, are oriented largely in the direction of increasing production per unit of land and labor. Innovations of this type concentrate upon the control of insects and pests, modification of the structure and of the plant food content of the soil, and improved functioning of the biological processes of plant and animal growth. The amount and quality of product per plant and per animal are increased. In the process, however, chemical innovations also enhance the productivity of labor and increase the amount of farm products which man can produce.

Perhaps the most important determinant of changes in the structure of agriculture has been mechanical innovation. The development and application of machine methods in the production and harvesting of farm products have greatly increased the amount of product which can be produced by a farm worker. Machine methods also have provided strong incentives to increase the size of farms. New machinery typically requires rather large outlays of capital. In view of these large investments, unit costs of production increase unless output is expanded to spread the overhead costs over a larger volume. In most instances, it is not profitable to purchase newly developed machinery and equipment unless the size of the business unit is expanded.

It should be emphasized that biological, chemical, and mechanical innovations tend to be specialized. Typically, they are applicable to the production of only one commodity or to the performance of only one task in the production of a commodity. For example, a mechanical cotton harvester can be used for cotton harvesting only. It cannot be used to harvest other commodities. Furthermore, if cotton is to be harvested mechanically, it should be planted and cultivated with this in mind. If new techniques are to be used efficiently in one phase of production, their use must be harmonized with technology employed in other phases. The results obtained from new technology depend importantly upon the use of complementary technology. Successful adoption of many innovations, therefore, requires specialized management and increases the premium placed upon the development of managerial skills.

Agricultural innovations generally are labor-saving and capital-using. They increase the productivity of capital relative to labor and encourage the substitution of capital for labor in the production and marketing of agricultural commodities. These changes have been so pronounced in U. S. agriculture that it has been possible to increase output greatly even though the use of labor has been decreased dramatically.

Economic development generates another set of forces which contribute to the adoption of labor-saving technologies. Economic development is characterized by relatively rapid increases in production as compared with consumption and, therefore, by increases in savings. Capital is accumulated and becomes more plentiful relative to the supply of labor. Consequently, the cost of obtaining capital, the interest rate, falls in comparison with the wage rate paid for labor. Since farmers seek to keep costs low, the fall in the price of capital relative to the price of labor provides them with an incentive to adopt labor-saving innovations. Furthermore, the increased availability of capital enables farmers to make this substitution. Economic development of agriculture is accompanied by increased capital investment per farm and by the employment of increased amounts of capital relative to the land and labor used in producing farm products.

In the early stages of agricultural development, a high proportion of the milk, eggs, fruits, and vegetables consumed on the farms is produced there. As agriculture develops, the increase in capital requirements and the growing complexities of management associated with biological, chemical, and mechanical innovations encourage greater specialization in the production of agricultural commodities. Production for commercial markets is emphasized. Farmers decrease the number of commodities produced and increase the size of each production unit. There are inherent, therefore, in modern technological progress strong forces which provide incentives for the farm firm to increase in size and to specialize in the production of a few commodities. This tendency toward specialization also is accompanied by a transfer of functions from farms to non-farm firms. Specialized firms develop which produce items used by farmers. Other specialized firms develop which process and market farm products. Farmers tend to concentrate upon certain tasks of production and depend upon others to perform other tasks. As a consequence of this specialization, the productivity of farm labor and management is greatly enhanced.

In the process of achieving greater specialization of production on farms, the structure of agriculture is radically changed. The size of the farm is increased, the number of farms is decreased, and there is a growing interdependence between farm and non-farm sectors of the economy. The lines between farm and non-farm plants become blurred. The separation of physical aspects of production and marketing increases the difficulty of co-ordinating production and marketing decisions. In some cases, that of broilers, for example, vertically integrated systems of production and marketing develop to facilitate co-ordination of decisions made at various levels. Farm and non-farm decisions become intertwined and planning is co-ordinated at all levels of production and marketing.

Changes in organizational structure, like other types of innovations, tend to be labor-saving. Specialization of function is encouraged by these changes, and the productivity of labor is increased. Innovations of an organizational nature especially increase the productivity of management, thereby enabling the farmer to expand output per unit of managerial time.

In summary, technological innovations of a biological, chemical, or mechanical nature, and innovations in the organizational structure of agriculture, all set in motion forces which provide incentives to increase the size of the farm firm. Furthermore, each of these innovations provides incentives to substitute capital for labor in the production of farm commodities. In this process the size of the farm not only is increased but it becomes more specialized and more directly related to non-farm sectors of the economy.

2

Since 1940, agricultural development has taken place at an unprecedented rate in the United States. Dramatic increases in farm output have been accompanied by rapid growth in farm supply, food processing, and marketing industries. This rapid development, however, has not been uniformly distributed among farmers nor among regions. Some regions have been favored by relatively low production costs, increased productivity, and improvements in income. Other regions and farmers have seen their competitive position degenerate as the result of the introduction of new technology, the development of new areas of production, or the development of competition from new products.

If a region had a monopoly on natural resources suitable for the production of a particular commodity and there were no close substitute products, it might safely disregard potential competition from other regions. The facts are, however, that intense competition is present or potentially present for all of the major farm commodities produced in the South. The region, therefore, is affected by developments which enhance the relative productivity of resources in other regions.

Agricultural development has taken place more rapidly in other regions than in the South. The nature of the development also has been somewhat different. The resource conditions in the South were not conducive to early mechanization of production. Much of the South is characterized by large amounts of labor, a preponderance of small land holdings, poor soils, and a climate which is conducive to rather heavy damage from insects, pests, and diseases. Initial emphasis in research and technological change in the southern region, therefore, was placed upon biological and chemical improvements which would enable the region to cope with the major impediments to increasing the productivity of agricultural land. Topographic and economic conditions provided a greater incentive for the mechanization of agricultural production in other regions.

The South lagged behind the rest of the nation in making agricultural adjustments in the 1920's and 1930's. The decline in workstock numbers took place much earlier and at a more rapid rate in the non-South than in the South. This earlier substitution of mechanical power for workstock gave a strong impetus to additional commercial production of farm products in other regions of the country. Labor productivity increased rapidly in other regions relative to the productivity of agricultural labor in the South. From 1939 to 1949 labor productivity per man-hour of farm work in the United States increased 62 per cent compared with an increase of 33 per cent in the Appalachian region and 55 per cent in the Southeast.[1] The greatest gains in productivity per man-hour were made in the wheat producing regions.

The earlier mechanization of production in other regions contributed to the rapid commercial development of agriculture in another important respect. The conversion from workstock to mechanical sources of power made it possible to transfer millions of acres of cropland and millions of man-hours of labor from the

1. *Changes in Farm Production and Efficiency, A Summary Report* (U.S. Department of Agriculture, Statistical Bulletin No. 233 [Washington, D. C., 1961]).

production of feed for workstock to the production of commercial farm products. In fact the major source of increase in farm output during the period 1920 to 1940 was the shift from workstock to mechanical power.[2] Since early machine methods favored other regions, their adoption weakened the competitive position of the South.

Many of the government agricultural programs instituted during the 1930's also strengthened the economic position of farmers in other regions relative to the South. This was particularly true of those programs which provided farmers with subsidies which increased directly with the size of the farm business. Since the South is characterized by small farms, the government payments to farmers in the region were small in comparison to payments made to farmers in other regions. Hence, the windfall gains received by farmers in other regions were more favorable to adjustment.

During the 1930's and 1940's southern agriculture also was subjected to increased competition from land reclamation and irrigation. Vast areas were reclaimed and irrigated especially in the West. A recent analysis suggests that "the main effects of western reclamation have been in the South, where perhaps $480,000,000 worth of production has been displaced . . . one farm worker for every twenty remaining in southern agriculture has been displaced by western reclamation."[3]

Over time, therefore, the competitive position of the agriculture of the South was weakened through changes in technology which increased the productivity of other regions relative to that of the South, by government policies and programs which encouraged the development of new regions of production for major commodities of the southern region, by a system of government payments based upon size of farm, by the development of new products which offer strong competition for some of the commodities traditionally produced in the South, and by the growth of competition from foreign producers.

Many farmers found it difficult, indeed, often impossible, to maintain the reorganizational capacity necessary to reorganize their

2. D. D. Durost et al., Changing Sources of Farm Output (U.S. Department of Agriculture, Production Research Report No. 36 [Washington, D. C., 1960]), p. 2.

3. G. S. Tolley, "Reclamation's Influence on the Rest of Agriculture," Land Economics, XXXV (1959), 180.

operations to take advantage of the constantly growing stream of improved technology. Farmers generally are frugal people. They have depended heavily upon internal financing for reorganization and expansion of their operations.[4] As capital requirements for modern farming skyrocketed, it became increasingly difficult to finance adjustments out of internal savings. The small undercapitalized farms of the region were subjected to particularly severe economic pressure. These farms found it impossible to maintain the rate of growth in income which characterized much of the U. S. economy. Consequently, during the 1930's and 1940's net income from agriculture per farm-operator family in the South fell rapidly relative to the net income per farm-operator family in the rest of the United States. It became increasingly apparent that extensive restructuring of southern agriculture was a necessary condition for increasing the returns for farm labor to a par with those received by comparable labor in other sectors of the economy. Faced with the complexities of modern management, the necessity to borrow relatively large amounts of capital for reorganization and expansion of farm size, and with prospects for comparatively low returns for resources employed in agriculture, farmers turned in large numbers to non-farm employment.

3

The increased competition from other regions exerted heavy pressures upon the agriculture of the South. Between 1939 and 1960, acreage of cropland used for crops in the South decreased 24 per cent. During the same period acreage of cropland used for crops in other regions increased 8 per cent. The Corn Belt, Northern Plains, and the Mountain areas all had large increases in cropland used for crops.

The prolonged period of relatively low returns for labor in agriculture encouraged heavy out-migration. Migration was heavier from the South than from other regions of the country. In each decade since 1920 the South has accounted for more than one-half of the migration from farms. Migration has been especially heavy from the low-income areas of the region. The rate of migration from

4. A. S. Tostlebe, *Capital in Agriculture—Its Formation and Financing Since 1870* (Princeton: Princeton University Press, 1957).

farms in low-income areas is about 20 per cent greater than the rate of migration from agriculture as a whole.[5]

The average annual rate of net migration from farms declined sharply from the decade of the 1920's to the 1930's but increased rapidly thereafter. During the 1950's migration from farms in the South increased rapidly and averaged 6.5 per cent of the population during the decade.[6]

The heavy out-migration of labor from agriculture during the 1950's was a major factor contributing to an alteration in the structure of southern agriculture. As the number of workers engaged in agricultural production decreased, there was extensive substitution of machinery for manpower. Commercial farming developed rapidly. Many farmers reorganized production, reduced labor supply, improved production and marketing efficiency, and greatly increased their income. During this decade the number of commercial farms producing $10,000 or more of products for sale increased 84 per cent. Meantime, the number of commercial farms selling less than $2,500 of products decreased 76 per cent.

During the 1950's the South made other significant improvements in its agriculture. It made gains relative to the rest of the nation in such important respects as a greater increase in farm output per man-hour of farm labor employed, a greater adjustment in transferring labor from farms to non-farm employment, rapid mechanization of some phases of farm production, and an improvement in the income position of farm families in the South as compared with farm families in other regions.

Capital investment per farm increased rapidly as farmers shifted to mechanical methods of production. During the 1950's the transition from workstock to tractors in the South was conducted with such speed that by the end of the decade the number of tractors per hundred workstock in the region was greater than for the rest of the nation. Mechanization greatly increased the productivity of labor, and sharecroppers were released in unprecedented numbers.

5. Gladys K. Bowles, *Farm Population, Net Migration from the Rural Farm Population, 1940-1950* (U.S. Department of Agriculture, Statistical Bulletin No. 176 [Washington, D. C., 1956]).

6. Vera J. Banks et al., *Farm Population Estimates for 1910-62* (U.S. Department of Agriculture, Economic Research Service Report No. 130 [Washington, D. C., 1963]).

The number of tenants also declined while the number of full owners and part owners increased.

These changes in resource use were associated with pronounced changes in the product mix in southern agriculture. The relative importance of crops decreased and the relative importance of livestock and poultry products increased sharply. There was a pronounced increase in the net production of all major classes of livestock and livestock products. Expansion in broiler and egg production was phenomenal. The region now produces a larger share of the poultry, eggs, beef, and pork than it did twenty years ago.

Production of corn and oats declined in the South, while the production of wheat and grain sorghum increased rapidly, especially in the Southwest. Production of soybeans increased in the Delta and in the Southeast. Cotton acreage and production moved from the Southeast to the West. Average annual production of cotton in the South during the period 1950-1960 was 6.4 per cent less than in 1940-1942. Average annual production outside the South increased more than two million bales per year during the same period. The acreage seeded to pasture increased sharply as livestock production expanded. This transition also was encouraged by the development of improved grasses which were adapted to the soils and climate of the region. More emphasis was placed upon the development of timber and wood products industries, and millions of acres were planted in trees during the decade of the 1950's.

In spite of the relative improvements that have been made in the South, the region experienced a smaller increase in agricultural output than the rest of the nation. The Appalachian region had the smallest increase in output of any region in the United States. Moreover, the gap in dollar per capita incomes of the South and in other regions widened, and the South now has a higher proportion of low-income, low-production farms than it had in 1950. Seventy per cent of the farms which produced less than $2,500 of products for sale are located in the South. Furthermore, one-fourth of all of the farms in the region sell less than $2,500 of product annually.

The productivity of labor in the production of the major commodities of the South remains comparatively low. The average size of farm business also is small. In 1959, 93 per cent of the tobacco farms and 78 per cent of the cotton farms sold less than $10,000 of products. These commodities, which represent the major cash commodities of the region, have not been subjected to the same degree of adjustment from technological and organizational innovation as have other commodities. Farms of these types will remain small and will be characterized by low incomes until the major jobs involved in production and harvesting of these commodities have been mechanized.

4

In spite of the high rate of out-migration from the South, the region still has a high replacement ratio compared with the rest of the nation. These high replacement rates will mean that the South will continue to be an area characterized by a large amount of underemployment of farm labor. The productivity of labor in the region remains low. If the income gap between farm families in the South and in the rest of the nation is to be closed, the kinds of adjustments which have been in process in the region during the past decade must be continued and even enhanced.

Capital accumulation on farms and farm adjustment are related to the age of the farm operator. A relatively high proportion of the farms which produced $10,000 of products for sale are operated by farmers in the older age groups. For the nation as a whole, it is expected that 150,000 farms of this size will become available to other operators during the present decade as a result of the retirement or death of farm operators. There will be approximately ten potential young farmers for each of these farms. In the South, however, there will be 17 potential young farm operators for each farm of $10,000 or more of marketings which will be vacated by its present operator through death or retirement during this decade. The potential supply of farm operators in the South, therefore, is quite high in relation to the number of high production commercial farms which will become available. Extensive transfers of labor from farm to non-farm occupations will continue during the 1960's.

On the basis of past experience it is possible to make regional projections to 1970 for the males who will remain on farms and who will migrate. There were 2.2 million males living on farms in the South in 1960 who were between five and sixty-five years of age.

Table 1. Regional Projections to 1970 for Males Remaining on Farms and Migrating off Farms (thousands).

Age in 1960	Number of 1960 rural farm males surviving to 1970	Number expected to be rural farm males in 1970	Implied off-farm migration
South, white			
5-14	470	188	282
15-24	338	59	279
25-34	178	112	66
35-44	248	194	53
45-65	457	414	44
Regional totals	1,691	967	724
South, non-white			
5-14	221	70	151
15-24	131	8	124
25-34	49	21	28
35-44	55	37	17
45-65	93	67	26
Regional totals	549	203	346
South totals	2,240	1,170	1,070

Source: C.E. Bishop and G. S. Tolley, "Manpower in Farming and Related Occupations," *Education for a Changing World of Work* (U.S. Department of Health, Education, and Welfare, Publication No. OE-80025, 1963), Appendix II.

Of these, 1.2 million are expected to be in the farm population in 1970, implying off-farm migration of 1.0 million.[7] See *Table 1.*

It is known that reduction of entry into farming in younger age groups is the predominant adjustment to a decline in total number of farms. Heaviest out-migration takes place among the group in the 15-24 age bracket. Consider, for example, the farm males in the South who were 15-24 years old in 1960. Only one in six of the persons in this age group who were farm residents in 1960 are expected to be on farms in 1970. On the other hand, more than 90 per cent of those who were forty-five years of age and older in 1960 are expected to be on farms in 1970.

The transfer of non-whites from agriculture will be at a more rapid rate than the transfer of whites. Only one in fifteen of the non-whites who were in the farm population and who were between 15-24 years of age in 1960 is expected to remain in the farm population in 1970.

The projected decline in the farm population and in farm

7. C. E. Bishop and G. S. Tolley, "Manpower in Farming and Related Occupations," *Education for a Changing World of Work* (U.S. Department of Health, Education, and Welfare, Publication No. OE-80025, [Washington, D. C., 1963]), Appendix II.

operator numbers in the South is greater than for other regions. This relatively heavy out-migration is expected to continue through the 1970's as labor is transferred from farms. The number of croppers and tenants will be decreased; mechanization of production will be increased; consolidation of units will be enhanced and the size of farm business will be enlarged.

Continued alteration of the structure of farming in the South also will be accompanied by additional changes in the product mix and by changes in marketing and processing. Shifts in the product mix of agriculture will continue to emphasize livestock products and other foods in comparison with the traditional commodities of the South. As these changes occur, greater emphasis will be placed upon marketing and processing.

The changes which have been outlined have their roots in technological progress, economic growth, increased incomes of consumers, and changes in the way consumers use their income. As long as society continues to make rapid changes in these important respects, agriculture will experience a need for adjustments. In view of the low-income position of agriculture in the South, adjustments in the region will be more extensive here than in the rest of the nation.

XII. EDUCATION AND THE NEW SOUTH /
Solon T. Kimball

Nations or regions which are committed to a pattern of self-sufficient, subsistence agriculture, or to a system of hand-labor, plantation production, do not create surplus wealth in sufficient quantities to pay the cost of a modern educational program for their children. These were the two methods of farming which dominated economic production in the South until recent decades. In retrospect, King Cotton may be viewed as a tyrant who depleted the soil resources and kept his subjects poor and badly educated.

The industrialism that began with the spread of textile mills in the 1890's and received new impetus from each of the two world wars in other areas of manufacturing triggered a transformation of certain portions of the South which is still accelerating. Among the consequences stemming from this change was the creation of economic resources which permitted the expansion of many public services, including education, but more importantly, the need and the desire for a modern educational system.

In recent years economists have been attempting to assess the contribution of education to economic development. There is agreement among them that it is considerable and essential and one of them, Galbraith, contends that much larger portions of our affluence should be channeled into education and other public services. The message is clear. Education, above all other functions, is the instrument through which the capabilities of a citizenry are developed that they may contribute to and participate in the material prosperity and cultural advancement of an urban, industrial world and in their own self-fulfilment.

But there are other consequences of these changes. Society is shaken up by the new organizational forms and cultural practices which come with an urban-industrial mode of life. In the South and elsewhere, the inequalities of race, occupation, and cultural ancestry which a traditional, agrarian system tolerated and perpetuated are challenged. But the educational system which fits the needs of a modern society discriminates on the basis of ability and motivation only. That some of these older distinctions linger on is to be as expected as it is that remnants of older agarian practices may be found in isolated areas, or that change in the educational system will also be uneven.

No problem, including the educational one, can be considered apart from the internal differences which divide the South into its contrasting and even antithetical cultures. They range from the primitive backwashes of the isolated pockets of humanity along coasts, rivers, swamps, and mountains to the ultra-modern industrial complexes of Atlanta or Houston. Within the cities themselves is a range which stretches from the areas of massed slum shacks to the suburban, split-level developments. These cultural distinctions express economic, educational, occupational, racial, and geographic divisions and for this reason no set of figures which attempts to set forth the condition of the South in any area of life can be interpreted other than as a gross but hardly adequate statement of fact for comparative purposes. Only when we begin to seek out the cultural clusterings will it be possible to view accompanying problems with clarity. The effort which such a detailed analysis entails is greater than the scope which the present presentation necessitates, but some broadly sketched differences will help to illuminate the internal intricacy of the problem.

Let us take soil fertility as the single criterion upon which we erect a superstructure of interpretation, knowing full well that in so doing we both oversimplify and distort reality, but that we also gain the advantage of a sharp perspective from which to view the present. The South was heir to two polar and antithetical cultural traditions from the old world. One of these, plantation culture, took root and flourished on the deep, rich soils of coastal plain, river valley, and delta. In its economic pattern of production for a world market and its division of labor into owner-overseer and worker, formal education for the unskilled majority of its members was unnecessary, and absent. That this untutored population was largely Negro was a consequence of slavery; that a large portion of the population in these localities continues today to be economically depressed and socially backward is a heritage of this past.

In contrast, the thin-soiled, rugged uplands of the Appalachians and the pine barrens of the sandy plains became home to another culture and another breed of men. These were the self-sufficient, subsistence farmers and appropriators of natural resources whose way of life was already deeply embedded in their European ancestry. That provisions for formal education among them were largely absent in the beginning, and eventually developed as a result of external pressures and with resources from outside the areas of their concentration, could lead us to conclude that here too there was little value in formal learning.

In neither of these two contrasting and divergent agrarian patterns could the acquisition of widespread formal education be counted as a significant cultural value. The consequence of this aspect of the cultural tradition extends, of course, into the present day. These are the areas of low educational expenditure and achievement, of endemic poverty, of outward migration, and of the possible absence or loss of the capacity to institute those measures by which their inhabitants can construct a viable way of life and enter into the mainstream of American culture. Consider for a moment the effect upon those averages which express per capita income, level of educational attainment, relief expenditures, and other evidences of the ill- or well-being of a population, if the population in these two subregions could be excluded from compilation of Census data for the southern states.

As we are only now beginning to recognize, the solution to the problems of this remnant population from an agrarian past resides as much within the orbit of national responsibility and policy as it does in states or localities. Fortunately, attention has now been directed toward the deplorable state of the primarily rural segments of Appalachia. The destitute of the older plantation areas deserve equal attention.

It is this older South which, in its stagnant and depressed state, has been and will continue to be a drag upon the whole until effective remedial measures can be instituted. These include capital for development, organization for planning and programs, and personnel with both social and technical skills. The educational problem here is of a different order than elsewhere and cannot be met outside general rehabilitative steps. But the contribution which education can make has been demonstrated in a number of experiments. Notable among these was the now-forgotten "Project in Applied Economics" in Kentucky, Florida, and Vermont, of the

Sloan Foundation of two decades past.[1] The principles applied and results achieved are as possible today as then. What would be of even greater value, however, would be to learn why a method that successfully used education for community improvement was also so quickly forgotten.

Statistical measures can tell us something about the educational pattern of a nation, region, or locality. Educators have long assumed that the major factor in producing quality education is the amount of money available. It is usually granted that adequate funds can provide good school buildings and equipment, attract better qualified teachers and administrators, and in other ways contribute to the excellence of educational opportunity. But it is also recognized that other factors intervene to affect the response of a school population to learning opportunities. Chief among these is the motivation children bring into the classroom. Motivation is a psychological quality which can be traced largely to community tradition and family background. The capacity to learn is another variable which is a function of the relation between genetic inheritance and cultural environment. There is every reason to believe that the population of the southern states possesses the same capabilities for successful response to formal education as that of any other population; thus any adverse or favorable manifestations of educational attainment are primarily an expression of the social environment and opportunity. It is within this context of understanding that statistics on education should be interpreted.

When we come to examine the indexes which express the existing situation, we discover that the southern states almost invariably fall at the lower end of any array of the states. This is a well publicized fact and has served as a goad to southern educators to wrest greater financial support from reluctant legislators. We have already warned, however, that such statistical averages can obscure the cultural divergencies and historical explanations embedded in the social reality of the present.

Let us select from the mass of available statistics a few that seem highly relevant to the present condition of the educational enterprise and to its future state. When we examine the listing, by states,

1. Clara M. Olson and Norman D. Fletcher, *Learn and Live* (New York: Alfred P. Sloan Foundation, 1946).

of the percentage of Selective Service registrants failing the mental test in 1961, we discover that fifteen southern and border states all exceed the national average of 23 per cent. Six of these—Arkansas, Georgia, Alabama, Louisiana, Mississippi, and South Carolina—had rates in excess of 40 per cent. In contrast, the fifteen states with the lowest percentage of failure were clustered in the upper Middle West—the central, mountain, and northwestern states with Utah, Washington, and Wyoming all having fewer than 5 per cent in the failing category.

Any attempt to explain this distribution would have to examine a great many variables including some for which the evidence is not at hand. But we cannot dismiss lightly the fact that the same group of southern states also claims the lowest ranking in those arrays which present years of schooling, per capita expenditures, personal income, etc. Since it is also likely that this relatively poor showing in the Selective Service mental test may be attributed to the larger proportion of Negroes in the sample population, a group that averages two years less formal schooling, it should be pointed out that West Virginia with a Negro population of 4.8 per cent ranked 39, and Kentucky with just over 7 per cent Negroes was 41. As further evidence that educational achievement is a primary factor in test performance, we note that these two states ranked 48 and 49, respectively, in an array based upon median school years completed by persons twenty-five years old and older as of 1960.

The real measure of the future, however, might be derived from an examination of those statistics which express the intent of a people to support and utilize the educational enterprise. The evidence here is not conclusive. In all respects the southern states show real improvement over previous years but when factors are examined on a comparative and nation-wide basis there is no consistent pattern and, in general, they seem to be barely keeping abreast of changes which are everywhere prevalent in the nation. *Table 1* demonstrates the wide variability.

This table is helpful as a rough measure of the existing situation. But it does not reveal the differential rate in years of schooling due to outward or inward migration, and the fact remains that the ten low-ranking states in median school years completed are all southern.

Table 1. Increase in Educational Attainment of Population 25 Years Old and Older, 1950 to 1960.

Order of ranking	Years
11. Virginia	1.4
14. Florida	1.3
17. Alabama	1.2
20. Georgia	1.2
24. Louisiana	1.2
28. South Carolina	1.1
29. Texas	1.1
30. North Carolina	1.0
39. Mississippi	.8
43. Arkansas	.6
47. Tennessee	.4
48. Kentucky	.3
49. West Virginia	.3

Source: Adapted from Research Division, National Education Association, *Rankings of the States,* 1963 (Washington, D.C.: National Education Association, 1963), Table 40.

The relatively unfavorable position of southern education is shown again in the expenditure per pupil in elementary and secondary schools. None approximates the national average of $432.00, and the nine states with expenditures below $300 are all southern. But, when the percentage increase over the past ten years is figured, we discover that Arkansas, Mississippi, and Alabama lead all other states and on the whole the South comes off rather well in the distribution as *Table 2* shows.

But when comparison is made with the period of the 1920's the transformation is nearly miraculous. The dollars available per pupil have increased between five and seven times over what was spent in 1929-1930.

When we come to examine the allocation of tax monies to education relative to other needs, and the amount spent on education in relation to personal income, the picture is far more encouraging. Southern states range widely when all expenditures for public education are expressed as a percentage of the expenditures for all purposes. North Carolina with 42.5 per cent and West Virginia with 40.9 per cent rank fourth and sixth respectively in the nation. Louisiana and Florida, the lowest, are 41 and 42, respectively.

Salaries paid to teachers continue to show great discrepancies. In general, those states that are more highly industrialized and urban pay the higher salaries. The southern states with a larger

Table 2. Per Cent of Increase in Estimated Current Expenditure per Pupil in ADA, 1952-1953 to 1962-1963.

Rank order	Per cent increase
1. Arkansas	153.8
2. Mississippi	128.2
3. Alabama	125.7
10. Virginia	95.9
11. Kentucky	89.7
12. Tennessee	87.7
13. North Carolina	81.1
23. West Virginia	72.0
24. Florida	71.8
25. Georgia	70.3
29. Louisiana	67.9
32. Texas	65.8
43. South Carolina	50.0

Source: Adapted from Research Division, National Education Association, *Rankings of the States, 1963* (Washington, D.C.: National Education Association, 1963), Table 83.

rural population, much of it economically depressed, pay lower salaries. Those in Mississippi are only 62 per cent of the national average (1962-1963), but over the past ten years the same state has led the nation in percentage increase, slightly more than double what they were in 1952-1953. All states with the exception of South Dakota have increased salaries by at least 50 per cent, and with the exception of West Virginia (53.9), the other southern states show respectable increases.

Comparatively, the brightest portion of the educational picture is found in the support of higher education. Louisiana, Mississippi, and West Virginia, all spend more per capita on higher education than the national average; and six states fall below Tennessee which expends the least of any southern state. Six southern states allocate a higher proportion of total state expenditures to education than the national average and none falls among the lowest ten.

But the direction of change in which an educational enterprise linked to urban-industrialism has been set may be expected to continue undiverted. All of the indexes which in the past have stirred southern educators and a supporting public to press for reform will continue to show the gradual improvement which comes from concerted effort. The illiteracy rate will be pushed to the vanishing point; per pupil expenditures will increase as new funds are made available for salaries, buildings, and materials. A larger proportion of students will graduate from high school and the number entering college will increase. Statistics such as the one which reveals that over the past decade southern universities have increased the proportion of awarded Ph.D.'s from 10 to 15 per cent of the national total may be expected to be commonplace. Nor may we expect that this accumulating evidence of progress will breed complacency.

The vital question is, however, are these evidences of continued advance good enough? Other sections of the nation are also deeply concerned about the educational system, and the energy and wealth that are being directed toward its improvement are enormous. There is the prospect of being forced to push ever harder just to keep up. The far more important question to consider, however, is whether or not it may be necessary to make some extensive changes, additions, and deletions in what we are now doing.

Anyone who has given attention to the turmoil which has surrounded the public discussions over education since the end of World War II can hardly do less than wonder what is happening. It is my own belief that we are in the throes of a largely unplanned and undirected reshaping (I hesitate to use the term revolution since it sounds too ominous) of our beliefs about the purposes of education, of our expectations of it for ourselves and our children, and of its modification in organization and operation. Perhaps if we recall some of the happenings in the recent past it will help in establishing a perspective to judge the present situation and a base upon which we might project the future.

During the decade of the 1950's a great hue and cry was raised about the adequacy of the education provided by the public schools. The consequences of the attack are nowhere better symbolized than in the precipitous decline of the esteem in which John Dewey was held. In 1949, a dinner honoring his 90th birthday brought testimonials of praise from around the world. Ten years later, he had been judged the evil genius who had insidiously permeated American education with progressive notions that made teachers soft on kids and the educational leaders soft on communism and soft in the head. But in all fairness we must also grant that there were men of knowledge and responsibility whose pungent criticisms of Dewey and the schools revealed weaknesses and exposed silliness that deserved concern and censure. Except for the occasional cry of alarm made by the radical right, the attacks have subsided and in their place we now have the serious analyses and proposals of a John Gardner, a James Conant, or a Martin Mayer.

However valuable the findings and comments of these men may be in correcting abuses and bringing desirable improvements in existing practices and in shaping public understanding, there are other forces at work which, in the long run, may prove more powerful as agents of change. The academicians, mostly men of science, have finally assumed a responsible concern for what happens in our high schools, and exploratory ventures have been directed toward the elementary grades. The physicists, led by Jerrold Zaccaharias, the mathematicians through the School Mathematics Study Group, and the biologists through the American Institute of Biological Sciences, have received the greatest publicity and had the most effect through the preparation of text materials and in the retraining of teachers in summer institutes. Through their professional societies, other disciplines have climbed aboard the band wagon and have received or petitioned for funds to institute similar programs.

Two aspects of this movement deserve particular note. Almost all of the funds which have supported these endeavors have been provided by the National Science Foundation. In an indirect and hardly publicized way the most significant modification in education in decades has been the responsibility of the federal government. The other important point is that professional educators have been largely excluded from initiating, promoting, or directing the changes. The consequences of their sidelines silence have yet to be evaluated.

This excursion onto the national scene has been a preliminary step to any specific consideration of the South, since in greater or lesser measure university people and educators of the southern states will also contribute to and be affected by the currents which are of nation-wide sweep. But there are some areas in which foresight and statesmanship will permit the South to capitalize on the forces now operating and to assume leadership. Being first is an honor that in most instances those of us who are competitive will relish. To be first in this instance is not just for that purpose, but because the demands and the potentialities of an industrial society point in this direction. The reorganization of education will require imaginative, aggressive, and dedicated leaders who unite men from many segments of the society in common endeavor. If efforts are successful it will require adjustments in the educational enterprise and in its relation to community and institution. Some of the realignments, particularly in the universities, may be painful, but since institutions of higher learning are pivotal in our kind of society in a way that was not true in the past, it is they who must carry the greatest responsibility and burden.

Those who are engaged in the educational enterprise in the South have an unusual opportunity to contribute to its further development. These efforts include much more than eliminating the deficiencies inherited from an agrarian past. They should include striking out in directions which are clearly indicated by current trends but where desirable goals have not yet been clearly formulated. I wish to draw attention to four areas which I believe to be crucial and which offer opportunities for accomplishment.

Sufficient evidence has now accumulated to allow us to believe that most of the learning acquired during the first two years of college can become a responsibility of the high schools. In other words, the coverage of the present twelve-year program should be extended to include what is now considered equivalent to a junior college education. The basis for such a conclusion is contained in a recent study which summarizes results from many sources.[2] These show that a program which combined the advantages of technological advance with increased expenditure, lengthened school year, the methods of teaching which hundreds of experiments have shown to be effective, and the requirement for greater student effort outside formal course work, can bring a gain of as much as 30 to 40 per cent in the quality of education which might be realized.

My second proposal is related to the problems which arise when a society is in transition from agrarian to industrial organization. On the one hand there are the rural rejects whose simple manual skills are unneeded, and on the other there is the demand for skilled technicians, semiprofessional, and professional workers in great numbers. The shortage of those with skills impedes further develop-

2. Harold F. Clark, *Cost and Quality in Public Education* (Syracuse, New York: Syracuse University Press, 1963).

ment and the surplus of the unskilled acts as a drag on the whole system.

The problem has not gone untended and the establishment of vocational training schools and introduction of agricultural and home economics training, in the past, into the high school curriculum have all helped some. But the situation has changed since the days when these programs were initiated. What is needed now is something quite different. Vocational training courses should be relegated to the do-it-yourself category for preparing boys and girls to assume the household chores they will face after marriage. Training that prepares for jobs must be of a different kind. It should be primarily technical and should be organized in conjunction with types of local industries.

High school training, however, is only the first step in the production of the skilled workers which industry and public services need. The answer to this problem is the establishment of residential, two-year, post-high school technical institutes that would give training in mechanics, electronics, vehicle maintenance, medical technology, and other such subjects. Today the nation possesses only a handful of such institutions, partly because industry has assumed some responsibility in training, and partly because of the difficulties of overcoming the older vocational tradition.

If that cadre of skilled workers which is necessary to the operation of services and industrial processes in the new South is to be available, then the educational system must be organized to provide this new form of training.

The third proposal is one which capitalizes upon a movement that has already gone far. Many public universities and a few of the private ones are no longer exclusively, nor even primarily engaged in the education of students. Through legislative appropriation and mandate, foundation and federal grant, and privately arranged consultation, their staffs do research in and sponsor programs in all areas of life and across the face of the globe. The organizational restructuring to accommodate these new functions is expressed in the bureaus, centers, services, and institutes which have flourished. Equally important, the regular instructional staff of each institution harbors a wealth of talent in the arts, humanities, and professions. Together these specialists constitute a cultural, scientific, and professional resource that no community, except the largest metropolitan center, could otherwise support. There is probably no group in the world that gives so generously of its time and talents to the requests of a surrounding region. It is my contention that we should consciously recognize the situation for what it is. Universities possess two major functions, that of providing graduate and undergraduate education, and that of providing centers for scientific, intellectual, and cultural development. In fact, it is the only organizational type (except museums) which provides an alternative to the commercialized entertainment and cultural influences which flow through the mass media concentrated in the great population centers. It seems to me that the conscious development of this public function, fully recognizing the problems and the costs, is not only an opportunity but a responsibility.

My last proposal is perhaps more crucial than the others because its consequences can be more far-reaching and fundamental than the more specific programmatic ideas advanced earlier. Stated simply, it is that a comprehensive and massive program of research be launched in the field of education. There is little need to argue the value of research to social scientists but its value is less clearly seen by many lay and professional people, including educators. In other sectors of American life, relatively greater attention is given to research than in education. Research and development funds in industry now exceed 15 billion per year, and the figure of 5 per cent of the gross income of an industry has been set as an optimum figure for expenditures in this area. The total estimated amount spent on education in this country exceeds twenty billion dollars a year, 5 per cent of which would be one billion. In contrast, the amount now spent from all sources in educational research probably does not exceed ten million dollars or just one one-hundredth of the sum which should be available if we approximate the industrial segment. Our national experience has proved that sums spent in research in health, agriculture, and industry return far greater dividends than any other form of investment. It is reasonable to expect that the same proportionate attention given to education would bring about comparable improvement in the quality and effectiveness of the educational enterprise.

I should like to suggest some specific areas in which there is great need for study, but first I would like to comment upon the kinds of research which have attracted educators in the past. Educators share with those in the professions of medicine, law, and religion, a great innocence about the concepts and procedures of research and experimentation. This naïveté is quite understandable if we consider that their training emphasizes the practice of an art, not its investigation. Nevertheless, a good many hundred researches in education have been made on such subjects as the relation of class size to learning; methods of teaching spelling, mathematics, reading, foreign languages, and other subjects; the relation between cost and quality of education, and between quality and size of community. Although the findings are oftentimes confusing and contradictory, the results, nevertheless, have given a sanction of "scientific" authority to those who advocate one method or another. Most of what may be labeled sophisticated educational research has been the work of psychologists who have concentrated almost completely on problems of learning in the tradition of E. L. Thorndike.

If educators are naïve about research procedures, they are not unenthusiastic about what they think research can do for them. In fact, some school budgets now assign a modest sum of 1 per cent of the total budget to what is labeled a research function. However valuable the activities which are carried on under this heading may be, most of us would hardly consider the results as scientifically sound. My point is that the need is great and that a warm welcome awaits those who will venture into this field. I think, however, that the problems we choose should be other than those which have been most popular with educators. Our attention should be directed to fields in which we are most competent, the cultural and social aspects of education. Let me suggest a few broad areas in which we might produce some startling and significant findings.

In a society such as ours, which depends so heavily upon an organized and deliberate education of the young, we really ought to know a great deal about the process of the transmission of culture. For example, what are the optimum conditions for learning? What is the difference between the rote acquisition of knowledge, a process that creates the quiz-kid mentality, and the development of understanding? The point has long been accepted that with cleverly applied rewards and punishments any animal can be trained to do almost anything. The conditioned reflex of Pavlov and the reinforcement theory of Skinner are based upon sound empirical research. But no matter how hard Skinner tries, he can never train a pigeon to construct an experimental situation which rewards or punishes a Skinner. There is real danger that if we accept this model of learning teachers will act like miniature Skinners and their students like pigeons. Gregory Bateson has made the point that the capacity to learn is itself learned, and the mysteries of this process still await our efforts at unravelling it and translating the findings to the teaching process and classroom materials.

A second major problem has usually been defined as one of determining the differentials by which children of varying social classes respond to formal education. Our attention was first directed to this area by Warner, Havighurst, and Loeb, in their *Who Shall be Educated*. Subsequent research by members of the Committee on Human Development at the University of Chicago has added greatly to our knowledge. The studies by Davis, Havighurst, and Hollingshead are among those which have attracted attention, but other than making educators aware of the problem relatively little has been transferred to the teacher-training process or to the work in the classroom.

The easy explanation has been that children from the lower classes find the environment of the schools, a middle-class institution, an unfavorable one. One proposed solution has been to create an educational formula for each social class, although no one has really dared to do so since this would immediately raise cries of discrimination and unequal treatment. Furthermore, there are too many exceptions to accede to this easy solution. There are middle-class children who also find the schools a punishing situation, and there are some slum schools where the academic results are startling.

If we accept the premise that success in academic training is essential for success in our kind of world, then the objective should not be to create a lower-class curriculum which in its de-emphasis of cognitive learning would perpetuate the values of that class. The problem is to determine what is there within the middle-class culture which favors the child from that group in the classroom, and what is in the cultural pattern of the working class which inhibits the success of their children. For those who come from the culture of poverty there is need to learn how to pierce the barrier which prevents these children from almost all learning except to identify teachers with a hostile world. Recently an experiment in Montgomery County, Maryland, has shown how complex and difficult is the problem of lifting the children of poverty from their slough of perpetual ignorance, but progress has been made and we may be on the right track.[3]

The school, as an ongoing institution, offers a third research area. Of the half-dozen major studies we now possess, not one was conducted in the South, and in those we do have, the emphasis is upon students rather than upon the total situation. Although the organizational terrain of education now remains largely unexplored, when we become ready to explore systematically its dimensions our research methods utilized in industry and hospitals will be fully applicable.

My concern with new research in school organization is not based on intriguing theoretical problems but upon the need of educators to learn what is happening to the educational process as a result of rapid expansion of administrative control in education. We can do no more than speculate at the moment on the effect which the rigid bureaucratic structure of New York and Chicago has upon the functioning of the teacher in the classroom, but a school system and its community, in which one-third of the students become truants each year, is not healthy.

One should not exclude the university as a suitable locale for organizational study, but any criteria for determining urgency do not give a high priority to this field.

Finally, social scientists should join with educators in research and experimentation of the effect of new technological devices. Visual aids, radio, television, and teaching machines have yet to be programmed into the objectives of education. Trial and error is a

3. Carla Eugster, "Field Education in West Heights," *Human Organization*, 23 (1964), 235-244.

slow and costly process and our approach should yield more effective understanding.

The program which I have sketched here is an ambitious one. It will require substantial sums of money, trained personnel, and facilities, all of which are in short supply. What then can be said about how to organize and plan?

Several successful co-operative ventures in education in the South offer models that might be copied, or applicable segments of each might be joined in a new combination. For example, the Southern Regional Education Board offered an opportunity for institutions of higher learning to share common problems. In the Research Triangle Institute several institutions jointly possess facilities which under ordinary circumstances could not have been acquired by any one of them alone. The medical centers at several universities bring together teaching, laboratory, and research facilities which range the gamut of biological, physical, and social science. Enough instances have been cited to show the possibility.

To sum up, we may expect that educational development in the South will be much the same as for the rest of the nation. That is because the newly emergent, metropolitan-scientific society is one which calls for a curriculum emphasizing the capacity to solve problems and a school organization which guarantees great autonomy in the teacher-learner relationship. But the situation is also different. There is no need to repeat some of the mistakes which have attended the monstrous growth of bureaucracies in some of the larger cities, and there is the unfinished business of an inferior education predominant in the traditional agrarian population. Extra efforts calling for resources beyond those available on the local level must be directed toward these depressed areas. Within the period of a single decade the improvement could be remarkable.

Meanwhile, an organized and consciously directed program should be gotten under way which would assist in the modernization of the curriculum and the teaching process. Some of the objectives of such a program have already been presented as proposals. These include the intensifying of educational effort in the first twelve years to achieve a level of attainment equal to that of the junior college, the conversion of presently constituted vocational courses for other purposes, and the creation of new, two-year, post-high school, technical institutes.

The academic aspects of higher education have not been a concern of this analysis. Relatively, the public institutions have received a generous share of tax monies, and medical and scientific education has been especially favored. It is contended here that the undeveloped contribution of the universities is in the use of their personnel and facilities as cultural and intellectual resources for the benefit of the people of the region. There is no desire to detract from the considerable efforts now being made, but to call attention to the potentiality.

Finally, educational change should no longer be a product of copying what is being done elsewhere, nor of intelligent insight to known needs, but should be based in the solid results of research. Research alone cannot provide answers to all the educational problems that need attention, but for health, agriculture, and industry, it has proved to be the most powerful instrument we possess to provide the basis from which intelligent change can be initiated. Social scientists occupy a particularly strategic position from which this effort may proceed, for they possess the experience and the research methods that are needed.

                                   ·   ·   ·

To discuss education in the South without extensive analysis of the changes which are necessary in order to conform with the Supreme Court decision which declared segregated schools illegal, and of the related civil rights movement among Negroes, seems hardly realistic. That problem is related to but not central to the transformation of the South. Denial of equal access to preparation for or participation in the new and emergent society has no relevancy in sex, race, age, or other comparable attribute. It has been assumed that such discriminations as still linger on from an agrarian past will gradually be dissipated, for the broad course of development has already been set and will not be denied.

XIII. THE ROLE OF HIGHER EDUCATION IN THE CHANGING SOUTH / Allan M. Cartter

1

"The university is a social instrument for investment in Man," wrote Sir Eric Ashby in his presidential address to the British Association for the Advancement of Science in 1963. A discourse on the role of higher education and the evolution of social organization might add to Ashby's dictum: Higher education is also a human instrument for investment in society. These two tenets broadly define the function of the higher learning in modern society—its role in passing on to contemporary man the essence of knowledge, both practical and humane, garnered through the ages, and its role in preserving and perfecting society through the preparation of successive generations for the performance of a complex society's myriad tasks.

A nation's colleges and universities have three major tasks to perform, dealing with the past, present and future: (a) to assemble, store and transmit the accumulated knowledge of the past, (b) to distribute practical contemporary knowledge through the development of skills and the training for professions, and (c) to shape the future through the encouragement of free inquiry, experiment, and innovation.

The first of these tasks is identified with the great liberal traditions of education, the education of the whole man. Emphasis is placed upon the classical disciplines, the study of earlier cultures, the language, history, literature, philosophy, and science which constitute our intellectual heritage. This education in the scholastic tradition aims at the formation of those qualities of mind and spirit which will enhance man's *humanitas*. Such an education, in the words of Cardinal Newman, "gives man a clear conscious view of his own opinions and judgments, a truth in developing them, an eloquence in expressing them, and a force in urging them." Liberal education, concluded Newman, "makes not the Christian, not the Catholic, but the gentleman."

The second task of education, in developing and transmitting contemporary knowledge and skills, is essentially utilitarian. It may be broad and "liberal," in the sense of training the well-rounded man, or it may be narrower in preparing for particular vocations or professions, but its justification is its usefulness for meeting the more mundane tasks of life. At its highest, utilitarian education trains man's faculties of judgment, not just his memory of factual knowledge; it emphasizes the ability to grasp problems, to pose searching questions, and to meet new situations.

The third major task of higher education is to foster creativity; in the words of Alfred North Whitehead, "The task of the university is to create the future." In this role the college or university must be the home of free inquiry, of critical thought, of research and scholarship. Professor and student are involved in the real process of discovery, of molding the future from the materials of the past and present. This is by far the most demanding role, the most difficult to perform, and the most sensitive to the aspirations and climate of opinion of the society of which colleges and universities are an integral part.

Every institution of higher learning performs each of these roles in some degree, whether it be the vast multipurpose university, the private liberal arts college, or the public teachers' college. In the university they are "indissolubly united," in the words of Karl Jaspers. "One cannot be cut off from the others without destroying the intellectual substance of the university, and without at the same time crippling itself. . . . By isolating them, the spirit of the university perishes."[1] The liberal arts college may give primacy to the first of these tasks, or the teachers' college or institute of technology to the second, but no single task can be well performed without attention to the other two.

2

Historically the role of higher education in the South can be analyzed according to the functions outlined above: the roles of colleges and universities as transmitters of tradition, instructors in the serviceable arts, and as creators of the future. In various nations and regions in various historical periods, higher education has performed these tasks ill or well in light of the evolving needs of society. Oxford and Cambridge of the seventeenth century and the late nineteenth century, Glasgow in the last half of the eigh-

1. Karl Jaspers, *The Idea of the University* (London: Peter Owen, 1960), p. 54.

teenth century, Göttingen, Berlin, and Bonn in the nineteenth century, the French universities in the late Middle Ages, all left distinctive marks on contemporary society and helped to shape the subsequent development of their nations or regions. Harvard and William and Mary in the early eighteenth century were the alma maters of many of the most distinguished statesmen of the Revolutionary period, although the latter just after the turn of the nineteenth century and the former at mid-century were of more dubious distinction.[2]

In the South, the history of the impact of higher education on the social and political structure of the region can be divided into three major periods: 1694-1830, when collegiate education was both fostered and respected, 1830-1920, when higher education rather passively reflected the withdrawal of the South from the main currents of American intellectual thought, and 1920 to the present, representing the new emergence of education symbolized by the growth of major universities. Even a decade ago it might have been too early to identify the most recent period as an intellectual renaissance, but it now seems apparent that the root-system of southern university tradition is sufficient in most states to withstand the present racial difficulties.

3

In the period prior to 1830 the South made fine beginnings in developing collegiate institutions. Just fifty years after the founding of Harvard College, after many years of proposals and plan, a royal charter for a college was granted in response to a petition of 1691 by the General Assembly of the Virginia colony. The second college of the American colonies, the College of William and Mary, opened shortly after 1693. Founded primarily for the training of ministers of the Gospel in the established church of the motherland, it attracted students from a wide area during most of the eighteenth century.[3] When college instruction was added to the lower schools,

2. See the extensive correspondence of Jefferson covering the period 1805-1815 when William and Mary was in dire straights and sought to move to Richmond, and *The Education of Henry Adams* (Boston: Houghton Mifflin Co., 1961).

3. The College of Philadelphia founded in 1740 (later the University of Pennsylvania), was frequently thought of as an Anglican college in colonial days, although it did not have official ties. The majority of the Board of Trustees were Anglicans, although the original Board also included a Roman Catholic priest.

shortly after the reorganization culminating in the Statutes of 1727,[4] William and Mary became noted as one of the foremost of the nine colonial colleges.

William and Mary is of particular interest to the academic historian. In the period from the revised Statutes of 1727 to 1776 it was essentially an institution self-administered by the faculty senate, perhaps the only college in this country to have experienced this degree of autonomy. After its reorganization at the close of the Revolution, control by the Board of Visitors was re-established, although the college never regained its relative position of eminence. Owing to a combination of unimaginative leadership, poor climate during the five or six hot months, removal of the seat of government to Richmond, and its reputation as a college for wealthy Episcopalians, the College of William and Mary declined notably after the turn of the century. Jefferson opposed the proposed move of William and Mary to Richmond, and felt that a new beginning would have to be made to create a leading southern institution of higher education.

The boldest educational venture of the new nation—and perhaps the most noteworthy attempt to create a major university from scratch in this country until the founding of the Johns Hopkins University and the University of Chicago in the latter part of the nineteenth century—was the founding of the University of Virginia in 1819. Jefferson's plans for a truly national university, based on a broad liberal curriculum with alternative programs of study, estimated to cost $300,000, and intended to attract a distinguished faculty from Europe, were visionary. Jefferson hoped that he would be remembered in the annals of history as the founder of the nation's first university even more importantly than as President of the United States. Although the University of Virginia did not fulfil all of Jefferson's dreams, it remained the most distinguished institution in the South for nearly a century.

Shortly after the Revolution, two southern states, Georgia and North Carolina, founded state universities. The dominant pattern that prevailed in the Middle and Far West seventy-five years later had its small beginnings in Athens, Georgia, in 1785 and in Chapel

4. See Richard Hofstadter and Wilson Smith, *American Higher Education: A Documentary History* (Chicago: University of Chicago Press, 1961), I, 33.

Hill in 1789. (The University of Georgia did not receive appropriated funds from the state government until 1881, and therefore was not fully a public university in the modern sense.) The South, which at the end of the century became a strong supporter of public education, thus set the stage at an early date. Referring to public education in the nineteenth century, Howard Odum has noted that "Its [the South's] failure to reach a higher level than it did, or to excel in the development of great universities, is in character with its relative achievements in other cultural fields. . . . Before the Civil War the South got a slow start toward public education because its aristocracy did not believe in education for the Negro and for the masses."[5]

During the colonial period and the first fifty years of nationhood, the history of southern collegiate education is very similar to that of the Middle Atlantic and New England states. In this period there was little that was peculiarly "southern" about its colleges, and students moved North and South with relative ease. Church affiliation was probably more important in the choice of a college than was geography; until the turn of the century the Unitarian, Congregational, or Presbyterian young college student, regardless of his home, journeyed to Cambridge, New Haven, or Princeton for his advanced education. It was only as the northern states became more democratic in their traditions and the southern traditions became more aristocratically entrenched that the early unity of educational ideals and practices was lost.

4

After 1830 the South rapidly developed a sense of regional homogeneity which separated it from its northern neighbors. At root the separatist movement reflected southern agrarianism, as opposed to the growing commercialism and industrialism of the North, as well as the growing dependence upon an economically justified biracial class structure. Increasingly the wealthier families of the South distrusted education of their sons in the unsympathetic environments of Cambridge or New Haven and sought to expand educational opportunities closer to home. During the 1840's and 1850's

5. Howard W. Odum, *The Way of the South: Toward the Regional Balance of America* (New York: The Macmillan Company, 1947), p. 215.

the South erected what might be called an intellectual protective tariff, giving greater stimulus to the founding of new academies and collegiate institutions within their region. Even a casual reading of the charters and early documents of southern colleges founded in this period indicates the growing feeling of isolation from the Middle Atlantic and New England states and a distrust of non-indigenous intellectual currents.

A generation earlier Jefferson had advocated the founding of colleges in the new United States so that American youth could be spared the "disillusioning" and "corrupting" experience of university education in the Old World. The student returning to the Old World

> learns drinking, horse racing and boxing. . . . He acquires a fondness of European luxury and dissipation, and a contempt for the simplicity of his own country; he is fascinated with the privileges of the European aristocrats, and sees, with abhorrence, the lovely equality which the poor enjoy with the rich, in his own country; he contracts a partiality for aristocracy or monarch; . . .[6]

After 1830 similar sentiments (with less emphasis upon dissipation, and more on unsympathetic political views) were expressed in relation to sending young southern men north for their college years. Bishop Leonidas Polk of Louisiana, in stating the case for the establishment of an Episcopal university in the South (the University of the South, at Sewanee, Tennessee) stressed in 1856 the common complaint that "our children are expatriated or sent off to an inconvenient distance [for their college education]; beyond the reach of our supervision or parental influence, exposed to the rigors of an unfriendly climate, to say nothing of other influences not calculated, it is to be feared, to promote their happiness or ours."[7]

The North Carolina *Standard* in 1856 carried a bitter essay noting that

> The importance of emancipating our young men from the baneful influences of the North—and nowhere is this influence more zealous-

6. Thomas Jefferson to J. Bannister, Jr., on Education in Europe, 1785. See E. W. Knight, *A Documentary History of Education in the South Before 1860* (Chapel Hill: University of North Carolina Press, 1950), II, 4-5.

7. Statement in New Orleans, July 1, 1856, quoted in Rev. Telfair Hodgson (ed.), *Reprints of the Documents and Proceedings of the Board of Trustees of the University of the South Prior to 1860* (Sewanee, Tennessee: University of the South Press, 1888), pp. 4-14.

ly exerted and powerfully felt than in the Northern colleges . . . has taken firm hold on our people; . . . Can North Carolina tell the world that her seminaries of learning are free from the corrupting influences of black Republicanism, and Southerners can receive Southern education unmixed with instructions hostile to the feelings and opinions their parents have instilled into them? . . . *We must have certain security, under existing relations of North with South, that at State Universities at least we will have no canker worm preying at the vitals of Southern institutions.*[8]

In the first decade of the nineteenth century probably half of the college graduates in the South had attended northern colleges; by the time of the Civil War this proportion was apparently less than a quarter. Until 1860 about 15 per cent of the students enrolled at Harvard were from the states which later constituted the Confederacy. At Yale in 1830, 72 of the 555 students enrolled were southerners, although the number dropped to 33 by 1860. At Princeton nearly half of the student body were southerners, 98 out of 227 in 1840, 115 out of 236 in 1850, and 113 out of 312 in 1860.[9] The strength of the Presbyterians, and the high value they traditionally placed on education, accounted for the continued popularity of the College of New Jersey at Princeton up to the eve of the outbreak of war.

Hofstadter has described the impact of social change in the North and western frontier on the democratization of education.

With the development of an open society during the early decades of the nineteenth century and with the coming of greater social, political and geographic mobility—with the development of all those tendencies that have been roughly and rather inaccurately designated as Jacksonian democracy—the inherited educational system began to be challenged. American society was too democratic to accept completely the idea of a gentleman's education, too practical and perhaps too philistine to accept complacently its classical content, too dynamic and competitive to accept indefinitely its static character.[10]

Despite Jefferson's early plans for the University of Virginia with its greatly liberalized curriculum and its appeal to a broader

8. Letter by John A. Englehard, a law student at the University of North Carolina, reprinted in Hofstadter and Smith, *op. cit.*, pp. 466-469.
9. See E. W. Knight, *op. cit.*, pp. 248-249.
10. Richard Hofstadter and C. DeWitt Hardy, *The Development and Scope of Higher Education in the United States* (New York: Columbia University Press, 1952), p. 22.

class of young men, southern education after 1830 became in many
ways less democratic. In the generation preceding 1860, southern
collegiate education, with a few notable exceptions, turned inward
and increasingly became a bulwark protecting the social and political *status quo*; it became more aristocratic, placing greater emphasis
on the education of a social elite and on conformity of thought and
behavior. As Nicholls puts it, the finer old traditions of the Tidewater aristocracy "went into a rapid decline, carrying with it the
last barriers to a spirit of conformity and intolerance already incipient in the South."[11]

After 1830 the greatest expansion in higher education in the
South was in the newer church colleges. As Philip Lindsley, president of the University of Nashville during the 1830's, complained:
"Almost every sect will have its college, and generally one at least
in each state. Of the score of colleges in Ohio, Kentucky and Tennessee, all are sectarian except two or three; and of course few of
them are what they might and should be; and the greater part of
them are mere impositions on the public. This is a grievous and
growing evil."[12] Only a few years earlier Jefferson had expressed
his concern for the effects of religious intolerance on education,
noting that the atmosphere "is charged with a threatening cloud of
fanaticism, lighter in some parts, denser in others, but too heavy in
all."[13]

The combination of the expanding influence of the churches in
higher education and the growing intensity of the slavery/abolition
issue acted as deterrents to freedom of inquiry and of expression in
southern colleges. The trial of President Thomas Cooper of the
University of South Carolina in 1832 for his anticlerical and Jeffersonian political views and the dismissal of the professor of
chemistry by the trustees of the University of North Carolina in
1856 for supporting Colonel Fremont, are but two outstanding
examples. The latter, Benjamin Hedrick, a North Carolinian by
birth, pleaded in his defense:

When I was a student in college [the University of North Carolina

11. William H. Nicholls, *Southern Traditions and Regional Progress* (Chapel
Hill: University of North Carolina Press, 1960), p. 133.
12. From the baccalaureate address in 1829, reprinted in Hofstadter and Smith,
op. cit., p. 233.
13. Letter to Thomas Cooper, November 2, 1822, Jefferson Manuscripts, Volume
223, Library of Congress, Washington, D. C.

about 1850], a few years ago, the young politicians used to debate
in the "Halls" of the societies, the same questions which the old
politicians were debating in the Halls of Congress. The side which
opposed slavery in the abstract, generally had the books in their
favor, and as the records of the societies will show, they had quite
often "the best of the argument." ... So that when Colonel Fremont
said that he was "opposed to slavery in the abstract" ... he but ut-
tered the sentiments of four-fifths of the best Southern patriots from
the Revolution down to the present day; and I may add the majority
of the people among whom I was born and educated.[14]

The concepts of faculty tenure and academic freedom were not
commonly accepted (or at least not strongly protected) in the
nineteenth century. The strength of feeling in the South on the
issue of slavery was so great by mid-century that the intellectual
nonconformist had no place in the southern college or university.
As social, religious, and political tolerance waned, so higher education languished. The only safe college subjects were the classical
curricula, the only "safe" historian was one who could discover
"the romantic message of the Old South." The new traditions were,
in the words of Ronald Howell: "to seal off the South as a vacuum
package, to reject all that seemed 'alien' or 'subversive,' to despise
and fear 'efficiency' and 'newness' and 'industrialism' and 'progress'
as diseased imports from the North—these were the sentiments that
then permeated the Southern campus, no less than the Southern
home, church, courthouse, and marketplace."[15]

The right of dissent, self-criticism, and tolerance were common
to the principles on which the colonies were founded, to Jeffersonian
democracy, and to Christian ideals. Yet the South, rich in its colonial
heritage, Jeffersonian in its ideals of statehood, democratic (in the
pre-Jacksonian sense), and devoutly Protestant, in the space of
hardly more than a generation became distinctive for its conform-
ism in behavior and political thought and its intolerance in spirit.

5

The War and its immediate aftermath, including the dismissal of
old faculties and the substitution of unwelcome "Reconstruction

14. *James B. Sprunt Historical Publications*, ed. J. G. Hamilton and H. M. G.
Wagstaff, Vol. X, No. 1 (Chapel Hill; University of North Carolina Press, 1910),
pp. 13-14.
15. Louis D. Rubin and James J. Kilpatrick (eds.), *The Lasting South: Fourteen
Southerners Look at Their Home* (Chicago: Henry Regnery Co., 1957), p. 152.

professors," left higher education in the South in an almost non-existent state. It was 1875 before the University of North Carolina finally reopened, 1880 at the University of South Carolina, and 1881 before the University of Georgia was reorganized under the auspices of the state government. Until the turn of the century growth was slow, and the colleges and universities chiefly reflected the desire of southern society to recapture the traditions of its earlier "golden period." This period, insofar as it was truly southern and not merely colonial or early nation-state, had lasted hardly more than a generation (roughly 1820-1860); it had actually been a period of rapid transition, both economically and politically, but it became enshrined as a fixed image of an age which the South wished nostalgically to recapture.

Until nearly World War I, higher education in the South suffered from a combination of forces—lack of money, reflecting the lower levels of per capita income and wealth in the region, lack of understanding of the function of the higher learning, lack of experience, lack of motivation—resulting in what Howard Odum called regional immaturity.[16] He noted that a particular southern characteristic was that "education reflects far more of the effect of politics, religion, and sectionalism than it appears as modifying influence upon them."[17] The colleges and universities played little creative role in molding the cultural and intellectual life of the postwar South; it would be closer to the truth to say that they mirrored society's (a narrow, regionally defined society) concern with its past rather than helped it to face its future.

One of the few exceptions to this generalization was the experience of Washington College (now Washington and Lee), which is one of the rare instances in the history of American higher education where a former military officer has made a significant contribution as a college president. Robert E. Lee's brief five years as an educator stand out as a beacon in an understandably intemperate South of the Reconstruction period. "I consider the proper education of (the South's) youth one of the most important objects now to be attained," Lee wrote in a letter to be used in soliciting funds for Washington College, "and one from which the

16. See *Southern Regions of the United States* (Chapel Hill: University of North Carolina Press, 1936), p. 503.
17. *Ibid.*, p. 507.

greatest benefits may be expected. Nothing will compensate us for the depression of the standard of our moral and intellectual culture, and each state should take the most energetic measures to revive its schools and colleges, and, if possible, to increase the facilities of instruction, and to elevate the standard of living."[18]

During Lee's brief tenure, Washington College introduced departments of agriculture, chemistry, commerce, and journalism, and expanded engineering into civil, mechanical, and mining. The plan for work in commerce, organized around studies in the basic social sciences, was a half-century ahead of its time, and the small college inaugurated the first "working" school of journalism in the United States. If the South had followed Lee's pattern in the postwar decades, as it had during the war, the history of collegiate education in the region might have differed greatly.

From the viewpoint of the three major functions of higher education discussed earlier, the period from roughly 1830 to 1920 saw great emphasis upon tradition (although not necessarily the traditions of classical thought), little emphasis upon training in the utilitarian arts, and almost no concern with the creation of the future. One might have thought that technical training in the various scientific and technological fields would have been a "safe" alternative, for the South greatly lagged behind in education for science, engineering, and agriculture, but these remained the weakest areas of education in all but a few institutions (e.g., Washington and Lee).

The South had fought Morrill's proposals for educational land grants in the 1850's, and it was only after the secession of the South that Congress finally enacted such legislation. The southern state universities were ultimately to be among the major beneficiaries of these land grants, but the grants were accepted with little enthusiasm in the latter third of the nineteenth century. Despite the heavy commitment of the southern economy to agriculture, no land-grant college of major stature emerged in the South until after World War I. And despite its great need to develop technological awareness and know-how among its best educated young people,

18. Letter of March 20, 1866, quoted in Douglas S. Freeman, *R. E. Lee: A Biography* (New York: Charles Scribner's Sons, 1949), IV, 258.

no university of national stature in the sciences emerged until nearly the middle of the present century. As late as 1936 Odum could write that: "Until very recently there was nowhere in the whole region a college or university science building or laboratory equal to many of the high school laboratories in the larger and better school systems of the country."[19]

In the fifty years following the close of the Civil War, the South wasted its best intellectual resources. Its colleges, acquiescing to immediate social and political pressures, by and large accepted only those on their faculties who would conform to local modes of thought. As Nicholls notes, "the result [was] 'safe' enough, but only at the expense of analytical ability, social conscience, and personal courage—all desirable attributes in a superior university faculty."[20] State universities had little choice in view of the political sentiments of their immediate constituencies; most private colleges and universities were equally narrow in their sectarian views. Not atypical of contemporary religious pressures was the famous case at Vanderbilt University in 1878 when the church intervened to dismiss Professor Alexander Winchell, a famous biologist of the day, because of his views on evolution. The Winchell case caused Andrew White, the President of Cornell to remark: "What an idea of a University those trustees must have! What was tragical in Galileo's case is farcical in this. . . . Very hard to see that the world progresses any, if, instead of being in the hands of a Roman Catholic Cardinal, we are to fall into the hands of a Methodist Bishop."[21]

Summarizing the ninety-year period ending with World War I, it could be said that higher education played a passive role in the evolving attitudes and culture of the South. By and large the colleges were the servants of society, not its tutors; they were a link with the past, not a gateway to the future. Not until the beginning of the twentieth century did the South begin to muster its resources to support education at all levels, and only gradually did the climate for free intellectual inquiry begin to prosper.

19. Odum, *op. cit.*, pp. 516-517.
20. Nicholls, *op. cit.*, p. 149.
21. Hofstadter and Smith, *op. cit.*, p. 848. It is interesting to note that a public institution, the University of Michigan, came to Winchell's rescue and offered him a chair. He later organized and was president of the Geological Society of America.

6

The modern history of higher education in the South begins only
in the second or third decade of the twentieth century. Within a
period of twenty years the South began to emerge from its provincialism, as evidenced by a number of aspiring universities. The
University of Virginia, which for one hundred years had managed
without any strong central administration, appointed its first president and began to rise above its finishing-school-for-gentlemen
reputation. The University of North Carolina emerged as a university of recognized national stature, "the home of liberal traditions" in the South. The magnificent bequest of James B. Duke in
1926 to Trinity College laid the foundation for a major private university in the region. Vanderbilt, freed of its restrictive sectarian
ties, moved rapidly to the fore with imaginative leadership. Emory
moved to Atlanta and became a university, and the Rice Institute
opened in Houston. The University of Texas began to develop
strong departments of graduate instruction. In many other areas
considerable progress was made, even though by comparative
standards the gap between the major national universities and many
of the state universities in the South remained great.

The credit for setting the pace in the development of southern
universities goes to the University of North Carolina, which under
the able leadership of President Francis P. Venable moved from
a sleepy little inbred public college of some repute, hardly larger
in 1900 than in the decade before the Civil War, to a small scale
but full-fledged university of quality and reputation by the beginning of World War I.

During the presidency of H. W. Chase (1919-1930) the University of North Carolina came to the fore as *the* outstanding southern university, a position it held without challenge until the last
decade. Under Chase's leadership, and that of his able successor
Frank P. Graham, the University clearly set its sights on the attainment of high national standards. "For him [Chase], to attain 'the
best in the South' fell far short of the mark. He was convinced that
if the South was ever to compete successfully with other parts of
the country in dealing with the complex problems of the Nation it

would have to provide training for its youth equal in every way to that which was available to youth elsewhere."[22]

Despite marked progress, however, as late as 1936 Howard Odum could observe:

Here are the facts, which, for the most part, the educational South appears not only unwilling to face but continues resentful of their presentation. It is not only that the region has no university of the first ranking, but it lacks college and university scholars and administrators of topmost distinction, measured by the usual standards of achievement and recognition . . . it lacks a reasonable number of endowed institutions sufficiently free from state or church dominance to function independently in the best manner of university standards and sufficiently well endowed to set the pace for other regional universities and to keep interregional and national influences and participation constantly on the scene. . . . The region has no educational administrative leaders who participate freely in the nation's councils of learning or who have access to its larger sources of endowment and support.[23]

Looking back from the vantage point of 1963 it is apparent that rapid progress has continued since 1936, and most particularly in the last five or ten years. Six of the forty-one members of the Association of American Universities are southern institutions: North Carolina, Virginia, Texas, Duke, Vanderbilt, and Tulane. While none of these would rank among the first fifteen universities in the nation in overall quality and prestige, all are strong and aspiring second-rank institutions (see below). The five major southern *private* universities have each selected new presidents within the last five years, and in each case they have searched for the most outstanding prospect regardless of regional or religious affiliation. It would have been inconceivable a generation ago that Tulane would have chosen a scientist from the University of Illinois, Rice a distinguished physicist (and member of the National Academy) from the University of California, Emory a biologist who was provost at Cornell, and Duke a humanist from Lawrence College (and formerly Yale). Only Vanderbilt chose a southerner as its new chancellor, and he is a scholar of national distinction who was concurrently being sought for a major northern presidency. At another level, the recently

22. Louis R. Wilson, *The University of North Carolina, 1900-1930: The Making of a Modern University* (Chapel Hill: University of North Carolina Press, 1957), p. 596.

23. Odum, *op. cit.*, pp. 513-517.

selected president of the American Council on Education, which represents all the universities and colleges in the country, was formerly chancellor at the University of Texas. To name only one professional area with which the author is well-acquainted, Duke and Vanderbilt have provided three presidents of the American Economic Association within the last ten years. One could continue to cite instances of progress in southern higher education, not only at the university level, but in the rising stature of many of the South's liberal arts colleges. These evidences do not yet add up to a conviction that the South has fully attained desirable national standards in all areas, but they are evidences of a marked renaissance.

7

Granted that considerable progress has been made in raising the quality of higher education in the South since World War II, what is the situation at present? How far must it go to close the gap between it and the rest of the nation?

The South, with just over a third of the nation's college-age youth, had only a quarter of them in college in 1960. Of the 219 universities offering the doctorate in 1960, fifty-seven were in the sixteen southern states represented in the Southern Regional Education Board. The most recent study of graduate education grouped institutions by quality and reputation.[24] The only institution among the top two groups, totalling twenty-two universities, was Johns Hopkins (hardly to be classified as a "southern university"). But interestingly, in the next category of twenty-seven institutions there were ten southern universities. Of the eleven institutions from the SREB area among these first forty-nine, eight are private universities, and only North Carolina, Texas, and Virginia represent public institutions. These figures suggest that, by and large, the southern states until recently have not been willing to make a sufficient investment in public higher education or to make an adequate commitment to quality.

In many of these states large investments have been made in facilities, which are physical monuments to education, but far too

24. Bernard Berelson, *Graduate Education in the United States* (New York: McGraw-Hill, 1960), p. 126.

little has been invested in the faculties—the human capital—which represent the bloodstream of the university.

Few pay their collegiate faculty much better—if as well—as some public school systems do in other regions of the country. For example, the average compensation of full-time faculty at the Universities of Alabama, Arkansas, Kentucky, Mississippi, and South Carolina was less than $8,250 in 1962-1963.[25] Only one institution in the entire South achieved an "A" rating on the AAUP "average faculty salary scale" in that year, and only Virginia and Rice achieved a "B" rating. Among the "C's" were only Florida, Georgia, L.S.U., North Carolina, Tennessee, Texas, Tulane, and Vanderbilt universities, and only Davidson, Hollins, Sewanee (University of the South), and Washington and Lee among the colleges. The average full-time faculty compensation for the state universities of the Old South (i.e., former Confederate states) was $8,690; for the state universities of the Midwest it was $10,070.[26] Only Duke University (with average compensation of $12,296) has fully accepted the challenge to meet national salary standards, recognizing that this is the only means of attracting and maintaining distinguished scholars.[27]

Few state universities in the South spend as much each year on acquisitions for their libraries as they do putting their football teams on the field. (Somewhat ironically, it is only in varsity athletics that southern universities have fully met or surpassed national standards.)[28] Only Duke, Texas, North Carolina, and Virginia have

25. For this, and the following data, see "The Economic Status of the Profession, 1962-63," *AAUP Bulletin*, 49 (Summer, 1963), 141-187.
26. This figure was $11,170 for Berelson's first ten institutions in the nation.
27. The next ranking universities in the South were: Virginia ($11,020), Rice ($10,518), Vanderbilt ($10,084), Tulane ($9,628), and Texas ($8,944). North Carolina would fall within this group, but salary data are not publicly available. The situation is bleaker in the class of liberal arts colleges. The South has approximately two hundred of the roughly eight hundred liberal arts colleges in the nation. On the AAUP average salary scale these institutions rank as follows:

| | Number of Colleges: | |
AAUP Salary Rank	United States	South
A	6	0
B	28	0
C	76	4

More than 62 per cent of faculty members in the country were in institutions with an average scale of "C" and above; not more than 5 per cent of southern college and university faculties were in such institutions.
28. This is not an economic argument, for football may show a financial profit, while a library has only the knowledge gained by students and the scholarship of the faculty to show for its cost. Rather this is a comment on the relative scale of

university libraries today that are fully adequate for high quality graduate education and research across the spectrum of disciplines (and each has weaknesses in a few areas), although the joint library of Vanderbilt-Peabody-Scarritt, Florida, Kentucky, L.S.U., Tulane, and Rice (in its areas of specialization) are strong in most disciplines. In a recent year Duke, Rice, Emory, and Vanderbilt among the major private universities, and Virginia, Texas, and North Carolina among the public institutions, spent between $30 and $50 per student on library acquisitions, while a few of the private and half of the public universities spent less than $20 per student.[29] (In the same year Harvard spent $56 per student, and Princeton over $100.)

In 1957 Hayward Keniston of the University of Pennsylvania queried department chairmen in twenty-five leading universities (including Duke, North Carolina, and Texas) asking them to rank order the strongest institutions in their field of study.[30] In the overall ratings no southern university appeared among the first twenty listed, although North Carolina had been eighteenth in a similar study conducted by R. M. Hughes in 1925.[31] In the division ratings Duke was fifteenth and Texas nineteenth in the biological sciences; and North Carolina nineteenth in the social sciences; no southern institution ranked among the first twenty in the physical sciences.[32]

In a recent unpublished study attempting to measure the quality of approximately eight hundred liberal arts colleges using a number of quantitative indexes, no southern college was among the first

values placed on the two enterprises. About half a dozen state universities in the South spend no more than $15 per student on annual library acquisitions.

29. See American Universities and Colleges (8th ed.; Washington: American Council on Education, 1960). The southern liberal arts colleges fare somewhat better on this measure; of the 157 colleges spending more than $15 per student on library acquisitions, 39 were from the South.

30. Graduate Study and Research in the Arts and Sciences at the University of Pennsylvania (Philadelphia: University of Pennsylvania Press, 1959); see Appendix, pp. 115-150.

31. A Study of the Graduate Schools of America (Oxford, Ohio, Miami University, 1925); summarized in American Universities and Colleges (1st ed.; Washington: American Council on Education, 1928). See also his follow-up studies: "Report of the Committee on Graduate Instruction" of the American Council on Education, printed in the Educational Record XV (1934), 192-234, and A Study of American Graduate Schools Conferring the Doctorate, 1937-38 to 1941-42 (Ann Arbor: Edwards Brothers, 1946).

32. By discipline Duke ranked eleventh in botany, twelfth in economics and fifteenth in political science; North Carolina ranked eleventh in classics, eleventh in music, eighth in romance languages, and eighth in sociology; Texas ranked ninth in German and tenth in linguistics.

group of thirty-six, although five of the next twenty were from the South (interestingly, two of the five were predominantly Negro colleges).

Another reflection of the quality of undergraduate education is provided by the percentage of undergraduates who go on to earn the doctorate in some academic field. For the better liberal arts colleges in the country this percentage is currently about 10 per cent, and about 7½ per cent for the better universities.[33] In a recent study the leading southern universities came out as follows: Rice 13.5 per cent, North Carolina 5.8 per cent, Duke 4.9 per cent, Texas and L.S.U. 4.5 per cent. The average for the southern universities was approximately 4 per cent. Among the liberal arts colleges no southern college approached the 10 per cent level, although twenty had more than 5 per cent of their graduates who went on to earn the doctorate (as compared with 113 colleges in other regions of the country).

Even as late as a generation ago it might not have mattered too greatly if a region lagged considerably in academic salaries and physical facilities. The "hardware" fields of science and technology, where laboratories and equipment are so essential to quality education and research programs, had not risen to their present eminence nor appeared as critically necessary to the economic development of a region. Academicians had not yet quite become "twentieth-century nomads," and their sense of allegiance was frequently more to their native region and its institutions than to the nation. All this has changed markedly with improved transportation and communication, with the great expansion of higher education, and with rapid economic development.

Today few public universities in the nation have as many as half of their graduate students from within their own state, or as many as three-quarters from within their region; few private (other than

33. The raw data for doctorates by baccalaureate origin have recently been published by the National Academy of Sciences—National Research Council in *Doctorate Production in United States Universities: 1920-1962*, publication #1142 (1963). A study has been made by the present author comparing doctorales granted in 1960-1962 with baccalaureate degrees granted seven years before, by institution. To allow for the varying proportion of women in undergraduate colleges, and the considerably smaller number who go on to advanced study, women graduates have been divided by five before calculating the percentages. See also Robert H. Knapp and Joseph J. Greenbaum, *The Younger American Scholar: His Collegiate Origins* (Chicago: University of Chicago Press, 1953), for a similar measure.

urban) universities have a quarter of their students from within their state or half from their own region. Upon completion of graduate studies the young teachers, scholars, and researchers disperse to the four winds, since the market for these specialized talents today is truly national rather than regional. Despite the fact that the South is a "net importer" of these specialized talents, producing about 7 per cent of the nation's doctorates and employing between 10 per cent and 12 per cent of persons who have recently obtained the doctorate, in many of its universities more than half of the new Ph.D.'s take posts outside the region.

The mobility of academic talent is of major importance in the creation of a national culture—of a national, rather than purely sectional economic, social, and political milieu. An institution in any region of the country which aspires to excellence must actively enter the national market for outstanding faculty, for promising graduate students, and to some extent (although of lesser import) for undergraduate students. It must be willing to meet national norms for academic salaries, to meet national standards in the protection of academic freedom and the right of free inquiry, and to compete on the national level for grants and fellowships from national agencies. The day of the outstanding regionally-oriented college or university disappeared with the coming of jet plane travel, national telephone service, national television networks, and national professional associations. While many persons may grieve over the implicit costs imposed on society by these evidences of rapid material advance, this is the world in which we live, and the world for which our colleges and universities must prepare the next generation of students.

8

The South has retained a sense of regional separateness from the rest of the nation longer than other regions for many reasons— among others, its particular congeries of physical resources, the memory of its earlier attempt to secede, the continuing problem of its biracial social structure. Until the end of World War I, higher education in the South did little to counteract these factors; indeed, it by and large acted as an intellectual buffer against change.

The South tended to live in its past, and the colleges and universities did little to point the path to a new future.

The picture changed sharply after World War I, and much of the tribute must go to three or four successive presidents of vision at the University of North Carolina, and the support which their faculty and the state legislature were willing to give them. Similar aspirations for a great university were soon evident in Texas, and the bequest of James B. Duke created overnight the potential for a great private university. Over the ensuing decades the climate gradually changed in most of the southern states as an increasing number of both public and private universities aspired to become nationally recognized institutions.[34] These developments helped to create a climate for the rapid progress of the smaller colleges of the region.

To a considerable extent institutions of higher education are mirrors of the society which they serve, but they can reflect the worst aspects of their environment as well as the best. With restricted financial support, suspicion of intellectual endeavors, and dictation of policies by external groups, no college or university will prosper or make a significant contribution to the culture or the economy of its region. However, given generous support, the encouragement of intellectual freedom, and a sufficient degree of autonomy and protection from external constraints, higher education can provide the requisite human resources and attitudes of both mind and spirit essential to meeting the challenges of the future. Only in recent decades have the evolving social attitudes of the South begun to foster, rather than to hamper, the development of higher education in a manner which would both permit and encourage its significant contribution.

In the decade of the sixties there will be five or six private universities and an equal number of public universities in the South vying for a place on the national scene. It is a tribute to this new spirit that the best of the southern colleges and universities have

34. Perhaps the one person who most clearly illustrates this evolution in aspirations is Howard W. Odum, the most constructive—and often severest—critic of the South he loved. The organization which receives major credit, not only for support of Odum's work (through the Social Science Research Council) but for lifting the sights of educators and citizens and helping materially many of the developing universities, is the General Education Board throughout its long history of activity in the South. This heritage has now passed to the Southern Regional Education Board.

taken desegregation in stride with hardly a ripple. There remain a few "closed societies," but these are islands in the South, no longer the mainland. In most states the foundations of higher education are now firmly enough implanted not only to withstand the buffeting of immediate social pressures, but to provide the precept and example for the constructive resolution of such problems.

As a new and vigorous South emerges, it is nowhere so evident as in its colleges and universities. In a progressive society aspirations always exceed accomplishments, but Jefferson's dream a century and a half ago for the higher learning in the South is now on its way to fulfilment.

XIV. THE SOUTH IN POLITICAL TRANSITION / Allan P. Sindler

As of this writing in late 1963,[1] it is widely believed that if Senator
Barry Goldwater of Arizona becomes the Republican presidential
nominee in 1964, his ensuing election strategy would be to attempt
to carry most southern states together with enough others, mostly
west of the Mississippi, to garner the required majority of electoral
votes. Major-party conventions carefully assess the election prospects of competing aspirants in determining their nominees. Therefore, when we find that the Senator generally is conceded to have a
good chance of gaining the Republican nomination, we have
emphatic confirmation of the changed position of the South in
national politics. The change is not so extreme as to suggest that
the region today is ready to follow Frederick Douglass' exhortation
of the last century that "the Republican party is the island; all else
is the sea." But the change is sufficient to conclude that the intense
regional commitment to the Democratic party that gave rise to the
term "the Solid South" has been profoundly altered in our time.
In this essay, we focus on this changed and still-changing political
position of the South.

1

The historic alliance between the eleven former Confederate states
and the national Democratic party was forged in the fires of the
Civil War and took fixed shape in the decades following Reconstruction and the withdrawal of federal troops from the South. Insofar
as the Civil War imposed sectional political alignments throughout
the nation the South was not unique in its response. In terms, however, of the number of states involved and their geographic spread
and of the durability and intensity of attachment to one national
major party, the South properly came to be regarded as the outstanding American example of political sectionalism.

The pursuit by eleven states of so persistently similar a course in

1. This essay was completed just prior to the assassination of President John F.
Kennedy. Whether President Johnson will diverge markedly from the policies of his
predecessor on those matters that greatly agitate the South as a region remains to be
seen. On the assumption that such will not be the case, no revision of the initially-
completed paper has been undertaken.

national politics presupposes a felt consensus throughout those
states on one or more public issues deemed overriding. Certain
shared characteristics of southern states and populations contributed importantly to a common policy outlook, e.g., the unity of a
section defeated in a sectional civil war, of a low per capita income,
of an agrarian economy, often of a one-crop nature, of an ethnic
homogeneity markedly divergent from that of the rest of the
country, and of an economy inadequately sharing in the industrial
and material progress manifest elsewhere in the nation. Even more
determinative than these supportive factors, however, was the
common response by whites to *the* regional problem of the presence
of large numbers of Negroes relative to that of whites. (It might be
recalled that from 1870 through 1910, 80 per cent of American
Negroes lived in the former secessionist states, and that in many
counties in the region Negroes were in the majority.) In committing
themselves to the doctrine of white supremacy as their solution to
the race problem in their midst, the majority of whites in the
southern states found that their common racial anxieties not merely
facilitated, but indeed required, their unified stance in national
politics. Thus the bedrock on which the Solid South was built was
the imperative of white political unity in the face of what was conceived to be the racial threat of the southern Negro.

The marriage between the South and the national Democrats
did appear to serve the racial goals of white southerners well for
many decades. The Republican party, confirmed of its majority
standing in the nation after the 1896 election, indifferently wrote
off the South as the territory of the enemy party. Most of the non-
South, apparently wearying of the less than effective struggle to
improve the lot of the Negro, acquiesced passively in the South's
providing its own solutions. The Democratic party, clearly the national minority party after 1896, depended heavily on its southern
heartland for both congressional seats and electoral votes, and posed
no threat whatsoever to the states' rights position of southern whites
on the Negro issue. Thus left to their own devices, one southern
state after another, through constitutional revision, legislation, and
elaborated tradition and custom, imposed its version of Negro
subordination on the institutions and practices of its biracial society.
The victimized Negro, for his part, either condoned such arrange-

ments through the millennial gradualism espoused by a Booker
T. Washington, or if he protested, in the manner of the NAACP
advocating a federal anti-lynching law, found that the parliamentary
skills of southern legislators, together with the opportunities for
obstructionism and minority vetoes inherent in congressional procedures, frustrated enactment of the desired racial reforms.

In American politics generally, a dedicated sectionalism in
national politics tends to breed within the region an even more
pervasive attachment to the same party in the conduct of state and
local politics. So it was in the case of the South. State and local
two-party rivalry in a southern state would not only give aid to the
state affiliate of the sectional enemy in national politics, but would
run the grave risk of opening the door to Negro voter influence as
an unwitting consequence of the parties' competitive quest for
support. Hence a Democratic monopoly of state-local politics inevitably accompanied the development of the Solid South in national politics. The threatening possibility of a Negro vote was
handled by a variety of devices which, in effect, barred Negroes
from membership in the Democratic party and/or excluded them
from the ranks of registered voters, thereby depriving them of any
influence at the critical points of the election process.

Given this deliberate adherence to one-partyism, would a viable
Democratic factionalism among whites develop within southern
states to serve effectively as the region's functional substitute for
two-party competition? There did exist within many states sufficient diversity of interests to permit voters and leaders to organize
politics in the mold of a meaningful and persistent factionalism, e.g.,
hill against delta, city against country, class antagonisms, and the
like. To the extent that such conflicting interests did in fact find
political expression, the actual patterns of southern state politics
were far more varied than their common attachment to the one-
party system implied.[2] In this sense, the analyst's reliance on the
imagery of a Solid South obscures political realities more than it
clarifies. Still, allowing for these variations, it may fairly be concluded that in the main the one-party system thwarted effective
political translation of these diverse interests and imposed on the

2. The definitive presentation of this thesis, together with the state-by-state details, is that of V. O. Key, Jr., *Southern Politics* (New York: Alfred A. Knopf, 1949).

South a political structure functionally inferior to that of two-party jurisdictions elsewhere in the nation.

When one-partyism takes the form of a loose multifactionalism, as it so often has in the South, its inadequacies as a political structure stand starkly revealed.[3] Candidacies tend to be individualistic, without reference to any collective slate. Factions tend to be transient, without a clear genealogy and with little hope of posterity. Under such conditions, voters are deprived of those elementary guideposts to candidate selection which by definition are supplied by party labels and party tickets in a two-party setting. Aspirants to state office, not being able to draw on the strength of a continuing organization, are forced to rely on their own initiative to develop state-wide voting support. Small wonder that some succumb to the temptation, which in two-party areas would be checked by the pressures of a party organization sensitive to its long-range interests, to gain a state-wide reputation rapidly and cheaply by employing one or another of the attention-getting tactics making up the armory of the demagogue. Such personalized and short-run perspectives on politics often carry over to the officeholding stage as well, so that southern governors have less incentive to concern themselves with long-range programs and have greater incentive to treat public office as private plunder than do their counterparts in two-party systems.

Where a situation of persistent Democratic bifactionalism obtains, as in the example of the Long and anti-Long forces in Louisiana, the gross defects of multifactionalism just noted are remedied but the system still falls short of a well-functioning two-partyism.[4] For instance, the scope of guidance to voters provided by bifactionalism typically is confined to state-office contests unless, in the manner of Huey and Earl Long, the reach of bifactionalism is enlarged because of the effects that new and questionable gubernatorial concentrations of power have on the political life of localities and districts. Again, factional leaders enjoy a greater freedom to switch from one faction to the other—and thereby to bewilder voters—than do party leaders. Numerous other adverse tendencies

3. See Key, *op. cit.*, especially chapters 5 and 14.
4. For a fuller exposition of the nature of Louisiana's Democratic bifactionalism, see Allan P. Sindler, *Huey Long's Louisiana: State Politics, 1920-1952* (Baltimore: The Johns Hopkins Press, 1956), especially the concluding chapter.

of bifactionalism and multifactionalism could be cited, but enough
has been said to affirm that factionalism within the one Democratic
party has not given to southern states a satisfactory functional
equivalent of the competition between Democratic and Republican
parties existent in most of the other American states.

A politics that lacks coherence, i.e., that is insufficiently structured to give voters a meaningful choice or to impose responsibility
to the voters on candidates both when campaigning and when in
office, tends to impede the formation of aggressive popular ma-
jorities and to play into the hands of the adherents of the status quo.
Consequently, the principal beneficiaries of southern one-partyism
have been those groups and interests which are cohesive, alert, in-
formed, well-organized, well-financed, and capable of effective
action, and which have a tangible material stake in governmental
policies to impel them to political activity. The adverse effects of
the one-party structure on state politics, in short, have been borne
most heavily by the disadvantaged elements of the population, by
"have-not" persons who score low on the characteristics just cited.
It is well to remember, in connection with subsequent analysis in
this paper, that economic conservatives have a considerable stake
in maintaining politics at a low level of clarity and coherence.

The deficiencies of its one-party system have made the South
over the years the target of repetitious exhortations for it to conform to national norms by adopting two-partyism. Pundits have
pored through southern election returns in the hope of uncovering
bits of evidence that might be heralded by them as signs of a
rejuvenated party rivalry. More than a few premature funeral ora-
tions have been conducted at the bier of the Solid South. These
well-meaning reformers were sound enough in their judgment that
party competition would promote political health better than one-
party factionalism, but they were guilty of the folly that so often
overtakes the ideologue, namely the naive optimism that the right-
ness of one's cause guarantees the conversion of the audience. Any
party system, after all, by developing vested interests and psychological loyalties over the decades, generates impressive mechanisms for self-perpetuation and for resisting change. With more
specific reference to the southern situation, these exhortations overlooked the instrumental character of southern one-partyism: it

served the racial needs of the majority of whites and, incidentally but importantly to its maintenance, it served the needs of top-drawer economic groups as well. Only when these purposes were no longer satisfied by continuance of the southern commitment to the Democratic party would conditions for important regional political change be at hand.

2

The national predominance of the Democratic party, accomplished during the 1930's, necessarily involved the party's pursuit of new policy directions and of new sources of voter support. The compatibility of these trends with the retention by the South of its controlling influence within the party on those salient matters that gave to the region its solidarity became increasingly questionable, and ultimately provoked sectional revolt against the Democrats. On the economic side, southern conservatives not only disliked much of the content of the New Deal and Fair Deal programs, but feared as well the marked expansion of national governmental authority that went with these policies. Perceptive conservatives further realized that the emerging alignments in national politics might well sharpen the clarity with which economic conflict was expressed within southern state and local politics. Many lower-class whites, although their traditional party loyalty was reinforced by the aid and welfare elements of Democratic policy, nonetheless viewed with suspicion and distaste the complexion of other groups with which they were harnessed in the grand majority coalition forged by FDR: urban machines and bosses, organized labor, and religious and ethnic minorities. Most offensive to regional sensibilities was the recruitment of the northern Negro as a partner with the Democrats, the course of mass Negro defection from the party of Lincoln over to the party of the New Deal having taken place by 1936. For the masses of white southerners, then, the emergence of race anxieties took precedence over class perspectives, and the region's capacity for popular revolt against the Democrats hinged on the latter's handling of the Negro issue.

The outcome, as we all know, was that the national Democratic party confirmed the fears of the South by increasingly committing itself to the cause of the Negro. While outraged southerners might decry this development as perfidy and cast about in baffled anger for ways to purify the party or protect the region, the lesson that all too many refused to learn was the increasing isolation of the South from the mainstream of national thought and policy. The Democratic support accorded the Negro, allowing for the overstatement typical of political rhetoric, proceeded generally from the same blend of ideological, moral, and practical political reasons that have moved much of the non-South in our time to be receptive to Negro demands for equal rights and opportunities.

The Negro quest for equality benefited greatly, for example, from a sense of humanitarian concern for the welfare of underdog groups and that of willingness to utilize governmental authority to alleviate social ills—both attitudes being characteristic of the New Deal and subsequently becoming an accepted part of our national thinking. Further, southern racist beliefs were placed ever more on the lonely defensive in the wake of public awareness of the mass murder of European Jewry undertaken by Hitler in the name of master-race concepts and of scientific findings invalidating previous notions about the innate inferiority of Negroes. Again, the democratic ideals heavily emphasized by us in defining our war aims and in distinguishing our way of life from that of our enemies in World War II not only rekindled the hopes of Negroes but sensitized many other Americans to the gap between our preachment and our practice, i.e., to what Gunnar Myrdal aptly termed "an American dilemma."[5] During the current Cold War period our leadership of the non-Communist bloc and our need to make effective appeal to African and Asian countries have placed American race relations in high visibility to the world and have given Negroes a powerful lever in their agitation for full citizenship rights. Landmark judicial decisions, such as the invalidation of the white primary in 1944 and the prohibition of racial segregation in public education in 1954-1955, helped affirm in a most prestigious and public way that Negro aspirations were fully supported by the rights embodied in the United States Constitution.

The intensified Negro claim on the American conscience was accompanied by domestic political pressures sparked by the mili-

5. This was the title of Myrdal's major study of the American Negro, financed by a Carnegie Corporation grant and published in 1944 by Harper & Brothers, New York.

tancy of Negro spokesmen and the rising influence of Negro voting power. Racial leaders talked far less of accommodation and far more of protest, and the goal of full equality was pushed as one realizable in the immediate future. Negro leaders understood that the greatest gains for their race often had been achieved in war and crisis periods, e.g., the threat of a mass march on Washington was skilfully used to wring from a less-than-enthusiastic FDR an executive order in mid-1941 establishing a national Fair Employment Practices Committee. This rising tide of Negro protest reflected and was reinforced by a new factor in the race question, a Negro vote of impressive size and strategic distribution. The large-scale migration of Negroes from the South, which had begun about the World War I period, had proceeded apace to the point that the 1950 Census reported that 60.2 per cent of all Negroes lived in the former Confederacy, and by 1960 the figure was down to 52.3 per cent. The settlement of most of these migrating Negroes in the urban-industrial states considered pivotal to the outcome of presidential elections, together with the increasing tendency of Negroes to vote in line with what they or their leaders perceived their racial interests to require, assured the Negro of maximum political influence and kept both major parties sympathetic to his demands.

Thus, even though the bulk of the Negro vote has remained Democratic in presidential contests since 1936, the Democrats have not been able to assume that it is an in-the-bag vote in the manner the party could in the case of the South prior to 1948, and the Republicans to date have not given up the hope of attracting much of the Negro vote either through positive appeal or through capitalizing on Negro disaffection with the southern wing of the Democratic party. Although the Republican position on the Negro question, being more concerned about private property rights and the fear of inflating the authority of the federal government, tends to be more moderate than that of the Democrats, the fact that the positions of the two major parties are far more similar than dissimilar lays bare the political dilemma facing the South with regard to the race issue.

On the race component of the contemporary southern revolt against the Democratic party, the pressures have been generated primarily by changes external to the region. Whereas national politics and policy on the Negro problem have undergone sharp transformations in the past three decades, much of the South retained older racial perspectives, the accommodation of which by any major party seeking national victory was increasingly unlikely. The southern rebellion against the Democrats, with reference to the race-based aspects, should be broadly understood as a sectional protest against the times being out of joint, with the Democratic party, as the historic ally of the region, bearing the brunt of the discontent. Since, however, the forces productive of these external changes in the race issue give no sign of abating, the South currently can be interpreted as being in a period of political transition, one in which it will have to move from negative protest to patterns of durable adjustment to the racial realities of America in the latter half of the twentieth century. We will consider the nature of this political transition in greater detail after we next review the sequence of party revolt as it actually occurred in the South.

3

The initial cracking of the Solid South in the presidential election of 1928 should be seen less as the first in a straight-line series of regional revolts continuing to the present than as an ad hoc response which provided no certain base for predicting the recurrence of party rebellion in the immediate future.[6] It is true that the 1928 experience could be said to demonstrate in a general way the capacity of the region to defect under conditions deemed sufficiently adverse and, in that sense, it provided a predictive warning to the national party. Moreover, the voting elements newly appealed to by the Democrats were those which at one and the same time gave offense to the South and yet provided the party with its major chance to gain election victory nationally. These elements were visibly personified, if not almost caricatured, in the single figure of the presidential candidate himself. New York Governor Alfred E. Smith

6. A related though more difficult problem is whether to interpret the 1928 contest as the real turning-point election, in preference to 1932 and/or 1936, in which new electoral alignments appeared which were subsequently merely affirmed by the New Deal. The sticky part of the judgment is that there can be no assurance that the novel 1928 alignments would have proved durable in the absence of a Great Depression, or that these alignments would not have been just the same and as firm because of the Depression even in the absence of the events of 1928. On the instant matter of comparing the 1928 revolt to the mainstream of regional rebellion, the differences between the two simplify the problem of judgment—or so it seems to this writer.

was everything the South was not: a big-city product and ally of
Tammany Hall, a Catholic of recent Irish immigrant stock, and a
"wet" on the liquor issue. Even though the Democrats as a majority
party were subsequently to take on a similar coloration, the assertion of a close parallel between the South's adverse reaction to
Smith and its later hostility to FDR and Truman would appear to
be more obvious than exact. The 1928 response turned little on
matters of race or economics, but on the "exotic" issues of liquor
and religion. The region's biases on those issues were intense enough
to induce party desertion in 1928, but once the prohibition issue had
died and the Democrats again put up Protestant presidential candidates, would not the 1928 defection prove to be transient and without structuring force for subsequent regional behavior? Highly relevant in this regard was the fact that all the five southern states carried by Hoover—North Carolina, Virginia, Tennessee, Florida, and
Texas—were rim-South states. The Deep South and black-belt areas,
which were the most sensitive to the problem of race relations and
most adamant on the need to maintain white supremacy, but which
presumably were no less exercised by the Catholic and liquor issues,
remained loyal to the Democratic party. Since contemporary southern political rebellion is intimately associated with the question of
race and the defection of Deep South states, the 1928 election cannot be located fully in the mainstream of sectional revolt nor made
to serve clearly as a predictor of things to come.

The increasing restiveness of the South under Roosevelt and
the New Deal lies closer to the heart of the contemporary regional
position, although the aggravated tensions between region and
party from 1932-1945 did not produce defection on the scale of that
of 1928. The practical ability of southerners to chastise the Democratic party in presidential elections was severely circumscribed by
FDR's national popularity. For example, had the eleven-state South
gone Republican throughout the period of Roosevelt's four elections, and had all other states remained unchanged in the direction
of their presidential vote, he nonetheless would have won office
each and every time. Further, the willingness of much of the South
to support party rebellion was dampened during the many years
either of major depression, the threat of war, or the actual conduct
of war. In so unfavorable a setting, the persistence with which

regional hostility to the Democrats was expressed testified to the emergence of a durable strand of sectional discontent.

Symptomatic of rising southern resentments, for example, were the actions of various southern delegations at Democratic national conventions. In 1936, most of the losing opposition to repeal of the two-thirds nomination rule, which had offered protection since 1832 to minority interests such as the South, came from the South. In 1940, the large majority of southern delegates opposed the convention's endorsement of Henry A. Wallace as the running mate of FDR. Again in 1944 the South, in combination with other influential forces, was able to bring about the rejection of Wallace as vice-presidential nominee in favor of Harry S Truman—a result not without its ironies in the light of subsequent events. Additional expressions of regional hostility were made in presidential elections, e.g., third-party slates of electors were put on the ballot in open opposition to FDR in Texas in 1936, in South Carolina in 1940, and in both those states and Mississippi in 1944. By way of final illustration, the emergence of an informal working alliance between southern Democratic conservatives and Republican legislators to block enactment of parts of the New Deal program was observable in the Congress by the late 1930's.

These upthrusts of regional grievance were motivated for the most part by the economic concerns of conservatives. The antipathy of southern conservatives to the trends of New Deal policies mirrored that of conservatives around the nation, and their willingness to shift allegiance from the Democrats in light of changed external realities was in keeping with the political characteristics of such high-status groups as noted earlier. This economic strand of southern rebellion, then, clearly antedates the Truman period and serves to link the contemporary situation back to its origins in the New Deal period. If, however, the fact of economic-induced defection was a reality by the latter part of FDR's incumbency, the accelerated rate of such defection derives from events during and since the presidency of Truman. Similarly, the enlarged scope and mass appeal of recent regional revolt cannot be accounted for in terms of economic resentments. The sensitive nerve of the white South has been the race issue, and with the exacerbation of that issue came large-scale sectional rebellion against the national Democratic party.

Truman's vigorous endorsement of civil rights measures and of the Fair Deal aroused and provided a common focus for the racial fears and economic anxieties of many southerners, and the apparent weakness of his candidacy in 1948 persuaded dissident southern leaders to retaliate against him and the party. Thus emerged the States' Rights or Dixiecrat movement which, operating solely in regard to the presidential election, sought as its immediate goal to deprive Truman of the bulk of the South's electoral vote. The achievement of that goal would serve, depending upon how the rest of the country voted, either to increase Truman's margin of defeat, to deadlock the electoral college and give over to the House the choice of president, or to provide the critical loss of support bringing about his defeat. Whichever way it came out, the Dixiecrats believed that the presidential and non-southern camps of the national Democratic party would be compelled to modify their indifference to southern interests. The Dixiecrat revolt may be considered, therefore, as pursuing a politics of revenge, but one aimed not at the alienation of region from party but rather the opposite: the purification of party so as to promote the reuniting of region and party on terms laid down mostly by the region. That such an ultimate aim was deemed realizable provides a measure of how distortedly southern dissidents perceived the realities of their time.

Other facets of the Dixiecrat rebellion help illuminate the general character of contemporary sectional defection.[7] The altered relationship between the South and the national Democratic party was dramatically demonstrated by the fact that the impetus for the party revolt came from the Deep South states and black-belt leaders —the loyalists of 1928 became the defectors of 1948. Conservative economic interests financed the movement, but though their doctrines of states' rights and "constitutionalism" were voiced by the Dixiecrats, main reliance for attracting voters was placed on the exploitation of the race concerns of whites. And although on paper

7. Analysis of the Dixiecrat movement may be found in Alexander Heard, *A Two-Party South?* (Chapel Hill: University of North Carolina Press, 1952), especially pp. 20-33, 251-278, and in Allan P. Sindler, "The Unsolid South: A Challenge to the Democratic National Party," in Alan F. Westin (ed.), *The Uses of Power* (New York: Harcourt, Brace & World, 1962), pp. 240-246.

the Dixiecrats claimed to be a national rather than a regional party, its effort and appeal were virtually restricted to the southern region alone.

As their method of revolt, the Dixiecrats chose to exploit the federal character of American government and of the party structure so as to run their presidential and vice-presidential nominees as the Democratic candidates in the southern states. Since this tactic necessitated control of the machinery of the state Democratic party in each state, the critical phase of the Dixiecrat rebellion turned on the attempt to take over the governing bodies of the state parties in order to determine which electors were to appear on the ballot, and under what party designation. In Alabama, Louisiana, Mississippi, and South Carolina, the Dixiecrats captured the state Democratic emblem for their candidates, and in the first-named state the Truman-Barkley ticket was completely excluded from the ballot. In Florida, neither the Dixiecrats nor the national Democratic ticket was assigned possession of the state party label. In the remaining six southern states, the party emblem was given to the Truman-Barkley slate, and Dixiecrat electors had to operate as a true third party.

In the election, nearly all of the 1,169,312 votes received by the States' Rights ticket came from the South, and more than half came from the four states in which the Dixiecrats ran as Democrats. Capture of those four states yielded 38 electoral votes to the Dixiecrats, but the overall southern strength of the movement was far from impressive: Truman secured 50 per cent of the region-wide popular vote, Dewey 26.6 per cent, and Governor J. Strom Thurmond of South Carolina, the Dixiecrat candidate, 22.6 per cent. Of the seven southern states lost by the Dixiecrats to Truman, their vote was less than that accorded the Republican candidates in all but Georgia. Much of the backing that the States' Righters did secure stemmed from the Negrophobia of whites: "in state after state the Dixiecrats won their greatest support among the whites who live closest to large numbers of Negroes."[8]

The Dixiecrat defection made use of two of the logically possible routes of party revolt. In the four states they won, the Dixiecrats literally took the name and place of the Democrats on the state

8. Heard, *op. cit.*, p. 27.

ballot. While this brought to the Dixiecrat ticket the support of thousands who habitually voted Democratic, it exposed them to the charge that their strength derived as much from subterfuge as from popular appeal. Moreover, the Dixiecrats' extreme insistence on a purely confederate view of national party structure invited retaliation against disloyal state party delegations by the national convention and ran the further risk of the national party fostering a rival loyalist faction in state politics. In the other seven southern states, the Dixiecrats had to operate in the usual manner of third parties in an overall political system uncongenial to third parties— and they lost by a wide margin in each. These defects of the Dixie- crat technique help explain why most of the South has not resorted to it since 1948, and underscore how alienated from the contem- porary political situation are those states—Mississippi and Alabama —which did rely on a variant of that tactic in 1960 and for a time threatened to do so again in 1964.

Eisenhower's election in 1952 and re-election in 1956 may be considered jointly in light of the similarity of southern response in both contests. These elections demonstrated the staying power of southern defection since the race issue was not agitated in the overt manner of 1948 and Stevenson was more moderate than Truman or the militantly liberal wing of national Democrats with regard to economic and racial policy. The appeal of the Republican candidate was felt in the South as well as in the rest of the nation, and helped not only to sustain party revolt but to channel it. On the ballot of every southern state in both elections the Stevenson slate was assigned the emblem of the state Democratic party; most state Democratic organizations did not openly defect and many, in fact, worked hard for the national party's ticket. The antipathy of southern dissidents to Stevenson's candidacy thus took the form of various influential leaders' defecting on an individual basis and heading ad hoc movements designed to promote Eisenhower's cause, as sharply distinguished from the Republican party's cause. For example, Governor Shivers of Texas and Governor Kennon of Louisiana led a "Democrats for Eisenhower" movement in support of presidential Republicanism, while Governor Byrnes of South Carolina took the alternative route of initiating an "Independents for Ike" group which placed its own electors on the ballot. As still another variation, Senator Harry F. Byrd, the leader of Virginia's Democratic organization, publicly assumed a position of neutrality in the 1952 and 1956 presidential elections, a stand which necessarily implied pro-Eisenhower leanings and facilitated party defection in that state.

The impressive backing given Eisenhower by the South affirmed that presidential Republicanism had become an acceptable avenue of protest for southerners disaffected with the presidential camp of the Democratic party. The region shared in the greatly increased turnout registered by the nation at large, supported the Republican candidate in every state at a much higher level as compared to 1948, and gave to Eisenhower the electoral votes of Florida, Tennessee, Texas, and Virginia in 1952 and again in 1956, as well as those of Louisiana in 1956. Critical to the understanding of the current political position of the South is the fact that the region's receptivity to Eisenhower, though doubtless partially accounted for by the high appeal of his personality, also derived from more enduring factors. Analysis has shown that the new sources of presidential Republican strength tapped in the South were not distributed uniformly across the status spectrum, but rather came disproportionately from higher-status sections within metropolitan, urban, and suburban areas.[9] With reference to presidential elections, then, many southern conservatives joined their counterparts elsewhere in the nation in mutual support of the Republican party.

Although analysis of the Kennedy-Nixon contest of 1960 is greatly complicated by the presence of the religious issue which induced presumably transient discontinuities of voter behavior, several observations relevant to our focus can be made with confidence. Regional disaffection with Kennedy's candidacy and the national party platform proceeded from racial and economic concerns no less than from religious animosity, and the strength of southern antipathy was implicitly acknowledged by Kennedy's choice of Senator Lyndon B. Johnson of Texas as his running mate. After the election, most commentators were in agreement that Johnson's dedicated campaign labors in the South were responsible for keeping most of the region in the Democratic fold, albeit by only

9. See, for example, Donald S. Strong, *Urban Republicanism in the South* (University, Ala.: Bureau of Public Administration, University of Alabama, 1960).

a slightly higher percentage of the Southwide vote than had been given to Stevenson. Despite this careful attention accorded the region and the unwillingness of most regional leaders to defect openly from the national party, Florida, Tennessee, and Virginia continued their behavior of 1952 and 1956 by going for Nixon and two Deep South states, Alabama and Mississippi, withheld electoral votes from both Kennedy and Nixon. This latter situation, involving an abortive attempt to revive Dixiecrat-style revolt throughout the region, merits further commentary.

By 1960 dedicated white segregationists had good reason to feel that all branches of the national government had turned against their position: the Supreme Court in its educational desegration rulings of 1954-1955 and subsequent decisions in Negro civil rights cases, the Congress in its passage of the Civil Rights Act of 1957 and of 1960, and President Eisenhower in his dispatching of federal troops to handle the Little Rock, Arkansas, school crisis in 1957. Their unwillingness to accede to what was clearly developing as a national consensus on the Negro problem shared by both major parties led these segregationists to turn (or return) to third-party tactics. The particular device employed was that of running a slate of "free" or "uncommitted" presidential electors in opposition to the tickets of the major parties. Initially, the "free" electors were to be located on the ballot under the state Democratic emblem, but as events turned out they ran as third parties. If victorious, they then were to decide whom to support in light of the outcome of the election in the rest of the country. Originally intended to attract at least the six Deep South states (with a total of 57 electoral votes), the movement in fact was able to secure only the eight electoral votes of Mississippi and six of the eleven of Alabama. Since Kennedy won by a margin of only 34 electoral votes, extreme southern dissidents sought to persuade presidential electors in other southern states to withhold their votes from Kennedy in order to throw the election into the House. That attempt came to naught, and the fourteen "free" electors consummated their futile protest by voting for Senator Harry F. Byrd of Virginia. Thus the most recent of southern attempts to become a balance of power between the major parties in presidential elections ended again in failure.

4

It has here been argued that changes in the drift of broad national policy and of the issue positions of the national Democratic party have aggravated the racial fears of many whites and the economic anxieties of relatively fewer whites in the region to the extent of bringing about a rupture of the long-standing alliance between region and party in presidential politics. It is admittedly somewhat artificial, as often logical analysis must be, to treat racial and economic motivations as separately as we have, since in actuality the two motives interact for specific individuals in ways ranging from mutual support to severe conflict. It would be too simple, for example, to explain the Deep South's turn to third parties in terms of the race factor and that of the rim-South to presidential Republicanism in terms of the economic factor. Yet, as this very example suggests, it remains analytically useful to distinguish between the two motives and to probe the quite different implications of each for the character and durability of southern political protest.

The far greater pervasiveness, gravity, and intensity of the race issue in the South than elsewhere in the nation means that the race issue has the capacity to mold new political alignments in its image even in the face of other forces moving the region in other political directions. Were we to suppose, for example, that one of the major parties chose to endorse the Negrophobic views of white segregationists, we would have to acknowledge that such a move could and most probably would restructure partisan attachments within the region, and we would have no great difficulty in predicting the directions these shifts would take. Yet even as we grant the primacy of the race issue, we must also admit the impossibility of predicting with confidence whether and in what form the race question may suddenly erupt in ways different than in the recent past. As a consequence, estimates of the likely future shape of southern politics are implicitly contingent upon the analyst's assumptions on the future course of the race issue, and are offered on the understanding that events which cannot be predicted may undercut those assumptions. The assumption operative here is that the race issue in the foreseeable future will continue in the form it has exhibited in recent years. More specifically, it is assumed that the race-oriented white southerner will continue to find it difficult to act on that motive in any choice between the major parties. The similarity in racial positions of the national Republican and Democratic parties has earlier been commented on, and the factors productive of that agreement are likely to increase in influence in the years ahead.

If aggressive political implementation of southern white racist views continues, therefore, it likely will take the form of presidential third-party activity in the pattern of 1948 and 1960. Several Mississippi and Alabama Democratic leaders are already on record, for example, as urging southern states to adopt the "uncommitted" presidential elector tactic in 1964 to attempt to increase the region's influence within the national Democratic party. Such a deliberate choice to operate outside the two-party system may properly be labeled a politics of desperation, one symptomatic of the extent to which rigid advocacy of what was the orthodox race position of the South has now become intransigence leading several Deep South states into political homelessness. When it is further considered that our political system discourages the maintenance of any serious third-party movement, it may be concluded that there is no long-range future to this tactic. Doubtless its futility will not prevent its recurrence in 1964 or beyond, so strong is the race feeling, but ultimately even the most unreconstructed of Deep South states must make its peace with the rest of the country, and in so doing, re-enter the mainstream of two-party presidential politics.

The contribution of economic motivations to regional political change offers less hazardous ground for prediction. The defection of southern conservatives from support of Democratic presidential candidates began, as we have seen, during the New Deal and has persisted since. Although the capacity of conservatives to shift partisan moorings in presidential politics undoubtedly was fortified and accelerated by the region's racial animosities against the Democrats after 1947 and by the appeal of Eisenhower in 1952 and 1956, this strand of disaffection appears durable and productive of the maintenance of a level of regional support for Republican presidential candidates markedly higher than that evident in 1944 and earlier. As the South continues to advance economically and as the salience of the race problem slowly declines, this political trend cannot help but be sustained and enlarged.

The interplay of economic and race factors thus has freed the South from its historic one-party attachment in presidential politics, and the recent turn to the Republicans marks the region's increasing participation in the "nationalizing" trends of American politics. Naturally, the pressures generating political change have not operated uniformly in the region. The urbanized, industrializing, and retirement areas (omitting consideration of the traditional areas of mountain Republicanism) have led the region in rising support of Republican presidential candidates. On a state basis, Florida, Tennessee, Texas, and Virginia now seem to qualify as competitive two-party states in presidential politics. Overall, the strength of presidential Republicanism in the region justifies the judgment that the Solid South may be considered a pattern of the past.[10] By no means, however, may it then be suggested that Republican presidential nominees are likely to carry a majority of the southern electorate with any regularity in the near future. Indeed, in the absence of such special factors as those of candidate personality or religious issue which existed in the three most recent contests, it is quite probable that region-wide support of the Republican aspirant will be lower than it has been. In concentrating on the impressive upsurge of presidential Republicanism in the section, it should not be forgotten that both the pull of party loyalty and the relative backwardness of the regional economy, to mention but two factors, should serve to persuade a majority of southerners to continue to favor Democratic presidential candidates.[11]

10. There is ample room for disagreement in estimating the likely rate of presidential Republican gains in the South in the immediate future, particularly when different measures of political change are used. For example, the southern presidential Republican vote in recent elections has been about 13 percentage points higher than the proportion of southern samples declaring themselves as Republicans in response to the interviewer's questions (about 48 and 35 per cent respectively). For a spirited exchange of views on this point, see Donald S. Strong, "Durable Republicanism in the South" and Philip E. Converse, "A Major Political Realignment in the South?" in Allan P. Sindler (ed.), *Change in the Contemporary South* (Durham: Duke University Press, 1963), pp. 174-194, 195-222.

11. Much the same observations could be offered with reference to the enlarging Negro vote in the South. This aspect of southern politics has not been treated in this paper partly because of space limitations and partly because at least two other chapters in this volume focus on the Negro. It may generally be said that the Negro vote is likely to be of a bloc nature and oriented to race goals, to stick with the national Democratic party if that party satisfactorily handles the civil rights problem, and to be aligned with liberal factions in state and local politics. It need not be added that unexpected developments on the race issue would upset any current calculations on the direction and effects of the Negro vote.

5

Does the emergence throughout much of the South of persistent party competition in presidential contests herald the same directional shift in the conduct of state and local politics within the region? If, as earlier argued, sectional solidarity in presidential politics promotes a more intense partisan uniformity in state politics, will not the abandonment of the former necessarily lead in the foreseeable future to a like abandonment of the latter? Many a commentator has so urged, but the asserted parallel is fundamentally in error.

To be sure, the attempt to pursue at the same time one-party state and local politics and two-party presidential politics breeds tensions which over a long time push in the direction of analogous party systems at both levels.[12] Further, as the Republicans rejuvenate their party organizations within the region, develop ambitious leaders desirous of public office, and contest more regularly for more elective posts, it is inevitable that in the years immediately ahead their electoral strength and overall vigor will notably increase. Ongoing institutional reforms push in the same direction in that a more equitable allotment of legislative seats to urban and suburban districts, the centers of Republican sentiment, is certain to follow in the wake of the Supreme Court's 1962 decision in *Baker* v. *Carr*. Finally, it is also true that in many southern states Democratic factional alignments are paralleling to a greater degree party alignments in presidential contests, a development which would facilitate the transition from one-party factionalism to two-party competition. Allowing for these factors, it nonetheless is here maintained that the chances in the near future of a regional restructuring of state-local politics in the image of its presidential politics are quite remote.

Once the assumption is made that the revitalization of Republicanism depends upon the support of economic conservatives, including some who are now major Democratic figures in state politics, the basic error in the asserted parallel between presidential and

12. Historical evidence suggests that any attempt to maintain a state political structure unrelated to or sharply at variance with national political alignments within that state produces strains ultimately resolved in the direction of a greater articulation of state and national political alignments. Perhaps the best example is the rise and fall of the Nonpartisan League of North Dakota.

state-local developments becomes apparent. Conservatives turned to presidential Republicanism only when dissatisfied with the presidential wing of the Democrats. Where is the counterpart dissatisfaction with the Democratic monopoly of state-local politics that would move conservatives to support Republicans in that arena? The answer is, of course, that in the main conservatives are content, for reasons advanced in the first section of this essay, with their influence over and with the policy product of one-party factionalism, as well as with the more confused structure of politics stemming from the coexistence of presidential two-partyism and state-local one-partyism. It would be highly relevant to note, in this regard, the tenacity with which southern Democratic leaders have insisted, even as they gave their backing to non-Democratic presidential candidates, that they remained true Democrats in good standing. As long, therefore, as conservatives are convinced of the advantage of their retaining the Democratic label in state-local politics, they will resist recruitment by or volunteering for the Republican party. The problem thus becomes one of devising ways of coercing such leaders and voters—we may call them Republicrats —into abandoning their nominal Democratic status and into adopting the Republican label.

The ability of leading southern Democrats to proffer open support for presidential Republicanism without thereby jeopardizing their own party status owes much to the loose federative character of the American party system. It is true that serious intra-Democratic disputes on the proper relationships between state and national party followed in the wake of past actions of southern Dixiecrats and Republicrats, and that the resolution of those conflicts added slightly to the slim armory of weapons with which the national party apparatus can attempt to resist or punish flagrant defection.[13] But it still remains fair to say that the odds are very much in favor of the defectors when the party revolt has constituency backing, as obviously has been the situation in the South. Would-be Republicrats, therefore, can feel free to continue their dual partisan behavior in the absence of effective party pressure making for consistent partisanship at both presidential and state-local election levels.

13. See Sindler, "The Unsolid South," in Westin, *op. cit.*, pp. 229-281 for a full account of this intra-party conflict from 1948 through 1960.

The position of conservative southern Democratic congressmen provides an apt illustration of some dimensions of the problem under discussion. Chamber and party rules give to members of this group disproportionate influence within the all-important committee structure, on the basis of which southerners have been pressing a far from ineffective form of party disaffection in the sense of opposing much of the liberal legislation advocated by Democratic presidents. This strategic influence within the Congress constitutes a major source of regional self-protection, and its continuance depends heavily on southern legislators' remaining Democratic. Consequently, these conservatives do not wish to shift to the Republican party nor to run the risk of being deprived of their committee posts by decision of a party caucus because of actions considered disloyal to the Democratic party. In terms of current concepts of the obligation of a legislator to his national party, conspicuous support of the opposition party's presidential candidate permits punishment whereas deviation from the party line in legislative voting does not. It is no accident, therefore, that conservative southern Democratic legislators express their defection seldom by openly endorsing presidential Republicanism (or Dixiecrat-style third parties) and often by voting across the aisle with Republican legislators within the Congress. If, to complete the logic of the point, deviance in legislative voting did become grounds for Democratic denial of important committee assignments to such a dissident, the southern conservative legislator would no longer be able to commit himself to Republican positions as a Democrat but instead would have to choose between his party label and his policy inclinations.

Another vantage point on the same problem may be had by considering state-local politics proper, where the conditions for restraining the emergence of Republicrats are obviously less developed than in the Congress. For conservatives to turn Republican voluntarily on the state level would presuppose that Democratic politics had been taken over by truly liberal factions promoting policies disadvantageous to conservative interests. In the absence of such a development, the Republicrat behavior of conservative Democratic leaders could be challenged if such behavior itself became a controversial issue in state politics and worked to the

detriment of the dissidents. That is, a Democratic leader intending
to take a Republicrat position, knowing that his presidential Republicanism might harm him in state politics, would then have to
choose a more consistent partisan course of action. The chances of
this situation's developing, however, would seem to depend once
again on the existence of a truly liberal faction willing to raise and
exploit the issue of party disloyalty. The emergence of liberal factions in southern states is far from an impossibility, as witness
recent events in Texas,[14] but it would be foolhardy to expect such
factions to be in assured control of Democratic politics soon in
many southern states.

A final consideration, so far implicit, merits emphasis as the ultimate handicap to any contemporary attempt to convert Republicrats into Republicans. We have argued that Republicrats will continue to implement their interests by remaining Republicrats until
certain conditions require them to be loyal to the same party in
both presidential and state-local elections, and we have not been
sanguine about the likelihood of the imminent development of
those conditions. Moving beyond that point and pushing the argument to its conclusion, we must ask for which party would most
Republicrats opt if such a choice did become necessary. The answer
seems reasonably clear in the case of those Republicrats who are
influential Democratic figures in the politics of their state and whose
actions are crucial to discouraging or hastening the trends of state
and local Republicanism in the South. Most such leaders would
choose to remain Democratic in order to protect their high influence
within the majority party, rather than to assume leadership in the
minority party, and then to indulge their hostility to Democratic
presidential candidates by methods short of open endorsement of
the Republican candidate. In sum, if the effort to compel Republicrats to make a clear party choice is undertaken in the name of
promoting two-party competition in the South, it may well have the
boomerang effect of transforming Republicrats back into Demo-

14. A "Democratic Coalition," composed of Latin-Americans, Negroes, trade
unionists, and liberals, is currently making a serious bid for control of Texas Democratic politics. If that Coalition becomes the major influence within the Democratic
party, there is no question but that the flight of Texas conservatives to the Republican party will be accelerated. See Ronnie Dugger, "3 'Parties' of Texas," *New
York Times* (Western edition), November 5, 1963, p. 9.

crats, and thereby depressing Republican strength in presidential as well as in state-local elections. The Republican party, therefore, will have to settle for some time for gains in presidential politics that will not be closely matched by a commensurate upturn in strength in state and local politics.

XV. THE FUTURE OF THE COLOR LINE/
Herbert Blumer

My approach to the topic of the changing relations between Negroes and whites in the American South is from the standpoint of the common concept of the "color line." This is an exceedingly apt and discerning term which helps to pinpoint what is crucial in the relation of the two racial groups. The term does not cover all of the ways in which Negroes and whites meet nor does it refer to all of the important relations between their respective institutions and modes of life. Instead, it singles out a central dimension of their interconnection—a dimension along which the "racial problem" lies and is formed. The distinction is of considerable importance. Extensive changes may take place in broad areas of the relationship of the two racial groups without appreciable effect on the color line; this may be seen, for example, in the preservation of the color line in the face of the profound transformations wrought by industrialization or by demographic change. It is a mistake to construe the broad social changes which are taking place in institutional areas in the South as necessarily portending some notable transformation in the basic relationship of the two racial groups. Change in this basic relationship must be sought, instead, in what happens to the color line.

The ostensible meaning of the color line is clear. It is a line which separates whites and Negroes, assigning to each a different position in the social order and attaching to each position a differential set of rights, privileges, and arenas of action. It defines the approach of each racial group to the other, it limits the degree of access to each other, and it outlines respective modes of conduct toward each other. The color line stems from a collective sense held by whites that Negroes as a racial group do not qualify for equal status, and that because of their racial difference Negroes have no claim to being accepted socially. Thus, the color line expresses and sustains the social positions of the two groups along two fundamental dimensions—an axis of dominance and subordination, and an axis of inclusion and exclusion.

Three important features of the color line should be noted. First, it represents a positioning of whites and Negroes as abstract or generalized groups; it comes into play when members of the two races meet each other not on an individual basis but as representatives of their respective groups. It is only when the encounters between whites and Negroes are controlled by an identification of their respective racial membership that the color line is set. Second, the color line is a collective definition of social position and not a mere expression of individual feelings and beliefs. Whites may have, and do have, a wide and variable range of feelings toward Negroes, from profound hostility to deep kindness and sympathy, yet adhere to the color line when and where the social code requires its application. The sense of group position is the central ingredient in the color line. Third, as a metaphor, the color line is not appropriately represented by a single, sharply drawn line but appears rather as a series of ramparts, like the "Maginot Line," extending from outer breastworks to inner bastions. Outer portions of it may, so to speak, be given up only to hold steadfast to inner citadels. We will have occasion in the subsequent discussion to indicate the relevance of these three points to the present and imminent changes in race relations in the South.

It is well to keep in mind that the color line has grown up as a primary basis for the organization of southern life. The color line was forged through many generations of critical experience in which the self-identity and survival of the whites as a given kind of group were at stake. The collective definition or social code elaborated from this experience came to be deeply embedded in the mores. The color line came to be felt by whites as natural, proper, and sacred, and as such to be zealously guarded against trespass by Negroes and preserved from disrespect by whites.

It is also desirable to keep in mind the impotent position of southern Negroes under the historic relationship with whites. The color line forced into being among them a posture of concealment of strong feelings of resentment and bitterness. The color line stood fundamentally for a denigration of Negroes as inferior and a rejection of them as alien. Yet it was not wise for Negroes to express before whites their feelings as they experienced affronts, indignities, and the various forms of exploitation which went with their inferior and impotent status. It was precisely this area of feelings, and of the sentiments and thoughts built up in it, that was typically unknown to southern whites under the operation of the color line. This condition, even more than the separation of the races into two communities with disparate areas of interaction and universes of discourse, was the major bar to communication and understanding between the two racial groups.

The foregoing remarks provide a suitable background for considering the present and proximate status of the color line. The color line in the South is under considerable attack. It is undergoing transformation, although so far more in a symbolic than in an actual sense. The attack, to re-employ our previous metaphor, is taking place chiefly at the outer battlements; it has scarcely entered into the intermediate fortifications, and of course has not touched inner citadels. It is currently being waged chiefly at certain points in the public area of civil rights; only rarely has it begun to enter the crucial area of economic position, and it is remote from the inner field of private association. How widespread will be the attack, how deeply it will penetrate and with what degree of success depends on a variety of forces, some currently in operation and some on the horizon. I wish to direct my discussion to this latter matter.

The initial forces which have operated to bring about changes in the color line can scarcely be thought of as having arisen indigenously from the cultural and social structure of the South. The powerful and deeply embedded code of the color line plus the impotency of the southern Negro have effectively prevented this from happening. It is commonly thought that the rather profound social transformation undergone by the South during the last few decades under the impact of industrialization, agricultural changes, demographic changes, educational advancement, and similar developments is responsible for undermining the color line. The evidence gives little support for this view. It appears, instead, that in this transformation the color line was carried over from the old situations to the new situations—from the plantation to the factory, from the rural area to the city, from the old institutional settings to the new institutional settings. The Negro was subjected to essentially the same subordination and exclusion. In the new industrial structure the Negro, as of old, was confined to low-status jobs; in the cities he had the poorest housing and other facilities; and he continued to be barred from white institutions and allocated to a separate world of association. The color line persisted with vigor, changing in form as it adapted to new conditions such as the use of the automobile, but preserving essentially intact the social positions of the two racial groups. This characterization should not be construed as denying such developments as the scattered formation of new liberal attitudes among southern whites, the emergence here and there of outstanding spokesmen of such attitudes, and the activity of an occasional southern organization seeking to ameliorate racial tensions. Insofar as such developments were able to exercise influence, their effect was more in the direction of improving conditions on the Negro side of the color line or of softening the harshness of treatment in the case of infractions of the color line, than in changing the color line itself. To these observations one should add that Negro residents in the South, individually and collectively, were negligible in initiating attacks on the color line. While their resentments and dissatisfactions with the color line were extensive and acute, the impotency and insecurity of their position restrained them from challenging the color line.

The import of these observations is to call attention to the fundamental fact that the significant agents of change of the color line have been located outside of the arena of southern life. We easily see this as we identify the more conspicuous ones which through law, administrative decree, judicial determination, policy, and action have exerted direct and indirect pressure to change the color line. Thus, we think of (a) the federal government in its many divisions—administrative acts of the executive branch, desegregation decisions in the armed services, judicial interpretation by the federal courts, legislation by Congress, and enforcement acts by appropriate federal agencies; (b) the policies and posture of a host of national organizations and institutions such as churches, educational associations, labor unions, and professional associations espousing stands contrary to different features of the color line; (c) national media of communication—periodicals, the press, television, and radio—presenting definitions which challenged the color line in different ways; (d) national political parties which through their platforms staked out official aims which, even though semi-ceremonial, were in conflict with the color line; and (e) a variety of national action groups, such as the NAACP, spearheading frontal attacks on the color line.

This identification of the major forces which are in play highlights a matter of central importance for an understanding of what is happening to the color line in the South. It is that changes in the color line are an expression and result of *the increasing incorporation of the South into the life of the nation.* This may seem to be a trite observation, scarcely worthy of mention. Yet it goes, I think, to the very heart of the problem of the color line in the South. It calls our attention to several facts. It points out that the change of the color line is both a consequence and a part of a massive movement toward national integration and not a result of scattered and disparate lines of regional activity. The pressures on the color line are not to be thought of as the machinations of questionable officials high in the circles of the federal government, or as incitement by outside agitators, or as the misguided efforts of innocent but uninformed northerners. Instead, the pressures are those of bringing the South increasingly within the body of laws, standards, principles, policies, and institutional arrangements which prevail generally in the nation. One may easily fail to see this fundamental fact when one views singly such events as a decision of a federal court, or a resolution of a religious conference, or the efforts of a team of outsiders to register Negroes on voter rolls in a southern county. However, these events, like a large number of congruent happenings, are but the manifestations of a vast process of embracing the South within a national pattern.

All sections of the nation are becoming increasingly welded into a large polity and entity under the play of such forces as increasing economic interdependency, mobility of people, extension of communication, the dissemination of sanctioned professional standards, the growth of national organizations and the elevation of their importance, the interlocking of institutions on a national basis, and the growth of federal direction and control. The South is already caught up in this massive movement of national integration. There are no tenable grounds for assuming that the South will halt, or be able to halt, this process of its increasing incorporation into national life. It is this perspective which provides us with solid grounds for forming a judgment on the status of the color line in the South in the proximate future.

The incorporation of the South into the national pattern will bear heavily on it in the case of the color line, especially in the Deep South where the color line is most rigidly set. Unquestionably, intense resistance will be offered to making accommodations to the national pattern of Negro-white relations since such accommodations strike, especially in their symbolic character, against the sense of identity and social position which the white group has forged in its historic past. Yet, however bitter and lingering may be the resistance, however dramatic may be acts of opposition at this or that part, however fearsome may be acts of violence and counter-violence, and however contrived the resort to evasion and token accommodation, the resistance can scarcely be viewed as likely to be successful in the face of the ponderous process of incorporation which is in play. We may expect far more, not less, pressure to bring the area of Negro-white relations in the South under the laws and standards of the nation. The South is being edged bit by bit in this direction. There is nothing on the horizon to suggest that this movement will not continue and indeed pick up increasing momentum.

The recognition that the South is being brought abreast of the rest of the nation leads to a significant conclusion, namely, that the fate of the color line in the South will depend increasingly on what happens to Negro-white relations in the nation as a whole. The gaining by southern Negroes of the rights which they enjoy generally elsewhere in the nation—even though this is and will be a strenuous and dramatic struggle in itself—is but an initial stage of the much larger shifting of the social positions of Negroes and whites in the nation. To understand the destiny of the color line in the South, it is necessary to view it from the larger perspective of what is happening to the alignment of Negroes and whites generally in the nation. The problem of Negro-white relations is becoming more and more a nation-wide problem and less and less a problem localized in a given geographical area. To understand the fate of the color line in the South, we must accordingly shift the forces of analysis to this broader arena of Negro-white relations in which the course of the future lies.

The discussion should begin with the recognition that a color line exists not only in the South but in all sections of the nation. In the North and West it is drawn differently from the manner characteristic of the traditional South; nevertheless, it is present extensively and set profoundly. It expresses the fact that in these sections the two racial groups occupy different social positions along the axes of dominance-subordination and exclusion-inclusion. Historically in these sections Negroes were barred, by tacit agreement if not by law, from equal access to many parts of the public arena; they were restricted predominantly to the lower levels of industrial occupation; they were scarcely ever allowed to enter the area of white management; they were subjected to strong residential separation; and they were excluded generally from private circles of white association. That, in comparison to the South, there was less exploitation of them, less hostile attacks on them, less overt denigration of them, and much less conventional "prejudice" shown toward them, does not alter the fact that a strong color line has been drawn against them. Northern and western whites have been much less aware of their color line and much less sensitive about it, but Negroes have felt its impact keenly.

Today Negroes are engaged in a struggle throughout the nation against their subordinate position—not merely in the South toward which dramatic events have focused attention. At present this struggle is taking place primarily in the outer band of the color line, seeking to gain what is customarily referred to as "civil rights," that is to say, to remove the segregated position of Negroes *in the public arena.* What is sought, chiefly, are such rights as free access to public accommodations and public institutions, the enjoyment of the franchise, the equal protection of laws, and equal rights as consumers. Since these rights stem from the legal status of Negroes as citizens and since the exercise of such rights has become a national imperative under the play of the huge forces which are welding the nation into a polity and entity, there is full reason to believe, as previously mentioned, that the rights will be gained. This has already happened in given regions of the North and West. That this will happen generally throughout the nation, even though at a much slower pace in the South, is the reasonable, indeed certain, prospect of the future.

The acquisition of civil rights by Negroes in the South will thus have two stages, so to speak—first, being brought abreast of the general level of enjoyment of such rights as exists elsewhere in the nation, and then sharing in the further struggle to extend those rights that is occurring on a national basis. This assertion may seem blithe in view of the bitter resistance and formidable obstacles set up in the South, particularly in the Deep South, against granting Negroes the round of civil rights which they enjoy elsewhere in the nation. Yet, as I have remarked, the major forces of our epoch are working steadily to weave the South into the national pattern. The border states are already being detached from what was previously a much larger isolated region and this same movement toward national incorporation is clearly at work in the states in the Deep South. The very fact that the resistance in such states to granting civil rights has become such a pronounced matter of *national* concern is itself indicative of the broad movement which is in play to bring the South inside of national patterns. It is this movement, and not the separate acts of resistance to it, which spells out the future of the color line in the South. The movement derives its momentum from the shaping forces of the contemporary age; the acts of resistance, however much they stimulate each other, gain their sustenance from a weakening traditional structure. The maintenance of the color line as it existed traditionally in the South would require a retention of the previous condition of regional isolation of the South in its social, organizational, and legal life. This isolation is breaking down and all signs indicate that it will break down much more rapidly in the future. Despite a lag, especially in rural regions, in extending to Negroes the rights of citizenship under the laws of the land and the standards of the nation, the course of the movement is clear.

It is a serious mistake, however, to regard the achievement by Negroes of civil rights, as presently defined, as equivalent to removing the color line. Whites are generally disposed, it is true, to view the matter in this way. They believe that if Negroes can vote, enter into politics, eat in any restaurant, go to any theater, ride on any public conveyance, have access to any hospital, attend any public function, enroll in any public school, apply for any job, and freely enter government employment, in short enjoy the ostensible rights of citizenship, the color line will have disappeared. However, the area of civil rights constitutes only a part, even though a highly significant part, of the larger region from which the Negro has been barred by the color line. The contested area of civil rights is, as previously stated, but the outer band of the color line. Inside of it lies the crucial area of economic subordination and opportunity restriction—an area of debarment of Negroes which is exceedingly tough because it is highly complicated by private and quasi-private property rights, managerial rights, and organizational rights. Still further inside of the color line are the varied circles of private association from which the Negro is grossly excluded. Thus, the successful achievement of civil rights merely peels off, so to speak, the outer layer of the color line. By itself, it does not alter significantly the social positions of the two racial groups. It raises somewhat the position of the Negro on the dominance-subordination axis but leaves this axis of relationship essentially intact. Its effect on the inclusion-exclusion axis is negligible.

That the satisfaction of demands for civil rights will neither dissolve the color line nor lessen the struggle waged against it can be appreciated further by recognizing how the struggle for civil rights has intensified racial consciousness. Such intensification of racial consciousness has been particularly pronounced in the case of the Negro. The struggle has released, aroused, and mobilized the feelings of bitterness and resentment which Negroes experience as a result of their objectionable social position. Their attitudes, even though largely concealed, have hardened against the whites as a group—against "the Man." Evidence of this may be seen in their increased militancy, in their disparagement of "Uncle Tom" types in their own ranks, in the pressure on their leaders to take a more decisive and militant posture, and in an increasing suspicion of whites extending even to liberal sympathizers. The struggle for civil rights is leading Negroes to a renewed assessment of their disadvantaged social status, bringing into sharper focus the illegality and injustice of their social position, making them chafe under the seeming insensitivity of whites to their plight, and with their increased sense of common identity making them writhe with bitterness over publicized instances of wanton indignity and cruelty occurring in the resistance of whites. They have become increasingly sensitive and touchy with regard to the posture and intentions of whites. To sum up, we are presented with the seemingly anomalous situation in which the struggle for civil rights, even as it moves ahead toward achievement, intensifies the Negro's sense of his disadvantaged position and reinforces his feelings that white society is lined up against him.

We may expect, then, a continuation of assault on the color line but it will shift, as it is now shifting, to a different and inner band. This band, as suggested previously, consists of the barriers confronting the Negro in his efforts to improve his economic lot. These barriers are extensive, varied, and formidable. To specify them is to recite the obvious—the difficulties of the Negro in getting employment, his assignment to lower paying jobs, the ceilings placed on his movements upward in the job structure, his difficulties in entering the areas of management, especially middle and upper management, his difficulties in gaining the training necessary to qualify for higher level jobs, and the formidable restrictions placed on him in the field of private entrepreneurship. Much of the debarment of the Negro, represented by such barriers, springs from feelings of dislike; additionally, much of it occurs through a tacit collective recognition that it is "not the thing to do" to give him entrance to given posts; and part of it results from a lack among Negroes of the training and experience needed to qualify for given posts. Whatever be the causes—and they are indeed complex and intertwined—this general area of debarment of the Negro is extensive, solidly structured, and deeply set. It constitutes a much more formidable part of the color line than is represented by the debarment of the Negro from the exercise of civil rights in the public arena.

What are the prospects of a change in this important part of the color line? We are witnessing today a large variety of scattered efforts to penetrate or remove the barriers which confine the Negro to an inferior economic position and to a sphere of markedly limited opportunity. They take such forms as pressure for fair employment legislation, widening of civil service to Negroes, administrative acts by branches of the federal government on behalf of equal opportunities in employment, greater admission of Negroes to labor unions, scattered voluntary efforts by large business corporations to increase the number of Negro employees and to open higher positions to them, direct demands by Negro groups supported by picketing and boycotts, inauguration of programs of vocational training, development of opportunity programs for Negro youth, and improvement of public education for Negro children. Without discounting the noticeable effects, here and there, of such efforts one must conclude that they have done comparatively little to improve the economic and opportunity base of Negroes in American society. As of the present they are more than offset by two prodigious developments taking place in the life of the Negro. These are, first, the well known demographic movement which is massing Negroes in the deteriorated or deteriorating areas of our large cities, and, second, the technological changes which are closing the doors to conventional fields of Negro employment. To recite the disabilities that flow from each of these two developments would require a lengthy chapter. It is sufficient to state that the combination of the two is producing a vast urban Negro proletariat with a high incidence of unemployment, with no secure foothold in the occupational structure, with restricted opportunities to escape or rise, and largely shut off from white society. The formation of such an urban Negro proletariat is currently proceeding at a pace which far outstrips the totality of the scattered remedial efforts referred to above.

It is not easy to determine or assess how the formation of this urban Negro proletariat will affect the color line. The formation is a new element in the positioning of the two races; its probable effects on their relationship are obscure. Certain conditions and ingredients of the new urban Negro population can be noted. It is an ecologically segregated and socially ingrown community; it is a poor and underprivileged group; it is marked by considerable community and family disorganization; it suffers a considerable loss of its better trained and economically successful members through migration; and its economic sights and hopes are low. This set of conditions might suggest that the urban Negro, like many underprivileged groups in history, would settle into, and accept, an inferior even though miserable position. But we have to recognize another set of conditions in the new urban Negro community—free discussion and movement within it, an increasing sensitivity of

Negroes in it to their plight, a placing of the blame for this plight on white society and hence a generation of increased bitterness toward whites, a stronger disposition to fight back, a fuller appreciation of their civic rights and a greater readiness to use them, a conduciveness to agitation and to formation of protest movements, and the possession of strategic political power. These conditions point to the probability that the urban Negro proletariat, unlike Negroes at the bottom of the social and economic ladder in the past, will not humbly accept this position but be poised to protest and rebel in some fashion. Such a posture introduces great uncertainty as to the status of the color line in the proximate future. The great unknowns are whether the urban Negro proletariat will be mobilized to act with some concert on behalf of a cause, whether its great political potential will be effectively used, and whether the larger white society will be led to undertake a massive program for the improvement of the position of the urban Negro.

A few words should be said about the latter possibility. It is obvious that national attention is increasingly being drawn to the situation of the urban Negro. A number of separate lines of great concern converge on this situation. Let us take note of them. In itself the general concern today with the increasingly pressing question of Negro-white relations leads more and more to the urban setting of these relations. The mounting concern with unemployment in our society, especially as a result of automation, focuses on the urban Negro since he is the chief sufferer from it. The looming concern with urban slums and urban renewal comes to be largely centered on the urban Negro. The mounting problem of delinquency and crime and the growing efforts to cope with the problem direct major concern to the urban Negro. The huge problems which have arisen to confront public education in our large cities, highlighted by the questions of drop-outs, discipline, and de facto segregation, bring the urban Negro centrally into the focus of attention. The augmenting financial difficulties of large cities in providing the services demanded of them have made the position of the Negro a matter of central municipal concern. And, finally, the growing political power of the urban Negro on the municipal, state, and federal levels evokes an order of political responsiveness that makes the urban Negro community an object of sensitive consequence. Given these formidable lines of concern, each of which is likely to increase in magnitude, it is well conceivable that a massive attack will have to be made, chiefly under federal auspices, to improve the economic and community position of the urban Negro.[1] Such an attack would arise less from racial considerations and more from the dictates of national interest.

If such a massive attack is not made and if conditions among urban Negroes are allowed to continue as they are now developing, the prospects are indeed high that discord and overt strife will be persistent marks of the color line. There is no conceivable likelihood that a social code would or could be developed to hold the disparate social positions of the two racial groups in an orderly relation such as was achieved under the color line now breaking down. If, in contrast, a massive attack is undertaken that raises significantly the economic position of the Negro, opens to him all doors in the occupational structure, makes available to him the level of training and preparation to enter such doors, and allows him free residential movement, this would be basically equivalent to eliminating the color line in the intermediate area in which it is now most massively entrenched.

The South will not escape, of course, the struggle that will center on the area of economic position and social opportunity of the urban Negro. The significant signs point to the preponderant likelihood that the struggle will be national in sweep and in character. The major battlegrounds—to use this expression—will be chiefly in the large cities of the North and West, in the headquarters of national organizations, and in the seats of government, particularly the federal government. But the South will be brought into the pattern that emerges and develops on the national scene. What this pattern may be, as foregoing remarks suggest, is a matter of pronounced conjecture. That there will be struggle is certain, since Negroes will be too aroused to accept an economic and social status of such disability and since, out of its own interests, the nation cannot ignore the problems that converge on a depressed urban Negro proletariat. The forces that may be brought into play in the struggle are far too lacking in shape to foreshadow the outcome of

1. Since this article was written (December, 1963), the federal government has shown an increasing interest in such a move, especially in its prospective anti-poverty program.

the struggle. The future of the color line in this intermediate band remains a highly problematic matter.

There remains for consideration the question of the status and fate of what was previously referred to as the inner citadel of the color line. This position of the color line must be recognized as very different from the outer layers represented respectively by denial of civil rights in the public arena and by exclusion of Negroes from economic and social opportunity. This "inner" line of separation is drawn along the inclusion-exclusion axis of the relationship between the two racial groups. It arises from a feeling that the Negro is alien and different and thus needs to be distinguished from those parts of the color line that reflect a sense that the Negro is inferior or subordinate. Its presence can be noted most clearly among whites who are willing to accept Negroes as having equal social status yet who are not disposed to admit them into intimate and private circles, represented by social sets, cliques, private clubs, friendship sets, family circles, courtship, and marriage. Even though this line of exclusion is woven into the lines of separation that stem from a sense of different status position and is obscured by these other lines of separation, it is unquestionably of powerful influence and of great import in the structure of the color line. It comes to vivid expression in that ultimate emotional shibboleth, "Do you want your daughter to marry a Negro?"

Despite its important place in the color line this form of exclusion has largely escaped scholarly study. We know little about it, analytically. But some observations are in order. First, it seems reasonable to expect it to decline in influence were the status positions of the two racial groups in American society to become equalized; however, even in this event there are no grounds to expect it to disappear. Second, it lies outside of the formal controls of a society; it is a matter of personal attitude and thus falls inside of the area of individual determination. Edicts, decrees, and laws cannot direct this line of separation as they may do in the case of other parts of the color line; it is peculiarly immune to outer assault. The two foregoing observations call attention to the fact that an erasing of the color line in the area of civil rights and in the area of economic position and social opportunity does not signify its elimination in this inner band. Third, it is entirely conceivable that even in a situation of equal social status the Negro group would accommodate to exclusion as a separate racial group—as, indeed, Jews have done in large measure. Such an accommodative relation is fully tenable without being a source of tension and discord in a social order.

XVI. RACE RELATIONS AND SOCIAL CHANGE / M. Elaine Burgess

1

Long a dormant giant, the Negro community is now astir, and dramatic alterations characterize southern race relations. News media are saturated with discussions of the "Negro Revolution." Boycotts in Montgomery, sit-ins in Greensboro, riots in Birmingham, freedom rides in New Orleans, and marches on Washington fill the headlines, leaving little doubt of a quickening pace so far as Negro protest is concerned.

In spite of rising tension and intermittent violence, to date the drama has been played largely within the existing social order—legislative enactments, court decisions, executive decrees, and non-violent demonstrations. Martin Luther King states the dominant Negro position in this fashion: "We are a nation of laws, not of men ... but we must present our very bodies, if necessary, to make certain our laws are just and that they are implemented."[1] Most Negroes leading the fight for change in racial patterns have not lost faith in the existing social system so much as in officials of the white community who have refused to provide equality within that system. They are seeking to make the nation aware of these inequalities, hopefully without a trail of blood. Indeed, one student of race relations has hypothesized that stress on non-violent resistance to segregation has developed among southern Negroes primarily as an effort to mediate between the conflicting traditions of the former accommodative patterns and the new militant protest patterns. For the rapidity of change in recent decades has caused most Negroes to be caught between two contradictory ways of life, the old second-class versus the new first-class citizenship. The underlying philosophy of the protest movement bridges the gap between these ways of life by legitimatizing "passive aggression" within the framework of our normative code.[2]

Thus far the Negroes' energetic push for equality, in spite of the fears of some alarmed whites and some voluble Negroes, is not so

1. As quoted in: Louis Lomax, "What Mass Protests Can't Do," *Saturday Review* (July 6, 1963), p. 12.
2. James Vander Zanden, "The Non-Violent Resistance Movement Against Segregation," *American Journal of Sociology*, LXVIII (March, 1963), 544-550.

much a revolution as it is a fast-moving reform movement. Their
goals do not seek to overcome the basic structure of government or
other fundamental institutions. What they are demanding in ever
louder voices is admission to a closed white society which has
denied full access to its protection and benefits. In short, as scholars
of race relations have emphasized, the American Negro is now
striving to become a *Negro American*. Whether the present shifts in
Negro-white relations remain at this level depends upon a number
of complex and interrelated factors, but for now the patterns of
change exist, in part, in social continuity.

The Negro is not simply becoming more and more a protagonist
of change. He is now, as he has always been, a symbol of change.
The new militancy in civil rights is a vital part of a generalized
social transformation throughout the South, and the nation as a
whole. Every major change in the status and role of the Negro in
the past has been a reflection of important modifications in other
parts of the social system.[3] And nothing of what is happening today
in race relations in the South and elsewhere can be understood
apart from all of the small- and large-scale modifications taking
place. The obvious legal changes of recent decades come to mind,
but other changes, frequently unnoticed, have played a vital part
in weakening the foundations of segregation. Demographic alterations, shifts in the economy, expanded communication, and increased urbanization, mechanization, industrialization, migration,
and political participation have all wrought changes in Negro-
white relations. Each contributor to this volume, therefore, has
something important to add to our understanding of shifting race
relations in the South.

We do not believe that changing racial patterns can be understood by studying the South alone. It is true that the southern experience with racial problems is in many ways unique, and that the
focus of the "American Dilemma" has until recent years been
primarily in the South. But the southern experience is unique only
in detail and degree, and Negro-white relations have always been a
national problem. This has become increasingly obvious as Negroes
have moved out across the nation to settle in the ghettos of the

3. See: Charles U. Smith, "Race, Human Relations and the Changing South,"
Phylon, XXIII (Spring, 1962), 66-72.

large urban centers of the North and West. Furthermore, the South has grown less and less isolated from other regions of the country and ever more occupied with national affairs.

Yet despite these facts there remains a constellation of socio-cultural characteristics peculiarly southern. A sense of history and identity continues to set the South apart. The very fact that there has been, and still is, a special quality surrounding southern Negro-white patterns, and that it was here that the boycotts, the picketing, and the sit-ins began, means that we can deal with regional race relations. For, unlike other regions of the United States, much of what the South has been, is now, and is presently to become can be understood only in terms of its biracial nature. V. O. Key illustrates this idea most succinctly:

> In its grand outlines the politics of the South revolves around the position of the Negro. It is at times interpreted as a politics of cotton, as a politics of free trade, as a politics of agrarian poverty, or as a politics of planter and plutocrat. Although such interpretations have a superficial validity, in the last analysis the major peculiarities of Southern politics go back to the Negro. Whatever phase of the southern political process one seeks to understand, sooner or later the trail of inquiry leads to the Negro.[4]

Thus, while our first concern is with race relations in the South, we are ever mindful that these relations influence, and in turn are influenced by, race relations throughout America.

The *South* as used throughout this analysis will ordinarily follow the definition of the Census of the United States, including the states of the South Atlantic, East South Central, and West South Central areas. Occasionally, we shall speak of the *Southeast*, following the delineation of Howard Odum. In such cases Louisiana, Tennessee, Virginia, Georgia, South Carolina, Arkansas, Kentucky, Mississippi, Alabama, North Carolina, and Florida are included in the definition. The time limits of this study will be somewhat narrowly drawn. To be sure, present trends in biracial patterns have their roots in the ante bellum period. A case can also be made for beginning with the events of the depression years and the New Deal. However, it is the very significant alterations in Negro-white relations that evolved during and following World War II which

4. V. O. Key, *Southern Politics in State and Nation* (New York: Alfred A. Knopf, Inc., 1949), p. 5.

seem most pertinent. Therefore special attention will be paid to the changing status of the Negro from the decade of the 1940's to the present.

2

Students have observed that the central fact of social change appears to be alterations in the individual or group positions of members of a society. Consequently, what is presently happening in race relations in the South can best be understood in terms of changing status and power aspirations.[5] Without denying the cogency of these arguments we would be remiss if we did not underscore a fundamental change in attitudes and values of Negroes which make these efforts toward status shifts possible. The objectives of every movement for change, whether or not such movements are revolutionary, have in common the fact that they represent interests and values that have failed to find full recognition in the existing power and status system.[6]

Segregation in the South and elsewhere has symbolized the inevitable inferiority of Negroes. It has "kept the Negro in his place," not only on buses and streetcars, in hospitals and restaurants, but to a great extent in the total socio-economic system. Resistance to any modification of this symbol of inferiority has been predicated, in many instances, on the fear that if the Negro were allowed to escape from his inferior position the status of the white man would thereby be jeopardized—the very prestige that "whiteness" has provided would be automatically abrogated. Nevertheless, the recent gains Negroes have realized as the result of shifts in the socio-economic structure have made many of them increasingly aware of the variance between the "ideal" values implicit in democracy and the "real" values explicit in discrimination and desegregation. They have become painfully conscious of the discrepancy between their

5. Edgar T. Thompson, "The South and the Second Emancipation," in Allan Sindler (ed.), *Change in the Contemporary South* (Durham: Duke University Press, 1963), pp. 93-118; Ruth Searles and Allen Williams, "Participation in Sit-Ins," *Social Forces*, XL (March, 1962), 215-220; M. Elaine Burgess, *Negro Leadership in a Southern City* (Chapel Hill: University of North Carolina Press, 1962); Daniel C. Thompson, *Negro Leadership Class* (Englewood Cliffs, N. J.: Prentice-Hall, Inc., 1963).

6. See for example: Kurt Lang and Gladys Lang, *Collective Dynamics* (New York: Thomas Y. Crowell Co., 1960), p. 492.

ascribed status of race and their achieved status of high school or college graduate, skilled, white-collar, or professional worker.

Where has this status inconsistency[7] been felt more keenly? The answer seems to lie within the rising new middle and lower-middle class, nourished and trained within the urban black belts. The slow but steady gains made by middle-class Negroes have (as we shall discuss in more detail later), prompted more, not less, dissatisfaction with their position in the power and status system. It is here, we propose, that some explanation can be found concerning the agitation for change in patterns of race relations, particularly since the Supreme Court decision of 1954.

The above assertions give rise to two basic questions: (1) what are the evidences of a significantly large and growing middle class among Negroes? and (2) why has this growth made a difference in expressions of racial conflict and change? Let us examine first the evidence attesting to an emerging Negro middle class.

3

While most students of race relations would agree that there is a sizeable Negro middle class in America today, the average layman may still find it hard to believe that most Negroes are not inherently lower class. It is, of course, difficult to define "middle class" with any exactness, and sociologists continue to disagree over the best means for differentiating social class in general. As in the white community, the class structure of the Negro community is fluid. There are no precise lines among strata, and social mobility is apparent. Yet we have continued to refine measures of class strata, and such measures provide some validity for the delineation of various class levels.

Among the current indexes of class position *occupation, education, class identification,* and *income* seem to be the most useful. Numerous revisions of earlier works place more or less emphasis on these variables as the most reliable measures presently available to the social scientist.[8] The relative importance of these symbolic

7. For a discussion of "status inconsistency" and similar concepts, see Elton F. Jackson, "Status Consistency and Symptoms of Stress," *American Sociological Review*, XXVII (August, 1962), 469-482; Gerhard Lenski, "Status Crystallization: A Non-vertical Dimension of Social Status," *American Sociological Review*, XIX (August, 1954), 405-413.

8. August B. Hollingshead and Fredrick C. Redlich, *Social Class and Mental*

characteristics of class status varies slightly between the white and the Negro community. A recent review of a number of studies done on Negro prestige and social class contends that while occupation is considered to be the single most important predictive class characteristic for whites, education continues to rank above occupation for Negroes.[9] Regardless of the weight attached to these criteria, however, there is ample support for their use as objective measures of class, and the author shall employ them to illustrate important advances made by the Negro middle class during the past two decades.*

It was implied earlier that the emergence of the Negro middle class was concurrent with an expanding Negro urban population. A brief discussion of Negro urban migration is therefore pertinent, for it is in the larger cities of the South, and more especially the North and West, that we find unmistakable evidence of the growth of class divisions and a sizeable middle stratum.

Following emancipation Negroes began their slow migration into the cities, although in 1890 four out of five Negroes still lived in rural areas. Those who moved went largely to southern cities, and as late as 1910 nearly 69 per cent of the urban Negro population still resided in the South. Between 1910 and 1917 urban centers of the South experienced a new influx of Negroes in response to the demand for labor in railroad building and new commercial and industrial enterprises. Thereafter the large Negro ghettos throughout the country began a very slow process of occupational and educational differentiation. A small group of pre-war freedmen and a small number of business and professional men provided the nucleus for an upper and a middle class. The latter gradually came to be separated from the mass of lower-class Negroes by greater stability of family life and by closer integra-

---

Illness (New York: John Wiley and Sons, Inc., 1958), pp. 387-397; Robert A. Ellis and W. Clayton Lane, "The Index of Class Position: An Improved Intercommunity Measure of Stratification," *American Sociological Review*, XXVIII (April, 1963), 272-277; Joseph Kahl and James A. Davis, "A Comparison of Indexes of Socio-Economic Status," *American Sociological Review*, XX (June, 1955), 317-325; Charles B. Nam, "Nationality Groups and Social Stratification," *Social Forces*, XXXVII (May, 1959), 328-333.

9. Norval D. Glenn, "Negro Prestige Criteria: A Case Study in the Bases of Prestige," *American Journal of Sociology*, LXVIII (May, 1963), 645-657; Burgess, *op. cit.*

* "Class identification" as an index of class status is implicit throughout Part 4, and shall not be dealt with as a separate variable in this section.

tion with the institutional life of the sub-community. Most of this group were skilled and semiskilled workers, and the more responsible domestic and service workers.[10] Still the climb up the class ladder was painfully slow and the middle class, as well as the upper class, remained very limited.

It was not until the decades of the 1940's and 1950's when we witnessed the most explosive growth of urban population in our history—particularly Negro—that a significant rise in the Negro middle class took place. While the native white urban population increased by 22.6 per cent (old urban-rural definition) between 1940 and 1950, the Negro urban population increased by 43.2 per cent (or at a rate almost twice that of whites) during this time. The rural South lost a million Negro residents in the years of the forties alone. Many migrated West or North, but a large number moved into southern cities as well.[11] A rapid rise in industrial employment facilitated this movement which continued through the 1950's. If we look only at the eleven states comprising the Southeast we find that 61 per cent of the nation's non-white population resided here in 1940; by 1960 the percentage had dropped to 44.8 per cent. In 1940 these southern states contained 32.8 per cent urban non-white population. In 1950 this proportion had risen to 42.9 per cent and by 1960 it was 52.9 per cent. By 1960 nearly 14 million of the approximately 19 million Negroes were living in urban areas of the United States.[12]

What do these migration patterns mean with regard to changing Negro class structure? Hylan Lewis explains their significance in the following way:

10. E. Franklin Frazier, *The Negro in the United States* (New York: The Macmillan Co., 1949), p. 190; Alvin Boskoff, "Negro Class Structure and the Technicways," *Social Forces*, XXIX (December, 1950), 124-131.

11. Donald Bogue, *The Population of the United States* (Glencoe, Illinois: The Free Press, 1959), p. 127; George Simpson and Milton Yinger, "The Sociology of Race and Ethnic Relations," in Robert K. Merton, Leonard Broom, and Leonard S. Cottrell, Jr. (eds.), *Sociology Today* (New York: Basic Books, Inc., 1959), p. 385.

12. Selz C. Mayo and C. Horace Hamilton, "Current Population Trends in the South," *Social Forces*, XLII (October, 1963), 80. Because Negroes make up approximately 98 per cent of the non-white population of the Southeast, 95 per cent of the non-white population of the Census South, and 92.1 per cent of the non-white population for United States as a whole, *Negro* and *non-white* have been used here and throughout the rest of paper as roughly coterminous. U. S. Bureau of the Census, *United States Census of Population: 1960, Subject Reports, Non-white Population by Race*, PC(2)-1C (Washington, D. C.: United States Government Printing Office, 1963).

The normal economic, political, and social imperatives of urban life are such that the Negro in the cities of the South gets an automatic increment in his struggle for status and power merely by the fact of being there. The urban premium on freedom, impersonality, efficiency and profits, voluntary organizations and participation by representation provides for Negroes and whites a new frontier for shaping of a common destiny.[13]

It is in the city that the greatest educational opportunities have become available to the Negro. It is here that expanding occupational opportunities have been possible, and that a rise in income and standard of living have gradually been realized. In the urban black belts, Negro institutions such as the church, the schools and colleges, business and professional associations, labor and political organizations, the Urban League, and the National Association for the Advancement of Colored People have flourished. These social institutions provided the breeding ground for a new kind of citizen and a new kind of leadership trained in the values and skills of the middle class. In what do they believe and what do they value? Primarily they believe in themselves and their future, in respectability, family stability, economic security, a "decent standard of living," and in responsible participation in community (i.e., Negro protest) affairs. Education and occupational achievement are highly valued. Education is the avenue to necessary training and skills for getting ahead, for inculcating the youth with the "right democratic values," the right motivations, the right commitments to the future, and the right patterns of behavior. A high school diploma is increasingly essential, and sacrifice to send children on to college is a positive good. Aspirations are for the professional, semiprofessional, white-collar, and skilled occupations—and the chance for a respectable style of life dictated by ability, not race. In sum, the new Negro middle class is distinguishable because it adheres to the predominant American value system of equality and is militantly determined to share in the "American Dream."[14]

Despite the characteristics we posit for the new middle class we do not assume that the members of this or any other stratum—Negro or white—are completely homogeneous. There is, of course,

13. Hylan Lewis, "Innovations and Trends in the Contemporary Negro Community," *Journal of Social Issues*, X (1954), 22-24.
14. Joseph Kahl, *The American Class Structure* (New York: Rinehart and Co., Inc., 1957), pp. 193-205; Burgess, *op. cit.*, pp. 34-35.

variation in behavior and in the degree to which they are committed to these middle-class goals and aspirations. Nevertheless, members of the Negro middle class, like other social class members, share significant traits in common and the social scientist can make generalizations about them.

A resumé of occupational shifts among Negroes during the past two decades illustrates important advances despite continued gaps between Negro and white attainment. Relatively little progress was made in permitting non-white workers to enter white-collar and skilled occupations prior to the 1930's. It was not until the labor shortages, the expansion of many occupations, and the effects of mass urban migrations began to be felt in the early 1940's that the growing occupational differentiation in the Negro population began to appear. Between 1940 and 1950 Negro occupational gains were very large compared to gains of previous decades. Utilizing an intracohort analysis to measure changes in occupational status of Negro males relative to education, Nathan Hare found that significant gains were made in the occupational groupings of proprietors, managers and officials; craftsmen and foremen; clerical and sales workers; and operatives and kindred. White males evidenced an increase in proportion among the first two categories, but the Negro representation changed at a relatively faster rate than it did for whites. Among the latter two occupational groups Negroes increased rapidly while whites showed a net loss. While Negroes are still overrepresented in the lower levels of the occupational structure and underrepresented in the upper strata, they have succeeded in leaving occupations of overrepresentation. Negro male college graduates made greater strides toward parity with whites than did those at any other educational level during the period from 1940 to 1950, but during the 1950's, unlike the 1940's, education in general was found to be much more effective in helping Negroes leave occupations of overrepresentation.[15]

Although the most important modifications in Negro occupational status occurred in the decade of the 1940's, substantial gains have continued to the present. During the first eight years of the

15. Nathan Hare, "Changes in Occupational Status of Negroes, 1930-1960: An Intracohort Analysis," paper read at the American Sociological Association, Los Angeles, California, August, 1963, pp. 9-13. See also: Norval Glenn, "Changes in the American Occupational Structure and Occupational Gains of Negroes during the 1940's," *Social Forces*, XLI (December, 1962), 188-195.

1950's the number of non-white male farmers (largely sharecroppers in the South) was estimated to have dropped by 55 per cent, and the number of farm laborers dropped by 21 per cent. The proportion of Negroes in certain higher status jobs has increased since 1950 as follows: professional and technical workers, 49 per cent; clerical and kindred workers, 69 per cent; sales workers, 24 per cent; craftsmen, 20 per cent. Discussions of growth rates can be misleading, since they can exaggerate the amount of change if the number of Negroes in a given occupation is initially very small. Nevertheless, a comparison of the proportion of non-white workers in each occupation with the average per cent who are non-white among all workers does illustrate that important shifts have taken place. In no one of the upper and middle occupational groups is the proportion of non-whites negligible, and there have been concrete additions in the proportion who are non-white in almost all categories. In 1940, 10.0 per cent of the non-white labor force were in professional, managerial, clerical, sales, or craftsmen occupations; 12.2 per cent were operatives. By 1960 these proportions had almost doubled with 22.2 per cent non-whites in the top five occupational groupings and 24.4 per cent listed as operatives.[16]

Within the South the same general trend has taken place, although at a slower pace. While there remains a high concentration of Negroes in the lower-status "Negro" jobs and a low proportion in the high-status "white" jobs, in the *broad middle range* of the occupational system of the Southeast there has been convergence among Negroes and whites.[17] These and similar findings lend support to the contention that a clearly defined and sizeable Negro middle class has evolved during the last two decades.

The gap between educational attainment of Negroes and whites has also narrowed during the past twenty years. In 1940 white persons twenty-five years of age and over had completed 8.7 median years of schooling in contrast to 5.8 for non-whites. By 1960 the medians had risen to 10.8 for whites and 8.2 for Negroes. An analysis of the young adult Negro population in the United States shows

16. Bogue, *op. cit.*, pp. 503-505, 506-507; U. S. Department of Labor, *The Economic Situation of Negroes in the United States, Bulletin* S-3 (Washington, D. C.: U. S. Government Printing Office, 1960).

17. Munro S. Edmonson and David R. Norsworthy, "Industry and Race in the Southern United States," New Orleans, Louisiana, Tulane University, 1963, p. 3. (Mimeographed.)

where the most striking gains have been made in educational advancement. The average level of attainment has risen more rapidly among the young non-white than it has among the young white population. The median school years completed for the white population between the ages of twenty-five to twenty-nine in 1940 was 10.7, compared to 7.0 for non-whites of this age, or a difference of 3.7 median years. In 1960 the difference in median school years completed had narrowed to 1.5, with the whites having completed 12.3 median years of schooling in contrast to 10.8 for non-whites. Similar achievements were made for non-whites in the thirty to thirty-four age group as well.[18]

By observing the changing proportion of Negro high school and college graduates we find an analogous trend. Only 9 per cent of the non-white population in the United States twenty-five years of age and older had completed four years of high school or beyond, or received a college degree in 1940. By 1960, 25.3 per cent in this age category had done so. Among those twenty-five to twenty-nine years of age in 1940, 13.9 per cent had graduated from high school, gone on to college, or finished at least four years of higher education. The proportion had jumped to 44 per cent by 1960.[19]

Increased educational attainment is further reflected in data on school enrollment, as Table 1 illustrates:

Table 1. Per Cent of School Age Youth Enrolled in School, by Color: 1940, 1950, and 1960.

Census year	7 to 13 year olds		14 and 15 year olds		16 and 17 year olds	
	White	Non-white	White	Non-white	White	Non-white
1940	95.5	91.3	91.0	82.8	70.6	52.9
1950	95.9	93.9	93.6	89.0	75.9	64.3
1960	97.8	95.9	94.7	90.1	81.9	73.3

Source: U.S. Bureau of the Census, *U.S. Census of the Population: 1960, United States Summary*, Table 169. U.S. Bureau of the Census, *U.S. Census of the Population: 1950, United States Summary* (Washington, D.C.: 1954), Table 110. Charles P. Nam, "Race and Educational Advancement," *Columbia University Seminar on Population and Social Change*, November 12, 1963 (New York: Columbia University Press, 1964), Table 1.

18. U.S. Bureau of the Census, *U.S. Census of the Population: 1960, Characteristics of the Population, United States Summary* (Washington, D. C.: U.S. Government Printing Office, 1964), Table 173. U.S. Bureau of the Census, *U.S. Census of the Population: 1940, United States Summary* (Washington, D. C.: U.S. Government Printing Office, 1944), Table 18. Bogue, *op. cit.*, p. 343.

19. Charles B. Nam, "Race and Educational Advancement," paper read at Columbia University Seminar on Population and Social Change, New York, November 12, 1963, Table 8.

The South still lags behind other regions of the country in the median number of school years completed, in the proportion of persons completing high school, attending or graduating from college, and in the proportion of youths enrolled in school. Yet the same general trend of educational advancement for Negroes and whites is found. For example, the median number of school years completed for the total population of the South rose from 8.6 in 1950 to 9.9 in 1960. In southern urban areas the median number of school years attained by Negroes jumped from 6.7 in 1950 to 8.4 in 1960. Similar improvements were evidenced for rural Negroes of the South.[20]

One final note with regard to education and the Negro in America. Recent research provides evidence that the plans and ambitions of Negro youths are becoming more similar to those of their white peers. In one instance it was found that Negro high school student educational aspirations exceed those of whites, as do their mobility aspirations.[21] While such studies do not indicate what subsequent educational achievements actually are, a survey made by the Census Bureau on plans and actions of high school seniors reveals that a slightly higher proportion of non-white seniors indicate that they plan to attend college than do whites. But a slightly higher proportion of the white seniors who plan to attend college actually do so than do non-whites.[22] Such studies, although merely suggestive, do indicate that Negro aspirations have greatly increased in recent years, and although their actual achievement of further education remains below that of white youth, differences are diminishing.

The divergence in income contingent upon race has narrowed substantially since 1939 when the median wage and salary income of non-white primary families and individuals was only 37 per cent of that of the corresponding white group. Between 1947 and 1962 non-white families enjoyed about the same relative increase in aver-

20. U.S. Bureau of the Census, *U.S. Census of the Population: 1950, Characteristics of the Population*, II, 363-364; *U.S. Census of Population: 1960, Subject Reports, Nonwhite Population by Race.*

21. Noel P. Gist and William S. Bennett, Jr., "Aspirations of Negro and White Students," *Social Forces*, XLII (October, 1963), 40-48.

22. Charles B. Nam and James D. Cowhig, "Factors Related to College Attendance of Farm and Non-Farm High School Graduates," in U.S. Bureau of the Census, *Farm Population*, ERS (P-27), 32 (Washington, D. C.: U.S. Government Printing Office, 1961).

age income as white families did (although in absolute terms the rise was considerably larger for white families). The median income rose from $1,600 in 1947 to $3,300 in 1962 for non-white families throughout the United States, representing an increase of 106 per cent. For white families income rose from $3,200 to $6,200, or by 98 per cent. The relative gains made by non-white families were more substantial in the first part of this period. The highest ratio of non-white to white income came in 1952, when it was .57. In subsequent years the ratio has fluctuated between .51 and .56, and in 1962 it was .53.[23] Of special interest for our purposes, however, is the fact that in 1949 only 6.1 per cent of the non-white families in this country had incomes ranging from $3,000 to $6,999, while in 1962 the proportion having incomes in this range jumped to 25.5 per cent. Furthermore, in 1962 the proportion of non-white families in the middle income group of from $4,000 to $6,000 was 21 per cent, about the same as the proportion of white families within this range, which was 22 per cent. The great disparity in income distributions between whites and non-whites is now found in the lower and higher income brackets.[24]

Alterations in income distribution in the South over the past twenty years show a trend similar to that for the entire country, although it remains behind the rest of the United States in this index as it does with others. The relatively low income of the southern rural Negro population, as well as the continued heavy concentration of Negro workers in the lower paid service and labor jobs, and the hazards of irregular employment influence Negro family yearly income in the South particularly. Yet median family income as well as per capita income of the Negro has moved upward here, too. In 1949 the median income per person fourteen years of age and over was $739 for Negroes in the South. By 1962 it had risen to $1,604.[25]

23. For regions outside the South, the ratio was approximately two-thirds in 1962, whereas in the South it was less than one-half. U.S. Bureau of the Census, *Current Population Reports, Consumer Income: Income of Families and Persons in the United States: 1962*, P-60, 41 (Washington, D. C.: U.S. Government Printing Office, 1963), pp. 5-11.

24. *Ibid.*, p. 33; U.S. Bureau of the Census, *U.S. Census of Population: 1950, United States Summary*, p. 298.

25. U.S. Bureau of the Census, *Current Population Reports, Consumer Income,* P-60, p. 36. U.S. Bureau of the Census, *U.S. Census of Population: 1950*, Table 162, p. 413.

Another interesting permutation in the Negro economic position can be seen in data on annual purchasing power. In 1939 Negro purchasing power in the Southeast was less than $1 billion. By 1950 this figure had grown to approximately $3.5 billion. For the United States as a whole the Negro purchasing power was slightly less than $15 billion in 1950. A recent market survey indicates that by 1964 this purchasing power will pass $28 billion annually, not quite double what it was in 1950, and approximately equal to Canada's entire consumer market.[26] These data demonstrate in a slightly different way that the overall economic status of the Negro has been improving.

We are not unmindful that the occupational advances made by Negroes have been slowing down during recent years and that the majority of Negroes remain at the lower levels of the occupation ladder, making them particularly susceptible to unemployment and other problems created by increased automation and technology. Nor are we unaware that Negro youths continue to represent the highest proportion of school dropouts. Their level of educational attainment and the quality of education for large numbers is far below that of their white peers. We are also conscious of the fact that 60 per cent of the Negroes continue to be represented at the lower levels of income and that the median income of Negro families is only about half of that for whites. Nevertheless, important changes have occurred. Growing numbers of Negroes are securing high school and college education; there has been a striking increase in professional, managerial, white-collar, and skilled occupations; and there is ample evidence of a rising standard of living. These phenomena have had their most dramatic influence at the middle levels of the Negro population, testifying to the appearance of a sizeable Negro middle class within and without the South.

4

Why has an expanding Negro middle class made a difference in the tempo and tone of American race relations in general and southern race relations in particular? The answer lies, I believe, within

26. Lucile Chambers, *America's Tenth Man* (New York: Twayne Publishers, Inc., 1957), p. 261; Richard L. Tobin, "The Negro and the Advertiser," *Saturday Review* (November 9, 1963), pp. 67-68.

sociological theory on change, collective behavior, and reference groups. Much of the literature dealing with social protest movements has given emphasis to the expressions of frustration and hostility felt by the deprived lower classes toward those in power, as well as toward themselves. Alienated from the larger society, they are driven by a sense of common fate into mass movements that provide release from the tension and psychological disturbance of their deprived status.[27] If this be the sole explanation one might well ask why then did not the militant activities of the Negro begin long ago when their conditions were, by present standards, much harsher. Kurt and Gladys Lang provide a partial answer when they observe that, although the alienated are composed of the "have-nots," they are not identical with the underprivileged lower classes. Rather, they may best be typified by the disaffected new middle classes and minorities whose expectations have been aroused but who somehow are blocked in the fulfilment of these expectations.[28]

Wilbert E. Moore holds a similar point of view but expands on it by turning to the concept of relative deprivation and reference group theory. He first makes the point that status and prestige systems may endure for considerable periods without causing rebellion because of the very nature of the differential distribution of power, resources, and knowledge. The question of how the poor and powerless will come to react against inequality can be answered only if we note that it is not always the most downtrodden members of the system that lead movements of protest or form the spearheads of discontent. Rather the overt manifestations of discontent are likely to occur among those who have not fared badly, but also have not fared well. Even Marx, whose capacity as a social analyst was frequently obscured by his political ideology, recognized the differences between "leading elements" and what he called the *Lumpenproletariat*. This characteristic of protest by those who have escaped the very lowest positions has been observed in the newly developing areas of the world such as Africa, and we derive from this evidence a kind of cross-sectional confirmation of

27. See for example: R. M. McIver and C. H. Page, *Society* (New York: Rinehart and Co., Inc., 1949), p. 372; Robert K. Merton, *Social Theory and Social Structure* (rev. ed.; Glencoe, Illinois: The Free Press, 1957), pp. 155-156.

28. Lang and Lang, *op. cit.*, pp. 324-343.

dynamic processes of order and change.[29] Therefore, concludes Moore:

> The *"relative deprivation"* [italics mine] of those fairly fully incorporated into the values associated with new modes of social placement, but thereby more envious of complete success than their less fortunate compatriots provides the explanatory key to the source of discontent in systems of social inequality.[30]

Neither the Negro lower class nor the upper class could have mounted the resistance movement we are now witnessing throughout the South. The former does not possess the resources, either internal or external, essential for such a movement, and the latter is much too small and, very frequently, too far removed from the masses to do so. Such activity had to wait upon the development of an ample middle class that was motivated to push for validation of a hard-won class position, thus far denied by the white social structure. The question of unequal distribution of status and power between Negroes and whites would consequently appear as a special case of the more basic problem of order and change. By no means are we saying that all challenges to established social structures or power distributions are class oriented, or directly concerned with relative social position. Nevertheless, it is true that one of the major sources of tension and therefore of change and potential change in the South, as in the broader society, stems from the new middle-class Negro's disbelief in past rationales for inequality and the desire for substitution of new rationales.[31]

Although the middle-class Negro has arisen in segregated urban sub-communities he has not been unmindful of his counterpart in the white community. It is not simply a matter of his having been educated to the democratic values of equality that has made him acutely aware of discrepancies in his status. The gradual changes in his occupation and other socio-economic positions have permitted certain kinds of communication and interaction with middle-class whites, at least on a formal level. Contact via community welfare and service agencies, professional contacts in such fields as education, religion, government, and law, and interaction within labor

29. Wilbert E. Moore, *Social Change* (Englewood Cliffs, New Jersey: Prentice-Hall, Inc., 1963), pp. 83-84.
   30. *Ibid.*
   31. *Ibid.*

unions, the creative arts, the armed services, and other such areas have grown considerably during the past twenty years. He no longer looks about him and says "I am better off than my parents were," or "I am better off than the mass of Negroes." Rather, he compares himself to, and identifies with, persons of similar position and training within the white community and finds his own position "wanting" in contrast to this new reference group. Nor does the old reference group of the upper-class Negro any longer obtain. With the changing networks of social relations and his increasing integration into the larger community, the middle-class Negro has sought to escape the obligations and pressures of "keeping up" the requirements of upper-class behavior in the Negro group, while acting in the role of middle-class white-collar worker in the community at large. Instead he seeks to orient his behavior with reference to the middle class of the broader community.[32] As he observes his white counterpart he finds reason for feeling deprived, and this sense of relative deprivation has proved the catalyst for militancy and mass protest against segregation and discrimination. Recent alterations in Negro tactics from passive accommodation to active demonstration can be seen, therefore, as a direct consequence of a shift from evaluating his status primarily in terms of his own (Negro) membership group to evaluating it in terms of the (white) non-membership group.[33] Incidental to this permutation in reference group has been, of course, "creeping legal desegregation," culminating in the Supreme Court decision of 1954, which has provided legitimacy to his desire for equal rights. It has given him the self-respect and the moral support needed in his push for complete realignment of his place in the American social system.

Hence an articulate and responsible citizenry has evolved in Negro sub-communities throughout the urban South. A proliferation of Negro organizations has emerged, such as the Southern Christian Leadership Conference and the Student Non-Violent Coordinating Committee, to take their place alongside the Urban League, the National Association for the Advancement of Colored People, and a myriad of other local and national religious, political, economic, and educational associations concerned with racial advancement.

32. Frazier, *op. cit.*, pp. 299-300.
33. Searles and Williams, *op. cit.*, pp. 216-217; Merton, *op. cit.*, pp. 242-269.

From the ranks of the articulate citizenry and the various organizations in city after city has come a new kind of leadership. The traditional Negro leadership roles have been replaced by a spirit of equalitarianism. The new leader fights, not acquiesces. No more can a single spokesman, a "white man's Negro," an apathetic or fearful leader, exercise influence. In spite of occasional assertions by some within the Negro ranks that vital leadership is still lacking, at no time in the history of the Negro in America has there been such a reservoir of qualified leaders as those now heading the push for equal rights.[34] The fact that they do not always agree on the means and/or the short-term goals involved in their crusade for equality does not alter this fact. Some diversity of purpose, some specialization of function are to be expected here as in other areas of society. The various protest programs within and among various Negro communities must, of course, realize a degree of harmony in order to be effective. But here again, never before has communication and interaction among Negroes, North and South, been more evident.

It is true that in some instances leaders, such as those within the Black Muslim movement, reflect goals and employ means which run counter to the mainstream of Negro aspiration. Responsible southern leaders are aware of, and do not discount, the sentiments expressed by groups like the Black Muslims, but thus far they have rejected their tactics and goals and strive for "Christian" action in obtaining full participation in the larger society. Furthermore, a new generation of Negro leadership is now coming from the colleges throughout the South—young people already skilled in leading marching columns of protest. Their determination and freedom of spirit, made possible by the changes we have been discussing, pay honor to present day Negro leadership, many of whom the young Negro will soon shoulder aside. It would seem, therefore, that the stage has been set for increasingly aggressive leadership in programs geared to the removal of barriers surrounding the black belts in the immediate future.

34. See for example: Daniel C. Thompson, *op. cit.*; Lewis Killian and Charles U. Smith, "Negro Protest Leaders in a Southern Community," *Social Forces*, XXXVIII (March, 1960), 253-257; Burgess, *op. cit.*; Louis Lomax, *The Negro Revolt* (New York: Harper and Row, 1963).

5

One is tempted to search for parallels in the experiences of the Negro and early immigrant groups, parallels which may shed light on the prospective course of Negro-white relations. As wave after wave of immigrants came to America they brought with them aspirations for the future. Beginning at the bottom they gradually moved up the status ladder as they acquired skills, capital, land, and eventually acceptance. Each group, in time, added something to the culture and meaning of America. They repeatedly illustrated that the uniqueness of America is a common hope, not a common past. Eventually, as Edgar Thompson has so eloquently pointed out, each of the groups could look back and say "We Americans— we did it."[35] Now the Negro, breaking out of the ghettos as did the immigrants in time past, desires to say "We Americans—we did it." He yearns for a future America that he too will have a part in building, a part quite different from that allotted him until now. To this extent an analogy exists.

There are some important differences, however, between the aspiring foreign-born white and the aspiring Negro. It was the European peasant coming to America who held pride in achievement. Although his standard of living in Europe may have been nearly as low as the Negro slave's, he came to our cities better equipped to move upward. He had had an opportunity in the Old World to market his produce, to manage his small stock of goods and money. Contrarily, Negroes emerging from slavery, or later from sharecropping, had little experience with money and little occasion to develop skill in planning and saving. Furthermore, Negroes have differed from European immigrant groups in that they did not develop the same kind of clannishness in the city. They did not have the same close family ties or strong family structure that in other groups provided a pool of resources upon which to rely, until such time as individuals "could make it on their own." It has been difficult for the Negro to develop the notion of "sticking together," of building a common life within the ghetto in order to get ahead in the broader society. Only gradually did Negro institu-

35. Edgar T. Thompson, "The South and the Second Emancipation," *op. cit.*, p. 108. The author has benefited immeasurably from a number of provocative ideas present in Thompson's article.

tions gain strength to provide a cohesive force for the black belts.[36] Thus pride in achievement, aspiration for full participation in American life, did not begin with the oft-times hopeless lower-class Negroes. These had to await the development of the lower-middle and middle classes.

There is, of course, a more significant difference between the Negro and the European immigrant. The Negro, no matter how successful he may become, cannot hide his membership in a group that has for so long symbolized inferiority in the minds of whites. Desire for advancement does not erase color. Whereas European ethnic groups were easily assimilated, posing little lasting threat to the basic status system of America, the Negro is not, and thus continues as a threat. And so long as there remains a color line there is much the Negro must continue to fight for, including achievements that the offspring of white immigrants realized much more rapidly.

What then of the future of Negro-white relations throughout the South and the country as a whole? The walls of discrimination have not yet come tumbling down. Advances made have also brought new problems needing urgent attention. Changes in Negro rights have to date been more symbolic than revolutionary. The occupational and economic advancement of the Negro has, for the time being at least, slowed down. The mass of lower-class Negroes suffer most from the threat of automation and unemployment. The problem of housing for urban Negroes has yet to be faced squarely in most communities. School desegregation in southern and northern communities alike is complicated by tokenism, overcrowding, poor preparation, lack of equipment and teachers, lack of motivation, and housing segregation. A hard core of white resistance to Negro advancement has appeared, and must be met. The mass of Negroes must develop responsibility for implementing their new rights and privileges.

Truly, the concentration of multiple problems in the Negro sectors of our cities remains exceptional, but low income, poor housing, and lack of education can explain only so much. The uprooting caused by urban migration creates new problems from

36. Nathan Glazer and Daniel Moynihan, *Beyond the Melting Pot* (Cambridge, Massachusetts: M.I.T. Press and Harvard University Press, 1963), pp. 32-33.

which even the best organized and integrated immigrant groups suffered. When the basic core of organization, the family, is still weak as it is for many Negroes, the magnitude of the problems can be staggering. What slavery began, prejudice and discrimination have continued to keep alive.

This, in essence, is the situation in many Negro communities today; it will likely remain so for some time. Hence the Negro middle class suffers greatly from the burden of its people's social problems. Frequently the dilemmas of the lower-class Negro are so great that the middle class is unable to deal with them. Too, their own image is still greatly affected by the lower-class problem element. Often the middle-class Negro is separated only by a thin line from the lower class and is too busy maintaining his own precarious adaptation to offer the necessary assistance. Furthermore the Negro, unlike other ethnic groups, has had few values and little culture explictly his own to guard. He is an American and because he is a product of America his needs are everyone's dilemma.[37]

There is no doubt but that the Negro will continue to win a greater share in American life, and at an ever increasing pace. Yet within and without the South the change in Negro status is confined by social systems with a limited amount of flexibility. Traditional value systems, problems of economic and technological development, lack of political and social maturity still pose barriers and, although the Negro is asking for equality *now* it seems most likely that his aspirations will continue to surpass actual attainment. Nevertheless, the South must realize that changing Negro status and demands are reflections of social change at many levels and cannot be handled without regard for this fact. Just how far the white community is willing to co-operate with the Negro in solving his problems and in realizing first-class citizenship will determine in large measure the future tenor of Negro protest. Certainly the Negro is no longer willing to accept "gradualism" as defined by the South. Without tangible advances there will surely come a point when faith in negotiation and non-violent activity will break down into extensive violence. However, the demagogues and racists, whether white or black, need not gain ascendency, thereby reversing dominant social trends and values within the American social order. The

37. *Ibid.*, pp. 52-53.

growing maturity of the Negro middle class and the continued development of Negro institutions and organizational life have thus far guided Negro action under the process of change in a responsible and disciplined way. Hopefully, a stable and emotionally healthy leadership and a co-operative followership in both the Negro and white communities will continue to search for ways to bring about a transformation of the color line in as peaceful a manner as possible.

XVII. RELIGION IN THE SOUTH, OLD AND NEW* / Joseph H. Fichter and George L. Maddox

Almost every observer of the South has, sooner or later, recorded impressions about the pervasiveness and peculiarity of religious behavior and institutions in the region. The dominant impression is that, historically and currently, there is a "southern religion," the essence of which is the distinctive, relatively stable, and culturally integrated Protestantism of the region's native-born whites. The South's religious minorities—its Negro Protestants, its Catholics, its Jews—have been less adequately and more impressionistically described, but on the basis of limited evidence, they too are said to reflect a discernable regional character.

We have attempted to summarize and evaluate some of the evidence which underlies the dominant impression about the distinctly regional character of southern religious behavior and organization. Since the sources which we have found most useful are not always conveniently available to the social scientist, we have used footnotes extensively to supplement our necessarily brief and, consequently, sometimes bold presentation of our impressions. Our disproportionately brief treatment of the regionally dominant Protestantism is intentional. The material to be presented on Catholicism and Judaism in the region is less conveniently available elsewhere than is the comparable material on Protestantism. Moreover, both Catholicism and Judaism, as they appear in the South, provide interesting studies of the impact of social and cultural forces in the region on religious behavior and organization.

1

Religion in the South has been largely a Protestant affair, characterized by high visibility, conservatism, and emotionalism. In the nineteenth century, the South presented perhaps the most solidly Protestant population in the world.[1] Louisiana was the only south-

---

* Professor Fichter assumed primary responsibility for the material on Catholicism and Professor Maddox for Protestantism and Judaism. The southern states considered in this paper include: Virginia, North Carolina, South Carolina, Georgia, Florida, Kentucky, Tennessee, Alabama, Mississippi, Arkansas, and Louisiana.

1. For convenient summations of the relevant historical material, see Charles S.

ern state in which a Protestant monopoly was not clearly established, and in all southern states Protestants were overwhelmingly
concentrated in two denominations, Southern Baptist and Methodist.[2]

Spectacular growth in church membership, the sheer number of
church buildings, the frequency of religious gatherings, and the
prominence of clergymen and churchmen in positions of leadership
combined to make religious behavior in the South highly visible.[3]
During the latter part of the nineteenth century, Protestant clergymen were acknowledged leaders in the region, enjoying an unchallenged and unparalleled position. In fact, following the Civil
War, southern Protestant clergymen remained vocal proponents
of the Confederate cause even after the defection of its secular
defenders. Southern churches became centers of conservative political sentiment and of resistance both to the invasion of northern
culture and to the doctrine of the New South.

Theological fundamentalism and an individualistic ethic were
the hallmarks of southern religious conservatism. In the nineteenth
century, uncritical literal interpretations of the Bible as the authoritative source of God's will predominated. So did a conception
of religion which emphasized a particularistic, pietistic morality and
the non-perfectability of human institutions. Religious conservatism
helped immunize southern Protestants against social as well as
religious influences from the outside and, in this way, contributed
to the survival of a distinctive regional culture. Southern Protestant-

---

Sydnor, *The Development of Southern Sectionalism: 1819-1848* (Baton Rouge:
Louisiana State University Press, 1948); Vann Woodward, *Origins of the New
South: 1877-1913* (Baton Rouge: Louisiana State University Press, 1951); and
Francis D. Simkins, *The History of the South* (New York: Knopf, 1959).

2. For example between 1820 and 1850 in Virginia, the Carolinas, and Georgia,
affiliation with Methodist churches increased by 240 per cent and with Southern
Baptist churches by 250 per cent, while the population increased only 33 per cent.
Also, in the last quarter of the nineteenth century, Methodists and Southern Baptists
alone comprised more than 90 per cent of the total church membership reported in
Alabama, Mississippi, Georgia, Florida, and South Carolina, and more than 80
per cent of church memberships in North Carolina and Virginia.

3. An English traveler in the South in the nineteenth century wrote, "In other
countries men are apt to make a private matter of their religion . . . ; but the Southerner wears his upon his sleeve." Also, there are reports from the Civil War period
of mass conversions of Confederate troops, among them such prominent persons as
Generals Joseph Johnston, John Hood, and William Hardee. The Reverend William
Pendleton was Lee's chief of artillery, and other ministers who became active
generals in the Confederate Army were Bishop Polk of Louisiana and the Reverend
Lowrey, a Mississippi Baptist.

ism successfully withstood three tendencies clearly discernible in American Protestantism outside the South in the last quarter of the nineteenth century: a concern for unity of the church, a liberalizing of theology, and an increasing emphasis upon social aspects of religion. The "old-time religion" prevailed, and the advance of industry, urbanization, and education in the nineteenth century neither hindered appreciably the advance of religious organization in the South nor disturbed its basically conservative orientation. This cannot be said with equal confidence about any other section of the United States.[4]

Even in the last quarter of the nineteenth century, evangelistic revivalism, largely abandoned in the nation as a whole, continued to flourish in the South. The southern Protestant persistently insisted that his religion be immediate and expressive, or as Samuel Hill phrases it, "straight from God,"[5] and has remained consistently indifferent or hostile toward reflectiveness. The region produced no eminent theologians to protect it intellectually against the pressure of liberal theological and scientific thought which increasingly assaulted it. For most Protestant folk in the South, their commitment to conservative, expressive religion apparently was strong enough to insulate them from the religious modernism which was sweeping the nation outside.

A survey of material on southern Protestantism in the twentieth century calls attention more to continuity than to change. Religion in the region has continued to be largely a Protestant affair characterized by high visibility, conservatism, and emotionalism. As in the nineteenth century, Southern Baptists and Methodists continue to dominate among southern religious organizations. For example, while approximately 31 per cent of the population of the United States is found in the southern region as defined by the 1950 Census, about 40 per cent of persons affiliated with Protestant churches are there. Among affiliated Protestants in the region, 73 per cent identify themselves as either Southern Baptists or Methodists, as compared with 43 per cent who identify with these two churches in the

4. For additional comments on religious conservatism in the South, see Thomas Ford (ed.), *The Southern Appalachian Region: A Survey* (Lexington: University of Kentucky Press, 1962), Chapters 2 and 12. See also Twelve Southerners, *I'll Take My Stand* (New York: Harper and Brothers, 1930).

5. "The South's Culture—Protestantism," *Christian Century* (Sept. 12, 1962), pp. 1094-1096.

nation as a whole.[6] In all southern states, Methodists and Southern Baptists still constitute at least two-thirds of the reported Protestant membership; and in Georgia, Tennessee, Alabama, Mississippi, Arkansas, and Louisiana, these two denominations account for more than eight out of ten Protestants. There are as yet no convincing indications of decline in the numerical strength of the Protestant church in the region or, within Protestantism, in the monopoly enjoyed by Methodists and Southern Baptists.

Religion in the contemporary South continues to be highly visible. This visibility is reflected in the large percentage of the population reported to be affiliated with a church, the large number of churches per unit of population, and the prominent social position of clergy. Statistics of the National Council of Churches Study of Churches and Church Membership in the United States (1952) indicate that, in the southern region, approximately 66 per cent of the total population were affiliated with some church. In eight

6. For a critical evaluation of the best available sources of statistics on religious affiliation and the limitations of their use, see Benson Y. Landis, "A Guide to the Literature on Statistics of Religious Affiliation with Reference to Related Social Studies," *Journal of the American Statistical Association*, XXIV (June, 1959), 335-337. Among the primary sources most useful to a sociologist are the Bureau of Census *Survey of Religious Bodies in 1936*, which includes comparative data from 1926, 1916, and 1906; and the survey of churches and church membership (1952) of the Bureau of Research and Survey, National Council of Churches of Christ in the U.S.A. While these two sources provide the most comprehensive statistics available on church affiliation, both of them are based solely on the official reports of religious bodies. In these sources, problems are posed by differences in the definition of membership used by various religious bodies and also by the failure of some religious groups to report. Rather consistently, for example, there are inadequate reports from more sect-type churches and from groups whose members are predominantly Negro. These limitations are discussed in some detail in the introductory statements of both sources and by a church statistician associated with the National Council of Churches survey (see B. Y. Landis, "Confession of a Church Statistician," *National Council Outlook*, 7 [1957]). It should be noted further that, while for the southern region both of these limitations tend to result in underreporting of religious affiliation, Douglass and Brunner have found that churches in the southern region carry almost twice as high a proportion of inactive members (30 per cent) on their rural church rolls as do all other regions combined and three times the proportion found in the Middle West. The result in this case would be overreporting for participating churches. See their *The Protestant Church as a Social Institution* (New York: The Institute of Social and Religious Research, 1935), p. 243.

Basis for confidence in the reported statistics of the National Council of Churches Survey is provided by two studies of religious preference summarized by Donald J. Bogue, *The Population of the United States* (Glencoe: The Free Press, 1959), pp. 693 ff. One is a report of a Census sample survey (*Current Population Reports*, Series P-20, No. 79 [Washington, D. C.: U.S. Government Printing Office, 1958]) and the other a secondary analysis of survey data provided by the National Opinion Research Center, Jacob J. Feldman, Sr., Study Director. Characterization of religious affiliation patterns in the South does not differ appreciably in the various reports.

Summaries of the material in most of the sources cited above are found in Leo Rosten (ed.), *Religions in America* (New York: Simon & Schuster, 1963).

southern states (Virginia, North Carolina, South Carolina, Georgia, Tennessee, Alabama, Mississippi, and Louisiana) the proportion of persons affiliated with churches (72 per cent) was well above the proportion affiliated in the nation as a whole (61 per cent). In the remaining three southern states (Florida, Kentucky, and Arkansas) the mean proportion of persons affiliated with churches was 55.6.

The sheer number of Protestant churches in the region also suggests the continuing visibility of religion there. In 1952, there were 4.1 Protestant churches per 2,000 population in the South as compared with 1.4 in the Northeast, 2.4 in the North Central Region, and 1.5 in the West. Churches are currently not only more visible in the southern region than in the rest of the country, but surveys indicate they also are more likely to be attended. In spite of these indications of religious activity, there is evidence of uneasiness among Protestant folk in the South, especially in the rural areas, with regard to the continuing importance of religion in the life of the region.[7] This uneasiness may reflect a realistic reading of signs and symptoms on the part of a people who have been peculiarly sensitive about and preoccupied with a highly visible type of social behavior. There are as yet, however, no obvious indicators of dramatic decline in the importance of organized religion in the life of the contemporary South.

While as late as 1955 clergymen appeared to have more influence and prestige among southern Protestants than among other Protestants, there is general consensus among observers that the position of Protestant clergymen has been declining gradually in this century. Social leadership in the region has increasingly passed to non-clerical editors, educators, and businessmen. Church leaders within the region have tended to lose to the universities and to scientists within them that intellectual leadership which pre-Civil War ministers of the gospel wrested from Jeffersonian liberals.[8] In

7. For example, in a secondary analysis of AIPO (Gallup) Poll No. 580 (1957) 52 per cent of the southern Protestants in the sample in contrast to 42 per cent of other Protestants reported having attended a religious service during the previous week. The same poll data, however, shows that 23 per cent of southern Protestants in comparison with 14 per cent of those outside the region viewed religion as losing influence. These regional differences continue to hold when place of residence is controlled within the regions. Southern Protestant urbanites were, for example, more likely than urban Protestants in other regions to attend church.

8. Simkins, op. cit., p. 414; Hill, op. cit., passim; see also Alfred O. Hero. In an unpublished manuscript entitled "Protestants, Catholics and Their Clergy," Hero

spite of indications of the clergyman's declining influence in the South, the ministry continues to be a relatively attractive occupation within the region. For instance, the ratio of clergymen to the population is higher in the South than in any other region. According to the U. S. Census report on occupational distribution, in 1950, 6.7 per cent of all white professionals in the labor force in the region were clergymen in contrast to 3.7 per cent in the Northeast and West and 5.5 per cent in the North Central region. Similar data from the 1960 Census indicate that in three southern states (Arkansas, Mississippi, South Carolina) white clergymen constitute more than 10 per cent of all white professionals in the labor force.[9]

The characteristic conservatism of the dominant Protestants in the South in the nineteenth century has also persisted, without dramatic modification, into this century, and ranks with traditional racial attitudes as a significant factor in the South's retention of its regional distinctiveness. The region's conservative orientation continues to value the past as much as—if not more than—the future, the fundamentalistic theological beliefs more than any of their modern alternatives, and a particularistic more than a universalistic interpretation of ethical imperatives. Thomas Ford's study of values and religious beliefs in the Southern Appalachians presents a case in point.[10] While one might expect, Ford argues, that the religion of the region would tend to lose its conservative character in those places where the greatest social and economic change has occurred, this has not been the case. Vestiges of fundamentalistic religion—the core of which is "biblicism" and a "Puritan" moral orientation—persist quite strongly today in the Appalachians, even among religious groups that have moved far along the classical route from sect to church. As expected, religious conservatism was found to be considerably stronger in the rural than in the urban parts of the region; however, this tradition was also found to persist quite strongly in the most highly urbanized areas. Urbanization has only

---

reports data suggesting that, in spite of indications of declining prestige, clergymen in the South maintain a position relatively better than their counterparts in other regions.

9. See Ernest Campbell and Thomas Pettigrew, *Christians in Racial Crisis* (Washington, D. C.: Public Affairs Press, 1959), for additional comments on the status of the southern clergyman.

10. "Status, Residence, and Fundamentalistic Religious Beliefs in the Southern Appalachians," *Social Forces*, XXXIX (Oct., 1960), 41-49. See also his "The Passing of Provincialism," in *The Southern Appalachian Region: A Survey*, Chapter 2.

tempered the Appalachian region's highly individualistic ethic and anti-fun morality, and has had even less effect on its fundamentalistic theology.[11]

In the absence of research comparable to the Appalachian survey in other areas of the South, one can only guess at the extent to which Appalachia caricatures or misrepresents the current religious orientation of the region and the potentialities for change. While religion in the contemporary South is too complex to capture in any single, simple formula, the essence of the situation appears to be reflected fairly well by the Appalachian study. An anti-fun, highly individualistic moral orientation and fundamentalistic theology continue to predominate.[12]

Just as the southern Protestant's designation of alcohol as a prime moral evil persistently reflects a peculiarly regional emphasis in his ethic, so does his hostility to the idea of racially integrating his churches and having his church take an active part in racial desegregation within the region. Southern churches have no monopoly on segregated religious facilities.[13] Individual Protestant churches, in spite of the official pronouncements to the contrary by the establishments to which they belong, have not consistently been leaders in promoting racial desegregation in any region of the

11. Earl Brewer ("Religion and the Churches," in *The Southern Appalachian Region: A Survey*, Chapter 12) reads the evidence somewhat differently. He reports finding more indications than Ford of the emergence of a non-religious, secular value orientation within the Appalachian region.

12. The conservative religious orientation of the southern region continues to be reflected in indications of a distinctly regional antagonism toward the National Council of Churches, toward belief in biological evolution, and toward feminism. See the summary of relevant public opinion poll data in Hero, *op. cit.* There are also indications, based on a secondary analysis by region of data from AIPO (Gallup) Poll No. 580 (1957), that southern Protestants are more likely than Protestants in other regions, even when control for rural or urban residence is introduced, to believe in the existence of a devil, in life after death, and that to be a Christian one must believe every word in the Bible and go to church. Both urban and rural religious folk in the region generally continue to express more concern about the use of alcoholic beverages than their counterparts in other regions. Protestants in the South, as compared with those in other regions, are considerably more likely to report themselves as abstainers, to object to having women drink in public, and to favor national prohibition. In a study among Methodists in the United States, Stotts and Deats, *Methodism and Society: Guidelines for Strategy* (Nashville: Methodist Publishing House, 1959), Vol. 4, Appendix A also found that 74 per cent of the respondents in the southeastern jurisdiction—which is roughly comparable to the southeastern states—prefer total abstinence, national prohibition, or both; as compared with 65.6 per cent of Methodists generally.

13. In 1953, Dwight Culver, *Negro Segregation in the Methodist Church* (New Haven: Yale University Press, 1953) estimated that only a fraction of 1 per cent of the total membership of the Methodist church and less than 5 per cent of the Negro membership were in churches outside a special jurisdiction for Negroes only.

United States. Yet even when this is admitted, southern Protestants have shown themselves more reluctant than Protestants in other regions to accommodate themselves to official denominational positions outlining the theological origins and implications of a doctrine of brotherhood.[14] In sum, although there are indications that religious conservatism in the South has been modified in this century as compared with the previous century, religious orthodoxy and a highly particularistic ethic continue to be the hallmarks of southern religion.

The historic southern preference for expressive religion unhampered by rational concerns has persisted strongly into the twentieth century. The lack of intellectual defense of orthodoxy, often cited as one of the great weaknesses of conservative religion in the region, was dramatically illustrated in the Scopes trial in Tennessee in 1925. In the intervening quarter of a century since this act of desperation on the part of conservative religious forces, indications of the change in the southern religious temper have been in evidence. Reconciliation of the two essentially different value systems represented by religion and science has become a possibility, perhaps a probability, if not a reality in the region.[15] Middle-status church members in the South, as elsewhere, have increasingly introduced ritual into their services and have added facilities in their churches clearly designed for social enjoyment and recreation.[16] But religious emotionalism, while showing signs of decline in the region, has certainly not disappeared. Southern Protestants continue to display a pronounced interest in evangelism, Biblical preaching, and other expressive religious activities.[17]

Thus, now as in the past, the religious establishments of southern Protestants have, for the most part, reflected the conservative social and political commitments of their members. In the latter part of the nineteenth century, southern Protestantism became the center of resistance to the emergence of a New South. A repetition of this state of affairs cannot be eliminated as a very real possibility in the

14. For example, in a national study of Methodism by Stotts and Deats (op. cit.) members of the church in the southeastern jurisdiction were less likely than those in other jurisdictions to accept the proposition that all discrimination and forced segregation should be abolished in the church.

15. Ford, "The Passing of Provincialism."

16. Simkins, op. cit.

17. Murray Leiffer, The Layman Looks at the Minister (Nashville: Abingdon Press, 1947). See also Hill, op. cit.

latter half of the twentieth century. Protestant churches in the region may prove increasingly to be centers of refuge for the most conservative social and political forces in the region and of resistance to the integration of the region into the mainstream of American life.[18] While there are some indications that some contemporary Protestant leaders in the South would like to associate the region with the political, social, and economic aspirations of the nation,[19] such leaders, both lay and clerical, within the region have been few, and have spoken with uncertain voices to congregations whose members have many reasons for not listening.

2

The religious behavior of Negro Protestants in the South warrants more detailed attention than can be given here. It is not possible in this brief survey to describe the origin of separate Negro churches within the region following the Civil War, and the development of Negro religious life within these churches during the nineteenth and twentieth centuries. There is compensation for this omission, at least in part. Gunnar Myrdal's *An American Dilemma*[20] and, more recently, Franklin Frazier's *The Negro Church in America*[21] summarize a number of references for those who would like to pursue the matter. For our purposes it is sufficient to report Myrdal's conclusion that the dominant pattern of Negro religious life has paralleled that of the dominant white community, although in this respect as in others, the Negro seems to present an exaggerated version of his model. In brief, religious life among Negroes in the South is most accurately described as almost exclusively Protestant, usually Baptist or Methodist, highly visible, conservative, and emotional.

Negro churches have been and continue to be the best and most successfully organized Negro institutions in the South, as well as in

18. On this point see Samuel Hill, Jr., "The Southern Baptists," *Christian Century* (Jan. 9, 1963), pp. 39-42. See also Campbell and Pettigrew, *op. cit.*; James Sells, *The South and Christian Ethics* (New York: Association Press, 1962); and Waldo Beach, "Ecclesiology and Race," *Union Seminary Quarterly Review*, XIV (Jan., 1959), 19-26.

19. For a forceful argument that the southern region has had a stronger identification with the national ethos than ordinarily believed, see Grady McWhiney, "Reconstruction: Index of Americanism," in C. G. Sellers, Jr., ed., *The Southerner as American* (Chapel Hill: The University of North Carolina Press, 1960).

20. (New York: Harper & Brothers, 1944), pp. 863 ff.

21. (New York: Schocken Books, 1963).

the nation as a whole. Now, as in the past, organized religion among Negroes within the region operates as an agency of social control, particularly in regard to maintaining family stability. It also functions as an organizational context in which economic co-operation is fostered, educational activities are supported, and political experience is gained, and as a refuge from a hostile social environment. As one indication of the continued importance of organized religion in the South, Frazier estimates that probably one-half of all Negro male professionals in the South are ministers.[22]

There are indications that the influence of Negro clergymen and churches is declining, certainly outside and probably inside the South. As racial barriers are weakened and as expectations, if not the realization, of social integration increase among Negroes, the traditional organization of Negro life is seriously undermined. In the immediate future, the church will remain the most important institution in the Negro community. In fact, Frazier believes, the Negro church will, in the short run, constitute the most important barrier to integration and the assimilation of Negroes.[23] In the long run, however, he argues that:

> The strength of the Negro church as a barrier to integration of Negroes into the main currents of American life should not be overestimated, especially since the process of integration has not progressed very far. Moreover, it is necessary to differentiate the situation in the North from that in the South.... The church can no longer serve as a refuge, as it did in the past, when the majority of Negroes lived in the South under a system of racial segregation and the majority of Negroes in the South lived in rural areas.... The Negro church has lost much of its influence as an agency of social control. Its supervision over the marital and family life of Negroes has declined, and the church has ceased to be the chief means of economic cooperation. New avenues have been opened to all kinds of business ventures in which secular ends and values are dominant. The church is no longer the main arena for political activities, which was the case when Negroes were disenfranchised in the South. Negro political leaders have to compete with white political leaders in the machine pockets of the cities. In a word, the Negroes have been forced into competition with whites in most areas of social

22. For an elaboration of this characterization, see Frazier, *op. cit.*, Chapters 3 and 4; and E. U. Essein-Udom, *Black Nationalism* (New York: Dell Publishing Company, 1962), Chapter 2.

23. *Op. cit.*, pp. 70 ff.

life, and their church can no longer serve as a refuge within the American community.[24]

3

The history of the South is told with an emphasis that is Protestant, fundamentalist, and conservative. There is only a vague recollection that Catholic priests were doing missionary work as early as 1565 at St. Augustine, the first permanent settlement in the United States.[25] While there were Catholics in the Southeast from the beginning of colonization, they remained so small a minority that most books on the region hardly mention them.[26] As the population grew over the centuries, the Catholics stayed mainly on the territorial fringes of the area, with the French influences in Louisiana, the Spanish along the Gulf Coast into Florida, and with settlements of English Catholics in Maryland and German Catholics in Kentucky.[27]

The entire new country was the diocese of the first Catholic bishopric erected in 1789 at Baltimore.[28] Four years later, in 1793, the New Orleans diocese was established as the episcopal see of Louisiana and the Two Floridas.[29] In the first half of the nineteenth century, eight new dioceses were established in the old South. The first was at Bardstown (1808), now the Louisville diocese, then two in 1820 at Charleston and Richmond, one in Mobile in 1829, two at Nashville and Natchez in 1837, Little Rock in 1843, and Savannah in 1850. Even before the Civil War, a second Louisiana diocese was set up at Alexandria (1853), and a second in Kentucky at Covington in the same year.

24. *Ibid.* For a reappraisal which counters Frazier's negativism, see Horace Cayton, "E. Franklin Frazier: A Tribute and a Review," *Review of Religious Research*, 5 (Spring, 1964), 137-142; and Liston Pope, "The Negro and Religion in America," *Review of Religious Research*, 5 (Spring, 1964), 142-152; the latter remarks that "the Negro ministry is on the ascendency in the eyes of all Americans" (p. 147).

25. Theodore Maynard, *The Story of American Catholicism* (New York: Macmillan, 1941), gives a popular account of these early years.

26. See the few words of Edwin McNeill Poteat, "Religion in the South," in W. T. Couch, ed., *Culture in the South* (Chapel Hill: University of North Carolina Press, 1935), p. 251.

27. See Howard Odum, *Southern Regions of the United States* (Chapel Hill: University of North Carolina Press, 1936), p. 145.

28. Peter Guilday, *The Life and Times of John Carroll, Archbishop of Baltimore* (New York: Encyclopedia Press, 1922), I, 384-385.

29. See Charles Gayarre, *History of Louisiana, The Spanish Domination* (New York: Redfield Press, 1854), p. 377.

It is assumed that some of the early Irish Catholic immigrants were "lost to the faith,"[30] and were absorbed by the dominant Protestant denominations. Yet there were signs of Catholic vitality. Two native religious sisterhoods were founded in Kentucky as early as 1812, and the first Catholic weekly newspaper was begun in 1822 by Bishop John Ireland, of Charleston. Bishops, priests, and nuns worked in the region, but Catholics remained a social minority in some ways dissimilar to the Protestant majority.

Adaptation occurred, but the basic doctrinal differences remained throughout the century. Catholic liturgical worship and sacramental practices differed sharply from the relatively simple church services of Methodists and Baptists. The characteristic garb of the priests and of the religious sisters gave high visibility to Catholic functionaries.[31] Catholics suffered the handicap of "alienism" even to the extent of being excluded from civil office.[32] Even southern-born Catholics were the object of anti-foreign sentiments and propaganda by the Know-Nothings, the American Protective Association, and the Ku Klux Klan.

Southern Catholics always remained a numerical minority, but so did southern Episcopalians and Presbyterians, without the same social effects. What made them a social minority were these several characterizations as subjects of a foreign power, as people with different worship services, having religious functionaries who dressed differently, were not hired by their congregations, and did not marry. The celibacy of the Catholic clergy and nuns probably seemed an odd kind of moral self-discipline, quite in contrast with the fact that Catholics did not consider smoking, drinking, cardplaying, and dancing as sinful activities. Catholic Temperance Societies and parish missions seemed to be less aggressive than their counterparts among the Protestants.[33]

But southern Catholics were not altogether different from south-

30. See the attempt to reconstruct population figures by Gerald Shaughnessy, *Has the Immigrant Kept the Faith?* (New York: Macmillan, 1925).

31. Many Confederate soldiers probably saw nuns for the first time on the battlefield. See the autobiographical description of the Nursing Sisters in Virginia in John Tracy Ellis, *Documents of American Catholic History* (Milwaukee: Bruce, 1956), pp. 376-379.

32. In spite of this, William Gaston was appointed to the State Supreme Court of North Carolina in 1833. See Ellis, *Documents*, pp. 248-252.

33. Contrast this with the mass hysteria of religious revival. See Alice Felt Tyler, *Freedom's Ferment* (New York: Harper and Brothers, 1944).

ern Protestants. As a matter of fact, the two ideological issues, racism and secession, which long characterized and still torment the South, found Catholics quite thoroughly acculturated. "The bishops of the South were not unionists, but defenders of the rights of States and abettors of the Confederacy."[34] Catholics apparently had a strong proof of their loyalty to the South, and played it for its propaganda value, when they insisted that the abolition movement was a Protestant movement, fomented and promoted mainly by New England Protestant clergymen.

Bishop Verot, of Savannah, was well-known as a dedicated rebel, who publicly and frequently placed much blame upon the Protestant clergy who "brought about this deplorable state of things." The ecclesiastical spokesman for Catholic Confederate enthusiasts was Bishop Lynch, of Charleston.[35] Bishop Martin of Natchitoches (Alexandria) belittled the horrors of slavery and exulted over the Confederate victories. Bishop Quinlan of Mobile was convinced of the justice of the southern cause, and publicly prayed for the victory of the Confederacy. Bishop McGill of Richmond was enthusiastic about the Confederacy, and promoted enlistments in the rebel army. Bishop Elder of Natchez was so outspoken and active for the South that he was for a while put under military guard as a traitor to the Union. There is only ambiguous evidence about the attitudes of Bishop James Whelan of Nashville,[36] and of Bishop Richard Whelan of Wheeling. Archbishop Odin of New Orleans seems to have remained politically aloof, but he had several fiery Confederate partisans among his clergy, who got into trouble with Union General Butler.[37]

The differences of opinion on abolition, the slavery question, and secession between northern and southern Catholics were probably as sharp as those between northern and southern Protestants. When Father Edward Purcell published an article in the *Catholic*

34. Benjamin J. Blied, *Catholics and the Civil War* (Milwaukee: St. Francis Seminary, 1945), p. 69.

35. See Ellis, *Documents*, pp. 356-365. In 1865, Jefferson Davis commissioned Bishop Lynch to go to Rome to win recognition for the Confederacy from Pope Pius IX.

36. Although Ellis, *American Catholicism* (Chicago: University of Chicago Press, 1956), p. 95, accepts the version that the Bishop was a northern sympathizer.

37. See Blied, *op. cit.*, "The Bishops of the South," pp. 53-69. Prominent Catholics were Generals Pierre Beauregard and James Longstreet and Admiral Raphael Semmes. The poet, Father Abram Ryan, is not listed among the twenty-eight known Catholic chaplains in the Confederate forces. See Blied, p. 123.

Telegraph of Cincinnati (April 8, 1863), observing that "the Church and slavery could never get along well together," Catholics in the North supported him, and those in the South attacked him.[38] While the official stand of the Catholic Church on slavery was strong and clear, just as it would later be on segregation, the southern mores were also strong among many Catholics.[39]

From the point of view of social continuity, however, it is important to note that there was never any hint of organizational schism, like that which began as early as 1845 among Protestant churches.[40] This continuity of structure was exemplified the year after the War, when forty-five bishops from every section of the country met in Baltimore for the Second Plenary Council. The assembled bishops manifested great concern about the spiritual care of the emancipated Negroes. They called for priest volunteers and money to carry on this ministry,[41] but they also had another large problem on their hands. They were then faced with the overwhelming immigration of European Catholics, and had to direct most of their personnel and resources to these people. For about a century, the "missionary" prospects of Catholicism among southern Negroes had to take second place to the problem of absorbing Catholic immigrants.

While it is a notable fact that the Catholic Church did not split into two separate branches, north and south, it seems equally remarkable that there was no denominational split into southern white and southern Negro churches. As early as 1829, the Oblate Sisters of Providence, the first religious community of Negro nuns, was founded in Baltimore. In 1842 another colored community, the Sisters of the Holy Family, was established in New Orleans. The Josephite Fathers, originally an English group started by Cardinal Vaughan, began work with the American Negroes in 1871. Twenty years later, Mother Katherine Drexel founded the Sisters of the Blessed Sacrament, who have since established a network of schools.[42]

38. This editorial is in Ellis, *Documents*, pp. 387-392.

39. For a study of North-South differences, see Madeleine H. Rice, *American Catholic Opinion in the Slavery Controversy* (New York: Columbia University Press, 1944).

40. See Ellis, *American Catholicism*, pp. 91-92.

41. See the remarks of Blied, *op. cit.*, p. 34, and also the *Decreta Concilii Plenarii Baltimorensis* (Baltimore: John Murphy, 1868), Title 10, ch. 4, pp. 243-247.

42. John Gillard, *Colored Catholics in the United States* (Baltimore: Josephite

The erection of separate parishes for Negro Catholics was discussed in 1866 by the Second Plenary Council of Baltimore, but was left to the decision of each bishop in his own diocese.[43] In Louisiana, where most of the Negro Catholics lived, Archbishop Janssens was reluctant to segregate them because the colored Catholics opposed it, and very few of the clergy favored the experiment.[44] The policy of segregated Negro and white parishes seems to have been accepted around the turn of the century. This soon included a whole separate system of orphanages, schools, hospitals, as well as religious organizations and societies within the Catholic Church in the South. The segregated system was always criticized by some Negroes, and did not begin to break down until the general civil rights movement following World War II.

Between 1870 and 1960 the Catholic population in the eleven southern States multiplied itself five-and-a-half times (from 438,700 to 2,423,413). Throughout these ninety years Louisiana has accounted for about 50 per cent of all the Catholics in the southern States.[45] The early large concentrations of Catholics were in the New Orleans and Louisville dioceses. By 1960 three other large centers had built up in the dioceses of Richmond, Miami, and Lafayette. The dioceses of St. Augustine and of Mobile also contained over one hundred thousand Catholics in each.

The population expansion after World War II was not an exclusively Catholic phenomenon, and the Catholic proportion of the total southern population increased only from 4 per cent in 1940 to 6.6 per cent in 1960. Whatever relative change there is between two populations is usually attributed to differentials in birth and death rates, and also to internal migration. In the case of religious populations, however, there is also the factor of adult conversion to a church. Clark writes that "the Catholic Church has under way a campaign to break the Protestant grip on the sprawling and rock-ribbed cotton belt."[46]

Press, 1941), pp. 123-126, reports also on other clergy groups and sisterhoods working among the Negroes.

43. *Ibid.*, p. 113, where this point is discussed.

44. *Ibid.*, p. 122.

45. The earlier census figures on Catholics seem to have been simple estimates, and are derived from the *Official Catholic Directory*, first published by Sadlier, and then taken over by Kenedy in New York.

46. Thomas D. Clark, *The Emerging South* (New York: Oxford University Press, 1961), pp. 255-256.

Whether or not any of the southern dioceses have made a special effort to convert Protestants to the Catholic Church, the conversion rate seems also to be a function of the population itself. The adult conversion rate per thousand was 3.5 in 1930 and 4.8 in 1960. Generally speaking, the rate is highest in those dioceses where the Catholic population is smallest and where the percentage of mixed marriages is highest. Alabama, Georgia, and the Carolinas are examples of this trend. In 1960 the Lafayette diocese, in Louisiana, had the highest proportion of Catholics (62.6 per cent) in the population, the lowest percentage of mixed marriages (16.5 per cent), and the lowest rate of conversions (1.1 per thousand).

In a speech given in 1940, Archbishop O'Hara of Atlanta said that "the Catholic Church has an attraction for Southerners." Non-Catholics come to Catholic services; priests are invited to address non-Catholic gatherings; and there is a higher conversion rate in the South than in any other section of the country.[47] The statistics we have been able to gather do not indicate any significant "success" in the effort to bring non-Catholics into the Church. Although accurate religious statistics are hard to come by, it is probably true to say that "the Pentecostals, rather than the Catholic Church, are at present making the deepest inroads in the statistical ranks of traditional southern church affiliation."[48]

When we have combined the increases to the Church by conversions and births, and subtracted the losses due to deaths, we are able to approximate the net rate of growth of the Catholic population in each of the southern states. There are, however, no available statistics on Catholic migration into and out of these areas. It is probable that gains in places like Richmond, Miami, and Mobile between 1930 and 1960 were in part the result of in-migration of Catholics from other places. Some of these seem to be refugees from Castro's Cuba. The fast growth in southern Florida probably also contains Catholics from other parts of the country. Statistics on the net increase of Catholic population in eleven southern states are presented in *Table 1*.[49]

47. *Catholic Conference of the South* (Richmond: Executive Headquarters, 1941), p. 26.
48. Clark, *op. cit.*, p. 524.
49. These statistics are computed from Kenedy's *Official Catholic Directory* and must be accepted only tentatively. The population figures for each diocese come ulti-

Table 1. Factors in Net Increase of Catholic Population in the Eleven Southern States, 1930-1960.

	1930	1940	1950	1960
Catholic percentage of total population	4.0%	4.0%	4.6%	6.6%
Birth rate per 1,000 of Catholic population	34.3	26.1	39.3	34.0
Conversion rate per 1,000 of Catholic population	3.5	5.0	5.8	4.8
Death rate per 1,000 of Catholic population	11.1	10.3	9.8	7.6
Net rate of increase of Catholic population	26.7	20.8	35.3	31.2

One of the indexes of acceptance of a social minority is intermarriage between its members and those of the social majority. In this case, however, the Church officially prefers that Catholics marry their coreligionists, and in granting a dispensation places certain moral obligations on both spouses. Approximately four out of ten Church marriages entered into by Catholics in the South are contracted with non-Catholics. This proportion reaches six or more out of ten in the Carolinas, Georgia, and Alabama, where the Catholic population is smallest. In contrast to these places, the diocese of Lafayette, in southwestern Louisiana, reports only one mixed marriage out of every six.[50] It is quite probable that some Catholics in the South marry Protestants "outside" the Church and consequently defect from their religion. There is no available source of data, however, by which this can be measured.

Threats to orthodoxy and Protestantism were seen also in urbanism and labor organizations, both of which "sheltered the foreign immigrant who brought with him either a strong attachment to the Catholic Church or was tainted with poisonous 'foreign atheism.' "[51] Perhaps more dreadful "threats were envisioned in the South when Alfred Smith ran for the presidency on the Democratic ticket in

mately from the census submitted by each pastor. If these are accurate then all of the rates given in the table are accurate. The absolute figures for marriages, infant and adult baptisms, and deaths, are most likely correct since the pastor is obliged to submit a record of these annually to his bishop.

50. In the "Southern Parish" study we found that three-quarters of the converts came into the Church because of marriage with a Catholic. See Joseph H. Fichter, *Dynamics of a City Church* (Chicago: University of Chicago Press, 1951), p. 40.

51. Clark, *op. cit.,* p. 252.

1928. The Klan rose again and Senator Tom Heflin of Alabama constantly harangued against Rome."[52]

The burning of crosses and the flood of anti-Catholic pamphlets were by no means confined to the South during the Smith election campaign. Ogburn analyzed the election results and concluded that the issue of prohibition was three times as important as the religious issue in defeating Smith.[53] The solid South was fundamentalist, rural, and dry, and one would expect its opposition to a Catholic, urban, and wet candidate. Yet Smith did get most of his electoral votes from the region—Alabama, Georgia, Louisiana, Mississippi, and South Carolina.

If it is true that the majority of American Catholics vote the Democratic party, Catholics should be politically at home in the South. Yet the South still considered the Catholic an alien even in the late 1950's when there was serious suggestion of John Kennedy as a presidential aspirant. In 1958, Baptists in Georgia and Alabama passed convention resolutions aimed at Kennedy.[54] In 1959 Alabama Methodists declared against the "political machinations of a determined, power-hungry Romanist hierarchy."[55] In 1960 the President of the Southern Baptist Convention felt that he had to speak up against a man "under control of the Roman Catholic Church."[56]

Prohibition and Tammany Hall were the important complicating factors in the Al Smith campaign. Liberal social principles and the race question complicated the Kennedy campaign, but these factors were most clearly revealed *after* Kennedy entered the White House. From 1960 and until the President's assassination, the "Kennedy issue" split the Democrats in all of the eleven southern states. This issue was not the Catholic Church. Indeed, many southern Catholics also became anti-Kennedy on the administration proposals for racial integration and for other programs that offended the social conservatism of the South. The extent to which Catholicism was linked

52. Berton Dulce and Edward Richter, *Religion and the Presidency* (New York: Macmillan, 1962), p. 88. See also the brief remarks in his autobiography by Alfred E. Smith, *Up to Now* (New York: Garden City Publishers, 1929), pp. 412-418.
53. The alien, or foreign-born, influence was found to be quite negligible. William F. Ogburn and Nell Talbot, "A Measurement of the Factors in the Presidential Election of 1928," *Social Forces*, VIII (Dec., 1929), 175-183.
54. *New York Times* (Nov. 14, 1958), p. 14.
55. *Ibid.* (June 25, 1959), p. 16.
56. *Ibid.* (Feb. 11, 1960), p. 29.

to these un-southern principles must be looked at from another point of view.

One of the most enthusiastic attempts to bring Catholic influence to bear on southern people and culture was the formation of the Catholic Committee of the South in 1939. Paul Williams, the Secretary of the Committee, pointed out that only those who are steeped in regionalism and the social teachings of the Church can be of real assistance in the creation of the New South.[57] Its specific objective was "to unify and coordinate Catholic endeavor in the Southland so as to restore all things to Christ."[58] A later convention, in 1951, spelled out its resolutions favoring labor unions, opposing right to work laws, approving the United Nations, and urging racial desegregation.[59]

In speaking before this organization, Archbishop Samuel Stritch praised southern family life as a preservative against "ugly industrialism. The South will remain, please God, a place of village, town and farm homes. There is no individual more individualistic than the Southerner. But he knows how to temper this individualism with something which we might call neighborliness—that something that is sometimes called Southern hospitality."[60]

Obviously, this kind of ideological "adaptation" was futile in a region which harbored rural peonage, racial violence, political anachronisms, anti-labor attitudes, illiteracy, and wide-spread poverty. In its annual meetings the Catholic Committee of the South made vigorous denunciations of these social evils, but in the early 1950's it began to lose its region-wide drive. Social action was localized mainly in Louisiana, where its members supported the strike of sugarcane workers in 1953, and with a grant from the Ford Foundation conducted an educational campaign on school integration throughout 1956.[61]

The so-called ecumenical movement of the postwar period has

57. *The Catholic Conference of the South* (Richmond: Executive Headquarters, 1941), p. iv.

58. *Ibid.*, p. 14.

59. *The Catholic Committee of the South*, Brochure of Resolutions of January, 1951, Convention at Columbia, South Carolina.

60. *The Catholic Committee of the South*, Richmond, April 26, 1942 (Richmond: Executive Headquarters, 1943), p. xv.

61. This campaign produced a pamphlet, *Handbook of Catholic School Integration* (New Orleans: Commission on Human Rights, 1956), which is still the only program of its kind suggested by southern Catholics.

certainly engaged the attention of southern Catholics, and has probably helped greatly to alleviate Protestant-Catholic tensions in the region. The fascinating question still remains concerning the cultural adaptation of this social and religious minority. Is there any current evidence that southern Catholics are culturally similar to other southerners, and therefore culturally dissimilar to their coreligionists in other parts of the country?

The key distinction between liberal and conservative social attitudes generally turns on the problem of race. A national poll sponsored by the *Catholic Digest* in 1956 found that three-quarters of southern white respondents were in favor of keeping the races apart, and there was no percentage difference between Catholics and Protestants.[62] Only three out of ten (32 per cent) non-southerners favored the separation of the races.[63] Those with a college education in the South are five times (34 per cent) more likely to favor integration than those with a grammar school education (7 per cent). Differences of region and education are more important factors than differences of religion.

In a nation-wide sample of young Catholics in military training, a small but consistent difference was found in the religious habits and attitudes of young men from the eleven-state South. More of the southerners (37 per cent to 28 per cent) pray daily, and more of them pray the Rosary (52 per cent to 48 per cent) frequently or sometimes. More of them (48 per cent to 42 per cent) said that they once thought about studying for the priesthood, and more of them (75 per cent to 70 per cent) have friendly personal relations with the clergy.[64] These data reflect the general notion that southerners are more likely to be prayerful, church-going folk than are other Americans.

In another nation-wide study of active Catholic parishioners, some expected differences were found between southerners and

62. See "The Negro-White Problem," *Catholic Digest* (June, 1956), pp. 2-5. This was the first of a series of articles reporting a nation-wide poll on the race question.

63. The "South" of this survey goes beyond the eleven-state region, on which we have been basing data, and includes Texas, Oklahoma, West Virginia, Maryland, and the District of Columbia.

64. These data are derived from an unpublished study of 4,171 Catholic young men trainees for the Air Force. The data were collected in 1962 and processed at Loyola University of the South.

other Catholics.[65] More of the southern Catholics (65 per cent) than of the others (51 per cent) regularly vote the Democratic ticket in national elections. They seem to have closer personal relations with the clergy, since more of the southerners (26 per cent) than of the others (18 per cent) say that the parish priest often visits their home.

On some of the broader issues of national life there is a consistent, but sometimes small difference of opinion between southern Catholics and other American Catholics. About the same proportion of both (63 per cent) evidence a growing interest in international affairs, but slightly more of the southerners (43 per cent) than of the others (39 per cent) are in favor of expanding the foreign economic aid program of the United States. More of the southerners (60 per cent) than of the others (55 per cent) say that their interest in the racial problem is increasing. Both categories agree that the maintenance of the basic civil rights of all Americans is the most important social goal of this country. But more of the southerners (19 per cent) than of the others (15 per cent) say that they have never had any interest in the problems of organized labor.

How do southern priests differ from their parishioners and from Catholic priests in the rest of the country?[66] In a national survey of diocesan parish priests it was found that about four out of ten (43 per cent) lean toward the Democratic party in national elections. Southern priests resemble other American priests more closely in this regard than they do their southern parishioners. Many more of them claim to be independent voters. About the same proportion (41 per cent) of southern priests are in favor of expanding the foreign economic aid program. Like their parishioners, the southern priests think that the first social goal of this country is to protect the civil rights of all citizens. Priests in other parts of the country put in first place the solution of the problems of crime and delinquency.

The southern priests have slightly more interest (53 per cent) than the other priests (49 per cent) in international affairs. Like the

65. This is taken from the data of a survey sample of 2,216 Catholic lay persons, representative of all dioceses in continental United States. See Joseph H. Fichter, *Priest and People* (New York: Sheed and Ward, 1965).

66. This nation-wide survey of 2,183 diocesan parish priests is parallel to that of the Catholic Laity mentioned above, and also represents every Catholic diocese in the continental United States.

laity, one-fifth (19 per cent) have never been interested in the
problems of organized labor. As may be expected, more of the
southern priests (83 per cent) than of the others (71 per cent) have
a continuing or growing interest in race relations. In all of these
comparisons neither clergy nor laity were asked whether they are
native-born southerners. It is probable that a higher proportion of
southern priests than of lay persons had been born outside of the
eleven-state South.

In summary of these materials, it may be said that southern
Catholics represent both a continuing and a changing social minority. Their "alienism" has never been ethnic, as was the case with the
large flood of European Catholic immigrants to other parts of the
country. The basic "foreign" characteristics which Catholics never
adapted to the prevailing Protestant culture lie in their doctrinal
and liturgical patterns. These involved the fundamental belief in a
unified, hierarchical church which survived the dramatic disagree-
ments of the Civil War. The one, holy, catholic faith did not separate
into two or more holy, regional faiths as a result of these sectional
controversies.

In other areas of attitudes and practices, southern Catholics are
very similar to southern Protestants. The two large issues of race
relations and labor organizations show very little difference among
the rank-and-file membership of the Christian churches in the
South. This fact, however, does not indicate gradual *adaptation* of
Catholics to the southern culture. It simply means that in these and
other areas of social issues southern Catholics have always been
southern. Like southern Protestants, they are the children of their
culture.

4

The history of Judaism in the South is difficult to reconstruct. This
difficulty reflects the limited number and the dispersion of Jews in
the region. It also reflects the experience of Jews within the region,
experience which encouraged them to conceal their identity. As a
consequence, many southern Jews did not maintain a synagogue
affiliation, and it was common for them to intermarry with Christians and rear their children in this faith.[67]

67. Very useful sources of information on Judaism in the South are J. R. Marcus,
Early American Jewry: The Jews in Pennsylvania and the South, 1655-1790

The accommodation of southern Jews to the culture and social structure of the region is suggested by the tendency among Gentiles in the North during the Civil War period to label Jews as enemies of the Union, secessionists, copperheads, and rebels.[68] The fate of Judah P. Benjamin, a Jew who was married to a Christian and who subsequently became an active political figure in the Confederacy, also reflects both the pressures on Jews to accommodate themselves to the peculiarities of the region and the limits of their success in doing so. As the Civil War ground to a close, Benjamin was frequently and publicly blamed for all the problems of the Confederacy, its defeats in military spheres while he was Secretary of War and its failures in diplomacy while he was Secretary of State. Furthermore, a sizeable number of references in contemporary diaries and memoirs, as well as in the columns of Confederate newspapers, attests to the widespread belief that Jews were the chief sources of the Confederacy's economic troubles. Stories of difficulty between Jewish officers and their men in the Confederate Army were also current.[69]

The proportion of Jews in the total population of the South in the nineteenth century is not known, but by the middle of the twentieth century an estimated two hundred thousand Jews were in the region, concentrated primarily in Tennessee, Georgia, Virginia, and Southern Florida. They currently constitute a little over one-half of one per cent of the population of the South.[70] Jews are perhaps more visible in the region in this century than in the past,

(Philadelphia: The Jewish Publication Society of America, 1953); B. W. Korn, *American Jewry in the Civil War* (Philadelphia: The Jewish Publication Society of America, 1951); and Alfred O. Hero, "Southern Jews," (unpublished manuscript).

68. In this connection it is interesting to read Korn's (*op. cit.*) account of General Order No. 11, which came to be known as the Jew Order, issued under the command of General Grant. In this order Jews along with cotton speculators and "other vagrants without honest means of support except trading on the misery of the country" were expelled from the command.

69. Korn attributes this tendency to scapegoat the Jews in the South to the general regional dislike of all aliens and foreigners, to the widespread suspicion of merchants and storekeepers typical of a society dominated by plantation owners and farmers, to a deep commitment to fundamentalistic Bible Christianity which was rampant in the region, and to the frustrations needing displacement which increased as the war dragged on and Confederate chances for victory became slight.

70. Estimates are based on statistics from the *American Jewish Yearbook, 1961* (New York: American Jewish Committee, 1961). See also Bureau of Research and Survey, National Council of Churches, *Churches and Church Membership in the United States*, Series A:4, 1957.

yet low visibility continues to characterize them.[71] While there are
surface indications that Jews have been fairly well integrated into
predominantly Gentile communities within the region, there is also
evidence that this acceptance depends on continuous public manifestations of accommodation by Jews, whatever their private opinions, to the regional culture, especially in regard to race relationships.[72]

5

This brief historical overview indicates that the sociological phenomenon of American religious pluralism is not fully reflected in the
eleven-state Southeast. Among both white and Negro southerners,
Protestant fundamentalism continues to the present day, but not
with the rigidity and dominance it once exhibited. Obvious theological and ritual differences remain among the major religious
bodies—Protestant, Catholic, and Jewish—and variants of religious
adherence can be detected within each of these major segments.
The sociological distance, however, between conservatives and
liberals within each large denomination is probably not so significant as it is elsewhere in America.

The ecological approach to American regionalism reveals that,
in spite of postwar changes of some magnitude, the Southeast is
still characterized by rural, racial, and religious factors, and that the
term "Bible Belt" is more than an epithet. The manner in which the
religious influences have helped to maintain the rural and racial
features of the region suggests that the religious factor has been
responsible more for continuity than for change.

This theme emerges from the present chapter. The southern
subculture, however one defines it, has run like a vital force through
the decades of history, and it is nurtured in one manner or another
by the variant religious categories. If southern Jews and Catholics
supported secession and the Confederacy, southern Protestants tried

71. Harry Golden, editor of the *Carolina Israelite*, made an informal survey of
synagogue membership in 1955 in eleven southern states. On the basis of reasonably
complete returns, it appears that only one in five Jews in the region was affiliated
with a synagogue. When the proportion of Jews in synagogues and the total Jewish
population are ranked for each state, there is a significant negative correlation of
—.82 between them. That is, the larger the number of Jews in a state, the smaller
the number affiliated with a synagogue.

72. See Joshua A. Fishman, "Southern City," *Midstream* (Summer, 1961), pp.
39-56; also Alfred O. Hero, "Southern Jews."

to restore and maintain the old traditions after Reconstruction. Negro Protestants too, since there appears to have been no alternative, found survival in accommodation and submitted to the folkways. From this point of view, religion was the pivotal institution of the regional subculture.

But our data do not leave us satisfied with this simple unilateral interaction. When we turn the coin we are constrained to note that the religious institution functioned as it did because it was southern. Baptists, Catholics, Jews, Methodists, and the other religionists of the area, are distinctively southern when compared with their co-religionists in other parts of America. To be a southerner (of either race) means to be a member of an organized religion (the statistics still show higher affiliation here than elsewhere). But it means also to be religious with a southern accent. The behavior patterns of southern religionists of all persuasions seem to be an ineluctable consequence of the regional cultural experience.

It may be said without disrespect that the churches seem to employ God to maintain and retain the Old South. The conserving function of religion seems to be socially and culturally more effective than its prophetic or forward-looking functions. From these observations one may argue that the South would move more rapidly into the dominant stream of American culture if it were not so religious. Or one may argue with more cogency that what the South needs more than anything is a dynamic and progressive religious leadership.

These speculations still leave the vexing problem of institutional interaction. We have not been able clearly to disentangle the relation of cause and consequence in this chapter. Nevertheless, there is no question that a distinctive, relatively culture-bound "southern religion" does exist, and that its regional flavor is shared across the major denominational lines. In this sense, then, southern religionists have contributed more to stability and continuity than to change and advance.

XVIII. A CYCLE OF CHANGE IN SOUTHERN LITERATURE* / C. Hugh Holman

In 1917, H. L. Mencken looked at the literary and artistic life of the southeastern United States and called the region "the Sahara of the Bozart."[1] The succeeding two score years of literary activity in the South stripped the appropriateness from Mr. Mencken's remark and left it an amusing definition of the beginning of a period of growth. During the past forty years "the Sahara of the Bozart" has had a literary movement, commonly called "The Southern Renascence."[2] Its magnitude probably has been unrivaled in the history of the United States, except during those wonderously fruitful years in the middle third of the nineteenth century in New England.

The most obvious characteristic of this Southern Renascence has been the appearance within the region of a plethora of writers of considerable talent and of at least a handful who, by almost any definition, were writers of genius.[3] These writers have worked in a variety of fields: poetry, criticism, long and short fiction, and the drama. The easiest proof of so seemingly extravagant a statement is simply a list of some of these writers: James Agee, Doris Betts, Cleanth Brooks, James Branch Cabell, Erskine Caldwell, Truman Capote, Donald Davidson, Ralph Ellison, William Faulkner, Ellen Glasgow, Caroline Gordon, Shirley Ann Grau, Paul Green, Lillian Hellman, Randall Jarrell, Andrew Lytle, Carson McCullers, Flannery O'Connor, Frances Gray Patton, Katherine Anne Porter, John Crowe Ransom, Elizabeth Madox Roberts, Jesse Stuart, William Styron, Allen Tate, Peter Taylor, Robert Penn Warren, Eudora Welty, Tennessee Williams, Thomas Wolfe, Stark Young. Such a list could be multiplied several times if we also included the writers

---

* A small portion of this essay appeared in different form as "Literature and Culture: The *Fugitive*-Agrarians," *Social Forces*, XXXVII (October, 1958), 15-19. It is here used by the permission of the editors.

1. "The Sahara of the Bozart," *Prejudices: Second Series* (New York, 1920). This essay was first published in the New York *Evening Mail*, November, 1917.

2. See, for example, *Southern Renascence: The Literature of the Modern South*, ed. Louis D. Rubin, Jr., and Robert D. Jacobs (Baltimore, 1953), or John M. Bradbury, *Renaissance in the South: A Critical History of the Literature, 1920-1960* (Chapel Hill, 1963).

3. The best brief guides to most of these writers are the bibliographies in James B. Meriwether, "For Further Reading: A Selected Checklist," *South: Modern Southern Literature in Its Cultural Setting*, ed. Louis D. Rubin, Jr., and Robert D. Jacobs (Garden City, N. Y., 1961), pp. 392-433.

of novels, short stories, plays, and poems who have practiced their
arts with success but a lesser distinction. Truly the southeastern
United States in the second and third quarters of the twentieth century has produced and is producing a literature distinctive enough
to have earned it special regional designation, and original enough
to give it importance in American literary history. Furthermore,
however great their differences may be, these writers form a group
in its way as self-contained as the New England group which
dominated the literature of the 1830's, '40's, and '50's, or as the
midwestern group that placed its imperishable stamp upon American literary realism.

The ultimate importance of southern writing in our time, however, is the result of the inexplicable occurrence in one region of
many men and women of remarkable talent. Talent seems to seek
its own vehicles and locales, finding such unlikely targets as an
apothecary's apprentice in London, the son of a middle-class
burgher in Stratford-on-Avon, and an ex-school teacher and journalist in Brooklyn. However much Hippolyte Taine's theory of literature as the product of "race, epoch, and era"[4] may help us understand the direction that talent takes and follow its implications with
greater certainty, we cannot explain talent itself in terms of historical, cultural, or environmental factors.[5] The issue is crucial to
an examination of a regional literature. In an attempt to clarify it,
it may help to distinguish among three by no means mutually exclusive elements in an author's work: his *talent*, which is not only
his remarkable ability to make and transmit imaginative worlds but
which includes his technical skills, literary conventions, linguistic
attitudes and aptitudes; his *subject*, which is the materials his talent
utilizes and which includes, in addition to the world he imitates, his
plots, structures of images, and patterns; and finally, his *theme*,
which is the ultimate union of *talent* and *subject*, the usually non-
conceptualized intention, realized through the play of *talent* upon
subject. These divisions are an extension of assertions about the

4. Section V of the Introduction, *Histoire de la litterature anglaise* (Paris, 1864).
Translated into English by H. Van Laun (New York, 1871).

5. See, for example, the debate regarding southern writing in these terms in
Donald Davidson, "Why the Modern South Has A Great Literature," *Vanderbilt
Studies in the Humanities*, I (1951), 1-17; Howard W. Odum, "On Literature and
Southern Culture," and John Maclachlan, "No Faulkner in Metropolis," in *Southern
Renascence*, pp. 84-100; 101-111.

nature of literature which Robert Penn Warren made in *Who Owns America?*, where, discussing Milton, he says, "... the subject of *Paradise Lost* is the story of the Fall of Man, the story of what happened to Adam and Eve. But the theme is the nature of justice, the relation of the human will to the Divine Will, the relation of Good to Evil.... It is conceivable that Milton might have used another subject ... for the vehicle of his theme."[6] Thus Thomas Wolfe used his own experiences as a subject through which to state his theme of what it means to be an American, and William Faulkner exployed his talent to imprison in stories of impotent perverts, homicidal Negroes, Snopses, and gallant Confederate soldiers a theme sufficiently close to Milton's to allow us, in one sense at least, to call his sprawling legend of Yoknapatawpha County a southern *Paradise Lost*.

If such distinctions as these have validity in discussing southern literature, we are, in fact, attempting to define how the special characteristics of the region have shaped the *subjects* of writers of *talent*, and thus have modified their *theme*. Yet, even in this limited sense, it would be futile to claim that twentieth-century southern literature has at any time been consistent throughout its parts, or that it reflects today the same attitudes or has the same bases with which it began three or four decades ago. There has been a startling continuity of talent; there has been a consistency in the choice of varying aspects of the South as subject; there has been a deep, perhaps a penetrating and profound, search in the historical past for the roots of meaning by which the present can be understood. There has often been a seeking after the symbols and symbolic actions by which the cosmic nature of the universe may be seen "in a grain of sand." There has been a common "voice" shared by many of these writers. They are indeed a special group, and yet their special value rests on their individual talent.

Now the seeds of change, sown in the South by two major wars, an industrial-economic revolution, and a social transformation, are producing a harvest which has not left this literary heritage untouched. One of the clearest ways of seeing the extent to which the literature of the twentieth-century South has undergone major change is to examine two collections of southern short stories made

6. *Who Owns America?*, ed. Herbert Agar and Allen Tate (Boston, 1936), pp. 268-269.

by one of the South's finest poet-critic-novelists, Robert Penn Warren. In 1937 in the anthology *A Southern Harvest*, Mr. Warren said of the "literary ferment in the South" that "it is not an isolated thing; it is part of a general cultural ferment in the region ... the new literature of the South is then but a part of this general ferment a part of the process of self-scrutiny and self-definition."[7] He added that the twenty-two writers whose work he assembled in this anthology of southern fiction shared a serious commitment to the problems of their region and that they were "incurably and incorrigibly historical-minded."[8] Twenty years later Mr. Warren, with the assistance of Albert Erskine, edited *A New Southern Harvest*, presenting fiction by twenty-three southern writers, only four of whom were represented in the earlier anthology. The editors, expressing their own surprise at this fact, said, "We had assumed a continuity which simply does not exist."[9] Eighteen stories in the first anthology had had rural settings and all but two of the twenty-two had had southern locales, but the editors observe that "In the new collection over half the stories have urban settings. ... Some are not set in the South at all, and in others the Southern background has no necessary relation to the meaning of the story."[10] Clearly, if there has been a continuity of talent, there has also been a pattern of change. John T. Westbrook, in a not very fond farewell to southern regional writing, said "... an old South, already too minutely autopsied in prose and poetry, should be left to rest in peace, forever dead and (let us fervently hope) forever done with."[11] If this is true, it is because, in one sense at least, it is time, in Harry Ashmore's words, to write an "epitaph for Dixie";[12] for in a continuity of talent, there has been a change in subject.

The literature of the southeastern United States has always had distinctive characteristics, typical of the region; and it is the presence of these recognizable regional qualities which since the 1830's has justified the term "southern literature." The South has produced a self-conscious literature from the first days of its awareness of the

7. (Boston, 1937), pp. xiii-xiv.
8. *Ibid.*, p. xiv.
9. (New York, 1957), p. vii.
10. *Ibid.*, p. viii.
11. "Twilight of Southern Regionalism," *Southwest Review*, XLII (Summer, 1957), 234.
12. *An Epitaph for Dixie* (New York, 1958).

differences that set the region apart. The writers of the section have sometimes presented their views of experience primarily for outside consumption, utilizing the region's distinctive virtues as ideals to be held before the eyes of the world and using its unique historical experience as exemplum and warning to the nation at large. They have sometimes addressed their fellow southerners in apology or reprobation or sentimental escape. Their writing has reflected a variety of attitudes toward the region and toward the outside world. It has found in the relatively consistent and caste-conscious ideals of the southern ruling classes a fruitful subject for romanticizing, a philosophical basis for demanding tradition and order, and a ready target for satiric and realistic attack; and at no time in its history has the South failed to use itself in all three ways, although in each period in its history one has been predominant.

Thus southern writing can be said to exist primarily because of the region's self-conscious distinctiveness. And, indeed, throughout much of its history, the writers of the South have believed that the highest art is imbedded in its regional fidelities. In 1856, William Gilmore Simms said of a collection of his stories: "One word for the material of these legends. It is local, sectional—and to be *national* in literature, one must needs be sectional."[13] And in 1945, Allen Tate, the almost official articulator of the aesthetic credo of the twentieth century southern traditionalist, said, ". . . no literature can be mature without regional consciousness."[14] The South has looked upon itself through long periods of its history as different from the remainder of the nation.[15] The most obvious of these differences, the one leading to the most intense statements and resulting in the greatest violence of action, has been connected with the fact that the southern climate and southern agricultural mode of life resulted in its becoming a slaveholding section of the Union and then intransigently retaining that way of life long after it had ceased to be morally acceptable to the rest of the nation. But there are other differences. The distinctive agrarian aspect of southern culture as opposed to the growing industrial capitalistic system of

13. *The Wigwam and the Cabin* (New York, 1856), pp. 4-5.
14. "The New Provincialism," *The Man of Letters in the Modern World* (New York, 1955), p. 322. This essay originally appeared in *The Virginia Quarterly Review* in April, 1945.
15. Ashmore, *An Epitaph for Dixie*, pp. 172-189.

the Middle Atlantic and New England states was a significant reality before the turn of the nineteenth century. It resulted in some brilliant exchanges between Thomas Jefferson and John Adams.[16] It was defined with considerable force in Thomas Jefferson's *Notes on the State of Virginia* as early as 1781.[17] In 1803 John Taylor of Caroline in *The Arator* essays defended the agricultural way of life against the growing tendency of the government to support manufacturers; and in his *Inquiry Into the Principles and Policy of the Government of the United States* (1814), he belatedly replied to John Adams' theory of government and asserted that the cultural and moral well being of America rested with its agricultural people and was being endangered by those who supported capitalistic industrialism, which he called "a system of paper and patronage." These fundamental differences wrote a long narrative of tariff fights and slave-free compromises across the first half of our national history, and when the efforts at compromise finally failed in 1861, the issue of the war was partly between these differing concepts of man and his society.

During this period, the South increasingly saw itself as surrounded by a *cordon sanitaire* within which it defended itself as a region and its institutions as practice against all attacks from the outside.[18] But perhaps as fundamental as these differences is the fact that the South was developed by a group of people who, however remote their own ancestry may have been from the Cavalier nobleman of England, embraced the Royalist position as the ideal for an aristocratic way of life. In contrast, the inhabitants of New England, the South's logical opponents on matters of policy and morality, came to America with moral and political commitments that were distinctly Roundhead; the Puritan conscience and the Puritan commitment to absolute good deeds defined the ideal of one segment of American life, while a more worldly commitment to an easier, more relaxed, Episcopal, and, they believed, more gentlemanly way of life defined that of another. These differences, perhaps more apparent than real, were a part of the intellectual

16. A dominant theme in *The Adams-Jefferson Letters*, ed. Lester J. Cappon (2 vols.; Chapel Hill, 1959).

17. See Thomas Jefferson, *Notes on the State of Virginia*, ed. William Peden (Chapel Hill, 1955), pp. 164-165, 292.

18. Clement Eaton, *Freedom of Thought in the Old South* (Durham, N. C., 1940), traces in detail this defensive attitude in the ante bellum South.

commitment and the emotional response of most of the writers of the South.

Before the Civil War, the bulk of southerners pursued the vocation of planter or the profession of law, and literature was likely to languish as an avocation of men of substance and affairs. Ellen Glasgow said that the Old South "suffered less from a scarcity of literature than from a superabundance of living. . . . Over the greater part of the Old South . . . a top-heavy patriarchal system . . . offered little hospitality to the brooding spirit of letters."[19] The southerners who were writers presented their region to the world at large as solidly centered in the Cavalier tradition. Nowhere is this more obvious than in the sometimes strident gallantry of poets like Philip Pendleton Cooke[20] and Edward Coote Pinkney,[21] in the strain of Byronesque which runs through most ante bellum southern poetry, and in the elevated grandeur of Henry Timrod's odes. The South embraced the theater while New England was still shuddering at the thought of it,[22] and it saw fiction as a desirable mode for literary expression while other regions still looked upon it with scorn. The popular reading of a young gentleman in Mr. Jefferson's University at Charlottesville, Virginia, included Henry Fielding's *Tom Jones* and Lawrence Sterne's *Tristam Shandy*.[23] The belletristic writing of the pre-Civil War South was deeply indebted to Sir Walter Scott and his British imitators, and it tried to create out of the historical events of the southern settlement and the Revolution an image of a feudal order.[24] William Alexander Caruther's *The Knights of the Horse-shoe* and John Pendleton Kennedy's *Swallow Barn, Horse-shoe Robinson*, and *Rob of the Bowl* are works which indicate the pervasiveness of this effort; for Caruthers opposed slavery and Kennedy supported the North in the Civil War, although both described their region in the Romantic terms of chivalry and caste. William Gilmore Simms, the most prolific and

19. *A Certain Measure* (New York, 1943), pp. 133-134.

20. In poems like "Life in the Autumn Woods" and his collection, *Froissart Ballads and Other Poems* (1847).

21. In poems like the famous "A Health," beginning "I fill this cup to one made up of loveliness alone."

22. Williamsburg, Va., had a theater in 1716. A. H. Quinn, *A History of the American Drama from the Beginning to the Civil War* (New York, 1923), pp. 6-7.

23. See Jay B. Hubbell, *The South in American Literature 1607-1900* (Durham, N. C., 1954), p. 182.

24. *Ibid.*, pp. 188-193.

representative of ante bellum southern writers, in more than eighty volumes of poetry, drama, criticism, biography, and fiction, created an image of society that established firmly on southern soil the ideals of Scott's essentially Tory view of life.[25]

In the period after the Civil War, southern authors rejoined the stream of American writing through the local color movement. They found in mountain and bayou the eccentric, the remote, and the whimsical; and they exploited it for a national audience suddenly dazzled by the variety and the richness of life in the large nation. George Washington Cable, "Charles Egbert Cradduck," and many others found in the varieties of speech, life, and strange custom a rich lode for commercial fiction. Other writers dedicated themselves to the construction of apologias for a vanished world, and, as Thomas Nelson Page did, tried in their fiction to show the Old South to be a world ideal in its dedication to honor, tradition, loyalty, and integrity. Short stories, such as Page's in *In Ole Virginia*, and novels, such as his *Red Rock*, simply assert that the Old South was the most glorious single realization of human aspiration and the finest social order which man has ever conceived. Page declared that that order "partook of the philosophic tone of the Grecian, of the dominant spirit of the Roman, and of the guardfulness of individual rights of the Saxon civilization. And over all brooded a softness and beauty, the joint product of Chivalry and Christianity."[26] This was essentially an export literature committed to celebrating the region and apologizing for it in terms that grew increasingly sentimentalized. When one of these writers turned his critical attention inward to discuss with the region itself the nature of its problems, he found, as George Washington Cable did after his famous "Freeman's Case in Equity" essay, that the South was not ready for serious comment and bitterly resented criticism. During this period the literature of the South became "sicklied o'er with the pale cast" of sentiment, and it glowed with the faint phosphorescence of decay. Ellen Glasgow was certainly accurate when she said that the South needed "blood and irony."[27]

25. See C. Hugh Holman, "The Influence of Scott and Cooper on Simms," *American Literature*, XXIII (May, 1951), 203-218; and the Introduction to William Gilmore Simms, *Views and Reviews of American Literature, History and Fiction*, ed. C. Hugh Holman (Cambridge, Mass., 1962), pp. xxxi-xxxvi, and the essays in that volume on "The Epochs and Events of American History," pp. 30-127.

26. *The Old South, Essays Social and Political* (New York, 1927), p. 5.

27. *A Certain Measure*, p. 28.

In the years before World War I, Miss Glasgow valiantly worked to give the South realistic treatment and to subject its institutions to the criticism of irony. Her fellow Virginian, James Branch Cabell, through the creation of Poictesme, an ideal world complete with history, geography, and elaborate theme in Europe between the twelfth and the nineteenth centuries, substituted a dream of beauty for an untenable reality and found in wit, sarcasm, and an occasional tendency to the scurulous and pornographic, a means of indirect comment upon his world. Except for these, however, the literature of the South was reasonably well summed up in the collection, edited in 1907 by E. A. Alderman, President of the University of Virginia, in fourteen substantial, handsome, and ponderous volumes, *The Library of Southern Literature*. It was this kind of use of the region that made the South, indeed, "the Sahara of the Bozart."

The new generation of writers in the early 1920's formed more than a group possessed of unusual talent; they also shared a sharp revulsion against this southern writing of the past. They were self-conscious southerners, finding in their region much to love, much to respect, much to use as an example, and, at the same time, much to criticize. It was out of this peculiar mixture of affection and criticism, this sense of saying in one breath "Hail" and "Farewell," that the literature of the modern South came. Allen Tate expressed this idea well when he said, "With the War of 1914-1918, the South re-entered the world—but gave a backward glance as it stepped over the border: that backward glance gave us a Southern Renascence, a literature conscious of the past in the present."[28]

The new literature of this post-World War South was complex It included many writers and a great variety of modes. Its early success was in the drama, where Lula Vollmer established a brief fame with *Sun-Up* and *The Shame Woman* in 1923, where Hatcher Hughes won a disputed Pulitzer Prize in 1924 with *Hell-Bent for Heaven*, and where Paul Green won the Pulitzer Prize with *In Abraham's Bosom* in 1926. At the University of North Carolina, Frederick Koch, with his Carolina Playmakers, was teaching a group of young writers to make the materials of their region the

28. "The New Provincialism," *The Man of Letters in the Modern World*, pp. 330-331.

subject matter of social drama. This dramatic use of southern materials was revived later by Lillian Hellman, particularly in *The Little Foxes* (1939) and since the 1940's by the plays of Tennessee Williams, especially *A Streetcar Named Desire* (1947), *Cat on a Hot Tin Roof* (1955), and *Sweet Bird of Youth* (1959). In the decades of the 1940's and 1950's, Miss Hellman and Williams won five New York Drama Critics Circle Awards and Williams received the Pulitzer Prize twice.

In the twenties, too, a Southern Renascence of poetry and criticism got under way in Charleston, New Orleans, and Nashville. The Poetry Society of South Carolina, which had among its members Dubose Heyward, Hervey Allen, John Bennett, and Josephine Pinckney, published its *First Yearbook* in 1921. The same year in New Orleans appeared the first number of the literary magazine *The Double-Dealer*, which published some of the earliest works by William Faulkner, Allen Tate, Donald Davidson, John Crowe Ransom, and Robert Penn Warren, and Ernest Hemingway's first published sketch. Its editors declared, "It is high time, we believe, for some doughty, cleared visioned penmen to emerge from the sodden marshes of Southern literature. We are sick to death of the treacly sentimentalities with which our well-intentioned lady fictioneers regaled us."[29] In 1922 a group of young poets and critics associated with Vanderbilt University, including Ransom, Tate, Davidson, Warren, and Merrill Moore, began publishing a small magazine of poetry and brief critical comment called *The Fugitive*.[30] The group was rejecting what Davidson called "poet-laureating, the cheapness and triviality of public taste . . . the lack of serious devotion to literature, to the arts, to ideas."[31] The editors asserted that *The Fugitive* "fled from nothing faster than from the high-caste Brahmins of the Old South."[32] *The Double-Dealer* ceased publication in 1926 and *The Fugitive* in 1925, but the writers to whom they had given an audience were to go on to write

29. "Southern Letters," *The Double-Dealer*, I (1921), 214.
30. This group has been the subject of three book-length treatments: John M. Bradbury, *The Fugitives: A Critical Account* (Chapel Hill, 1958); Louis Cowan, *The Fugitive Group: A Literary History* (Baton Rouge, 1959); Rob Roy Purdy (ed.), *Fugitive's Reunion: Conversations at Vanderbilt, May 3-5, 1956* (Nashville, 1959).
31. From an unpublished letter of May 10, 1939, quoted in F. J. Hoffman, Charles Allen, and Carolyn F. Ulrich, *The Little Magazine: A History and a Bibliography* (Princeton, 1947), p. 121.
32. Bradbury, *The Fugitives*, p. 13.

a distinguished chapter in American literary history. Fresh and life-giving air had been let into the southern scene and the uses of literature in the region were not soon to be what they had for so long a period been.

The development of a serious prose fiction lagged behind that of drama and poetry, but by the mid-twenties Ellen Glasgow and James Branch Cabell had been joined by capable social realists, such as Edith Summers Kelley, whose *Weeds* (1922) is a grim picture of Kentucky rural life; Dubose Heyward, whose *Porgy* (1925) was, in an opera version, *Porgy and Bess,* to achieve long life; T. S. Stribling, whose *Teeftallow* came in 1926 and was followed by his trilogy, *The Forge* (1931), *The Store* (1932), a Pulitzer Prize novel, and *Unfinished Cathedral* (1934); Julia Peterkin, whose *Scarlet Sister Mary* won a Pulitzer Prize in 1928; Marjorie Kinnan Rawlings, whose *South Moon Under* (1933) was a grim record of a scrub country woman and whose gentler *The Yearling* (1938) won the Pulitzer Prize. Before the decade of the 1930's, Erskine Caldwell, the best and most prolific of the southern writers of harsh social realism, was already at work, and in 1932 came his *Tobacco Road,* in 1933 *God's Little Acre,* and in 1940 *Trouble in July.*

The popular historical novel also flourished, notably in James Boyd's *Drums* (1926), *Marching On* (1927), and *Long Hunt* (1930); in Evelyn Scott's *The Wave* (1929); in Caroline Miller's *Lamb in His Bosom* (1933), a Pulitzer Prize novel; and Margaret Mitchell's *Gone With the Wind* (1936), which won a Pulitzer Prize and established international sales records.

However, these writers who used the South as regional subject matter for works in the traditional modes of social realism or historical romance did not equal in quality the continuing performance of Ellen Glasgow. Her *Barren Ground* (1925) and *Vein of Iron* (1935) were impressive Hardyesque studies of Virginia rural life, and *The Romantic Comedians* (1926), *They Stooped to Folly* (1929) and *The Sheltered Life* (1932) were distinguished ironic studies of southern manners. In the late twenties and the thirties she was joined by an impressive group of novelists practicing a new and distinctive treatment of the South. The principal writers of this group, with the first important novel published by each and the best known when it is not also the first, are: Elizabeth Madox Roberts, *The Time of Man* (1926); Stark Young, *Heaven Trees* (1926) and *So Red the Rose* (1934); William Faulkner, *Soldier's Pay* (1926) and *The Sound and the Fury* (1929); Thomas Wolfe, *Look Homeward, Angel* (1929); Katherine Anne Porter, *Flowering Judas* (1930) and *The Ship of Fools* (1962); Caroline Gordon, *Penhally* (1931); Andrew Lytle, *The Long Night* (1936) and *The Velvet Horn* (1957); Robert Penn Warren, *Night Rider* (1939) and *All the King's Men* (1946). These writers were so distinctive in their use of their region that they created the bulk of the Southern Renascence and generated much of its energy. A host of writers emerged during the four decades which followed the founding of *The Double-Dealer* in 1921, and it would be futile to attempt in a short essay to give a sense of their variety, their richness, and their individuality.[33] It is more feasible to attempt to present what seem to be some of their common characteristics; and then to suggest some of the directions which they took away from their common position by looking at one group and at two special cases. The group is the collection of writers who assembled at Vanderbilt University and published *The Fugitive*. The two novelists are William Faulkner, the undisputed master of southern fiction, and Thomas Wolfe, the man who is after Faulkner the most important and the ablest writer which the South has produced in this century.

The Fugitive group began by attacking what Ellen Glasgow had called the "evasive idealism" of southern writing and by writing poetry that dealt wryly and astringently but also gracefully and decorously with the values of the pre-Civil War South. Their techniques came from T. S. Eliot, Hart Crane, the French *symbolistes*, and the English metaphysicals, but the controlled rage which gave them vigor came from a joint revulsion against both the South and the modern world. They represented a spirited aesthetic rejection of the contemporary South in much the same way that the Paris expatriates rejected the business culture of the Middle Atlantic states, and that midwesterners like Sinclair Lewis rejected the businesses and towns of his section. But the difference between the

33. John M. Bradbury, in *Renaissance in the South*, gives an invaluable listing of the writers and works produced in the South between 1920 and 1960.

expatriates or the midwestern satirists and the Fugitive group is one of direction. Both the expatriates and the midwesterners were moving on toward new ideals, were committed to a belief in progress, and espoused anti-traditional methods and attitudes. On the other hand, the Fugitive group sought in the past of their region for the bases of an ideal order.

This order was based on a belief that the agrarian way of life and an aristocratic order were preferable to a capitalistic way of life and an industrial order. The pattern of history had plainly gone against the South and its dream of an agrarian order. But the old order had other qualities which lingered in the memory of the region after the social fact of the order itself had been demolished, and which formed a powerful myth. Without attempting to demonstrate them, it can be asserted that some of the qualities that outlived in the mind the institutions with which they were associated include: the persistence of pessimism and the sense of evil and imperfection that are the most distinctive heritages of the Calvinism which, despite the Episcopal tenor of the coastal regions, forms the philosophical frame within which the South thinks and feels; a love for classical learning—a love which predated the devotion to the Greek state which southerners of the 1840's developed in justification of slavery; a sense of place and soil, which is associated with every agrarian literature and culture the world has known; a profound but seldom articulated awareness of the interpenetration of the past and the present, so that history becomes a record of inestimable value; a reverence for the family as the basic social unit; a deep sense of the individual dignity of man and a comparatively small reverence for his group relations; a tendency to examine the particular rather than to generalize; the ability to live at ease with an unresolved paradox; and a reverence for gracious living and good manners.

It was this legend of their land and its past virtues which the Fugitives chose as their antidote to progress and the theory of class conflict. Their motives were clearly expressed by Stark Young when he wrote in *I'll Take My Stand*:

> . . . we can never go back, and neither this essay nor any intelligent person that I know in the South desires a literal restoration of the old southern life . . . dead days are gone, and if by some chance they

should return, we should find them intolerable. But out of any epoch in civilization there may arise things worth while, that are the flowers of it. To abandon these, when another epoch arrives, is only stupid, so long as there is still in them the breath and flux of life. . . . It would be childish and dangerous for the South to be stampeded and betrayed out of its own character by the noise, force, and glittering narrowness of the industrialism and progress spreading everywhere, with varying degrees, from one region to another.[34]

Thus the Agrarian way which the Fugitives adopted was, in a sense, a myth of the good order of the past used as a weapon of attack against what they believed to be the bad order of the present.

In the poetry of John Crowe Ransom, Allen Tate, Robert Penn Warren, and Donald Davidson, this vision of the past was held before an audience that had itself to be cultured and sophisticated in order to understand. Astringent wit, philosophic depths clouded by obscurity, high technical skill, and an almost religious devotion to art and to its thoughtful and committed criticism were typical of the group. And combined with these qualities was also a mixture of the elegiac celebration of a past order with a hortatory address to an intolerable present. Perhaps the best examples of this combination are to be found in two of the finest poems of the movement: Allen Tate's "Ode to the Confederate Dead" and John Crowe Ransom's "The Harvesters."

It was much the same view of man and history which undergirded William Faulkner's vast body of work. In his twenty novels and four volumes of short stories, Faulkner portrayed a version of the history of the South. In that portrayal he asserted through archetypal pattern, through symbol, and through rhetoric, that the tragic experience which his region has had and through which its citizens individually have passed and are passing is but a microcosm of the seamless fabric of human history. His whole vast narrative is, like the ledgers in *The Bear*, a "chronicle which was a whole land in miniature, which multiplied and compounded was the entire South,"[35] and, then by obviously intended extension, the nation and the world and the Universe. This chronicle is one of guilt and expiation woven from the threads of southern history. It recounts a noble order in the Old South, damned by the sin of exploiting first

34. *I'll Take My Stand*, by Twelve Southerners (New York, 1930), p. 328.
35. *Go Down, Moses* (New York, 1942).

the Indian and then the Negro. It sees the Civil War as the act by
which the good order of the Old South is expelled for its sins from
its Paradise. Then in the New South, the old order compromises
with a material culture and a soulless acquisitiveness to exploit its
physical resources and its Negroes. The only hope rests finally with
the very young and the enduring Negro.

In many short stories and in *Sartoris* (1928), *The Sound and the
Fury* (1929), *As I Lay Dying* (1930), *Sanctuary* (1931), *Light in
August* (1932), *Absalom, Absalom!* (1936), *The Wild Palms*
(1939), *The Hamlet* (1940), *Go Down, Moses* (1942), *Intruder in
the Dust* (1948), *Requiem for a Nun* (1951), *The Town* (1957),
The Mansion (1959), and *The Rievers* (1962) he wrote the fictional
history, spanning more than two hundred years, of a mythical
Mississippi County, Yoknapatawpha. Thus, William Faulkner is in
a unique way a writer of the South. His talent is very great; he has
an imaginative vigor which has led him to the creation of one of the
greatest galleries of characters and actions and one of the most
ambitious projects ever formed by the mind of a novelist, a project
which approaches in magnitude that of Balzac's *Human Comedy*,
and he has a magnificent gift for rhetorical expression, a great command of language. These qualities would have produced distinguished fiction under whatever circumstances or skies he should
work—southern or otherwise. But to say this is to pay a tribute to an
innate quality of greatness in the writer, and in Faulkner's case this
great talent was shaped by the qualities of his own region in such
a way that he is peculiarly a novelist of the southern small town
and rural community. He is imbedded firmly in the essentially
Calvinistic Protestantism of that world, conceiving his eternal dilemmas in the broad, rather simple terms of that folk theology. He
finds the stage on which his cosmic dramas are to be acted out in
tiny hamlets, country stores, and in a small southern city. When
his characters reach a city of the size of Memphis they become be-
wildered and lost. Yoknapatawpha County is an epitomization of
the rural world. Jefferson, its county seat, never emerges from the
status of the small town, presented symbolically through its own
central small town square. Faulkner found in these materials a
sufficient area and an adequate scope for all that he wished to say
of the grandeur, of the responsibility, of the dignity, and of the

potential degradation of man. But he has said it in terms of the conflict of poor white and aristocrat, of Negro and white man, of the South torn by dissension, of an aristocratic order dedicated to the ideals of chivalry and courage and yet acquiring what it acquired at the too high price of the enslavement of the Negro. Thus, southern history becomes for him a fable of man's lot in an intolerable world, another record of an Eden lost through man's own depravity and to be won back painfully, if at all, by the efforts of the children.

This view of the South, which Faulkner has extended through the magic of his art into a permanent possession of the literary mind in the Western world, is, perhaps, one of the greatest contributions which the southern experience has made to man's understanding of himself, but it was an understanding of a South which was passing, of a South caught at one of the frontiers of historical and social change. The essential condition of Faulkner's tragic vision of the South which he loved with a passion that was intense and whose injustices, indignities, and enslavement he hated with a passion equally intense, was perhaps best expressed by the historian C. Vann Woodward when he said of the experience of southern history: "The South has had its full share of illusions.... But the illusion that 'history is something unpleasant that happens to other people' is certainly not one of them.... For the South had undergone an experience that it could share with no other part of America—though it is shared by nearly all the peoples of Europe and Asia—the experience of military defeat, occupation, and reconstruction. Nothing about this history was conducive to the theory that the South was the darling of divine providence."[36]

By contrast, Thomas Wolfe, who possessed much of the same intensity and rhetorical power which Faulkner had, was the annunciator of his own intense experiences, his sensory responses. He was more like Whitman than any other American novelist, for like the poet he sang himself in an effort to realize his land through its impact on him and to find through what happens to him the key to the human riddle, the answer to the perennial problems of man caught always in the lonely search for communion, for the lost key,

36. C. Vann Woodward, *The Burden of Southern History* (Baton Rouge, 1960), p. 170.

the "lost lane end" into heaven. Wolfe in his work and in his life was a figure of the New South rather than the Old. It is by no means surprising that Faulkner spent his college days at the University of Mississippi at Oxford and the Fugitive poets were clustered in their traditional southern point of view at Vanderbilt University. On the other hand, Thomas Wolfe was a part of the movement toward a New South that was centered in the work of a group of men in Chapel Hill, and he breathed the atmosphere of the University of North Carolina, where Koch's Carolina Playmakers were making socially significant drama of the South, and where before very many years had passed from the time that Wolfe was there, Howard Odum, Guy Johnson, Rupert Vance, Albert Coates, and many others had made Chapel Hill the citadel of the critical approach to the issue of regionalism and, under the leadership of Frank Porter Graham, had made it the voice and conscience of the liberal South.

Wolfe went on from Chapel Hill to Harvard and then to New York City, where he taught at New York University and wrote his four long novels: *Look Homeward, Angel* (1929), *Of Time and The River* (1935), *The Web and the Rock* (posthumously published, 1939), and *You Can't Go Home Again* (posthumously published, 1940), and two collections of shorter fiction, *From Death to Morning* (1936) and *The Hills Beyond* (posthumously published, 1941).[37] This large body of fiction is in several respects more directly autobiographical than any other fictional work of comparable value in American writings, and it follows in its loose plot the pattern of its author's life, with its movement from a small southern mountain city to a university and thence to the great world of the North and of Europe. Where Faulkner used a rural county to write a record of the South, Wolfe sought in his pages to show through the experience of one man what it was to be an American. Where Faulkner's characters are seen embedded in history, Wolfe's characters are dramatizations of an attitude that is national and epic rather than sectional and mythic. Where Faulkner's characters seem always to be hearing "the last ding-dong of doom,"[38] Wolfe's

37. Richard S. Kennedy, in *The Window of Memory* (Chapel Hill, 1962), traces Wolfe's development and his literary career with a thoroughness that has been afforded no other twentieth-century southern writer.

38. William Faulkner, speech accepting the Nobel Prize for Literature, in Stockholm, Sweden, December 10, 1950.

people have embraced the promise of the future, and can declare, "I believe that we are lost here in America, but I believe we shall be found. . . . I think the true fulfillment of our spirit, of our people, of our mighty and immortal land, is yet to come. I think the true discovery of our democracy is still before us. And I think that all these things are certain as the morning, as inevitable as noon."[39]

Wolfe was thoroughly a southerner and, like many thoughtful and observant southerners, he loved his region and despised many of its attributes and attitudes.[40] He became the novelist of youth in the South and of the southerner in the outer world.[41] A part of his difference from Faulkner is the result of his growing up among qualities which Arnold Toynbee found in North Carolina—"up-to-date industries, mushroom universities and a breath of the hustling, 'boosting' spirit"—in contrast to Virginia and South Carolina which seemed to him to be "living under a spell, in which time has stood still." Toynbee's explanation—a most partial one—is that North Carolina "has not been inhibited by the idolization of a once glorious past."[42] Certainly Wolfe was the novelist of the New South, where Faulkner was that of the Old South. This fact, perhaps as much as any other, accounts for the ignoring of Wolfe by many southern critics and for some of the attacks on him.

Both Faulkner and Wolfe shared many things—being "southern," verbal power, intensity, probing introspection, admiration for James Joyce, artistic seriousness and experimentation, a view of man as a responsible being. But they also shared another and important quality that led them to attempt to resolve what Raymond Williams recently called "the deepest crisis in modern literature . . . the division of experience into social and personal categories."[43] For both writers, committed by method and interest to the exploration of the inner selves of their characters, still found the meaning of

39. Thomas Wolfe, *You Can't Go Home Again* (New York, 1940), p. 741.
40. I have discussed at some length Wolfe's relation to the South in "The Dark, Ruined Helen of His Blood: Thomas Wolfe and the South," in *South: Modern Southern Literature in Its Cultural Setting*, pp. 177-197.
41. Two important discussions of Wolfe's writing of cities are: Blanche Housman Gelfant, *The American City Novel* (Norman, Okla., 1954), pp. 119-132; and Louis D. Rubin, Jr., *Thomas Wolfe: The Weather of His Youth* (Baton Rouge, 1955), pp. 96-116.
42. Arnold J. Toynbee, *A Study of History*, Abridgement of Vols. I-VI by D. C. Somervell (New York and London, 1947), pp. 315-316.
43. "Tolstoy, Lawrence, and Tragedy," *Kenyon Review*, XXV (Autumn, 1963), 633.

these persons in their place and fate in a social world. That world for Faulkner was always the rural South; for Wolfe it ultimately was a non-sectional America.

The Old South was doomed at the moment when it most brilliantly epitomized for the writers of the Southern Renascence an ideal of order, truth, and virtue, for the agrarian South was smoothed away by the tools of an industrial age. As C. Vann Woodward has observed, in the struggle between the bulldozer and the magnolia tree, the bulldozer is clearly winning.[44] The other essays in this volume document the magnitude and the nature of the change that the South is undergoing. Its literature inevitably reflects those changes, for its subject is no longer the same. In 1935, at the height of the Renascence, Allen Tate saw that this would be true and said: "The considerable achievement of southerners in modern American letters must not beguile us into too much hope for the future. The southern novelist has left his mark upon the age; but it is of the age. From the peculiarly historical consciousness of the southern writer has come good work of a special order; but the focus of this consciousness is quite temporary."[45]

The present-day southern writers of distinction, even where their subject matter is the South, plainly have a different focus from the Fugitives and Faulkner, a focus that Wolfe would have understood, for they have moved from the rural South to a broader world, and have lost much that was distinctively southern in the movement. Flannery O'Connor finds in the South materials for religious allegory; Ralph Ellison and Richard Wright almost reverse the telescope on the Negro question. William Styron's latest novel is laid in Italy and Katherine Anne Porter's on a boat closer to the fifteenth century *Narrenschiff* than to a Mississippi river boat. Doris Betts explores problems of personality in lower-middle-class industrial communities and in suburbia. Randall Jarrell, in poetry, fiction, and essays, displays his "sad heart in a supermarket" which is located in a completely de-sectionalized, asphalt-paved parking area. Frances Gray Patton writes charmingly of the social problems of a middle-

44. *The Burden of Southern History*, pp. 3-26.
45. "The Profession of Letters in the South," *The Man of Letters in the Modern World*, p. 319. This essay originally appeared in the *Virginia Quarterly Review* in 1935.

class intelligentsia that might be in Cambridge or Berkeley almost as well as in Durham, North Carolina. And so the record goes.

Its literature was perhaps the greatest contribution that the South made to America in the first half of this century. But in the 1960's, filled with burgeoning industrial development, increasing urbanization, expanding education and research, and the accelerating race revolution, the South as *subject* has changed, and many of the distinct qualities of a self-consciously regional literature have themselves now become a part of history.

XIX. SOCIAL CHANGE IN THE SOUTHERN APPALACHIANS / Rupert B. Vance

The Southern Appalachian Region, it is sometimes said, comprises the backyards of some seven southern states. In the brief compass of this book it was not possible to present all the subregional components that make up the South. For several reasons, however, the Southern Highlands deserve their own accounting. They are different, but this analysis is not presented as a portrait of quaint customs and surviving folklore. Rather, when the problem of continuity and change is examined, the serious question arises as to how and on what terms the region will be able to follow the South in its thrust to get back into the mainstream of American economic and cultural life. Examined in terms of its attitude toward industrial change sweeping over the rest of the South, the region's stance seems to partake more of a heritage from the frontier than from the Civil War. Social change has not dealt kindly with certain parts of this area.

Analysis of the Appalachians, we find, is no longer regarded as an academic exercise in delimiting subregions and subcultures; it has become a problem of social action and policy. "End the cycle of poverty," economic redevelopment, and the attempt to prevent large parts of the areas from becoming a back eddy of American life represent aspects of current policy. The present chapter, if unable to present sure solutions, will nevertheless be written in concern with what is unique and urgent about the region.

If the Appalachians are here presented as a problem area, it is only to point out that great variations exist. Cities in the area are like cities elsewhere in the United States, except that their slums are populated by recent migrants from the mountains rather than by Negroes and Puerto Ricans. The Great Valley is surrounded by mountains, but it stands out as one of the richest agricultural areas in the country. The truly mountainous areas, those over 2,000 feet in altitude, no longer offer serious problems. Scenery of pure beauty, often penetrated by magnificent highways, stretches across these highlands, and areas like the Great Smoky Park and the famous parkways have few or no permanent inhabitants left—only touring customers. Nevertheless, the Appalachian problem areas remain, mainly in the lower reaches of hills and dissected plateaus as we shall see. Vigorous studies of these areas have documented the problem.[1]

1

Without committing ourselves to geographic determinism, we can point out that the Southern Appalachians, as a part of the Eastern Mountain system running from the Laurentians of Canada to Alabama and Georgia, have the highest peaks and the most sharply dissected plateaus east of the Rockies. Beginning from the east, (1) the Blue Ridge Mountains comprise the highest ranges; (2) the Central Division has four valleys with alternating ridges; and (3) the Western Subregion consists mainly of three dissected plateaus, the Allegheny, the Northeastern Cumberland, and the Northwestern Cumberland areas.[2]

In its unfolding analysis the extent of this subregion has gradually been narrowed. From the first important survey, that of John C. Campbell in 1910[3] to the Appalachian survey of 1960, the region as depicted shrunk from 210 counties of 112,000 square miles to 190 counties of approximately 80,000 square miles and 5,600,000 population. This includes the six metropolitan areas formed by the cities of Charleston and Huntington, West Virginia; Roanoke, Virginia; Asheville, North Carolina; and Knoxville and Chattanooga, Tennessee.

It is agreed in our country's history that differing geography has gone along with differing types of settlement. Regional distinctions soon gave the Southern Tidewater its primacy with an aristocracy based on tobacco, rice, and indigo. The rest was back country, for the supremacy of the Piedmont was to be delayed until industrialization approached its zenith in the twentieth century. The

1. Thomas R. Ford (ed.), *The Southern Appalachian Region: A Survey* (Lexington: University of Kentucky Press, 1962), is the best overall analysis. Mary Jean Bowman, and W. W. Haynes, *Resources and People in East Kentucky* (Baltimore: The Johns Hopkins Press, 1963), is an excellent survey sponsored by Resources for the Future. Harry Candle, *Night Comes to the Cumberlands: A Biography of a Depressed Area* (Boston: Little, Brown and Co., 1962), is an excellent account by a journalist who is also a native of the area.

2. The U. S. Department of Agriculture, *Economic and Social Problems of the Southern Appalachians*, Misc. Publications 205 (Washington, D. C.: Government Printing Office, 1935), Chapters 7, 10-15.

3. John C. Campbell, *The Southern Highlander and his Homeland* (New York: Russell Sage Foundation, 1921), pp. 10-18.

image we have of the mountains is that of a frontier with "no indication that the people were shuttled into the mountains nor that they were of inferior stock." When D. H. Davis studied the mountain region for the State Geological Survey of Kentucky in 1928 he reported: "The stock is in all probability, in a large part, the same as that of the Kentucky Blue Grass [region] but it has been modified by long isolation in an area of lesser opportunity."[4]

2

The fluctuating trend lines of social change and continuity in these mountains are as baffling to the analyst as those of our national life—partly because they are inextricably intertwined. As it moved out of the frontier period, it must have required some time for the nation to realize that the mountain people were likely to be left isolated and underprivileged in the change. For a time good hunting, pasture on the free range, subsistence agriculture, and homespun living were adequate rewards. Finally, the breakdown of isolation made possible the comparison of regional and national standards of life. When the Great Depression introduced relief and public works in the 1930's, the application of federal standards made half the population in certain Appalachian areas eligible for relief—and this without any lowering of the customary "live-at-home" and "do-without" economy.[5]

As economic recovery proceeded, it became evident that the economic status and thus the social adequacy of the region would depend largely on its ability to participate in the nation's urban industrial complex. Any analysis along this line will point out the great diversity of the region in terms of (1) what communities have lost in economic competence and (2) what they never had.

Before 1900 most adult workers were employed in agriculture. Today (1960) two-thirds of the population live in rural areas but this figure exaggerates the region's social continuity with the frontier. Only 55 per cent of the employed who live on farms now work in agricultural occupations. Less than one-ninth of the employed males are farmers and farm managers. More persons work in industry than any other branch of economy, but manufacturing em-

4. D. H. Davis, *Geography of the Kentucky Mountains* (Frankfort, Ky.: Kentucky Geological Survey, 1928), pp. 157-158.
5. Ford, *op. cit.*, p. 5.

ploys only 21 per cent of the people. In 1957 the average number of miners working daily was 122,243—a drop of 40 per cent in six years. Now less than one-eighth of the working force in the area, the mining force continues to decline.

Without laboring the details, certain clear-cut conclusions are evident. (1) Coal mining is a sick industry, ruinous of men and natural resources of stream and soil. The worst areas in the Appalachians, the Kentucky Cumberlands, certain West Virginia areas and northern areas as in Pennsylvania, consist of stranded coal communities. With the finest reserves of bituminous coal, expected to last 1,000 years, with the chance of reaching again some of the peak years of physical production, the industry will never re-employ its stranded workers. Until the workers move out and the abusive practices of strip mining are abandoned these many coal camps have little hope beyond dire poverty.[6]

Much of (2) mountain agriculture has been subsistence farming—strictly limited in resources and furnishing very little cash income to the farmer's family. The mode of national agriculture today is one of extended operations, requiring capital and access to well-organized markets. Agriculture in the mountains can be improved and more commercial crops can be grown but only for fewer farmers cultivating larger acreage. Land is limited; slopes are steep; more lands should be put back into forests; and more people will be pushed off the farms. Subsistence farming today is an occupation in which no self-respecting parent should want to rear his children. Everytime the health authorities issue a new directive that fluid milk must be carried to market in glass-lined refrigerator trucks instead of milk cans, more hill farmers go out of the dairy business. Mountain agriculture produces few commercial staples, gets few subsidies for cutting back production—they underproduce not overproduce—but pays the increased prices for grain for feeder calves and hog production. Few government programs have been designed for this type of farming, and it is evident that many offer no hope at all for the mountain farmer. It seems safe to say that mountain agriculture is not only the stepchild of nature; it is the forgotten stepchild of the United States Department of Agriculture.[7]

6. *Ibid.*, pp. 103-114.
7. Roy E. Proctor and T. Kelly White, Chapter 6 in *ibid.*, pp. 87-101.

The mountains have the finest (3) national and state forests left in this country and more land can be reforested. Lumber production, however, has passed its peak and the new program is one of conservation and reduced yield with public and private employment in scientific forestry. The larger areas in corporate and private ownership must be given the same treatment, if timber is to remain a continuing resource. The frank truth is that not a large number of people are required "to watch trees grow." If a sizeable labor force is employed in speeding up the cut, they will have neither trees nor their employment very long! The United States Forestry Service and certain private owners are doing a magnificent work, but they offer no great hope of re-employing a population of any size.[8]

This analysis leaves (4) industrialization as the main hope of a reinvigorated Appalachia. There is a distinct industrial belt in the Appalachians as the survey showed; manufacturing employment has increased at a faster rate than in the nation; the region's cities generate markets and employment for their hinterlands.[9] The crucial point here is the amount of capital investment required to furnish employment for an industrial worker at a decent annual wage. If the farmer requires some $15,000 to $25,000 invested capital in land and equipment to furnish an annual return of $5,000 to $7,500 on his labor, the industrial worker depends on an equal or greater amount of capital investment—an investment that may be lost unless there exists access to a good market for the product. This usually means a national market. Every area in the country, it appears, is in competition with other areas for industrialization and for access to markets. All communities in the United States want to further industrialization and good, sound commercial agriculture, but since the localizing factor is anchorage to resources which may be developed and processed on the site or near it, industrialization has many choices of where to alight in its movement over the country. To expect corporate industry to function as a relief program to bail out stranded communities in the Southern Appalachians is futile. To attract national corporations and to break into competitive markets, areas must offer special advantages. This is a fair statement of what any region faces in competition in the national picture. It

8. *Ibid.*, pp. 115-118.
9. *Ibid.*, Chapter 8, gives an excellent account of the development of manufacturing in the region.

is also a fair statement of what other parts of the South have accomplished.

3

We can be more specific and more statistical. Agriculture and coal mining are the sick industries of Appalachia; the new hope is to be found in industrialization and urbanization. Of the 5,672,178 people enumerated in the subregion in 1960, one-third lived in some 157 urban places; two-thirds were still accounted among the rural population. The metropolitan centers have been listed; while not large by national standards, they include some 25 per cent of the region's population. In all there were only 13 cities of 25,000 population and over; 42 cities had from 10,000 up to 25,000 people. Over half the nation's working force are now employed in the services, distribution, the professions, etc., the so-called white-collar trades, located in urban centers. It is here that the great middle-class standard of living is developed and spread throughout the population. These occupations are hardly affixed to any specific source except that they represent central operations in and related to the urban complex. Here transportation, finance, and marketing tend to equal resources in importance.

All over the South great advances have been made by participating in the nation's industrial goals, adjusting commercial agriculture, and creating centers for the increased emphasis on the expansion of social and institutional services—educational, clerical, and professional. Here it is generally felt that portions of the Appalachians have not kept up with advances in the South. No part of the country needs these improved institutional services more; and certainly serious efforts must and will continue to be made toward reorganization of the area's basic economy.

To basic economic pressures, the inhabitants of this area have reacted by taking out-migration as the avenue of escape and self-help. From 1940 to 1960 almost 2,000,000 more people have left Appalachia than have settled there. A loss of 13 per cent from 1940-1950, and 19 per cent from 1950 to 1960, was balanced by a rate of natural increase—the excess of birth over death—of 21 and 16.2 per cent in 1940-1950 and 1950-1960 respectively. Kentucky lost over 500,000 by out-migration and West Virginia over 600,000 during this twenty-year period. The greatest out-migrations left the Cumberland and Allegheny Plateaus: 28.3 per cent in 1950-1960; the next greatest loss was from the Blue Ridge area: 14.7 per cent; the least from the Great Valley: 8.7 per cent. From 1940-1950 the six metropolitan areas gained 10,518 by migration; from 1950-1960 they lost 137,684. The only metropolitan area to show gain was Roanoke, Virginia.[10]

When the 190 counties were classified on the basis of major occupations, the regions' hard-pressed economies were easily identified. Mining counties had approximately 40 per cent loss by net out-migration; agricultural areas with mining and manufacturing lost 23 to 25 per cent. Only state economic areas characterized by manufacturing and mixed agriculture, or manufacturing and commercial showed gains, 8.3 and 5.4 per cent respectively from 1950 to 1960. Where population numbers have been maintained, it must be assigned to the natural increase, and here the trend is downward. Migration has a double effect. It removes a disproportionate number of people in the younger working ages and it reduces future population increase by the number of children these people would have had in their home communities. Here we are faced with an interesting question. If changed conditions have forced this amount of out-migration, what changes have they induced in mountain attitudes?

4

The older regional studies, more concerned with causation than social change, emphasized social continuity in the mountains. They looked back to physical limitations, and from physical resources and crude modes of making a living, the analysis moved forward to consider institutional adjustments and the attitudes of the people. Thus mountain isolation, which began as a physical limitation enforced by rugged topography, became mental and cultural isolation which causes people to remain in disadvantaged areas and resist the changes that would bring them into contact with the outside world. The effect of conditions thus becomes a new cause of conditions, but the cause is now an attitude, not a mountain. If we devote attention to religion in the mountains, we find it an effect of con-

10. J. S. Brown and C. A. Hillery, Chapter 4 in *ibid.*, pp. 54-78.

ditions under which people have lived. Not only is it an effect of conditions under which people live, but the particular attitudes of religion may then operate to perpetuate these conditions. Thus if hard lives have given rise to fatalism and fundamentalism, these attitudes may operate to perpetuate original conditions. The change from fatalism to the social gospel may actually go over into engineered change in breaking through limiting physical conditions. Since mountains are not likely to be moved, the new regionalism proceeds on the assumption that men can be moved.

How resistant to change are the mountain people in their sentiments and beliefs, the way they feel the world is, and should be, ordered? In a field survey the opinions and attitudes of a representative sample were secured. In attempting to measure the extent and influence of individualism and self-reliance, of fundamentalism and fatalism, the survey showed that attitudes are changing. The aspirations of our national life have penetrated the mountains and the people visualize a more equitable future for their children. They are now willing for them to leave the region in the search of a better life. In the main the population accepts the necessity of welfare and relief; they feel that the government should do more, but hesitate to give their support to the raising of taxes for these goals. They now recognize the advantage of group action, but think of government as "they" not "we." While they may not have yet reached the level of responsible organization for self-help, the people, as the survey showed, present a greater hope of improved social organization.

The much-criticized fundamentalism no longer appears as an obstacle to progress, for the people have assimilated much of the social gospel along with the belief in the ability of education and science to improve their lot. Professor Thomas Ford calls his analysis the passing of provincialism. While present attitudes show no passive acceptance of the *status quo*, they do not indicate that the people themselves yet know how to lead the way to change.[11]

Special attention was devoted in the Appalachian survey to the attitude of community leaders selected from interviews with the people themselves. The persons named as leaders—379 were inter-

11. T. R. Ford, "The Passing of Provincialism," Chapter 2 in *ibid.*, pp. 9-24.

viewed—were considerably ahead of the total population in education, property ownership, income, and age. Half were regarded by the criteria of the study as belonging to the region's upper class. The leaders were definitely ahead of the people, activists and progressive, pushing for change and development, receptive of national values and contacts. Although named by the people, they were not of the people in modal attitudes and opinions. Nevertheless, to find the professional and propertied people of the area with these new attitudes gave an indication that this can hardly be called a traditional society. Here is one indication that feasible plans and programs, if developed, will have the support of the community leaders. This whole trend of attitude toward change increases from the rural through the urban to the metropolitan populations.[12] Admitting it has required a long period for these attitudes to develop, the question now remains: Can the new attitudes clear the ground for a changeover in the more depressed areas of the Appalachians?

5

Change has been abroad in the land and the Appalachians are far from being a stagnant enclave. Population growth has tended to stabilize; nearly two million people have migrated elsewhere in the last twenty years. Since 1939 manufacturing employment and production have increased more rapidly than in the nation. Unprecedented aid from outside the region has pushed the development of new highways and of water resources as in the TVA. Schools have been improved; more students attend schools and for longer periods. Programs of public assistance, while inadequate, have developed to mitigate the harsher aspects of poverty. While change is by no means absent from the region, the nation has advanced at a more rapid rate, leaving the Appalachians still under a disadvantage. Moreover, certain areas like the Kentucky Cumberland have encountered serious damage. Schools have improved but it is less easy to repair the educational damage already inflicted on maturing populations.[13]

In public policy it is oftimes easier to agree on basic goals than

12. *Ibid.*, pp. 24-29.
13. *Ibid.*, pp. 289-290.

to reach consensus on how the goals may be attained. In the case at hand, the determination of objectives has been especially compelling. The Appalachians problem areas show no tendency to go away if they are simply left alone. However, since they also show little tendency to depress the normal trend line of our national prosperity, it has been suggested that they can be accepted as chronic pockets of poverty, and thus safely disregarded in the ordinary plans of business and government. The fallacy of this argument "is that it ignores the enormous human and social cost of the depressed areas and the danger to national policy in letting them fester." The continual wastage of human resources in depressed areas has thus been called "a social crime, an economic absurdity and a political menace."[14]

In the present climate of opinion, and with the resources of an affluent society, it may surprise some to find that it will prove less difficult to secure budgets for the development of Appalachia than to determine how best to use these budgets. In the problem of induced social change we have two main questions to answer: What is the strategy of regional development in an area like this? What type and kinds of social organization already exist and what others can be developed to carry through this strategy? Just as we have glanced at the new researches and the new knowledge developed about the Appalachians, let us recount the appearance of agencies and organizations devoted to redevelopment. Then we shall follow through by looking at the problem of strategy and tactics.

The Appalachians have long been the center of missionary and extension activity by private groups and agencies. Health services were first taken to the mountains by the Frontier Nursing Service. Nurses who rode horseback to deliver the babies of mountain mothers were the first to bring modern maternal and child health services to remote areas. Practically all of the national denominations have supported missionary activity in the area; and before the era of public schools, many staffed and supported a mountain academy. Berea College remains a fine example of an institution especially adapted to mountain culture and needs.

Recent events converging on this area have served to make in-

14. Melvin R. Levin, "What Do We Do With Depressed Areas?" *Iowa Business Digest*, April, 1960, p. 1.

duced change regarded as a social necessity. From the Southern Governor's Conference to President Lyndon Johnson's attack on poverty many agencies, governmental and private, are at work on plans for the region's development. The Conference of Governors of the Appalachian States issued an initial call for action at its meeting in Annapolis, Maryland, in May, 1960. The group sponsored an economic report, and agreed on programs of increased highway facilities, the development of water resources, and improved education.[15] On May 21, 1961, President Kennedy signed the Area Redevelopment Act—a measure to help stranded rural and urban communities overcome chronic unemployment by a series of studies, projects, and programs to be financed by grants-in-aid. The Area Redevelopment Administration was established in the Department of Commerce and given a sizeable budget with promise of other funds to come.[16] In the meantime, conditions became worse and the program of surplus foods was developed in order to feed hungry people in certain stranded communities. Much of the Cumberland Plateau of Eastern Kentucky, many of West Virginia's counties and other regions of the Appalachians were designated as redevelopment areas under the new act.

Certain other plans can also be pointed out. In West Virginia a group of core counties, organized under the combined Extension Services of the State University, have embarked on a program of development proposed and guided by core county committees. Under a grant from the Kellogg Foundation, the University of Kentucky is carrying integrated extension services to the thirty counties of the Cumberlands in an attempt to hasten redevelopment. The idea is to stimulate certain communities by offering these services, to encourage them to inventory their needs and work toward alleviation. The governor of North Carolina and his advisors organized a program entitled, "End the Cycle of Poverty in North Carolina," secured the support of the Ford Foundation and other groups, and established an agency embarking on a program of upgrading and developing an educational program geared to the underedu-

15. Maryland Department of Economic Development, *The Appalachian Region* (Annapolis, Md., 1960).

16. Public Law 87-27, 87th Congress, p. 1, May 1, 1961; Area Redevelopment Act Report of the Committee on Bonding and Currency, House of Representatives, 87th Congress, March 22, 1961.

cated. While this is mainly devoted to vocational education it involves an upgrading of all education. Other projects can be mentioned in various stages of development.

With administrative machinery at hand, with seed capital in sight, with favorable climate of public opinion, we come to a most important question: What alternatives should be set up and what choices will have to be made in the attempt to develop physical and human resources in a program of induced social change in the Southern Appalachians? The Appalachians and the nation have come to a point where they must ponder policy. Do we have any guide lines in such a program of deliberately breaking the trend line of continuity with tradition and embarking on a program of hastening social change?

Certainly, if this region or any other is to be more fully developed, it must be agreed that the program for its development will take place in the context of national growth and development. Not all areas in need of advance are equally capable of it. What America wants is the equitable and desirable development of physical and human resources. It appears, however, that inevitably a Spartan decision may have to be made. When the potential physical resources of a given area do not furnish a basis for further development, the resources to be conserved are the people themselves and their development must be put foremost. This conclusion means that for certain areas, the conservation and development of the human resources of the Appalachians must proceed elsewhere. Whether they know it or not, parents in the region should no longer rear their children to go into subsistence agriculture. And if only one-sixth to one-tenth of the males growing to adulthood in the mining camps can expect to find employment in the mines, these facts must be faced in the necessity for outward movement. Large contingents of mountain youth must be prepared to migrate to strange cities to engage in new trades and crafts, and the institutional agencies of the region must give them all the aid they can in this difficult adventure.[17]

In America, people have always moved in an effort to better themselves—this is the way America was settled. Sometimes they made mistakes, but it was these movements that settled the country

17. See the discussion in Chapter 19, Ford, *op. cit.*, pp. 289-299.

and balanced the economy. Such migrations will continue as our
changing agriculture and the shifting Appalachian populations
show. But it now seems that these movements can be guided and
speeded up for the benefit of the people and for the nation. The
development of growing pockets of poverty must be prevented
wherever they threaten to occur. This is hard doctrine for any
American community and one service of the subsidies of the Area
Redevelopment Administration is to test the chances for redevelopment of certain problem areas. Once satisfied that these communities are unsuited for industrial development, other plans can be
made that will get the support of community forces.

It would be well therefore to develop a sense of urgency about
the problems of the Appalachians and its people. Many subregions
will aid in carrying forward induced social change. The metropolitan areas and the Great Valley especially can be further developed.
Other urban centers will develop important functions. Certain areas
are severely limited in their opportunities and here social institutions, geared to a culture of poverty, have not only failed to solve
these problems but have contributed to their perpetuation. Many
people cannot and do not realize what has happened to them and
what goes on in the great world outside. In such situations the
schools have failed to provide the youth with the knowledge and
skills required for high-income employment. Local agencies operating in an atmosphere of poverty in which expenditures beyond
a bare minimum are luxuries cannot make the capital investments
necessary for cultural and economic development. Here the rule is
to conserve and develop the human resources. As the people move
to new opportunities, it will be realized that with its crowded industrial and urban areas, the nation stands in need of open spaces
for recreation and refreshment. It is here that many of the Appalachian areas will find their better utilization.

Once certain areas are opened up to the development of the
natural beauties of water, lakes, and forests, there will be a reorganized basis of support and a new social structure for an emerging
economy and culture. A better life for fewer people has proved
necessary in national agriculture; it is overdue in the mining areas
of the mountains; it can extend through the depressed areas of subsistence agriculture. Where resources are limited, population pres-

sure great, and failure endemic, outward movement will continue and should be aided and accelerated. If we are to confess to sentiment in this situation, we must be sentimental about people—not about territory. The value to be served is the better preparation of oncoming youth to take their place in American life, wherever they choose to go.

The Appalachians are located in one of the more advanced and dynamic countries of the world. Many natural processes work for change—growth, expansion, migration, and readjustment. It seems safe to contend that continuing readjustment and much shifting within the area will, over a period, enable the Appalachians to support as many people as they now have and at higher levels of accomplishment. Planning procedures accelerate certain processes here, retard others there, take up the slack elsewhere. This is a national challenge and the nation and the region have the resources, the skill, and the organization to bring it to pass. Here in induced social change we have a new approach, a new type of program, and a new urgency in its accomplishment.

XX. THE CHANGING STATUS OF THE SOUTHERN WOMAN / Guion Griffis Johnson

If one would understand a region, it is important to remember that the past lives on in the present, and that old political, economic, social, and racial rivalries become the basis for the tensions of the present. This truism is as important for an understanding of the changing role of the southern woman as for any other aspect of the changing South.

A hundred years ago the ideal southern woman was described as soft, gentle, self-effacing, with enough education to enable her to carry on a polite conversation of small talk and enough wisdom to know her place and keep it.[1] The hard facts both of law and social custom have decreed male supremacy down through the years, but the slowly expanding legal rights of women, the rapid flow of women into the labor force, the progress in the education of women, the impact of science and technology in reshaping domestic and social patterns, and the dynamics of women's voluntary organizations have all played a part in producing change.

On the eve of the Civil War the life of the southern woman, even that of the wealthy planter class, was a round of busy details which left little time for leisure. As Dr. James A. Norcom of Edenton, North Carolina, described it:

> ... if it is not managed with great ability, sobriety, and good sense, the duty of house-keeping is dirty, demoralizing and debasing in a high degree.... It confines one to a series of low pursuits, a course of filthy drudgery, and disgusting slovenliness, that have but little time for study or quiet meditation, and very little for improving conversation or refined society; and it is altogether unsuited to moral and religious enjoyment. It keeps one in a perpetual agitation, anxiety, and apprehension; and has no pleasure equal to the pains, the toil, the privations and the suffering, which it is almost sure to impose.[2]

A young married woman of eastern North Carolina confirmed Dr. Norcom's appraisal in a letter to a friend, saying, "One does

1. Guion Griffis Johnson, *Ante-Bellum North Carolina, a Social History* (Chapel Hill: University of North Carolina Press, 1937), pp. 228-229.
2. Quoted in *ibid.*, p. 237.

not always have a great deal of good humor to spare after marriage."

However much the ante bellum woman chose to appear as a lady of ease, few in the South could actually assume this role. In any successful family whose fortune was built largely on agriculture, regardless of the number of slaves at their command, "the feeble wife" was no less industrious or economical than her husband. Many a southern husband might have written to his wife as William Alston of Virginia did late in the 1850's, "I know that, accustomed to luxury, and capable of shining in society, you have cheerfully worked, economized, and shunned the world."

Wives of the yeomanry, as the small farmers were called, not only did the work associated with the maintenance of the household, but also assisted with the work in the field. They and their children performed the lighter tasks of farm work, dropping seeds, chopping cotton, hoeing corn, setting, worming, and curing tobacco, picking cotton. They even helped with the more strenuous work of plowing, clearing fields, and pulling fodder. Almost a hundred years later (1939) Margaret Jarman Hagood in a study of southern white tenant farm women found the same general conditions still prevailing: "From truncated childhoods, with meager preparation, they begin prematurely the triple role of mother, housekeeper, and field laborer."[3] Twenty-five years still later, the mechanization of agriculture has almost put an end to the farm tenant problem.

The life expectancy of women in the nineteenth century was considerably below that of men. "It is an appalling fact," wrote Dr. W. C. Lankford of Franklin County, North Carolina, "that there are more diseases, peculiar to women, which come to the knowledge of the physician, than of all the diseases which 'man is heir to'; and what is still more to be pitied, they are on a rapid increase." Most of the diseases were those incident to childbirth and the reproductive organs. Large families were the rule even among the gentry. The mother—rich or poor, black or white—bore a child every year or so until the process was stopped by age or ill health.

Despite the hardships of married life, the goal of every southern

3. *Mothers of the South* (Chapel Hill: University of North Carolina Press, 1939), p. 242.

woman was a husband, a home, and children. The unmarried female was an embarrassment to the family and the butt of many cruel jokes. Unless she possessed unusual courage and enterprise, she lived out her life as a drudge in the household of a relative or friend. Girls married at an early age, in some southern states as early as twelve years with parental consent, but society frowned upon a man's marrying until he was settled in a job or profession and could support his family.

Although the historian must be cautious in appraising the extent of premarital sex relations a hundred years ago because of the scanty records available on which to base a conclusion, from an examination of the bastardy cases arising in the county courts and the petitions coming before the legislature to legitimatize children, it would seem that illegitimacy was more prevalent in the nineteenth century than in the twentieth. For example, the bastardy cases arising in seven North Carolina counties between 1801 to 1805 amounted to 118, whereas thirty years later these cases had dropped to 63, and the next two decades continued to show a decline.[4] These figures rather well indicate what happens when a frontier society begins to stabilize.

The assumption that southern families closely guarded their young women, strictly chaperoned them, and permitted a minimum of contact during the courtship period is not borne out by the facts. In the early ante bellum period a young man wrote his sister, about to leave her home in the country for a visit in the city, that he hoped she could "associate with those who are called the polite and well bred, the gay and fashionable ladies of the present day, without assuming their manners, and adopting their free and forward airs, without, like them, admitting the gentlemen . . . to liberties, to familiarities, which, if they are not criminal, are at least inconsistent with that modesty, and chastity of manners, which constitute the first female charm. . . ."[5] He did not want his sister to deport herself like "those fashionable ladies . . . who in public companies suffered themselves to be clasped in our arms, seated on our knees, kissed, pressed and toyed with in the most familiar manner—with whom our hands scarce need restraint."

4. Johnson, *op. cit.*, p. 211.
5. *Ibid.*, pp. 208-209.

Legally the personality of the wife was merged in that of the husband. She could not sue or be sued alone. She could not hold property separate from her husband even in her savings unless her husband gave her permission to claim it as her own. She could not dispose of the lands which she brought to her husband in marriage without a legally executed document whereby he gave her this privilege. Marriage was itself an unqualified gift to the husband of all the wife was in possession of at the time and all that she should thereafter acquire whether he should survive her or not. The property which a woman possessed at the time of her marriage might be secured to her through a marriage contract entered into prior to the wedding and registered as a deed, but any wealth she might inherit thereafter became the sole property of her husband.

The southern husband a hundred years ago not only had control over his wife's property but he also was the master of her person. "The wife must be subject to the husband. Every man must govern his household," said Chief Justice Pearson of North Carolina in 1862.[6] The law also made the husband responsible for his wife's acts. If the wife should commit a criminal offense, less than felony, in the presence of her husband, he, not she, was held responsible. But the law also gave the husband "power to use such a degree of force as is necessary to make the wife behave herself and know her place."

With such legal restrictions thrown about the wife's ability to hold property, enter contracts, or otherwise to express herself as a person, it is a wonder that the nineteenth-century woman should have developed motivation or individuality. Actually, the meekness of a wife depended more upon her temperament than upon repressive customs. Many women, even of the upper classes, were able by frugality and good management to add something to the family income. For example, Mrs. John Croker, wife of a wealthy planter of eastern North Carolina, carried on a thriving business from her needlework, the sale of fowls, eggs, butter, and vegetables from her garden. She and her husband kept separate accounts at the stores, she lent her money on bond and took notes in her own name, and her husband even borrowed from her.[7]

6. *Ibid.*, p. 241.
7. *Ibid.*, p. 246.

Women set up millinery and dress shops, ran small bakeries, operated inns, taverns, and boarding houses. They also opened select boarding schools for genteel females and thereby often provided the only means by which a rural girl might obtain an education outside the home. When factories began to be established in the South a decade before the Civil War, the mill hands were almost exclusively young white women. The work most often resorted to by "destitute females" was domestic service, laundering, and sewing. The prevailing wage for a white housekeeper just before the Civil War was $4 a month.[8]

The humanitarian reform movement which began in western Europe in the middle eighteenth century swept across the Atlantic, stirred the American Revolution, and touched all aspects of life. It brought the benefits of education to the poor as well as the rich. It softened the criminal code. It broke the shackles of the Negro slave, and it eventually elevated the status of women.

But change in the legal status of women has come at snail's pace. Most of the state constitutions, revised during the Reconstruction period, were liberal documents which brought public education to the South, increased the civil rights of Negroes, and improved the position of women. For instance, the first significant change in the property and contract rights of married women in North Carolina came with the Constitution of 1868 which removed most restrictions. But, as Justice Walter Clark told the Federation of Women's Clubs in 1913, the Constitution of 1868 "had to be construed by judges who had been raised up in the old belief as to the total incapacity of the married woman." The result has been that successive legislative acts have been required gradually to bring the contract rights of married women within the provisions of the Constitution. In January, 1964, this constitutional protection was amended and the property rights of married women now rest in the hands of the legislature.

As the President's Commission on the Status of Women points out, "In many specific areas of State law, the disabilities of married women are considerable. . . . Single women enjoy equality of legal treatment with men in respect to property and contract law, the only general exception being the lower minimum age at which they

8. *Ibid.*, p. 247.

may contract to marry. But married women, over much broader legal ranges, are denied such equality."[9]

The piecemeal approach to the enlargement of women's legal rights has resulted in strange contradictions. As a result, some southern states may be in the most liberal position in the nation with respect to some rights and the most backward with respect to others.

For example, the Mississippi Constitution (Art. 4, Sec. 94) declares that the legislature may never create by law any distinction between the rights of men and women to acquire, own, enjoy, and dispose of property of all kinds, or their power to contract in reference thereto. "Married women are fully emancipated from all disability on account of coveture." No other southern state seems to declare so unequivocally the property rights of the married woman, but the common law still prevails in Mississippi with regard to property acquired by the co-operative efforts of both spouses after marriage. Nor are women in Mississippi eligible for service on juries. Alone among all the states in the nation, Mississippi and two other southern states—South Carolina and Alabama—deny this political right to women. Until 1956, Mississippi permitted common law marriages, and the age of consent to marriage in this state is, with the exception of South Carolina, the lowest of any southern state, fifteen years for the woman and seventeen for the man. Even this age limit may be waived if the written consent of the parent or guardian is presented to the clerk of the circuit court along with a statement of extenuating circumstances. Six southern states still recognize the validity of marriages under the common law.

Of all the southern states, Louisiana and Texas continue to impose disabilities on the married woman most nearly like those characteristic of the ante bellum South. In both states a premarital contract is necessary to protect the property which the wife owned prior to marriage. Property acquired by joint efforts of husband and wife during marriage are at the complete disposal of the husband in Louisiana, but in Texas the wife may have some relief by applying to the proper court for the right to the sole use of her wages. According to the Civil Code of Louisiana (Art. 2402), "The

9. The President's Commission on the Status of Women, *American Women* (Washington: U. S. Government Printing Office, 1963), p. 47.

husband is the head and master of the partnership or community of
gains; he administers its effects, disposes of the revenues which they
produce, and may alienate them . . . without the consent and permission of his wife."

The majority of southern states, in fact, do not permit the wife
to share equally and separately in a business which has been built
up by her joint efforts during marriage unless a contract has been
made to this effect. In a few states, a wife cannot collect damages
for personal injury inflicted on her by her husband on the assumption that the personality of the wife is still merged in that of her
husband.

All the southern states, however, declare "the right to hold
public office is open to both sexes alike,"[10] and Texas, despite its
unequal disposition of property and personal rights, gallantly pro-
claims, "An office is essentially a trust or agency for the benefit of
the public. The supreme qualification is unselfish fidelity to duty.
Who will say that her sex prevents a woman from displaying this
virtue in as marked a degree as the greatest of men?"[11]

The ever increasing number of southern women who are gainfully employed make these legal restrictions on their right to control
their property and their joint earnings anachronistic. But the right
to work outside the home, especially the right of the white middle-
class married woman to do so, has come as slowly as woman's improved legal status. In 1900 there was little expectation that women
would ever play a conspicuous role in public affairs. Like the Negro,
a woman had a fixed place in society, and the white woman's place
was in the home. It was a condition of slavery that the Negro woman
work outside the home. After her chattel status ceased to exist, social
custom as well as hard economic circumstances continued to sanction her working from ten to fourteen hours a day when she could
find steady employment.

Agriculture was still the dominant economic pattern in the South
despite the steady increase in textile manufacturing and the coming

10. *The Legal Status of Women in the United States of America: Report for
Alabama as of January 1, 1959* (U.S. Department of Labor, Women's Bureau,
Bulletin 157-1 [rev. ed.; Washington, 1959]), p. 13.

11. Dickson v. Strickland (1924), 114 Tex., 176, quoted in *The Legal Status
of Women in the United States of America: Report for Texas as of January 1, 1959*
(U.S. Department of Labor, Women's Bureau, Bulletin 157-42 [rev. ed.; Washington, 1959]), p. 14.

of some heavy industry such as the manufacture of steel in Alabama. The ranks of the planter aristocracy had been seriously depleted and a new aristocracy with wealth based on industry was rising.

World War I brought the first shock of rapid change. Negro labor began its movement from the South into industries of the North and West and continues to this day a migration which at last has given every one of the old slave states a white majority in the population. At the same time, more and more southern women, both white and Negro, became a part of the labor force. With men serving in the armed forces, women had their first real opportunity to fill the labor vacuum and they were reluctant to give up their new jobs when war ended. World War II accelerated the pace, and, when again the war was over, the expanding industrial growth of the nation permitted many more to remain in the labor force than had been able to do so in 1918.

In 1900 women composed 18 per cent of all workers in the labor force. By 1930 this percentage had increased to 22 and by 1962 it had climbed to 34 per cent of all women aged fourteen and over.[12] Today women compose about a third of the entire labor force in the United States. In July 1963 they numbered almost 25½ million.[13] By 1970 the Women's Bureau of the Department of Labor estimates that almost half of the new workers needed to produce the goods and services of the growing population will be women. This will result in a 25 per cent increase for women workers as compared with a 14 per cent increase for men.

In 1960 the South equalled the national average of 34 as to the percentage of all women in the population, fourteen years and over, gainfully employed. In the District of Columbia, 52 per cent of all women were in the labor force, the highest percentage anywhere in the nation. Six other areas in the South—Delaware, Florida, Georgia, Maryland, and North and South Carolina—exceeded the national average of 34 per cent.

When the Women's Bureau of the Department of Labor questioned a group of women workers about why they were employed,

12. *1962 Handbook on Women Workers* (U.S. Department of Labor, Women's Bureau, Bulletin 285 [Washington, 1963]), pp. 4-5.
13. "Background Facts on Women Workers in the United States, September 1963" (U.S. Department of Labor, Women's Bureau, Mimeographed Bulletin 64-78 [Washington, 1963]), p. 1.

most of them gave financial reasons.[14] With a few exceptions, the women without husbands were supporting not only themselves but dependents as well. Most working wives were adding essential income to the family budget. They were working to raise the family standard of living, to send their husbands or their children to college, and to help meet financial crises. Very few worked for the mere pleasure of the job or just to keep their skills sharpened.

In fact, 56 per cent of the total number of women workers in March, 1962, were married women living with their husbands, and only 23 per cent were single women. One southern state, Florida, had the third highest percentage of the number of working wives of all states in the country. The lower the husband's wage the more likelihood there is of the wife working. This fact accounts for the large number of married Negro women in the labor force and this also helps to explain the high percentage of married women in the South who are gainfully employed, 32 per cent as compared to 29 per cent in the North Central states and 30 per cent in the Northeast. One out of eight employed women in July, 1963, were non-white, while non-whites compose only about 10 per cent of the entire population in the United States.

Other important changes in the female work force since World War II have been the rise in the age of women workers, changes in women's occupations, and a corresponding rise in the earnings and income levels of women. An increased importance of older women in the work force has been found throughout the country. In 1950 the median age of women workers was thirty-six but today it is forty-one. Of all the Census regions, the South has the lowest median age, thirty-nine.[15] By 1970 the Women's Bureau estimates that the women in the age group from forty-five to fifty-four will have the highest percentage of employed workers of any of the age categories for women. It is also interesting to note that in the category of fifty-five and over, the Bureau estimates that slightly more than 52 per cent will also be employed by 1970.

Women are employed in a great variety of occupations, but the largest number in July, 1963, (7.3 million) had clerical jobs. This

14. *1962 Handbook on Women Workers*, Part I.
15. *Women Workers in 1960* (U.S. Department of Labor, Women's Bureau, Bulletin 284 [Washington, 1962]), p. 8.

category includes secretaries, stenographers, typists, bookkeepers, office-machine operators, and telephone operators. Women service workers totaled 3.7 million and factory workers 3.5 million. There were 2.7 million women professional and technical workers. This category includes teachers, nurses, accountants, librarians, social workers, doctors, lawyers, engineers, natural and social scientists, and technicians.

Changes in women's employment in the South in specific occupational groups were generally consistent with total occupational changes in the country. Specifically, three groups of occupations—clerical, service, and professional—attained added importance in the South. The majority of non-white southern women, however, continued to be employed in private-household or other personal service work. For the country as a whole, almost three-fifths work in this low-income bracket. Nevertheless, during the ten-year period from 1950-1960, the income level of non-white women improved in relation to that of all women, and was moving upward more rapidly than any other segment in the labor force. In 1949, non-white women with some income averaged only $590—less than three-fifths the amount for all women receiving income. Ten years later, this amount had reached $909 and was more than two-thirds that of all women. In 1962 their income level had edged even closer to that of white women as more and more entered professional and managerial work, but in the South the increase has come slowly and when it has come it has been in the large cities and in the border states.

In southern areas with a high concentration of Negroes in the population there are still Negro women who work 65 hours a week for $10 and rations. When it is remembered that the Negro family tends still to be matriarchal with the mother representing the core of stability, the grinding poverty of this low wage becomes all the more apparent. Here the culturally deprived family begets culturally deprived children who swell the list of school absenteeism, dropouts, illiteracy, and delinquency.

Nevertheless, ever since Emancipation, a Negro middle class has slowly been evolving with orientation and aspirations similar to those of southern white families. More often than not it has been the work of the Negro mother outside the home which has contributed to the upward movement. Even today her income often exceeds that of her husband, and this fact tends to put a strain upon what otherwise might be a normal husband-wife relationship. It also reinforces at the upper-class level the mother-dominated family system which the conditions of slavery fostered.

In areas where the labor of the non-white woman is undervalued and underpaid, the wages of white women tend also to be below the national average. Mississippi, for example, not only reported in 1962 the lowest income in the nation for non-white women but for white women as well. In all categories of labor the Southeast has the lowest average hourly earnings in the country, and the South Central Region is not far above this rate. The differential is not only to the disadvantage of the southern woman as compared to women in other regions but it is disadvantageous in relation to the median income of men. With all too few exceptions, women who do the same work as men are paid less for their efforts, and even in industries where the federal equal-pay-for-women law applies possible evasive techniques have already been suggested.[16]

The overall picture is not a bright one. In 1947 the average median income of all employed women was $1,017 as compared to $2,230 for men. By 1962, the median income of all male workers had jumped to $4,372, while that for women had risen to only $1,342. The highest incomes were paid female professional and technical workers—for professional workers, just under $5,000, and for clerical workers, a little more than $3,500.

The opportunities for women to enter the best paying jobs with a reasonable expectation of job advancement are strongly influenced by the amount and type of education they have received. In fact, the progress in the education of women is one of the most important factors in shaping the change in the status of the southern woman. In 1895, about 4 per cent of girls seventeen years old were high school graduates; today about 70 per cent have completed high school. In 1895, bachelor's degrees annually awarded women were less than 5,000. Today more than 125,000 yearly earn this degree. While slightly more than half the country's female population five to thirty-four years of age was attending school in the fall of 1961,

16. Emergency Bulletin from Prentice-Hall, Inc., "How the Newly Enacted Equal-Pay-for-Women Law will Skyrocket Your Payroll Costs—And What to Do About It" (Englewood Cliffs, N. J.: Prentice-Hall, Inc., n.d.) [1963] No. LL/DX-A-1. This federal law covers about 7 million of the 25½ million women in the labor force.

the number of dropouts is much sharper as college age approaches. This is not true, however, for non-whites. The non-white woman is more likely to finish high school and go on to college than the non-white man. In 1960, in the South, 291,439 non-white men had four years of high school education in comparison to 422,439 women and only 64,643 non-white men had four years or more of college as compared to 108,923 women. In the total population of the nation, however, only 6 per cent of the number of women attending school in the fall of 1961 were in colleges or professional schools. A little less than a third of these students under thirty-five years of age were enrolled in private trade schools and business colleges outside the regular school system.

Nevertheless, college enrollments for women have increased proportionately more than for men during the past six years. The percentage of women among all college students has moved steadily up from 34.6 per cent in 1956 to 37.7 per cent in 1961, and is again approaching the 40.2 per cent which women attained in 1939. These percentages are all the more significant when it is remembered that the women reported to be attending colleges in 1961 were more than twice the number in 1950, although the number of girls aged eighteen to twenty-four in the population was only 12 per cent higher in 1961.

As the scientific revolution speeds onward and automation is introduced into more and more phases of American industry, the opportunities for private-household employment may become greater and the opportunities for high-income, professional employment still greater and greater. If the gap in the differential between the income level of men and women is ever to be closed, women have no choice but to obtain the best possible education in the professional and technical categories or to drop down to lower brackets in the labor force. Indeed, some economists are predicting that by the turn of the century the engineer will be the laboring man and that there will be no room whatever for unskilled labor, not even for raking leaves.

The impact of science and technology in reshaping domestic and social habits and also in modifying customs accounts for the fourth major cause of the rapid change in the status of women. Although there are southern men today in responsible positions in education, for example, who still insist that women are innately inferior to men, not many voice this belief publicly. Two such men, however, stoutly maintained several years ago at a session of the Carolina Symposium at the University of North Carolina that women are good at rote learning but are not competent in creative endeavors. This ability to memorize and reproduce the exact words of the professor, they held, is responsible for the average higher grades for women students than for men.

Research on personality and individual differences is pointing out that the individual differences within one sex are as great as the differences between the two sexes, and this research is entering into the training and activities of both men and women.[17]

Perhaps two of the most potent scientific developments working in behalf of the emancipation of women—far more important than the electrical devices which ease the housekeeper's burden—have been, first, the development of antibiotics which can control and eradicate the venereal diseases that have been a plague to women for centuries and, in the second place, the development of effective contraceptives which have put an end to the yearly childbearing cycle. The result has been the increased life span of women, an expectancy now several years greater than that for men. A woman is no longer old at forty-five. The average woman can look forward to a stretch of twenty or thirty good years after she passes the child-bearing period, and the average married woman will spend from ten to twenty of these years as a widow. The Women's Bureau predicts that she will spend these years in the labor force instead of the chimney corner.

The development of an effective contraceptive, plus the drive for equality, has upset considerably woman's conception of her sex role. Society is now experiencing the tensions and anxieties which always accompany change. Since this particular aspect of the emancipation of women revolves around an important biological function and a threat to the family, the basic unit of society, it is now and will continue to be for another generation or so as traumatic as any aspect of change which American civilization is facing in this revolutionary century.

17. See for example, Ashley F. Montagu, *Education and Human Relations* (New York: Grove Press, 1958).

As a result of the scientific developments which have protected the health and lengthened the life span of women, southern intellectuals, as well as those elsewhere in the nation, are re-examining their sex roles and their place in civilization.[18] This new leadership analyzes the ideology of male supremacy and tends to assume a pragmatic rather than an egalitarian approach. Because of her biological function and the structure of the family system in Western culture, at least the married woman with children, if not the childless married woman and the single woman, must play many roles—sex partner, mother, breadwinner, companion, community leader, culture bearer. While pantaloons are more in favor among modern women than they were among the Bloomer Girls of a hundred years ago, and for reasons quite different, today's women make more demands upon their husbands for personal services—kitchen helper, assistance with the family marketing, care of the offspring—than did their counterparts of the nineteenth century.

This insistence upon a husband's sharing in the chores once considered entirely woman's work comes as a counter ideology to the cult of sex and "maleness" now prevailing in American advertising, fiction, to some extent in all the creative arts, and for a time in certain schools of thought for the treatment of the mentally ill and emotionally disturbed. The impact of this glorification of the sexual function has led to a relaxation of the standards of moral conduct and a general demand from adolescent youth for greater freedom from "captivity to the puritanical 'hatpin brigade.'" In the face of increasing rates of high school and college student marriages, educational institutions throughout the country have eased regulations controlling courtship customs. No southern university has yet permitted visiting hours for women in the rooms of men students as in some of the northeastern institutions, but the agitation for such a change is already under way in the South.

The issue on "Sex" published in the spring of 1963 by *New Wine*, a Christian journal produced by the Westminster Fellowship composed of students at the University of North Carolina at Chapel

18. See, for example, the statements of Margaret Menzel of Tallahassee, Florida, Kathryn Stone of Virginia, and Conchita Winn of Dallas, Texas, in Betty Friedan, "Women: The Fourth Dimension," *Ladies Home Journal*, LXXXI, No. 5 (June, 1964), 50, 51, 54-55. See also Betty Friedan, *The Feminine Mystique* (New York: W. W. Norton and Company, Inc., 1963).

Hill, points to the threat which this new emphasis on sex in American culture poses for the personal integrity of women. It reduces woman to "a simple female unit" as opposed to a complex individual with personality and character, emotion and intellect, passion and reason.[19]

Southern women who are thinking and writing about this rise of the cult of sex in relation to woman's changing status seem to be of the opinion that the basic needs of women are similar to those of men—self-acceptance, self-fulfilment, self-expression. These needs, they think, are as important as the sexual need with perhaps even more serious consequences when thwarted. They want, therefore, such a practical arrangement as a national educational program for women who seriously want to continue their education or who want retraining. They want maternity leaves, professionally run day-care centers, home nursing services so that a woman can meet her commitments to a profession, politics, or community leadership and to marriage and motherhood as well.[20]

It would not, of course, be possible for women to think in terms of a commitment to a role of wife-mother-housekeeper-career-community activity had not modern technology freed her from the weary round of housekeeping which circumscribed the life of the nineteenth-century woman. It is true that a housewife can now prepare in an hour or less a substantial meal which would have required her mother three hours of busy activity. Because of this some social scientists tend to think of American women, especially of the upper classes, as bored creatures with too much time on their hands. As automation progresses, leisure[21] may, indeed, become a problem for the American man as well as woman, but today the southern housewife finds herself as rushed as her mother ever was.

More important, however, than leisure is the change in woman's

19. See also *The Intercollegian* (Urbana: University of Illinois) quoted in O. Hobart Mowrer, "Pornography—Realism or Illusion?" *Concern*, VI, No. 11, p. 11. Marya Mannes of Washington, D. C., said in a discussion on "Portrayal of Women by the Mass Media," in The President's Commission on the Status of Women, *Report on Four Consultations* (Washington, D. C.: Government Printing Office, August 6, 1963), p. 22, that she felt "the 'bunny' and the entire Playboy psychology" was "degrading to women."

20. See, for example, The Governor's Commission on the Status of Women, *The Many Lives of North Carolina Women, The Report of the Governor's Commission on the Status of Women* (Raleigh: The Governor's Commission on the Status of Women, 1964).

21. *Cf.* James C. Charlesworth, ed., *Leisure in America: Blessing or Curse?* (Philadelphia: The American Academy of Political and Social Science, 1964. Monograph 4).

attitude toward physical labor and toward housekeeping itself. The
contempt for labor which was a concomitant of slavery has slowly
been eroded through the years, and, except in certain areas of the
Deep South, has almost wholly disappeared since World War II.
The average southern woman does most, if not all, her own house-
work but she is no longer compulsively tidy as in the days when
she had servants to command. Not long ago, an upper-class southern
woman said with an amused smile, "I used to insist that my maid
dust twice a day. Now I have a cleaning woman who comes in
once a week, and we clean the house whether it needs it or not."

The southern woman puts much of the leisure which she now
has gained into community activities, and this work has given her
a new power and status. In 1895 the Woman Suffrage Movement
was in full swing. The feminists of that era, like the early agitators
of the 1840's, loudly proclaimed their right to be considered independent personalities and responsible human beings.[22] Laws and
restrictive customs which denied these rights, they said, should be
abolished just as human slavery had been struck down. Some of the
leading feminists dressed like men and affected the mannerisms of
men, but today they have for the most part yielded to an entirely
different type of leadership among women. The early movement,
extreme perhaps as it had to be to triumph, did actually bring
about the ratification of the Nineteenth Amendment in 1919, usher-
ing in the day of women's suffrage.

Southern women organized and worked tirelessly to create an
opinion in their states favorable to ratification, but this last strong-
hold of chivalry was reluctant to subject its women to the "chicanery
and pollution of the polling place." The amendment became effective without the approval of several key southern states. Interestingly enough, the first woman to be elected a state governor came
from Texas; the first woman to serve in the United States Senate
came from Arkansas; and the fourth woman to serve on a state
supreme court was elected in 1962 in North Carolina.

It was the dream of the feminists who led the fight for suffrage
that the basic discrimination against women would soon cease to
exist once women had power at the ballot box. More than forty years

22. For a brief history of the movement see Robert E. Riegel, *American Feminists*
(Lawrence: University of Kansas Press, 1963).

later, it is clear that change does not come as rapidly in ancient customs as the suffragists had hoped. When a change in the status of women takes place, it often comes, like the Nineteenth Amendment, as the result of the work of women themselves. The rapid growth in women's organizations has been a phenomenon of the twentieth century. By 1810 there was a church sewing circle and at least one charitable society of women in every city and village of the Upper South. Then came the tract societies, the literary clubs which were the forerunners of the present-day exclusive book clubs, the social sororities one of the first of which grew from a club organized at Wesleyan Female College in Georgia in the ante bellum period, groups set up to accomplish a specific reform such as the Woman's Christian Temperance Union in 1888, and the Southern Association of College Women which later joined with two other similar regional groups to become the American Association of University Women. As early as the turn of the century, southern women were beginning to combine their strength in state federations of women's clubs, but groups of organized women did not gain or even realize their power until after World War I.[23]

All of the nineteenth-century organizations and most of those even today have segregated memberships. Organizations of Negro women came first in connection with religious work. As the Negro middle class expanded, women began to set up their own literary, professional, and social groups so that there is a Negro counterpart for almost every type of organized effort now being pursued by southern white women. Some of these organizations such as the Congress of Colored Parents and Teachers and the State Home Demonstration Councils have large and active memberships with as many as 650 local units in a state organization and a state membership of 20,000 or more. Most of the efforts of Negro women have been concentrated on self-improvement programs, raising scholarship funds, establishment of libraries, agitation in behalf of state institutions for juvenile correction, and establishment of summer camps for Negro children.[24]

23. For an example of how a southern regional organization of women joined with other regional groups to form a strong national association, see Marion Talbot and Lois R. M. Rosenberry, *The History of the American Association of University Women* (Boston: Houghton Mifflin Company, 1931).

24. For an account of the life and work of one southern Negro woman who has been described as "the most powerful of American Negroes while the Franklin D.

The efforts early in the twentieth century toward interracial co-operation led the way for organizations with memberships cutting across racial barriers, but few women, white or black, joined in these first efforts. The trend toward integrated organizations of southern women was not to come until after World War II, although southern white women had in a spirit of noblesse oblige been working to ease the lot of the Negro woman since ante bellum days. For example, the Georgia WCTU was concerned over the brutal treatment of Negro women prisoners in the convict camps and won the fight to segregate and protect them from the male prisoners. The work of the Association of Southern Women for the Prevention of Lynching, organized after World War I, all but stopped lynchings in fifteen southern states within a generation. Wilma Dykeman and James Stokely tell the story briefly in *Seeds of Southern Change*, "All over the South, ladies in their white gloves and navy silks and flowered cottons marched into sheriffs' offices ... and asked for a signed pledge that the keeper of the law would do all in his power to prevent any lynching in his county."[25]

The Young Women's Christian Association was a pioneer in the South in bringing white and Negro women together into co-operative working relationships for the general welfare of the community. Among other organizations which have removed racial restrictions on membership are United Church Women, the American Association of University Women, and the League of Women Voters.

When more and more women's groups are able to look beyond the stigma of caste, it is possible that the last ghosts of the troubled past may finally be laid to rest. Women's organizations have already been amazingly effective in promoting social legislation and educating the public to the need for protective laws affecting the family and its members. Among important measures which may be listed to the credit of organized groups of southern women are the creation of at least one State Department of Public Welfare and the establishment in several states of the programs for public assistance to the needy, aged, blind, and dependent children and laws

Roosevelts were in the White House," one who was also able to organize a powerful group of Negro women into the National Council of Negro Women, see Rackman Holt, *Mary McLeod Bethune* (New York: Doubleday and Company, 1964).

25. *Seeds of Southern Change: The Life of Will Alexander* (Chicago: University of Chicago Press, 1962), pp. 143-152.

to protect children against abuses in their adoption. They have worked for prison reform; for rehabilitation, probation, and parole; for abolition of flogging and replacement of county chain gangs with a more humane prison system. They have led and won the movements for the erection of county and district health units and the establishment of matching funds for the federal hospital construction act; for protective legislation for women and children in industry, the minimum wage law, the abolition of child labor, workmen's compensation acts, juvenile court systems, and a variety of legislation in behalf of public education. They have also worked to improve the educational opportunities for women, including raising the standards of education in small, private as well as public, colleges for women, and thus they have improved the opportunities for women to obtain and hold status positions in the professions.

The structure and goals of women's organizations have provided outlets for cultural and leisure time interests, for spiritual drives and self-expression and an opportunity for creativity in the larger context of community, state, and national affairs. At least one southern governor has within recent years given credit for his election to the organized women of his state and has rewarded them by appointment to public office.

As a result of the efforts of many dedicated women over a period of more than a hundred years, southern women today can enjoy a status undreamed of in 1800. Their area of freedom has greatly expanded; freedom to be recognized as self-determining personalities, freedom to get an education, freedom to work outside the home, freedom to vote and hold public office, but freedom to have equality of opportunities to advance in their professions or to be judged equally by social customs has yet to be attained.

XXI. THE PAST IN THE FUTURE OF THE SOUTH / John Hope Franklin

A deep consciousness of its past is as characteristic of the South as corn pone and cotton patches. Observe any generation in the South since 1820 and you will discover much more than a casual interest in the region's past. This interest is shared alike by the historian and the layman, the learned and the unlearned, the devotee of "The Lost Cause" and those southerners, black and white, who are deeply committed Americans. This is not to deny the obvious fact that peoples generally, and corporate groups especially, are prone to look back over their shoulders in order to see the course over which they have traveled. What one sees in the South is a rather excessive interest in this past, a somewhat exaggerated posture of examining and recapitulating. Perhaps nowhere else in the United States than in the South has the assertion been more true that every man is his own historian. This interest and general stance reflect an approach to the past that not only makes it seem authoritative but authoritarian as well.

Almost without exception the South's interest in the past has been motivated by practical if not ulterior considerations. Over the past century and a half if anything seemed clear to southerners, of whatever economic or intellectual orientation or racial or religious background, it was that history was an all-important factor in understanding existing conditions and in promulgating future policies. In this sense, the appreciation on the part of most southerners for the role of history in the life of a people was developed to an unusual degree. And from the time that they began to sense their own distinctiveness and became sensitive about their place in the Union, one can say that southerners *practiced* their history with a passion that one usually associates with a professional commitment.

This view of the past enabled southerners to use their past as an argument to bolster their claims not only to greatness but to major consideration in any expression of gratitude that the nation cared to make regarding the factors and forces that had contributed to its birth and growth. "As for our history," boasted William Lowndes Yancey before the Civil War, "we have made about all that has glorified the United States."[1] Even earlier, in 1844, the South's leading novelist, William Gilmore Simms, commented on the pervasive character of the history of the South, and especially of his native South Carolina. "It is already deeply engraven on the everlasting monuments of the nation. It is around us, a living trophy upon all our hills. It is within us, an undying memory in all our hearts. It is a record which no fortune can obliterate—inseparable from all that is great and glorious in the work of the Revolution."[2]

As the South witnessed the decline of her national position in the years before the Civil War, her professional and lay historians sought diligently to bolster that position by pointing to the South's contributions to the establishment of independence. In making claims on the basis of superior past performances, the South hoped that the nation would concede to her a larger voice in the determination of current and future policies. The Revolution in South Carolina, for example, was "conceived and organized by the native population," asserted Colonel Lawrence M. Keitt; "the constituted authorities of the State committed her, from the first, to the Revolutionary movement, and she neither waivered nor faltered throughout its progress."[3] In 1856 South Carolina's Senator Andrew P. Butler, answering the charges made by Charles Sumner regarding the South's dereliction during the War for Independence, shouted, "I challenge him to the truth of history. There was not a battle fought south of the Potomac that was not fought by Southern troops and Southern slave holders."[4]

If the South played a major role in the founding of the country—and this role was proved to the satisfaction of every Southerner—it was the height of injustice to deny to the South a major voice in national decision-making in, say, the eighteen-fifties. One writer after another and one politician after another argued that the South's claims were valid not merely because of the theory of

1. John W. DuBose, *The Life and Times of William Lowndes Yancey* (Birmingham: Roberts and Son, 1892), I, 376.
2. William Gilmore Simms, *The Sources of Independence: An Oration on the Sixty-Ninth Anniversary of American Independence; Delivered at Aiken, South Carolina, Before the Town Council and Citizens Thereof* (Aiken, 1844), p. 22.
3. Lawrence Massillon Keitt, "Patriotic Services of the North and South," *De Bow's Review*, XXI, 491-492.
4. *Congressional Globe*, 34th Congress, 1st Session (Washington, D. C.: J. C. Rives, 1956), pp. 627-628.

the equality of the states under the Constitution but also because
history supported her claims to a larger share in the counsels of the
nation. Southerners never permitted the rest of the country to for-
get that they had contributed the bulk of the manpower during
the Mexican War and that their strength and heroism were decisive factors in the winning of the war. Viewing with obvious satisfaction the "vast" contributions to that effort that southerners had
made, one of them said, "As a military people, none can deny that
we are fully equal, perhaps superior, to any other. Our renown for
skill, courage and indomitable energy in battle, humanity and mod-
eration after victory, has overspread the world."[5]

The South, then, had turned the tide of battle in the nation's
wars and had been the training ground for the soldiers of the
country. The South had given the nation more eminent statesmen
than any other section. Its leaders had helped shape the thinking
that had provided the political, social, and economic philosophy
of the country. If the nation's actions and policies were at variance
with those suggested by the South and her leaders, it was because
the nation had strayed from the proper path. And the nation's waywardness had, indeed, been considerable. The irony of it all was
that some of the waywardness had been started by southerners
themselves. Jefferson had said that all men were created equal; and
what was almost unbearable, many northerners had incorporated
his own words in their creed that was used to attack the South. It
remained, therefore, for southerners to repudiate this doctrine and
reiterate the doctrine of innate differences. "We talk a great deal
of nonsense about the rights of man," said Thomas Cooper of South
Carolina. "We say that man is born free, and equal to every other
man." Then, calling on history as his star witness, he added,
"Nothing can be more untrue: no human being ever was, now is,
or ever will be born free."[6]

The repudiation of the doctrine of equality in the natural rights
philosophy was only one of many ways in which southerners made
certain that ideas and actions of the past—as they saw them—were
to be used to support present and future policies. What would the

5. "The Conquest of California," *Southern Quarterly Review*, XV (July, 1849),
414.
6. Quoted in William S. Jenkins, *Pro-Slavery Thought in the Old South* (Chapel
Hill: University of North Carolina Press, 1935), p. 125.

nation's social and political system have become without the contributions by southerners, they asked. The reply was bold and
imaginative, to say the least. "The Southern states," one of them
asserted in 1860, "were settled and governed, in a great measure
. . . by and under the direction of persons belonging to the blood
and race of the reigning family, and belonged to that stock recognized as CAVALIERS."[7] This rather blatant claim, with little to
substantiate it, involved the rewriting of the history of the founding of the southern colonies; and this seemed not to trouble those
who did so. The total effect of such a claim was so great that extensive efforts to deny it and disprove it have not yet been altogether successful.[8]

In a similar vein southerners claimed that the civilization they
had developed by 1860 was not only different from but quite
superior to that which the northerners had developed. They
pointed with pride to what the institution of slavery had done for
the South, how it provided the leisure time in which the aristocrats
could pursue a healthy life of the mind and spirit. For slavery "was
not only God's commanded order, not only the most humane order,
but also the most natural order." Indeed, it was the "cornerstone"
of southern civilization. This civilization, they said, flourished in a
manner that no other civilization in the New World could possibly
match.

Their tracing of the history of slavery and their claims regarding
its benefits left unanswered numerous questions regarding its effectiveness as well as its validity. Was it really profitable? Was
there any significant culture and refinement in the South? If there
was any, did it improve as a result of the economic and social support provided by slavery? Did the barbarity of one man's having
dominion over another outweigh any cultural benefits arising out of
the master's enjoyment of leisure provided by slavery? As Wilbur
Cash has observed so convincingly, the southerners' claim to a superior civilization, with slavery at the center of it, "was perhaps the
least well founded of the many poorly founded claims which

7. "The Difference of Race Between the Northern and Southern People,"
Southern Literary Messenger, XXX (June, 1860), 407.
8. Wilbur J. Cash, *The Mind of the South* (New York: Alfred A. Knopf, 1941),
pp. 11-14.

Southerners so earnestly asserted to the world and to themselves in which they so warmly believed."[9]

When southerners began to fight for their own independence in 1861, they were sustained by a strong faith in the historical validity of their cause. In May, 1861, as the fighting began in earnest, Christopher G. Memminger, the Confederate Secretary of the Treasury, said, "The South has always exhibited the example of communities in which law prevails; and the secession of the Southern States gives to history a splendid illustration of peaceful revolution."[10] And as the war progressed many southerners assumed the task of writing the history of the "most glorious chapter" in all their experiences. Time was of the essence, and since some did not have time to write history, they merely recorded their experiences in the daily press and in such popular magazines as *Southern Field and Fireside*, the *Southern Illustrated News*, and *The Countryman*. Others, with a bit more time and insight, such as Edwin A. Pollard, H. C. Clarke, and John Esten Cooke, began to write their histories of the war and biographies of its heroes. If southerners had been slow to tell their side of the War for Independence, they would not be guilty of a similar dereliction in the great fratricidal conflict.

It was quite natural for a people so conscious of the importance of history as the southerners to devote a considerable amount of time and attention to stating and defending their case during the Civil War and the Reconstruction. Magazines such as *The Land We Love* and *The Southern Review* devoted their pages almost exclusively to recounting the experiences of the Confederate heroes of the war. Leaders such as Jefferson Davis, Alexander Stephens, and the rebel clerk John B. Jones wrote their memoirs with a view to vindicating the cause as well as their part in it. Groups such as the United Daughters of the Confederacy, the Confederate Survivors Association, and the Southern Historical Society undertook to keep alive the glories as well as the righteousness of "The Lost Cause." In every way and in many quarters the South was making certain that its past would get a full and fair hearing in the future.

If it is not remarkable, it is nevertheless worth noting that even as the events of Civil War and Reconstruction receded slowly into

9. *Ibid.*, p. 94.
10. Quoted in E. Merton Coulter, *The Confederate States of America* (Baton Rouge: Louisiana State University Press, 1950), p. 14.

the past, significant distortions and misrepresentations created myths that have persisted down to the present time. Surely the heat and passion of the period influenced the writing of the history that was something less than objective. Many who wrote the history of the period had been deeply and personally involved; and their point of view, their way of looking at the events, had been shaped by this involvement. One hastens to add, of course, that this was as true of northerners as of southerners. But special circumstances and conditions in the South fostered a view and interpretation of the past that, in turn, encouraged myth-making and distortion. One circumstance was the persistence of a considerable amount of the ingredient that Cash, Osterweis, and others have called southern romanticism.[11] During the generation before the Civil War, southerners were excessively romantic about themselves and their civilization; this seemed to make it difficult for them to look at themselves with any degree of objectivity and to examine critically their triumphs and their failures. After the war "there was naturally a great aversion . . . to surrender the glory which had been theirs under the *ancien régime*. And like many another people come upon evil days, the South in its entirety was filled with an immense regret and nostalgia; yearned backward toward its past with passionate longing."[12]

Another circumstance was the extreme sensitivity and anxiety that one could see almost everywhere that promoted a zealous advocacy of their cause and a strong determination to defend the position they had taken. It seemed to many that the haunting fear and uneasiness about the future would somehow be dispelled if any doubts about the validity of the South's position in the past could be dispelled. Still another circumstance was the persistence of the feeling that the South had been the victim of injustice at the hands of the North and of downright mistreatment and neglect at the hands of the federal government. These ways of reacting to their problems survived the Civil War and Reconstruction era and, if anything, were intensified by it. They had much to do with the manner in which southerners wrote about these shattering experiences.

Meanwhile, the North's relative neglect of these more un-

11. Cash, *op. cit.*, pp. 46-55 and Rollin G. Osterweis, *Romanticism and Nationalism in the Old South* (New Haven: Yale University Press, 1949), *passim.*
12. Cash, *op. cit.*, p. 127.

pleasant aspects of the nation's history seemed to be a part of the post-Reconstruction settlement. In the middle 1870's northerners, weary of the controversies of the Reconstruction period and eager to get on with other things, began to repeat the refrain, "Let the South alone." And as northerners became more interested in national political and economic questions, they seemed as willing to permit the South to write the history of the Civil War and other unpleasantries as to solve the race problem in its own way. Henry Adams, John Fiske, and other historians of the North seemed to care little for the matters that were of immediate and grave concern to southern historians. And whenever northern historians did turn their attention to historical problems where the role of the South loomed large, they tended to give the South the benefit of every doubt. The admonition, "Let us have peace," was followed as scrupulously by northern historians as by northern politicians.

The historians of the South, therefore, could and did give attention to matters close to their hearts without any undue interference by historians of the North. They gave attention to the ante bellum period, praising the "unmatched" excellence of southern civilization. They wrote about the Civil War, when southern heroism and gallantry went down to a noble and glorious defeat. They lamented the Reconstruction era, when the South was at the mercy of an embittered and vindictive North. Despite their zeal and industry, however, they did more than remind the South of the continuing importance of its past. Deploring the mediocrity of the contributions of the post-Reconstruction historians, Thomas Nelson Page said in 1892, "There is no true history of the South. In a few years there will be no South to demand a history."[13] Five years later John Spencer Bassett expressed a similar view. "No man with instincts for accuracy can be satisfied with our statement of our own case," he wrote. He was particularly contemptuous of the heroes, turned historians, who, having fought bravely with their swords, were now "tempted to make asses of themselves with the pen."[14]

At least some of the distress of Page and Bassett was relieved by certain developments that were taking place when they were writ-

13. "The Want of A History of the Southern People," in Thomas Nelson Page, *The Old South, Essays Social and Political* (New York, 1892), p. 253.
14. Wendell Holmes Stephenson, "John Spencer Bassett as A Historian of the South," *North Carolina Historical Review*, XXV (July, 1948), 299.

ing. In 1892, at the University of the South, William P. Trent had begun to edit *The Sewanee Review*. And he opened its pages to historians as well as literary critics. He maintained a very high standard in his own writings on the South, and he demanded that his contributors do the same. Ten years later at Trinity College Bassett himself launched the *South Atlantic Quarterly*, expressing the hope that the world would learn that "there is in the South at least one spot in which our history may be presented in all of its claims, and where it may receive a respectful and unimpassioned hearing."[15] Soon, Trent and Bassett had taken posts in northern institutions; and their departure was not unrelated to their view of the low state of southern culture in general and the mediocrity of southern historical scholarship in particular.

By the turn of the century at least some of the conditions that troubled Trent and Bassett had been changed. A fairly large group of southerners had become professional historians, with graduate training under Herbert Baxter Adams at the Johns Hopkins University and under William Archibald Dunning at Columbia. They wrote on southern themes of slavery, Civil War, and Reconstruction. Their monographs appeared in the Hopkins *Studies in Historical and Political Science* and in the Columbia *Studies in History, Economics and Public Law*. They took up posts in southern colleges and universities and trained several generations of young southerners to view the South's history very much as they did.

The Adams and Dunning students reflected in their monographs on the South the extensive and rigorous training they had received in their graduate seminars. They employed a wide variety of sources, ranging from legislative records to personal memoirs. They organized their materials with great care and wrote with the new "scientific" approach that was pervading the social sciences at the time. But their conclusions, couched in the most respectable and scholarly format, did not differ markedly from those of their intellectually underprivileged predecessors. If their investigations were broader and deeper, they invariably came to the defense of the white South and vindicated its conduct. In their studies of the Reconstruction, the black codes were defended, the Radical govern-

15. Quoted in Wendell Holmes Stephenson, *The South Lives in History* (Baton Rouge: Louisiana State University Press, 1955), p. 4.

ments were condemned as an unmitigated evil, marked by corruption and perfidy, and the Ku Klux Klan was excused as a natural consequence of Radical excesses. Soon, each state had its own Reconstruction authority; and if each presented variations in the use of materials and in organization, all of them were in general agreement on the main outlines.

The all-pervasive characteristic of these studies was their uncritical and unrealistic judgment of some of the facts while ignoring many other facts. Consequently, these histories did not provide the basis for a mature understanding of the South and its problems. They gave to the white South the intellectual justification for its determination not to yield on many important points, especially in its treatment of the Negro. Since they insisted that they were both scientific and impartial, the new southern historians even helped persuade many non-southerners that through the years the South had indeed been treated unjustly, that its own course of actions had been substantially right, and that its racial attitudes should be condoned if not imitated.

The writings of these historians also provided the intellectual support for others who undertook to popularize in fiction and film the view of the South's history that came to be accepted on a national scale. Thomas Dixon, Jr., became the most articulate and successful protagonist of the southern cause in essay and fiction. In 1903 his *The Leopard's Spots*, a most rabid attack on the Negro and a most vigorous defense of the white South, was a hit on the Broadway stage. A bit more than a decade later the first great American film epic, D. W. Griffith's *The Birth of A Nation*, was based on the writings of Dixon and had much to do with making almost permanent the view of the South as a land where white supremacy was thoroughly justified. The Dixons and the Griffiths had thus gone a step beyond even the historians in making the past a vital factor in the future of the South.

Consciousness of the past in the South was not confined to the whites; and since Negroes loomed so large in the interpretation of the past by white southerners, it was only natural that the Negroes' consciousness of the past would be quickened in response. Even before Dixon wrote, there were Negroes who had become quite apprehensive about the case that the white South was making for itself. It was a case that excluded the Negro altogether as a factor in the history of the South, except as a docile slave and a fool and knave during the Reconstruction era. Educated, articulate Negroes, therefore, began to attempt to modify the general view of the Negro that the whites were seeking to convey. Several Negroes, such as George W. Williams and E. A. Johnson, wrote histories of the Negro in the United States and presented masses of evidence to refute the charges that Negroes had contributed nothing to the development of the country. Several, such as Williams and J. T. Wilson, seemed to derive much satisfaction by publishing books on the role of the Negro soldier in the Union Army during the Civil War. In his *History of the Colored Race in America*, published in 1887, William T. Alexander argued with much force that Negroes were the intellectual equals of whites.

If the pioneer efforts to write of the Negro's part in the nation's history were made by persons of limited qualifications, later efforts— early in the twentieth century—were made by persons who had enjoyed educational opportunities similar to those of the white southern historians. W. E. B. Du Bois, with a doctorate from Harvard, described in his first book how slaves were smuggled into the South even after the foreign slave trade had been closed. In later works he was to treat other aspects of the history of the South with particular reference to the Negro. Carter G. Woodson, with a doctorate from Harvard, told of the disruption of Virginia in his first book; and then he went on to write numerous works on the role of the Negro in the history of the United States. W. H. Crogman, who taught Greek at a Negro college in Atlanta, Georgia, published in 1902 a book entitled *Progress of A Race*, a review of numerous ways in which Negroes had contributed to the development of the South. In time others followed—among them, Booker T. Washington, C. V. Roman, and John W. Cromwell—and added to the mounting evidence that histories by white southerners were, by and large, histories of white people regardless of the extent of involvement of others.

It is not without significance that when Carter G. Woodson launched the Association for the Study of Negro Life and History in 1915 the bulk of the support of the organization came from southern Negroes. Likewise, when "Negro History Week" was put into operation a decade later it was in Negro communities and Negro schools and colleges in the South that the idea first caught fire. The reasons for the southern Negro's intense interest in his own past were not difficult to discover. One reason was that in an almost totally separate world he was forced to examine his own origins and his own history in the attempt to understand the nature of the society in which he was forced to live, and at the same time to seek an identity for himself that was meaningful. (Negroes in other parts of the country would develop similar interests, but much more slowly.) Almost as important was the pervasive consciousness of the past that one felt virtually everywhere in the South. Negroes were as much a part of this as the whites. Perhaps Negroes cared little for Andrew Jackson's birthday or the anniversary of the Battle of New Orleans; but they had Lincoln's birthday and the anniversary of the Emancipation Proclamation on which to lavish their enthusiasm.

In the present century, and at the present time, the South's consciousness of history continues. This is reflected in the remarkable growth of historical societies, the widespread interest in preserving historical monuments of every conceivable kind, and in the generosity with which state and local governments have begun to support the collection and preservation of private manuscripts, public records, and the like. That much of this activity is in the hands of lay leaders may suggest the numerical inadequacy of trained personnel; but it also suggests the undeniable fact that southerners would never be willing to restrict historical activities to a relatively small coterie of trained historians.

This continuing interest in history on the part of the larger public in the South suggests, by implication at least, the continuing role of the past in the South's present and future. In the hands of laymen, who subscribe to the view that every man is, indeed, his own historian, history can be used as an effective weapon with which to shape the future. One early and characteristic result of the South's looking at its past was to express satisfaction with its institutions and its social order in general. In the nineteenth century this led to a rather general opposition in the South to reform and, indeed, to any significant change. Before the Civil War white southerners opposed industrialization because experience had taught them that an

agrarian way of life was better for them. They opposed the abolition
of slavery because history told them that slavery was the best state
of existence for Negroes and, incidentally, the best form of labor for
the southern economic order. In the post-Civil War years they
opposed the franchise for Negroes because they saw no historical
counterpart for the enfranchisement of an "ignorant, illiterate
people."

In the twentieth century many white southerners continued to
resist change. They summoned history to support their arguments
that age-old practices and institutions could not be changed overnight, that social practices and customs could not be changed by
legislation. There could be no racial desegregation, they argued,
because such a move would break down long established customs
and bring instability to a social order that, if left alone, would have
no serious racial or social disorders. After all, southern whites
"knew" Negroes; and their knowledge had come from many generations of intimate association and observation. It would be folly and
utter irresponsibility to change the basic relationship of the races,
they insisted, for it would improve neither the condition nor the
happiness of whites and Negroes.

In like manner white southerners have summoned history to
support them in their resistance to federal legislation designed to
secure the civil rights of Negroes. At every level—in local groups,
state governments, and in the Congress of the United States—white
southerners have asserted that federal civil rights legislation in
1964 was an attempt to turn the clock back to the Reconstruction
era, when federal intervention, they claim, imposed a harsh and unjust peace. To make effective their argument, they use such emo-
tion-laden phrases as "military occupation," "Negro rule," and
"blackout of honest government."

It would be incorrect to assert that those who resist change in
the South have a monopoly on historical interests or the use of the
historical experience. In the South as well as in the North, students
of southern history have, in recent years, been making it more difficult to use the South's past as a weapon to resist change. As early
as 1941, Wilbur J. Cash, himself a white southerner, effectively
challenged the South's claim to a superior civilization; and he made
a shambles of all arguments that had at any time claimed that the

South favored change of any significant kind.[16] Many students of the Jackson period have clearly proved that the resistance to granting the franchise to illiterate citizens was never substantial, except when the prospective voters were Negroes.[17] Bell I. Wiley of Emory University, some years ago, pointed out that southern whites did not "know" the Negro. He did so by describing how, to the utter disappointment and distress of the whites, Negroes deserted their masters during the Civil War.[18]

Southern whites are more and more embarrassed in their effort to use history to resist change. This is especially true of their claim that segregation is such an ancient institution that it is deeply ingrained in the mores of southern culture. C. Vann Woodward has proved, to the satisfaction of reasonable people, that segregation is neither ancient nor honorable. He has pointed out that most segregation legislation came shortly before the end of the nineteenth century and that perhaps its political motivations were greater than its social justifications.[19] Several historians have established the facts that during the Reconstruction era there was no great military occupation of the South, no Negro rule, and that respectable southern whites were involved in the corruption of the time.[20] And Woodward has given numerous examples of the continuation of corrupt practices after southern whites had "redeemed" the southern states with the promise that they would give the southern states clean, honest government.[21]

Examples of these "new viewpoints" of the history of the South could be multiplied. They suggest that there are fresh winds of change blowing across the southern scene, changes in the way history is being written as well as in other ways. They indicate that history, which for many generations has been a special weapon enlisted in the battle against change, is finding new sponsors and new uses. The increasing number of persons desiring change in the South

16. Cash, *op. cit.*, pp. 94-102.
17. Arthur M. Schlesinger, Jr., *The Age of Jackson* (Boston: Little Brown, 1945).
18. Bell Irvin Wiley, *Southern Negroes, 1861-1865* (New York: Rinehart and Company, 1953).
19. C. Vann Woodward, *The Strange Career of Jim Crow* (New York: Oxford University Press, 1955).
20. John Hope Franklin, *Reconstruction After the Civil War* (Chicago: University of Chicago Press, 1961).
21. C. Vann Woodward, *Origins of the New South, 1877-1914* (Baton Rouge: Louisiana State University Press, 1951).

—significant and far-reaching change—are discovering that much of the South's history is "on their side." It illustrates both the folly and irresponsibility of resisting change by the distortion and misrepresentation of the past. It also illustrates the value and importance of the past in laying a solid foundation on which to build a better South.

XXII. THE SOUTH IN OLD AND NEW CONTEXTS / Edgar T. Thompson

In this age of global thinking it is important that we try to understand our corner of the world, the South, in a frame much larger
than we are accustomed to employ. It is no longer sufficient to study
the South in terms of its own unique history; that way arouses sentiment but yields very little knowledge. Nor is it sufficient to study
it within the context of the United States only. The South is part
of a world organization which is not exactly a machine but which
runs and shakes like a machine, and the South is being shaken along
with the rest of it. The units now in competition are entire regions
and continents as well as local corporations and populations, and
the laws and administrative regulations of the state are obstacles,
such as mountains and seas once were, that are being crossed in the
widening competition for goods and markets. The very competitions
and conflicts between the peoples of the world have, in a sense, as
Hans Kohn has pointed out,[1] given an impetus to the unification of
mankind, so that for the first time we live in a world community
and a great society which are coextensive with the inhabited globe.
The South is a differentiated part of this demographic, economic,
political, and moral order that extends far beyond the immediate
area within which its own historic values and ideals are held and
shared.

The South is a unit of territory and humanity which can be
viewed as a sociological unit or object, and to look at it as such is
probably what we mean by being objective. It is an object because
we point to it and talk about it as such. To be sure it is an object
not always easy to bound. The problem of identifying and separating it from other territorial areas or objects poses serious questions
when it comes to making definite statements and to comparing
statements different students and data-collecting agencies make
about it. We sorely need some agreed-upon conception if only so
that all can be sure they are talking about the same thing. As readers
will note, no such consensus has been established among the score
of contributors to this book. There is the further complication that

1. "Education for the World," *Adult Education Journal*, VI (July, 1947), 129-
133.

the South as an object is, like every object, a somewhat different thing when placed in different relational and historical contexts. It is the purpose of this chapter to suggest what the thing we call the South has been and is in the various contexts in which it has existed. It is hoped that from this perspective the various chapters in this book, each the work of different authors, will find a place in a frame which may help integrate them into a more systematic whole.

1

The South is first of all a physical habitat which sustains a population. For all practical purposes the geography of the world as men have known it through historical time has been its most immutable element. Throughout this time the South is geographically where it has always been and physically what it has always been. There has always been an Appalachian-Ozark core bordered by piedmont areas to the east, south, and west. Beyond this the clay soils gave way, as they do now, to loamish and sandy soils to the very edge of the Atlantic Ocean, the Gulf of Mexico, and the Mississippi River. The present fairly heavy rainfall, the relatively mild winters, and the long growing season were facts about the geography and climate of the South long before the first Europeans ever saw this country. The same rivers, then as now, ran down from the same mountains to the same seas. The distribution of the South's mineral, land, climatic, and other resources will remain constant but, of course, the nature and extent of the exploitation of these resources are subject to change.

All the changes—past, present, and future—discussed in this book, and many not discussed, have taken place and will take place against the background of the physical geography of the South. Geography separated this area by large water bodies from Europe and South America. Geography attached it to the southeastern part of the North American continent, but geography failed to separate it by any effective natural barrier from areas to the north and west of it. In the opinion of many southerners this was a mistake on the part of the Creator. Geography does not favor secession.

Because geography does not argue, because it simply is, because it presents us with that which stays, it is necessary for people either to move away or come to terms with it. When he was Director of the

Tennessee Valley Authority, David Lillienthal said of the Tennessee
River, "A river has no politics." Perhaps most, if not all, so-called
national and regional historical policies, such as the Monroe Doctrine of the United States, Russia's persistent effort to get to the sea,
and the southern and South African determination to maintain
white supremacy, have continued in one form or another under the
vicissitudes of even opposing régimes and ideologies because many
successive generations have to make substantially the same adjustment to the permanent elements of the physical environment. There
have been, to be sure, many and important changes in southern
society from colonial days to the present, but the changes are not
beyond recognition. The abiding earth is the most elementary principle of certainty and social continuity.

In geographic nature there is, of course, no North, South, East,
or West. In their various cultures, men themselves structure space
in terms of their experiences with nature and in terms of their relations with neighboring people of other cultures. They do so because
some principle of spatial orientation is clearly needed if people are
to know where they are in the world and in which direction they
are moving.

South, of course, is a point on the compass—a direction. In the
most abstract and therefore the most universal cultural formulation
imposed upon the dimensions of the world, the world of the compass, the cardinal directions exhibit two polar antitheses—east-west
and north-south. The contrast between the lands of the rising sun
and the evening lands, between Orient and Occident, have in the
past suggested such cultural dichotomies as family and market place,
tradition and progress, sacred and secular, immobility and mobility,
continuity and change, and old countries and frontiers. The movement from east to west historically has symbolized a graduated
change from a higher to a lower degree of cultural development.

In the northern hemisphere, the hemisphere of world history, the
contrasts between the lands of the north and the lands of the south
have in the past suggested such contrasting ideas as cold climates
and hot climates, cold-blooded and hot-blooded peoples, peoples
of active energy and peoples of passive leisure, commercial-in-
dustrial economies and agricultural economies, and urban societies
and rural societies. The movement from north to south or from south

to north historically has symbolized contacts between one people and another so abrupt that they tend to be thought of as peoples of different stock or race. It is significant that the various climatic theories of society, from Aristotle to Huntington, are closely associated with the various racial theories of society. Along with race, climate has long been used to "explain" the South. In principle the North-South contrast is mainly geographic, but in reality it is in good part charged with ideas deeply held in the beliefs of the peoples concerned. Americans will recognize them as a mixture of fact and lore long accepted by the people of this country as they contemplate the differences between northerners and southerners,[2] but actually they tend to obtain over the whole of the northern hemisphere. In the southern hemisphere the north-south conceptualizations tend to be reversed.

South also is a place, and as such becomes "the South." To be south is necessarily to be south of *something* which is, of course, north or "the North." The south is often the more southernly part of an area bearing the same name such as South Dakota, South Carolina, South Africa, or South America. The assumption here has to do with an area thought to be sufficiently homogeneous geographically or historically to warrant a common name, but also sufficiently different to require separate designations. England has its north and south and so has France, Germany, Italy, India, and probably every other country. Perhaps because of the large size of the United States and the intensity and scale of the conflict between its two major historic areas eventuating in bloody war, the southern part of this country became known as "the South" in a special sort of way. To southerners themselves it is "South for sure," and no funny business such as "Southeast" or "Southwest" will do; it must be the South, the sunny South, the magnolia South, or nothing.

2

If, for all practical purposes, the South has always been located between the same latitudes and longitudes, a location which gives a certain indigenous and persistent quality to its society, it also

2. Thomas Jefferson was one of the first to give literary expression to our own contrasting North-South ideas in a letter to the Marquis de Chastellux in 1785. See John Richard Alden, *The First South* (Baton Rouge: Louisiana State University Press, 1961), p. 17.

has been subject, as every other area on earth has been subject, to periodic shifts in its position in the world community. Every area occupies a space complementary to every other area, and these complementary relations, or positions, are constantly changing. The world is shrinking, we are accustomed to saying, but a much more important fact is that it does not shrink evenly, and new alignments between its parts followed by new stresses and strains between them are continually developing. New routes of trade, new sources of raw materials, new modes of co-operation, and new political adjustments and compromises have to be worked out. This uneven shrinkage of the world is brought about principally by advances in the time and cost of transportation and communication.

It may be suggested that the area we now call "the South" was originally not south at all. It was north although it never became "the North." This area was originally differentiated as part of an economic region in an expanding world of commerce and production for commerce after the sixteenth century. Relatively cheap water transportation transformed the Atlantic Ocean into an inland sea, no larger than the Mediterranean once was, and gave the warmer lands in and surrounding the Caribbean and Gulf of Mexico territorial divisions of labor in the larger community of Western civilization as producers of agricultural staples for the markets of Europe. "The South," with outlets along the Atlantic coast and later the Gulf of Mexico,[3] became the northern part of a Caribbean-Gulf economic region which over the period from colonial days until now has included eastern Mexico, Middle America, northern and northeastern South America, and the islands of the West Indies.[4]

3. "The South is the only region of the United States that fronts the sea on two sides. From Virginia to Key West it looks to Europe across the Atlantic; from Key West to Brownsville, it looks to Latin America. The South's shoreline along the Atlantic is 1,099 miles; along the Gulf, 1,659 miles. It has a total shoreline of 2,758 miles. It has nearly four times the shoreline of the North, more than twice that of the Pacific coast, and nearly six hundred miles more seacoast than the North and West combined." Walter Webb, "The South's Call to Greatness," *The Graduate Journal of the University of Texas*, III (1960), Supplement, 304.

4. This region, of course, extended to the southwest from the distant markets of Western Europe across the Atlantic Ocean. But it might be considered a segment of a frontier describing one of von Thünen's concentric circles which had its counterpart, where soil and climatic conditions were favorable, to the east of these centers. J. H. von Thünen, *Der Isolierte Staat in Beziehung auf Land wirlhschaft und Nationalökonomie* (3 vols.; Berlin: Wiegandt, Hempel und Parey, 1875). Beyond the Elbe River in Germany there appeared large plantation-like estates producing

The cultivation of tobacco in this northern subregion was the first settled and specialized industry of any kind in mainland America, and for decades the South's cotton was the most important American product—measured both in terms of the number of people engaged in its production and in the value of the export. Until well into the present century, cotton was relied on to settle our balance of foreign trade and to conserve the gold of our domestic commerce. The dependent positions of the southern areas specializing in these and other staples provided an American market which contributed most significantly to calling into existence supporting industries and areas in other parts of the nation such as the wheat belt, the corn belt, and the cattle and meat belts. New England was culturally dependent upon Old England, but economically its manufacturing and shipping were dependent upon the southern market. From this point of view a good case might be made for the argument that southern commercial agriculture has been the central fact in the economic history of the United States.

The northern subregion of the Caribbean-Gulf plantation region also was an important influence in the economic history of Western civilization. The contrast between English settlements in this subregion and northern settlements seems to have been apparent somewhat earlier in England than in the settlements themselves. In England the northern settlements often were referred to as "our northern colonies," whereas the southern settlements were more frequently referred to as "our southern plantations." The agricultural economies of the southern plantations supplemented and complemented the economy of England, which therefore favored them against the more competitive economies of the northern colonies. It was in England, it appears, that the distinction between the American North and the American South was initially made. But not for long.[5]

On the international scene it was cotton, the plantation staple which required much more extensive processing after production

for the same market centers. Rüstow suggests that the New World plantations actually formed the model for these eastern estates, but it is possible they developed independently in response to ecological and historical circumstances similar to those from which the New World plantations sprang. Alexander Rüstow, *Ortesbestimmung der Gergenwart* (Erlenbach-Zurich: Eugen Rentsch, 1950), pp. 62, 171-172.

5. Alden, *op. cit., passim.*

than rice, indigo, or tobacco, that did most to transcend colonies and states and knit almost the entire area into a single economic system. Its development and extension would have been entirely impossible without the parallel development of processing machinery which could not take place in the areas of production but which did take place in England. In England, cotton imports from the American South, pressing against existing technology, led to a series of inventions in the textile industry and to those far-reaching changes in English economy and society which we since have called the Industrial Revolution. The American answer to each invention in England which increased the demand for cotton was, save in the case of the cotton gin, an expansion of the cotton-growing area toward the southwestern frontier.[6] The expansion reached around the northern rim of the Gulf of Mexico and by the time of the Civil War included eastern Texas. We may speculate that without the South's cotton there would have been no Industrial Revolution and without the Industrial Revolution there would have been no South. The heartland of the South became that great extent of cotton-exporting territory in southern and southwestern North America scooped out as by a great bulldozer based and energized in England.

The plantation could expand no further nor faster into the southwest than the necessity for maintaining market connections allowed. The area over which cotton could be grown in terms of soil and climate was larger than the area over which cotton had to be grown in terms of market and profits. Since no commodity enters the world market except by way of the oceans, and since the plantation is everywhere an institution which produces for distant markets, plantation societies of the world, the South among them, are characteristically grouped around the water's edge. Without the Gulf of Mexico the area now included in the Southwest would have been even more landlocked than the Old Northwest originally was and

6. Thomas Ellison, *The Cotton Trade of Great Britain* (London: E. Wilson, 1886, p. 29; Harold Rugg, *Changing Civilization in the Modern World* (New York: Ginn and Co., 1930), p. 62; M. B. Hammond, *The Cotton Industry* (Ithaca, N. Y.: American Economic Association, 1897), Appendix I; L. C. A. Knowles, *The Industrial and Commercial Revolutions in Great Britain During the Nineteenth Century* (London: Routledge and Kegan Paul, 1926), p. 51; F. V. Emerson, "Geographical Influences in American Slavery," *American Geographic Society Bulletin*, XLIII (January-March, 1911), 13-26, 106-118, 170-181; U.S. Bureau of the Census, *Eleventh Census: 1890, Progress of the Nation, 1790-1890*, Part I, pp. xviii-xxviii.

might very well have had a climate and a terrain much like that of New Mexico and Arizona today.

3

What kind of civilization is and has been southern civilization? Is the model manorial Europe, Old Testament Hebrew, the classic Greek state, or what? All these and other models have been employed, but the civilization of the South really has to be understood in terms of an institution that came significantly upon the world after the sixteenth century, the plantation. The plantation has been the molecular unit, the very quintessence, of the South and of southernism. In a sense the plantation is the South writ small and the South is the plantation writ large. It has given this society its fundamental principle of order and of continuity, and in it generations of southerners have found their identity. If now there are vital changes taking place in this society as it moves further and faster into the United States and the world, it is in large part because the plantation is being mechanized, consolidated into other types of enterprise, broken down into small farms, converted into a dude and hunting estate, abandoned, or otherwise disappearing. But whatever new order of social life may be in process of replacing it we shall not be able to escape entirely its heritage. Whether we conform to this heritage or revolt against it, the plantation norm will continue to glorify or to stain the culture and the attitudes of the South's people. If it is not with a dead ante bellum institution that we have to deal but with a living tradition, then its nature and development deserve a closer look.

The outcome of economic succession and population invasion which appear to follow shifts in the ecological position of areas, but which tend to be concealed in great masses of historical detail, is everywhere about the same. People of different race and culture find themselves occupying the same territory. In the absence of a self-distributing labor market in the South, and in a situation where there was more land than labor to till it, entrepreneurs turned planters could secure, hold, and move labor only by means of slavery, and the slavery was fastened upon the highly visible blacks who were imported cheaply from Africa and who were not motivated in the economic traditions of Western Europe. In addition to its industrial function the plantation arose in this area as a means of accommodating peoples of different race and culture to each other. Without it, two such different peoples as European whites and African blacks could not, in all probability, have lived together on the same soil.

If, as Walter Webb has demonstrated,[7] the civilization of the Great Plains was made by men who left the timber for the great open spaces of the West, the civilization of the South was produced by men who entered the seemingly everlasting forest that stretched westward. "It was not the Atlantic," John Peale Bishop remarks in one of his essays, "that separated Americans from the European tradition, but the woods of the Old West."[8] Beyond the line of English coastal plantations and towns moved a stream of Scotch, Scotch-Irish, Welsh, Germans, and Englishmen liberated from indentured servitude. Out there these diverse population elements squatted on the land and built a way of life based upon the small diversified farm with free family labor which brought them into conflict with the wealthier planters of the tidewater. It was a conflict characterized by mutual contempt and bitter words, a conflict between farm and plantation such as the conflict between North and South was later in part to be. In this context the plantation society considered itself and was considered East and not South. However, as plantation settlement moved inland as far as Texas, the stage was set for the line separating East and West to swing around on an axis provided by the boundary line between Maryland and Pennsylvania, the Mason and Dixon line.

As the South became the area below the Mason and Dixon line, it spawned a distinctive culture which came to characterize a very large territory. Whatever is distinctive about a culture appears to be an incident of isolation, and this was an area separated in high degree from the tides and currents of world thought in somewhat the same manner and degree in which South Africa has been isolated. It is interesting that the extreme northeastern part of the United States, New England, and the southern part of the country, Dixie, are the only parts which have achieved areal names other than points of the compass. The people of each of these areas have given

7. Walter Webb, *The Great Plains* (Boston: Ginn and Co., 1931).
8. John Peale Bishop, *Collected Essays* (New York: Charles Scribner's Sons. 1948), p. 171.

allegiance to entities intermediate between the states on the one hand and the nation on the other to a degree apparently stronger than have the people of any other region of the United States. There are sound historical reasons for this similarity; both underwent periods of avoidance by non-English-speaking white immigrants. In New England, 25,000 English immigrants settled in the thirty-year period between 1620 and 1650, and for a hundred years afterwards immigration into the area was negligible. Practically all of the 1,000,000 people in New England at the time of the first census in 1790 were descendants of the Englishmen who arrived before 1650. This isolation and the almost complete freedom from admixture during this period produced a distinctive American type, the New England Yankee. The South, too, has been comparatively unaffected by the great variety of stocks which occupied the middle colonies and states. Of the more than 2,500,000 aliens arriving in the United States between 1820 and 1850, only about 300,000 came to reside in the South. Before and after the Civil War the great tide of immigration from foreign countries swept around the plantation areas, thus avoiding competition with low-cost Negro labor. By so doing they helped define the northern and northwestern boundaries of the South and gave white southerners cause to boast of their "pure" Anglo-Saxon ancestry.

There was another and more local source of isolation in the development of southern culture. As farmers and planters moved further into the Southwest, their farms and plantations appeared as small clearings widely separated from each other by the forest. In the South, as in other plantation areas in the world, tales of wild beasts and wild game hunting form a substantial part of the lore of settlement and planting. The forest into which the planters went and to which outlaws and restless individuals could escape marked the boundary of effective control by the central authority of the colony or state. Since the type of organization in which authority resides seems to depend, ultimately, upon the means and extent of communication, each settlement and particularly each plantation became in some considerable measure a state in itself. As a state or as a subdivision of the state, the plantation developed a monopoly of authority within a closed territory. Law was such compulsion as the planter, himself a sort of settlement outlaw and the strongest power of the moment, chose to enforce. Under the circumstances that old conception inherited from England to the effect that it is better for the law to be consistent than for the law to be just did not always apply. Southern law became somewhat like Chinese law, that is, implicated in a network of personal relations and differentially enforced upon individuals according to social standing.[9]

On the isolated plantation in the forest whatever was and is distinctive about the culture of the South took form. The institution was and to some extent continues to be characteristically one of those aggregations of persons which, like the family, exists in the fact that people are reckoned as belonging to each other. It was this "reckoning together" that made the plantation, again much like the family, a unit of collective expectation and obligation, where social relations are so primary and personal that people do not talk of rights and duties; this kind of talk is reserved for the more formal relationships of the city and the larger state. On the plantation, in general, persons descended from or appended to the same individual were reckoned together and their characteristics attributed to that one from whom they are descended or to whom they belonged or upon whose "place" they lived. This "reckoning together" of the past with the present and of the black with the white means that, not only were persons counted together, but were designated as "belonging" to the plantation, the planter and his family no less than his slaves or tenants, as though the plantation were another something existing apart from the very members who made it up. It became a structure living in the mind and in culture, and fashioning the personalities and outlooks of those who lived upon it. To understand this fact is to understand much that is otherwise puzzling about the culture of the Old South, the base line from which we have to understand the present South. In this context words that meant one thing in the North meant something at least slightly different in the South. It is likely that the word *slave* came to have

9. In an Alabama county seat, according to a story remembered from the lectures of Robert E. Park, a sign at the entrance to the court house read: "No spitting—$100 fine for spitting." But all around was the evidence of vast expectoration. One morning an additional sign appeared which read: "If you don't stop this spitting we're going to enforce this law." For more on the history of the southern attitude toward law and its enforcement see Charles S. Sydnor, "The Southerner and the Laws," *Journal of Southern History*, VI (February, 1940), 3-23.

somewhat different meanings North and South, and northerners and southerners debating the issue were not always talking about the same thing. As late as 1945 Ruth Landes, an anthropologist, could write:

> My own experience taught me that one must live a while in the South with Southerners, in order to learn the key words and what they mean. Thus, one hears a familiar vocabulary, but the timbre echoes differently. To sense the implications, one must follow the tones of the voice, gather the things that are left unsaid, hear the eloquent silences, note the special actions. In very truth, these words serve another style of living.[10]

No wonder it is easier to *feel* the differences between North and South than it is to conceive them intellectually or to state them formally. Perhaps it is much like the feeling we have for the differences between Orient and Occident or the feeling that the Romans and the Greeks must have had for the differences between their respective social worlds.

4

The plantation was a small single-purpose enterprise which progressively mobilized several different layers of people upon the same territory and steadily got itself involved with others like it. Some amount of co-operation between individual despotisms for the solution of common problems such as transportation and marketing was necessary. Normally every institution survives by becoming part of a social system or by generating a social system around itself and controlling that system. The plantations of Brazil, numerous and important though they were, seem never to have centered an institutional system; an impression gained from the literature is that they never succeeded in subordinating the Catholic Church.[11] Hawaii developed a system of plantations but perhaps not a plantation system.

A plantation system did arise in the South, or, it might be better to say, the scattered plantations in this region systematized themselves into the South, for the plantation system and the South seem

10. Ruth Landes, "A Northerner Views the South," *Social Forces*, XXIII (March, 1945), 376.
11. Stanley M. Elkins, *Slavery: A Problem in American Institutional Life* (Chicago: University of Chicago Press, 1959).

to have been almost synonymous expressions. Because here the interdependency between most or all institutions was centered and held together by the plantation it became a plantation system, that is to say, a plantation survival system. The plantation centered the system in the South because it developed in this region unchallenged by any other established institutional interest, economic, political, or religious.[12] In time it formed the family, white and black, in its own image and according to its own requirements. Its planters dominated the state and filled its offices. The state universities and military academies trained their sons to succeed them as another generation of planters. The church gave moral sanction to the principle of rank order among kinds of men. Originally there was no manufacturing industry to compete for its labor; when such industry did develop it retained the paternalistic principle of the plantation. The small farm sometimes got in the way, but yeoman farmers and even poor whites aspired to become planters themselves.

In the southern system, orthogenetic cities such as Charleston and New Orleans grew up as plantation capitals. In these capital cities what Redfield[13] calls "the little tradition" of the individual and isolated plantations, each varying a little from every other, was reshaped and articulated by poets, novelists, theologians, scholars, and editors into a "great tradition" generally accepted all over the South and which gave southerners their stock clichés, platitudes, and rationalizations. The individual plantations fed their experiences, beliefs, problems, and lore to the wise men and prophets of the capitals; these experiences and this lore came back in standardized form as ideology and conviction.

If the capital cities of the southern plantation system belonged to the planters, the heterogenetic cities of the present South belong to the merchants and manufacturers. Atlanta and Dallas, according to Winsborough, have taken the place of Charleston and New Orleans and chambers of commerce have taken the place of planters' associations.

12. *Ibid.*
13. Robert Redfield and Milton B. Singer, "The Cultural Role of Cities," *Economic Development and Social Change*, III (October, 1954), 53-73.

5

The South became "the South" as a section, not, as we are distinguishing the words, as a region or subregion. It began as that part
of the Caribbean-Gulf plantation region settled principally by
whites of English origin as against the southern parts which were
settled, in the main, by whites of Latin origin. English-speaking
whites along coastal North America staged a common revolt
against the mother country which was successful and which paved
the way for a new nation. Consequently the northern part of the
Caribbean-Gulf region became part of a political entity, the United
States, to which other parts of the same region did not belong. It
was to become a politically conscious section of the new nation in
conflict with other sections. We have to understand the sectionally
conscious South, as southerners themselves came to understand it,
in terms of the enemies it acquired. Without a common enemy the
loose aggregation of states along the South Atlantic and the Gulf of
Mexico probably never would have become "the South" in anything more than a directional sense.

Political bipolarity is not unusual in the history of nations. A
northern area of strength and prestige in China stood repeatedly
against a southern area of lesser strength, and Upper and Lower
Egypt were set off against each other at various times historically.[14]
The fact that the South had its North as Carthage had its Rome,
had, in other words, cultural and political ties with the people of
another part of the same commonwealth with whom it was, nevertheless, in a state of tension and conflict, led the people of the South
to that degree of conscious reflection upon, and justification of, their
way of life as to generate a conception of themselves as a different
people. To know who we are it is first necessary to know who we
are not, and southerners came to know and to thank God they were
not Yankees. The North was stereotyped, as England once was, as
a nation of traders and peddlers, and southerners could, along with
General Lee, refer to Americans opposing them as "those people."
Thus it was that the people of the North and the people of the
South came to form conceptions of themselves as different peoples
but they were, of course, differentiated as counterparts of each other

14. J. H. Breasted, *A History of Egypt* (2nd ed.; New York: C. Scribner's Sons,
1912).

out of the same dialectical process. They do not and could not exist apart from each other. The South became that part of the nation regarded as the South by the people of the North and vice versa.

An order of society whose economy produced primarily for foreign markets and which consequently sought low tariffs, which was based upon unfree labor, and which pressed for *lebensraum* toward the west, inevitably aroused the opposition of economic competitors and ideological antagonists. Before about 1830 there was a great deal of such opposition in the western small farm areas within the South itself. This early opposition proposed change by way of reform. After about 1830 the opposition moved north and assumed a much more virulent and revolutionary character. Northern and southern newspapers began to take sides and to divide public opinion into two hostile camps. Revolutionary abolitionism in the North began with an attack upon the evils of slavery and the dark purposes of the slave power and later broadened out into a bitter and indiscriminate condemnation of the southern "way of life" generally. With John C. Calhoun, southerners moved from defense to attack on everything northern which became equally intemperate. Between 1830 and 1860 the North and the South engaged each other in a prolonged cold war, during which time the partisans of each side added to their cultures elaborate tissues of rationalizations and doctrines intended to naturalize and to sanction their own institutions. There is nothing exceptional about this process; it is the way the customs of every society enter the *mores* and come to be regarded as essential to societal survival. In a plantation society similar to that of the South, Brazil, this process did not occur, which fact probably accounts in considerable measure for the present differences between the two.

In the war that followed, southerners experienced what they fought for, the South, as northerners experienced what they fought for, the Union. "It was the war with the Yankee," says Cash, "which really created the concept of the South as something more than a matter of geography."

> The armies had brought men together from the four quarters, molding them to a common purpose for four years, teaching them more and more to say and think the same things, giving them com-

mon memories—memories transcending all that had gone before and sealed with the great seal of pain and hunger and sweat....

Local patriotism was far from being dead in them, but nobody remembered now that they had ever gone out to die merely for Virginia or Carolina or Georgia. In their years together, a hundred control phrases, struck from the eloquent lips of their captains in the smoke and heat of battle, had burned themselves into their brains —phrases which would ever after be to them as the sounding of trumpets and the rolling of drums, to set their blood to mounting, their muscles to tensing, their eyes to stinging, to call forth in them the highest loyalties and the most active responses. And of these phrases the great master key was in every case the adjective Southern.

Moreover, four years of fighting for the preservation of their world and their heritage, four years of measuring themselves against the Yankee in the intimate and searching contact of battle, had left these Southerners far more self-conscious than they had been before, far more aware of their differences and of the line which divided what was Southern from what was not. And upon that line all their intensified patriotism and love, all their high pride in the knowledge that they had fought a good fight and had yielded only to irresistible force, was concentrated, to issue in a determination, immensely more potent than in the past, to hold fast to their own, to maintain their divergencies, to remain what they had been and were.[15]

The American Civil War, like the similar Boer War in South Africa, was one of the last of the romantic wars and one of the first of the modern wars. For the South it ended in defeat, and for the establishment of the southern tradition this is perhaps the most important fact of all. Had the South been victorious there probably would have been no South today at all. Secession in America, like *apartheid* in South Africa, is not a principle upon which a strong unity can be built. It was not simply divergent economic and cultural interests that made the South a nation within a nation. More than anything else, perhaps, it was a common emotion and a common loss that bound the people of the South together. Walter Ratheneau, speaking of Germany after World War I, remarked that only those nations which have known defeat have souls. It was the defeat of 1865 that gave the South something like a national soul and a conception of a past finer, in its own opinion, than its present. Both

15. W. J. Cash, *The Mind of the South* (New York: A. A. Knopf, 1941), pp. 103-104.

New England and the South have Golden Age traditions, but it has to be asserted that the tradition in the South seems much the stronger.[16] In this connection there comes to mind the volume contributed to by twelve nostalgic southerners three decades ago entitled *I'll Take My Stand*,[17] and the popular literature issued by the devoted ladies who belong to the United Daughters of the Confederacy.

In all the racial strife and turmoil of today perhaps the thing that rankles and embitters most is what appears to be the bland assumption on the part of the outlanders that the natives of the Deep South, like the natives of Deep Africa, are benighted and primitive enough to be urgently in need of conversion. Now if there is one thing certain about the inheritors of an old and proud tradition it is the fact that they strongly resist conversion as they resist any other assault upon their identity. Southerners experienced such an assault during the post-Civil War period when northern victory was felt to justify the imposition of the principles and the way of life for which the North had fought and won as well as a military peace treaty. As Sherman was about to march to the sea, the Reverend Lyman Abbot wrote, "We have not only to conquer the South, we have also to convert it."[18] So following the war it was inevitable that the South be "reconstructed," a northern effort which the people of this section never felt the need for and never really accepted. Along with northern armies of occupation and carpetbaggers came teachers and missionaries,[19] as along with federal marshals they are coming now and with very much the same southern reaction against them. Because of them, in part, the intersectional cold war continues, but whether southerners like it or not it is well to remember that in the kind of mutual watching and listening world in which we live today, the process of passing judgment over other people is inevitable and will continue. The missionaries may not do the South justice but they

16. See Francis P. Gaines, *The Southern Plantation: A Study in the Development and Accuracy of a Tradition* (New York: Columbia University Press, 1924).

17. Twelve Southerners, *I'll Take My Stand: The South and the Agrarian Tradition* (New York: Harper and Brothers, 1930).

18. *New Englander*, XXIII (October, 1864), 701.

19. See, among other books on the Reconstruction period, Harry Lee Swint, *The Northern Teacher in the South, 1862-1870* (Nashville: Vanderbilt University Press, 1941).

may do the South good. At any rate, Reconstruction, then as now, had for its principal object the transformation of racial attitudes.

6

We are brought now to the Great Division, superseding all others, which runs like a thread through about all that has been said in this book and which everyone thinks of when the South is mentioned in ordinary conversation. No matter where or in what form questions of race arise anywhere in the United States and in much of the rest of the world, always in the background the South is there. It is by no means, of course, the only assortment of human oddities in the world. Relations between odd lot peoples, called minorities, and their hosts are implicated in the persistent problems of most if not all modern societies. Every such society must have problems peculiarly its own, or believed to be its own, with which it must live, if only because its problems distinguish it from all other societies. There are no problems like our problems, and a certain indignation is aroused in us when others dare compare their problems with our own. The long-time problem of the South, the one which does most to identify it, is its race problem. It is a problem now in process of changing its character, as it has changed its character several times before, and the change is an earnest of another orientation which the South is undergoing in the United States and in the world.

As race and race relations are commonly considered, the most general assumption is that from the very beginning there is race. But race has to be accounted for and not assumed as an original fact. Races are made in culture, not found in nature. We have only human aggregations to begin with, which, when welded together by crucial events of history, select out certain characteristics held or alleged to be held in common, and become "peoples" of a certain sort—nations, nationalities, religious communities, linguistic communities, folks, or races. These terms represent something more than mere categories; they are wholes or totalities large enough or old enough to be more or less self-contained and to have a self-perpetuating social system. A people is a socially or culturally defined emergent from a society and not just a demographic component of it. What kind of people a collectivity will become will be determined by the history and circumstances of the situation it is in and by the kind of other peoples with which it is in contact and interaction. A people, every people, is constantly changing its limits and its constitution; in no one form does it last forever if it lasts at all. Old peoples are constantly being replaced by new peoples.[20]

The plural society, that is, a group of peoples, is by its very nature localized in particular areas occupied by particular peoples who have particular relations with each other. It is found, for example, not in the relations between Christians and Moslems in general but in Lebanon, not in the relations between Jews and Gentiles in general but in Germany, not in the relations between whites and Negroes in general but in the South. Negroes are not Negroes in general but blacks under various names vis-à-vis other peoples in particular areas. Their names are not just the names of entities but of the relationships that each people has with other people in the same general area. No people can come to consciousness as a people against other people in general but only against particular other people in the context of a particular society. One does not know how to take the others into account in general; one knows or learns how to take the other into account in actual situations. Thus the events out of which a people come and the actions it is engaged in must be understood in terms of the particular concatenation of peoples of which it is a part at a given time and place and in a given situation.

Peoples now regarded as racial in character were not necessarily always so nor are they necessarily destined to remain so. In early Virginia, African blacks appear to have been regarded as religiously different, that is, as non-Christians sometimes called Moors. As the color of their skin merged with religious ideas about them, they were sometimes called blackamoors or tawnymoors. With the development of the slave trade and plantation slavery they came to be regarded as labor battalions in an industrial army of occupation. It was during the course of this development that the conception of whites and blacks as different races took form in the South.[21] Here it functioned first to naturalize and to rationalize

20. Everett C. Hughes, "New Peoples," in Andrew W. Lind, *Race Relations in World Perspective* (Honolulu: University of Hawaii Press, 1955), Ch. V.

21. Edgar T. Thompson, "The Plantation as a Race-Making Situation," in Leonard Broom and Philip Selznick, *Sociology* (Evanston, Illinois: Row, Peterson and

slavery but with abolition it has turned into an end-value in itself, and was politically used to disenfranchise the Negro and to segregate him in separate areas and institutions.[22]

The Negroes of the United States now are a vastly different people from their African ancestors, not only because they have mixed their blood with Indians and whites, but principally because they now are realizing themselves in mass action. They now are speaking and acting for themselves through their own writers, politicians, and institutions. In her chapter, Burgess calls attention to the large and growing Negro middle class, a class which barely existed in 1860, in changing American Negroes into a different people with an entirely different conception of themselves. With the change in the Negro people, southern whites are becoming a new people also. It is very important in understanding recent white behavior in the South to realize that native whites born of native parents who in the past grandly or reluctantly made concessions of rights to the Negro minority now constitute a minority group themselves. They are seeking to convert old customs into "rights."

7

The dominant white people of the South structured society upon the premise that Negro people are a subordinate group immutably confined to their condition. This assumption made the South, like the White Highlands of Kenya and the cities of South Africa, a "white man's country," a phrase which carries with it the unspoken corollary that it is not a black man's country even in areas where blacks outnumber whites. A white man's country would appear to be any part of the world where white men can live and breed and control its institutions.

In the South there were and are the institutions directly controlled by the white majority but which included or serviced members of both races. Foremost among these is the plantation, which intermixed whites and blacks on the land albeit in different stations

Company, 1955), pp. 506-507. Elsewhere I have tried to account more specifically for the rise and operation of various factors leading up to the definition of the relations between whites and blacks in the South as "race relations." "The South and the Second Emancipation," in Allan P. Sindler (ed.), *Change in the Contemporary South* (Durham: Duke University Press, 1963).

22. C. Vann Woodward, *The Strange Career of Jim Crow* (New York: Oxford University Press, 1955).

within it. After the Civil War, white and Negro sharecroppers often worked the land side by side. Another common institution which became especially important in the postwar period was the country store, about which relatively little has been written. Because of the impersonal and symbiotic character of trade generally, the full force of the local community's population, white and Negro, focused upon it as upon no other institution. Consequently community life tended to center around it and southern villages and towns, especially in the plantation areas, developed from it and around it. The southern country store could effect the exchange of goods and services with a minimum amount of hard money, since for most of its people the South's economy was traditionally non-pecuniary and the times did not favor the possession of much money anyway. Indeed, there was a certain contempt for money and for the monied class; there were too many values and sentiments that "money can't buy," and that only a Yankee would think of trying to buy.[23] In addition to general merchandise the country store was often the post office, the funeral parlor, the railway depot, the news-paper, and sometimes the place where the fraternal orders, religious groups, and even school classes met. It was also a bank because it was about the only institution around possessing an iron safe. As the merchant became affluent and cashed in on his mortgages and crop liens he often became a planter, entering into or taking the place of the old planter class. Or he might become a banker and often did. As money and credit became a new basis for power and control, as banks and diversified businesses proliferated, as money and goods circulated as landed property could not, the South be-came more and more regionally as well as sectionally oriented to-ward the great financial and commercial centers of the North and became, in fact, a colonial province of the North. Finance, even more than politics, has made the United States one community and has, of course, drawn the South into a tighter integration with the rest of the nation. But the southern masses remain, perhaps, less pecuniary-minded than the generality of people in any other part of the nation. No one section of the country has a monopoly over improvidence (there are other words for it), but the people of the

23. See W. F. Ogburn, "Southern Regional Folkways Regarding Money," *Social Forces*, XXI (March, 1943), 297-299.

South have more than their share of it. Here it is not just a fact but
a tradition.

Industrial institutions, particularly textile manufacturing,
emerged in the post-Civil War period out of a social movement
intended to solve the "poor white" problem of the South by af-
fording new occupational opportunities to them. The poor whites
were that class of whites said to have a lot of kinfolks but no ancestors, or hardly conscious of any. As the plantation economy had
earlier almost completely eliminated all except Negro labor, the
initial program of industry omitted almost all except white labor.
In non-textile industry this pattern of ethnic segregation did not
prevail, although the distinction between skilled and unskilled work
generally held to the color line. As is true of colonial territories
generally, some capital for the development of industrial institutions
in the recent and present South originated in the great investment
markets of England, but mainly it came from the North. Contrary to
the general assumption that the industrialization of colonial areas is
everywhere a major force in transforming race relations and in undermining the traditional order, southern industry, stemming from
northern as well as southern capital and management, has until
now accommodated itself to the plantation pattern and to the prevailing racial mores.[24] Nevertheless, these institutions, controlled as
they are by finance capital centered outside the South, have been
instrumental in launching southern society into the general complex
economy of America and the world subject to all the varied forces
playing upon that economy, and have helped transform the race
problem into a more impersonal and indirect affair in which unionism and automation will progressively play an important part.

Between peoples, so long as they are separate peoples, there
appears always to be some institutional segregation, voluntary or
involuntary, complementary or parallel, enforced by law or enforced by custom. Segregation appears as a spatial and/or institutional division of labor, and of course carries with it some kind and
degree of isolation. Some peoples have preferred their institutions
segregated, others have protested against it, and at times and places
peoples have changed their preference. It was when segregation be-

24. Herbert Blumer, "Industrialisation and Race Relations," in Guy Hunter (ed.),
Industrialisation and Race Relations (London: Oxford University Press, 1965).

came a matter of public policy as it did in the South after the 1880's, with the aim of consolidating old social differences between the races, that the stage was set for a change in preference on the part of Negroes leading to the present revolt. The present drive is for what is called an "open society," and it may be expected to change or eliminate certain old forms of segregation; but it may just as well institute new forms.

The present drive was launched against the maintenance of separate schools for the two major races, but it has broadened out into an assault on the principle of racial segregation generally. Southern whites have not strongly objected to education for Negroes so long as it was defined as a way of improving the "condition" of underlings, but they have strenuously objected to any form of status education which threatened "our schools." Now our school, our personal school, our almost private school, the school from which we get the news and gossip of the community, is being invaded, or threatened with invasion, by Negroes. It is shocking to realize that it no longer is our school but an impersonal institution of the state over which we no longer have complete control and in which classes have to begin on time because it has ceased to be a common community of family gossip. In the course of time, however, the desegregation and impersonalization of the schools may lead us to talk somewhat less about better white schools or even better Negro schools and somewhat more about just better schools.

Actually, southerners will have to do this because the problem of education in the South, as elsewhere, is itself changing with changes in the nation and in the world. In the stable agricultural society of the pre-twentieth century South, it was not really necessary that the generality of men have much formal education. Many men became great landholders and members of the legislature without any at all. Other men knew a little Latin and Greek and wore this kind of learning like medals on their chests. The real educational forces derived from the forces of production; men were and still are educated by what they are making and doing. The men who had to buy fertilizer, keep the commissary accounts of their tenants, and negotiate the selling of their cotton or tobacco had necessarily to pick up enough reading, writing, and arithmetic in

order to get along.[25] In the relatively simple world in which white
and black southerners of the past have lived and worked, they
acquired about all the education they could use. But that kind of
world is rapidly passing as the chapters in this book testify, and to
win their bread and rear their families in the complex world already
upon us it will be necessary, absolutely necessary, for them to gear
their minds and hands to new and higher levels of endeavor. The
forces actually desegregating education in the South derive from
something more than idealism and pathos and Supreme Court decisions. Rather they stem from a complex of forces that are fundamentally economic and cultural and world-wide. Barbara Ward,
surveying the present world scene from the standpoint of race relations, has pointed out that "the common denominator of the sense
of equality, where it has appeared, has been education."[26]

The drive to educate the children of everybody does not stop
with the public schools. It does not stop even with undergraduate
education at the college level. In the South as elsewhere in the
nation it presses on to higher quality education in the colleges and
universities, not just college by college and university by university,
but into a complex of colleges and universities qualified to meet
the demands of modern science and research. We shall continue to
call it education but actually the drive is for survival, societal
survival.[27]

Most southerners have known for two hundred years or more
that the South is God's country, that the favored land of God is the

25. "Education, like other aspects of culture, is a condition for the satisfaction
of the elementary needs of individuals and groups of individuals. Like intelligence,
it is in considerable measure a response to a problematic situation that requires
reflection and energy and struggle. The fundamental educational process is therefore
a kind of biological adaptation." Edgar T. Thompson, "Comparative Education in
Colonial Areas," American Journal of Sociology, XLVIII (May, 1943), 93. The
point is supported by the following observation by Lynn Smith, "... there is a much
greater tendency for Negroes to be able to read and write when they independently
operate small farms, for themselves, or if a family or so of them work for a single
white family, than there is if they are grouped together in large numbers as wage
hands, croppers, or share tenants on the plantation." The Population of Louisiana,
Louisiana Bulletin No. 293 (Baton Rouge: Louisiana State University, November
1937), 67.
26. Barbara Ward, "Race Relations as a World Issue," The New York Times
Magazine, November 11, 1956, p. 12.
27. Perhaps this is what Whitehead had in mind when he wrote: "In the conditions of modern life, the rule is absolute. The race which does not value trained
intelligence is doomed. There will be no appeal from the judgment which will be
pronounced on the uneducated." Alfred North Whitehead, The Aims of Education
and Other Essays (New York: The Macmillan Company, 1929), pp. 22-23.

land of His most faithful followers, leading outside scoffers to term it the Bible Belt. In the South itself God seems often to have appeared as a great Planter in somewhat the same way He appeared as a great Lord in the early days of manorial England. The people worshipped Him in churches erected for the purpose according to their station in life, and in time adherence to a church, especially in the Protestant denominations, tended everywhere to be an ethnic, class, and standard-of-living affair. Today its professional leadership is often trained in liberal outlooks but the laity of all faiths and both races tend to cling to fundamentalism and to carry on the ceremonials of the traditional past which do not now meaningfully relate to the daily lives and hopes of the people or give expression to their actual experiences on the land and with each other. Unlike the school, which has moved out into the hinterlands from the towns and cities, the southern church, white and Negro, continues to be a rural institution even when it is located in the city. This is why, perhaps, the mores of southerners are more completely embodied in it than in any other institution except the family, and in this respect the differences between Protestant and Catholic faiths appear negligible. The churches of both faiths functioned well within the culture of the plantation system which placed the stamp of southernness upon most of them.[28]

The plantation movement originally was more or less at war with the traditional European and African family, and ended by shaping the family life of both peoples to its own requirements. This was particularly true of the Negro family.[29] But the white family too, high and low, was largely reconstituted by the plantation and became in fact the mechanism whereby its customs and attitudes were transmitted to future generations. The southern family, particularly the white family of the planter class, was established in a system of related families in which a member was almost as much at home in the home of a kinsman as in the home of his parents and with almost as many liberties. "You all" is an expression of this familism.

28. In this connection it is interesting to recall the conclusion of Will Herberg in *Protestant—Catholic—Jew* (Garden City, New York: Doubleday and Company, 1955), *passim*, that in America generally these three "communions" developed an underlying unity beyond their European origins as they responded to the American environment.

29. E. Franklin Frazier, *The Negro Family in the United States* (Chicago: The University of Chicago Press, 1939).

That which does most to sustain and continue a people is perhaps that which is most deeply rooted in its family values, and a people will not change from one form to another until these primary group values are assaulted and changed. If we wish to know why Brazil, almost alone among the plantation societies of the world, is not dominated by the idea of race, the answer probably will be found in the nature and values of Brazilian family life. It is difficult, if not impossible, in Brazil to draw a color line, because such a line would cut across families.[30] Family life in Brazil cannot be defined in racial terms; but this is precisely how it is defined in the South. White and Negro southerners do have kin across the color line but they are not publicly recognized, and we may not expect the fundamental social structure of southern society to change appreciably until and unless the family finally yields to desegregation.

"The Southern white woman and the Negro man," says Charles H. Fairbanks, are psychologically the focal points of the South's fear of desegregation."[31] It is at this point that American values represented by racial equality run head-on into values that represent sex equality. Everywhere, it seems, an approximate equality between the sexes is taken to be a requisite to what the world is coming to understand by "modern." In Moslem countries women are dropping the veil, and in India women are coming out of purdah. In Japan women are mingling more freely with men. These countries are becoming, as we say, "modern," and freer association between men and women is generally taken as sign and symbol of the fact. In regions where race relations are a problem, as in South Africa and the American South, the racial restrictions that have been placed upon and accepted by white women, and the racial restrictions that have been placed upon Negro men, may be of the same order of traditional phenomena resisting modernization and final emancipation. We have our own versions of purdah and the veil.

8

Although they arise out of social movements and change, it is in the nature of institutions, once established, to resist change and

30. E. Franklin Frazier, "A Comparison Between Negro White Relations in Brazil and in the United States," *Transactions of the New York Academy of Sciences*, Series II, VI (May, 1944), 266.

31. *The Negro in American Society* (Tallahassee: Florida State University Studies No. 28, 1958), p. 13.

uphold old ways of life. This is less true of industrial and financial institutions than it is of others, but as the world shifts and changes around them, all institutions at different tempos have to change also. In the South there are geographical shifts in agriculture and occupational changes in the racial division of labor as well as in the economy generally. All these changes are bound up with the re-placement of the plantation system by a metropolitan system in which southern cities link up with each other as well as with the cities of the nation and of the world. It is by reason of its cities that the South is now experiencing its first general emancipation from its geographical locus. Even in the most isolated rural communities in the South, communities like Possum Trot, Alabama,[32] places where readjustments are made with most difficulty, changes are taking place which cumulatively build up into major changes in the life of the region and the nation. Radio, television, and electric lights are being introduced into the humblest tenant homes, and electric bills have to be paid regularly each month. Almost for the first time, these tenants are entering into the decision-making process along with farmers and planters as to how the land shall be used and how and when the products shall be marketed. Incidental-ly, our social scientists are not adequately taking these local changes into account; it appears that we know more now about the South at federal and state levels than we know at the grass-roots level.

Behind the urbanization of the South and the shift in position of this region in the nation and in the world are the great advances in transportation and communication made during the past century and especially during the past few decades. Recent advances in road, railway, bus, truck, and air transportation and forms of mass communication such as radio, newspapers, and television as well as person-to-person communication such as telephone and postal service are incorporating the South into the life of the nation at an ever faster pace. The South may still be rooted in the same old soil, but the airplane has put its people under the same sky all other people live under. More detailed studies of the place of communi-

32. H. C. Nixon, *Possum Trot* (Norman: University of Oklahoma Press, 1941). As local people are realigned into new and wider group relationships there is, among other things, a loss of a shift in group loyalties. "It is hard," Prof. Nixon says, "to be loyal to a highway, a rural route, or a bus line. It is hard to be loyal to a consolidated school which is located somewhere else."

cation and transportation in reorienting the South in the modern world are urgently needed.

In the urban landscape of the South, as elsewhere, the most striking objects are moving objects, such as automobiles and trucks. Mobility by means of such media of transportation is greatest in the cities and recedes as one moves away from them, but through them the influence of the cities is being extended along the highways and power lines into the remotest rural areas. These modern forms of capillary transportation have, by reducing the scale of local distance, introduced intercity competitions and new local divisions of labor, both agricultural and industrial, within the South itself. They are changing traditional patterns of local life far more than the railroads ever did. For one thing, many villages and towns are languishing while towns and cities more widely spaced are flourishing.

The rise of great cities within the South is contributing to the secularization and the impersonalization of its society. A new type of man is emerging in them, a man more ready to face the facts of the modern world and to seek to understand them more objectively. The city everywhere is the natural habitat of the liberal mind, and the southern liberal is increasing in number and making himself heard. Here, too, the conservative is finding a rationale upon which to base the conservatism which formerly he took for granted, but which now may require him to change his traditional political party allegiance. It is interesting to note that the southern liberal, like the southern conservative, tends to hold tenaciously to the body of southern culture even while trying to reform it.[33]

The new southern man is more urban and is becoming more urbane. He is ripe for scientific advance as Western man is generally. The Brahmans of southern science, as elsewhere, are mathematicians and physical scientists, because they are most immediately and obviously useful to industry and agriculture. In the area of social scholarship he has given first place to the field of history, especially southern history, perhaps because until relatively recently the historian was himself a sectional type who not only interpreted the past from a sectional point of view but who also often took an

33. Leslie W. Dunbar, "The Changing Mind of the South," in Avery Leierson (ed.), *The American South in the 1960's* (New York: Frederick A. Praeger, 1964), p. 7.

active part in the sectional struggle. The modern southern historian, however, is writing not simply of the past as something past but as a point of view from which to come back at the present. He can investigate and reconstruct a past to which he never belonged. Social scientists in the South investigate a society to which they do belong. These scientists do not yet belong to the high caste, but the value of their contributions is being recognized. They are bringing the study of southern society within the discipline of rigorous scientific procedure. However, we have to understand the development of social science in the South, as we have to understand the development of science generally, as something not entirely born in the minds of its professional exponents, within or without the area, but as a situational imperative inherent in the processes of social change itself. No longer can the facts and the events of this society be looked upon as something imposed either by God alone or the legislature; we now have the disposition and we are acquiring the means for examining and better understanding ourselves objectively without apology or flattery. We now are in one of those historical situations where society, in the South as elsewhere, appears over against a population aggregate, over against the state, and over against the territory it occupies. The social sciences show society itself thrown against the screen in such manner that its members may become conscious of what it includes and what it does not include. It is suggested that such a development comes at a predictable stage in social evolution and that the South has reached this stage.

Before 1860 the South was something like medieval Europe, a theological swampland, and its intellectuals and men of letters sought in what they then called "social science" a body of doctrine justifying the existing order of things and resisting change in that order. These men produced the first literature described as "sociology" that appeared in the United States. After the Civil War, the social sciences, and sociology in particular, became identified with carpetbag movements to reform the social system and to some extent this is what sociology popularly means in the South today. When our social scientists began to discover the South as a social object their disposition was to treat it as a more or less unique and incomparable society. The members of the old Southern Sociological Congress and the early Southern Sociological Society were so disposed. Today the tendency is to study behavior in the social system we call the South as representative of human nature and social process generally.[34] Southern social scientists can now be more detached about the phenomena they study in this area because they are more attached to a larger human unity. We can now join the nation and the world and use common humanity, the human nature that underlies all cultures, as a means of communication and of understanding ourselves as well as others. In this context there is no North or South nor an East or West. Simply to know this fact, and to act upon it, can be a factor in changing the South. Social change is bringing about the means for a better understanding of our society, and to better understand a society is itself a factor in bringing about further change. By advancing what we know about our society we contribute to changing the society we know.

34. Edgar T. Thompson, "Sociology and Sociological Research in the South," in Howard W. Odum and Katherine Jocher (eds.), *In Search of the Regional Balance of America* (Chapel Hill: University of North Carolina Press, 1945), pp. 114-123.

THE CONTRIBUTORS

JOHN C. McKINNEY was born in Velasco, Texas, in 1920; educated at Colorado State College and Michigan State University (Ph.D.). He is currently Professor of Sociology and Chairman of the Department of Sociology and Anthropology at Duke University. Mr. McKinney is the author of *Constructive Typology and Social Theory*, and coauthor of *Introduction to Social Research*. He has had a long-time interest in macro-sociology, the problems of large-scale systems in development, continuity, and change.

HALLIMAN H. WINSBOROUGH was born in St. Louis, Missouri, 1932; educated at the University of Chicago (Ph.D.). An Assistant Professor of Sociology at Duke University, Mr. Winsborough is co-author of *Metropolis and Region*, as well as various articles on population, the ecology of cities, and statistics. Much of Mr. Winsborough's recent research has involved studies of changing spatial organization of human groups.

CHARLES HORACE HAMILTON was born in McClennon County, Texas, in 1901; educated at Southern Methodist University, Texas A. and M. College, Harvard University, and the University of North Carolina (Ph.D.). He is now William Neal Reynolds Professor of Rural Sociology at North Carolina State University. He is the author of numerous professional papers and research monographs in rural sociology and demography. As Director of Sociological Research with the Commission on Hospital Care he contributed a number of chapters to *Hospital Care in the United States*. During his career he has done sociological research in demography, land tenure, health and medical care, and rural life. Most recently he participated in the Southern Appalachian Regional Study and wrote the chapter on Health and Health Services. He is currently engaged in a study of educational selectivity in internal migration.

LEONARD REISSMAN was born in Cleveland, Ohio, 1921; educated at Wayne State University, the University of Wisconsin, Princeton University, and Northwestern University (Ph.D.). He is currently Professor of Sociology and Favrot Professor of Human Relations at Tulane University. Mr. Reissman has held a senior postdoctoral fellowship from the National Science Foundation and has spent a year as a Fellow at the Center for Advanced Study in the Behavioral Sciences. He is the author of *Class in American Society, The Urban Process*, and monographs and articles on political sociology, community organization, suburbanization, and the professions. He has been engaged in a broad study of urbanization in the underdeveloped as well as the developed nations, and the effects of such massive changes upon society.

JOSEPH J. SPENGLER was born in Piqua, Ohio, 1902, and educated at Ohio State University (Ph.D.). Mr. Spengler, now James B. Duke Professor of Economics, Duke University, has published a number of essays on southern economic and demographic problems and ante bellum southern economists. He has also published books and articles on the demography of France, economic development, population problems, and social and economic theory and its history. He is a past president of the Population Association of America, and currently serves as president of the American Economics Association. Mr. Spengler's publications include coeditorship of *Population Theory and Policy*, and *Essays in Economic Thought; Aristotle to Marshall*.

JOE SUMMERS FLOYD, JR., was born in Arcadia, Florida, in 1920; educated at the University of Florida and the University of North Carolina (Ph.D.). Mr. Floyd, who is now Professor of Finance in the Graduate School of Business Administration at the University of North Carolina, has published the *Effects of Taxation on Industrial Location*, *The Changing South* (with J. M. Maclachlan), and *Financing Industrial Growth: Public and Private Sources of Capital for Industry* (with Mr. L. H. Hodges, Jr.). He has served as a member of the Board of Editors of the *Southern Economic Journal*. As an expert on the effects which taxation and finance have upon industrial growth, he has served as a consultant to the North Carolina Department of Tax Research and the Committee of State Finance Officers, and is currently working with the Advisory Commission for Intergovernmental Relations on a study of the influence which state and local taxes have upon economic growth.

DANIEL OLIVER FLETCHER was born in Oberlin, Ohio, in 1930; educated at Oberlin College and the University of Michigan (Ph.D.). An Associate Professor of Economics at Ohio State University, Mr. Fletcher has contributed various journal articles in the general area of transportation and government and business relations. He spent the 1963-1964 academic year on leave with the United States Department of Commerce.

E. WILLIAM NOLAND was born in Romney, West Virginia, in 1912; educated at West Virginia University, the University of Chicago, and Cornell University (Ph.D.). He has held academic positions at Cornell University, Yale University, the University of Iowa, and the University of North Carolina. Mr. Noland's business experience includes a vice-presidency in R. S. Dickson & Company, investment bankers, and service as Coordinator of Industrial and Personnel Relations, American and Efird Mills. He has served as organizational consultant to numerous business firms and the United States Air Force. Author of numerous journal articles, he is the coauthor (with E. W. Bakke) of *Workers Wanted,* and (with R. P. Calhoon and A. M. Whitehill) *Human Relations in Management.* He is currently Professor and Head, Department of Sociology, Purdue University.

RICHARD L. SIMPSON was born in Washington, D. C., 1929; educated at Cornell University and the University of North Carolina (Ph.D.). He is now Associate Professor of Sociology, University of North Carolina at Chapel Hill. Mr. Simpson is coeditor, with Ida Harper Simpson, of *Social Organization and Behavior,* and the author of articles and chapters in various sociological journals and symposia. His most recent research has dealt with occupational careers and professional orientations of public school teachers.

DAVID R. NORSWORTHY was born in Florien, Louisiana, 1931; educated at Louisiana State University and the University of North Carolina (Ph.D.). He has engaged in research on occupations and social change in North Carolina and on regional development in western Louisiana. This paper was written while he was an Assistant Professor of Sociology at Tulane University. Now an Assistant Professor of Sociology at the University of Michigan, Mr. Norsworthy is especially interested in the effects of population composition and trends upon the course of social and economic changes.

DONALD F. ROY was born in Spokane, Washington, in 1909; educated at the University of Washington and the University of Chicago (Ph.D.). While at the University of Chicago, he engaged in industrial research with the Committee on Human Relations in Industry. He is currently an Associate Professor of Sociology at Duke University. He is the author of several articles on the industrial worker, including "Goldbricking," "Efficiency and 'The Fix,'" and "Banana Time." In recent years Dr. Roy's research interest has centered, in the main, on the study of union organizing campaigns in southern industry.

CHARLES EDWIN BISHOP was born in South Carolina, in 1921; educated at Berea College, the University of Kentucky, and the University of Chicago (Ph.D.). Mr. Bishop has been at North Carolina State since 1950 and is now Reynolds Professor and Head of the Department of Agricultural Economics. He also serves as Executive Director of the Agricultural Policy Institute. Mr. Bishop has conducted extensive research on the problems of agriculture in the United States and in other countries. He has written numerous research publications and is the coauthor of *Introduction to Agricultural Economic Analysis*. His major interests are in agricultural policy, agricultural development, rural adjustments to changes in technology, and labor mobility.

SOLON T. KIMBALL was born in Manhattan, Kansas, in 1909; educated at Kansas State University and Harvard University (Ph.D.). Mr. Kimball has been Professor of Anthropology and Education at Teachers College, Columbia University, since 1953. From 1948 to 1953 he was Chairman of the Department of Sociology and Anthropology at the University of Alabama. He is coauthor of *Education and the New America, The Talladega Story*, and *Family and Community in Ireland*. Mr. Kimball's interests in education include Latin America, where he served for a year as technical consultant on community education to the Brazilian Center for Educational Research, and in Peru, where he has helped organize a program to assist the Peruvian Ministry of Education in educational development.

ALLAN MURRAY CARTTER was born in Westfield, New Jersey, 1922; educated at Colgate University, Cambridge University, and Yale University (Ph.D.). Formerly Professor of Economics and Dean of the Graduate School at Duke University, he is now vice-president of the American Council on Education. Mr. Cartter is author of *The Redistribution of Income in Postwar Britain, Theory of Wages and Employment*, coauthor of *Indonesia: Perspective and Proposals for United States Economic Aid*, and editor of *American Universities and Colleges, 1964*. He is currently conducting a major research project on the changing character of American universities, and serves as director of the Commission on Plans and Objectives for Higher Education.

ALLAN P. SINDLER was born in Brooklyn, New York, in 1928; educated at Harvard University (B.A. and Ph.D.). Recently an Associate Professor of Political Science at Duke University, he is now Professor of Government at Cornell University. His principal interest is in the field of American party politics and voter behavior. This paper was written during his fellowship year at the Center for Advanced Study in the Behavioral Sciences. Several of his writings reflect a special concern for southern politics: *Huey Long's Louisiana: State Politics, 1920-1952*; "The Unsolid South: A Challenge to the National Democratic Party," in A. F. Westin (ed.), *The Uses of Power*; and *Change in the Contemporary South* (editor, with contributing essay).

HERBERT BLUMER was born in St. Louis, Missouri, 1900; educated at the University of Missouri and the University of Chicago (Ph.D.).

He is currently Professor of Sociology and director of the Institute of Social Sciences, University of California, Berkeley. He is past president of the American Sociological Association and the Society for the Study of Social Problems, and is currently vice-president of the International Sociological Association. From 1940 to 1952 he served as editor of the *American Journal of Sociology*, and in 1954 was co-organizer of a World Congress on Race Relations held in Honolulu, Hawaii. He is the author of many papers in the area of race relations, social psychology, industrial sociology, and methodology of research.

M. ELAINE BURGESS was born in Walla Walla, Washington, 1927; educated at Washington State University and the University of North Carolina (Ph.D.). She is now an Associate Professor in the Department of Sociology and Anthropology at the University of North Carolina at Greensboro. Miss Burgess is author of *Negro Leadership in a Southern City*, and coauthor of *An American Dependency Challenge*, as well as various articles on community, poverty, and social change. Her special areas of interest include social structure, stratification, and race relations; and she is currently conducting research on Negro and white lower-class family patterns.

JOSEPH H. FICHTER was born in Union City, New Jersey, 1908; educated at St. Louis University and Harvard University (Ph.D.); entered the seminary of the Jesuit Order in Louisiana in 1930 and was ordained priest in 1942. He is Professor of Sociology and Head of the Department at Loyola University of the South, active in sociological, religious, and interracial organizations. Author of research studies: *Religion as an Occupation, Parochial School, Social Relations in the Urban Parish*, and *Southern Parish*. He has been visiting professor at University of Muenster (Germany), Notre Dame University, and the Catholic University of Chile, and has held summer appointments at Fordham University, Universidad Ibero-Americana (Mexico), and Sir George Williams University (Montreal).

GEORGE L. MADDOX was born in McComb, Mississippi, in 1925; educated at Millsaps College, Boston University, and Michigan State University (Ph.D.). Now Professor of Sociology, Departments of Sociology and Psychiatry, Duke University, Mr. Maddox has published a number of articles, particularly on drinking behavior among adolescents and on social aspects of human aging. He is the coauthor of *Drinking Among Teenagers: A Sociological Interpretation*. Mr. Maddox is a member of the Kent Fellowship Advisory Committee, Danforth Foundation, and of the Research Utilization Committee, National Institute of Mental Health.

C. HUGH HOLMAN was born in Cross Anchor, South Carolina, 1914; educated at Presbyterian College (S.C.), New York University, and the University of North Carolina (Ph.D.). He is now Kenan Professor of English and Dean of the Graduate School at the University of North Carolina at Chapel Hill. He has specialized in the study of the American novel and of southern American literature. He revised and enlarged *A Handbook to Literature*, by Thrall and Hibbard. He is the author of *Thomas Wolfe*, and is a coauthor of *The Development of American Literature Criticism*, *The Southerner as American*, and *Southern Writers: Appraisals in Our Time*. He has edited works by Thomas Wolfe and William Gilmore Simms.

RUPERT B. VANCE was born in Plummervill, Arkansas, in 1899, and educated at Vanderbilt University and the University of North Carolina (Ph.D.), where he is Kenan Professor of Sociology. Population, ecology, and regionalism are his special fields. For thirty-five years he has done work on the regional South. Among his sixty titles are books on *Human Factors in Cotton Culture*, *Human Geography of the South*, *The Urban South* (coeditor), *All These People*, and *New Farm Homes for Old* (coauthor). He is past president of the Southern Sociological Society, the American Sociological Association, and the Population Association of America. He is the recipient of the University's Thomas Jefferson award, the North Carolina Society's Mayflower Cup, and the Lord and Taylor American Design award for work on the regional South.

GUION GRIFFIS JOHNSON was born in Wolfe City, Texas, in 1900; educated at Mary-Hardin Baylor College, the University of Missouri, and the University of North Carolina (Ph.D.). In 1960 she served as Lecturer in Sociology, Rhodes University, Grahamstown, South Africa. Mrs. Johnson is a past member of the Executive Committee of the North Carolina Council of Women's Organizations, serving as president from 1952-1958. She is the author of *A Sociological History of the Sea Islands*, and *Ante-Bellum North Carolina: A Social History*.

JOHN HOPE FRANKLIN was born in Rentiesville, Oklahoma, in 1915; educated at Fisk University, and Harvard University (Ph.D.). He is currently Professor of History at the University of Chicago. He was the recipient of a Guggenheim Fellowship in 1950-1951, and was the President's Fellow at Brown University in 1952. He has published numerous books and articles dealing with the history of the South and of American Negroes, including *The Militant South*, *From Slavery to Freedom*, and *Reconstruction after the Civil War*. In the past Mr. Franklin has served on the United States National Commission for UNESCO and the Board of Directors of the American Council on Human Rights.

EDGAR T. THOMPSON was born in Little Rock, South Carolina, in 1900; educated at the University of South Carolina, the University of Missouri, and the University of Chicago (Ph.D.). He is now Professor of Sociology at Duke University. Mr. Thompson was a member of the Ford Foundation Conference on Race Relations in World Perspective, Honolulu, 1954, and participated in the Pan American Union Seminar on New World Plantations in San Juan, Puerto Rico, in 1957. He was Hugh le May Fellow at Rhodes University, Grahamstown, South Africa, in 1956, and served as president of the Southern Sociological Society in 1961. He is the author of *Race and Region*, and *The Plantation: A Bibliography*, edited (with contributions) *Race Relations and the Race Problem* and *Race: Individual and Collective Behavior* (with Everett C. Hughes), contributed chapters to several published symposia, and is the author of numerous papers principally dealing with race relations and plantation societies.

INDEX